Financial Accounting

A Business Process Approach

Jane L. Reimers

Rollins College, Crummer Graduate School of Business

THIRD EDITION

Prentice Hall

Boston   Columbus   Indianapolis   New York   San Francisco   Upper Saddle River
Amsterdam   Cape Town   Dubai   London   Madrid   Milan   Munich   Paris   Montréal   Toronto
Delhi   Mexico City   São Paulo   Sydney   Hong Kong   Seoul   Singapore   Taipei   Tokyo

Editorial Director: Sally Yagan
Editor in Chief: Donna Battista
AVP/Executive Editor: Jodi McPherson
Product Development Manager: Ashley Santora
Editorial Project Manager: Rebecca Knauer
Development Editor: Karen Misler
Editorial Assistant: Christina Rumbaugh
Director of Marketing: Kate Valentine
Senior Marketing Manager: Maggie Moylan
Director of Digital Development: Lisa Strite
Media Development Manager: Cathi Profitko
Editorial Media Project Manager: Allison Longley
Senior Managing Editor: Cynthia Zonneveld
Project Manager: Lynne Breitfeller
Senior Operations Specialist: Diane Peirano

Senior Art Director: Jon Boylan
Text and Cover Designers: Jon Boylan and Anthony Gemmellaro
Cover Image: iStockphoto.com
Manager, Visual Research: Beth Brenzel
Manager, Rights and Permissions: Zina Arabia
Image Permission Coordinator: Craig A. Jones
Manager, Cover Visual Research & Permissions: Karen Sanatar
Full-Service Project Management: GEX Publishing Services
Composition: GEX Publishing Services
Printer/Binder: Courier Kendallville
Cover Printer: Phoenix
Text Font: 10/12 Times Roman

Credits and acknowledgments: pp. 24, 25 Reprinted by permission of Dell. All rights reserved; p. 73 Reprinted by permission of *Wall Street Journal*, Copyright © 2009 Dow Jones & Company, Inc. All Rights Reserved Worldwide; p. 529 Reprinted by permission of Books-A-Million. All Rights Reserved.

Photo Credits: p. 4 Paul Sakuma\AP Wide World Photos; p. 10 Studio M\Stock Connection; p. 10 Michael Newman\PhotoEdit Inc.; p. 10 Spencer Grant\PhotoEdit Inc.; p. 10 David Young Wolff\Getty Images Inc. - Stone Allstock; p. 27 Emile Wamsteker/Bloomberg News /Landov; p. 27 AP Wide World Photos; p. 27 Mike Derer\AP Wide World Photos; p. 27 Susan Walsh\AP Wide World Photos; p. 27 David J. Phillip\AP Wide World Photos

Library of Congress Cataloging-in-Publication Data
Reimers, Jane L.
  Financial accounting : a business process approach / Jane L. Reimers. — 3rd ed.
      p. cm.
  Includes bibliographical references and index.
  ISBN-13: 978-0-13-611527-4 (casebound : alk. paper)
  ISBN-10: 0-13-611527-6
  1. Accounting. 2. Financial statements. I. Title.
  HF5636.R45 2010
  657--dc22

                    2009047951

10 9 8 7 6 5 4 3 2 1

Prentice Hall
is an imprint of

www.pearsonhighered.com

ISBN 13: 978-0-13-611527-4
ISBN 10: 0-13-611527-6

For my son

Brief Contents

Contents

Chapter 6   Acquisition and Use of Long-Term Assets   267

Chapter 7   Accounting for Liabilities   317

With
Financial Accounting:
A Business Process Approach
Student Text, Study Resources,
and MyAccountingLab
students will have more
"I Get It!"
moments.

A Business Process Approach

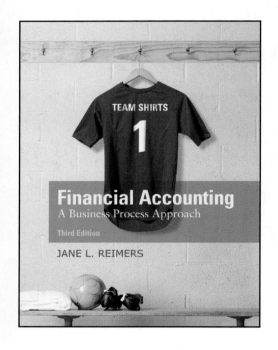

Financial Accounting: A Business Process Approach, Third Edition, explains accounting concepts in a way all majors can understand by organizing the material around how a business works. The business process approach in this text presents a business topic and then shows the accounting concepts behind that topic—rather than solely explaining accounting concepts based on the balance sheet order, a difficult approach for students who have yet to learn about the balance sheet. Overall, this text reinforces the big picture of how businesses operate while showing students how the corresponding accounting concepts work in context.

Jane Reimers' Unique Business Process Approach, in her own words...

More Important to Business Than Ever Before

In the past, one of the biggest challenges we have faced as accounting professors has been motivating our students to learn accounting. However, the business failures of the past decade, particularly those involving accounting irregularities and fraud, have done a great deal to provide needed motivation. In addition, the economic recession of 2008–09 has continued to keep accounting in the news. Most of our students today have no doubt that accounting is important to business. My approach to the first course in accounting is based on emphasizing this relationship between business and accounting.

Make Financial Statements Relevant to All Majors.

With a focus on what a business does and less of a focus on bookkeeping, the business process approach helps all majors understand financial statements. Although the mechanics of debits and credits are included in an appendix for professors who want to use this tool, the fundamental accounting equation and the path from business transactions to financial statements are at the heart of this approach.

Offer Hands-On Practice in Preparing Statements: Color-Coded Accounting Equation.

To become effective users of financial statements, students must understand how the statements are prepared—and nothing helps them understand this more than having them prepare the statements themselves. Students have had extremely positive reactions to the color-coded accounting equation, which enables them to see exactly how business transactions are summarized and presented on each of the four basic financial statements.

Color-Coded Accounting Equation

This color-coded accounting equation is a tool you will use throughout your financial accounting course. Fully explained in Chapter 1, this tool is so important that we have put it here for quick reference. You may find this helpful when preparing your homework assignments. Each financial statement has a unique color. You will see these colors throughout the chapters when we present a financial statement.

| | | Assets | | = Liabilities | | + | Shareholders' Equity | |
| | | | | | | | Contributed Capital | Retained Earnings |
Transaction	Cash	All other assets	(Account)	All liabilities	(Account)		Common stock	(Account)
1.	$250						$250	
2.	850			850	Notes payable			
3.	(650)	650	Property, plant, and equipment					
4.	(25)							(25) Operating expenses
5.	(300)	300	Property, plant, and equipment					
6.	800							800 Service revenue
7.	(480)							(480) Salary expense
8.		20	Supplies	20	Accounts payable			
9.	(5)							(5) Dividends
	$440	+ $970		= $870		+	$250	+ $290

■ Income Statement ▬ Statement of Changes in Shareholders' Equity ▬ Balance Sheet ▬ Statement of Cash Flows

■ Red identifies the income statement. The transactions that affect the income statement will have an amount in the red section on the accounting equation worksheet.

■ Yellow identifies the statement of shareholders' equity. The transactions that affect shareholders' equity will have an amount in the yellow section.

■ Blue identifies the balance sheet. Only the summary of the transactions—the ending balances in each account—will be shown on the balance sheet.

■ Green identifies the statement of cash flows. The cash inflows and outflows are all found in the cash column of the accounting equation worksheet. These inflows and outflows are explained in the statement of cash flows.

All of our students—both accounting and non-accounting majors—need to understand the basic relationship between business transactions and the financial statements. Overall, the approach in this text provides a strong foundation for accounting majors while keeping the content relevant for all majors. I hope this textbook provides your students with all of the tools they will need to truly understand accounting.

— *Jane L. Reimers*

New to the Third Edition

Understanding the Latest Potential Shift in Reporting Standards: International Financial Reporting Standards (IFRS).

Awareness of IFRS—including what it is, what it means, and when it's coming—is becoming increasingly important in our global economy. In the third edition, IFRS is introduced and explained in the first chapter. Then, throughout the book, differences between U.S. GAAP and IFRS are noted as they apply to the chapter's topic. A section on IFRS has been added to the capstone chapter (11), along with some examples of financial statements prepared according to IFRS.

Learning in the Right Sequence: Reordered Coverage of Operating and Investing Activities.

Operating topics, such as sales and inventory, are covered before the acquisition and use of long-term assets, consistent with a renewed emphasis on operating, investing, and financing activities by the FASB. This new order helps students because it's consistent with the statement of cash flows and the lifeblood of all business. This reorganization will also help prepare students for convergence with IFRS because it reflects how IFRS statements are organized.

Making Practice Easier: Revised Color-Coded Accounting Equation Worksheet.

We modified the color-coded accounting equation worksheet to make it easier to use. Rather than having a column for every asset and liability account used in a problem, there are just two asset columns—cash and all other assets—and just one column for liabilities. The new format provides space to include the name of the account next to each entry in the general asset and liability columns, making the worksheets larger and easier to read.

Panel A: Clean Sweep

		Assets		=	Liabilities	+	Owner's Equity		
							Contributed Capital	Retained Earnings	
	Cash	All other assets	(Account)	All liabilities	(Account)				(Account)
Beginning Balances	$ 900	$ 200	Supplies	$400	Notes payable		$700		
Transaction									
1. Earns revenue and collects fees in cash	750							$ 750	Revenue
2. Makes loan payment	(440)			(400)	Notes payable			(40)	Interest expense
3. Adjusts for supplies used		(175)	Supplies					(175)	Supplies expense
Ending Balances	$1,210	+ $ 25		= 0		+	$700	+ $ 535	

—Income Statement —Statement of Changes in Owner's Equity —Balance Sheet —Statement of Cash Flows

Panel B: Maids-R-Us

		Assets		=	Liabilities	+	Owner's Equity		
							Contributed Capital	Retained Earnings	
	Cash	All other assets	(Account)	All liabilities	(Account)				(Account)
Beginning Balances	$900	$200	Supplies	$400	Notes payable		$700		
Transaction									
1. Earns revenue and extends credit		750	Accounts receivable					$750	Revenue
2. Makes loan payment	(140)			(100)	Notes payable			(40)	Interest expense
3. Adjusts for supplies used		(175)	Supplies					(175)	Supplies expense
Ending Balances	$760	+ $775		= $300		+	$700	+ $535	

ETHICS Matters

Paying for Silence

With just two weeks until the start of his trial, Computer Associates International's former CEO, Sanjay Kumar, pleaded guilty to securities fraud and obstruction of justice. Not only did Kumar engage in a conspiracy to inflate the firm's 2000 and 2001 sales revenue, but he also authorized a $3.7 million payment to buy the silence of potential witnesses. In November 2006, he was sentenced to 12 years in prison and fined $8 million for his part in the $2.2 billion fraud.

As you will learn in this chapter, precisely *when* revenue is included on the income statement is one of the most crucial timing issues in accounting. Computer Associates included revenue on its income statement *before* the company actually earned the revenue. This violates one of the most significant accounting principles that forms the basis of U.S. GAAP and IFRS. Revenue must be earned before it can be included on the income statement for the period.

Emphasizing How Ethics Matters.

With the current scandals occurring in today's economy, ethics is one aspect of accounting that truly does matter. To help students avoid potential pitfalls and complications involved with ethics, this edition opens each chapter with a current, relevant example stressing the importance of ethics in accounting and business.

Including the Coverage You Want: Revised Time Value of Money Coverage.

Due to extensive reviewer feedback, time value of money and calculating proceeds from a bond issue have been moved to a chapter appendix. Now Chapter 7, long-term liabilities, can be covered without prior knowledge of present value concepts. The appendix, however, can easily be integrated into chapter coverage for those who prefer to include it.

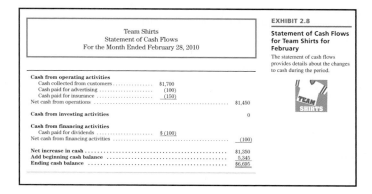

EXHIBIT 2.8

Statement of Cash Flows for Team Shirts for February

The statement of cash flows provides details about the changes to cash during the period.

Connecting Accounting to Business: Continuing Case Example.

Seeing one example carried throughout the entire business process is a great way to help students connect accounting to the big picture of business. The previous edition's example, Tom's Wear, has been updated to Team Shirts, and the computations for depreciation, prepaid expenses, and cost of goods sold are easier to follow. The slow build of the continuing case and its computations in each chapter help students follow the progression of the calculations they're learning.

Keeping Up with the Trends: Updated Examples.

The third edition includes many opportunities to discuss the economic issues facing firms today. For example, in Chapter 3, the Understanding Business feature discusses the cost savings of "going green." Throughout the book, examples like this help students see how the changes in the economy are reflected in a firm's financial statements.

Promoting Practice: A Second Set of Short Exercises.

Included in each chapter of this edition, every Short Exercise, Exercise, and Problem in the Set "A" material has a "matching" exercise or problem in the corresponding Set "B" material. This provides students with even more practice to enhance their skills.

Student Resources

www.myaccountinglab.com

MyAccountingLab is Web-based tutorial and assessment software for accounting that gives students more "I Get It!" moments. **MyAccountingLab** provides students with a personalized, interactive learning environment where they can complete their course assignments with immediate tutorial assistance, learn at their own pace, and measure their progress.

In addition to completing assignments and reviewing tutorial help, students have access to the following resources in **MyAccountingLab**:

- Pearson eText
- Study Guide
- Excel in Practice
- PowerPoints
- Working Papers in both Excel and PDF
- Flash Cards

Study Guide
This chapter-by-chapter learning aid helps students learn financial accounting while getting the maximum benefit from study time.

Student Resource Website www.pearsonhighered.com/reimers
- Excel in Practice
- Working Papers

Student Reference Cards

International Financial Reporting Standards Student Reference Card

This four-page laminated reference card includes an overview of IFRS, why it matters and how it compares to U.S. standards, and highlights key differences between IFRS and U.S. GAAP.

Math for Accounting Student Reference Card

This six-page laminated reference card provides students with a study tool for the basic math they will need to be successful in accounting, such as rounding, fractions, converting decimals, calculating interest, break-even analysis, and more!

Instructor Resources

The primary goal of the Instructor Resources is to help instructors deliver their course with ease, using any delivery method—traditional, self-paced, or online. *Every instructor and student resource has been either written or reviewed by the author.*

www.myaccountinglab.com

MyAccountingLab is Web-based tutorial and assessment software for accounting that not only gives students more "I Get It!" moments, but also provides instructors the flexibility to make technology an integral part of their course or a supplementary resource for students. And, because practice makes perfect, **MyAccountingLab** offers all the Set A end-of-chapter material found in the text along with algorithmic options that instructors can assign for homework. **MyAccountingLab** also replicates the text's exercises and problems so that students are familiar and comfortable working with the material.

Instructor's Manual

The Instructor's Manual, available electronically or in print, offers course-specific content including a guide to available resources, a road map for using **MyAccountingLab**, a first-day handout for students, sample syllabi, and guidelines for teaching an online course, as well as content-specific material including chapter overviews, teaching outlines, student summary handouts, lecture outline tips, assignment grids, ten-minute quizzes, and more!

Instructor Resource Center www.pearsonhighered.com/reimers

For your convenience, many of our instructor supplements are available for download from the textbook's catalog page or from **MyAccountingLab**. Available resources include:

- **Solutions Manual** containing the fully worked-through and accuracy-checked solutions for every question, exercise, and problem in the text.
- **Test Item File with TestGen Software** providing over 1,600 multiple choice, true/false, and problem-solving questions correlated by Learning Objective and difficulty level as well as AACSB and AICPA standards.
- **Author-Reviewed PowerPoint Presentations.** There are 508 Compliant Instructor PowerPoints with extensive notes for on-campus or online classes, and Student PowerPoints.
- **Excel in Practice**
- **Image Library**
- **Working Papers and Solutions**
- **Instructors' Manual**

Course Cartridges

Course Cartridges for BlackBoard, WebCT, CourseCompass, and other learning management systems are available upon request.

Provide More "I Get It!" Moments.

New! End-of-Chapter Material Integrated with MyAccountingLab at: www.myaccountinglab.com
Students need practice and repetition in order to successfully learn the fundamentals of financial accounting. The **MyAccountingLab** course for *Financial Accounting: A Business Process Approach, third edition*, now contains book-match and algorithmic Short Exercises, Exercises, and Problems. This makes it easy to assign homework, and provides practice that's relevant to each chapter. In addition, IFRS coverage has been added so students can see how IFRS will impact decisions in accounting.

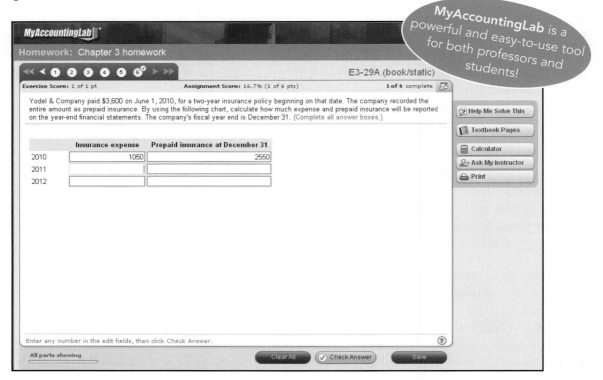

Powerful Homework and Test Manager
Create, import, and manage online homework assignments, quizzes, and tests that are automatically graded, allowing you to spend less time grading and more time teaching. Create assignments from online exercises directly correlated to the textbook. Homework exercises include guided solutions and other tools to help students understand and master concepts.

Comprehensive Gradebook Tracking
MyAccountingLab's online Gradebook automatically tracks your students' results on tests, homework, and tutorials, and gives you control over managing results and calculating grades. All **MyAccountingLab** grades can be exported to a spreadsheet program, such as Microsoft® Excel. The **MyAccountingLab** Gradebook provides a number of views of student data and gives you the flexibility to weight assignments, select which attempts to include when calculating scores, and omit or delete results for individual assignments.

About the Author

For the past six years, Jane Reimers has been a member of the faculty at the Crummer Graduate School of Business at Rollins College. Previously, she taught at Florida State University and Duke University.

Professor Reimers grew up in the Orlando area, earning her bachelor's degree at the University of Florida. She worked as a high school math teacher and as an auditor with a national accounting firm in Orlando before going on to the University of Michigan where she earned a Ph.D. in accounting. In 2009, she won the Cornell Outstanding Faculty in Crummer Award. She has published research in the *Journal of Accounting Research*, *The Accounting Review*, *Auditing: A Journal of Practice and Theory*, *Accounting Horizons*, *Decision Sciences*, and *Accounting, Organizations and Society*.

Acknowledgments

Instructors from colleges and universities across the country helped with the revision of *Financial Accounting: A Business Approach*. Their suggestions and comments were invaluable. All of the Prentice Hall people who worked on this edition also deserve my thanks. At the top of that list is Karen Misler, the developmental editor for this edition. Her skill, insight, and patience were astounding. I want to give special thanks to Christopher Evans, a friend and former graduate student of mine, for his invaluable help with this revision. I am grateful to all of the following people for their help.

Reviewers of the third edition:

Robert Derstine, Villanova University

Anthony Greig, Purdue University

John Hathorn, Metropolitan State College

Jeff Hillard, Baltimore County Community College

Nancy Lynch, West Virginia University

Joyce Middleton, Frostburg State University

Susan Minke, Indiana University – Purdue University Fort Wayne

Aamer Sheikh, Quinnipiac University

Pavani Tallapalli, Slippery Rock University of Pennsylvania

Craig Vilhauer, Merced College

Accuracy checkers:

Anthony Greig, Purdue University

Joyce Middleton, Frostburg State University

Richard J. Pettit, Mountain View College

Carolyn Streuly

To the loyal users of previous editions of my book: Your support has made this revision possible. You have inspired me with your dedication to finding the best ways to teach introductory financial accounting. Special thanks to the hundreds of students over the past 20 years who have inspired me to strive to be a better teacher and a better person. Thanks, too, for your specific suggestions for the book.

To my family and friends, including all of my colleagues at Rollins, thank you for all of the opportunities and support you have given me. I am grateful to a handful of special friends who, year after year, continue to go above and beyond anything I could expect from friends. You know who you are. Thank you.

Finally, to my son, thank you for the support and encouragement you have always given me. I continue to learn so much from you and the way you live your life. This book is definitely for you!

Jane L. Reimers
Professor, Crummer Graduate School of Business
Rollins College

1

Business: What's It All About?

LEARNING OBJECTIVES

When you are finished studying Chapter 1, you should be able to:

1. Describe what a business does and the various ways a business can be organized.

2. Classify business transactions as operating, investing, or financing activities.

3. Describe who uses accounting information and why accounting information is important to them.

4. Identify the elements of the four basic financial statements—the income statement, the statement of changes in shareholders' equity, the balance sheet, and the statement of cash flows, explain the purpose of each, and be able to use basic transaction analysis to prepare each statement.

5. Identify the elements of a real company's financial statements.

6. Describe the risks associated with being in business and the part that ethics plays in business.

ETHICS Matters

Ethical Decisions—As Easy as 1-2-3

When you are asked to do something you believe may be unethical, ask yourself the following questions: (1) Is it legal? (2) Will it harm anyone? (3) Would you mind reading about your decision in the morning newspaper? These are not ambiguous or theoretical questions. They are questions that should be part of everyone's decision-making process. An example follows of what can happen if you ignore them.

In 2009, Bernie Madoff pleaded guilty to 11 felony charges associated with a $50 billion Ponzi scheme that lasted for decades. In his own words, Madoff does a pretty good job of explaining what a Ponzi scheme involves:

> The essence of my scheme was that I represented to clients and prospective clients who wished to open investment advisory and individual trading accounts with me that I would invest their money in shares of common stock, options and other securities of large well-known corporations, and upon request, would return to them their profits and principal. Those representations were false because for many years up until I was arrested on December 11, 2008, I never invested those funds in the securities, as I had promised. Instead, those funds were deposited in a bank account at Chase Manhattan Bank. When clients wished to receive the profits they believed they had earned with me or to redeem their principal, I used the money in the Chase Manhattan Bank account that belonged to them or other clients to pay the requested funds. (Source: Document #09-Cr-213(DC) filed with the United States District Court Southern District of New York on March 12, 2009.)

1

Madoff's auditing firm, Friehling & Horowitz, CPAs, has been charged with failing to conduct meaningful, independent audits of Madoff's firm while falsely certifying that it had done so. As you will read later in this chapter, investors depend on auditors to provide an unbiased evaluation of a firm's financial position and performance. As in the big scandals of the early 2000s, such as Enron and WorldCom, people are asking why the auditors didn't find the problems.

Madoff's failure to address our initial three questions, combined with the auditor's failure to do a competent audit, resulted in thousands of people losing their life savings. Madoff's sentence of 150 years in prison will keep him in jail for the rest of his life. As of this writing, the case against the auditor has not been resolved. See if you can find out what happened.

Do you think accounting is important? Anyone who has a television or reads a newspaper is reminded almost every day of the importance of accounting. Now more than ever, it is crucial for people in business to understand basic accounting. In this chapter, you will start with a simple company to learn the basic ideas of how a business works and why the financial reporting for a business is so important to its success. As you learn about accounting, you will understand more and more about what has been happening in our economy and how it relates to accounting information. First, you must understand what a business is all about.

Purpose and Organization of a Business

L.O.1
Describe what a business does and the various ways a business can be organized.

Sara Gonzales loved to play basketball. She also wanted to start her own business. During years of playing on various teams organized by local recreation departments, she noticed that the teams did not have any identifying clothing—no matching outfits or T-shirts. She began her business by ordering T-shirts with a logo monogrammed on them, and the other teams in the area wanted matching T-shirts, too. Today, Sara runs a large Web-based T-shirt business that specializes in shirts for groups of any type. Her company, Team Shirts, has been growing every year in both sales and profit.

How does a business get started and, once started, how does it succeed? Generally, a business is formed to provide goods or services for the purpose of making a profit for its owner or owners. It begins by obtaining financial resources—and that means money. Team Shirts began as a business with $5,000 of Sara's own money and a $500 loan from her sister. The financial resources to start a business—called **capital**—come from the owners of the business (like Sara), who are investors, or from creditors (like Sara's sister), who are lenders.

Capital is the name for the resources used to start and run a business.

Why buy T-shirts from Team Shirts rather than from somewhere else? It's all about value. We order clothes from J.Crew because the company provides added value to us. Instead of going to the mall to buy our clothes, we may prefer the convenience of mail-order delivery. J.Crew's customers find value in this service. What all businesses have in common is that they provide their customers with something of value. A business may start from scratch and create something of value or it may simply add value to an existing product or service. For some customers, the value that J.Crew adds to the product may be its easy order and delivery procedures. For other customers, the added value may be in the specific styles available. Businesses create or add value to earn money for the owners.

A **for-profit firm** has the goal of making a profit for its owners.

An enterprise—another name for a business organization—with this goal is called a **for-profit firm**. In contrast, a firm that provides goods or services for the sole purpose of helping people instead of making a profit is called a **not-for-profit firm**. A not-for-profit firm is more likely to be called an organization or agency than a business. Even though it is called not-for-profit, this type of organization does not mind making a profit. The difference is that a not-for-profit organization uses any profit to provide more goods and services to the people it serves rather than distributing profits to its owners. Both for-profit organizations and not-for-profit organizations provide value. Throughout this book, we will be dealing primarily with for-profit organizations—businesses.

A **not-for-profit firm** has the goal of providing goods or services to its clients.

To be a viable business, Team Shirts needed to provide customers with something of value. Sara found a supplier to make shirts to order and then provided them to her customers.

What Is a Business All About?

A simple model of the firm is shown in Exhibit 1.1.

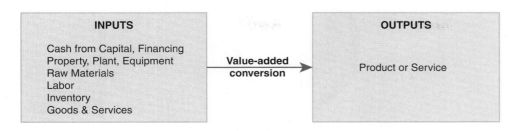

INPUTS		OUTPUTS
Cash from Capital, Financing Property, Plant, Equipment Raw Materials Labor Inventory Goods & Services	Value-added conversion →	Product or Service

EXHIBIT 1.1

The Firm

A firm takes inputs, adds value, and provides the output to its customers.

The inputs in a firm include capital, equipment, inventory, supplies, and labor. The firm acquires goods and services and pays for them. The firm then takes these inputs and converts them into outputs by adding value. The outputs of a firm are its products or services. As the firm carries out these activities—acquiring inputs, converting them to outputs, and providing those outputs to customers—information about these activities is recorded in the company's information system. Both insiders (the owners and the firm's employees) and outsiders (the creditors, governmental agencies, and potential investors) use the information.

A business must successfully plan, control, and evaluate its activities. If it does these activities well, the business will survive. If it does them very well, it will make a profit. Profit is the difference between the revenue—the amount a business earns for the goods it sells or the services it provides—and the expenses of selling those goods or providing those services. When a company takes all of its revenue and subtracts all of the expenses of earning that revenue, the difference is called **net income**. This is a number and a concept that we will focus on throughout this book because of its importance to firms and to investors. The complexity of a company's planning, control, and evaluation processes depends on the type, size, and structure of the business. You will see this as we look at businesses in two ways: the nature of their operations and who owns them.

Net income equals all revenues minus all expenses for a specific period of time.

The Nature of Business Operations

The operation of a business depends on what the business has been formed to do. From that perspective, there are four types of businesses: service, merchandising, manufacturing, and financial services. Although most businesses can be classified as one of these four types, many large businesses are a combination of two or more.

A **service company** provides a service—it does something for you, rather than sells something to you. Services range from activities you cannot see, such as the advice provided by lawyers or tax consultants, to activities you can see, such as house cleaning or car washing. During the past two decades, our economy has been producing more services than goods. Google is an example of a service firm.

A **service company** does something for its customers.

A **merchandising company** buys goods, adds value to them, and then sells them with the added value. It does not make the goods, and it does not buy them to use. Instead, a merchandising business buys the goods for the purpose of adding its own particular value to them and, after adding value, sells them to another company or person.

A **merchandising company** sells a product to its customers.

There are two types of merchandising companies:

- A wholesale company buys goods, adds value, and sells them to other companies (business to business).
- A retail company buys goods, adds value, and sells them to customers who consume them, which is why you will see these customers referred to as "final consumers" (business to consumer). Target, shown in the photo on the following page, is an example of a retail company.

Both wholesale and retail merchandising companies add value to the goods they buy. Wholesale companies are often not familiar to us because we do not buy things from them. Typically, a wholesale firm sells to another business, like a company that sells computer chips to Dell or Apple. A retail firm, on the other hand, sells its products to the final consumer. However, as a result of the ability of firms to sell their products on the Internet, the line between wholesale and retail firms has become blurred. A decade ago you would have purchased this textbook from

Target is an example of a retail firm. It buys goods and sells them to the final consumer.

your school's bookstore—a retail business—and the bookstore would have purchased it from Pearson Education, operating in the role of a wholesale company. Now you can also buy your book directly from Pearson Education's Web site.

A manufacturing company makes the goods it sells.

A **manufacturing company** makes the products it sells. Manufacturing companies vary in size and complexity. Making clay pots and vases in a space no larger than a garage is a manufacturing business. Manufacturing giants such as Boeing and Lockheed Martin, owned by many thousands of people and employing hundreds of thousands of workers at all levels in enormous factories all over the world, are large and complex manufacturing businesses.

Financial services companies deal in services related to money.

Financial services companies do not make tangible products, and they do not sell products made by another company. They deal in services related to money. Banks are one kind of financial services company; they lend money to borrowers to pay for cars, houses, and furniture. Another type of financial services company is an insurance company, which provides some financial protection in the case of loss of life or property. Financial services firms, like Countrywide Mortgage and Merrill Lynch, have been at the center of the 2008 financial crisis.

Your Turn 1-1

1. What is the main purpose of a business?
2. Describe the four general types of businesses and what each does.

Ownership Structure of a Business

No matter what type of product or service it provides, a business must have an owner or owners. The government owns some businesses, but in the United States, an individual or a group of individuals owns most businesses. Business ownership generally takes one of three general forms: a sole proprietorship, a partnership, or a corporation.

SOLE PROPRIETORSHIPS. If a single person owns a business, like the clay pot maker in his garage, it is a **sole proprietorship**. A new business often starts as a sole proprietorship. In the course of running the business, a sole proprietorship accumulates financial information—such

A **sole proprietorship** is a company with a single owner.

Business

Starting A New Business: The Business Plan Includes Financial Statements

Have you ever considered starting your own business? According to the Small Business Administration (SBA*), small businesses—those with fewer than 100 employees—

- represent more than 99.7% of employer firms.
- employ half of all private-sector workers and 41% of workers in high-tech jobs.
- have provided 60%–80% of the net new jobs annually over the last decade.

The SBA was established by Congress in 1953 to assist small businesses. In addition to the many contributions SBA makes to ongoing businesses, the SBA provides information and guidance for starting a business. For example, before Sara started her T-shirt company, she found some terrific information on the SBA Web site, like the fact that she needed to start with a business plan. The SBA describes four sections to be included in the body of the business plan: the business description, marketing, finances, and management.

The business description is the foundation for the rest of the business plan. It should give the form of your business enterprise—a sole proprietorship, a partnership, or a corporation. The business description should also describe the nature of your business—manufacturing, merchandising, or service. Then, more specific details should be explained—goals and objectives, operating procedures, location, personnel, marketing, licenses and insurance, and financing plans. Sara learned about many issues she needed to address before she could start her business, including state and local licensing requirements.

The section on finances should include a start-up budget and a detailed operating budget. The financial statements are prepared based on the budgets. The financial statements are a significant part of a business plan. Sara was lucky enough to learn about the financial statements in an accounting course she took in college. Fortunately, she still had the book on her shelf for reference.

A good business plan is essential for starting a successful company. For more information on the SBA and creating a business plan, visit the SBA Web site at www.sba.gov.

---

*Sources: U.S. Bureau of the Census; Advocacy-funded research. Data provided by the SBA.

---

as the cost of materials, equipment, rent, electricity, and income from sales—but is not required by law to make any of that financial information available to the public. That means the average person is not privy to this information. Naturally, the Department of Revenue in the states where the company operates will receive some of this information from the company's sales tax return.

A business in the form of a sole proprietorship is not separate from its owner in terms of responsibility and liability—the owner is personally responsible for all the decisions made for the business. For example, the income from the business is included as income on the owner's individual income tax return. The business does not have its own tax return.

Also, as a sole proprietor, you are responsible for your company's debts. Your company's bills are your bills; if there is not enough money in your company's "pockets" to pay its bills, then you must pay the bills from your pockets. Moreover, you own the company's assets, and your personal assets are the company's assets—even if those personal assets are the only way of paying your company's bills.

Even though the financial records of a business—the company's books—should always be kept separate from the owner's personal financial records, there is no separation of the sole proprietorship's books and its owner's books for tax and legal purposes. For example, your business checking account should be separate from your personal checking account, but the income you earn from your business and the income you earn from other sources must both be included on your individual, personal tax return.

You will see in Exhibit 1.2 on the following page that there are more sole proprietorships in the United States than any other form of business. Notice, however, that profits for sole proprietorships do not come close to the enormous profits earned by corporations.

PARTNERSHIPS. A business **partnership** is owned by two or more people, although it is similar to a sole proprietorship in the sense that the income both partners earn (or lose) from the business partnership is included on their own personal tax returns. When two or more people form a

> A **partnership** is a company owned by two or more individuals.

EXHIBIT 1.2

Types of Firms and Their Profits

Although over two-thirds of U.S. firms are sole proprietorships, more than two-thirds of firm profits are made by corporations. Source: Internal Revenue Service Web site (www.irs.gov).

Types of Firms

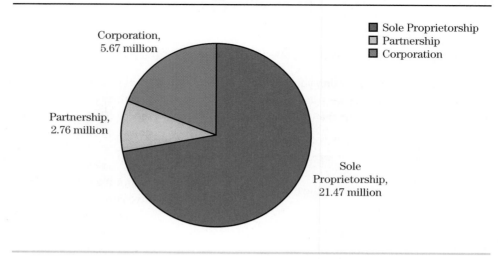

Corporation, 5.67 million
Partnership, 2.76 million
Sole Proprietorship, 21.47 million

- Sole Proprietorship
- Partnership
- Corporation

Profits by Type of Firm

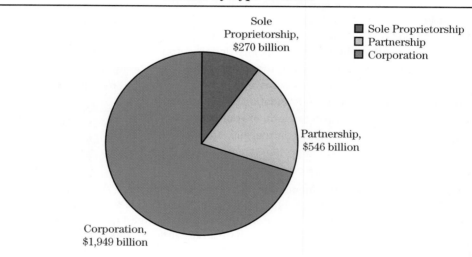

Sole Proprietorship, $270 billion
Partnership, $546 billion
Corporation, $1,949 billion

- Sole Proprietorship
- Partnership
- Corporation

business as partners, they usually hire an attorney to help them define the specific terms of their business relationship. Details regarding how much work each will do and how they will divide the profits from the business are specified in a document called a partnership agreement. Like a sole proprietorship, the owners—each of the partners—are responsible for everything the company does. For example, if the company is sued for violating an employee's civil rights, then the partners are legally liable. The company's assets are the partners' assets, and the company's debts are the partners' debts. Even so, as with a sole proprietorship, the financial records of a partnership should be separate from the partners' personal financial records.

CORPORATIONS. A **corporation** is legally separate and financially separate from its owners. Individual states control the rules for forming corporations within their boundaries. A company must have a corporate charter that describes the business, how the business plans to acquire financing, and how many owners it will be allowed to have. Ownership in a corporation is divided into units called **shares of common stock**, each representing ownership in a fraction of the corporation. An owner of shares of stock in a corporation is called a **stockholder** or a **shareholder**. Most corporations have many shareholders, although there is no minimum number of owners required. A corporation whose shares of stock are owned by a very small number of people is called a closely held corporation.

As legal entities, corporations may enter into contracts just like individuals. A corporation pays taxes on its earnings. A corporation's owners do not include the corporation's income in

A **corporation** is a special legal form for a business in which the business is a legal entity separate from the owners. A corporation may have a single owner or a large number of owners.

Shares of common stock are the units of ownership in a corporation.

Stockholders or **shareholders** are the owners of the corporation.

their personal tax returns—unlike the owner of a sole proprietorship or the partners in a partnership. Each individual corporation owner does not have individual legal responsibility for the corporation's actions, as is true for the owners of a sole proprietorship or partnership. For example, a shareholder cannot be sued for the illegal actions of the corporation. The managers are held responsible for the actions of the corporation, and only the corporation's assets are at risk.

Dell Inc. is one of America's best-known corporations. Dell Inc. was founded in 1984 by Michael Dell, currently the computer industry's longest-tenured chief executive officer, on this simple concept: By selling computers directly to customers, Dell Inc. could get a clear picture of its customers' needs and then efficiently provide the most effective products to meet those needs. The company has offered new shares of stock to anyone who is able and willing to invest in the company by making them available for sale on a stock exchange. A **stock exchange** is a marketplace for buying and selling shares of a publicly-traded corporation.

After the shares are issued—sold for the first time to the public—investors who want to become owners of a corporation may purchase the shares from people who want to sell the same shares. The buyers and sellers get together, usually through a stockbroker, by using a stock exchange. Stockbrokers represent people who want to buy shares and the people who want to sell shares of a corporation. Stockbrokers work for firms like Charles Schwab. There are several stock exchanges—known collectively as the **stock market**—in the United States; the New York Stock Exchange is the largest. If you wanted to be one of the owners of Dell Inc., you could purchase shares by contacting a stockbroker.

Another way to buy or sell shares of stock—also known as *trading*—is to use the Internet. Many companies now provide a way for investors to buy and sell stock without a stockbroker. As Internet usage continues to grow at an incredible pace, more and more people are taking advantage of electronic trading in shares of stock.

Regulation Shareholders usually hire people who are not owners of the corporation to manage the business of the corporation. This separation of ownership and management can create problems. For example, there may be a large number of owners, and they may be far away from the location of the business. How can the owners be sure that the managers are running the corporation the way the owners want it to be run? How do the owners monitor the managers to be sure they are not taking advantage of the power of being a manager of a large company, for example, buying expensive items like country club memberships and luxury cars for the business?

To protect the owners with respect to issues like these, the government created the **Securities and Exchange Commission (SEC)** to monitor the activities and financial reporting of corporations that sell shares of ownership on the stock exchanges. The SEC sets the rules for stock exchanges and for the financial reporting of publicly-traded corporations for the entire United States. The degree of regulation for corporations depends on the size and nature of the business. A business that provides an essential product or service, such as electric power generating companies, has more rules to follow than a business that provides something not essential, but discretionary, such as toys. Large companies have more rules than smaller companies because large companies provide more opportunities for managers to take advantage of the owners. Due to the financial crisis that began in 2008, financial firms like banks and mortgage companies will be subject to many new regulations in the future.

Advantages of a Corporation Advantages of the corporate structure of a business organization include the following:

- Investors can diversify their financial risk. Being able to buy a small share in a variety of corporations means that persons are able to balance the risks they are taking as business owners. For example, an investor may own shares in a soft drink company and also own shares in a coffee company. If coffee companies have a bad year due to a shortage of coffee beans, people will be likely to buy more soft drinks. By owning a little of each type of company, an investor reduces overall risk.
- Owners have limited liability. Individual owners risk only the amount of money they have invested in the company, that is the amount they paid for the shares of stock. If the corporation is found legally responsible for injury to an employee or customer, or if the business fails, only the corporation's assets are at risk—not the owner's personal property. (In contrast, there is no limit to the legal liability of a sole proprietor or a partner. Both the assets of the business and the personal assets of the owner or owners are at risk.)

A **stock exchange** is a marketplace where buyers and sellers exchange their shares of stock. Buying and selling shares of stock can also be done on the Internet.

The **stock market** is the name for a collection of stock exchanges. It is a term generally used to designate any place where stock is bought and sold.

The **Securities and Exchange Commission (SEC)** is the governmental agency that monitors the stock market and the financial reporting of the firms that trade in the market.

Disadvantages of a Corporation   Disadvantages of the corporate structure of a business organization include the following:

- Separation of management and ownership creates a difference in knowledge about the operations of the business. Suppose you own 100 shares of Dell Inc. stock. The managers of Dell will know many details of the business that you do not know. For example, the managers are aware of all possible investment options for the company's extra cash. They may select the option that minimizes clerical work, whereas an owner might prefer an option that involves more work but would secure a higher return.

  There are literally thousands of such details that owners do not know, many of which they do not even want to know. However, the owners want some assurance that managers are acting in the best interests of the shareholders. Owners need information about how well the business is doing to assess how the actions and decisions of the managers are affecting the business. The owners need some assurance that managers are providing complete and accurate information about the business. Both the individual states and the SEC at the federal level set rules for the financial reporting of corporations. A corporation's type of business and its size determine how extensive its reporting requirements are. We will come back to this subject many times throughout our discussions of financial accounting, especially given the current economic environment and the new reporting regulations that are certain to be developed in the next few years.

Dividends are the earnings of a corporation distributed to the owners of the corporation.

- Corporate income is taxed twice. Unlike a sole proprietorship or partnership, a corporation pays income taxes on its net income. Then, net income (or at least a part of it) may be divided by the number of shareholders of the corporation and distributed among shareholders as **dividends**. The shareholders must include the dividend income on their personal tax returns. This amounts to double taxation on the same income. The income of the corporation—which is owned by shareholders—is taxed as corporation income, and then the amount passed on to owners as dividend income is again taxed as personal income. (Current tax laws do allow some special treatment for dividend income to the shareholder, so this disadvantage can be reduced by a change in the tax law.)

LIMITED LIABILITY PARTNERSHIPS (LLP) AND CORPORATIONS (LLC). In the past 10 years, new business forms with some characteristics of a partnership and some characteristics of a corporation have become commonplace. Both LLPs and LLCs have the tax advantages of a partnership and the legal liability advantages of a corporation.

An LLP is a business form mostly of interest to partners in professions such as law, medicine, and accounting. An LLP's owners—who are the partners—are not personally liable for the malpractice of the other partners. They are personally liable for many types of obligations owed to the LLP's creditors, lenders, and landlords. Owners of an LLP report their share of profit or loss on their personal tax returns. The LLP form of business organization is not available in all states, and it is often limited to a short list of professions—usually attorneys and accountants. You will notice that the four largest international accounting firms have all taken this organizational form. The letters LLP will appear after the firm's name.

An LLC is a corporation that has characteristics of a partnership. It has the advantage of limited liability like a regular corporation with the tax advantage of a partnership. It generally requires less paperwork and documentation than a regular corporation.

Your Turn 1-2

1. What are the three major forms of business ownership?
2. From the owners' point of view, what are the advantages and disadvantages of each form of ownership?

L.O.2
Classify business transactions as operating, investing, or financing activities.

Business Activities and the Flow of Goods and Services

A person who takes the risk of starting a business is often called an *entrepreneur*. Our entrepreneur, Sara, started a T-shirt business. Exhibit 1.3 shows the events for Team Shirts that followed. Identifying those events and analyzing the transactions are the first steps in understanding how a business works.

EXHIBIT 1.3

How a Business Works

These business transactions show Team Shirts' first month of business.

We can classify each step in the process of developing a business in terms of exchanges—who gets what and who gives what in return. One of the important functions of accounting is to provide information about these economic exchanges, also known as business transactions. In accounting, we often classify transactions as operating activities, investing activities, or financing activities. Operating activities are transactions related to the general operations of a firm—what the firm is in business to do. Investing activities are transactions related to buying and selling items that the firm will use for longer than a year. Financing activities are those that deal with how a business gets its funding—how it obtains the capital needed to finance the business.

The first exchange starts the business—Sara invests her own $5,000 in the business. From the perspective of the business, this is called a contribution. It is often called **contributed capital**. As with all transactions, we look at this from the point of view of the business entity. This transaction is the exchange of cash for ownership in the business. Because this transaction deals with the way Team Shirts is financed, it is classified as a financing transaction.

> **Contributed capital** is an owner's investment in a company.

You may need to think about it to see the *give* part of this exchange—it is the business giving ownership to Sara. Because Sara has chosen to organize her business firm as a corporation, this share of ownership is called stock. For a sole proprietorship or a partnership, the ownership has no special name. Sara has chosen the corporate form of organization because of the limited legal liability of a corporation. The *get* part of the exchange is the business getting the $5,000 cash. Because Sara is the only shareholder, she owns 100% of the stock.

The second transaction is between Team Shirts and Sara's sister. The business borrows $500 from Sara's sister. Team Shirts gets an economic resource—cash—and in exchange Team Shirts gives an I-owe-you (IOU). From the perspective of Team Shirts, this transaction involves a cash receipt. Borrowing money to finance a business is the get side of the exchange. The give side is the IOU to Sara's sister. Technically, it is not really the give side until Sara repays the loan with cash. The IOU is useful for describing the timing difference between the time of the get and give sides of the exchange. We will see a lot of examples of this type of timing difference in accounting for business events. Again, this transaction is a financing activity.

The next transaction is the company's purchase of 100 T-shirts with unique logos on them. The get part of the exchange is when Team Shirts gets the shirts for the inventory. The give part of the exchange is when Team Shirts gives cash to the T-shirt manufacturer. Remember, the exchange is seen through the eyes of Team Shirts. The transaction would look different if we took the perspective of the T-shirt manufacturer. In business problems, we take one point of view throughout a problem or an analysis. This transaction is an operating activity.

The next transaction is the acquisition of a service. The economic resources exchanged in this transaction are advertising and cash. The get part is the acquisition or purchase of advertising brochures. The give part is a cash disbursement transaction. Again, this is an operating activity.

Team Shirts now sells the T-shirts, exchanging T-shirts for cash. Once again, the activity is an operating activity, precisely what Team Shirts is in business to do—sell T-shirts.

Finally, Team Shirts repays the $500 loan from Sara's sister plus interest. The company gives the economic resource of cash (amount of the loan, called the **principal**, plus **interest**, a cost of borrowing the money) to Sara's sister. Recall that the actual get part of this exchange occurred near the beginning of our story. The second transaction was when Team Shirts took the cash, as a loan, from Sara's sister. The IOU was a sort of marker, indicating that there would be a timing difference in the get and give parts of this transaction. Repayment of the principal of a loan is a financing activity. Payment of interest, on the other hand, is considered an operating activity.

> The **principal** of a loan is the amount of money borrowed.

> The **interest** is the cost of borrowing money—using someone else's money.

Your Turn 1-3

1. What are the two sources of financing for a business, both used by Team Shirts?
2. What do you call the cost of using someone else's money?

L.O.3
Describe who uses accounting information and why accounting information is important to them.

Revenue is the amount the company has earned from providing goods or services to customers.

Expenses are the costs incurred to generate revenue.

Information Needs for Decision Making in Business

To start a new business, Sara had many decisions to make. First, how would she finance it? What organizational form should it take? How many T-shirts should she buy? From whom should she buy them? How much should she pay for advertising? How much should she charge for the shirts?

After the first complete operating cycle, shown in Exhibit 1.4—beginning with cash, converting cash to inventory, selling the inventory, and turning inventory sales back into cash—Sara has more decisions to make. Should she buy T-shirts and do the whole thing again? If so, should she buy more T-shirts than she bought the first time and from the same vendor? To make these decisions, Sara must have information. The kind of information usually provided by accountants will provide the basis for getting a good picture of the performance of her business.

* What was the **revenue** from sales during the accounting period? An accounting period is any length of time that a company uses to evaluate its operating performance. It can be a month, a quarter, or a year.
* What **expenses** were incurred so those sales could be made?
* What was net income—the difference between revenues and expenses?
* What goods does Team Shirts have left at the end of the period?
* Should Sara increase or lower the price of the T-shirts she sells?

In addition to this kind of financial information, there is other information that can help Sara make decisions about her business. For example, Sara would want information on the reliability of different vendors and the quality of their merchandise to decide which vendor to use next time.

EXHIBIT 1.4

The Operating Cycle

The operating cycle shows how a firm starts with cash and, after providing goods to its customers, ends up with more cash.

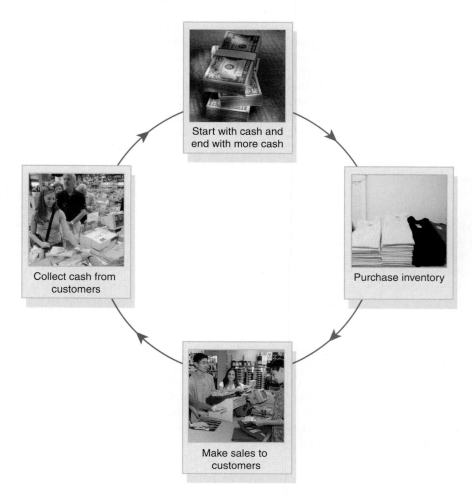

Start with cash and end with more cash

Purchase inventory

Make sales to customers

Collect cash from customers

Before the advances in computer technology that have enabled us to collect, organize, and report huge quantities of information, a company had only the basic financial information to help make its business decisions. Today, financial information is just a part of a firm's information system.

A modern supermarket is a great example of a business that collects a tremendous amount of information. With a simple, swift swipe of the grocery item bar code past the checkout scanner, the store information system collects product data, recording and tracking information about vendors, product shelf life, customer preferences and buying habits, and the typical financial information such as price and quantity of each item sold. As we look at business processes and the information needed to run a business, we will pay attention to the information reflected in the basic financial statements—the income statement, the balance sheet, the statement of changes in shareholders' equity, and the statement of cash flows. You will learn more about each of these statements soon.

---

1. What are revenues and expenses?
2. What are the four basic financial statements?

Your Turn 1-4

Who Needs Information about Transactions of the Business?

No part of any business can operate without information. The functions of the management of a company are to plan, to control, and to evaluate the operation of the business. To perform these functions effectively, management must have information about what the business has done, about what it is currently doing, and about where it looks like it is going or should be going. Traditionally, the accounting information system has provided only very general data about the past transactions of a business firm. A business firm used to keep at least two sets of records, each for specific purposes: one set for financial reporting and one set for internal decision making. Now, with modern computers and software that can organize information in a variety of ways with a few simple commands, one information system can accumulate and organize all data of a company. The managers of each business area—usually referred to as a department—can obtain and use whatever information is relevant to the decisions they make. Accountants, too, can obtain the information they need for preparing the basic financial statements.

SETTING GUIDELINES. The financial statements are based on a set of guidelines called **generally accepted accounting principles (GAAP)**. These guidelines are not exact rules. As you learn more about accounting, you will see that the amounts on the financial statements are not exact. To make the financial statements useful, we need to understand the guidelines and the choices used to construct them. Who sets the guidelines for financial reporting? As shown in Exhibit 1.5 on the following page, at the top of the authority chain is the Securities and Exchange Commission.

In the 1930s, Congress established the SEC to set the rules for corporations that trade on the public stock exchanges. The SEC has delegated much of the responsibility for setting financial standards to an independent group called the **Financial Accounting Standards Board (FASB)**. This is a group of professional business people, accountants, and accounting scholars who have the responsibility of setting current accounting standards. Accounting standards dictate the way business events are reported, so it makes sense that businesses are very interested in what the FASB does. The newest player in the rule-setting game is a group called the **Public Company Accounting Oversight Board (PCAOB)**. Mandated by the Sarbanes-Oxley Act in 2002, this independent board was created to oversee the auditing profession and public company audits.

INTERNATIONAL FINANCIAL REPORTING STANDARDS. Although U.S. GAAP are currently the set of standards used by U.S. firms, there is another widely used set of accounting standards called the **International Financial Reporting Standards (IFRS)**. These standards, similar in many ways to GAAP, are used in many other places around the world. They are set by a group called the **International Accounting Standards Board (IASB)**, similar to the FASB. As a matter of fact, there is a member of FASB who also sits on the IASB. In 2008, the SEC published a "roadmap to IFRS" that details how and when U.S. GAAP should converge with IFRS so that one global set of standards is used by all major economies. The SEC plan calls for implementation of IFRS in the United States by 2014. Currently, there is some resistance and a great deal of uncertainty regarding this change. Throughout this book, we will look at some of the ways GAAP and IFRS differ and the implications for firms' financial statements. This is an ongoing issue, so you should look for developments in the popular business press.

Generally accepted accounting principles (GAAP) are the guidelines for financial reporting.

The **Financial Accounting Standards Board (FASB)** is the group that sets accounting standards. It gets its authority from the SEC.

The **Public Company Accounting Oversight Board (PCAOB)** is a group formed to oversee the auditing profession and the audits of public companies. Its creation was mandated by the Sarbanes-Oxley Act of 2002.

The **International Financial Reporting Standards (IFRS)** are international guidelines for financial reporting, used in many places around the world.

The **International Accounting Standards Board (IASB)** is the group that sets international financial reporting standards.

EXHIBIT 1.5

Who Sets the Guidelines for Financial Reporting?

The U.S. Congress established the Securities and Exchange Commission (SEC) in 1934. Auditing standards are set by the Public Company Accounting Oversight Board (PCAOB), and accounting standards (GAAP) are set by the Financial Accounting Standards Board (FASB).

Securities and Exchange Commission (SEC)

Public Company Accounting Oversight Board (PCAOB)

In response to the 2001–2002 discovery of accounting scandals, the SEC created the PCAOB to oversee the auditing profession and the audit of public companies.

Financial Accounting Standards Board (FASB)

The SEC has delegated much of the standards-setting responsibility to the FASB. The SEC retains and sometimes exercises the right to set accounting standards.

In many industries, there are regulatory agencies that require specific information from companies, particularly corporations. For example, the SEC requires corporations that trade on the stock exchanges to file many different kinds of reports about the company's transactions. We will come back to this topic near the end of the chapter when we turn our attention to real company financial statements.

For all businesses, payroll taxes and sales taxes must be reported and paid to state revenue agencies. The **Internal Revenue Service (IRS)** requires information from businesses concerning income and expenses, even if the income from the business flows through to the owners as it does for sole proprietorships and partnerships.

When a company wants to borrow money, creditors—the people and firms who lend money—require information about the company before they will lend money. Banks want to be sure that the loans they make will be repaid. The creditworthiness—a term indicating that a borrower has in the past made loan payments when due (or failed to make them when due)—of a business must be supported with information about the business. This information is usually very specific and very detailed.

The **Internal Revenue Service (IRS)** is the federal agency responsible for federal income tax collection.

OTHER USERS OF ACCOUNTING INFORMATION. Who else needs information about the business? Potential investors are information consumers. Suppose Sara wanted to find additional owners for her T-shirt business. That means she would be looking for someone who wanted to invest money in her T-shirt business in return for a portion of ownership in the company. A potential owner would want some reliable information about the business before making a financial investment. Publicly-traded corporations—whose shares are traded on the stock exchanges—invite anyone willing and financially able to become an owner by offering for sale shares of stock in the corporation. Buying the stock of a corporation is investing in that corporation. Investors want information about a company before they will buy that company's stock. The SEC requires that the information provided by companies whose stock is publicly traded be accurate and reliable. That means the information in their financial statements must be audited. Audited information means it has been examined by professional accountants, called **certified public accountants (CPAs)**. We will talk more about that when we turn our attention to real company financial statements.

Finally, current and potential vendors, customers, and employees also need useful information about the company. They need to evaluate a company's financial condition to make decisions about working for, or doing business with, the company.

Accounting Information: A Part of the Firm's Information System

Have you ever filed an address change with a company only to find later that one department uses your new address, while another department of that same company continues to use your old address? Even with such common data as customer names and addresses, the information is often gathered and maintained in several different places within the same organization. As computers and databases become more common, central data information systems are replacing departmental systems and eliminating their inefficiencies.

Because accountants have traditionally been the recorders and maintainers of financial information, it makes sense that they have expanded their role as the keepers of business information systems to include more than financial information. The cost of obtaining and storing business information has decreased rapidly in the past few years. The financial accounting information a company reports is now just a part of the total available business information. For example, the information a firm uses to file its tax return is not the same information that shareholders need. People who know very little about accounting often think that accounting means taxes. This is not true. Tax accounting and financial accounting are very different. The goal of reporting to the IRS is usually to minimize the amount of taxes owed (within the law), and the goal of financial reporting is to provide useful information to the shareholders and other external parties (not including the IRS) to make investment and credit decisions. Financial accounting information is provided in four basic financial statements and supporting notes.

Generally, accounting is divided into two major areas: financial accounting and managerial accounting. Financial accounting deals with the financial reporting primarily for those outside the firm, like creditors and shareholders. Managerial accounting, on the other hand, deals with information needs and uses inside the firm. Managerial accounting is addressed in another course. In this textbook, we will be studying financial accounting.

Overview of the Financial Statements

There are four financial statements a company uses to report its financial condition at a point in time and operations for a period of time.

1. Balance sheet
2. Income statement
3. Statement of changes in shareholders' equity
4. Statement of cash flows

A company's set of financial statements includes these four basic statements as well as an important section called **notes to the financial statements**. These notes, sometimes referred to as *footnotes*, are an integral part of the set of financial statements. The notes describe the company's major accounting policies and provide other disclosures to help external users better understand the financial statements. As you learn about the four statements, remember that you will be able to find additional information about each in the notes.

In this chapter, we will look at each financial statement briefly. Later chapters will go into each in detail.

Balance Sheet

A **balance sheet** describes the financial situation of a company at a specific point in time. It is a snapshot that captures the items of value the business possesses at a particular moment and how the company has financed them. A balance sheet has three parts:

• Assets
• Liabilities
• Shareholders' equity

A **certified public accountant (CPA)** is someone who has met specific education and exam requirements set up by individual states to make sure that only individuals with the appropriate qualifications can perform audits. To sign an audit report, an accountant must be a CPA.

L.O.4
Identify the elements of the four basic financial statements—the income statement, the statement of changes in shareholders' equity, the balance sheet, and the statement of cash flows, explain the purpose each, and be able to use basic transaction analysis to prepare each statement.

Notes to the financial statements are information provided with the four basic statements that describe the company's major accounting policies and provide other disclosures to help external users better understand the financial statements.

The **balance sheet** shows a summary of each element of the accounting equation: assets, liabilities, and shareholders' equity.

Assets—economic resources owned or controlled by the business.

Liabilities—obligations of the business; amounts owed to creditors.

Shareholders' equity—the owners' claims to the assets of the company. There are two types: contributed capital and retained earnings.

Retained earnings is the total of all net income amounts minus all dividends paid in the life of the company. It is descriptively named—it is the earnings that have been kept (retained) in the company. The amount of retained earnings represents the part of the owner's claims that the company has earned (i.e., not contributed). Retained earnings is *not* the same as cash.

Assets are economic resources owned or controlled by a business. They provide future benefits to the firm. Cash and equipment are common assets. When a business has an asset, someone has the rights to, that is, a claim to, that asset. There is a claim on every asset in a business. There are two groups who might have claims to a company's assets—creditors and owners.

The claims of creditors are called liabilities. **Liabilities** are amounts the business owes to others outside the business—those who have loaned money to the company and have not yet been fully repaid. For example, the amount of a loan—like your car loan—is a liability.

The claims of the owners are called **shareholders' equity**. Stockholders' equity and owners' equity are other names for the claims of the owners. Shareholders' equity is also called net assets because it is the amount left over after the amount of the liabilities is subtracted from the amount of the assets. Another way to say this is that liabilities are netted out of assets.

There are two ways for the owners to increase their claims to the assets of the business. One is by making contributions, and the other is by earning a net income. When the business is successful, the equity that results from doing business and is kept in the company is called **retained earnings**. We will see the difference between contributed capital and retained earnings more clearly when we go through the first month of business for Team Shirts.

Together, assets, liabilities, and shareholders' equity make up the balance sheet, one of the four basic financial statements. The second equation below is called the accounting equation, and it is the basis for the balance sheet:

$$\text{Assets} = \underbrace{\qquad\qquad \text{Claims} \qquad\qquad}$$
$$\text{Assets} = \text{Liabilities} + \text{Shareholders' equity}$$

Each transaction that takes place in a business can be recorded in the accounting equation. In other words, every transaction changes the balance sheet; but the balance sheet must stay in balance. Look at the transactions for Team Shirts for January and see how each one changes the accounting equation.

Date	Transaction
January 1	Sara contributes $5,000 of her own money to start the business in exchange for common stock.
January 1	Team Shirts borrows $500 from Sara's sister for the business.
January 5	Team Shirts buys 100 T-shirts for inventory for $400 cash.
January 10	Team Shirts pays a public relations firm $50 cash for advertising brochures.
January 20	Team Shirts sells 90 of the T-shirts in inventory for $10 each (cash).
January 30	Team Shirts repays Sara's sister the $500 plus $5 interest.
January 31	Team Shirts declares and pays a $100 dividend.

Before the first transaction, there are no assets, no liabilities, and no shareholders' equity. So the accounting equation is as follows:

Assets	=	Liabilities	+	Shareholders' equity
0		0		0

Sara starts her company as a corporation. That means the owner's equity will be called shareholder's equity (note the singular form because there is only one owner), and her initial contribution will be classified as common stock. We will discuss the details of shareholder's equity in Chapter 8. This is how the first transaction affects the accounting equation:

Assets	=	Liabilities	+	Shareholder's equity
$5,000 cash		0		$5,000 common stock

Also on January 1, Team Shirts borrows $500. This is how the second transaction affects the accounting equation:

Assets	=	Liabilities	+	Shareholder's equity
$500 cash		$500 notes payable		0

A balance sheet can be prepared at any point in time to show the assets, liabilities, and shareholder's equity for the company. If Team Shirts prepared a balance sheet on January 2, 2010, these two transactions would be reflected in the amounts on the statement. Exhibit 1.6 shows the balance sheet at that time. With every subsequent transaction the balance sheet will change.

Team Shirts
Balance Sheet
At January 2, 2010

Assets		Liabilities and Shareholder's Equity	
Cash	$5,500	Note payable	$ 500
		Common stock	5,000
Total assets	$5,500	Total liabilities and shareholder's equity	$5,500

EXHIBIT 1.6

Balance Sheet for Team Shirts at January 2, 2010
This shows a balance sheet after just two days of business for Team Shirts. Notice that the accounting equation is in balance: assets = liabilities + shareholder's equity.

There are several characteristics of the balance sheet that you should notice in Exhibit 1.6. First, the heading on every financial statement specifies three things:

- The name of the company
- The name of the financial statement
- The date or time period covered by the statement

The date on the balance sheet is one specific date. If the business year for Team Shirts, also known as its **fiscal year**, is from January 1 to December 31, the balance sheet at the beginning of the first year of business is empty. Until there is a transaction, there are no assets, no liabilities, and no shareholder's equity.

The balance sheet in Exhibit 1.6 for Team Shirts is dated January 2, 2010. Team Shirts has been in business for only two days. Even though a business would be unlikely to prepare a balance sheet just two days after starting the business, this is what the balance sheet for Team Shirts would look like on January 2, 2010. The balance sheet shows the financial condition—assets, liabilities, and shareholder's equity—at the close of business on January 2, 2010. At this time, Team Shirts had received $5,000 from the owner, Sara, and had borrowed $500 from Sara's sister. The total cash—$5,500—is shown as an asset, and the liability of $500 plus the shareholder's equity of $5,000 together show who has claim to the company's assets.

Because the balance sheet gives the financial position of a company at a specific point in time, a new, updated balance sheet could be produced after every transaction. However, no company would want that much information! When a company presents its revenues and expenses for an accounting period, the information makes up the income statement. The company must show the balance sheet at the beginning of that period and the balance sheet at the end of that period. Those two balance sheets are called **comparative balance sheets**. For Team Shirts, the first balance sheet for the fiscal year is empty. That is, at the beginning of the day on January 1, 2010, the accounting equation was 0 = 0 + 0. Before we look at the balance sheet at January 31, 2010, we need to see the income statement for the month of January. We need the information on the income statement to see what happened during the time between the two balance sheets.

> A **fiscal year** is a year in the life of a business. It may or may not coincide with the calendar year.

> **Comparative balance sheets** are the balance sheets from consecutive fiscal years for a single company. The ending balance sheet for one fiscal year is the beginning balance sheet for the next fiscal year.

---

1. What are the two parts of shareholders' equity?
2. What is a fiscal year?

Your Turn 1-5

Before we prepare an income statement for January for Team Shirts or a balance sheet at January 31, 2010, we will look at each transaction that took place in January and see how each affects the accounting equation. This analysis is shown in Exhibit 1.7 on the following page.

EXHIBIT 1.7

Accounting Equation Worksheet for Team Shirts for January

All of a firm's transactions can be shown in the accounting equation worksheet. The income statement is made up of the transactions in the red box—everything that is in the retained earnings column EXCEPT dividends. The income statement transactions (revenues and expenses) are then condensed into one number (net income), which becomes part of the statement of changes in shareholder's equity, indicated by the yellow box. Then, the information from the statement of changes in shareholder's equity is summarized as part of the balance sheet, shown in blue. All of the transactions have directly or indirectly affected the balance sheet. The balance sheet reports the condensed and summarized information from the transactions, indicated by the amounts in the last row (balances at 1/31/2010). The fourth statement, the statement of cash flows, indicated by the green box, shows how the company got its cash and how it spent its cash during the accounting period.

Date	Transaction	Assets			= Liabilities		+ Shareholder's Equity	
							Contributed Capital	Retained Earnings
		Cash	All other assets	(Account)	All liabilities	(Account)	Common stock	(Account)
1/1/2010	Company receives $5,000 contribution from Sara in exchange for common stock.	$5,000					$5,000	
1/1/2010	Company borrows $500 from Sara's sister.	500			500	Notes payable		
1/5/2010	Company buys 100 shirts for inventory for $4 each.	(400)	400	Inventory				
1/10/2010	Company purchases advertising for $50 cash.	(50)						(50) Advertising expense
1/20/2010	Company sells 90 shirts for $10 each, cash. (Inventory goes down.)	900	(360)	Inventory				900 Sales revenue / (360) Cost of goods sold
1/30/2010	Company pays off $500 loan plus $5 interest.	(505)			(500)	Notes payable		(5) Interest expense
1/31/2010	Company declares and pays $100 dividend.	(100)						(100) Dividends
Balances 1/31/2010		**$5,345**	**+ $ 40**		**= 0**		**+ $5,000**	**+ $385**

━ Income statement　━ Statement of changes in shareholder's equity　━ Balance sheet　━ Statement of cash flows

When a business is started, it begins with an empty balance sheet. For Team Shirts, there are no assets, and therefore no claims at the start of business on January 1, 2010. The first two trans-actions that started the business, Sara's contribution of $5,000 and the loan from Sara's sister for $500, occurred on January 1, 2010. First, Sara's contribution increases assets by $5,000 and share-holder's equity by $5,000, because the owner, Sara, has claim to the new asset. Then, the loan increases assets by $500 and liabilities by $500. The company receives an asset (cash) and a cred-itor (Sara's sister) has claim to it. Following these two beginning transactions, the operations of the business begin. Each transaction that takes place during the month is shown as it affects the balance sheet. Study each transaction in Exhibit 1.7 as you read the following descriptions:

- On January 5, cash is decreased by $400 and inventory is increased by $400. This is called an asset exchange, because the company is simply exchanging one asset (cash) for another asset (inventory). Notice the entire effect of this exchange on the accounting equation is on one side of the equation. That is perfectly acceptable. Also notice an asset exchange has no effect on shareholder's equity. Sara still has claim to the same dollar amount of assets.

- On January 10, Sara pays $50 for advertising brochures. This is a cost Team Shirts has incurred to generate revenue. Assets are decreased and retained earnings, a component of shareholder's equity, is decreased. Why is retained earnings decreased? Because when assets are decreased by $50, someone's claim must be reduced. In this case, the shareholder's claims are reduced when assets are decreased. Retained earnings is the part of shareholder's equity that reflects the amount of equity the business has earned. (Throughout this book, as you study the transactions that take place in a business, you will see that all revenues increase retained earnings and all expenses decrease retained earnings.)

- On January 20, Team Shirts sells 90 T-shirts for $10 each. This sale increases assets (cash) by $900. Who has claim to this asset? The shareholder has this claim. Revenues increase retained earnings. At the time of the sale, an asset is reduced. The company no longer has 90 of the original 100 T-shirts in the inventory. Because each shirt costs $4 (and we recorded the T-shirts at their original cost), the firm now must reduce the asset inventory by $360. That reduction in assets is an expense and so shareholder's claims—via retained earnings—are reduced by the amount of that expense.

- On January 30, Team Shirts pays off the $500 loan with $5 interest. The repayment of the $500 principal reduces cash and eliminates the obligation that had been recorded as a liability. In other words, that liability is settled. The $500 reduction in assets is balanced in the accounting equation with a $500 reduction in the claims of creditors. However, the interest represents the cost of borrowing money. For a business, that is called interest expense. Like all expenses, it reduces the shareholder's claims by reducing retained earnings.

- On January 31, Team Shirts pays a $100 dividend. A dividend is a distribution paid to the shareholders of a corporation. That reduction in cash reduces the shareholder's claims to the assets of the firm, shown by the decrease in retained earnings. The $100, after it is distributed, is now part of Sara's personal financial assets, which are entirely separate from the business.

Using the accounting equation to keep track of the transactions of a business is a useful way to see how the financial statements are put together. Exhibit 1.8 shows how the statements are related to the basic accounting equation.

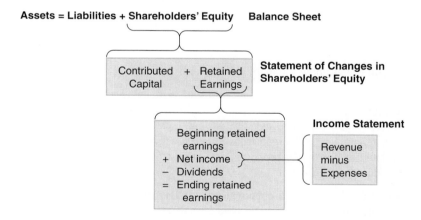

EXHIBIT 1.8

The Accounting Equation
This shows how the accounting equation forms the foundation of the financial statements.

The actual way a company keeps track of its financial transactions and its records—commonly called its **books**—can vary from a simple manual record-keeping system to a complex computerized system. No matter how a company keeps its records, the financial statements will look the same. The accounting equation is the basis for accumulating accounting information and communicating that information to decision makers. A company starts the year with a balance sheet (empty only at the start of the business firm), engages in business transactions during the year, and ends the year with a new, updated balance sheet. After a year of operations, the first statement a firm prepares is the income statement.

The **books** are a company's accounting records.

Income Statement

The most well-known financial statement is the **income statement**, also known as the statement of earnings, the statement of operations, or the profit and loss statement (P&L). The income statement is a summary of all the revenues (from sales or services) a company earns minus all the

The **income statement** shows all revenues minus all expenses for an accounting period—a month, a quarter, or a year.

expenses (costs incurred in the earning process) associated with earning that revenue. It describes the performance of a company during a specific period, which is called a fiscal period. Most often, the term fiscal period is used to describe the business year, which may or may not coincide with the calendar year. A fiscal year (not physical year) for a company may, for example, begin on July 1. That means the fiscal year of the business runs from July 1 of one year to June 30 of the next calendar year. Sometimes a company will end a fiscal year at a specific point in time that may result in slightly different dates for its year end from year to year. For example, Dell Inc. defines its fiscal year as the 52- or 53-week period ending on the Sunday nearest January 31.

Recall that the balance sheet gives the amount of assets, the amount of liabilities, and the amount of shareholders' equity of a business at a specific date. However, the first statement a firm prepares after completing an accounting period is the income statement. The income statement describes the operating performance of a company during a period. Look at the income statement for Team Shirts in Exhibit 1.9. It shows the amount of sales the company made during the month, from January 1, 2010, through January 31, 2010. The expenses shown are also for the same period. As noted earlier, the difference between the revenues and expenses is called net income, or net earnings.

EXHIBIT 1.9

Income Statement for Team Shirts for January

The income statement for the month of January shows all of the revenue and all of the expenses for the month.

Team Shirts
Income Statement
For the Month Ended January 31, 2010

Revenue		
Sales		$900
Expenses		
Cost of goods sold	$360	
Advertising	50	
Interest	5	
Total expenses		415
Net income		$485

Notice several things about the income statement:

- First, only the cost of the T-shirts that were sold is included as an expense—cost of goods sold, also called cost of sales. The cost of the T-shirts that were not sold is shown as an asset called inventory on the balance sheet.
- Second, the repayment of the loan from Sara's sister is not shown as an expense. The only expense related to borrowing money is the interest owed to the lender. The repayment of principal is not an expense.

Also notice that dividends, a corporation's distribution to owners, are excluded from the income statement. Sara could have paid herself a salary for running the business. That salary would have been an expense, but she decided not to do that. Instead, she decided to take cash out of the business as a dividend. Dividends are not a component of earnings; they are a distribution of earnings.

The Difference between the Balance Sheet and the Income Statement

You should get a better idea of the difference between the balance sheet and the income statement by thinking about your own personal finances. If you were asked to prepare a personal balance sheet, you would list all your assets, such as your cash on hand (no matter how little) and the cost of your car, clothes, computer, and cell phone. Then, you would list all the people to whom you owe money and how much money you owe to each. This might include some credit card companies and perhaps a bank for a car loan. All these assets and liabilities are measured in dollars. The specific point of time associated with a balance sheet must be given. For example, if you were listing your assets and liabilities on the last day of 2010, your balance sheet date would be December 31, 2010. Remember the accounting equation:

$$\text{Assets} = \text{Liabilities} + \text{Shareholder's equity}$$

If you subtract the amount of your liabilities—what you owe to others—from your assets, the difference is your equity. Shareholders' equity is sometimes called the residual, indicating that it is the amount left over after the claims of creditors are deducted from a company's assets.

In contrast, if you constructed a personal income statement, it would cover a period of time. For example, what was your net income total during the year 2010? You would list all revenue you received during the year and then subtract all your expenses during the same year. The difference would be your net income for the year. There is no equation to balance. The income statement lists all of your sources of revenue and subtracts the related expenses, leaving a difference, hopefully positive, called net income. If the subtraction of expenses from revenues results in a negative number, that amount is called a net loss.

Your Turn 1-6

1. What is included on the income statement? What is included on the balance sheet?
2. Describe the difference in the time periods captured by the income statement and the balance sheet.

Statement of Changes in Shareholders' Equity

As its name suggests, the statement of changes in shareholders' equity shows the changes that have taken place in the amount of shareholders' equity during a period. For a corporation, the statement is called the **statement of changes in shareholders' equity** because the owners are known as shareholders. (When there is only one owner, use the singular "shareholder's equity." When there are two or more owners, use the plural "shareholders' equity." If you don't know the number of owners, using the plural is the accepted practice.) The statement starts with the amount of contributed capital on a given balance sheet date and summarizes the additions and subtractions from that amount during a specific period, usually a year. In this course, we will not see deductions from contributed capital. Contributed capital is reduced in only very special circumstances, and those will be studied in more advanced accounting courses. The second part of the statement starts with the beginning balance in retained earnings and then shows the additions (net income is the most common) and the deductions (dividends are the most common). Contributed capital and retained earnings are then added to show the total amount of shareholders' equity at the end of the accounting period. For demonstration purposes, we will look at monthly financial statements for Team Shirts throughout this book.

The statement of changes in shareholder's equity for Sara's first month of business is shown in Exhibit 1.10.

The **statement of changes in shareholders' equity** starts with the beginning amount of contributed capital and shows all changes during the accounting period. Then the statement shows the beginning balance in retained earnings with its changes. The usual changes to retained earnings are the increase due to net income and the decrease due to dividends paid to shareholders.

EXHIBIT 1.10

Statement of Changes in Shareholder's Equity for Team Shirts for January

This statement shows all of the changes to shareholder's equity that occurred during the period.

Team Shirts
Statement of Changes in Shareholder's Equity
For the Month Ended January 31, 2010

Beginning contributed capital	$ 0	
Stock issued during the month	5,000	
Ending contributed capital		$5,000
Beginning retained earnings	$ 0	
Net income for the month	485	
Dividends	(100)	
Ending retained earnings		385
Total shareholder's equity		$5,385

The statement starts with the contributed capital at the beginning of the month. Team Shirts has nothing on the first day of the month, because the company is just getting started. Then, capital contributions—the owner's contributions to the business—made during the month are listed. Sara contributed $5,000 to the business. In a corporation, contributions take the form of shares of stock. Next, the statement shows beginning retained earnings, the equity that owners have as a result of the business earning income, rather than the equity from contributions. The beginning retained earnings balance is zero because January was the company's first month of doing business. Net income for the period—$485—is shown as an increase to retained earnings. The dividends of $100 are shown as a decrease to retained earnings. The amount of retained earnings at the end of the period is then added to the amount of contributed capital at the end of the period to give the total shareholder's equity at the end of the period.

After preparing the income statement for the month and the statement of changes in shareholder's equity for the same month, you will be able to prepare the end-of-the-month balance sheet. If you set up the balance sheet horizontally in the accounting equation format as shown in Exhibit 1.7, you can view the changes in assets, liabilities, and shareholder's equity from the beginning to the end of the month, with each transaction keeping the accounting equation in balance. The balance sheet for Team Shirts at January 31, 2010, is shown in Exhibit 1.11.

EXHIBIT 1.11

Balance Sheet for Team Shirts at January 31, 2010

After a month of transactions, this is the balance sheet for Team Shirts. Notice how all the information from the income statement and statement of changes in shareholder's equity is incorporated in the totals shown on the balance sheet.

The **statement of cash flows** shows all the cash collected and all the cash disbursed during the period. Each cash amount is classified as one of three types:

1. **Cash from operating activities**—cash transactions that relate to the everyday, routine transactions needed to run a business.
2. **Cash from investing activities**—transactions involving the sale and purchase of long-term assets used in the business.
3. **Cash from financing activities**—transactions related to how a business is financed. Examples include contributions from owners and amounts borrowed using loans.

Team Shirts
Balance Sheet
At January 31, 2010

Assets		Liabilities and Shareholder's equity	
Cash	$5,345	Notes payable	$ 0
Inventory	40		
		Common stock	5,000
		Retained earnings	385
		Total liabilities and	
Total assets	$5,385	shareholder's equity	$5,385

Statement of Cash Flows

The **statement of cash flows** is needed to form a complete picture of a company's financial health. This statement is, in theory, the easiest to understand, and many people consider it the most important. It is a list of all the cash that has come into a business (its cash receipts) and all the cash that has gone out of the business (its cash disbursements) during a specific period. In other words, it shows all the cash inflows and all the cash outflows for a fiscal period. Compare the cash inflows and cash outflows for a specific period with the revenues and expenses for the same specific period on the income statement. Accountants measure revenue as what the company has earned during the period, even if it is not equal to the amount of cash actually collected. Accountants measure expenses as the costs incurred to generate those revenues, even if they are not the same as the amounts actually paid in cash. Because this way of measuring revenues and expenses may not have an exact correspondence to the amount of cash collected and disbursed, the statement of cash flows is necessary to get a complete picture of the business transactions for the period.

The statement of cash flows is divided into three sections:

- **Cash from operating activities**
- **Cash from investing activities**
- **Cash from financing activities**

These represent the three general types of business activities. Exhibit 1.12 shows some common transactions and how they fit into these classifications. Remember that the transactions must be cash transactions to be shown on the statement of cash flows.

	Operating Activities	Investing Activities	Financing Activities
Cash inflows...	From customers who purchase products From interest or dividend income earned from bank deposits	From sale of property and equipment	From issuing long-term debt From issuing stock
Cash outflows...	To suppliers for the purchase of inventory To employees in the form of salaries	To purchase plant and equipment To purchase investments in other firms	To repay long-term debt principal To pay dividends to owners

EXHIBIT 1.12

Types of Cash Flows

All transactions can be classified as one of these three types. When the transactions are for cash, they appear on the statement of cash flows.

Cash inflows and outflows from operating activities pertain to the general operating activities of the business. For Team Shirts, purchasing T-shirts is an operating activity. Look at the other cash flows from operations on the statement of cash flows in Exhibit 1.13.

Team Shirts
Statement of Cash Flows
For the Month Ended January 31, 2010

EXHIBIT 1.13

Statement of Cash Flows for Team Shirts for January

The statement of cash flows shows all of the cash inflows and outflows during the period. At the end of the statement, the beginning cash balance is added to the change in cash to give the ending cash balance.

Cash from operating activities:		
Cash collected from customers	$ 900	
Cash paid to vendors	(400)	
Cash paid for advertising	(50)	
Cash paid for interest	(5)	$ 445
Cash from investing activities:		0
Cash from financing activities:		
Contributions from owners	$5,000	
Cash from loan	500	
Cash to repay loan	(500)	
Cash paid for dividends	(100)	4,900
Increase in cash		$5,345
Add beginning cash balance		0
Ending cash balance		$5,345

Cash inflows and outflows from investing activities are the cash flows related to the purchase and sale of assets that a firm uses for more than a year. If Sara decided to purchase a piece of equipment to silk screen her own shirts, that purchase would be an investing activity—not an operating activity—because Team Shirts is not in the business of buying and selling equipment. The purchase and sale of assets that last longer than a year—often called long-term assets—are investing activities.

Financing activities are related to a company's sources of capital. The two sources of capital, usually in the form of cash, for financing a business are contributions from owners and loans from creditors. Any cash inflows related to these transactions are classified as cash inflows from financing activities. Financing outflows include repayment of the principal of loans and distributions to owners. Team Shirts' repayment of the $500 loan is an example of a financing cash outflow.

You should begin to see the relationship between the four financial statements. Study Exhibit 1.14, where all of the statements for Team Shirts for January are shown with arrows

EXHIBIT 1.14

Summary of Team Shirts' Financial Statements and Their Relationships

This shows how the four financial statements are related.

> **Team Shirts**
> **Income Statement**
> **For the Month Ended January 31, 2010**

Revenue	
Sales	$900
Expenses	
Cost of goods sold	(360)
Advertising expense	(50)
Interest expense	(5)
Net income	$485

> **Team Shirts**
> **Statement of Changes in Shareholder's Equity**
> **For the Month Ended January 31, 2010**

Contributed capital		
Beginning balance	$	0
Stock issued during the month		5,000
Ending balance		5,000
Retained earnings		
Beginning balance	$	0
+ Net income		485
– Dividends		(100)
Ending balance		385
Total shareholder's equity		$5,385

> **Team Shirts**
> **Statement of Cash Flows**
> **For the Month Ended January 31, 2010**

Cash from operating activities:		
Cash collected from customers ...	$ 900	
Cash paid to vendors	(400)	
Cash paid for advertising	(50)	
Cash paid for interest	(5)	$ 445
Cash from investing activities: ...		0
Cash from financing activities:		
Contributions from owners	$5,000	
Cash from loan	500	
Cash to repay loan	(500)	
Cash paid for dividends	(100)	4,900
Increase in cash		$5,345
Add beginning cash balance		0
Ending cash balance		$5,345

> **Team Shirts**
> **Balance Sheet**
> **At January 31, 2010**

Assets	
Cash	$5,345
Inventory	40
Total assets	$5,385
Liabilities & Shareholder's Equity	
Liabilities	
Note payable	0
Shareholder's Equity	
Common stock	5,000
Retained earnings	385
Total liabilities and shareholder's equity	$5,385

indicating the relationships between the statements. All four financial statements will be discussed in detail in the chapters to follow. By the time you are finished, you will be able to read and understand what is on most financial statements. You will also be able to analyze business transactions and understand how they affect the financial statements of a business.

---

1. Refer to Exhibit 1.14. How is the income statement related to the balance sheet? In other words, how does the amount of net income affect the balance sheet?
2. Why is it necessary to have both an income statement and a statement of cash flows? Look at the statements for Team Shirts and explain why they are different.

Your Turn 1-7

Flow of Information and the Financial Statements

A company records and uses a large amount of information about its transactions. The amount of data and the way the information is collected and stored vary widely from company to company. The information contained in the four financial statements is a specific, well-defined part of the information available from a company's overall information system. The purpose of these four financial statements is to provide the financial information needed to represent and evaluate the transactions of the business. Investors, regulators, vendors, customers, and creditors rely on financial accounting information as a critical input for decision making.

Real Company Financial Statements

L.O.5
Identify the elements of a real company's financial statements.

All publicly-traded corporations—ones that sell their stock in the public stock exchanges such as the New York Stock Exchange (NYSE)—must prepare the four basic financial statements every year. Even though these statements are much more complicated than those of Team Shirts, they have all of the basic financial statement elements that were on the statements for Team Shirts.

The SEC requires these companies to regularly supply information about what is happening in their firms. Check out the SEC's Web site at www.sec.gov. Explore the links to see if you can find some recent corporate filings. One of the most important filings a company must make is the 10-K, an important report that companies file with the SEC. It provides a comprehensive overview of the registrant's business. An important part of a 10-K is a company's audited financial statements, without the company's sales pitch and story found in its glossy annual report. The 10-K report includes information you simply will not find in most annual reports, such as insider stock holdings and brief biographies of the management team. The report must be filed within 60 or 75 days after the end of the company's fiscal year (depending on the company's filing status).

Beginning in June 2009, firms that are required to file 10-K reports with the SEC will do so using a computer language called **XBRL (Extensible Business Reporting Language)**. This is a technology that enables firms to report information in a standardized way that makes the data immediately reusable and interactive. Take a test drive at www.sec.gov/spotlight/xbrl/viewers.shtml; click on *Interactive Financial Reports*. According to the SEC, the interactive data encoded with XBRL will make analyzing financial information more efficient and effective.

XBRL (Extensible Business Reporting Language) is a technology that enables firms to report information in a standardized way that makes the data immediately reusable and interactive.

Interactive data can create new ways for investors, analysts, and others to retrieve and use financial information in documents filed with us. For example, users of financial information will be able to download it directly into spreadsheets, analyze it using commercial off-the-shelf software, or use it within investment models in other software formats. Through interactive data, what is currently static, text-based information can be dynamically searched and analyzed, facilitating the comparison of financial and business performance across companies, reporting periods, and industries. (Source: SEC Release Nos. 33-9902; 34-59324; 39-2461.)

Look at the comparative balance sheets of Dell Inc., formerly called the Dell Computer Corporation (see Exhibit 1.15 on the following page). Notice the similarities between the real

EXHIBIT 1.15

Comparative Balance Sheets for Dell Inc.

This is Dell's balance sheet, taken from its annual report.

Dell Inc.
Consolidated Statements of Financial Position
(in millions)

> Statement of Financial Position is just another name for the balance sheet.

> Assets are shown first on the balance sheet.

Assets	January 30, 2009	February 1, 2008
Current assets:		
Cash and cash equivalents	$ 8,352	$ 7,764
Short-term investments	740	208
Accounts receivable, net	4,731	5,961
Financing receivables, net	1,712	1,732
Inventories, net	867	1,180
Other current assets	3,749	3,035
Total current assets	20,151	19,880
Property, plant, and equipment, net	2,277	2,668
Investments	454	1,560
Long-term financing receivables, net	500	407
Goodwill	1,737	1,648
Purchased intangible assets, net	724	780
Other non-current assets	657	618
Total assets	$26,500	$27,561

> Liabilities and Stockholders' Equity are shown together.

Liabilities and Equity	January 30, 2009	February 1, 2008
Current liabilities:		
Short-term debt	$ 113	$ 225
Accounts payable	8,309	11,492
Accrued and other	3,788	4,323
Short-term deferred service revenue	2,649	2,486
Total current liabilities	14,859	18,526
Long-term debt	1,898	362
Long-term deferred service revenue	3,000	2,774
Other non-current liabilities	2,472	2,070
Total liabilities	22,229	23,732
Commitments and contingencies (Note 10)		
Redeemable common stock and capital in excess of $.01 par value; shares issued and outstanding: 0 and 4, respectively (Note 4)	–	94
Stockholders' equity:		
Preferred stock and capital in excess of $.01 par value; shares authorized: 5,000; shares issued and outstanding: none	–	–
Common stock and capital in excess of $.01 par value; shares authorized: 7,000; shares issued: 3,338 and 3,320, respectively; shares outstanding: 1,944 and 2,060, respectively	11,189	10,589
Treasury stock at cost: 919 and 785 shares, respectively	(27,904)	(25,037)
Retained earnings	20,677	18,199
Accumulated other comprehensive income (loss)	309	(16)
Total stockholders' equity	4,271	3,735
Total liabilities and equity	$26,500	$27,561

> The balance sheet actually balances.

The accompanying notes are an integral part of these consolidated financial statements.

world of Dell and the fictitious world of Team Shirts—the balance sheets for both actually balance. Both companies list assets first, then liabilities and stockholders' equity. Both companies have used dollars to measure their balance sheet items. There are differences between the balance sheets of the real-world example and our not-so-real-world example that we will discuss in later chapters.

Dell's income statement (consolidated statements of income in Exhibit 1.16) does not look exactly like the Team Shirts' income statement (Exhibit 1.9). First, Dell Inc. provides three years of comparative income statements. Both Dell Inc. and Team Shirts have revenues and expenses, but the two companies have presented the data in a different order. Team Shirts lists revenue first and then groups all the expenses together. This is called a **single-step income statement**. Dell Inc. lists its largest revenue first and then subtracts the largest expense related to the revenue, *cost of revenue* (also known as *cost of goods sold*), which gives a subtotal called gross margin. This is called a **multistep income statement**. If we were to recast Team Shirts' income statement into a multistep income statement, we would subtract the cost of goods sold of $360 from the sales revenue of $900 to get a subtotal of $540 for the gross margin. Although Dell Inc. and Team Shirts have arranged their revenues and expenses differently, net income for each company is still the difference between all revenues and all expenses. Net income is always the same no matter how the revenues and expenses are grouped on the statement.

A **single-step income statement** groups all revenues together and shows all expenses deducted from total revenue.

A **multistep income statement** starts with sales and subtracts cost of goods sold to get a subtotal called gross profit on sales, also known as gross margin. Then, other operating revenues are added and other operating expenses are deducted. A subtotal for operating income is shown before deductions related to nonoperating items and taxes are deducted. Then, income taxes are subtracted, leaving net income.

EXHIBIT 1.16

Dell's Income Statements
This shows the income statements for Dell Inc. for three consecutive years.

Dell Inc.
Consolidated Statements of Income
(in millions, except per share amounts)

	Fiscal Year Ended		
	January 30, 2009	February 1, 2008	February 2, 2007
Net revenue	$61,101	$61,133	$57,420
Cost of revenue	50,144	49,462	47,904
Gross margin	10,957	11,671	9,516
Operating expenses:			
Selling, general, and administrative	7,102	7,538	5,948
In-process research and development	2	83	–
Research, development, and engineering	663	610	498
Total operating expenses	7,767	8,231	6,446
Operating income	3,190	3,440	3,070
Investment and other income, net	134	387	275
Income before income taxes	3,324	3,827	3,345
Income tax provision	846	880	762
Net income	$ 2,478	$ 2,947	$ 2,583
Earnings per common share:			
Basic	$ 1.25	$ 1.33	$ 1.15
Diluted	$ 1.25	$ 1.31	$ 1.14
Weighted-average shares outstanding:			
Basic	1,980	2,223	2,255
Diluted	1,986	2,247	2,271

The accompanying notes are an integral part of these consolidated financial statements.

A complete set of annual financial statements includes the four basic statements—balance sheet, income statement, statement of changes in shareholders' equity, and the statement of cash flows—as well as the Notes to the Financial Statements. Accompanying the annual financial statements in a public company's 10-K is an audit opinion. Exhibit 1.17 on the following page shows the audit opinion from the most recent annual report of Dell Inc. Independent auditors play a crucial role in making sure the financial statements provide data that investors can rely on.

EXHIBIT 1.17

Report of the Independent Auditor

Every public company is required to have an audit. Only part of the audit report is shown here.

Report of Independent Registered Public Accounting Firm

To the Board of Directors and Shareholders of Dell Inc.

In our opinion, the consolidated financial statements listed in the accompanying index present fairly, in all material respects, the financial position of Dell Inc. and its subsidiaries ("Company") at January 30, 2009 and February 1, 2008, and the results of their operations and their cash flows for each of the three years in the period ended January 30, 2009 in conformity with accounting principles generally accepted in the United States of America. In addition, in our opinion, the financial statement schedule listed in the accompanying index presents fairly, in all material respects, the information set forth therein when read in conjunction with the related consolidated financial statements. Also in our opinion, the Company maintained, in all material respects, effective internal control over financial reporting as of January 30, 2009, based on criteria established in *Internal Control — Integrated Framework* issued by the Committee of Sponsoring Organizations of the Treadway Commission (COSO). The Company's management is responsible for these financial statements and the financial statement schedule, for maintaining effective internal control over financial reporting, and for its assessment of the effectiveness of internal control over financial reporting included in Management's Report on Internal Control Over Financial Reporting appearing under Item 9A. Our responsibility is to express opinions on these financial statements, on the financial statement schedule, and on the Company's internal control over financial reporting based on our integrated audits. We conducted our audits in accordance with the standards of the Public Company Accounting Oversight Board (United States). Those standards require that we plan and perform the audits to obtain reasonable assurance about whether the financial statements are free of material misstatement and whether effective internal control over financial reporting was maintained in all material respects. Our audits of the financial statements included examining, on a test basis, evidence supporting the amounts and disclosures in the financial statements, assessing the accounting principles used and significant estimates made by management, and evaluating the overall financial statement presentation. Our audit of internal control over financial reporting included obtaining an understanding of internal control over financial reporting, assessing the risk that a material weakness exists, and testing and evaluating the design and operating effectiveness of internal control based on the assessed risk. Our audits also included performing such other procedures as we considered necessary in the circumstances. We believe that our audits provide a reasonable basis for our opinions.

PricewaterhouseCoopers LLP
Austin, Texas
March 26, 2009

> Consolidated means that any firms controlled by Dell are included in Dell's financial statements.

> What do you think it means for the statements to "present fairly"?

> What is a reasonable basis for an opinion?

Business Risk, Control, and Ethics

Starting a business is more than having a good idea about what it should be and obtaining the financing to get it going. Both are a good beginning, but they must be followed with sound business planning for acquiring goods and services and selling the company's products or services. Part of that planning is identifying the risks involved. Before we discuss the details of the business activities in the chapters to follow, we consider the risks of being in business and how we can minimize the negative consequences of those risks.

> A **risk** is a danger—something that exposes a business to a potential injury or loss.

A **risk** may be generally defined as anything that exposes us to potential injury or loss. In business, risks can turn into significant losses, scandals, or total company failure. There are hundreds of risks that any business faces. Some examples are

- the risk of product failure that might result in the death of consumers.
- the risk that someone will steal assets from the company.
- the risk that poor-quality inventory will be purchased and sold.

What losses could result? For a serious product failure, such as the Firestone tires on the Ford Explorers in the early 2000s, the financial losses of the business could amount to millions of dollars in lawsuit settlements. For employee theft, the potential losses range from significant financial losses to the loss of a company secret that could cause a business to fail. Poor-quality inventory could result in the loss of customers and reputation.

Risks relate to all aspects of the business, including the following:

- General strategic risks—for example, should we market our cigarettes to teenagers?
- Operating risks—for example, should we operate without a backup power supply?
- Financial risks—for example, should we borrow the money from the bank or get it from our shareholders?
- Information risks—for example, should we use a manual accounting system?

The potential losses from taking on business risks may be the loss of reputation, loss of customers, loss of needed information, or loss of assets. All the losses translate into monetary losses that can put the company at risk for total failure.

It is difficult to think of business risk without considering the relationship of risks to ethics. When the risks of business result in losses or legal exposure, a firm's managers want to minimize the damage to the firm. In such cases, the ethical standards of the firm and its managers become paramount. A manager must always put good ethical behavior above putting a good face on the firm's financial position or performance. Failure to do this has resulted in huge losses for employees and investors. See how many of the faces you recognize in Exhibit 1.18.

EXHIBIT 1.18

Accounting Frauds

Company	What Happened	The Legal Events	
Enron, an energy company	Firm filed for bankruptcy protection in December 2001, after massive fraud was uncovered by the SEC.	Andrew Fastow, former CFO, was sentenced to 10 years in prison; Jeff Skilling, former CEO and president, was sentenced to 24 years in prison.	
WorldCom, a telecommunications company	Firm filed for bankruptcy protection in July 2002 after disclosing it overstated profits by $3.8 billion.	Bernie Ebbers, former CEO, was sentenced to 25 years in prison.	
Computer Associates (CA), a computer company	Former CEO Sanjay Kumar was indicted in April 2004 for $2 billion fraud and obstruction of justice.	Kumar pleaded guilty in May 2006 and was sentenced to 12 years in prison.	
Monster Worldwide, Inc., a global online career company	Monster executives secretly backdated stock options granted to officers, directors, and employees, and overstated the company's annual earnings between 1997 and 2005 by $339.5 million (pretax).	Without admitting or denying liability, Monster agreed to pay a $2.5 million penalty. According to the SEC complaint, Monster cooperated with the investigation.	
Countrywide Financial, a mortgage lender	Countrywide Financial executives are charged with deliberately misleading investors about the credit risks they were taking in an effort to build the company's market share and maintain the stock price.	On June 4, 2009, the SEC filed fraud charges against former Countrywide Financial CEO, Angelo Mozilo, former COO and president, David Sambol, and former CFO, Eric Sieracki. These cases are pending.	

Why do people take risks? Every risk brings a potential reward. The reward is why we are in business. An entrepreneur like Sara has put her money and her reputation at risk to start a business. Why? For the potential of developing a successful business. To deal with the risks and increase the chances to reap the rewards, a firm must establish and maintain control over its operations, assets, and information system. A control is an activity performed to minimize or eliminate a risk. As we study the business processes that Team Shirts will be engaged in during its first year in business, we will look at how the firm can control the risk involved in each process.

Chapter Summary Points

- A business is started when investors are willing to risk their money to start a business—to provide something of value for customers and to make a profit.
- Investors, vendors, customers, and governmental agencies require financial information about businesses. There are four basic financial statements that provide the information: the income statement, the balance sheet, the statement of changes in shareholders' equity, and the statement of cash flows.
- The financial statements are based on a set of guidelines called generally accepted accounting principles (GAAP). The SEC and the FASB are currently the important players in the rule-setting game.
- The accounting equation, assets = liabilities + shareholders' equity, is the basis of the balance sheet. It is a snapshot of the business at a specific point in time.
- The income statement shows all revenues and expenses for a period of time, resulting in net income.
- The statement of changes in shareholders' (owners') equity shows the changes in shareholders' equity—both contributed capital and retained earnings—for a period of time.
- The statement of cash flows presents all the cash inflows and outflows for a period of time. It accounts for the difference between the balances in cash on the balance sheets at the end of two consecutive accounting periods.
- Notes to the financial statements are an important part of the financial information provided with a firm's four financial statements.

Chapter Summary Problems

Suppose the following transactions occurred during Lexar Computer's first month of business:

a. Two friends together contributed $50,000 from their savings to start Lexar Computer, Inc. In return, the corporation issued 100 shares of common stock to each of them.
b. The company paid $20,000 cash for parts for new computers that it planned to make during the next few months.
c. The company rented office space for the month for $350 cash.
d. The company hired and paid employees for work done during the month for a total of $1,500.
e. The company sold computers for $40,000 cash. (These computers were made from the parts the company purchased in item (b).)
f. The company declared and paid $400 in dividends to its shareholders.
g. On the last day of the month, the company purchased $12,000 worth of office furniture and equipment on credit. (Lexar signed a 60-day note—that is, borrowed the money—from the furniture company.)

Instructions

1. For each transaction, tell whether the related accounting information will be shown on the income statement, the balance sheet, or both. If it is on the income statement, tell whether it increases or decreases net income.
2. For each transaction, tell whether it is an operating, investing, or financing activity.
3. For each transaction, identify an asset or a liability that is affected by the transaction, and tell whether it is an increase or a decrease to the asset or liability you named.

Solution

Transaction	Which financial statements are affected?	Which type of activity is it?	Which asset or liability is affected?
a. Two friends together contributed $50,000 cash to start Lexar Computer, Inc. In return, the corporation issued 100 shares of common stock to each of them.	Balance sheet	Financing	Asset: Cash—increased
b. The company paid $20,000 cash for parts for new computers that it planned to make during the next few months.	Balance sheet	Operating	Assets: Inventory—increased; Cash—decreased
c. The company rented office space for the month for $350 cash.	Balance sheet and income statement (decreases income)	Operating	Asset: Cash—decreased
d. The company hired and paid employees for work done during the month for a total of $1,500.	Balance sheet and income statement (decreases income)	Operating	Asset: Cash—decreased
e. The company sold computers for $40,000 cash. (These computers were made from the parts the company purchased in item (b).)	Balance sheet and income statement (increases income)	Operating	Asset: Cash—increased; Inventory—decreased
f. The company declared and paid $400 in dividends to its shareholders.	Balance sheet	Financing	Asset: Cash—decreased
g. The company purchased $12,000 worth of office furniture and equipment on credit. (Lexar signed a 60-day note with the furniture company.)	Balance sheet	Investing	Asset: Office Furniture—increased; Liability: Notes payable—increased

Key Terms for Chapter 1

Assets (p. 14)
Balance sheet (p. 13)
Books (p. 17)
Capital (p. 2)
Cash from financing activities (p. 20)
Cash from investing activities (p. 20)
Cash from operating activities (p. 20)
Certified public accountant (CPA) (p. 13)
Comparative balance sheets (p. 15)
Contributed capital (p. 9)
Corporation (p. 6)
Dividends (p. 8)

Expenses (p. 10)
Financial Accounting Standards Board (FASB) (p. 11)
Financial services company (p. 4)
Fiscal year (p. 15)
For-profit firm (p. 2)
Generally accepted accounting principles (GAAP) (p. 11)
Income statement (p. 17)
Interest (p. 9)
Internal Revenue Service (IRS) (p. 12)
International Accounting Standards Board (IASB) (p. 11)

International Financial Reporting Standards (IFRS) (p. 11)
Liabilities (p. 14)
Manufacturing company (p. 4)
Merchandising company (p. 3)
Multistep income statement (p. 25)
Net income (p. 3)
Not-for-profit firm (p. 2)
Notes to the financial statements (p. 13)
Partnership (p. 5)
Principal (p. 9)
Public Company Accounting Oversight Board (PCAOB) (p. 11)

Answers to YOUR TURN Questions

Chapter 1

Your Turn 1-1

1. The main purpose of a business is to make a profit, increasing the value of the company for the owners.
2. The four general types of businesses are as follows:
   a. Service company: provides a service—it does something for its customers rather than selling them a tangible product.
   b. Merchandising company: buys goods, adds value to them, and then sells them with the added value.
   c. Manufacturing company: makes products and sells them to other companies and sometimes to the final consumers.
   d. Financial services company: provides services related to money—insurance, banking, etc.

Your Turn 1-2

1. The three general forms of business ownership are (1) sole proprietorships (single owner), (2) partnerships (multiple owners), and (3) corporations (potential for widespread ownership often with separation of ownership and management).
2. Some advantages and disadvantages of each business form are as follows:

	Sole Proprietorship	Partnership	Corporation
Advantages:	Owner control Taxes flow to proprietor's income	Owners control Taxes flow to partners' income	Limited liability for owners Often easier to raise capital For owners, they may diversify their investments across many different companies, often for a very small investment
Disadvantages:	Owner is liable for all business decisions Often difficult to raise capital	Partners are liable for all business decisions Often difficult to raise capital	Often, management and owners are separate, creating a conflict of interests Corporation pays taxes and then owners pay taxes again on the dividends they receive (unless the tax law provides special treatment for dividends)

Your Turn 1-3

1. The two sources of financing for a business are investments by owners (contributed capital) and loans from outsiders (liabilities).
2. Interest is the cost of using someone else's money.

Your Turn 1-4

1. Revenues are the amounts a company earns from providing goods or services to its customers. Expenses are the costs to earn those revenues.
2. The four statements include the income statement, balance sheet, statement of changes in shareholders' equity, and the statement of cash flows.

Your Turn 1-5

1. The two parts of shareholders' equity are contributed capital and retained earnings (earned capital).
2. A fiscal year is a year in the life of a business for financial reporting purposes. It may begin at any time and ends a year later.

Your Turn 1-6

1. The income statement contains revenues and expenses. The balance sheet contains assets, liabilities, and shareholders' equity.
2. The time period captured by the income statement is an accounting period, often a fiscal year. The statement covers a period of time. On the other hand, the balance sheet describes the financial position of a company at a given point in time.

Your Turn 1-7

1. The income statement gives the revenues and expenses for the period. The net amount, net income, is added to retained earnings. So the income statement number becomes part of the retained earnings total on the year-end balance sheet.
2. The income statement shows all revenues and expenses for a period of time—all the revenues that have been earned and expenses incurred to earn those revenues. The statement of cash flows simply lists the cash inflows and outflows during the period. The income statement and the statement of cash flows for Team Shirts are different because Team Shirts paid cash for some inventory that was not sold, so the cost of that inventory is not included in the income statement's cost of goods sold. Also, any transactions with owners (contributions and dividends) are not included on the income statement.

Questions

1. What is the purpose of a business?
2. Is the goal of all organizations to make a profit?
3. Name the three types of activities that make up most business transactions.
4. What are the possible ownership structures for a business?
5. What are the advantages of the corporate form of ownership?
6. What are the disadvantages of the corporate form of ownership?
7. Who are some of the people in need of business information and for what purposes?
8. What is the relationship between the information available to a business and the information provided in financial statements?
9. What are the basic financial statements? Describe the information that each provides.
10. What makes the income statement different from the statement of cash flows?
11. What is XBRL and why is the SEC mandating its use?

Multiple-Choice Questions

1. What type of activities relate to what the firm is in business to do?
   a. Investing activities
   b. Operating activities
   c. Financing activities
   d. Protection activities
2. Which financial statement is similar to the accounting equation?
   a. The income statement
   b. The balance sheet
   c. The statement of changes in shareholders' equity
   d. The statement of cash flows
3. The Pets Plus Superstore, Inc., acquires 50 doggie beds from a supplier for $500 in cash. What is the give portion of this transaction?
   a. Pets Plus giving the doggie beds to customers in return for cash
   b. The supplier giving the doggie beds to Pets Plus
   c. Pets Plus giving $500 in cash to the supplier
   d. The supplier giving $500 to Pets Plus

4. The two parts of shareholders' equity are
   a. assets and liabilities.
   b. net income and common stock.
   c. contributed capital and retained earnings.
   d. revenues and expenses.
5. Which financial statement is a snapshot of the financial position of a company at a specific point in time?
   a. Income statement
   b. Balance sheet
   c. Statement of changes in shareholders' equity
   d. Statement of cash flows
6. Online Pharmacy Company borrowed $5,000 cash from the National Bank. As a result of this transaction,
   a. assets would decrease by $5,000.
   b. liabilities would increase by $5,000.
   c. equity would increase by $5,000.
   d. revenue would increase by $5,000.
7. Accounting information is
   a. useful in profitable businesses only.
   b. considered the most important part of a company's information system by all managers.
   c. an integral part of business.
   d. used only by CPAs.
8. During its first year of business, West Company earned service revenues of $2,000. If the company collected $700 related to those sales, how much revenue would be shown on West's income statement for the year?
   a. $2,000
   b. $700
   c. $1,300
   d. Cannot be determined with the given information
9. Interest is the cost of
   a. purchasing inventory.
   b. making a sale.
   c. being in business.
   d. using someone else's money.
10. The balance sheet of United Studios at December 31 showed assets of $30,000 and shareholders' equity of $20,000. What were the liabilities at December 31?
    a. $30,000
    b. $10,000
    c. $20,000
    d. $50,000

MyAccountingLab

All of the A exercises can be found within MyAccountingLab, an online homework and practice environment.

Short Exercises
Set A

SE1-1A. *Classify business transactions. (LO 2).* For each of the following cash transactions, identify whether it is better described as an operating, financing, or investing activity.

1. An entrepreneur contributes his own money to start a new business.
2. The business buys a machine.
3. The business purchases inventory.
4. The business sells inventory to customers.
5. The business repays a loan.

SE1-2A. *Identify balance sheet items. (LO 4).* Classify the items listed (1 to 6) under the following balance sheet headings:

A - Assets
L - Liabilities
SE - Shareholders' equity

1. _____ Cash
2. _____ Common stock
3. _____ Equipment
4. _____ Notes payable
5. _____ Retained earnings
6. _____ Accounts receivable

SE1-3A. *Calculate owners' equity. (LO 4).* Doughnut Company shows $130,000 worth of assets on its December 31, 2009, balance sheet. If the company's total liabilities are $55,800, what is the amount of owners' equity?

SE1-4A. *Calculate liability. (LO 4).* Given the following items on Tiffany Restoration Company's June 30, 2009, balance sheet, how much did the company owe its creditors on June 30, 2009?

Cash	$ 1,725	Liabilities	???
Inventory	205		
Equipment	10,636	Common stock	$7,600
Other assets	8,135	Retained earnings	7,450
Total	$20,701		

SE1-5A. *Income statement analysis. (LO 4).* For each of the following, calculate the missing amount:

1. Revenues $560; Expenses $300; Net Income = _____
2. Net Income $700; Expenses $485; Revenues = _____
3. Expenses $600; Revenues $940; Net Income = _____
4. Revenues $1,240; Net Income $670; Expenses = _____
5. Net Income $6,450; Expenses $3,500; Revenues = _____

SE1-6A. *Calculate owners' equity. (LO 4).* Pasta Enterprises has $42,000 in cash, $20,000 in inventory, $17,000 balance due to creditors, and $21,000 balance due from customers. What is the amount of owners' equity?

SE1-7A. *Calculate retained earnings. (LO 4).* Super Shop had a retained earnings balance of $1,000 on December 31, 2010. For year 2011, sales were $14,000 and expenses were $7,500. Cash dividends of $1,000 were declared and distributed on December 31, 2011. What was the amount of retained earnings on December 31, 2011?

Set B

SE1-8B. *Classify business transactions. (LO 2).* For each of the following cash transactions, identify whether it is better described as an operating, financing, or investing activity.

1. A firm pays dividends to its shareholders.
2. A firm provides services to its customers.
3. A firm sells inventory.
4. A firm pays its employees for work completed.
5. The business takes out a loan from the local bank.

SE1-9B. *Identify balance sheet items. (LO 4).* Classify the items listed (1 to 6) under the following balance sheet headings:
A - Assets
L - Liabilities
SE - Shareholders' equity

1. _____ Inventory
2. _____ Notes payable
3. _____ Cash
4. _____ Accounts payable
5. _____ Accounts receivable
6. _____ Common stock

SE1-10B. *Calculate owner's equity. (LO 4).* Breck Company shows $180,000 worth of assets on its December 31, 2011, balance sheet. If the company's total liabilities are $103,200, what is the amount of owners' equity?

SE1-11B. *Calculate liability. (LO 4).* Given the following items on Baldwin Company's December 31, 2011, balance sheet, how much did the company owe its creditors on December 31, 2011?

Cash	$ 2,000	Liabilities	???
Inventory	1,500		
Equipment	10,400	Common stock	$ 5,000
Other assets	8,100	Retained earnings	12,450
Total	$22,000		

SE1-12B. *Income statement analysis. (LO 4).* For each of the following, calculate the missing amount:

1. Revenues $860; Expenses $500; Net Income = _____
2. Net Income $300; Expenses $185; Revenues = _____
3. Expenses $360; Revenues $1,040; Net Income = _____
4. Revenues $2,240; Net Income $1,670; Expenses = _____
5. Net Income $5,450; Expenses $1,500; Revenues = _____

SE1-13B. *Calculate owners' equity. (LO 4).* Lasting Enterprises has $82,000 in cash, $30,000 in inventory, $37,000 balance due to creditors, and $11,000 balance due from customers. What is the amount of owners' equity?

SE1-14B. *Calculate retained earnings. (LO 4).* M Company had a retained earnings balance of $4,200 on June 30, 2010. For the fiscal year ended June 30, 2011, sales were $24,000 and expenses were $12,500. Cash dividends of $2,500 were declared and distributed on June 1, 2011. What was the amount of retained earnings on June 30, 2011?

MyAccountingLab

Exercises
Set A

E1-15A. *Business exchanges. (LO 1, 2).* Identify the transactions from the following story. For each, identify the transaction as operating, investing, or financing.

Latasha Jones decided to go into business for herself. As a talented Web designer, she decided to open a small consulting firm with $5,000 of her own money, for which she received common stock. Latasha borrowed $500 from her best friend to help get the business started, and in exchange she gave her friend an I-owe-you (IOU). The company bought a state-of-the-art desktop computer, complete with the accessories and software needed to get the business off the ground, at a total cost of $6,000. The business required a separate phone line, which cost $450. Then, the company put an advertisement in the local newspaper, at a cost of $45 per month for weekly ads. The company was ready to go. All of the payments were cash.

E1-16A. *Analyze business transactions using the accounting equation. (LO 4).* John Weiss recently started a lawn care service named "The Grass Is Always Greener, Inc." The following transactions occurred during the company's first month of business. Enter each of the following transactions into the accounting equation and identify an increase or decrease to assets, liabilities, shareholder's equity, revenues, or expenses.

1. John contributed $16,500 of personal savings in exchange for common stock to start the business.
2. The company purchased $7,500 of inventory (plants and shrubs) from a gardening whole-saler in Kansas.
3. The company purchased three riding lawn mowers at a cost of $5,000 each.
4. The company paid rent expense of $500 the first month.
5. The company earned service revenue of $9,000 and sold the entire $7,500 of inventory it had purchased to customers for $13,250 cash.

All the transactions were for cash. Use the following format:

			Shareholder's equity		
Total assets	=	Total liabilities	+	Contributed capital	+ Retained earnings
Transaction 1: _____		_____		_____	_____

E1-17A. *Classify business transactions. (LO 2).* For each of the transactions in E1-16A, tell whether the transaction was an operating, investing, or financing activity.

E1-18A. *Analyze the balance sheet. (LO 3, 4).* Use the balance sheet for Leatherheads Football Gear, Inc., at August 31, 2010, to answer the following questions:

Leatherheads Football Gear, Inc.
Balance Sheet
At August 31, 2010

Assets		Liabilities and Shareholder's Equity	
Cash	$ 7,250	Accounts payable	$ 4,575
Short-term investments	400	Notes payable	11,570
Accounts receivable	275		
Inventory	490	Contributed capital	4,450
Prepaid insurance	345	Retained earnings	3,040
Prepaid rent	875		
Equipment (net)	14,000		
	$23,635		$23,635

---

1. List the assets the company had on August 31, 2010. Who has claim to these assets?
2. List the liabilities the company had on August 31, 2010.

E1-19A. *Analyze business transactions using the accounting equation. (LO 4).* Enter each transaction below into the accounting equation. Then, calculate (1) the amount of assets owned by Tommy's Irish Pub, Inc., at the end of its first month of business, and (2) the amount of net income for the month. All these transactions took place during the first 30 days of business.

1. Tommy started the pub by contributing $17,000 in exchange for common stock, and the business borrowed $12,750 from the bank.
2. The pub purchased $4,000 worth of beer and other items (its inventory) with cash.
3. The pub hired a bartender to assist Tommy and help run the new company. For this service, the pub paid $100 each day for 30 days.

4. The pub was popular with the local college and sold half of its inventory for total cash revenues of $8,500.
5. The pub paid rent expense of $725 the first month.
6. The pub repaid $1,500 of the bank loan along with $50 of interest for the first month.

E1-20A. *Classify business transactions. (LO 2).* Classify each of the transactions in E1-19A as an operating, investing, or financing activity.

E1-21A. *Business transactions effects on shareholders' equity. (LO 4).* For each of the transactions given, tell whether it increases, decreases, or has no effect on shareholders' equity. Consider both shareholders' equity components—contributed capital and retained earnings.

1. Two friends get together, each contributing $7,125, to start the Swing Right Golf Supplies Corporation in exchange for common stock.
2. Swing Right purchases equipment for $6,250 cash.
3. Swing Right purchases $3,000 worth of inventory for cash.
4. Swing Right pays expenses of $800 for electricity and phone for the month.
5. Swing Right makes cash sales to customers of $4,685 during the month.
6. Swing Right pays employees $2,000 for hours worked during the month.
7. Swing Right declares and pays $500 dividends to each of its owners at the end of the month.

E1-22A. *Classify cash flows. (LO 2, 4).* Classify each transaction as an operating, investing, or financing activity. Assume all transactions are for cash.

1. Jackie Benefield makes a contribution of $95,000 to start the Horse Trails & Stables from her personal funds in exchange for common stock.
2. The company purchases three horses and some equipment for $25,000 in cash.
3. The company purchases $5,000 worth of advertising with the local newspaper.
4. The company pays rent of $15,000 for barn and pasture space as well as use of 50 acres of land for riding trails.
5. The company hires several people to clean stables at a cost of $600 for the month.
6. The first customers pay Horse Trails & Stables $4,225 for six months' worth of riding lessons.

E1-23A. *Analyze business transactions using the accounting equation. (LO 4).* Enter each transaction into the accounting equation and identify its increase or decrease to assets, liabilities, shareholder's equity, revenues, or expenses of Green Trees & Lawn Corp.

1. Green Trees & Lawn earned and collected the cash for $15,000 in service revenues.
2. The business paid $2,000 cash for supplies.
3. Green Trees & Lawn paid $1,500 of a $4,000 note payable to creditors.
4. The company paid $1,100 for rent expense.
5. The company's owner provided $7,500 in additional financing in exchange for common stock.
6. The business declared and paid $2,100 in dividends.
7. Green Trees & Lawn loaned $2,225 cash to another company.

Use the following format:

					Shareholder's equity		
Total assets	=	Total liabilities	+	Contributed capital	+	Retained earnings
Transaction 1: _____		_____		_____		_____

E1-24A. *Changes in net income. (LO 4).* For each of the following transactions, determine if there is an increase, decrease, or no change on net income for Fun Movie Productions, Inc.

1. Fun Movie earned $10,000 in monthly sales.
2. The firm recorded a decrease in inventory of $6,000 due to the monthly sales.
3. The company paid current month's rent of $1,500.
4. The company paid employees $2,500 for work done in the current month.

5. The company purchased land for $7,500.
6. Fun Movie invested $4,000 in another company's stock.
7. The firm paid $1,000 in cash dividends.

E1-25A. *Relationship between income statement and balance sheet. (LO 4).* Fill in the amounts for X, Y, and Z in the following table. (The company started business on January 1, 2009.)

	December 31, 2009	December 31, 2010
Assets	$4,550	$5,225
Liabilities	X	$1,500
Contributed capital	$1,300	$1,300
Retained earnings	Y	Z
Revenue	$1,250	$2,575
Expenses	$ 225	$1,175

E1-26A. *Revenues and the statement of cash flows. (LO 4).* Bob started a pool cleaning business on the first day of March. He cleaned 15 pools in March and earned $225 for each cleaning. Most of his customers paid him at the time of cleaning, but one customer, Jeremy Thompson, asked Bob to mail him a bill and he would then send Bob a check. Bob sent Jeremy an invoice but had not yet received the payment by the end of March. When Bob prepares his first monthly income statement, how much will the statement show for revenue for the month ended March 31? How much will be shown on the statement of cash flows as cash collected from customers for the first month?

E1-27A. *Expenses and the statement of cash flows. (LO 4).* Naida decided to open a candle shop. During her first month of business, she purchased candles from the supplier for a total of $500 and paid in cash. She sold half of those candles during the month. On the income statement for the month, what amount would appear for the cost of goods sold expense? On the statement of cash flows for the month, what amount would appear as the cash paid to suppliers?

E1-28A. *Retained earnings and cash. (LO 4).* Checkmate Games, Inc., started business on April 1, 2011, with $7,500 cash contribution from its owners in exchange for common stock. The company used $2,225 of the cash for equipment for the new shop and $2,750 on games for its inventory. During the month, the company earned $4,275 of revenue in cash from the sale of the entire inventory. On April 30, 2011, the owners then spent $3,000 cash on more games for the inventory. What is the retained earnings balance on April 30, 2011? How much cash does the company have on hand on April 30, 2011?

E1-29A. *Classify cash flows. (LO 2, 4).* For E1-28A, what amounts would Checkmate Games show on its statement of cash flows for the month ended April 30, 2011? Classify each as an operating, investing, or financing cash flow.

Set B

E1-30B. *Business exchanges. (LO 1, 2).* Identify the transactions from the following story. For each, identify the transactions as operating, investing, or financing.

   Bonnie Lawhon decided to start a business for herself breeding AKC miniature dachshunds. As a talented breeder who gave puppies to her friends and family, she decided to open a small kennel with $6,500 of her own money. She received common stock in exchange. The business had concrete poured and fences installed to give the dogs and puppies shelter at a cost of $3,250, paid in cash. Then, Bonnie's business hired a consultant to design and maintain a Web page for the company at a cost of $200 for the original design and $25 per month maintenance. She paid for the design and one month's maintenance fee. The business required a separate mobile phone to be purchased at a cost of $169 cash. Then, the business put an advertisement in the local newspaper, at a cost of $20 per month for weekly ads. The business paid cash for one month's advertising. The business was ready to go.

E1-31B. *Analyze business transactions using the accounting equation. (LO 4).* Joe Evans opened a fishing supply store named Evans Bait & Tackle, Inc. The following transactions occurred during its first month. Enter each transaction into the accounting equation and identify an increase or decrease to assets, liabilities, shareholder's equity, revenues, or expenses.

1. Joe Evans used $100,000 of personal savings in exchange for common stock, and the business borrowed $50,000 from the bank to start the business.
2. The business purchased a small building for $75,000.
3. The business purchased $10,500 worth of inventory.
4. The business paid operating expenses of $1,315 the first month.
5. Evans Bait & Tackle, Inc., sold $5,250 of its inventory to customers for $7,875.

All the transactions were for cash. Use the following format:

	Total assets	=	Total liabilities	+	Shareholder's equity		
					Contributed capital	+	Retained earnings
Transaction 1:	_____		_____		_____		_____

E1-32B. *Classify business transactions. (LO 2).* For each of the transactions in E1-31B, tell whether the transaction was an operating, investing, or financing activity.

E1-33B. *Analyze the balance sheet. (LO 3, 4).* Use the balance sheet for Specialty Party Supplies, Inc., at December 31, 2011, to answer the following questions:

Specialty Party Supplies, Inc.
Balance Sheet
At December 31, 2011

Assets		Liabilities and Shareholders' Equity	
Cash	$ 5,000	Accounts payable	$ 1,770
Short-term investments	300	Notes payable (van)	12,500
Accounts receivable	465		
Inventory	825	Paid-in capital	4,000
Prepaid insurance	500	Retained earnings	4,120
Prepaid rent	300		
Mobile grooming van (net)	15,000		
	$22,390		$22,390

1. List the assets the company had on December 31, 2011. Who has claim to these assets?
2. List the liabilities the company had on December 31, 2011.

E1-34B. *Analyze business transactions using the accounting equation. (LO 4).* Enter each transaction into the accounting equation. Then, calculate the (1) amount of assets owned by Izzy's Ice Cream Shop at the end of its first month of business and (2) the amount of net income for the month. All transactions took place during the first month; Izzy's was open for 25 days.

1. Izzy started the business by contributing $5,500 in exchange for common stock, and the firm borrowed $3,500 from the bank.
2. Izzy's Ice Cream Shop purchased an ice cream delivery truck for $4,500 cash.

3. The business purchased $1,200 worth of ice cream and other items (its inventory) for cash.
4. Izzy hired a delivery driver to work two days a week for a total of eight days the first month to help deliver ice cream for the new company. For this service, Izzy's paid $25 each day worked.
5. The ice cream delivery service was popular and Izzy's sold two-thirds of its inventory for total cash revenues of $3,600.
6. Izzy's paid operating expenses of $215 the first month.
7. Izzy's repaid $100 of the bank loan along with $5 of interest for the first month.

E1-35B. *Classify business transactions. (LO 2).* For each of the transactions in E1-34B, tell whether the transaction was an operating, investing, or financing activity.

E1-36B. *Business transactions effects on shareholders' equity. (LO 4).* For each of the transactions given next, tell whether it (1) increases, (2) decreases, or (3) has no effect on shareholders' equity. Consider both shareholders' equity components—contributed capital and retained earnings.

1. Two friends get together, each contributing $25,000 in cash, to start Luna's Pet Luau in exchange for common stock.
2. Luna's purchases a company van for $30,000 cash.
3. Luna's buys $2,250 worth of supplies for cash and uses them all right away.
4. Luna's pays cash expenses of $2,150 for gas and auto insurance.
5. Luna's earns service revenue from customers of $8,150 during the month and receives payment in cash.
6. Luna's pays its employees $465 cash for hours worked during the month.
7. Luna's declares and distributes $360 cash dividends to each of its owners at the end of the month.

E1-37B. *Classify cash flows. (LO 2, 4).* Classify each cash transaction for the statement of cash flows as an operating, investing, or financing activity.

1. William makes a contribution of $75,000 from his personal funds to start the Cookie Dough & More Ice Cream Co. and received common stock in exchange.
2. The company purchases a building and some equipment for $45,000 in cash.
3. The company purchases $5,500 worth of advertising time on a local television station for cash.
4. The company pays electricity and insurance expenses of $1,500 for the month.
5. The company hires several people to help make ice cream at a cost of $350 for the month and pays them in cash.
6. The National Bank pays $2,500 for ice cream and catering services for its grand opening.

E1-38B. *Analyze business transactions using the accounting equation. (LO 4).* Enter each transaction into the accounting equation and identify an increase or decrease to assets, liabilities, shareholders' equity, revenues, or expenses of Captured Memories Photography, Inc.

1. Captured Memories collected and earned $16,150 in sales revenues.
2. The firm paid $1,500 cash for supplies.
3. Captured Memories paid $1,000 of a $3,000 note payable to creditors.
4. The company paid $1,750 for operating expenses.
5. The company's owner provided $6,500 in additional financing in exchange for common stock.
6. The firm declared and paid $1,020 in dividends.

Use the following format:

| | | | Shareholders' equity | | |
Total assets	=	Total liabilities	+	Contributed capital	+	Retained earnings
Transaction 1: ————		————		————		————

E1-39B. *Changes in net income. (LO 4).* For each of the following transactions, determine if there is an increase, decrease, or no change on net income for Gardenia Lane Productions, Inc.

1. Gardenia Lane earned $12,000 in monthly sales.
2. The firm recorded a decrease in inventory of $7,500 due to the monthly sales.
3. Supplies were purchased for $50, and all of them were used.
4. The company paid employees $1,715 for current work done.
5. The company purchased land for $26,500.
6. Gardenia Lane paid rent of $2,500 for the current month.
7. The firm paid $1,000 in cash dividends.

E1-40B. *Relationship between income statement and balance sheet. (LO 4).* Fill in the amounts for X, Y, and Z in the table. The company started business on July 1, 2008.

	June 30, 2009	June 30, 2010
Assets	$2,000	$4,250
Liabilities	X	$2,500
Contributed capital	$ 500	$ 700
Retained earnings	Y	Z
Revenue	$ 800	$7,200
Expenses	$ 250	$6,700

E1-41B. *Revenues and the statement of cash flows. (LO 4).* Frank Frock started a consulting business on the first day of July. He provided consulting services for 30 hours in July and earned $150 per hour. Most of his clients paid him at the time he provided the services, but one customer, Ray Linch, asked Frank to send him a bill for the 5 hours he worked for him and he would then send the company a check. Frank sent Ray an invoice but had not received his payment by the end of July. When Frank prepares his first monthly income statement, how much will the statement show for revenue for the month? How much will be shown on the statement of cash flows for the month as cash collected from customers?

E1-42B. *Expenses and the statement of cash flows. (LO 4).* Lisa owns a jewelry shop. During her second month of business, she paid $150 of principal and $10 of interest on a loan from the bank. On the income statement for the month, what amount would appear as an expense? On the statement of cash flows for the month, what amount would appear as the loan payment to principal? Would each of these activities be classified as operating, financing, or investing?

E1-43B. *Retained earnings and cash. (LO 4).* Cookies & Pastries, Inc., started business on July 1, 2010, with a $16,000 cash contribution from its owners in exchange for common stock. The company used $7,500 of the cash for equipment for the new shop and $3,500 for cookies and pastries for its inventory. During the month, the company earned $7,000 cash revenue from the sale of the entire inventory. On July 31, 2010, the owners spent $5,000 for more cookies and pastries for the inventory. What is the balance in retained earnings on July 31, 2010? How much cash does the company have on hand on July 31, 2010? Use the accounting equation to help answer the questions.

E1-44B. *Classify cash flows. (LO 2, 4).* For E1-43B, what amounts would Cookies & Pastries, Inc., show on its statement of cash flows for the month ended July 31, 2010? Classify each as an operating, investing, or financing activity.

Problems
Set A

P1-45A. *Analyze income statement and balance sheet. (LO 4).* A set of financial statements for Gator Company follows:

Gator Company
Income Statement
For the Year Ended December 31, 2012

Sales	$600,000
Cost of goods sold	?
Gross profit on sales	375,000
Administrative expenses	54,000
Operating income	?
Interest expense	6,000
Income taxes expense	94,500
Net income	?

Gator Company
Balance Sheet
At December 31, 2012

Cash	$?		Accounts payable	$ 13,350
Accounts receivable	13,024		Notes payable	9,830
Inventory	43,271			
Equipment	972,684		Contributed capital	605,000
			Retained earnings	?
Total	$1,129,780		Total	?

Requirement

Fill in the missing amounts (indicated with question marks).

P1-46A. *Analyze business transactions using the accounting equation. (LO 3, 4).* The following transactions apply to Molly's Maid Service during April 2012:

a. Molly started the business by depositing $5,000 in a business checking account on April 1 in exchange for common stock.

b. The company provided services to clients and received $4,215 in cash.

c. The company borrowed $1,200 from the bank for the business by signing a note.

 d. The company paid $1,125 of operating expenses.
 e. The company purchased a new computer for $3,000 cash to use to keep track of its
    customers, starting next month.
 f. The company declared and distributed $1,050 to the owner as dividends.

Requirements

 1. Enter the transactions into the accounting equation.
 2. What are the total assets of the company at April 30, 2012?
 3. Prepare a statement of cash flows for the month ended April 30, 2012.
 4. What was net income for the month ended April 30, 2012?

P1-47A. *Analyze business transactions and the effect on the financial statements. (LO 2, 4).*
The following business transactions occurred during Buck's Hunting Gear, Inc.'s first month
of business:

 a. Buck began his business by depositing $25,000 into the business checking account. He
    received common stock in exchange.
 b. The company provided services to customers for $30,000 cash.
 c. The company paid travel expenses in the amount of $1,000 cash.
 d. The company borrowed $5,000 from the bank for operating capital.
 e. The company purchased $275 worth of office supplies (for future use) from Office
    Market for cash.
 f. During the month, the company paid cash of $5,000 for operating expenses.
 g. The company paid monthly rent on the retail space in the amount of $1,250.
 h. The company paid the staff $4,200.
 i. The company declared and paid a dividend of $1,000 to the owner, John Buck.
 j. On the last day of the month, Buck's purchased equipment costing $6,250 by signing a
    note payable with the bank.

Requirements

For each transaction in items (a)–(j), do the following:

 1. Identify whether it is an operating, investing, or financing transaction.
 2. Determine whether there is an increase, decrease, or no effect on the total assets of the business.
 3. Determine whether there is an increase, decrease, or no effect on net income.
 4. Indicate on which financial statement each amount would appear: the income statement (IS),
    the balance sheet (BS), the statement of changes in shareholder's equity (SE), or the state-
    ment of cash flows (CF). (Some will be shown on more than one statement.)

P1-48A. *Analyze business transactions and the effect on the financial statements. (LO 4).* Using
transactions a–j in P1-47A, answer the following questions:

Requirements

 1. What is the cash balance at the end of Buck's first month of business?
 2. Does the company have any liabilities at the end of the first month of business? If so, how much?
 3. Which assets will appear on the balance sheet at the end of Buck's first month of business?
 4. Did the company generate a net income or a net loss for its first month of business? How much?

P1-49A. *Analyze effect of transactions on accounting equation. (LO 2, 4).* What will be the
effects (increase, decrease, or no effect) on total assets, total liabilities, and total stockholders'
equity in each of the following situations? When shareholders' equity changes, note whether it is
contributed capital or retained earnings that changes. Identify whether each transaction is an operating, investing, or financing transaction.

	Total assets	=	Total liabilities	+	Shareholders' equity Contributed capital	+	Shareholders' equity Retained earnings
a. Received cash and issued shares of common stock	_____		_____		_____		_____
b. Purchased equipment with cash	_____		_____		_____		_____
c. Received cash from customers for services rendered	_____		_____		_____		_____
d. Borrowed money from the bank	_____		_____		_____		_____
e. Received a utility bill and paid cash for it	_____		_____		_____		_____

P1-50A. *Analyze business transactions and prepare the financial statements. (LO 4).* The following cash transactions took place during July 2010, the first month of business for Stay Bright Cleaning Supplies, Inc.:

    a. Bill Lunden started a business, Stay Bright Cleaning Supplies, Inc., by contributing $7,500 cash. He received common stock in exchange.

    b. The company earned and collected cash revenue of $2,500.

    c. The company paid expenses of $1,250 in cash.

    d. The company declared and paid dividends of $500.

    e. On July 31, the company borrowed $4,375 from the local bank by signing a three-year note.

Requirements

1. Show how each transaction affects the accounting equation.
2. Prepare the income statement, statement of changes in shareholder's equity, and statement of cash flows for the month ended July 31, 2010, and the balance sheet at July 31, 2010.

P1-51A. *Retained earnings portion of the statement of changes in shareholders' equity. (LO 4).* The following information is for Rick's Bed and Breakfast:

    a. Retained earnings on February 1, 2011, were $150,000.

    b. In February, revenues were $35,000 and expenses were $65,000.

    c. In March, revenues were $89,000 and expenses were $74,000.

    d. In April, revenues were $73,000 and expenses were $62,000.

    e. The only dividends declared and paid were in April for $5,000.

Requirements

1. Calculate the retained earnings balance for the three months ended April 30, 2011, for Rick's Bed and Breakfast.
2. Show the retained earnings portion of the statement of changes in shareholders' equity for the three months ended April 30, 2011.

Set B

P1-52B. *Analyze income statement and balance sheet. (LO 4).* A set of financial statements for Shelby's Music, Inc., follows:

Shelby's Music, Inc.
Income Statement
For the Year Ended June 30, 2012

Sales	?
Cost of goods sold	375,000
Gross profit on sales	525,000
Administrative expenses	?
Operating income	419,000
Interest expense	?
Income taxes	142,450
Net income	$264,550

Shelby's Music, Inc.
Balance Sheet
At June 30, 2012

Cash	$158,592	Accounts payable	$ 14,070
Accounts receivable	18,621	Notes payable	12,520
Inventory	?		
Equipment	895,895	Contributed capital	?
		Retained earnings	425,000
Total	?	Total	$1,231,000

Requirements

Fill in the missing amounts (indicated with question marks).

P1-53B. *Analyze business transactions using the accounting equation. (LO 3, 4).* The following transactions apply to Bostic's Auto Detail Service during November 2012:

    a. Xavier Bostic started the business by depositing $3,350 in a business checking account on November 1 in exchange for common stock.

    b. The company purchased a vacuum cleaner for $1,145 cash.

    c. The company borrowed $1,575 from the bank for the business by signing a note.

    d. The company provided services to clients and received $5,705 in cash.

e. The company paid $535 of operating expenses.

f. The company declared and made a distribution of $200 to the owner.

Requirements

1. Enter the transactions into the accounting equation.
2. What are the total assets of the company at November 30, 2012?
3. Prepare a statement of cash flows for the month ended November 30, 2012.
4. What was net income for the month ended November 30, 2012?

P1-54B. *Analyze business transactions and the effect on the financial statements. (LO 2, 4).* The following business transactions occurred during Heidi's Smoothy Shop, Inc.'s first month of business:

a. Heidi began her business by depositing $22,000 into the business checking account in exchange for common stock.

b. The shop paid travel expenses in the amount of $325.

c. The shop borrowed $12,000 from the bank for operating capital.

d. The shop purchased $600 worth of office supplies (for future use) from Office Supermarket for cash.

e. During the month, the shop earned revenue of $10,000 cash.

f. The shop paid the monthly rent on the retail space in the amount of $1,100.

g. The shop paid the staff $2,000.

h. Other operating expenses for the month were $1,375, which were paid in cash.

i. On the last day of the month, the shop purchased equipment costing $10,000 by signing a note payable with the bank.

j. The company declared and paid a dividend of $235 to Heidi, the firm's only shareholder.

Requirements

For each transaction in items (a)–(j), do the following:

1. Identify whether it is an operating, investing, or financing transaction.
2. Determine whether there is an increase, decrease, or no effect on the total assets of the business.
3. Determine whether there is an increase, decrease, or no effect on net income.
4. Indicate on which financial statement each amount would appear: the income statement (IS), the balance sheet (BS), the statement of changes in stockholder's equity (SE), or the statement of cash flows (CF). (Some will be shown on more than one statement.)

P1-55B. *Analyze business transactions and the effect on the financial statements. (LO 4).* Using transactions (a)–(j) in P1-54B, answer the following questions:

Requirements

1. What is the cash balance at the end of Heidi's Smoothy Shop's first month of business?
2. Does the shop have any liabilities at the end of the first month of business? If so, how much?
3. Which assets will appear on the balance sheet at the end of the shop's first month of business?
4. Did Heidi's generate a net income or a net loss during its first month of business? How much?

P1-56B. *Analyze effect of transactions on accounting equation. (LO 2, 4).* What will be the effects (increase, decrease, or no effect) on total assets, total liabilities, and total shareholders' equity in each of the following situations? When shareholders' equity changes, note whether it is contributed capital or retained earnings that changes. Identify whether each transaction is an operating, investing, or financing transaction.

	Total assets	=	Total liabilities	+	Contributed capital	+	Retained earnings
					Shareholders' equity		
1. Purchased land with cash	_____		_____		_____		_____
2. Performed services and received cash from customers	_____		_____		_____		_____
3. Received cash from the issue of shares of common stock	_____		_____		_____		_____
4. Paid cash for inventory	_____		_____		_____		_____
5. Sold inventory for cash	_____		_____		_____		_____

P1-57B. *Analyze business transactions and prepare the financial statements. (LO 4).* The following cash transactions took place during August, the first month of business for Comfy Cushions Cleaning, a corporation:

    a. Justin Snyder started the company by contributing $30,000 cash and received common stock in exchange.
    b. The company earned and received $10,000 cash in service revenue.
    c. The company paid employees $3,000 cash.
    d. Miscellaneous expenses paid amounted to $725 cash.
    e. The company declared and paid cash dividends of $975.
    f. On August 31, the company borrowed $13,300 from the local bank, to be repaid at the end of December.

Requirements

1. Show how each transaction affects the accounting equation.
2. Prepare the income statement, statement of changes in shareholder's equity, and the statement of cash flows for the month ended August 31 and the balance sheet at August 31.

P1-58B. *Retained earnings portion of the statement of changes in shareholders' equity. (LO 4).* The following information is for Larry's Book Store:

1. Retained earnings on January 1, 2010 were $127,000.
2. In January, revenues were $15,000 and expenses were $10,000.
3. In February, revenues were $17,500 and expenses were $20,000.
4. In March, revenues were $19,225 and expenses were $13,000.
5. The company declared and paid dividends in March of $1,000.

Requirement

Calculate the ending balance in retained earnings, and then prepare the retained earnings portion of the statement of changes in shareholders' equity for the quarter (three months) ended March 31, 2010.

Financial Statement Analysis

FSA1-1. *Identify items from the balance sheet. (LO 5).* Use Apple Inc.'s balance sheets given here to answer the questions that follow.

Apple Inc.
Consolidated Balance Sheets
(in millions, except share amounts)

Assets:	September 27, 2008	September 29, 2007
Current assets:		
Cash and cash equivalents	$11,875	$ 9,352
Short-term investments	12,615	6,034
Accounts receivable, less allowances of $47 in each period	2,422	1,637
Inventories	509	346
Deferred tax assets	1,447	782
Other current assets	5,822	3,805
Total currents assets	34,690	21,956
Property, plant, and equipment, net	2,455	1,832
Goodwill	207	38
Acquired intangible assets, net	285	299
Other assets	1,935	1,222
Total assets	$39,572	$25,347
Liabilities and Stockholders' Equity		
Current liabilities:		
Accounts payable	$ 5,520	$ 4,970
Accrued expenses	8,572	4,310
Total current liabilities	14,092	9,280
Non-current liabilities	4,450	1,535
Total liabilities	18,542	10,815
Commitments and contingencies		
Stockholders' equity:		
Common stock, no par value; 1,800,000,000 shares authorized; 888,325,973 and 872,328,972 shares issued and outstanding, respectively	7,177	5,368
Retained earnings	13,845	9,101
Accumulated other comprehensive income	8	63
Total shareholders' equity	21,030	14,532
Total liabilities and shareholders' equity	$39,572	$25,347

Requirements

1. What date marks the end of Apple's most recent fiscal year?
2. Did Apple earn a net income or net loss during the most recent fiscal year? How can you tell?
3. Did the owners of Apple make any capital contributions during the most recent fiscal year (or did Apple get some new owners)?
4. Did Apple buy or sell any property, plant, or equipment during the most recent fiscal year? How can you tell?
5. On the last day of the most recent fiscal year, did Apple have any debts? If so, what was the total amount?

FSA1-2. *Identify items from the statement of cash flows. (LO 5).* Use the statement of cash flows for Apple Inc. for the year ended September 27, 2008, given here to answer the questions that follow.

Apple Inc.
Statement of Cash Flows
For the Year Ended September 27, 2008

(in millions)	
Cash and cash equivalents, beginning of the year	$ 9,352
Operating Activities:	
Net income	4,834
Adjustments to reconcile net income to cash generated by operating activities . . .	4,762
Cash generated by operating activities	9,596
Investing Activities:	
Purchase of short-term investments	(22,965)
Proceeds from maturities of short-term investments	11,804
Proceeds from sales of short-term investments	4,439
Purchase of property, plant, and equipment	(1,091)
Other	(376)
Cash (used in) generated by investing activities	(8,189)
Financing Activities:	
Proceeds from issuance of common stock	483
Other financing activities (net)	633
Cash generated by financing activities	1,116
Increase in cash and cash equivalents	2,523
Cash and cash equivalents, end of the year	$11,875

Requirements

1. Did Apple purchase any property, plant, or equipment during the year?
2. If you were to examine Apple's balance sheet at September 27, 2008, what amount would be shown for cash and cash equivalents?
3. Was cash generated from operations or used by operations? By what amount?
4. Did Apple receive any new contributions from owners during the year? How can you tell?
5. What was the primary source of cash for Apple for the year ended September 27, 2008? What does this say to you about Apple's operations for this year?

FSA1-3. *Examine financial statements. (LO 2, 3, 5).* Use the selected pages from the annual report from Books-A-Million found in Appendix A to answer the following questions:

Requirements

1. What type of business is Books-A-Million and how is it organized?
2. Suppose you inherited $10,000 when your great-uncle passed away and you want to invest in a promising company. Would you invest in Books-A-Million? What information in the annual report would be useful in your decision? Be specific. Is there any information that is not provided in the annual report that you would want to have before making your decision?
3. What is your opinion of the information in the annual report? For example, do you think it is accurate? Useful? Interesting? Informative? Why or why not?

Critical Thinking Problems

Risks and Controls

Being in business is risky. Imagine that you are starting a business. What type of business would you start? What are the most significant risks you face with your business? What controls would you put into effect to minimize those risks?

Group Problem

Look at the four basic financial statements for Books-A-Million, found in Appendix A at the back of this book. Find the total assets, liabilities, and shareholders' equity for the two most recent years. As a group, discuss the change in the company's financial position without looking at the income statement. Jot down your opinions. Then, study the income statement for the most recent year. Do the results support your opinions about the balance sheet changes? What information do these statements provide for your analysis? What additional information would be useful? After answering these questions as a group, look at the notes to the financial statements. Do the notes help answer any of your questions?

Make a list of 10 questions you have about the financial statements. Try to answer them and discuss why you would like answers to these questions. Save the list so you can check to see how many of the questions you are able to answer at the end of the course.

Ethics

Does your school have an honor code? If it does, it very likely addresses the issue of cheating on assignments or exams. Have you ever cheated on an exam? Have you ever "borrowed" a friend's assignment and used it to help you complete yours? Have you ever been a witness to a violation of the honor code by your peers? Compare Target's code of ethics (called Business Conduct Guide and found at http://investors.target.com/phoenix.zhtml?c=65828&p=irol-govConduct) to your school's honor code. How are they similar in purpose and scope?

Internet Exercise: Disney Corporation

The Walt Disney Company is a diversified worldwide entertainment company with interests in ABC TV, ESPN, film production, theme parks, publishing, a cruise line, Infoseek, and the NHL Mighty Ducks. By using the Disney Web site, you can explore vacation options and get Disney's latest financial information.

Please go to the Disney Web site at http://corporate.disney.go.com/investors/

IE1-1. What is the Walt Disney Company's key objective?

Go to Financial Information and click on the most recent annual report.

1. What are the key businesses of the Walt Disney Company? Identify whether you think the primary business activity is manufacturing, merchandising, or servicing for each key business segment.
2. Use the site map to find Financial Highlights. Identify the amount of total revenues and operating income for the most recent year. On which financial statement will you find these amounts reported? Is the Walt Disney Company a proprietorship, a partnership, or a corporation? How can you tell?
3. Use the Site Map to find Financial Review. What key business segment was the largest driver of operating revenue and operating income growth for the past year? Does this order surprise you? Explain why or why not.

Please note: Internet Web sites are constantly being updated. Therefore, if the information is not found where indicated, please explore the annual report further to find the information.

2

Qualities of Accounting Information

LEARNING OBJECTIVES

When you are finished studying Chapter 2, you should be able to:

1. Define generally accepted accounting principles and explain why they are necessary.

2. Explain the objective of financial reporting and the qualities of financial information necessary to achieve this objective.

3. Identify the elements of the financial statements and describe their characteristics.

4. Explain how accrual basis accounting differs from cash basis accounting, and identify examples of accrual basis accounting on actual financial statements.

5. Compute and explain the meaning of the current ratio.

6. Identify the risks and potential frauds related to financial accounting records, and explain the controls needed to ensure their accuracy.

ETHICS Matters

Paying for Silence

With just two weeks until the start of his trial, Computer Associates International's former CEO, Sanjay Kumar, pleaded guilty to securities fraud and obstruction of justice. Not only did Kumar engage in a conspiracy to inflate the firm's 2000 and 2001 sales revenue, but he also authorized a $3.7 million payment to buy the silence of potential witnesses. In November 2006, he was sentenced to 12 years in prison and fined $8 million for his part in the $2.2 billion fraud.

As you will learn in this chapter, precisely *when* revenue is included on the income statement is one of the most crucial timing issues in accounting. Computer Associates included revenue on its income statement *before* the company actually earned the revenue. This violates one of the most significant accounting principles that forms the basis of U.S. GAAP and IFRS. Revenue must be earned before it can be included on the income statement for the period.

Why would a smart and wealthy man falsify accounting records, taking the risk of a long prison sentence? Sometimes people in power begin to feel invincible. It is important for every individual to have a strong sense of ethical behavior and to apply high moral standards to every business decision, no matter how small. Too often a number of seemingly small decisions can add up to one big crime.

L.O.1
Define generally accepted
accounting principles
and explain why they
are necessary.

Net profit equals all revenues
minus all expenses.

Information for Decision Making

After Sara sold her first batch of T-shirts, she had some decisions to make. The biggest one was whether or not to continue in business. What she needed to know to evaluate that decision was whether or not the company made a profit in January. **Net profit**, also known as net income, is the amount left after all expenses are deducted from all revenues.

For Team Shirts, the accounting period is the first month of doing business, January 1 through January 31. Information about the month's operations is summarized on the income statement—one of the four basic financial statements. The revenues for the period amounted to $900; this is the total amount the company earned when it sold 90 shirts. The expenses were the cost of the T-shirts sold, the cost of the advertising, and the interest paid on the loan from Sara's sister. The cost of the 90 T-shirts sold was $360, advertising expense was $50, and the cost of borrowing the money—interest expense—was $5. When those expenses, totaling $415, are deducted from the sales revenue of $900, the remaining $485 is net profit. Team Shirts added value by ordering shirts with a special logo and providing them to customers at a convenient time and place. And Team Shirts achieved its goal—to make a profit.

On the income statement in Exhibit 2.1, you will see $485 shown as net income, another name for net profit. The term profit can be applied to a single sale, a group of sales, or all the transactions for a period of time of business activity, whereas net income is a more specific term for describing a company's entire profit for a specific time period. The company made a gross profit of $540 ($900 sales − $360 cost of goods sold) on the sale of 90 T-shirts, and Team Shirts' net income for its first month of business activity was $485.

EXHIBIT 2.1

Income Statement for Team Shirts for January

This is a simple income statement for one month of business.

Team Shirts		
Income Statement		
For the Month Ended January 31, 2010		

Revenue		
Sales		$900
Expenses		
Cost of goods sold	$360	
Advertising expense	50	
Interest expense	5	
Total expenses		415
Net income		$485

Financial reporting provides information for decision making. An income statement, like the one shown for Team Shirts, is one source of information. When the second month of business activity is complete, Sara will prepare another income statement and will be able to compare the two statements. To make such a comparison meaningful, Sara needs to use the same rules for preparing the two statements. If Sara wanted to compare her company's performance to the performance of another T-shirt company, she would need to be sure that the other company was using the same rules to prepare its income statement. For financial information to be useful for evaluating the performance of a business across time or for comparing two different companies, the same rules must be used consistently.

As you learned in Chapter 1, there is a set of guidelines called generally accepted accounting principles (GAAP) that a company must follow when preparing its financial statements; this helps ensure consistency. These guidelines—usually known as accounting principles—were historically developed through common usage. A principle was acceptable if it was used and acknowledged by most accountants. Today the process of establishing GAAP is more formal, with the SEC and the FASB responsible for setting accounting standards.

Setting accounting standards has become a widely discussed topic since the beginning of the 2008 financial crisis. As you read in Chapter 1, there is an international body called the International Accounting Standards Board (IASB) that sets international accounting rules and guidelines called International Financial Reporting Standards (IFRS). The general characteristics and qualitative characteristics of accounting information you are about to study are the same for U.S. GAAP and IFRS. Most differences that arise apply to specific assets and liabilities as well as to classifications of some transactions. Overall, U.S. GAAP are detailed and technical, with over 160 standards and even more interpretations and related guidance. It is often characterized as rule-based. IFRS, on the other hand, has much less detailed instruction and is often characterized as concept-based. Applying IFRS will require much more judgment and interpretation of circumstances than is required in the application of GAAP. As you learn more about these topics in the chapters to come, you'll read about some specific differences in the two sets of standards.

Most people who prepare and who use financial statements believe that having a single set of standards used worldwide is a good idea. With the technological advances of the past few decades, the world has become a global business market. Consider Fiat's 2009 purchase of Chrysler, formerly one of the big three U.S. automakers. As a member of the European Union, Italy, the home of Fiat, uses IFRS, while Chrysler has used GAAP for decades. If both companies had used the same set of accounting standards, the analysis that was done in the execution of this purchase could have been significantly easier. Relationships between U.S. businesses and businesses in the rest of the world have become the norm, and these relationships result in an obvious need for the use of the same accounting standards. Recall that the SEC has set forth a time table for the convergence of U.S. GAAP and IFRS, with the complete adoption of IFRS by the United States possible by 2014. For this reason, it is a good idea to stay abreast of the differences in the two sets of standards and how those differences will be reconciled in the next several years.

---

1. What does GAAP stand for? What does IFRS stand for?
2. Why are guidelines needed for financial reporting?

Your Turn 2-1

Characteristics of Accounting Information

What Makes Information Useful?

The most general and the most important objective of financial reporting is to provide useful information for making decisions. What makes information useful? According to the FASB, the information must be relevant, reliable, comparable, and consistent.

RELEVANT. For information to be *relevant*, it needs to be significant enough to influence business decisions. The information should help confirm or correct the users' expectations. No matter how significant the information is, however, it must be timely to be relevant. For example, the price of fuel is extremely important information to an airline such as Southwest or JetBlue, and a manager needs this information to make decisions about ticket prices. However, if the firm reports fuel prices only monthly, the information will not be timely enough to be relevant. To be relevant, information must be useful in predicting the future. Currently, the SEC requires most firms to submit their financial information within 60 days of the end of the firm's fiscal year.

RELIABLE. When information is *reliable*, you can depend on it and you can verify its accuracy. The information is completely independent of the person reporting it. To be reliable, the information in the financial statements must be a faithful representation of what it intends to convey. For example, Darden Restaurants, Inc., parent company of Red Lobster and Olive Garden, reported $6.63 billion in sales for its fiscal year ended May 25, 2008. This amount must be true and verifiable; otherwise, the information could be misleading to investors. As you learned in Chapter 1, it is part of the auditors' job to make sure Darden has the documentation to confirm the accuracy of its sales amount. Anyone who examines Darden's sales records should come up with the same amount.

COMPARABLE. In addition to being relevant and reliable, useful information possesses *comparability*. This means investors will be able to compare corresponding financial information between two similar companies—how one company's net income compares with another company's net income. In putting together financial statements, accountants must allow for meaningful comparisons. Because there are often alternative ways to account for the same

L.O.2
Explain the objective of financial reporting and the qualities of financial information necessary to achieve this objective.

transaction within GAAP, companies must disclose the methods they select. The disclosures allow educated investors to adjust the reported amounts to make them comparable between different companies. As we learn more about the accounting choices involved in preparing the financial statements, you'll see how important comparability is to those who use financial statements.

CONSISTENT. To be useful, accounting information must be consistent. *Consistency* is the characteristic that makes it possible to track a company's performance or financial condition from one year to the next. Only if a company uses the same accounting methods from period to period are we able to make meaningful comparisons. For example, total revenues for Darden Restaurants were $6.63 billion for the fiscal year ended May 25, 2008, and $5.57 billion for the fiscal year ended May 27, 2007. Only when these two numbers are based on the same set of accounting methods can investors determine why sales increased. If the increase was caused partly or solely by the change in the way the company measured sales, then investors would be misled about the company's actual performance. Financial statement users want to rely on the firm's consistent application of accounting standards. Exhibit 2.2 summarizes the desired qualitative characteristics accounting information must have to be considered useful by GAAP.

EXHIBIT 2.2

Qualitative Characteristics of Accounting Information

Relevance: Information that will provide a basis for forecasts of future firm performance by the CEO and CFO, among others. What's ahead for this company?

Reliability: Information that is neutral and verifiable. Is the information independent of the specific person who prepared it?

Comparability: Different companies use the same set of accounting rules. Does the information allow meaningful comparisons of two different companies?

Consistency: A company uses the same rules from year to year. Does the information allow meaningful comparisons of a company's performance at different points in time?

Your Turn 2-2

1. What is the purpose of financial statements?
2. What four characteristics explain what GAAP mean by "useful" information?

Assumptions Underlying Financial Reporting

The **separate-entity assumption** means that the firm's financial records and financial statements are completely separate from those of the firm's owners.

The **monetary-unit assumption** means that the items on the financial statements are measured in monetary units (dollars in the United States).

Financial information pertains to only the firm, not to any other parties such as the firm's owners. This distinction between the financial information of the firm and the financial information of other firms or people is called the **separate-entity assumption**. It means that the financial statements of a business do not include any information about the finances of individual owners or other companies. Suppose Sara took a vacation to Hawaii at a cost of $3,000. No part of that transaction would be part of Team Shirts' financial reports because of the separate-entity assumption. Look at the income statement in Exhibit 2.1 on page 52, which summarizes the revenues and expenses for Team Shirts. You will notice that the items on the financial statements are expressed in amounts of money. This is called the **monetary-unit assumption**. Only items measured in monetary units, like dollars, are included in the financial statements.

At a minimum, firms prepare new financial statements every year. For internal use, financial statements are prepared more frequently. The SEC requires publicly-traded firms to prepare a new set of financial statements each quarter, which enables users to compare the company's performance from one quarter (every three months) to the next. Accountants divide the life of a business into time periods so they can prepare reports about the company's performance during those time periods. This creation of time periods is called the **time-period assumption**. Although most companies report financial information every three months, only the annual financial information is audited. Most companies use the calendar year as their fiscal year.

> The **time-period assumption** means that the life of a business can be divided into meaningful time periods for financial reporting.

Accountants assume a company will continue to remain in business for the foreseeable future, unless they have clear evidence it will either close or go bankrupt. This is called the **going-concern assumption**. With this assumption, financial statement values are meaningful. Would the bank lend money to a firm if the firm were not going to continue operating in the foreseeable future? If the firm expects to liquidate, the values on the financial statements lose their meaning. If a company is not a going concern, the values on the financial statements would need to be liquidation values to be useful.

> The **going-concern assumption** means that, unless there is obvious evidence to the contrary, a firm is expected to continue operating in the foreseeable future.

Principles Underlying Financial Reporting

In addition to these assumptions, there are four crucial principles that guide financial reporting. The first is called the **historical-cost principle**. Assets are recorded at their original cost to the company at the time of purchase. Accountants use cost because the cost of an asset is a reliable amount—it is unbiased and verifiable. After their original purchase, however, some assets and liabilities are revalued for the financial statements. You'll learn about assets that are originally recorded at historical cost but later adjusted to their fair market value—the amount the asset could be sold for in the marketplace under normal conditions—for presentation on the balance sheet. So, while the historical cost principle is still a basic accounting principle, both GAAP and IFRS have been increasing the use of fair value in the financial statements. The trade-off here is between information that is reliable (historical cost is exact and can be documented) and information that is relevant (fair value is often more useful to investors but may be harder to document and may not be exact).

> The **historical-cost principle** means that transactions are recorded at actual cost.

The second principle is called the **revenue-recognition principle**. When should revenue be included on an income statement? GAAP say that revenue is **recognized** when it is earned—meaning that is when revenue should be recorded and included on the income statement. Recall that this is where Computer Associates went wrong. When Team Shirts delivers a shirt to a customer, the company has earned the revenue. When one of Sara's friends simply says she is going to buy a T-shirt next week, no revenue is recognized. When an exchange actually takes place, or when the earnings process is complete or "virtually complete," that is the time for revenue recognition. When Team Shirts and a customer exchange the cash and the T-shirt, there is no doubt the transaction is complete. However, even when Team Shirts only delivers the T-shirt and the customer agrees to pay for it later (the sale is on account), the company will consider the earnings process virtually complete. Team Shirts has done its part, so the sale is included on the income statement. The cash for the sale does *not* have to be received in order to recognize the revenue.

> The **revenue-recognition principle** says that revenue should be recognized when it is earned and collection is reasonably assured.

> **Recognized revenue** is revenue that has been recorded so that it will show up on the income statement.

What about expenses? When an expense is recognized depends on when the revenue that results from that expense is recognized. Expenses are recognized—included on the income statement—when the revenue they were incurred to generate is recognized. This is the third principle, called the **matching principle**, and it is the basis of the income statement. Expenses are matched with the revenue they helped to generate. An example is the cost of goods sold. Only the cost of the T-shirts *sold* is recognized (e.g., included as an expense on the income statement). The expense is matched with the revenue from the sale of those shirts. The cost of the unsold T-shirts is not an expense—and will not be an expense—until those shirts are sold. An expense is a cost that has been used to generate revenue. If a cost has been incurred but it has not been used up, it is classified as an asset until it is used.

> The **matching principle** says that expenses should be recognized—shown on the income statement—in the same period as the revenue they helped generate.

The fourth principle is called the **full-disclosure principle**. It essentially says that companies should disclose any circumstances and events that would make a difference to the users of the financial statements. As you might guess, there is a lot of judgment involved in applying this principle to the financial statements.

> The **full-disclosure principle** means that the firm must disclose any circumstances and events that would make a difference to the users of the financial statements.

As you have read about the four financial statements and the notes to the statements, you have learned about the qualities of financial information and the assumptions and principles that provide the foundation of financial reporting. Without these assumptions and principles, managers, investors, and analysts could not rely on the information to make decisions.

To complete the foundation for financial reporting and to enable you to gain a full understanding of the information contained in the financial statements, you will need to know about two constraints that apply to the preparation of the statements. A *constraint* in financial accounting is a limit or control imposed by GAAP. There are two types of constraints: materiality and conservatism.

Materiality refers to the size or significance of an item or transaction in relation to the company's overall financial performance or financial position. An item is material if it is large enough to influence investors' decisions. For example, the cost of fuel, the amounts paid to employees, and the cost of buying or leasing airplanes are all material items for JetBlue or Southwest Airlines. In contrast, an item is considered immaterial if it is too small to influence investors. GAAP do not have to be strictly applied to immaterial items (measured in total). For example, suppose JetBlue Airlines made an isolated error and failed to record the revenue from your $350 ticket purchased and used in 2008. Because JetBlue's total revenue was over $3.38 billion for its fiscal year ended December 31, 2008, the company would not need to correct this single error. The item is considered immaterial. (However, if there were lots of these errors, the total amount could be material and JetBlue would have to investigate the errors and correct them.)

Conservatism refers to the choices accountants make when preparing the financial statements. When there is any question about how to account for a transaction, the accountant should select the treatment that will be least likely to overstate income or assets. Accountants believe it is better to understate income or assets than it is to overstate either. As you learn more of the specific ways GAAP are applied, you will see how this conservatism constraint is embedded in many accounting principles. You'll learn, for example, that under specific circumstances a firm has to review its assets before a balance sheet is prepared to make sure none is valued at more than it is actually worth. For example, JetBlue's December 31, 2008, balance sheet shows total property and equipment of $4.47 billion. Under certain conditions, GAAP require JetBlue to evaluate these assets to make sure they are not overstated with respect to their future revenue-generating potential.

L.O.3
Identify the elements of the financial statements and describe their characteristics.

Elements of the Financial Statements

As you learned in Chapter 1, a complete set of financial statements includes the following:

1. Income statement (sometimes called the statement of earnings)
2. Balance sheet (sometimes called the statement of financial position)
3. Statement of changes in shareholders' equity (sometimes called the statement of changes in stockholders' equity)
4. Statement of cash flows
5. Notes to the financial statements

GAAP describe the individual items that are included in the financial statements. To learn what is shown on each financial statement, we will look at the second month of business for Team Shirts. We will take the second month's transactions and see how they affect the accounting equation and the financial statements. Then, we will relate the statements to the qualitative characteristics described by GAAP.

At the beginning of the second month, on February 1, 2010, Team Shirts has a balance sheet that is identical to the balance sheet dated January 31, 2010. Recall that the company's assets, liabilities, and shareholder's equity balances roll forward when the new period starts.

Transactions for the Second Month of Business

The transactions for Team Shirts' second month of business are shown in Exhibit 2.3.

The first transaction in February is the purchase of 200 T-shirts, costing $4 each. Last month, Team Shirts paid cash for the purchase of the T-shirts. This month, the company buys them on credit, also known as **on account**. This means Team Shirts will pay for them later. The purchase increases the company's assets—$800 worth of T-shirts—and the $800 claim belongs to the vendor. When a company owes a vendor, **accounts payable** are the amounts the company

On account means *on credit*. The expression applies to either buying or selling on credit.

Accounts payable are amounts that a company owes its vendors. They are liabilities and are shown on the balance sheet.

Date	Transaction
February 1	1. Team Shirts purchases 200 T-shirts for inventory at $4 each. They are purchased on account.
February 5	2. Team Shirts buys advertising for $150, paying $100 in cash and the remainder on account. The brochures are distributed and used up in February.
February 14	3. Team Shirts purchases three months' worth of insurance for $150 cash, with the policy beginning on the date of purchase.
February 23	4. Team Shirts sells 185 T-shirts for $10 each; 170 of these are sold for cash and the remainder on account.
February 28	5. Team Shirts declares and pays a dividend of $100.

EXHIBIT 2.3

Transactions for Team Shirts for February

owes. This is the first transaction shown in Exhibit 2.4 on the following page, where the transactions are presented in the accounting equation worksheet.

Next, Sara hires a company to advertise the business immediately. This cost is $150 for a service. Team Shirts pays $100 when the service is provided, so the company still owes $50. Like the first transaction, this one also postpones payment. However, in this transaction, Team Shirts has incurred an expense. In the first transaction—when the inventory was purchased—Team Shirts gained an asset. The cost of the shirts will become an expense when the shirts are sold. In contrast, the work done related to the advertising is complete, and that signals an expense. (The timing of recognizing expenses can be tricky; the next chapter will discuss timing in detail.) The $150 expense, like all expenses, reduces the owner's claims to the assets of the firm. Assets decrease by $100 (the cash paid for the advertising), and the remaining $50 increases creditors' claims (liabilities) because it will be paid later. It is shown as other payables because accounts payable is generally reserved for amounts a firm owes its vendors. This is the second transaction shown in Exhibit 2.4. Notice that the expense is recorded even though all of the cash has not yet been paid.

As her business grows, Sara decides the company needs some insurance. Team Shirts pays $150 for three months' worth of coverage, beginning February 14. When a company pays for something in advance, the item purchased is something of future value to the company. Because such an item provides future value, it is classified as an asset. Some items purchased in advance may seem like unusual assets, and often have the word *prepaid* with them to provide information about what sort of assets they are. Common prepaid items are insurance, rent, and supplies. In this case, Team Shirts has purchased an asset called **prepaid insurance**. Cash is decreased by $150, and the new asset—prepaid insurance—is increased by $150. Notice that insurance expense has not been recorded. Until some of the insurance is used up—and it can be used up only from one point in time to a subsequent point in time—there is no expense. Sometimes companies call these prepaid items *prepaid expenses*. Even though the word *expense* is used in its name, a prepaid expense is not an expense as we define it. In accounting, an expense is an item on the income statement. A prepaid expense is an asset, shown on the balance sheet. This is another case of the cash flow being different than the expense on the income statement. We'll cover this topic in more detail in the next chapter, but this should help you begin to think about the difference between spending cash for something for the business and actually recognizing an expense on the income statement.

The company's success continues with the sale of 185 more T-shirts at $10 each. Although Transaction 4 shows these sales as a single transaction, this is just the total of all of the month's sales. They are grouped together here to make the presentation simple. Of the 185 shirts sold, 170 were sold for cash of $1,700 (170 shirts at $10 each) and 15 were sold on account for $150 (15 shirts at $10 each). When a sale is made on account, **accounts receivable**, the amounts owed to the firm by customers, are recorded. Accounts receivable are assets—resources with economic value to a business. This is the fourth transaction shown in Exhibit 2.4. Notice that the rest of this transaction includes the decrease in inventory of $740 (185 shirts at $4 each) with a corresponding expense (cost of goods sold of $740), which decreases retained earnings by $740.

Prepaid insurance is the name for insurance a business has purchased but not yet used. It is an asset.

Accounts receivable are amounts customers owe a company for goods or services purchased on credit.

EXHIBIT 2.4

Accounting Equation Worksheet for Team Shirts for February

All of a firm's transactions can be shown in the accounting equation worksheet. The income statement is made up of the transactions in the red box—that is everything in the Retained Earnings column except the beginning and ending balances and dividends. The income statement transactions (revenues and expense) are then condensed into one number (net income), which becomes part of the statement of changes in shareholder's equity, indicated by the yellow box. Then, the information from the statement of changes in shareholder's equity is summarized as part of the balance sheet, shown in blue. All of the transactions either directly or indirectly affect the balance sheet. The balance sheet reports the condensed and summarized information from the transactions, the totals indicated by the amount in the last row (balances at 2/28/2010). The fourth statement, the statement of cash flows, indicated by the green box, shows where the company got its cash and how it used its cash during the accounting period. Don't forget the beginning balances carried over from the end of January.

	Assets			= Liabilities		+	Shareholder's Equity		
							Contributed Capital	Retained Earnings	
	Cash	All other assets	(Account)	All liabilities	(Account)		Common stock		(Account)
Beginning Balances	$5,345	$ 40	Inventory				$5,000	$ 385	
Transactions									
1		800	Inventory	800	Accounts payable				
2	(100)			50	Other payables			(150)	Advertising expense
3	(150)	150	Prepaid insurance						
4	1,700	150 (740)	Accounts receivable Inventory					1,850 (740)	Sales revenue Cost of goods sold
Adjustment		(25)	Prepaid insurance					(25)	Insurance expense
5	(100)							(100)	Dividends
Balances at 2/28/2010	$6,695	+ $375		= $850		+	$5,000	+ $1,220	

━ Income Statement   ━ Statement of Changes in Shareholder's Equity   ━ Balance Sheet   ━ Statement of Cash Flows

Details of Ending Balances:

Non-cash assets:		Liabilities	
Prepaid insurance......................	$125	Accounts payable	$800
Account receivable...................	150	Other payables	50
Inventory.....................................	100	Total...	$850
Total...	$375		

At the end of the second month of business, Team Shirts pays a dividend of $100 to its only stockholder, Sara. This transaction reduces assets—cash—by $100, and it reduces retained earnings by $100. This is Transaction 5 in Exhibit 2.4. Notice that it is not recorded with the other transactions. Because dividends are not a component of net income, we have to record a dividend payment *outside* the red (income statement) box.

The financial statements for February can be prepared with the information from these transactions. However, there is still one more step before accurate financial statements can be prepared. This step is called **adjusting the books**. A company must review the amount that has been recorded for each asset and each liability to make sure every amount correctly reflects the financial situation of the company on the specific date of the balance sheet—the last day of the fiscal period (month, quarter, or year). After reviewing the transactions for Team Shirts during the month, can you identify any amount that seems incorrect to you? Start at the beginning of the accounting equation worksheet in Exhibit 2.4 and look at each item that has been recorded. The assets are cash, $6,695; accounts receivable, $150; inventory, $100; and prepaid insurance, $150. Are these amounts accurate at February 28, 2010, the end of the second month of business? Is any asset likely to communicate incorrect information?

> **Adjusting the books** means to make changes in the accounting records, at the end of the period, just before the financial statements are prepared, to make sure the amounts reflect the financial condition of the company at that date.

Yes—prepaid insurance, as it currently appears in the company's records, will not express what it should. Because the balance sheet will have the date February 28, 2010, Team Shirts wants the amount of prepaid insurance to be accurate at that date. What is the amount of the asset—insurance that is still unused—at the date of the balance sheet? It is the $150, paid on February 14, applied to three months. On February 28, half a month's worth has passed. So, approximately one-sixth (half a month's worth) of the prepaid insurance has been used. An adjustment must be made to make sure the correct amount of prepaid insurance is shown on the balance sheet. Like routine transactions, adjustments must keep the accounting equation in balance. To record this adjustment in the accounting equation, subtract $25 (1/6 × $150) from the prepaid insurance column, reducing the amount of prepaid insurance, and then reduce owner's claims by the same $25 amount. This reduction in the owner's claims is an expense—insurance expense—so it will be shown in the red-boxed area in the accounting equation worksheet. This adjustment is shown on the worksheet in Exhibit 2.4. The correct amount of the asset—the unused portion—will be shown on the balance sheet at February 28, 2010, as $125.

A review of the other items on the balance sheet does not reveal any other needed adjustments on this particular balance sheet date. In the next chapter, you will learn about other situations requiring adjustments before the financial statements can be prepared. For now, this adjustment makes the accounting records ready for the preparation of the financial statements at the end of February.

The income statement, prepared first, lists the revenues and expenses for the period; you can find those in the red-boxed area in Exhibit 2.4. All revenues increase retained earnings; all expenses decrease retained earnings. The only item that we regularly find under retained earnings that is *not* included on the income statement is a distribution to the owners, *dividends* in a corporation. GAAP say that distributions are not expenses, so we will never record them in the income statement area (red box).

All of the items for the income statement are in the red-boxed area of the worksheet. We can simply take the amounts in the red box in the retained earnings columns and group the transactions into revenues and expenses to form an income statement. The accounts are considered income statement accounts, not balance sheet accounts, even though the amounts will eventually be included in the retained earnings balance. They are income statement accounts because we will see the individual accounts on the income statement. The first item on the income statement is revenue. For Team Shirts, the sales revenue, often simply called *sales*, is $1,850.

There are three types of expenses listed. One is the cost of goods sold—also known as cost of sales. Recall that this is the expense associated with selling something purchased from someone else. Team Shirts has cost of goods sold of $740. The other two expenses are $150 for the advertising and $25 for insurance. Be sure you see and understand that the insurance expense is not the amount Team Shirts actually paid to the insurance company. Instead, it is the cost of the insurance that was used during the period. The amount that has not been used as of February 28 remains on the balance sheet as an asset.

The net income for the period is $935—revenues of $1,850 minus expenses of $915. Check it out in Exhibit 2.5, the income statement for Team Shirts for the month of February.

EXHIBIT 2.5

Income Statement for Team Shirts for February

This is the income statement for the second month of business for Team Shirts.

Team Shirts
Income Statement
For the Month Ended February 28, 2010

Revenue		
Sales		$1,850
Expenses		
Cost of goods sold	$740	
Advertising expense	150	
Insurance expense	25	
Total expenses		915
Net income		$ 935

The statement of changes in shareholder's equity is prepared next (shown in Exhibit 2.6).

EXHIBIT 2.6

Statement of Changes in Shareholder's Equity for Team Shirts for February

The statement of changes in shareholder's equity shows how all of the equity accounts have changed during the month.

Team Shirts
Statement of Changes in Shareholder's Equity
For the Month Ended February 28, 2010

Beginning common stock	$5,000	
Common stock issued during the month	0	
Ending common stock		$5,000
Beginning retained earnings	$ 385	
Net income for the month	935	
Dividends declared	(100)	
Ending retained earnings		1,220
Total shareholder's equity		$6,220

This statement provides the details of the changes in shareholder's equity during the year. The information for this statement is found in the shareholder's equity columns of the worksheet in Exhibit 2.4, shown in the yellow-boxed area. Team Shirts began the month with $5,000 in contributed capital. No new stock was issued during the month. That means no new contributions were made during the month. Retained earnings began the month with a balance of $385. Net income of $935 increases retained earnings, and the dividend of $100 decreases retained earnings. Because we have already prepared the income statement to summarize what happened in the red-boxed area in the retained earnings column, we do not need to list all of the individual items again on the Statement of changes in shareholder's equity. We just need to add net income as a single amount. The amount of retained earnings at the end of the period is $1,220 ($385 + 935 − 100).

Next, Team Shirts prepares the balance sheet. The balance sheet was really prepared as the transactions were put in the accounting equation worksheet, but not in a way to communicate the information most effectively. The transactions need to be summarized and organized to communicate the information clearly and effectively. The total amounts at the end of the accounting equation worksheet will be the foundation for the balance sheet. Each asset owned at February 28 is listed, along with the claims to those assets. Notice the similarity between the list of transactions on the worksheet in Exhibit 2.4 and the balance sheet in Exhibit 2.7.

The assets are listed at their amounts on February 28, 2010. There is $6,695 cash. (The details of how this number was calculated will be shown on the statement of cash flows.) Team Shirts also

EXHIBIT 2.7

Balance Sheet for Team Shirts at February 28, 2010

The balance sheet at February 28 has incorporated the new retained earnings balance.

Team Shirts
Balance Sheet
At February 28, 2010

Assets		Liabilities and Shareholder's Equity	
Cash	$6,695	Accounts payable	$ 800
Accounts receivable	150	Other payables	50
Inventory	100		
Prepaid insurance	125	Common stock	5,000
		Retained earnings	1,220
		Total liabilities and	
Total assets	$7,070	shareholder's equity	$7,070

has accounts receivable of $150—the amount customers still owe the company for T-shirts purchased during the month. There are 25 shirts left in the inventory, each having a cost of $4, for a total of $100.

The last asset is prepaid insurance, and the amount shown is $125—the unused portion at February 28. The adjustment reduced prepaid insurance by $25 for the amount used up during the last half of February.

There are two liabilities at February 28, 2010—accounts payable of $800 and other payables of $50. These are amounts that Team Shirts still owes to creditors.

The last item is the amount of shareholder's equity. Because we have already prepared the statement of changes in shareholder's equity, we know that $5,000 is the total contributed capital—in the form of stock—and $1,220 is the amount of retained earnings. Together, the liabilities plus shareholder's equity add up to $7,070—the same amount as the total assets.

The statement of cash flows (shown in Exhibit 2.8) shows every cash collection and every cash disbursement for the month. Sometimes several cash flows are summed rather than individually listed if there are lots of cash transactions. Each cash transaction is classified as one of three types: operating, investing, or financing.

To prepare this statement, you need to use the items from the transactions in the cash column of the worksheet in Exhibit 2.4, shown in the green-boxed area. For each cash amount, ask yourself if it pertains to operating activities, investing activities, or financing activities.

EXHIBIT 2.8

Statement of Cash Flows for Team Shirts for February

The statement of cash flows provides details about the changes to cash during the period.

Team Shirts
Statement of Cash Flows
For the Month Ended February 28, 2010

Cash from operating activities		
Cash collected from customers	$1,700	
Cash paid for advertising	(100)	
Cash paid for insurance	(150)	
Net cash from operations		$1,450
Cash from investing activities		0
Cash from financing activities		
Cash paid for dividends	$ (100)	
Net cash from financing activities		(100)
Net increase in cash		$1,350
Add beginning cash balance		5,345
Ending cash balance		$6,695

The first cash amount in Exhibit 2.4 is the payment of $100 in cash for advertising; that was the second transaction. This $100 is an operating cash flow because it is a cash expense related to routine business activities.

The next cash transaction is the $150 paid to the insurance company. The purchase of insurance is an operating cash flow. Notice that the statement of cash flows shows the cash paid—with no regard for when the insurance is used.

Transaction 4 involves cash inflows, for a total of $1,700. This transaction was a sale, which is an operating cash flow. Notice the cash in Transaction 4 is $1,700, representing 170 T-shirts sold for cash. Although 185 were actually sold, the cash for 15 of them has not been collected yet. In the statement of cash flows, every item must be cash only.

The final cash transaction is the distribution of $100 to the owner as dividends. This is classified as a financing cash flow because it relates to how the business is financed.

Be sure you see that the statement of cash flows includes every cash inflow and every cash outflow shown on the accounting equation worksheet. Also notice that nothing else is included on this financial statement. The net amount is the change in the amount of cash during the period. The bottom of the statement of cash flows adds the beginning cash balance of $5,345 to the increase of $1,350 to get the ending cash balance of $6,695, shown on the February 28, 2010, balance sheet.

Notes to the financial statements are not included here for Team Shirts, but you should never forget that they are a crucial part of the financial statements. Look at the notes in the financial statements of Books-A-Million in the appendix of the book. The notes are longer than the statements! As you gain an understanding of the complexity of the choices accountants make in preparing financial statements, you will see the need for notes to give the financial statement users information about those choices. Remember that one of the four basic principles under GAAP is full disclosure.

Your Turn 2-3

Is prepaid insurance an expense or an asset? Explain.

Assets

Looking at the balance sheet at February 28, 2010, for Team Shirts, Exhibit 2.7, you see the company's assets, also referred to as economic resources, on the left. According to GAAP, *assets* are those items of value that belong to or are controlled by the company. They are on the balance sheet as a result of past transactions, but they do have value, which they will provide in the future when they will be used to help the business produce revenue.

The first asset on Team Shirts' balance sheet is cash. The amount has been determined by past transactions, and the money has value because of what it can buy in the future. Other common assets include accounts receivable (amounts owed to the company by customers) and inventory (items purchased for sale). The last asset shown is prepaid insurance. This is the unused portion of the insurance—it still has value on February 28.

Liquidity is a measure of how easily an asset can be converted to cash. The more liquid an asset is, the more easily it can be turned into cash.

Assets are listed on the balance sheet in order of **liquidity**. Liquidity refers to how easily an asset can be converted into cash. The assets that the firm expects to use within a year are called **current assets**. The assets that will not be used within a year are called **noncurrent assets**, or **long-term assets**. So far, Team Shirts has only current assets. Look at the balance sheet of The Home Depot, Inc., in Exhibit 2.9. The asset section of the balance sheet shows both current and long-term assets.

Current assets are the assets the company plans to turn into cash or use to generate revenue in the next fiscal year.

Assets are one of three classifications of items on the balance sheet. The other two classifications tell who—creditors or owners—has claim to these assets. Recall that the balance sheet is essentially the accounting equation:

$$\text{Assets} = \text{Liabilities} + \text{Shareholders' equity}$$

Noncurrent assets, or **long-term assets**, are assets that will last for more than a year.

Liabilities

The January 2, 2010, balance sheet, shown in Exhibit 1.6, indicated that Team Shirts owed $500 to Sara's sister. On February 28, 2010, that is no longer the case. The debt was paid off in January. On February 28, 2010, the only liabilities Team Shirts has are accounts payable and other payables. *Liabilities* are amounts that the business owes. The word *payable* indicates a liability. Liabilities are the claims of creditors. Usually, these claims will be paid to creditors in

EXHIBIT 2.9

Comparative Balance Sheets for The Home Depot

Here are comparative balance sheets taken from The Home Depot's recent annual report.

The Home Depot, Inc., and Subsidiaries
Consolidated Balance Sheets

amounts in millions, except share and per share data	February 1, 2009	February 3, 2008
Assets		
Current assets:		
Cash and cash equivalents	$ 519	$ 445
Short-term investments	6	12
Receivables, net	972	1,259
Merchandise inventories	10,673	11,731
Other current assets	1,192	1,227
Total current assets	13,362	14,674
Property and equipment, at cost:		
Land	8,301	8,398
Buildings	16,961	16,642
Furniture, fixtures, and equipment	8,741	`8,050
Leasehold improvements	1,359	1,390
Construction in progress	625	1,435
Capital leases	490	497
	36,477	36,412
Less accumulated depreciation and amortization	10,243	8,936
Net property and equipment	26,234	27,476
Notes receivable	36	342
Goodwill	1,134	1,209
Other assets	398	623
Total assets	$41,164	$44,324
Liabilities and Stockholders' Equity		
Current liabilities:		
Short-term debt	$ —	$ 1,747
Accounts payable	4822	5,732
Accrued salaries and related expenses	1,129	1,094
Sales taxes payable	337	445
Deferred revenue	1,165	1,474
Income taxes payable	289	60
Current installments of long-term debt	1,767	300
Other accrued expenses	1,644	1,854
Total current liabilities	11,153	12,706
Long-term debt, excluding current installments	9,667	11,383
Other long-term liabilities	2,198	1,833
Deferred income taxes	369	688
Total liabilities	23,387	26,610
Stockholders' Equity		
Common stock, par value $0.05; authorized: 10 billion shares; issued 1.707 billion shares at February 1, 2009 and 1.698 billion shares at February 3, 2008; outstanding 1.696 billion shares at February 1, 2009 and 1.690 billion shares at February 3, 2008	85	85
Paid-in capital	6,048	5,800
Retained earnings	12,093	11,388
Accumulated other comprehensive income (loss)	(77)	755
Treasury stock, at cost, 11 million shares at February 1, 2009 and 8 million shares at February 3, 2008	(372)	(314)
Total stockholders' equity	17,777	17,714
Total liabilities and stockholders' equity	$41,164	$44,324

See accompanying Notes to Consolidated Financial Statements.

cash. Liabilities, like assets, are the result of past transactions or events. For example, a purchase of inventory items on account creates a liability called accounts payable. The balance sheet on February 28, 2010, was prepared after the purchase of the shirts but before the company paid for them, so the balance sheet shows the cost of the shirts as accounts payable. Once incurred, a liability continues as an obligation of the company until the company pays for it. The accounts payable amount for the T-shirts remains on the balance sheet until Team Shirts pays the bill for the shirts. Often, liabilities involve interest—payment of an additional amount for the right to delay payment. When Team Shirts repaid Sara's sister in January, the company paid $5 interest for the use of her money.

Liabilities can also be current or noncurrent. If a liability will be settled with a current asset, it is called a **current liability**. For practical purposes, you can think about a current liability as a liability that will be paid off in the next year. **Noncurrent liabilities**, or **long-term liabilities**, will be paid off over a period longer than one year. Most balance sheets show a subtotal for current assets and a subtotal for current liabilities. That format is called a **classified balance sheet**. Look at the balance sheet for Home Depot, shown in Exhibit 2.9. See if you can find the subtotals for current assets and current liabilities. This is a classified balance sheet because it has two classifications of assets and liabilities—short- and long-term.

> **Current liabilities** are liabilities the company will settle—pay off—in the next fiscal year.
>
> **Noncurrent liabilities**, or **long-term liabilities**, are liabilities that will take longer than a year to settle.
>
> A **classified balance sheet** shows a subtotal for many items, including current assets and current liabilities.

Your Turn 2-4

1. What is the difference between a current asset and a long-term asset?
2. What is a classified balance sheet?

Shareholders' Equity

Shareholders' equity, sometimes called net assets, is the owners' claims to the assets of the company. There are two ways owners can create equity in a company. The first way is by making capital contributions—*contributed capital*. Usually, the capital is cash, but it could be equipment or other items of value. When Sara started her T-shirt business, she invested $5,000 of her own money. Sometimes this is called the owner's investment in the company. The term *investment* may be confused with investments that the company itself makes with its extra cash. For example, Apple may invest some of its extra cash in the stock of Google, which Apple would call an investment. To avoid that confusion, we will refer to owners' investments in the firm as capital contributions.

The second way to create equity in a business is to make a profit. (That is the preferred way.) When Team Shirts sells a shirt, the profit from that shirt increases the owner's equity in the company. In general, revenues increase shareholders' equity and expenses reduce shareholders' equity.

In corporations, the two types of equity are separated on the balance sheet. The first type of equity is contributed capital, also known as **paid-in capital**, while the second is *retained earnings*. In a sole proprietorship or partnership, both types of equity are together called *capital*. Separating these amounts for corporations provides information for potential investors about how much the owners have actually invested in the corporation.

> **Paid-in capital**, another name for contributed capital, is the owner's investment in the business.

Measurement and Recognition in Financial Statements

We will now take a closer look at some of the features of the balance sheet and income statement. Recall that the balance sheet is simply a summary of the transactions from the accounting equation: **Assets = Liabilities + Shareholders' equity**. The three elements are major categories, each divided into subcategories.

MEASURING ASSETS. We will start with assets. The most well-known asset is cash. It is listed first on the balance sheet. As you will notice on Home Depot's balance sheet, all other assets are listed in order of their liquidity—how easily they can be converted to cash. A monetary value is computed for each asset. Cash, for example, is the total amount of money in checking and savings accounts. The next asset could be short-term investments, ones the company can easily sell for cash at any time. The next asset on the balance sheet is usually accounts receivable—the total amount that customers owe the company for credit sales. Inventory is another asset, measured at its cost. We saw that Team Shirts' balance sheet included the cost of the T-shirts still in the inventory on the balance sheet date. Statements prepared under GAAP almost always list assets in order of liquidity, starting with cash. However, under IFRS, the balance sheet often *ends* with current assets. This type of formatting difference is quite common between GAAP and IFRS financial statements.

Earlier you learned two characteristics of the way things are measured for the financial statements. First, they are measured in monetary units. For us, that means dollars. For example, the actual number of T-shirts in the inventory is not shown on the balance sheet; only the cost of the inventory is shown. Second, the items on the financial statements are reported at historical cost—what the company paid for them. They are not reported at the amount the company hopes to sell them for. Some assets continue to be shown at cost on the balance sheet, and others are revalued to a more current amount for each balance sheet. You will learn the details of which assets are revalued and which assets are not revalued in the chapters to come.

RECOGNIZING REVENUES AND EXPENSES. As you know, revenue is recognized when it is earned. Must the customer actually pay the company in cash before a sale can be counted as revenue? No. Notice that the sales of all the shirts are included in the sales total, even though 15 of the shirts have not been paid for yet. When a customer purchases an item on account, the earnings process is considered virtually complete, even though the cash has not been collected. Similarly, a cost incurred in the generation of revenue need not be paid to be included on the income statement. In calculating the revenue and expenses for an income statement, accountants do not follow the cash. Instead, they record revenue when the "economic substance" of the transaction is complete.

Accountants use the expressions *virtually complete* and *economic substance* to describe the same idea—that a transaction does not need to be technically complete to recognize the resulting revenue. If the transaction is substantially complete, the revenue is recognized. This is the revenue-recognition principle we discussed earlier. When Team Shirts sells T-shirts, delivering them and receiving the customers' promise to pay are considered the economic substance of that transaction. Cash may come before the transaction is complete or it may come afterward. This way of accounting for revenues and expenses—using the economic substance of the transaction to determine when to include it on the income statement instead of using the exchange of cash—is called **accrual basis accounting**. Exhibit 2.10 summarizes the assumptions, principles, and constraints of financial reporting.

> **Accrual basis accounting** refers to the way we recognize revenues and expenses. Accountants do not rely on the exchange of cash to determine the timing of revenue recognition. Firms recognize revenue when it is earned and expenses when they are incurred—no matter when the cash is received or disbursed. Accrual accounting follows the matching principle.

EXHIBIT 2.10

Assumptions, Principles, and Constraints of Financial Reporting

Assumptions:	Time-period assumption	The life of a business can be divided into artificial time periods for financial reporting.
	Separate-entity assumption	Financial statements of a firm contain financial information about only that firm.
	Monetary-unit assumption	Only items that can be measured in monetary units are included in the financial statements.
	Going-concern assumption	A company will remain in business for the foreseeable future.
Principles:	Historical-cost principle	Assets are recorded at cost.
	Revenue-recognition principle	Revenue is recognized when it is earned and collection is reasonably assured.
	Matching principle	Expenses are recognized in the same period as the revenue they helped generate.
	Full-disclosure principle	A company should provide information about any circumstances and events that would make a difference to the users of the financial statements.
Constraints:	Materiality	Materiality refers to the size or significance of an item or transaction on the company's financial statements.
	Conservatism	When there is any question about how to account for a transaction, the accountant should select the treatment that will be least likely to overstate income or overstate assets.

When to recognize revenue is easy for some businesses and extremely difficult for others. There is a lot of disagreement among accountants about the timing of revenue recognition. Everyone agrees that the accounting standards say that revenue should be recognized when the revenue has actually been earned and it is reasonable to assume the customer will pay. That is, the transaction is virtually complete. But people often cannot agree on exactly when that has happened. This is an important topic that is regularly debated in the financial community. Unfortunately, improper revenue recognition has caused serious problems for many companies. Many of the accounting scandals in the last decade are related to revenue recognition.

Your Turn 2-5

Give an example of the matching principle from the income statement for Team Shirts for February.

L.O.4
Explain how accrual basis accounting differs from cash basis accounting, and identify examples of accrual basis accounting on actual financial statements.

Accruals and Deferrals

Accrual Basis Accounting

The term *accrual basis accounting* includes two kinds of transactions in which the exchange of cash does not coincide with the economic substance of the transaction. The revenues and expenses are recognized at a time other than the time when the cash is collected or paid.

One kind of accrual basis transaction is an **accrual** and the other is a **deferral**. The meaning of each kind of accrual basis transaction is shown in Exhibit 2.11.

EXHIBIT 2.11

Accrual Basis Accounting

Accrual basis accounting involves both accruals and deferrals.

An **accrual** is a transaction in which the revenue is earned or the expense is incurred before the exchange of cash.

A **deferral** is a transaction in which the exchange of cash takes place before the revenue is earned or the expense is incurred.

When the action comes before the cash, it is an *accrual*. When Team Shirts made a credit sale, it was an accrual. To accrue means to "build up" or "accumulate." In accounting, we are building up our sales or our expenses even though the cash has not been exchanged. The sale is completed first—merchandise is delivered to the customer—and the cash payment will come later. Instead of receiving the asset *cash* from the purchaser, the company records an asset called *accounts receivable*—meaning *cash* due from the purchaser. Accounts receivable is the amount owed to the company by customers. Because GAAP are based on accrual accounting, the necessary part of the transaction for recording the revenue is the actual sale of goods or services—that is the "action," not the cash receipt from the customers.

When the dollars come before the action, it is called a *deferral*. When Team Shirts paid for the insurance, it was an advance purchase—as we all pay insurance premiums up front, not after the expiration date of the policy. But the amount paid for the insurance was not considered an expense until it was actually used as indicated by time passing. To defer something, in common language, means to put it off—to delay or postpone it. In the language of accounting, a deferral means that the company will postpone recognizing the expense until the insurance is actually used. When Team Shirts paid the cash in advance of the period covered by the insurance, the company recorded the cash disbursement. In other words, Team Shirts recorded it in the business records as cash that had been spent. However, the expense was not recognized when the cash was paid. It will be recognized—and remember, that means included on the income statement—when the cost is actually used. That use is the "action" that signals expense recognition.

Cash Basis versus Accrual Basis Accounting

Cash basis accounting is a system based on the exchange of cash. In this system, revenue is recognized only when cash is collected, and an expense is recognized only when cash is disbursed. This is not an acceptable method of accounting under GAAP.

There is another type of accounting called **cash basis accounting**; revenue is recognized only when the cash is collected, and expenses are recorded only when the cash is paid. This is *not* a generally accepted method of accounting according to the FASB and the SEC. Using the exchange of cash as the signal for recognizing revenue and expense does not communicate the performance of the business in a way that allows us to evaluate its achievements. The cash flows are important, but alone they do not provide enough information for decision makers. This does not stop some businesses from using it as the basis of their own accounting records. Remember, some businesses are not required to follow GAAP. For example, doctors who are sole proprietors may use cash basis accounting in their businesses. This means they recognize only the cash they receive as revenue. If they provide services to someone who has not yet paid for those services at the time an income statement is prepared, they would not include the fee not yet received as revenue for that income statement. That is not GAAP. If the doctors were following GAAP, they would count it as revenue and as a receivable (accounts receivable).

Accounting Periods and Cutoff Issues

Why does it matter (for accounting purposes) if there is a difference between the time when the goods or services are exchanged (the economic substance of the transaction) and the time when the cash related to that transaction is received or disbursed? If a company makes a sale on account and the cash is collected later, why does it matter when the sale is recognized—included as revenue on the income statement? Studying Team Shirts will help you answer these questions.

When Sara began her business in 2010, she chose the calendar year as the company's fiscal year. Each of the company's annual income statements will cover the period from January 1 to December 31 of a specific year. It is important that what appears on the income statement for a specific year is only the revenue earned during those 12 months and only the expenses incurred to generate that revenue. What is included as a sale during the period? Accountants have decided to use the exchange of goods and services, not the cash exchange, to define when a sale has taken place. Expenses are matched with revenues, also without regard to when the cash is exchanged. This makes the financial statements of all companies that follow GAAP consistent and comparable.

Recall that the balance sheet is a snapshot view of the assets, liabilities, and shareholders' equity on a specific date. For a company with a fiscal year end on December 31, that is the date of the balance sheet. Remember, the end-of-the-year balance sheet for one year becomes the beginning-of-the-year balance sheet for the next year. When you are out celebrating New Year's Eve, nothing is happening to the balance sheet. When Sara goes to sleep on December 31, 2010, the cash on the December 31, 2010, balance sheet of Team Shirts is exactly the amount of cash that the company will have on January 1, 2011. So the final balance sheet amounts for one year simply roll forward to the next year.

Then, transactions start happening—exchanges take place. The revenues and expenses for the period of time are shown on the income statement. The income statement covers a period of time. A company may construct weekly, monthly, quarterly, or annual financial statements. Many companies prepare monthly and quarterly financial statements; all companies prepare annual financial statements. The income statement for a specific year gives the revenues and expenses for that year. It gives information about how the balance sheet has changed between the beginning of the year and the end of the year. The revenues increase owners' claims; expenses reduce owners' claims. If the difference between revenues and expenses is positive—if revenues are greater than expenses—the company has a net income. If the expenses are greater than revenues, the company has a net loss. The net income or net loss is sometimes called the *bottom line*.

What is the difference between cash basis and accrual basis accounting? **Your Turn** 2-6

How Investors—Owners and Creditors—Use Accrual Accounting Information

Owners and creditors can both be considered investors in a business. Both invest their money to make money, and they both take a risk in investing their money in the business. In this context, you can think of risk as the uncertainty associated with the amount of future returns and the timing of future returns. Some investments are riskier than others. For example, when a bank makes a loan to a company, the banker evaluates the ability of the company to repay the loan amount—the principal—plus interest—the cost of borrowing the money. If the bank makes a loan to a company that does not do well enough to repay the debt, the company may need to sell noncash assets to raise cash to pay off the loan plus interest due. When lending money, the bank must compare the risk with the expected return.

Most often, the risk and return of an investment change value in the same direction—we say they are positively correlated. *Positively correlated* means they move in the same direction— higher risk means higher expected return for taking the higher risk; lower risk means lower expected returns. For higher investment risk, the potential for a higher return is needed to attract investors.

Investing in a company as an owner is riskier than investing as a creditor. A creditor's claim to the assets of a company has priority over an owner's claim. (Creditors have first claim to the assets.) If a company has just enough money either to pay its creditors or to make a distribution to its owner or owners, the creditors must be paid, and *they always must be paid* before anything—if there is anything left—is distributed to the owners. That translates into less risk for a creditor. The owner's risk is that the company will go out of business.

However, the owner, who takes more risk, has the right to share the profit. So the risk for the owner is accompanied by the potential for a higher return. A creditor, on the other hand, will never receive more than the amount of the loan, plus the amount of interest that is agreed on when the loan is made.

Financial information is useful for someone deciding whether or not to invest in a company. Suppose Team Shirts wanted to borrow money to expand. A bank would want to examine the company's income statement, balance sheet, and the statement of cash flows. The reason is to evaluate potential risk—the company's ability to make the required principal and interest payments.

The balance sheet shows a company's assets and who has claim to them. A bank loan officer would use the information on the balance sheet to evaluate Team Shirts' ability to repay the loan. He or she would want to be sure that the company did not have too many debts. The more debt a company has, the more cash it must generate to make the loan payments.

The information on the balance sheet would not be enough to assure the bank loan officer that Team Shirts would be able to repay the loan. Because a loan is repaid over several months or years, information about the future earning potential of the business is important. Studying the past performance of a business helps predict its future performance. That makes the profit the company earned during the past year relevant to the banker. Details about the sales revenue and expenses incurred to generate that revenue would help the bank evaluate the company's potential to generate enough cash to repay a loan.

Still, the information on these two financial statements, no matter how relevant to the bank's evaluation, would not be enough. Another piece of the puzzle is the way the company manages its cash. A company may have little debt and lots of earning potential. However, if the company does not have enough cash, the loan payments cannot be made. Because cash collection is the bank's primary concern, the statement of cash flows provides additional information for the bank.

An Example to Illustrate the Information Financial Statements Provide

We will compare two companies, each starting its fiscal year with an identical balance sheet. Then, during the first month of the year, they have very similar transactions. We will look at only a few of the transactions, and we will see that their income statements for the first month are the same. As you study the companies, try to figure out why their income statements are the same. Their ending balance sheets and statements of cash flows are not the same. Where do the differences show up in the financial statements?

The two companies are Clean Sweep and Maids-R-Us. Both are cleaning businesses and both are sole proprietorships. Judy Jones owns Clean Sweep, and Betty Brown owns Maids-R-Us. On January 1, 2011, the two companies have identical balance sheets. Look at each item on the balance sheet in Exhibit 2.12 and be sure you know what it means. Do this before you go on.

EXHIBIT 2.12

Beginning Balance Sheet for Clean Sweep and Maids-R-Us

At the beginning of the month, both companies have the same balance sheet.

Clean Sweep or Maids-R-Us
Balance Sheet
At January 1, 2011

Assets	
Cash	$ 900
Supplies	200
Total assets	$1,100
Liabilities	
Notes payable	$ 400
Owner's equity	
Capital, Owner's name (Jones or Brown)	700
Total liabilities and owner's equity	$1,100

Study each transaction and look at its effect on the accounting equation. Follow along using Exhibit 2.13 and 2.14 (on the following page).

Both Clean Sweep and Maids-R-Us	Clean Sweep	Maids-R-Us
1. Clean 10 houses for a fee of $75 per house	Collects the fees in cash at the time the services are rendered	Agrees to extend credit to the customers; fees will be collected after 30 days
2. Make a loan payment plus interest	Pays off the entire loan plus $40 interest	Pays only $100 of the loan plus $40 interest
3. Count the supplies on January 31 and find $25 worth left on hand	Both will make an adjustment to show $175 worth of supplies used	

EXHIBIT 2.13

Transactions for January 2011 for Clean Sweep and Maids-R-Us

Be sure to study how the transactions are different for the two companies.

Transaction 1: Each company earns $750 worth of revenue. Clean Sweep collects the cash, but Maids-R-Us extends credit to its customers. Clean Sweep records the asset cash, whereas Maids-R-Us records the asset *accounts receivable*. Both companies have earned the same amount of revenue, so each will show $750 revenue on its income statement for the month.

Transaction 2: Each company makes a loan payment. Clean Sweep pays the entire amount of the note payable, $400, plus interest of $40. Maids-R-Us pays only $100 of principal on the note payable, plus interest of $40. The only expense in this transaction is the interest expense of $40. Both companies have incurred the same amount of interest expense, so each will show $40 interest expense on its income statement. The repayment of the principal of a loan does not affect the income statement.

Adjustment: At the end of the period, each company will record supplies expense of $175, leaving $25 as supplies on hand on the January 31 balance sheet. Both income statements will show supplies expense of $175.

We can construct an income statement for each company from the numbers in the red-boxed area in Exhibit 2.14. Revenues for the month of January amounted to $750 and expenses were $215, so net income was $535. This is the case for both companies, as shown

EXHIBIT 2.14

Accounting Equation Worksheets for Clean Sweep and Maids-R-Us

The differences in the transactions between the two companies are reflected in the accounting equation worksheet.

Panel A: Clean Sweep

	Cash	**Assets** All other assets	(Account)	**= Liabilities** All liabilities	(Account)	**+ Owner's Equity** Contributed Capital	Retained Earnings	(Account)
Beginning Balances	$ 900	$ 200	Supplies	$400	Notes payable	$700		
Transaction								
1. Earns revenue and collects fees in cash	750						$ 750	Revenue
2. Makes loan payment	(440)			(400)	Notes payable		(40)	Interest expense
3. Adjusts for supplies used		(175)	Supplies				(175)	Supplies expense
Ending Balances	$1,210 + $ 25			= 0		+ $700	+ $ 535	

▬ Income Statement   ▬ Statement of Changes in Owner's Equity   ▬ Balance Sheet   ▬ Statement of Cash Flows

Panel B: Maids-R-Us

	Cash	**Assets** All other assets	(Account)	**= Liabilities** All liabilities	(Account)	**+ Owner's Equity** Contributed Capital	Retained Earnings	(Account)
Beginning Balances	$900	$200	Supplies	$400	Notes payable	$700		
Transaction								
1. Earns revenue and extends credit		750	Accounts receivable				$750	Revenue
2. Makes loan payment	(140)			(100)	Notes payable		(40)	Interest expense
3. Adjusts for supplies used		(175)	Supplies				(175)	Supplies expense
Ending Balances	$760 + $775			= $300		+ $700	+ $535	

in Exhibit 2.15. Even though one company extended credit to its customers and the other collected cash for its services, the income statements are identical. The income statement is only concerned with revenues earned and expenses incurred, not with the timing of the related cash flows.

The balance sheet at January 31 for each company can be constructed by simply organizing the details of the ending balances of the accounting equation for each company in Exhibit 2.14. For a sole proprietorship, all owner's equity—contributed and earned—is added together and called *owner's capital*. Both types of equity—contributed capital and retained earnings—are shown on the worksheet, and their balances are added together when the balance sheet is prepared. The two balance sheets are shown in Exhibit 2.16. Notice the

Clean Sweep or Maids-R-Us
Income Statement
For the Month Ended January 31, 2011

Revenue		
Cleaning fees		$750
Expenses		
Supplies	$175	
Interest	40	
Total expenses		215
Net income		$535

EXHIBIT 2.15

Income Statement for Clean Sweep and Maids-R-Us for January

Look back at Exhibit 2.14 to the accounting equation worksheet, where you will see the transactions in the red-boxed area are the same for both companies. That means their income statements are identical.

EXHIBIT 2.16

Balance Sheets for Clean Sweep and Maids-R-Us at January 31, 2011

The balance sheets are not the same. The total assets are different because Clean Sweep paid $300 more than Maids-R-Us on the note payable. They have different assets also. Maids-R-Us has accounts receivable of $750, revenue it earned but did not collect in January.

Clean Sweep
Balance Sheet
At January 31, 2011

Assets		Liabilities and Owner's Equity	
Cash	$1,210		
Supplies	25	Capital, Jones	$1,235
Total assets	$1,235	Total liabilities and owner's equity ...	$1,235

Maids-R-Us
Balance Sheet
At January 31, 2011

Assets		Liabilities and Owner's Equity	
Cash	$ 760	Notes payable	$ 300
Accounts receivable ...	750		
Supplies	25	Capital, Brown	$1,235
Total assets	$1,535	Total liabilities and owner's equity ...	$1,535

differences. Assets and liabilities are different for the two companies, but the owner's equity amounts are the same.

It is important to understand why both companies have the same amount of owner's equity. Both had beginning equity of $700 plus net income for the month of $535, for a total of $1,235. That is the number you find on the January 31 balance sheet for owner's equity. The timing of cash receipts and disbursements does not affect owner's equity.

Finally, look at the statement of cash flows. As you have seen, the cash receipts and disbursements for the two companies were not the same. This shows up clearly on the statement of cash flows. The cash flows statement for each company shows all the cash received and all the cash disbursed for the month. The cash flows statements are shown in Exhibit 2.17 on the following page.

Your Turn 2-7

1. Explain how the revenues recognized on the income statement differ from the cash collected from customers shown on the statement of cash flows.
2. Suppose a company earns $50,000 in sales revenue, 20% of which is provided on account. How much revenue will be shown on the period's income statement? How much will be shown on the period's statement of cash flows? How much revenue will be included in the retained earnings total on the end-of-the-period balance sheet?

EXHIBIT 2.17

Statements of Cash Flows for Clean Sweep and Maids-R-Us

The differences in the cash transactions result in differences in the statements of cash flows.

Clean Sweep
Statement of Cash Flows
For the Month Ended January 31, 2011

Cash from operating activities		
Cash collected from customers	$ 750	
Cash paid for interest	(40)	
Net cash from operations		$ 710
Cash from investing activities		0
Cash from financing activities		
Repayment of loan	(400)	
Net cash from financing activities		(400)
Net increase in cash		$ 310

Maids-R-Us
Statement of Cash Flows
For the Month Ended January 31, 2011

Cash from operating activities		
Cash paid for interest	$ (40)	
Net cash from operations		$ (40)
Cash from investing activities		0
Cash from financing activities		
Repayment of loan	$(100)	
Net cash from financing activities		(100)
Net increase (decrease) in cash		$(140)

Putting It All Together—The Objectives of Financial Statements

Financial information should be useful. What makes it useful is the way the transactions of the business are organized into the four basic financial statements:

1. The income statement
2. The statement of changes in shareholders' equity
3. The balance sheet
4. The statement of cash flows

The ongoing life of a business is broken into discrete periods so that performance can be evaluated for a specific period. For our cleaning business example, the period is a month.

Income is measured in a way that captures the economic substance of earning revenue and incurring expenses; it is not based on cash collections and cash disbursements. Notice, the net incomes for Maids-R-Us and Clean Sweep for January are exactly the same, in spite of the differences in when the cash is collected and disbursed. Those timing differences are reflected on the balance sheet by the differences in cash and both receivables and payables; and differences are also shown on the statement of cash flows—the statement that provides the details of the timing of cash receipts and disbursements. The four statements have been designed to be relevant, reliable, consistent, and comparable.

In addition to these qualities, accounting information relies on the basic assumptions and principles we discussed earlier, shown in Exhibit 2.10. We can relate each of the assumptions and principles to the financial statements of Maids-R-Us.

- The separate-entity assumption means that only the business transactions of Maids-R-Us are shown in the financial statements—none of the owner's personal transactions are included.
- The going-concern assumption means we may assume that Maids-R-Us is an ongoing, viable business. According to GAAP, if it were not ongoing, the company would need to have all its assets appraised and listed at liquidation value.
- The monetary-unit assumption means everything shown on the financial statements is measured in monetary units; here we are using dollars.

UNDERSTANDING → # Business

Accounting Is Accrual but Cash Is Important

In this chapter, you have learned that financial statements are prepared on an *accrual* basis, but that does not mean *cash* is not important. As a matter of fact, in the current economic environment, having enough cash is more important than ever. Business owners prepare and use historical cash flows statements to gain an understanding about where all of the cash came from and where all the cash went. Smart business owners also develop annual or even multiyear cash flow projections to make sure they can meet ongoing business needs. The goal of cash budgeting is to always have enough cash to keep your business running smoothly. If it turns out that you have more cash than you need, then you must figure out how best to use that extra cash—how to invest it. That is a cash flow problem that you definitely want!

Even in tough economic times, some companies might have too much cash. According to a 2009 *Wall Street Journal* article:

> Tech companies have traditionally held lots of cash because of the risk in developing new technologies. And right now, maintaining a healthy cash balance is prudent for anyone.
>
> But much of the tech industry is now mature and generating lots of cash. Many big tech names should have a plan for using the money.

Having enough cash to run a business is crucial, but having too much cash could be a poor use of a firm's financial resources. How much cash is enough?

Source: "Tech Companies Need a Cash Plan," by Martin Peers. *Wall Street Journal*, Heard on the Street, March 20, 2009.

- The historical-cost principle means the items on the financial statements are valued at cost. For example, the supplies on the balance sheet are not valued at what they might be worth if resold or at the current cost, which might be higher than the amount that Maids-R-Us paid for them. They are valued at the price Maids-R-Us paid when they were purchased.
- The revenue-recognition principle means the revenue on the income statement has been earned. The related cash may not have been collected, but the work of earning it has been completed and collection of the receivables is reasonably assured.
- The matching principle means related revenues and expenses should be on the same income statement. Only the supplies that are used to earn the revenue during the period are counted as supplies expense. The unused supplies are reported on the balance sheet, as an asset, until they are actually used.

Accrual basis accounting is an accounting system in which the measurement of income is not based on cash receipts and cash disbursements. Instead, revenue is included in the calculation of income when it is earned, and expenses are included as they are matched to revenue. Timing differences between the economic substance of a transaction and the related cash flows do not affect income. That is why both companies have the same net income even though the timing of the cash flows is different.

Real Company Financial Statements

Even though Team Shirts is a small, start-up company, its financial statements include the same types of financial statement items as large, well-established corporations. When Team Shirts sold shirts to customers on account, the balance sheet showed accounts receivable. Look at the balance sheet of FOSSIL, Inc., shown in Exhibit 2.18 on the following page. In the asset section, FOSSIL's balance sheet shows accounts receivable of $205,973,000 at January 3, 2009 (fiscal year 2008), its fiscal year end. Customers owe FOSSIL this amount for products and services the company provided to its customers on account.

Can you find another asset on the balance sheet that reflects the use of accrual basis, rather than cash basis, accounting? In the current assets section, the balance sheet lists prepaid expenses (and other current assets) of $60,084,000. Although the details of FOSSIL's prepaid expenses are not shown, the included items will be similar to prepaid insurance or prepaid rent—items the company has paid for but has not used yet. On the other side of the balance sheet, FOSSIL has

EXHIBIT 2.18

Balance Sheet of FOSSIL, Inc.

Compare the balance sheet of FOSSIL to that of Team Shirts. See how many similarities you can find.

FOSSIL, Inc.
Consolidated Balance Sheets
(dollars in thousands)

Fiscal Year	2008	2007
Assets		
Current assets:		
Cash and cash equivalents.....................................	$ 172,012	$ 255,244
Securities available for sale...........................	6,436	12,626
Accounts receivable—net	205,973	227,481
Inventories—net..	291,955	248,448
Deferred income tax assets—net	27,006	24,221
Prepaid expenses and other current assets.....................	60,084	56,797
Total currents assets.....................................	763,466	824,817
Investments...	13,011	13,902
Property, plant, and equipment—net..........................	207,328	186,042
Goodwill	43,217	45,485
Intangible and other assets—net	60,274	52,382
Total assets	$1,087,296	$1,122,628
Liabilities and Stockholders' Equity		
Current liabilities:		
Short term debt...	$ 5,271	$ 9,993
Accounts payable	91,027	111,015
Accrued expenses:		
Compensation	34,091	44,224
Royalties...	17,078	22,524
Co-op advertising	21,869	17,769
Other...	30,306	32,833
Income taxes payable..................................	7,327	40,049
Total current liabilities...............................	206,969	278,407
Long-term income taxes payable	38,784	38,455
Deferred income tax liabilities	22,880	16,168
Long-term debt...	4,733	3,452
Other long-term liabilities	8,567	8,357
Total long-term liabilities.............................	74,964	66,432
Minority interest in subsidiaries.............................	3,219	6,127
Stockholders' equity:		
Common stock, 66,502 and 69,713 shares issued for		
2008 and 2007, respectively................................	665	697
Additional paid-in capital..................................	81,905	88,000
Retained earnings..	695,427	646,492
Accumulated other comprehensive income	24,147	36,473
Total stockholders' equity	802,144	771,662
Total liabilities and stockholders' equity........................	$1,087,296	$1,122,628

accounts payable of $91,027,000. This represents what the firm owes to vendors for inventory items the company has purchased but has not yet paid for.

Check out the other things you learned in this and the previous chapter about the balance sheet. First, it balances—assets = liabilities + shareholders' equity. FOSSIL has a classified balance sheet. Current assets are shown first, with a subtotal, and current liabilities are also shown with a subtotal. Look at the stockholders' equity section. There is common stock and additional paid-in capital—both contributed capital amounts. Then, the balance sheet shows retained earnings, the amount of equity the shareholders have earned (reduced by any dividends paid) by FOSSIL's operations. Also, there are two balance sheets shown, which you will recall are called *comparative balance sheets*. Take notice of the dates of the balance sheets. This financial statement shows the financial position of the company at a single point in time. For FOSSIL, the last day of the most recent fiscal year shown was January 3, 2009, which FOSSIL refers to as fiscal

2008. A company selects its fiscal year for convenience and ability to compare its results with others in the industry.

Applying Your Knowledge: Ratio Analysis

Every business must pay its bills. Suppliers, in particular, want to evaluate a company's ability to meet its current obligations. Simply looking at how much cash a company has does not provide enough information. Using ratios often provides additional insights. A financial ratio is a comparison of different amounts on the financial statements. Several ratios measure the short-term liquidity of a company. The most common is the **current ratio**, which accountants compute by dividing the total amount of current assets by the total amount of current liabilities. The ratio gives information about a company's ability to fund its current operations in the short run.

$$\text{Current ratio} = \frac{\text{Current assets}}{\text{Current liabilities}}$$

Using the current ratio, investors can compare the liquidity of one company to that of other companies of different types and sizes. Recall that liquidity is a measure of how easily a company can turn its current assets into cash to pay its debts as they come due. This information would be important to a supplier considering extending credit to a company. The current ratio also provides information about the liquidity of a company over time.

Look at the balance sheet for Home Depot in Exhibit 2.9 on page 63. The current ratio at February 1, 2009, was

$$\$13,362 \text{ million} \div \$11,153 \text{ million} = 1.20$$

The current assets at February 3, 2008, totaled $14,674 million, and the current liabilities were $12,706 million. So the current ratio at February 3, 2008, was

$$\$14,674 \text{ million} \div \$12,706 \text{ million} = 1.15$$

Another way to think about the current ratio is to say that Home Depot had, at February 3, 2008, $1.15 of current assets with which to pay off each $1.00 of its current liabilities. Can you see why companies often strive to have a current ratio of 1 or greater? That would mean a firm has enough current assets to pay off its current liabilities. When using ratio analysis, it is often interesting to compare a firm's ratios to those of a competitor in the same industry. Lowe's, for example, had a current ratio of 1.15 at January 30, 2009, and 1.12 at February 1, 2008. For both firms, the current ratio has increased slightly over time. Also, for both companies, the current ratio has been above 1 for the past two years, so no trouble is indicated with respect to this ratio.

Looking at the current ratio for two consecutive years gives some information about Home Depot or Lowe's, but you would need much more information to reach any conclusions. As you learn more about financial statements, you will learn additional ratios and several ways to analyze a company's financial statements.

You might be surprised to know that some firms actually try to keep their current ratio *below* 1. If a firm generates a great deal of cash from operations, it may know that it will generate sufficient cash to pay its current liabilities as they come due. Darden Restaurants, owners of Olive Garden, Red Lobster, and LongHorn Steakhouse, had a current ratio of 0.41 at May 25, 2008. Here's what Darden's management had to say about the current ratio in the firm's annual report:

> Cash flows generated from operating activities provide us with a significant source of liquidity, which we use to finance the purchases of land, buildings and equipment and to repurchase shares of our common stock. Since substantially all our sales are for cash and cash equivalents and accounts payable are generally due in five to 30 days, we are able to carry current liabilities in excess of current assets.

Business Risk, Control, and Ethics

Now that we have discussed the general characteristics of accounting information and the information shown on the four basic financial statements, we will take a look at how companies make sure the information in those statements is reliable.

L.O.5
Compute and explain the meaning of the current ratio.

Current ratio is a liquidity ratio that measures a firm's ability to meet its short-term obligations.

L.O.6
Identify the risks and potential frauds related to financial accounting records, and explain the controls needed to ensure their accuracy.

Internal Controls—Definition and Objectives

Internal controls are the policies and procedures the managers of a firm use to protect the firm's assets and to ensure the accuracy and reliability of the firm's accounting records. Internal controls are a company's rules to help it keep its assets safe and to make sure its financial records are accurate. By adhering to those rules, a firm minimizes the risks of being in business. These rules are called internal controls because they are put in place and controlled within the company. Controls imposed from outside the firm—laws and regulations, for example—are not internal controls because they are not rules that originated within the company.

Special Internal Control Issues Related to Financial Statements

Accountants are particularly concerned with the financial statements. Whether you are involved in preparing them or using them to make decisions, you must have confidence that the information in them is accurate and reliable. When you see cash on a company's balance sheet, you should be confident this is actually the amount of cash the company had on the balance sheet date. The sales shown on the income statement should be sales that have been completed—goods delivered to the customers.

Inaccurate information creates enormous problems. For example, the SEC filed charges against Computron for improperly recording more than $9 million in revenue on its financial statements contained in its reports to the SEC. Improperly recorded revenue was the focus of a recent SEC investigation of the Mexican unit of Xerox Corp. Xerox officials in Mexico failed to set up appropriate allowances for bad debts and improperly classified sales, leases, and rentals, violating GAAP. The causes cited were (1) failure (of the Mexican executives) to adhere to Xerox's corporate policies and procedures, and (2) inadequate internal controls.

Exhibit 2.19 summarizes three types of controls a company can use to minimize the risk of errors in the accounting system: preventive controls, detective controls, and corrective controls. This is just one possible way to classify internal controls.

EXHIBIT 2.19

Types of Internal Controls

A company's accounting information system consists of three major types of controls: ones that prevent errors, ones that detect errors, and ones that correct errors.

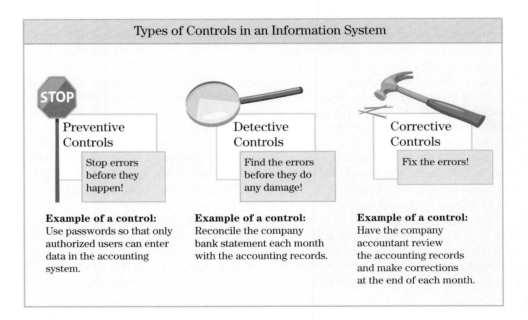

Types of Controls in an Information System

Preventive Controls

Stop errors before they happen!

Example of a control:
Use passwords so that only authorized users can enter data in the accounting system.

Detective Controls

Find the errors before they do any damage!

Example of a control:
Reconcile the company bank statement each month with the accounting records.

Corrective Controls

Fix the errors!

Example of a control:
Have the company accountant review the accounting records and make corrections at the end of each month.

PREVENTIVE CONTROLS. These types of controls help prevent errors in an accounting system. When you order something from Amazon.com, for example, the company gives you more than one chance to review and confirm your order. The computer program is designed to automatically insert the price of each item you order. These are controls that Amazon has put in place to help prevent errors from entering its accounting system.

DETECTIVE CONTROLS. Detective controls are those that help a company find errors. For example, at the end of every work day, a cashier at Target will count the money, ATM receipts, and credit card receipts in his or her drawer and compare the total to the total sales entered in the computer. This control will help Target find errors in its sales and receipts. Once the errors are found, they must be corrected.

CORRECTIVE CONTROLS. Corrective controls are policies and procedures that correct any errors that have been discovered. Target has a policy for handling cash shortages—perhaps the cashier must make up for any shortage.

As you learn more about accounting, you will see examples of preventive, detective, and corrective controls. Keep in mind that to be effective, a system of internal control must rely on the people who perform the duties assigned to them. An internal control system is only as effective as the people who execute it. Human error, collusion (two or more people working together to circumvent a policy or procedure), and changing conditions can all weaken a system of internal control.

Chapter Summary Points

- To make the financial statements useful, we need to understand the rules and the choices used to construct them. These rules are called generally accepted accounting principles (GAAP). In the future, the whole world may use a single set of standards known as International Financial Reporting Standards (IFRS).
- Accounting according to GAAP is accrual based. That means that revenues are recognized when they are earned (when the goods or services have been delivered), not when the cash is collected. Costs are matched to revenues so that they are recognized—put on the income statement as expenses—at the same time as the revenues they helped generate.
- Accrual basis accounting consists of two types of transactions—accruals and deferrals— in which the exchange of cash takes place at a different time than the exchange of goods or services.
- With accruals, the action takes place before the exchange of cash. An example is a credit sale. The sale is recorded, but the cash will be collected later. Remember, accrue means to "build up." When Team Shirts makes a sale on account, the company builds up sales, even though the cash has not been collected yet.
- With deferrals, the dollars are exchanged before the action occurs. An example is paying for something in advance. When Team Shirts paid for the insurance in advance, that was a deferral. Remember, defer means to "postpone." When Team Shirts purchases insurance in advance, prepaid insurance, the company postpones recognition of the expense. The action, in this case, is the passing of the time to which the insurance applies.
- Adjustments are made before financial statements are prepared. The amounts recorded throughout the year may need to be adjusted to make sure they accurately reflect the assets, liabilities, shareholders' equity, revenues, and expenses on the date of the statements. How we actually adjust the amounts to correctly reflect the financial position of a company depends on how we keep track of our business transactions.

Chapter Summary Problems

The following transactions took place during the first year of business for SW2 Company. (Dollars given are in millions. Use the numbers as shown, but make a note on your statements that the dollars are in millions.) The firm's year end is June 30.

a. Issued SW2 common stock (received contributions from owners) in the amount of $250
b. Borrowed $850 from a local bank with a 6-year note (ignore interest expense)
c. Purchased land for $650 cash
d. Paid $25 for operating expenses
e. Purchased new equipment for cash of $300
f. Collected $800 from customers for services provided
g. Paid salaries to employees of $480
h. Purchased supplies for $20 on account, to be used in the coming year
i. Declared and paid dividends to new shareholders of $5

Instructions

1. Set up an accounting equation worksheet like the one in Exhibit 2.4 and record each transaction on the worksheet. (Record the equipment purchase as an asset and ignore the fact that the equipment was probably used during the year. We will get to that topic in a later chapter. Also, ignore interest expense on the bank note.)
2. Prepare the four basic financial statements from the worksheet.

Solution

(dollars in millions)

| | | Assets | | = Liabilities | | + | Shareholders' Equity | |
| | | | | | | | Contributed Capital | Retained Earnings |
Transaction	Cash	All other assets	(Account)	All liabilities	(Account)		Common stock	(Account)
a.	$250						$250	
b.	850			850	Notes payable			
c.	(650)	650	Property, plant, and equipment					
d.	(25)							(25) Operating expenses
e.	(300)	300	Property, plant, and equipment					
f.	800							800 Service revenue
g.	(480)							(480) Salary expense
h.		20	Supplies	20	Accounts payable			
i.	(5)							(5) Dividends
	$440	**+ $970**		**= $870**		**+**	**$250**	**+ $290**

━ Income Statement   ━ Statement of Changes in Stockholders' Equity   ━ Balance Sheet   ━ Statement of Cash Flows

From the accounting equation worksheet, you can prepare the financial statements. Start with the income statement. The red box indicates the revenues and expenses. In this case, it is a very condensed income statement. That is, the company would have many types of revenue accounts and many more expense accounts in its internal recordkeeping:

SW2 Company
Income Statement
For the Year Ended June 30
(in millions)

Service revenue	$ 800
Expenses	505
Net income	$ 295

The next statement you prepare is the statement of changes in shareholders' equity. Notice how net income is used in this statement:

SW2 Company
Statement of Changes in Shareholders' Equity
For the Year Ended June 30
(in millions)

Contributed Capital:	
Beginning balance, common stock	$ 0
Common stock issued	250
Ending balance, common stock	$250
Retained Earnings:	
Beginning balance	$ 0
+ Net income	295
– Dividends declared	(5)
Ending balance	290
Total shareholders' equity	$540

These amounts will go to the equity section of the balance sheet.

The balance sheet is the next statement that you prepare. Notice that revenues, expenses, and dividends are *not* shown on the balance sheet. Those amounts have been folded into the retained earnings balance.

SW2 Company
Balance Sheet
At June 30
(in millions)

Assets		
Cash	$ 440	← The change in cash from the beginning of the year (0 in this example) to the amount on the year-end balance sheet ($440) will be explained by the statement of cash flows.
Supplies	20	
Property, plant, and equipment	950	
Total assets	$1,410	
Liabilities and Shareholders' Equity		
Liabilities		
Accounts payable	$ 20	
Note payable	850	
Shareholders' equity		
Common stock	250	← These amounts came from the statement of changes in shareholders' equity.
Retained earnings	290	
Total liabilities and shareholders' equity	$1,410	

Finally, you prepare the statement of cash flows. To do this, go down the list of transactions in the cash column of the worksheet and identify each as cash from operating activities, cash from investing activities, or cash from financing activities.

- All cash collected from customers and all cash paid for the expenses to run the day-to-day operations of the firm are cash flows from operations. For SW2, these are (d.) cash paid for operating expenses, (f.) cash collected from customers, and (g.) cash paid to employees for salaries.
- All cash paid for land and equipment (assets that last longer than a year) are cash flows from investing activities. For SW2, these are (c.) purchase of land and (e.) purchase of equipment.
- All cash used to finance the business—from owners and long-term creditors—are cash flows from financing activities. For SW2, these are (a.) issue of stock, (b.) receipt of proceeds from loan, and (i.) payment of dividends to shareholders.

Notice that Transaction 8, purchase supplies on account, does not affect the statement of cash flows. Why not? No cash is involved in the transaction. When the cash is paid in the next year, it will be an operating cash flow.

SW2 Company
Statement of Cash Flows
For the Year Ended June 30
(in millions)

Cash from operating activities:
Cash collected from customers	$ 800	
Cash paid for operating expenses	(25)	
Cash paid to employees	(480)	
Net cash from operations		$ 295

Cash from investing activities:
Cash paid for land	$(650)	
Cash paid for equipment	(300)	
Net cash used for investing activities		(950)

Cash from financing activities:
Cash from common stock issued	$ 250	
Cash proceeds from loan	850	
Cash paid for dividends	(5)	
Net cash generated by financing activities		1,095
Increase in cash		$ 440
Add beginning cash balance		0
Ending cash balance		**$ 440**

This is the cash balance found on the balance sheet.

Key Terms for Chapter 2

Accounts payable (p. 56)
Accounts receivable (p. 57)
Accrual (p. 66)
Accrual basis accounting (p. 65)
Adjusting the books (p. 59)
Cash basis accounting (p. 66)
Classified balance sheet (p. 64)
Current assets (p. 62)
Current liabilities (p. 64)
Current ratio (p. 75)
Deferral (p. 66)

Full-disclosure principle (p. 55)
Going-concern assumption (p. 55)
Historical-cost principle (p. 55)
Internal controls (p. 76)
Liquidity (p. 62)
Long-term assets (p. 62)
Long-term liabilities (p. 64)
Matching principle (p. 55)
Monetary-unit assumption (p. 54)

Net profit (p. 52)
Noncurrent assets (p. 62)
Noncurrent liabilities (p. 64)
On account (p. 56)
Paid-in capital (p. 64)
Prepaid insurance (p. 57)
Recognized revenue (p. 55)
Revenue-recognition principle (p. 55)
Separate-entity assumption (p. 54)
Time-period assumption (p. 55)

Answers to YOUR TURN Questions

Chapter 2

Your Turn 2-1

1. GAAP stands for generally accepted accounting principles. IFRS stands for International Financial Reporting Standards.
2. Guidelines are needed to ensure the usefulness of the information so that a firm's performance can be compared from period to period and compared to other firms' performances.

Your Turn 2-2

1. The purpose of financial statements is to provide information useful for decision making.
2. Useful information is relevant, reliable, comparable, and consistent.

Your Turn 2-3

Prepaid insurance is an asset until the time to which the policy applies has expired. Then, it becomes an expense.

Your Turn 2-4

1. A current asset is one that is expected to be converted to cash or used in the next year. A long-term asset is one that is expected to last longer than a year.
2. A classified balance sheet is one that has subtotals for both current assets and current liabilities.

Your Turn 2-5

An example of the matching principle is cost of goods sold and the related sales. The cost of the T-shirts sold is put on the same income statement as the sales revenue from the sale of those shirts.

Your Turn 2-6

The difference between cash basis and accrual basis accounting is the timing of recognizing revenues and expenses. Cash basis accounting recognizes revenue when the cash is collected and expenses when cash is disbursed. In accrual accounting, revenues are recognized in the period in which they are earned (by the completion of the work) and expenses are matched to the revenues they help create.

Your Turn 2-7

1. On the income statement, the revenues earned are shown. (That is called *recognizing* the revenue.) On the statement of cash flows, only the amount of cash collected from customers is included.
2. If a company earns $50,000 worth of revenue, then all of that will be recognized—included on the income statement. The amount of cash collected is given as 80%, so $40,000 would be shown on the statement of cash flows as cash collected from customers. The entire amount, $50,000, will be in the retained earnings balance because the retained earnings increase is the amount that is on the income statement.

Questions

1. What is GAAP? What is IFRS?
2. Name the four characteristics that help make accounting information useful.
3. What is the separate-entity assumption?
4. Why would the going-concern assumption be important to a bank giving a business a loan?
5. Explain materiality and give an example of both a material and an immaterial item.
6. What are the four basic financial statements?
7. Which financial statement pertains to a single moment in time?
8. What is a current asset? What is a current liability?
9. What are the two ways that shareholders' equity is generated in a business?
10. What does the income statement report about a firm? Name the types of accounts that appear on the income statement.
11. What is the purpose of the statement of cash flows? How are the cash flows categorized? What is the significance of classifying cash flows into these categories?
12. What is the full-disclosure principle?
13. What does *recognize revenue* mean in accounting?
14. What is the matching principle?
15. What is an accrual? What is a deferral?
16. Must a company collect the money from a sale before the sale can be recognized?
17. What is the cost of goods sold?
18. Explain the difference between cash basis accounting and accrual basis accounting.
19. How is the current ratio computed? What does it tell us about a company?
20. Define internal control and explain why it is important.
21. For each of the controls given, tell whether it is primarily a preventive control, a detective control, or a corrective control.
    a. Retro Clothing, Inc., has an online purchase system that automatically inserts the total price of each item a customer orders.
    b. The teller double-checks the account number on the loan payment before applying payment.
    c. External auditors are hired to audit the year-end financial statements.

Multiple-Choice Questions

1. If revenue exceeds expenses for a given period,
   a. total assets for the period will decrease.
   b. cash for the period will increase.
   c. the income statement will report net income.
   d. liabilities for the period will decrease.
2. The matching principle is best described as the process of
   a. matching assets to liabilities and owners' equity.
   b. recognizing a cost as an expense in the period in which it is used to generate revenue.
   c. matching cash collections to revenue.
   d. matching income to owners' equity.
3. Which of the following would never appear on a company's income statement?
   a. Prepaid insurance
   b. Cost of goods sold
   c. Interest expense
   d. Sales revenue
4. Which of the following statements is consistent with accrual basis accounting?
   a. Revenues are recorded when cash is received.
   b. Expenses are recorded when cash is paid.
   c. Expenses are recorded in a different period than the related revenue.
   d. Revenues are recorded when earned and expenses are matched with the revenues.
5. Sales revenue is most often recognized in the period in which
   a. the customer agrees to purchase the merchandise.
   b. the seller agrees to sell the merchandise to the customer at a specified price.
   c. the seller collects cash from the customer.
   d. the seller delivers the merchandise to the customer.
6. Which of the following is an example of a financing cash outflow?
   a. Borrowing money from a bank by signing a long-term note payable
   b. Financing the purchase of a new factory by issuing new shares of stock
   c. Paying a cash dividend to stockholders
   d. Purchasing a new delivery truck
7. How are assets reported in the balance sheet?
   a. Chronologically
   b. Alphabetically
   c. In the order of their liquidity
   d. In the order of their relative values
8. Which of the following financial statement elements is found on the balance sheet?
   a. Insurance expense
   b. Retained earnings
   c. Sales revenue
   d. All of the above
9. A company's current ratio is 1.85. You can safely conclude that
   a. the company is a good investment.
   b. the company will have no trouble paying its current obligations.
   c. the company has a short-term problem related to paying its bills.
   d. the company has a long-term problem related to meeting its obligations.
10. Which of the following is not a type of internal control?
    a. Preventive
    b. Corrective
    c. Collusion
    d. Detective

Short Exercises
Set A

SE2-1A. *Elements of the financial statements. (LO 3).* For each item that follows, tell whether it is an asset, a liability, or a shareholders' equity item.

1. Automobile
2. Prepaid insurance
3. Common stock
4. Unearned revenue
5. Accounts payable
6. Retained earnings
7. Accounts receivable
8. Inventory
9. Cash

SE2-2A. *Elements of the financial statements. (LO 3).* For each of the following line items, give the financial statement on which it would appear.

Operating expense	Accounts payable
Sales revenue	Accounts receivable
Cost of goods sold	Net cash from operations
Equipment	Prepaid rent
Long-term debt	Advertising expense

SE2-3A. *Revenue recognition. (LO 3, 4).* Public Relations, Inc., managed a grand opening party on behalf of a new restaurant on April 15, 2009. Public Relations charged the restaurant $2,100. The restaurant paid for $1,800 of the bill from Public Relations, Inc., on April 20, 2009. The remaining balance was paid on May 5, 2009. How did these transactions affect Public Relations' income statement for the month of April and the balance sheet at April 30, 2009?

SE2-4A. *Accrual accounting versus cash basis accounting. (LO 4).* Missy & Adele Ice Cream, Inc., purchased inventory for its ice cream shop in August 2009 for $55,000 cash to sell in August and September. The company sold inventory that cost $35,000 in August and the remainder in September. What is the cost of goods sold for August 2009 and the cost of goods sold for September 2009 if Missy & Adele uses GAAP? What is the cost of goods sold for each month if Missy & Adele uses cash basis accounting?

SE2-5A. *Recording credit sales. (LO 4).* Wasil Company provided services on account for a customer that amounted to $1,000. How would this transaction be shown in the accounting equation?

SE2-6A. *Accounts payable versus accounts receivable. (LO 4).* Bolo Company purchased inventory on account in the amount of $500. Then, Bolo sold the inventory to a customer for $1,000. Bolo extended credit to this customer. In other words, the sale was made on account. Related to these two transactions, how much did Bolo record as accounts payable? How much did Bolo record as accounts receivable?

SE2-7A. *Cash versus credit sales. (LO 3, 4).* Company A had sales of $1,500 during the year and collected them all in cash. Company B, on the other hand, had sales of $1,500 during the year but collected only $1,000 cash with the remaining $500 sales on account. Both firms had expenses of $700, all paid in cash by both firms. What was Company A's net income for the year? What was Company B's net income for the year? What was Company A's net cash from operating activities during the year? What was Company B's net cash from operating activities during the year?

SE2-8A. *Costs versus expenses. (LO 3).* The cost of supplies purchased by the Decker Company was $5,000 during the year. Decker used $4,000 worth of those supplies during the year and still had $1,000 worth of them left at year end. What was the amount of Decker's supplies expense for the year?

SE2-9A. *Interest payment and cash flows. (LO 4).* Suppose Miller Hardware borrowed $10,000 from the local bank, with payments of principal and interest due each month. For April, Miller paid the bank $1,000 of principal and $50 interest. How would these cash flows be classified on the statement of cash flows?

SE2-10A. *Compute and explain current ratio. (LO 5).* Given the following information, compute the current ratio for the two years shown. Explain the trend in the ratio for both years and what you think it means.

From balance sheet at	06/30/2010	06/30/2011
Current assets	$300,000	$360,000
Current liabilities	$200,000	$300,000

Set B

SE2-11B. *Elements of the financial statements. (LO 3).* For each item that follows, tell whether it is an asset, a liability, or a shareholders' equity item.

1. Prepaid insurance
2. Accounts receivable
3. Retained earnings
4. Cash
5. Notes payable
6. Supplies

SE2-12B. *Elements of the financial statements. (LO 3).* For each of the following line items, give the financial statement on which it would appear.

Salary expense	Service revenue
Sales revenue	Accounts payable
Cost of goods sold	Net cash from financing activities
Land	Prepaid insurance
Notes payable	Marketing expenses

SE2-13B. *Revenue recognition. (LO 3, 4).* Myadd, Inc., spent $3,000 on catering for its grand opening. Myadd paid the caterer half of the bill at the event, and requested a bill for the remaining half. The following day, Myadd's accountant had to record the transaction. Show what he or she recorded by using the accounting equation.

SE2-14B. *Accrual accounting versus cash basis accounting. (LO 4).* At the beginning of January, Conway Coffee Bean Shop purchased inventory for $5,000 cash to sell in January and February. The shop sold inventory that cost $2,100 in January and the remainder in February. What is the cost of goods sold for January and the cost of goods sold for February if Conway Coffee uses GAAP? What is the cost of goods sold for each month if Conway Coffee uses cash basis accounting?

SE2-15B. *Recording credit sales. (LO 4).* Jaybee Company provided services on account for a customer that amounted to $400. How would this transaction be shown in the accounting equation?

SE2-16B. *Accounts payable versus accounts receivable. (LO 4).* Renata Jewels purchased inventory on account in the amount of $10,000. Then, the store sold the inventory to customers for $17,500. Renata extended credit to its customers. In other words, all sales were made on account. Related to these two transactions, how much did Renata Jewels record as accounts payable? How much did Renata Jewels record as accounts receivable?

SE2-17B. *Cash versus credit sales. (LO 3, 4).* Company X had sales of $7,500 during the year and collected half of them in cash. Company Y, on the other hand, had sales of $7,500 during the year and collected all in cash. Both firms had expenses of $2,400, paid in cash by both firms. What was Company X's net income for the year? What was Company Y's net income for the year? What was Company X's net cash from operating activities during the year? What was Company Y's net cash from operating activities during the year?

SE2-18B. *Costs versus expenses. (LO 3).* The cost of supplies purchased by the Alpha Company was $1,000 during the year. Alpha used $460 worth of those supplies during the year and still had $540 worth of them left at year end. What was the amount of Alpha's supplies *expense* for the year?

SE2-19B. *Interest payment and cash flows. (LO 4).* Suppose Betty's Beauty Supplies borrowed $40,000 from the local bank, with payments of principal and interest due each month. For the month of August, Betty's paid the bank $4,000 of principal and $200 interest. How would these cash flows be classified on the statement of cash flows?

SE2-20B. *Compute and explain current ratio. (LO 5).* Given the following information, compute the current ratio for the two years shown. Explain the trend in the ratio for both years and what you think it means.

From balance sheet at	09/30/2010	09/30/2011
Current assets	$13,000	$11,000
Current liabilities	$10,000	$10,000

Exercises
Set A

E2-21A. *Elements of the financial statements. (LO 3).* The following accounts and balances were taken from the financial statements of Electronic Super Deals, Inc. For each item, identify the financial statement(s) on which the item would appear. Then, identify each balance sheet item as an asset, a liability, or a shareholders' equity account.

Equipment	$120,000
Accounts receivable	105,000
Inventory	225,000
Long-term notes payable	315,025
Net cash from operating activities	28,000
Common Stock	35,150
Land	575,000
Retained earnings	100,000
Cash	340,000
Interest payable	650
Long-term mortgage payable	85,000
Salaries payable	21,525
Net cash from financing activities	18,000

E2-22A. *Net income and retained earnings. (LO 3).* Jule's Dairy Farm, Inc., reported the following (incomplete) information in its records for 2010:

Net income	$ 25,000
Sales	115,000
Beginning balance—retained earnings	20,000
Cost of goods sold	45,000
Dividends declared and paid	2,250

1. If the sales revenue given is the only revenue for the year, what were the expenses for the year other than cost of goods sold?
2. What is the balance of retained earnings at the end of 2010?

E2-23A. *Elements of the financial statements. (LO 3).* Listed are elements of the financial statements discussed in this chapter. Match each element with the descriptions (use each as many times as necessary).

a. Assets
b. Liabilities
c. Shareholders' equity
d. Revenues
e. Expenses

1.	_____	Debts of the company
2.	_____	Economic resources with future benefit
3.	_____	Inflows of assets from delivering or producing goods or services
4.	_____	Things of value a company owns
5.	_____	The residual interest in the assets of an entity that remains after deducting its liabilities
6.	_____	The difference between what the company has and what the company owes
7.	_____	The owners' interest in the company
8.	_____	Outflows or using up of assets from delivering or producing goods and services
9.	_____	Costs that have no future value
10.	_____	The amount the company owes
11.	_____	Sales

E2-24A. *Balance sheet and income statement transactions. (LO 3, 4).* Unisource Company started the first year of operations with $2,000 in cash and common stock. During 2010, the Unisource Company earned $4,600 of revenue on account. The company collected $4,200 cash from accounts receivable and paid $2,850 cash for operating expenses. Enter the transactions into the accounting equation.

1. What happened to total assets (increase or decrease and by how much)?
2. What is the cash balance on December 31, 2010?
3. What is the total shareholders' equity on December 31, 2010?
4. What is net income for the year?

E2-25A. *Income statement preparation. (LO 3).* Use the following to prepare an income statement for Excel Technology, Inc., for the year ended June 30, 2011:

Service revenues	$62,675
Rent expense	12,000
Insurance expense	6,550
Salary expenses	18,625
Administrative expenses	5,720

E2-26A. *Classified balance sheet preparation. (LO 3).* The following items were taken from the December 31, 2012, financial statements of Whitehouse Corporation. (All dollars are in millions.) Prepare a classified balance sheet as of December 31, 2012.

Property and equipment	$15,225	Salaries payable	11,250
Common stock	15,895	Other noncurrent liabilities	1,445
Investment in land	13,215	Retained earnings	8,835
Short-term investments	1,900	Prepaid insurance	675
Cash	1,850	Other noncurrent assets	6,795
Accounts receivable	185	Interest payable	845
Supplies	110	Mortgage payable	1,685

E2-27A. *Current ratio. (LO 5).* Use the balance sheet you prepared in E2-26A to compute the current ratio at December 31, 2012.

E2-28A. *Current ratio. (LO 5).* The following data was taken from the 2009 and 2008 financial statements of Tasty Sweets Corporation. Calculate the current ratio for each year. What happened to the company's liquidity from 2008 to 2009?

	2009	2008
Current assets	384,728	385,642
Total assets	649,803	590,112
Current liabilities	151,084	157,990
Total liabilities	261,676	282,244
Total shareholders' equity	388,127	307,868

Set B

E2-29B. *Elements of the financial statements. (LO 3).* The following accounts and balances were taken from the financial statements of Books & Media, Inc. For each item, identify the financial statement(s) on which the item would appear. Then, identify each balance sheet item as an asset, a liability, or a shareholders' equity account.

Inventory	$ 81,250
Accounts payable	52,300
Cash	77,880
Short-term notes payable	32,200
Net cash from investing activities	49,300
Building	76,475
Common stock	105,000
Retained earnings	63,000
Net cash from financing activities	21,080
Accounts receivable	44,270
Long-term mortgage payable	54,000
Taxes payable	1,500
Net cash from operating activities	34,350

E2-30B. *Net income and retained earnings. (LO 3).* Donut Hole, Inc., reported the following (incomplete) information in its records for 2011:

Net income	$ 52,000
Sales	153,750
Beginning balance—retained earnings	15,445
Cost of goods sold	68,000
Dividends declared and paid	3,025

1. If the sales revenue given is the only revenue for the year, what were the expenses for the year other than cost of goods sold?
2. What is the balance of retained earnings at the end of 2011?

E2-31B. *Elements of the financial statements. (LO 3).* Listed are elements of the financial statements discussed in this chapter. Match each element with the descriptions (use each as many times as necessary).
   a. Assets
   b. Liabilities
   c. Shareholders' equity
   d. Revenues
   e. Expenses
   f. Retained earnings
   g. Common stock

1. _____ Note signed with a bank
2. _____ Rent paid a year in advance

3. _____ Items that make up net income that appear on the income statement
4. _____ Items that appear on the balance sheet
5. _____ A share of ownership in a corporation
6. _____ Equity that results from doing business and is kept in the company rather than paid out to stockholders
7. _____ Shareholders' interest in the company
8. _____ Costs of the daily operations of a business
9. _____ Salaries owed to employees
10. _____ Cost of inventory when it is sold
11. _____ Revenue received for services not yet provided
12. _____ Interest received on notes receivable

E2-32B. *Balance sheet and income statement transactions. (LO 3, 4).* Pet Caterers, Inc., started the first year of operations with $3,500 in cash and common stock. During 2012, Pet Caterers earned $6,500 of revenue on account. The company collected $5,900 cash from accounts receivable and paid $3,115 cash for operating expenses. Enter the transactions into the accounting equation.

1. What happened to total assets (increase or decrease and by how much)?
2. What is the cash balance on December 31, 2012?
3. What is the total shareholders' equity on December 31, 2012?
4. What is net income for the year?

E2-33B. *Income statement preparation. (LO 3).* Use the following to prepare an income statement for Grace's Landscape Service, Inc., for the year ended June 30, 2011:

Service revenue	$37,515
Rent expense	8,675
Insurance expense	2,125
Other operating expenses	12,075
Salary expense	10,650

E2-34B. *Classified balance sheet preparation. (LO 3).* The following items were taken from the December 31, 2012, financial statements of Organic Vegetables, Inc. (All dollars are in thousands.) Prepare a classified balance sheet as of December 31, 2012.

Land and building	$6,750	Accounts payable	4,125
Common stock	3,651	Other noncurrent liabilities	2,150
Long-term investments	2,175	Retained earnings	1,297
Short-term investments	615	Other current assets	1,100
Cash	1,260	Vehicles	3,267
Accounts receivable	575	Current portion of long-term debt	1,160
Inventories	505	Long-term debt	3,864

E2-35B. *Current ratio. (LO 5).* Use the balance sheet you prepared in E2-34B to compute the current ratio at December 31, 2012.

E2-36B. *Current ratio. (LO 5).* The following data was taken from the 2011 and 2010 financial statements of Shelby Pet Supplies Company. Calculate the current ratio for each year. What happened to the company's liquidity from 2010 to 2011?

	2011	2010
Current assets	105,000	142,000
Total assets	275,000	376,750
Current liabilities	55,000	115,000
Total liabilities	125,000	175,000
Total shareholders' equity	150,000	201,750

MyAccountingLab

All of the A problems can be found within MyAccountingLab, an online homework and practice environment.

Problems
Set A

P2-37A. *Relationships between financial statement items. (LO 3).* Use the information from Shane and Lane, Inc., for the year ended December 31, 2011, to answer the questions that follow. Assume that the shareholders made new contributions of $25 to the company during the year.

    a. Expenses for the year ended December 31, 2011 = $625

    b. Net income for the year ended December 31, 2011 = $415

    c. Beginning balance (December 31, 2010, balance) in retained earnings = $215

    d. Ending balance (December 31, 2011, balance) in retained earnings = $500

    e. Total liabilities and shareholders' equity at December 31, 2011 = $875

    f. Beginning balance (December 31, 2010, balance) in total liabilities = $260

    g. Ending balance (December 31, 2011, balance) in total liabilities = $275

Requirements

1. What were the company's total revenues during the year ended December 31, 2011?
2. What was the amount of the dividends declared during the year ended December 31, 2011?
3. What is the total that owners had invested in Shane and Lane as of December 31, 2011?
4. What were total assets on the company's December 31, 2011, balance sheet?

P2-38A. *Analyzing transactions. (LO 3).* Accounting Services Corporation entered into the following transactions during 2010:

    a. The company started as a corporation with a $14,700 cash contribution from the owners in exchange for common stock.

    b. Service revenues on account amounted to $8,250.

    c. Cash collections of accounts receivable amounted to $6,875.

    d. Purchased supplies on account for $125 and used all of them.

    e. On December 15, 2010, the company paid $6,000 in advance for leased office space. The lease does not go into effect until 2011.

Requirements

Put each of the transactions in an accounting equation worksheet. Then, answer the following questions:

1. What is the amount of cash flow from operating activities for 2010?
2. What amount of total liabilities would appear on the December 31, 2010, balance sheet?
3. What is the amount of contributed capital as of December 31, 2010?
4. What amount of net income would appear on the income statement for the year ended December 31, 2010?

P2-39A. *Analyzing transactions and preparing financial statements. (LO 3).* The following transactions occurred during MP Public Relations Firm's first month of business:

    a. Marlene and Pamela opened up MP Public Relations Firm by contributing $22,750 on July 1, 2009, in exchange for common stock.

    b. The firm borrowed $15,000 from the bank on July 1. The note is a 1-year, 10% note, with both principal and interest to be repaid on June 30, 2010.

    c. The firm prepaid a year of rent for $1,200 that started August 1, 2009.

    d. The firm paid $1,050 cash for operating expenses for the first month.

    e. The firm earned $10,500 in revenue the first month. Of that amount, $7,500 was collected in cash.

    f. The firm hired an administrative assistant and paid $525 cash in salary expense for the first month.

    g. The firm declared and paid distributions to owners in the amount of $2,250 for the first month.

    h. At the end of the month, $125 of interest payable is due but not yet paid on the note from item (b).

Requirements

1. Show how each transaction affects the accounting equation.
2. Prepare the income statement, statement of changes in shareholders' equity, and statement of cash flows for the month of July. Also, prepare the balance sheet *at* July 31.

P2-40A. *Analyze transactions from the accounting equation and prepare the four financial statements. (LO 3).* The following accounting equation worksheet shows the transactions for Data Services for its first month of business, May 2010:

		Assets		=	Liabilities	+		Shareholders' Equity	
							Contributed Capital	Retained Earnings	
Transaction	Cash	All other assets	(Account)		All liabilities	(Account)	Common stock		
a.	$ 5,000						$5,000		
b.	15,000				15,000	Notes payable (5-year)			
c.	(10,000)	10,000	Land						
d.		6,500	Accounts receivable					6,500	Revenue
e.	12,000							12,000	Revenue
f.	(8,000)	8,000	Land						
g.	3,500	(3,500)	Accounts receivable						
h.	(2,100)							(2,100)	Expense
i.	(750)							(750)	Dividends

Requirements

1. Analyze each transaction in the accounting equation worksheet and describe the underlying exchange that resulted in each entry.
2. Has the company been profitable this month? Explain.
3. Prepare an income statement for the month ended May 31, 2010.
4. Prepare a statement of shareholders' equity for the month ended May 31, 2010.
5. Prepare a statement of cash flows for the month ended May 31, 2010.
6. Prepare a balance sheet at May 31, 2010.

P2-41A. *Analyzing transactions and preparing financial statements. (LO 3, 5).* After Nate, Maggie, Nicol, and Lindsay finished medical school, they decided to open a new medical practice named New Beginnings. The graduates formed New Beginnings, Inc., as a corporation on January 1, 2011. Each graduate contributed $65,000 to the business in exchange for 2,500 shares of common stock. The company signed a note with Noble Bank for an additional $120,000. The company used available funds to purchase office space (building) for $216,000. The company also purchased medical equipment on account for $139,000, with payment due at the beginning of the following year.

• During the first year of business, New Beginnings earned $280,000 in service revenue, but collected only $215,000; the remaining $65,000 was due from customers early the next year.
• Salary expenses for the year were $115,000, of which $95,000 was paid in cash during the year; the remaining $20,000 was due to employees the first day of the next year.
• The company purchased an insurance policy for $40,000 cash of which $5,000 was for the current year and the remainder was for future years.
• The company paid operating expenses of $39,000 in cash during the year.
• The company sent a check during the last month of the year for $8,100 for interest expense due on the loan from Noble Bank.
• The company invested $22,000 of cash in short-term investments at the end of the year.
• New Beginnings declared and paid cash dividends of $10,500 during the year.

Requirements

1. Show how each transaction affects the accounting equation.

2. Prepare the income statement, the statement of changes in shareholders' equity, and the statement of cash flows for the year ended December 31, 2011. Prepare the balance sheet *at* December 31, 2011. Ignore depreciation expense on building and equipment.

3. Calculate the current ratio at December 31, 2011.

Set B

P2-42B. *Relationships between financial statement items. (LO 3).* Use the following information for Exotic Cruise Corporation for the year ended June 30, 2011, to answer the questions. Assume that the shareholders contributed $100 to the company during the year.

   a. Revenues for the year ended June 30, 2011 = $650
   b. Net income for the year ended June 30, 2011 = $215
   c. Beginning balance (June 30, 2010, balance) in retained earnings = $280
   d. Ending balance (June 30, 2011, balance) in retained earnings = $375
   e. Total liabilities and shareholders' equity at June 30, 2011 = $755
   f. Total liabilities at June 30, 2010 = $105
   g. Total liabilities at June 30, 2011 = $130

Requirements

1. What were Exotic Cruise's total expenses during the year ended June 30, 2011?
2. What was paid to shareholders during the year ended June 30, 2011?
3. What is the total that owners had invested in Exotic Cruise Corporation as of June 30, 2011?
4. What were total assets on Exotic Cruise's June 30, 2011, balance sheet?

P2-43B. *Analyzing transactions. (LO 3).* New Magazine Company entered into the following transactions during 2012:

   a. New Magazine Company started as a corporation with a $9,650 cash contribution from the owners in exchange for common stock.
   b. The company purchased supplies for $1,000 with cash and used all of them.
   c. Advertising revenues, all on account, amounted to $17,625.
   d. Cash collections of accounts amounted to $8,175.
   e. On October 15, 2012, the company paid $4,050 in advance for an insurance policy that does not go into effect until 2013.
   f. The company declared and paid dividends of $575.

Requirements

Put each of the transactions in an accounting equation worksheet. Then, answer the following questions:

1. What is the amount of net cash from financing activities for the year ended December 31, 2012?
2. What amount of total assets would appear on the December 31, 2012, balance sheet?
3. What amount of net income would appear on the income statement for the year ended December 31, 2012?
4. What is the amount of retained earnings as of December 31, 2012?

P2-44B. *Analyzing transactions and preparing financial statements. (LO 3).* The following transactions occurred during Bono Exterminators' first month of business:

   a. Joe Bono started a business, Bono Exterminators, by contributing $6,200 cash on January 1, 2010, in exchange for common stock.
   b. The company borrowed $18,000 from the bank in January. The note is a 1-year, 5% note, with both principal and interest to be repaid on December 30, 2010.
   c. The company paid $2,500 in cash for an insurance policy that begins February 1.
   d. The company earned $4,775 in revenues during January. Cash collections of revenue amounted to $4,270 during the month.
   e. The company paid operating expenses of $815 cash for the month of January.
   f. The company declared and made distributions to owners in the amount of $125 cash in January.
   g. At the end of January, $75 of interest payable is due on the note from item (b).

Requirements

1. Show how each transaction affects the accounting equation.
2. Prepare the income statement, statement of changes in shareholder's equity, and the statement of cash flows for the month of January and the balance sheet at January 31.

P2-45B. *Analyze transactions from the accounting equation, prepare the four financial statements, and calculate the current ratio. (LO 4, 5, 7).* The following accounting equation worksheet shows the transactions for Internet Advertising, a corporation, for the first month of business October 2009.

Transaction	Cash	All other assets	(Account)	All liabilities	(Account)	Common stock	(Account)
	Assets			**= Liabilities**		**+ Shareholders' Equity**	
						Contributed Capital	Retained Earnings
a.	$17,250					$17,250	
b.	16,900			16,900	Long-term notes payable		
c.	(4,500)						(4,500) Salary expenses
d.	1,500	1,500	Accounts receivable				3,000 Service revenue
e.		8,000	Supplies	8,000	Accounts payable		
f.	8,150	1,850	Accounts receivable				10,000 Service revenue
g.	1,000	(1,000)	Accounts receivable				
h.	(5,000)			(5,000)	Accounts payable		
i.	(4,100)						(4,100) Operating expenses
j.	(165)						(165) Dividends

Requirements

1. Analyze each transaction in the accounting equation worksheet and describe the underlying exchange that resulted in each entry.
2. Has the company been profitable this month? Explain.
3. Prepare an income statement for the month ended October 31, 2009.
4. Prepare a statement of shareholders' equity for the month ended October 31, 2009.
5. Prepare a statement of cash flows for the month ended October 31, 2009.
6. Prepare a balance sheet at October 31, 2009.
7. Calculate the current ratio at October 31, 2009.

P2-46B. *Analyzing transactions and preparing financial statements. (LO 3, 5).* Joanna Wu won a Web-designing contest and decided to start her own Web-design company. She contributed $200,000 in exchange for 1,000 shares of common stock and borrowed another $55,000 by signing a 4-year note with Quality Bank. She formed Wu Web Designs, Inc., on July 1, 2009. The business used available funds to purchase some land with an office building for $125,000 and office equipment and furniture for $25,000. The business also bought a computer system on account for $45,500; payment was due at the beginning of the following year.

• During the first year of business, Wu Web Designs earned $215,000 in service revenue, but had collected only $172,000; the remaining $43,000 was due early the next year.
• Salary expenses for the year were $95,000 of which the company paid $80,000 in cash during the year; the remaining $15,000 was due the first day of the next year.

- The company purchased an insurance policy for $24,000, of which $6,000 was for the current year and the remainder was for future years.
- The company paid operating expenses of $20,250 in cash during the year.
- Interest expense for the year was $7,175 but has not yet been paid.
- The company invested $20,000 of cash in a short-term investment at the end of the year.
- Wu Web Designs declared and paid dividends of $3,200 during the year.

Requirements

1. Show how each transaction affects the accounting equation.
2. Prepare the income statement, statement of changes in shareholder's equity, and statement of cash flows for the year ended June 30, 2010; and prepare the balance sheet at June 30, 2010. (Ignore depreciation.)
3. Calculate the current ratio at June 30, 2010.

Financial Statement Analysis

FSA2-1. *Identify items from the balance sheet. (LO 3, 5).* The balance sheets (adapted) for Tootsie Roll Industries, Inc., are shown here.

Tootsie Roll Industries, Inc.
Balance Sheet (adapted)
(in thousands)

	December 31, 2008	December 31, 2007
Assets		
Cash	$ 68,908	$ 57,606
Investments	17,963	41,307
Receivables	34,196	35,284
Inventory	55,584	57,402
Other current assets	11,328	8,127
Net property, plant, and equipment	217,628	201,401
Other noncurrent assets	406,485	411,598
Total assets	$812,092	$812,725
Liabilities and Shareholders' Equity		
Accounts payable	13,885	11,572
Dividends payable	4,401	4,344
Accrued liabilities	40,335	42,056
Deferred income taxes	631	0
Total current liabilities	59,252	57,972
Noncurrent liabilities	118,070	116,523
Total liabilities	177,322	174,495
Contributed capital	509,131	495,197
Retained earnings	142,872	156,752
Other shareholders' equity accounts, net*	(17,233)	(13,719)
Total shareholders' equity	634,770	638,230
Total liabilities and shareholders' equity	$812,092	$812,725

*This is an item you will learn about in a later chapter.

Requirements

1. What were the total current assets at December 31, 2007? December 31, 2008?
2. How are the assets ordered on the balance sheet?
3. What were the total current liabilities at December 31, 2007? December 31, 2008?
4. Calculate the current ratio at December 31, 2007, and December 31, 2008. What information do these numbers provide?

FSA2-2. *Evaluate liquidity from the balance sheet. (LO 3, 4, 5).* Selected information from the comparative balance sheets for Sears Holdings Corporation is presented here. Although some accounts are not listed, all of the current assets and current liabilities are given.

Sears Holdings Corporation
From the Consolidated Balance Sheets
(dollars in millions)

	January 31, 2009	February 2, 2008
Cash	$1,297	$ 1,622
Accounts receivable	839	744
Inventory	8,795	9,963
Other current assets	485	473
Property, plant, and equipment	8,091	8,863
Accounts payable	3,006	3,487
Other current liabilities	5,506	6,075
Long-term liabilities	7,450	7,168
Total shareholders' equity	9,380	10,667

Requirements

1. Provide the following values at the end of each given fiscal year:
   a. Current assets
   b. Current liabilities
   c. Current ratio
2. Based on your answers in part 1, discuss the change in liquidity between the two years.

FSA2-3. *Identify items from the statement of cash flows. (LO 3).* A condensed statement of cash flows for Apple Inc. for the year ended September 27, 2008, is shown here. Use it to answer the questions given after the statement.

Apple Inc.
Statement of Cash Flows (adapted)
For the Year Ended September 27, 2008
(in millions)

Cash and cash equivalents, beginning of the year	$ 9,352
Cash generated by operating activities	9,596
Investing Cash Flows:	
Purchase of short-term investments	(22,965)
Proceeds from maturities of short-term investments	11,804
Proceeds from sales of short-term investments	4,439
Purchase of property, plant, and equipment	(1,091)
Other	(376)
Cash (used in) generated by investing activities	(8,189)
Financing Cash Flows:	
Proceeds from issuance of common stock	483
Other (net)	633
Cash generated by financing activities	1,116
Increase in cash and cash equivalents	2,523
Cash and cash equivalents, end of the year	$11,875

Requirements

1. What was Apple's net cash flow related to operating activities during the year?
2. What was Apple's net cash flow related to investing activities during the year?
3. What was Apple's net cash flow related to financing activities during the year?
4. If you were to look at Apple's balance sheets for the two most recent fiscal years, what amount would be shown on each for cash (and cash equivalents)?

Critical Thinking Problems

Risk and Controls

Look at the information from the Books-A-Million annual report in Appendix A, paying special attention to the notes. What kinds of risks does Books-A-Million face? Use the information in the annual report and your own experience to answer this question.

Ethics

Ken Jones wants to start a small business and has asked his uncle to lend him $10,000. He has prepared a business plan and some financial statements that indicate the business could be very profitable. Ken is afraid his uncle will want some ownership in the company for his investment, but Ken does not want to share what he believes will be a hugely successful company. What are the ethical issues Ken must face as he prepares to present his business plan to his uncle? Do you think he should try to *emphasize* the risks of ownership to his uncle to convince him it would be preferable to be a creditor? Why or why not?

Group Assignment

Look at the four basic financial statements for Team Shirts in Exhibits 2.5, 2.6, 2.7, and 2.8. Work together to find numbers that show the links between the various financial statements. Then, write a brief explanation of how the statements relate to each other.

Internet Exercise: MSN Money and Merck

MSN Money offers information about companies, industries, people, and related news items. For researching a company, the Web site is a good place to start gathering basic information.
Please go to http://moneycentral.msn.com.

IE2-1. In the *Symbol* box, enter MRK for Merck and Co., Inc.

1. What type of company is Merck?
2. List three products manufactured by Merck.

IE2-2. Click on Financial Results, and then on Statements.

1. For the most recent year list the amounts reported for sales, cost of goods sold, and total net income. Does the amount reported for revenue represent cash received from customers during the year? If not, what does it represent? What does the amount reported for cost of goods sold represent? Is Merck a profitable company? How can you tell?
2. For the most recent year list the amounts reported for total assets, total liabilities, and total shareholders' equity. Does the accounting equation hold true? Are assets primarily financed with liabilities or shareholders' equity?
3. Does Merck use accrual-based or cash-based accounting? How can you tell?

Please note: Internet Web sites are constantly being updated. Therefore, if the information is not found where indicated, please explore the Web site further to find the information.

Accruals and Deferrals: Timing Is Everything in Accounting

ETHICS Matters

Cookie Sales Were Not So Sweet

Perhaps you've wondered what happened to the Archway cookies that used to be on your grocery store shelves. In 2008, daily sales reports looked pretty dismal. Then one evening, Keith Roberts, who had joined the Archway & Mother's Cookie Company in 2007 as the director of finance, found himself looking at some truly excellent sales figures. He was surprised, to say the least. After digging through the company's inventory, shipping, and sales records, Roberts determined that Archway had been recording fictitious sales.

You've read about Computer Associates recording sales before actually earning the revenue. Archway, in an even bolder fraudulent activity, simply made up sales that did not exist. According to one long-time distributor of Archway cookies, the company began billing him for $14,000 worth of cookies when they had only sent him $4,000 worth. He called it "hocus-pocus." You'll see in this chapter how Archway recorded this—by accruing revenue that did not exist.

Before this scandal resulted in Archway's bankruptcy, a private equity group owned the company. It was not traded on any stock exchange, so there was no need to produce false sales to maintain a stock price. Why, then, would a company simply falsify sales? Roberts concluded that it was done to maintain access to needed funds from its bank, Wachovia. After Roberts' discovery, the bank cancelled its funding of Archway, forcing the company into bankruptcy. Several members of Catterton Partners, the private equity firm that owned Archway, and former executives at Archway have been named in lawsuits brought by former employees and independent distributors.

Source: *"Oh, No! What Happened to Archway?" by Julie Creswell.* New York Times, *May 31, 2009.*

L.O.1
Define accrual accounting
and explain how income is
measured.

Measuring Income

After its first month, Team Shirts prepared a set of financial statements to measure and report the company's performance during that first month and to measure and report its financial position at the end of that month. Team Shirts did both again for the second month.

At different points of time in the life of a company, owners, investors, creditors, and other interested parties want to know the company's financial position and accomplishments in order to make all kinds of evaluations and decisions, including whether or not the company is meeting its goals. The main goal is usually to make a profit; so measuring the profit the company has made during a specified period plays a big role in evaluating how successfully a company has been doing its business.

THE INCOME STATEMENT. As you learned in Chapter 2, the income statement summarizes revenues and expenses for a period of time, usually a year. Net income can also be measured for a week, a month, or a quarter. For example, many companies provide quarterly financial information to their shareholders. That information would include net income for the quarter.

Accountants consider the continuous life of a business as being composed of discrete periods of time—months, quarters, or years. The way we divide the revenues and expenses among those time periods is a crucial part of accounting. That is why timing is everything in accounting. If revenue is *earned* (not necessarily *collected*) in a certain time period, you must be sure that it is included on the income statement for that period—not the one before and not the one after. If you have used some supplies during a period, then you need to include the cost of those supplies as part of the expenses on the income statement for that same period.

Sometimes you will see the income statement referred to as the *statement of operations* and other times as the *statement of earnings* or the *profit and loss statement*. However it is referred to, it will usually appear as the first financial statement in a company's annual report. Exhibit 3.1 shows the income statements for The Gap, Inc.

When you see total sales of $14,526,000,000 for the year ended January 31, 2009, you know that all the sales made in that fiscal year—a year of business for the company—are included in that amount, even if some of the cash has not been collected from the customers by January 31, 2009. Similarly, the expenses listed are only the expenses incurred in that fiscal year, whether or not the company has paid for those expenses by January 31, 2009. The Gap has to make sure the amounts are correct.

EXHIBIT 3.1

Income Statements for The Gap, Inc.

The Gap, Inc., had net sales of over $14.5 billion during the fiscal year ended January 31, 2009. Investors depend on that information, so The Gap works hard to get it right.

The Gap, Inc.
Consolidated Statements of Earnings
(dollars in millions)

	2008	Fiscal Year 2007	2006
Net sales..	$14,526	$15,763	$15,923
Cost of goods sold and occupancy expenses.....................................	9,079	10,071	10,266
Gross profit	5,447	5,692	5,657
Operating expenses...................................	3,899	4,377	4,432
Operating income	1,548	1,315	1,225
Interest expense	1	26	41
Interest income..	(37)	(117)	(131)
Earnings from continuing operations before income taxes...............	1,584	1,406	1,315
Income taxes..	617	539	506
Earnings from continuing operations, net of income taxes..................................	967	867	809
Loss from discontinued operation, net of income tax benefit..........................	—	(34)	(31)
Net earnings	$ 967	$ 833	$ 778

Timing differences in accounting are differences between

- the time when a company earns revenue by providing a product or service to customers and the time when the cash is collected from the customers,

and

- the time when the company incurs an expense and the time when the company pays for the expense.

You will see in this chapter how to identify timing differences and present them on the financial statements.

As discussed in the previous chapter, you can think of the timing problems in accounting in two simple ways:

- Action before dollars
- Dollars before action

Action refers to the substance of the transaction—the actual earning of the revenue or using the expense item. An example of action before dollars is when a sale is made *on account*. A customer buys on credit and agrees to pay later. The action of making the sale—the economic substance of the transaction—takes place before dollars are exchanged in payment. This type of transaction—action first, dollars later—is called an **accrual**.

In contrast, an example of dollars before action is when a firm buys insurance. By its nature, insurance must be purchased in advance of the time period to which it applies. Payment (when the dollars are exchanged) is made first, and the use of the insurance (the action provided by insurance protection) comes later. Dollars first, action later is called a **deferral**.

Accruals

When the substance of a business transaction takes place before any cash changes hands, the accountant includes that transaction in the measurement of income. That is, if a firm has earned revenue, that revenue must be included on the income statement. If the firm incurred an expense to earn that revenue, that expense must be included on the income statement. Accruals can pertain to both revenues and expenses.

Some accruals are the result of routine transactions like buying and selling items as you run your company. Other times revenue is earned or an expense is incurred without being captured by the accounting system in its everyday recordings. These will require an adjustment at the end of the accounting period, before the financial statements are prepared. First, let's talk about accruals related to revenue, and then we will turn our attention to accruals related to expenses.

Accrued Revenue

The most common accrual transaction is the *sale* of goods or services on account. You will recall that this transaction results in the firm recording revenue and accounts receivable. The cash will be collected later, but the revenue is recognized at the time the goods or services are delivered. Recording revenue with an increase to accounts receivable is called accruing revenue. In the chapter opener, you read about Archway recording fictitious revenue. This is how the company did it—with an increase in sales and an increase in accounts receivable. (Unfortunately, the company did not have valid sales to warrant recording revenue.) Recording revenue on account is a routine business transaction, not an adjusting entry in the accounting system.

However, there are other types of revenue that may have been earned but not recorded as a routine part of the accounting system. For example, interest revenue is an example of revenue that often must be accrued, recorded so that it will go on the income statement before the cash is actually collected at the end of the accounting period. Banks and other financial institutions make loans as a regular business activity, and other firms might lend money to another company or to an employee. A company that lends money earns interest revenue during the time the loan is outstanding. If the company has earned some interest revenue but not yet collected it at the date of the financial statements, the company will want to record that revenue. This is the formula for interest:

$$\text{Interest (I)} = \text{Principal (P)} \times \text{Rate (R)} \times \text{Time (T)}$$

Timing differences arise when revenues are earned in one accounting period and collected in a different accounting period. They also arise when expenses are incurred in one accounting period and paid for in another.

An **accrual** is a transaction in which the revenue has been earned or the expense has been incurred, but no cash has been exchanged.

A **deferral** is a transaction in which the cash is exchanged *before* the revenue has been earned or the expense has been incurred.

L.O.2
Explain *accruals* and how they affect the financial statements; describe and perform the adjustments related to accruals.

The amount of interest revenue will increase assets—interest receivable—and will increase retained earnings via interest revenue. Notice that making this accrual will have the same result that making a sale on account will have: Revenue is recorded along with a receivable.

Suppose a company lends $200 to an employee on October 1 at 10% interest, to be repaid on January 1 of the following year. The transaction on October 1 decreases assets (cash) and also increases assets (other receivables). Because firms generally use *accounts receivable* to describe amounts customers owe the company, we call the amounts owed by others—meaning anyone who is not a customer—*other* receivables.

Assets	=	Liabilities	+	Shareholders' equity		
				Contributed capital	+	Retained earnings
(200) cash						
+ 200 other receivables						

On December 31, the company will accrue interest revenue. Why? Because some time has passed and interest revenue has been earned during that period. With interest, the action is the passage of time, so the action has taken place, but the cash will not change hands until the following January 1. You would record interest revenue of $5 ($200 × 0.10 × 3/12). You would also record interest receivable of $5. By doing all this, the financial statements would accurately reflect the following situation on December 31:

- The company has earned $5 of interest revenue as of December 31.
- The company has not received the interest revenue at December 31.

Because all revenues increase retained earnings, the interest revenue will be recorded under retained earnings in the accounting equation:

Assets	=	Liabilities	+	Shareholders' equity		
				Contributed capital	+	Retained earnings
+ 5 interest receivable						+ 5 interest revenue

When the company actually receives the cash for the interest on January 1, along with repayment of the $200 principal, it will not be recorded as interest revenue. Instead, the total $205 cash is recorded as an increase in cash, a decrease in the asset *other receivables* by $200, and a decrease in the asset *interest receivable* by $5. The timing difference resulted in recording the interest revenue in one period and the cash collection in another.

There are other types of revenues that must be accrued at the end of the period so that the financial statements will accurately reflect the business transactions for that period. For example, if you have provided services for a customer during 2009 but have not recorded those services (perhaps because you have not billed the customer yet), you want to be sure to report the revenue on the 2009 income statement. Why report this on the 2009 income statement? Because the action of earning the revenue was completed in 2009. Even though you will not collect the cash until sometime in 2010, the revenue will be shown on the 2009 income statement.

To summarize, accrued revenue and receivables are often paired together in accruals. An increase in assets (accounts receivable) and an increase in retained earnings (revenue), both in the same amount, balance the accounting equation. Then, when the cash is actually collected—sometimes called **realized**—it is not recognized as revenue because it was already recognized in a previous period.

Realized means the cash is collected. Sometimes revenue is *recognized* before it is *realized*.

Exhibit 3.2 shows the current assets section of Talbots' balance sheet. At January 31, 2009, Talbots had accounts receivable amounting to $169,406,000. This is a significant amount of money! When you see receivables on a company's balance sheet, it means the related revenues have been earned and included on the income statement for that period even though the cash has not been collected yet.

EXHIBIT 3.2

Current Assets Section of Talbots' Balance Sheet

This is the current assets section of Talbots' balance sheet.

The Talbots, Inc., and Subsidiaries
From the Consolidated Balance Sheets

(amounts in thousands)

Assets	January 31, 2009	February 2, 2008
Current Assets:		
Cash and cash equivalents...	$ 16,718	$ 25,476
Customer accounts receivable—net	169,406	210,853
Merchandise inventories..	206,593	262,603
Deferred catalog costs...	4,795	6,249
Due from related party...	376	3,040
Deferred income taxes...	—	25,084
Income tax refundable	26,646	—
Prepaid and other current assets...	35,277	34,524
Assets held for sale—current...	109,966	84,018
Total current assets...	$569,777	$651,847

Your Turn 3-1

Suppose your firm loaned an employee $1,000 at 7% (interest rates are always assumed to be per year) on July 1. On December 31, the firm is preparing its year-end financial statements. What adjustment would the firm need to make to properly account for any interest revenue that had been earned prior to year end?

Accrued Expenses

If a firm buys goods or services from others (as opposed to selling them), and the firm uses those resources, an expense must be recognized even if the firm has not yet paid for the goods or services. Recording an expense along with an increase to a payable account, like salaries payable, is called accruing an expense.

Interest expense is often incurred before the firm actually pays the cash for it. Let's look at an example of borrowing money. Suppose you borrowed $500 from a bank on January 1, 2010, and agreed to repay it with 8% interest on January 1, 2011. On January 1, 2010, when you borrow the money, you get the $500 cash, an asset, and you increase your liabilities. The accounting equation is increased on both sides by $500.

Assets	=	Liabilities	+	Shareholders' equity		
				Contributed capital	+	Retained earnings
+ 500 cash		+ 500 notes payable				

When you get ready to prepare the financial statements for the year ended December 31, 2010, you see that this liability—notes payable—is still on the books and will be listed on the balance sheet. That is because on December 31, 2010, you still owe the bank the full amount of the loan. What about the $500 cash you received? You may still have it, but it is more likely you spent it during the year to keep your business running. That is why you borrowed it.

What about the cost of borrowing the money—the interest expense? On December 31, 2010, one full year has passed since you borrowed the money. The passing of time has caused interest expense to be incurred. Recall, however, that you aren't paying the interest until January when you repay the principal.

- Interest expense is the cost of using someone else's money.
- Time passing is the action related to interest expense.

Although the action of using someone else's money during the year has taken place, the dollars have not been exchanged—the interest payment for using that money. To make the December 31, 2010, financial statements correct, you must show the interest expense of $40 ($500 × 8% × 12/12, or $500 × 0.08 × 1) on the income statement. Also, you must show—on the balance sheet—the obligation called **interest payable**. It is a liability, indicating the bank's claim to the $40 as of December 31, 2010. The liability section of the balance sheet will show both the $500 loan and the $40 interest payable.

> **Interest payable** is a liability. It is the amount a company owes for borrowing money (after the time period to which the interest applies has passed).

Assets	=	Liabilities	+	Shareholders' equity		
				Contributed capital	+	Retained earnings
		+ 40 interest payable				(40) interest expense

Making this adjustment is called accruing interest expense; the expense itself is called an accrual. Sometimes a company will label the amount of interest expense accrued as *accrued liabilities* or *accrued expenses*. Each expression means the same thing—an expense that will be paid in the future. Notice that the interest expense will be on the income statement for the period, even though the cash has not been paid yet.

REPORTING INTEREST EXPENSE. Suppose you borrowed the $500 on July 1, 2010 (instead of January 1). In this case, you would have use of the money for only half of the year and therefore would have incurred only half a year of interest expense as of December 31, 2010. Remember that interest rates, like the 8% interest rate in this example, always pertain to a year. As of December 31, 2010, the interest payable on the note would be $500 × 0.08 × 6/12 = $20. The last part of the formula gives the time as a percentage of a year, or the number of months out of 12. Whenever you accrue interest, you must be careful to count the months that apply. That will help you make sure you put the right amount of interest expense on the income statement for exactly the period of time you had use of the borrowed money.

If you borrowed the $500 on January 1, 2010, for one full year, what would happen when you pay the bank on January 1, 2011? On one side of the accounting equation, you will reduce cash by $540. The equation will be balanced by a reduction of $500 in notes payable plus the reduction of $40 in interest payable. There will be no interest expense recorded when you actually pay the cash. Remember, the action has already taken place, and the action resulted in interest expense in 2010. There is no interest expense in 2011 because you paid off the loan on January 1, 2011.

This is how timing differences work. The expense is recorded in one period, but the cash is paid in another period.

Assets	=	Liabilities	+	Shareholders' equity		
				Contributed capital	+	Retained earnings
(540) cash		(40) interest payable (500) notes payable				

OTHER ACCRUED EXPENSES. In addition to interest, there may be other expenses that need to be accrued. When you get to the end of an accounting period—when you prepare financial statements—you examine your records and business transactions to find any expenses that might have been incurred but not recorded. These are the expenses you have not paid for yet. (If you paid for them, you would have recorded them when you gave the cash to pay for them.) When you receive a bill for some expenses such as utilities, you likely will record the expense and the related miscellaneous or other payable. If you already accrued the expense when you received the bill, you will not need to accrue it at the end of the period.

However, there are some typical expenses that companies do not record until the end of the period. These expenses will be accrued, recorded so that the result is an expense on the income statement and some sort of payable in the liabilities section of the balance sheet. These expenses have been recognized—shown on the income statement—but the cash has not been paid yet.

One of the most common accruals is salary expense. Typically, a company will record salary expense when it pays its employees. (In the accounting equation, that transaction would reduce assets—cash—and reduce retained earnings via salary expense.) What do you do if the end of an accounting period does not coincide with payday? You need to record the salary expense for the work that your employees have done since the last time you paid them. You want to be sure to get the correct amount of salary expense on the income statement for the period. This accrual will increase liabilities—salaries payable—and decrease retained earnings via salaries expense. The action—the employees performing the work—has already taken place; however, the cash will not be exchanged until the next payday, which will be in the next accounting period.

Suppose you are preparing the financial statements for the accounting period ended on December 31, 2012. That date is on a Monday. If you pay your employees every Friday, the last payday of the year is December 28, 2012. As of December 31, 2012, you will owe them for their work done on Monday, December 31, 2012. You will need to record the salary expense for that day, even though you will not pay the employees until Friday, January 4, 2013. Recording this salary expense so it is recognized on the correct income statement is called accruing salary expense. This adjustment will increase liabilities—salaries payable—and decrease retained earnings by increasing salary expense.

What happens when January 4, 2013, arrives and you actually pay the employees? You will pay them for the week from December 31, 2012, through January 4, 2013. (These employees are lucky enough to get paid for New Year's Day!) The expense for one day—December 31—was recorded on December 31, 2012, so that it would be on the income statement for the fiscal year ended December 31, 2012. The expense for the other four days—January 1, 2013, through January 4, 2013—has not been recorded yet. The expense for those four days belongs on the income statement for the fiscal year ended December 31, 2013. When you pay the employees on January 4, 2013, you will reduce liabilities—the amount of the salaries payable you recorded on December 31, 2012, will be deducted from that account—and you will reduce retained earnings by recording salary expense for those four days in 2013.

Putting numbers in an example should help make this clear. Suppose the total amount you owe your employees for a five-day workweek is $3,500. Look at the calendar in Exhibit 3.3—we are interested in the week beginning December 31.

EXHIBIT 3.3

Calendar for Accruing Salaries

If the firm's fiscal year ends on December 31 and payday is every Friday, then salary expense for December 31 must be accrued—even though it will not be paid to the employees until January 4.

Monday	Tuesday	Wednesday	Thursday	Friday
December 24	December 25	December 26	December 27	December 28
December 31	January 1	January 2	January 3	January 4

On December 31, you need to accrue one day's worth of salary expense. The $3,500 applies to five days, but you need to look at it as $700 per day. To accrue the salary expense for one day, you increase the liability salaries payable and decrease retained earnings via salary expense by $700. Why are you recording the salary expense and salaries payable even though you are not paying your employees until January 4? Because you want to have the expense for December 31 on the income statement for the year ended December 31, 2012. How does this adjustment affect the accounting equation? Both the income statement and the balance sheet are affected by this accrual.

Assets	=	Liabilities	+	Shareholders' equity		
					Contributed capital	+	Retained earnings
		+ 700 salaries payable				(700) salary expense

On January 4, when you actually pay the employees for an entire week, you will give them cash of $3,500. How much of that amount is expense for work done in the year 2012 and how much is expense for work done in 2013? We already know that $700 is expense for 2012. The other four days' worth of work done and salary earned—$2,800—applies to 2013. Here is how the transaction on January 4—paying the employees for a full week of work—affects the accounting equation:

Cash is reduced, salaries payable is reduced, and retained earnings is reduced via salary expense.

Assets	=	Liabilities	+	Shareholders' equity		
				Contributed capital	+	Retained earnings
(3,500) cash		(700) salaries payable				(2,800) salary expense

Review the example and make sure you know why the adjustment on December 31 was necessary and how the amount was calculated. When the employees receive their pay on January 4, notice that the salary expense recorded is only the amount of the January work.

Your Turn 3-2

Suppose ABC Company pays its employees a total of $56,000 on the 15th of each month for work done the previous month. ABC generally records salary expense when the employees are paid. If the ABC fiscal year end is June 30, 2010, does any salary expense need to be accrued at year end? If so, how much?

L.O.3
Explain *deferrals* and how they affect the financial statements; describe and perform the adjustments related to deferrals.

Deferrals

The word *defer* means "to put off or to postpone." In accounting, a deferral refers to a transaction in which the dollars have been exchanged before the economic substance of the transaction—the action—has taken place. Just like accruals, deferrals can apply to both revenues and expenses. As you read and study the examples that follow, remember that you are taking the point of view of the business.

Deferred Revenue

One of the most common deferrals is called unearned revenue. That's when money has been collected before the firm has earned the revenue. Suppose a company sells a monthly magazine subscription to customers who pay in advance. Suppose a customer pays $60 cash for a 12-month subscription. Here's how the company would record the receipt of the $60:

Assets	=	Liabilities	+	Shareholders' equity		
				Contributed capital	+	Retained earnings
+ 60 cash		+ 60 unearned revenue				

Unearned revenue is a liability. It represents the amount of goods or services that a company owes its customers. The cash has been collected, but the action of *earning* the revenue has not taken place.

Unearned revenue is a balance sheet account—a liability. It represents amounts a company owes to others—customers. This is called a *deferral* because the company is *putting off* the recognition of the revenue, that is, not showing it on the income statement until the revenue is actually earned. Please notice that the name of this liability is a bit unusual. It has the word revenue in it, but it is *not* an income statement account.

When the items sold are actually delivered, the company will recognize the revenue. This will be done by decreasing unearned revenue and increasing retained earnings via revenue. In this example, the $60 payment buys 12 magazines, so each magazine is $5. Here is how the accounting equation will be affected after the first month's magazine has been delivered to the customer:

Assets	=	Liabilities	+	Shareholders' equity		
				Contributed capital	+	Retained earnings
		(5) unearned revenue				5 sales revenue

Now that one month's worth of the payment has been earned, the company can recognize $5 worth of the revenue. The unearned revenue for the remaining 11 months, $55, remains as a liability on the balance sheet.

SUBSCRIPTIONS. Subscriptions are a very common deferred revenue. For example, the current liabilities sections of the balance sheet for Time Warner at December 31, 2008 and 2007, shown in Exhibit 3.4, show $1,169 million of unearned revenue at the end of 2008 and $1,178 million at the end of 2007. The company calls it *deferred revenue*. It represents amounts Time Warner has collected from customers but has not yet earned by providing the related services. As the company earns those revenues, the earned amounts will be deducted from the liability and recognized as revenue.

EXHIBIT 3.4

Deferred Revenue from Time Warner

Time Warner has had over a billion dollars of deferred revenue at the end of each of the past two years, highlighted in the portion of its balance sheet shown here.

Time Warner
From the Consolidated Balance Sheets
At December 31, 2008 and 2007
(amounts in millions)

	2008	2007
Liabilities		
Current liabilities		
Accounts payable	$ 1,341	$ 1,470
Participations payable	2,522	2,547
Royalties and programming costs payable	1,265	1,253
Deferred revenue	1,169	1,178
Debt due within one year	2,067	126
Other current liabilities	5,610	5,611
Current liabilities of discontinued operations	2	8
Total current liabilities	$13,976	$12,193

GIFT CARDS. Another common deferred revenue relates to gift cards. Almost all retail firms are happy to sell gift cards. Suppose you decide to purchase a $50 gift card at Best Buy to give your cousin for his or her birthday. You want something easy to mail, and you are not sure what sort of gift he or she would like. When you pay $50 to Best Buy for a gift card, Best Buy records the cash (an asset) and a liability (unearned revenue). Some firms combine their liability for gift cards with other liabilities on their balance sheet. Others have such a significant amount that the liability for gift cards is shown as a line item on the balance sheet. Look at Best Buy's balance sheet in Exhibit 3.5 on the following page. You will see the liability *unredeemed* gift card liabilities for $479 million at February 28, 2009. As the gift cards are redeemed or as they expire, Best Buy will recognize the related revenue.

Living Time Magazine collected $300,000 for 12-month subscriptions before it published its first issue in June 2010. How much revenue should the magazine company recognize for the fiscal year ended December 31, 2010? Explain what it means to *recognize* revenue in this situation.

Your Turn 3-3

EXHIBIT 3.5

Liabilities from Best Buy's Balance Sheet

The highlighted line shows that Best Buy had a significant amount of outstanding gift cards at the end of each of the fiscal years shown.

Best Buy
From the Consolidated Balance Sheets
(dollars in millions)

	February 28, 2009	March 1, 2008
Liabilities and Shareholders' Equity		
Current Liabilities		
Accounts payable	$ 4,997	$ 4,297
Unredeemed gift card liabilities	479	531
Accrued compensation and related expenses	459	373
Accrued liabilities	1,382	975
Accrued income taxes	281	404
Short-term debt	783	156
Current portion of long-term debt	54	33
Total current liabilities	8,435	6,769
Long-Term Liabilities	1,109	838
Long-Term Debt	1,126	627
Minority Interests	513	40
Shareholders' Equity		
Preferred stock, $1.00 par value: Authorized—400,000 shares; Issued and outstanding—none	—	—
Common stock, $.10 par value: Authorized—1.0 billion shares; Issued and outstanding—413,684,000 and 410,578,000 shares, respectively	41	41
Additional paid-in capital	205	8
Retained earnings	4,714	3,933
Accumulated other comprehensive (loss) income	(317)	502
Total shareholders' equity	4,643	4,484
Total Liabilities and Shareholders' Equity	$15,826	$12,758

Deferred Expenses

Four kinds of expenses are commonly paid in advance. We will first discuss expenses for insurance, rent, and supplies. The other is an advance payment for equipment used by a company for more than one fiscal period. All four expenses have in common that the timing of the cash disbursement precedes the actual use of the product or service purchased.

INSURANCE. Like any of us when we buy insurance, a company pays for insurance in advance of the service provided by the insurance company. In accounting, the advance payment for a service or good to be received in the future is considered the purchase of an asset. Recall from Chapter 2 that accountants call the asset for insurance paid in advance *prepaid insurance*. Remember, assets are items of value that the company will use up to produce revenue. Until it is actually used, prepaid insurance is shown in the current asset section of the balance sheet. Suppose a firm paid $2,400 for one year of insurance coverage, beginning on October 1, 2010, the date of the payment to the insurance company. Here is how the payment would affect the accounting equation:

Assets	=	Liabilities	+	Shareholders' equity		
				Contributed capital	+	Retained earnings
(2,400) cash						
+ 2,400 prepaid insurance						

Purchasing the insurance policy is an asset exchange: cash is exchanged for prepaid insurance. No expense is recorded when the payment is made because the benefit of the cost has not been used. The expense will be recognized when the company actually uses the insurance. The signal that the insurance is being used is the passing of time. As time passes, the insurance protection expires and the amount paid for insurance during that time becomes an expense. The firm will make the adjustment when it prepares the financial statements.

Suppose the firm wants to prepare the financial statements on December 31, 2010. How much of the insurance is still unused? That is the amount the firm must show as an asset on the December 31, 2010, balance sheet. How much has been used up? That is the amount the firm must show as an expense on the income statement.

Here is the adjustment the firm makes before preparing the December 31, 2010, financial statements:

Assets	=	Liabilities	+	Shareholders' equity	
				Contributed capital	+	Retained earnings
(600) prepaid insurance					(600) insurance expense

The firm has used up 3 months of the 12-month insurance policy already paid for. The firm paid $2,400 for the 12-month policy, so the monthly cost of insurance is $200. That means the total insurance expense for 3 months is $600, and the prepaid insurance remaining—insurance not yet used up—will be on the December 31, 2010, balance sheet in the amount of $1,800. Exhibit 3.6 shows how this works.

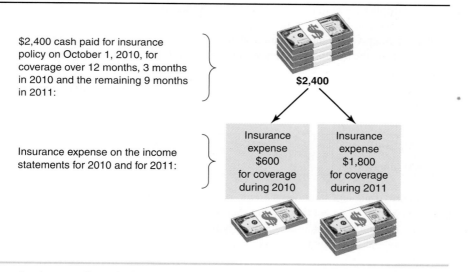

$2,400 cash paid for insurance policy on October 1, 2010, for coverage over 12 months, 3 months in 2010 and the remaining 9 months in 2011:

$2,400

Insurance expense on the income statements for 2010 and for 2011:

Insurance expense $600 for coverage during 2010

Insurance expense $1,800 for coverage during 2011

EXHIBIT 3.6

Deferred Expenses— Insurance

RENT. Rent is also usually paid in advance. In the accounting records, prepaid rent is treated exactly the same way as prepaid insurance. When the company pays the cash for rent in advance, an asset called **prepaid rent** is recorded. The disbursement of cash for prepaid rent is an asset exchange. Suppose a company paid $9,000 to rent a warehouse for three months, beginning on November 1, the date of the payment. The way it would affect the accounting equation follows:

Assets	=	Liabilities	+	Shareholders' equity	
				Contributed capital	+	Retained earnings
(9,000) cash					
+ 9,000 prepaid rent					

Prepaid rent is an asset. It represents amounts paid for rent not yet used. The rent expense is deferred until the rented asset has actually been used—when the time related to the rent has passed.

The asset *prepaid rent* is increased, and cash is decreased. Notice, no expense is recognized when the company makes the payment for the rent. Until it is actually used, prepaid rent is an asset. When would the rent expense be recognized, that is, when would it be put on the income statement? When the company prepares financial statements, it wants to be sure that the rent expense is shown correctly on the income statement. The amount paid was $9,000 for a period of three months, which is $3,000 per month. When the financial statements are prepared on December 31, two months of rent has been used—$6,000. To make sure the income statement reflects the expense for the period ended December 31, the company makes the following adjustment:

Assets	=	Liabilities	+	Shareholders' equity		
				Contributed capital	+	Retained earnings
(6,000) prepaid rent						(6,000) rent expense

Notice that rent expense is shown as a reduction in retained earnings, like all expenses. That leaves one month of rent, $3,000, on the balance sheet as prepaid rent. The rent expense for November and December—$6,000—will be shown on the income statement for the year ended December 31.

Your Turn 3-4

Advantage Company paid the annual rent on its new office space on March 1. The total for a year of rent was $3,600. How much rent expense would be shown on the Advantage December 31 income statement?

In general, **supplies** are not called inventory. Supplies are miscellaneous items used in the business. When purchased, supplies are recorded as an asset. Supplies expense is recognized after the supplies are used. *Inventory* is a term reserved for the items a company purchases to resell.

SUPPLIES. **Supplies** are commonly purchased in advance. A company buying supplies is exchanging one asset for another. The cost of the supplies is not recognized as an expense until the supplies are actually used. Suppose a company started March with no supplies on hand and purchased $500 worth of supplies during the month. Here is how the purchase affects the accounting equation:

Assets	=	Liabilities	+	Shareholders' equity		
				Contributed capital	+	Retained earnings
(500) cash						
+ 500 supplies						

If monthly financial statements are prepared, the company will count the amount of unused supplies on March 31 to get the amount that will be shown as an asset on the March 31 balance sheet. Only the amount of unused supplies will be an asset on that date. The difference between the amount available to use during March and the amount remaining on March 31 is the amount of supplies that must have been used. This amount, representing supplies used, will be an expense on the income statement.

Suppose the company counts the supplies on March 31 and finds that there is $150 worth of supplies left in the supply closet. How many dollars worth of supplies must have been used? Five hundred dollars of supplies on hand minus $150 supplies remaining = $350 supplies used. After supplies have been counted, the company must make an adjustment to get the correct amounts for the financial statements. This is the necessary adjustment:

Assets	=	Liabilities	+	Shareholders' equity		
				Contributed capital	+	Retained earnings
(350) supplies						(350) supplies expense

That will leave $150 for the amount of supplies to be shown on the March 31 balance sheet. The income statement for the month of March will show $350 in supplies expense.

Suppose that during April the company purchases an additional $500 worth of supplies. Then, on April 30 as the company is preparing financial statements for April, the supplies left on hand are counted. If $200 worth of supplies are on hand on April 30, what adjustment should be made? Recall that at the end of March, there were supplies on hand amounting to $150. That means that April started with those supplies. Then, $500 worth of supplies were purchased. That means that the company had $650 of supplies available to use during April. What dollar amount of supplies was actually used? Because $200 worth of supplies are left, the company must have used $450 worth of supplies during April. The adjustment at the end of April would reduce the asset supplies by $450 and would reduce retained earnings by $450 via supplies expense.

Check out Exhibit 3.7 for another example of deferring supplies expense.

EXHIBIT 3.7

Deferred Expenses—Supplies

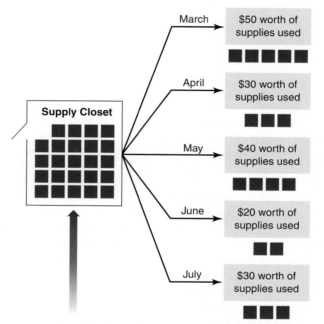

March	$50 worth of supplies used	Cost of supplies *used* in March will be on the income statement as **supplies expense of $50** for the month of March.
April	$30 worth of supplies used	Supplies expense for April will be $30.
May	$40 worth of supplies used	Supplies expense for May will be $40.
June	$20 worth of supplies used	Supplies expense for June will be $20.
July	$30 worth of supplies used	Supplies expense for July will be $30.

February 1: Company buys $240 worth of supplies and pays cash. This will be on the **statement of cash flows**.

Company puts the supplies in the supply closet. The cost of the supplies is recorded as an asset on the **balance sheet**. The company has something of value. Dollars have been exchanged before the action of using the supplies has taken place. This is a deferral: dollars first, action later.

As supplies are used, the cost of those used becomes supplies expense and will be on the **income statement** as an expense in the period the supplies are used.

There are supplies worth $70 in the supply closet at the end of July. That amount will remain on the balance sheet as an asset until the supplies are used.

Konny Company started April with $500 worth of supplies. During the month, Konny purchased $650 worth of supplies. At the end of April, supplies on hand were counted, and $250 worth of supplies was left.

Your Turn 3-5

1. What amount of supplies would Konny put on its balance sheet at April 30?
2. What amount of supplies expense would appear on its income statement for the month of April?

EQUIPMENT. When a company purchases an asset that will be used for more than one accounting period, the cost of the asset is *not* recognized as an expense when the asset is purchased. The expense of using the asset is recognized during the periods in which the asset is used to generate revenue. When a firm buys an asset—such as a computer or office furniture—it will record the purchase as an asset. It is an asset exchange because the firm is exchanging one asset—cash—for another asset—equipment. Then, the firm will recognize a portion of that equipment cost each accounting period in which the equipment is used, hopefully to generate revenue.

The matching principle is the reason the cost of equipment is spread over several periods. Expenses and the revenues they help generate need to be on the same income statement—that is the heart of the matching principle. When it is hard to make a precise match with specific revenue (such as sales and cost of goods sold), the next best match is to put an expense on the income statement in the period in which the related asset is used. That is what you do with equipment—allocate the cost of the equipment to the periods in which the equipment is used.

Suppose a company purchases a computer for $5,000 cash. When the purchase is made, the company will record the acquisition of the new asset and the cash payment.

Assets	=	Liabilities	+	Shareholders' equity		
				Contributed capital	+	Retained earnings
(5,000) cash						
+ 5,000 computer						

If the firm were to classify the purchase as an expense at this point, it would be doing a very poor job of matching revenues and expenses. The firm wants to recognize the expense of the computer during the years in which it uses the computer.

The terminology that accountants use with equipment is different than the terminology used with other deferrals. Instead of calling the expense related to using the computer something logical like "computer expense," it is called **depreciation expense**. Do not confuse depreciation in this accounting context with depreciation commonly used to mean decline in market value.

As the asset is used and the firm wants to reduce its amount in the accounting records, the accountant will not subtract the amount of the expense directly from the asset's purchase price. Instead, per generally accepted accounting principles (GAAP), the firm will show the subtractions separately on the balance sheet. Exhibit 3.8 shows how Best Buy presents this information.

Using real financial information to first learn an accounting concept can be difficult. An example with a fictitious company will help explain the accounting treatment of the cost of equipment and its depreciation expense over time. Sample Company purchased a computer for $5,000 on January 1, 2011, and recorded the asset exchange shown in the preceding accounting equation. Then, when Sample Company prepares its year-end financial statements, depreciation expense must be recognized. The shareholders' claims to the company assets are reduced via depreciation expense.

To calculate how much the asset cost should be reduced each year, Sample Company first must deduct the value it believes the asset will have—what it will be worth—when the company is finished using it. That amount is called the **residual value**. In this example, Sample Company plans to use the computer until it is worth nothing; that means the residual value is zero. The cost of the asset minus any residual value is divided by the number of accounting periods that the asset will be used. Usually, the time period for depreciation expense is a year. Because Sample plans to use the $5,000 computer for five years and has estimated its residual value to be zero, the annual depreciation amount will be $1,000.

The total reduction in the dollar amount of equipment, at any particular point in time, is called **accumulated depreciation**. Each year, accumulated depreciation gets larger. Accumulated depreciation is not the same as depreciation expense. Accumulated depreciation is the total depreciation expense taken over the entire life of the asset, and depreciation expense is the amount of depreciation for a single year. Accumulated depreciation is called a **contra-asset** because it is the opposite of an asset. It is a deduction from assets. Accumulated depreciation is disclosed separately somewhere in the financial statements so that the original cost of the equipment is kept intact.

On the balance sheet, the original cost of the equipment is shown along with the deduction for accumulated depreciation—the total amount of depreciation that has been recorded during the time the asset has been owned. The resulting amount is called the **book value**, or **carrying value**, of the equipment. The book value is the net amount that is included when the total assets are added up on the balance sheet.

The **depreciation expense** is the expense for each period.

Residual value, also known as *salvage value*, is the estimated value of an asset at the end of its useful life. With most depreciation methods, residual value is deducted before the calculation of depreciation expense.

The **accumulated depreciation** is the reduction to the cost of the asset. Accumulated depreciation is a contra-asset, deducted from the cost of the asset for the balance sheet.

A **contra-asset** is an amount that is deducted from an asset.

The **book value** of an asset is the cost minus the accumulated depreciation related to the asset.

Carrying value is another expression for book value.

EXHIBIT 3.8

Best Buy
From the Consolidated Balance Sheets
(dollars in millions)

Assets	February 28, 2009	March 1, 2008
Current Assets		
Cash and cash equivalents	$ 498	$ 1,438
Short-term investments	11	64
Receivables	1,868	549
Merchandise inventories	4,753	4,708
Other current assets	1,062	583
Total current assets	8,192	7,342
Property and equipment		
Land and buildings	755	732
Leasehold improvements	2,013	1,752
Fixtures and equipment	4,060	3,057
Property under master and capital lease	112	67
	6,940	5,608
Less accumulated depreciation	2,766	2,302
Net property and equipment	4,174	3,306
Goodwill	2,203	1,088
Tradenames	173	97
Customer Relationships	322	5
Equity and Other Investments	395	605
Other assets	367	315
Total assets	$15,826	$12,758

Assets from Best Buy's Balance Sheet

Best Buy has property and equipment that cost $6,940 million on February 28, 2009. The total amount of depreciation expense the firm has recorded over the life of these assets is $2,766 million.

Here is the year-end adjustment to record depreciation of the asset after its first year of use:

Assets	=	Liabilities	+	Shareholders' equity	
				Contributed capital	+ Retained earnings
(1,000) accumulated depreciation					(1,000) depreciation expense

The accumulated depreciation is shown on the balance sheet as a *deduction* from the cost of the equipment. The depreciation expense is shown on the income statement. The book value of the asset is $4,000 (cost minus accumulated depreciation) at the end of the first year.

After the second year of use, Sample Company would again record the same thing—$1,000 more recorded as accumulated depreciation and $1,000 as depreciation expense. The amount of accumulated depreciation will then be $2,000. The amount of depreciation expense is only $1,000 because it represents only a single year—the second year—of depreciation expense. The accumulated depreciation refers to all the depreciation expense for the life of the asset through the year of the financial statement. The book value of the computer at the end of the second year is $3,000—$5,000 cost minus its $2,000 accumulated depreciation. See Exhibit 3.9 on the following page for another example.

Your Turn 3-6

Tango Company purchased a computer on July 1, 2011, for $6,500. It is expected to last for five years and have a residual value of $500 at the end of the fifth year. How much depreciation expense would appear on the Tango December 31, 2011, income statement? What is the book value of the computer at the end of 2012?

EXHIBIT 3.9

Deferred Expenses—Depreciation

Truck purchased on January 1, 2007. The truck will last for seven years. Cost is $49,000. No residual value.

Cost of the truck will be spread over the income statements of the seven years the truck is used as depreciation expense. The expense is being **deferred**, that is *put off*, until the truck is actually used.

The cost of the asset is spread—as an expense—evenly (in this example) over the life of the asset.

Year ended December 31	2007	2008	2009	2010	2011	2012	2013
Depreciation expense	$7,000	$ 7,000	$ 7,000	$ 7,000	$ 7,000	$ 7,000	$ 7,000
Accumulated depreciation	$7,000	$14,000	$21,000	$28,000	$35,000	$42,000	$49,000

L.O.4
Construct the basic financial statements from a given set of transactions that include accruals and deferrals and recognize the effect of these transactions on actual financial statements.

Effects of Accruals and Deferrals on Financial Statements

Now that you have learned the details of accruals and deferrals you are ready to put it all together in the construction of a set of financial statements. We will take Team Shirts through its third month of business to see how timing differences affect the firm's financial statements. Then we will look at some real firms' financial statements to identify the effects of accruals and deferrals.

Team Shirts Transactions for March

In Chapters 1 and 2, Team Shirts completed its first two months of operations. Exhibit 3.10 shows the company's balance sheet at the end of the second month, which we prepared in Chapter 2.

EXHIBIT 3.10

Team Shirts' Balance Sheet at February 28, 2010

Team Shirts
Balance Sheet
At February 28, 2010

Assets		Liabilities and Shareholder's equity	
Cash...	$6,695	Accounts payable	$ 800
Accounts receivable.............	150	Other payables	50
Inventory................................	100		
Prepaid insurance.................	125	Common stock..............................	5,000
		Retained earnings.........................	1,220
		Total liabilities and	
Total assets............................	$7,070	shareholder's equity...............	$7,070

These are the amounts that are carried over to the next month, so this is the March 1, 2010, balance sheet, too. We will now take Team Shirts through the third month of business, with the transactions shown in Exhibit 3.11.

At the end of the third month, Team Shirts prepares its financial statements to see how the business is progressing. We will see how each transaction affects the accounting equation. Then, we will look at the accounting equation worksheet in Exhibit 3.12 at the end of the example to see all of the transactions together.

Transaction 1: Purchase of a long-term asset Team Shirts purchases a fixed asset that will last longer than one year; therefore, it will be classified as a long-term asset. Remember, current assets will be used up or converted to cash within one year. If the

Date	Transaction
1. March 1	Purchased computer for $4,000 with $1,000 down and a three month, 12% note for $3,000. The computer is expected to last for three years and have a residual value of $400.
2. March 10	Paid the rest of last month's advertising bill, $50.
3. March 15	Collected accounts receivable of $150 from customers from February.
4. March 20	Paid for February purchases—paying off the accounts payable balance of $800.
5. March 24	Purchased 250 shirts @ $4 each for inventory for cash, $1,000.
6. March 27	Sold 200 shirts for $10 each, all on account, for total sales of $2,000.

EXHIBIT 3.11

Transactions for Team Shirts for March

cost of an asset needs to be spread over more than one year, it is considered long-term. The actual purchase of the asset is recorded as an asset exchange, not as an expense. Do not worry about depreciation expense and interest expense right now. That will be considered when it is time to prepare the financial statements. Here is how the purchase of the $4,000 computer with $1,000 down and a note payable of $3,000 with an annual interest rate of 12%, due in three months, affects the accounting equation:

Assets	=	Liabilities	+	Shareholder's equity		
				Contributed capital	**+**	**Retained earnings**
(1,000) cash		+ 3,000 notes payable				
+ 4,000 computer						

The recognition of the expense related to the cost of the computer will be deferred—put off—until Team Shirts has used the asset and is ready to prepare financial statements. The cash portion of the payment for the computer will be shown as an investing cash flow on the statement of cash flows.

Transaction 2: Cash disbursement to settle a liability Last month, Sara hired a company to do some advertising for her business. On February 28, 2010, Team Shirts had not paid the full amount. Because the work was done in February, the expense was shown on the income statement for the month of February. In March, Team Shirts pays cash of $50 to settle—eliminate—the liability. Here is how the cash disbursement affects the accounting equation:

Assets	=	Liabilities	+	Shareholder's equity		
				Contributed capital	**+**	**Retained earnings**
(50) cash		(50) other payables				

The action took place during February, so the expense was shown on that month's income statement. The cash is now paid in March, but no expense is recognized in March because that would be double counting the expense. An expense is recognized only once. The cash payment is an operating cash flow for the statement of cash flows.

Transaction 3: Collection of cash to settle a receivable At the end of last month, Team Shirts had not received all the cash it was owed by customers. Because the sales were made during February, the revenue from those sales was shown on the income statement for the month of February. Because the cash for the sales was not collected at the time the sales were made, Team Shirts recorded accounts receivable. Accounts receivable is an asset that will be converted to cash within the next year. When customers pay their bills, Team Shirts records the receipt of cash and removes the receivable from its records. Here is how the collection of the cash affects the accounting equation:

Assets	=	Liabilities	+	Shareholder's equity		
				Contributed capital	+	Retained earnings
+ 150 cash (150) accounts receivable						

Revenue is not recorded when the cash is collected because the revenue was already recorded at the time of the sale. To count it now would be double counting. The cash collection is an operating cash flow for the statement of cash flows.

Transaction 4: Payment to vendor At the end of last month, the balance sheet for Team Shirts showed accounts payable of $800. This is the amount still owed to vendors for February purchases. Team Shirts pays this debt, bringing the accounts payable balance to zero. The cash payment is an operating cash flow for the statement of cash flows.

Assets	=	Liabilities	+	Shareholder's equity		
				Contributed capital	+	Retained earnings
(800) cash		(800) accounts payable				

Transaction 5: Purchase of inventory Team Shirts purchases 250 shirts at $4 each, for a total of $1,000 and pays cash for the purchase. The cash payment is an operating cash flow for the statement of cash flows.

Assets	=	Liabilities	+	Shareholder's equity		
				Contributed capital	+	Retained earnings
(1,000) cash						
+ 1,000 inventory						

Transaction 6: Sales Team Shirts sells 200 shirts at $10 each, all on account. That means the company extended credit to its customers and Team Shirts will collect the cash later.

Assets	=	Liabilities	+	Shareholder's equity		
				Contributed capital	+	Retained earnings
+ 2,000 accounts receivable						+ 2,000 sales revenue

At the same time sales revenue is recorded, Team Shirts records the reduction in inventory. The reduction in inventory is an expense called cost of goods sold.

Assets	=	Liabilities	+	Shareholder's equity		
				Contributed capital	+	Retained earnings
(800) inventory						(800) cost of goods sold

Notice that the sale is recorded at the amount Team Shirts will collect from the customer. At the same time, the reduction in the inventory is recorded at the cost of the inventory—200 shirts at a cost of $4 per shirt. This is a terrific example of the matching principle.

Notice that there is no explicit recording of profit in the company records. Instead, profit is a derived amount; it is calculated by subtracting cost of goods sold from the amount of sales. For this sale, the profit is $1,200. It is called the gross profit—also called gross margin—on sales. Other expenses must be subtracted from the gross margin to get to net profit, also called net income.

Up to this point, we have looked just at the routine transactions during the month ended March 31, 2010. At the end of the month, Team Shirts will adjust the company records for any accruals and deferrals needed for accurate financial statements. Look back over the transactions and see if you can identify the adjustments needed.

Adjustments to the Accounting Records

A review of the balance sheet at March 1 along with the transactions for March should reveal three adjustments needed at the end of March 2010:

1. Depreciation expense for the computer
2. Insurance expense for the month (recall that Team Shirts purchased three month's worth of insurance in the middle of February)
3. Interest expense on the note payable

We will now look at each of the adjustments and how the amounts for those adjustments are calculated.

Adjustment 1: Depreciation The computer purchased on March 1 must be depreciated—that is, part of the cost must be recognized as depreciation expense during March. To figure out the depreciation expense, the residual value is subtracted from the cost of the asset, and then the difference is divided by the estimated useful life of the asset. In this case, the residual value is $400, so that amount is subtracted from the cost of $4,000. The remaining $3,600 is divided by three years, resulting in a depreciation expense of $1,200 per year. Because we are preparing monthly statements, the annual amount must be divided by 12 months, giving $100 depreciation per month. The adjustment is a reduction to assets and an expense.

Assets	=	Liabilities	+	Shareholder's equity		
				Contributed capital	+	Retained earnings
(100) accumulated depreciation						(100) depreciation expense

The reduction to the cost of the computer accumulates each month, so that the carrying value of the asset in the accounting records goes down by $100 each month. In the accounting records, we do not simply subtract $100 each month from the computer's cost on the left side of the equation, because GAAP require the cost of a specific asset and the total accumulated depreciation related to that asset to be shown separately.

The subtracted amount is called *accumulated depreciation*. After the first month, accumulated depreciation related to this particular asset is $100. After the second month, the accumulated depreciation will be $200. That amount—representing how much of the asset cost we count as used—is a contra-asset, because it reduces the recorded value of an asset.

The cost of an asset minus its accumulated depreciation is called the *book value* or *carrying value* of the asset. Each time depreciation expense is recorded, the accumulated depreciation increases, and the book value of the asset decreases.

Depreciation expense represents a single period's expense and is shown on the income statement.

Adjustment 2: Insurance expense Remember that Team Shirts purchased three months' worth of insurance for $150, which is $50 per month, in mid-February. On the March 1 balance sheet, there is a current asset called prepaid insurance in the amount of $125. A full month of insurance expense needs to be recorded for the month of March. That amount will be deducted from prepaid insurance.

Assets	=	Liabilities	+	Shareholder's equity	
				Contributed capital	+ Retained earnings
(50) prepaid insurance					(50) insurance expense

Adjustment 3: Accruing interest expense On March 1, Team Shirts signed a three-month note for $3,000. The note carries an interest rate of 12%. (Interest rates are typically given as an annual rate.) Because the firm is preparing a monthly income statement, it needs to accrue one month of interest expense. The interest rate formula—Interest = Principal × Rate × Time—produces the following interest computation:

$$\text{Interest} = \$3,000 \times 0.12 \times 1/12 \text{ (1 month out of 12)} = \mathbf{\$30}$$

Assets	=	Liabilities	+	Shareholder's equity	
				Contributed capital	+ Retained earnings
		+ 30 interest payable			(30) interest expense

These are the needed adjustments at March 31, 2010, for Team Shirts to produce accurate financial statements according to GAAP.

Exhibit 3.12 shows all of the transactions and adjustments in the accounting equation worksheet. Notice how each financial statement is derived from the transactions.

Preparing the Financial Statements

First, Team Shirts prepares the income statement. Revenues and expenses are found in the red-boxed column on the accounting equation worksheet. Organized and summarized, they produce the income statement for Team Shirts for March, shown in Exhibit 3.13 on page 118. The income statement covers a period of time—in this case, it covers one month of business activity.

Second, Team Shirts prepares the statement of changes in shareholder's equity—a summary of what has happened to equity during the period. It is shown in Exhibit 3.14 on page 118. Like the income statement, the statement of changes in shareholder's equity covers a specific period of time—in this case, one month.

Third, Team Shirts prepares the balance sheet—composed of three sections: assets, liabilities, and shareholder's equity—with the amount of each on the last day of the period. The assets are arranged in order of liquidity—how easily the asset can be converted to cash. Remember that current assets will be used or converted to cash sometime during the next fiscal year, whereas long-term assets will last longer than one year.

Similarly, current liabilities are obligations that will be satisfied in the next fiscal year, whereas long-term liabilities are obligations that will not be repaid in the next fiscal year.

Shareholder's equity is shown in two parts—contributed capital and retained earnings. Because the balance sheet is a summary of all the transactions in the accounting equation, it should balance if there are no errors in your worksheet. The balance sheet is shown in Exhibit 3.15 on page 118.

Fourth, Team Shirts prepares the statement of cash flows. Because the first three financial statements (the income statement, statement of changes in shareholder's equity, and the balance sheet) are accrual based instead of cash based, these three financial statements do not provide detailed information about a company's cash—where it came from and how it was spent. The balance sheet gives only the total amount of cash on hand at the close of business on the last day of the fiscal period, and the income statement—the focus of financial reporting—gives no information about cash.

Notice, the residual value is deducted only in the calculation of the amount of depreciation expense. It is not deducted from the cost of the asset in the company's formal records.

Notice that the calculation of the interest expense does not take into consideration the length of the note. The interest expense would be the same if this were a six-month note or a two-year note, or a note of any other length of time. Interest expense is calculated based on the time that has passed as a fraction of a year because the interest rate used is an annual rate.

EXHIBIT 3.12

Accounting Equation Worksheet for Team Shirts for March

The income statement is prepared first. Then, the net income can be used on the statement of changes in shareholder's equity. The total contributed capital and retained earnings from that statement are then used on the balance sheet. Finally, the cash transactions are reorganized and summarized for the statement of cash flows.

	Assets		= Liabilities	+ Shareholder's Equity		
	Cash	**All other assets** (Account)	**All liabilities** (Account)	**Contributed Capital** Common stock	**+ Retained Earnings** (Account)	
Beginning Balances	$6,695	$150 Accounts receivable 100 Inventory 125 Prepaid insurance	$800 Accounts payable 50 Other payables	$5,000	$1,220	
Transaction						
1.	(1,000)	4,000 Computer	3,000 Notes payable			
2.	(50)		(50) Other payables			
3.	150	(150) Accounts receivable				
4.	(800)		(800) Accounts payable			
5.	(1,000)	1,000 Inventory				
6.		2,000 Accounts receivable			2,000	Sales
		(800) Inventory			(800)	Cost of goods sold
Adjustment 1		(100) Accumulated depreciation			(100)	Depreciation expense
Adjustment 2		(50) Prepaid insurance			(50)	Insurance expense
Adjustment 3			30 Interest payable		(30)	Interest expense
Ending Balances	$3,995	+ $6,275*	= $3,030	$5,000	+ $2,240	

*All other assets (details)

$2,000	Accounts receivable
300	Inventory
75	Prepaid insurance
4,000	Computer
(100)	Accumulated depreciation, Computer
$6,275	Total

— Income Statement   — Statement of Changes in Stockholders' Equity   — Balance Sheet   — Statement of Cash Flows

117

EXHIBIT 3.13

Income Statement for Team Shirts for March

Team Shirts
Income Statement
For the Month Ended March 31, 2010

Sales revenue		$2,000
Expenses		
Cost of goods sold	$800	
Depreciation expense	100	
Insurance expense	50	
Interest expense	30	980
Net income		$1,020

EXHIBIT 3.14

Statement of Changes in Shareholder's Equity for Team Shirts for March

Team Shirts
Statement of Changes in Shareholder's Equity
For the Month Ended March 31, 2010

Beginning common stock	$5,000	
Common stock issued during the month	0	
Ending common stock		$5,000
Beginning retained earnings	$1,220	
Net income for the month	1,020	
Dividends declared	0	
Ending retained earnings		2,240
Total shareholder's equity		$7,240

EXHIBIT 3.15

Balance Sheet for Team Shirts at March 31, 2010

Team Shirts
Balance Sheet
At March 31, 2010

Assets		Liabilities and Shareholder's equity	
Current assets		Current liabilities	
Cash	$ 3,995	Interest payable	$ 30
Accounts receivable	2,000	Notes payable	3,000
Inventory	300	Total current liabilities	3,030
Prepaid insurance	75	Shareholder's equity	
Total current assets	6,370	Common stock	5,000
Computer (net of $100		Retained earnings	2,240
accumulated depreciation)	3,900	Total shareholder's equity	7,240
		Total liabilities and	
Total assets	$10,270	shareholder's equity	$10,270

This is why the statement of cash flows is needed. Even though accrual accounting does not base the measurement of income on cash, there is no debate about the importance of the sources and uses of cash to a business. The statement of cash flows gives the details of how the cash balance has changed from the first day of the period to the last day. This statement is shown in Exhibit 3.16.

EXHIBIT 3.16

Statement of Cash Flows for Team Shirts for March

Team Shirts
Statement of Cash Flows
For the Month Ended March 31, 2010

Cash from Operating Activities:		
Cash collected from customers............................	$ 150	
Cash paid to vendors..	(1,800)	
Cash paid for advertising.....................................	(50)	
Net cash used by operating activities...		$(1,700)
Cash from Investing Activities:		
Cash paid for computer*..		(1,000)
Cash from Financing Activities:...		0
Net decrease in cash...		$(2,700)
Beginning cash balance...		6,695
Ending cash balance		$ 3,995

*Computer was purchased for $4,000. A note was signed for $3,000 and cash paid was $1,000.

Accruals and Deferrals on Real Firms' Financial Statements

The most apparent place on a set of financial statements to identify accruals and deferrals is the balance sheet. Most often, the transactions have been summarized in such a way that the income statement does not make accruals and deferrals obvious. For example, if a firm shows sales revenue on the income statement, the firm may or may not have collected the related cash. The place to find that information is on the balance sheet.

Take a close look at Hormel Foods Corporation's balance sheets in Exhibit 3.17 on the following page. Although there are many items on these statements that you are not familiar with, you should be able to see how much you have learned about financial statements in three short chapters. For example, you know that it is a classified balance sheet because there are subtotals for current assets and current liabilities. The assets are ordered by liquidity, with cash and cash equivalents at the beginning of the assets. As you look at more real firms' financial statements, you will find that each firm will use some unique terminology. Usually, you will be able to figure out what sort of account or amount it is. If you cannot, take a look in the notes to the financial statements for more information.

Look down the balance sheet and see if you can identify specific accruals and deferrals that the company probably recorded when it was preparing its year-end balance sheet. Here are a few examples:

1. *Prepaid expenses.* This is listed as a current asset. It represents goods or services that have been paid for but not used. Putting this amount on the balance sheet is deferring the expense until the period in which the items are used. It is rare for the word *expense* to be on the balance sheet. Here it is the word *prepaid* that makes this an asset on the balance sheet rather than an expense on the income statement.

2. *Allowance for depreciation.* Hormel Foods has several types of property and equipment. Notice that *accumulated depreciation* is called *allowance for depreciation* here, and it has been deducted from the recorded cost of the assets to give the total book value of the assets. In the firm's accounting records, accumulated depreciation (or allowance for depreciation) is a contra-asset, representing the amount of the assets the company has recorded as depreciation expense over the life of the assets to the date of the balance sheet.

3. *Accrued expenses.* As part of the current liabilities, accrued expenses are amounts that the company has recognized as expenses (i.e., put on the income statement). The company purchased these things on account. That is, the company still owes someone for these things. It could be things such as utilities payable or salaries payable—anything the company has used to generate revenue but has not yet paid for. Again, there is the word *expense* on the balance sheet. Here it is preceded by the word *accrued*, which indicates that it is a liability on the balance sheet rather than an expense on the income statement.

EXHIBIT 3.17

Hormel Foods Corporation's Balance Sheets at October 26, 2008, and October 28, 2007

The three shaded items are just a few examples of accruals and deferrals that can easily be picked out from Hormel's balance sheet.

Hormel Foods Corporation
Consolidated Statements of Financial Position

(In Thousands)	October 26, 2008	October 28, 2007
Assets		
Current Assets		
Cash and cash equivalents	$ 154,778	$ 149,749
Accounts receivable [net of allowance for doubtful accounts of 3,144 at October 26, 2008 and 3,180 at October 28, 2007]	411,010	366,621
Inventories	784,542	646,968
Deferred income taxes	45,948	52,583
Prepaid expenses and other current assets	41,900	15,804
Total Current Assets	1,438,178	1,231,725
Deferred Income Taxes	89,249	66,220
Goodwill	619,325	595,756
Other Intangibles	151,219	162,237
Pension Assets	91,773	99,003
Investments in and Receivables from Affiliates	93,617	102,060
Other Assets	155,453	170,048
Property, Plant and Equipment		
Land	52,940	48,663
Buildings	662,519	615,245
Equipment	1,275,175	1,192,481
Construction in progress	78,083	114,415
	2,068,717	1,970,804
Less allowance for depreciation	(1,091,060)	(1,004,203)
	977,657	966,601
Total Assets	$3,616,471	$3,393,650
Liabilities and Shareholders' Investment		
Current Liabilities		
Accounts payable	$ 378,520	$ 290,919
Notes payable/Short-term debt	100,000	70,000
Accrued expenses	72,192	66,000
Accrued workers compensation	26,825	27,372
Accrued marketing expenses	60,223	67,260
Employee compensation	106,225	111,051
Taxes, other then federal income taxes	6,979	5,454
Dividends payable	24,946	20,745
Federal income taxes	5,323	5,927
Current maturities of long-term debt	0	49
Total Current Liabilities	781,233	664,777
Long-Term Debt – less current maturities	350,000	350,005
Pension and Post-Retirement Benefits	386,590	440,810
Other Long-Term Liabilities	91,076	53,275
Shareholders' Investment		
Preferred stock, par value $.01 a share – authorized 80,000,000 shares; issued – none		
Common stock, nonvoting, par value $.01 a share – authorized 200,000,000 shares; issued – none		
Common stock, par value $.0586 a share – authorized 400,000,000 shares; issued 134,520,581 shares October 26, 2008; issued 135,677,494 shares October 28, 2007	7,883	7,951
Additional paid-in capital	0	0
Accumulated other comprehensive loss	(113,184)	(101,811)
Retained earnings	2,112,873	1,978,643
Total Shareholders' Investment	2,007,572	1,884,783
Total Liabilities and Shareholders' Investment	$3,616,471	$3,393,650

See notes to consolidated financial statements.

Side note (left margin): Even though it is unusual to see the term "expenses" used on the balance sheet, you will often find it with the word "prepaid." A prepaid expense is NOT an expense; it's an asset.

Side note (left margin): Again, the term "expenses" is found on the balance sheet, but accrued expenses are NOT expenses. They are liabilities.

Side note (right margin): PPE assets are shown at cost, and then the accumulated depreciation is deducted. Allowance for depreciation means the same thing as accumulated depreciation.

UNDERSTANDING → # Business

Does Going Green Help a Company's Bottom Line?

The goal of a corporation is to make money for its shareholders—that is, to increase shareholders' value. It is the job of financial statements to report the corporation's financial performance. Where does a corporation's social responsibility fit in? Is there a relationship between financial performance and a corporation's social performance? For any company, part of being socially responsible is finding ways to reduce its negative impact on the environment. Everyone, it seems, is talking about "going green."

In his book, *What Matters Most: How a Small Group of Pioneers Is Teaching Social Responsibility to Big Business and Why Big Business Is Listening*, Jeffrey Hollander argues that "introducing social responsibility into day-to-day business operations is an effective way of creating long-term sustainable growth and improved financial performance." Many organizations agree. Staples, for example, reports that its switching from three-amp to two-amp light bulbs added $4.2 million to its bottom line. Dell's plan to neutralize its carbon footprint saved the company $3 million in 2008. Dell Inc. plans to reduce its waste and reuse 99% of its waste by 2013.

According to a recent study by A.T. Kearney, firms with a true commitment to corporate sustainability practices are achieving above-average performance in the financial markets in the current economic recession. John Mahoney, CFO at Staples, told the CFO Green Conference in March 2009 that being socially responsible should continue to reap financial benefits.

"While the economy is reeling today, we can afford to maintain our sustainability programs because of their measurable impact on our financial performance. I think the economic environment is going to really represent a turning point for many companies in thinking about how sustainability works."

Source: "Staples CFO: Going Green Means Saving Green," by David McCann, April 1, 2009, CFO.com

As you continue to learn about the underlying business transactions that are included in a company's financial statements, you will see more examples of accruals and deferrals that are an integral part of GAAP.

Applying Your Knowledge: Ratio Analysis

Profit Margin on Sales Ratio

In this chapter, we have discussed how firms measure profit with accounting net income. To evaluate the firm's profitability over time, the firm might use a ratio called **profit margin on sales**. Sometimes it is called the *net* profit margin on sales ratio or simply the profit margin ratio. It measures how much of the firm's sales revenue actually makes its way to the bottom line—net income. To calculate this ratio, simply divide net income by net sales:

$$\text{Profit margin on sales} = \frac{\text{Net income}}{\text{Net sales}}$$

> **L.O.5**
> Compute and explain the *profit margin on sales* ratio.

> **Profit margin on sales** is a ratio that measures how much of the firm's sales revenue actually makes its way to the bottom line—net income. To calculate this ratio, simply divide net income by net sales.

As shown in Exhibit 3.18 on the following page, for its fiscal year ended October 26, 2008, Hormel Foods Corporation earned a net income of $285,500,000 with net sales of $6,754,903,000. That is a profit margin on sales ratio of 4.2%. Just a little over four cents of every dollar of sales makes its way to net income. Let's calculate the profit margin on sales ratio for the two prior fiscal years:

For fiscal year ended October 28, 2007: $301,892,000 ÷ $6,193,032,000 = 4.9%

For fiscal year ended October 29, 2006: $286,139,000 ÷ $5,745,481,000 = 5.0%

The trend shows that a smaller percentage of sales is making it all the way to net income each year. This means that a larger percentage of the firm's sales dollars are going toward covering the firm's costs. This is something that Hormel is definitely keeping an eye on, because it is a trend that the firm needs to either stop or reverse.

EXHIBIT 3.18

Income Statements for Hormel Foods Corporation

Hormel Foods Corporation
Statements of Operations

	Fiscal Year Ended		
(In Thousands, Except Per Share Amounts)	October 26, 2008	October 28, 2007	October 29, 2006
Net sales	$6,754,903	$6,193,032	$5,745,481
Cost of products sold	5,233,156	4,778,505	4,362,291
Gross Profit	1,521,747	1,414,527	1,383,190
Expenses:			
Selling and delivery	834,292	771,597	754,143
Administrative and general	178,029	162,480	182,891
Total Expenses	1,012,321	934,077	937,034
Equity in earnings of affiliates	4,235	3,470	4,553
Operating Income	513,661	483,920	450,709
Other income and expense:			
Interest and investment (loss) income	(28,102)	13,624	5,470
Interest expense	(28,023)	(27,707)	(25,636)
Earnings Before Income Taxes	457,536	469,837	430,543
Provision for income taxes	172,036	167,945	144,404
Net Earnings	$ 285,500	$ 301,892	$ 286,139
Net Earnings Per Share:			
Basic	$ 2.11	$ 2.20	$ 2.08
Diluted	$ 2.08	$ 2.17	$ 2.05
Weighted-Average Shares Outstanding:			
Basic	135,360	137,216	137,845
Diluted	137,128	139,151	139,561

Your Turn 3-7

Use the following information from Campbell Soup Company's income statements to calculate the company's profit margin on sales ratio. How does it compare with the ones calculated for Hormel?

Campbell Soup Company
(dollars in millions)

	For the year ended August 3, 2008	For the year ended July 29, 2007
Net sales	$7,998	$7,385
Net income	$1,165	$ 854

L.O.6

Explain the business risks associated with financial records and accounting information.

Business Risk, Control, and Ethics

In Chapters 1 and 2, we discussed the risks a business faces, particularly those risks associated with financial information. Now that you have learned how many transactions are reflected on the financial statements, we will look at the three most significant risks associated with this information:

1. Errors in recording and updating the financial accounting records
2. Unauthorized access to the financial accounting records
3. Loss of the data in the financial accounting records

No matter how transactions are recorded, the information system needs to address the risks of errors in recording the data, unauthorized access to the data, and potential loss of the data.

Errors in Recording and Updating the Accounting Records

Errors in recording transactions can lead to inaccurate records and reports. These errors can be costly, both for internal decision making and external reporting. The accuracy and completeness of the recording process are crucial for a firm's success. The controls that can minimize the risk of these errors include the following: (1) input and processing controls, (2) reconciliation and control reports, and (3) documentation to provide supporting evidence for the recorded transactions. These controls should be present in both manual and computerized accounting information systems.

- *Input and processing controls*. This control is designed to make sure that only authorized transactions are put into the system. For example, when a sales clerk enters a sale at a cash register, the clerk must put in an employee code before entering the data. Additional controls, such as department numbers and item numbers, help make sure that clerks enter the correct information. The computer program that controls this part of the accounting system may also have limits on the dollar amounts that can be entered. The design of the controls depends on the accounting information system and the business, but all firms should have controls to ensure the accuracy of the input and processing of the data that are recorded.
- *Reconciliation and control reports*. This control is designed to catch any errors in the input and processing of the accounting data. Computerized accounting systems are valuable because they make sure the accounting equation is in balance at every stage of the data entry. This type of equality with each entry is a control programmed into accounting software such as Peachtree and QuickBooks. Accounting software does not guarantee that all the transactions have been recorded correctly, but it does keep some errors from occurring.
- *Documentation to provide supporting evidence for the recorded transactions*. This control is designed to keep errors from occurring and also to catch errors that have occurred. The employee who puts the data into the accounting system will get that data from a document that describes the transaction. The information contained in the documentation can be compared to the data put into the accounting system. For example, when a book-publishing company such as Prentice Hall sends an invoice to Amazon.com for a shipment of books, Prentice Hall will keep a copy of this invoice to input the data into its accounting system. Prentice Hall may also use this invoice to verify the accuracy of the accounting entry by referring back to the original invoice.

Unauthorized Access to the Accounting Information

Unauthorized access is an obvious risk for any company's accounting system. Such access would expose a company to leaks of confidential data, errors, and the cover-up of theft. In manual systems, the records should be locked in a secure place so that they cannot be accessed by unauthorized employees. Computerized systems have user IDs and passwords to control access to the accounting system.

There are serious ethical issues related to a firm's data and computerized accounting systems. With the rapid expansion of the Internet and the development of wireless technologies, system-related fraud has been on the rise. Firms must carefully screen all employees, but particularly those who are involved with developing and securing the firm's computer systems. No system is totally safe from fraud.

Loss or Destruction of Accounting Data

Imagine that you are working for several hours on a report for your marketing class, and you save your work on your hard drive. You decide to step out for a coffee with friends before wrapping up. While you are gone, the computer shuts down, and you cannot reboot. If you backed up your file, you are okay. If you did not, you must start the report from scratch.

The accounting information system contains data that are crucial parts of a company's operations, so there must be a backup and disaster-recovery plan. According to the *Washington Post* (September 21, 2005, "Backups Enabled Systems to Survive," p. D05), disaster recovery related to computer records "has become a $6 billion share of the computer industry as companies and governments have taken to heart the lessons of lightning strikes, floods, and other incidents, such as the Sept. 11, 2001, terrorist attacks."

Chapter Summary Points

Accountants want the income statement to reflect the revenues and expenses for the period covered by the statement—none from the period before or the period after. Accountants also want the balance sheet to show the correct amount of assets and liabilities on the date of the statement. To do that, accountants must allocate revenues and expenses to the correct periods. This is done by making adjustments at the end of the accounting period.

- Sometimes a company purchases something and pays for it later. Sometimes a company earns revenue but collects the cash for that revenue later.
- Accountants do *not* base the recognition of revenues and expenses on the income statement on the collection of cash or on the disbursement of cash. Revenues and expenses are recognized—shown on the income statement—when the economic substance of the transaction has taken place. The economic substance of a transaction is the action of providing or receiving goods and services.
- When the action has been completed but the dollars have not yet changed hands, it is called an accrual. Action comes first, and payment for that action comes later. You accrue—build up or accumulate—revenue you have earned or expenses you have incurred, even though the cash has not been exchanged.
- In some situations, the payment comes first and the action for that payment comes later. Sometimes you pay in advance for goods or services; or sometimes your customers pay you in advance for those goods or services you will provide in a later period. These situations are called deferrals. Dollars are exchanged, but you defer recognition of the revenue or expense until the action of the transaction is complete.

Chapter Summary Problems

BB&B Decorating provides decorating services for a fee. Suppose BB&B Decorating began the month of January 2011 with the following account balances:

Cash	$200,000
Supplies	20,000
Equipment*	100,000
Accumulated depreciation	(10,000)
Total assets	$310,000
Miscellaneous payables	$ 40,000
Salaries payable	4,000
Long-term notes payable	50,000
Common stock	126,000
Retained earnings	90,000
Total liabilities and equity	$310,000

*Equipment is depreciated by $10,000 each year, which is $833 per month.

The following transactions occurred during January 2011:

- **a.** Purchased additional supplies for $12,000 on account (record the liability as miscellaneous payables)
- **b.** Paid salaries owed to employees at December 31, 2010
- **c.** Provided decorating services for $84,000 cash
- **d.** Paid entire balance in miscellaneous payables (including purchase in transaction (a))
- **e.** Purchased $15,000 worth of supplies on account (record as miscellaneous payables)
- **f.** Paid six months' worth of rent on buildings for $6,000, starting on January 1, 2011
- **g.** Made a payment on the long-term loan of $5,000, of which $4,950 was principal and $50 was interest for January

Additional information follows:

- There was $5,000 worth of supplies left on hand at the end of the month.
- The equipment is being depreciated at $833 per month.
- At month-end, the following expenses for January (to be paid in February) had not been recorded:
  Utilities $ 350
  Salaries $4,600

Requirements

1. Set up an accounting equation worksheet and enter the beginning balances. Then, record each transaction including the needed adjustments.
2. Prepare the four basic financial statements. For the statement of changes in shareholders' equity, prepare only the retained earnings portion of the statement.

Solution

	Assets			= Liabilities		+	Shareholders' Equity		
							Contributed Capital	Retained Earnings	
	Cash	All other assets	(Account)	All liabilities	(Account)		Common stock		
Beginning Balances	$200,000	$ 20,000 100,000 (10,000)	Supplies Equipment Accumulated Depreciation	$40,000 4,000 50,000	Misc. payables Salaries payable Long-term notes payable		$126,000	$90,000	
Transaction a.		12,000	Supplies	12,000	Misc. payables				(Account)
b.	(4,000)			(4,000)	Salaries payable				
c.	84,000							84,000	Revenue
d.	(52,000)			(52,000)	Misc. payables				
e.		15,000	Supplies	15,000	Misc. payables				
f.	(6,000)	6,000	Prepaid rent						
g.	(5,000)			(4,950)	Long-term notes payable			(50)	Interest expense
Adjustment 1		(42,000)	Supplies					(42,000)	Supplies expense
Adjustment 2		(833)	Accumulated depreciation					(833)	Depreciation expense
Adjustment 3				350	Misc. payables			(350)	Utilities expense
Adjustment 4				4,600	Salaries payable			(4,600)	Salary expense
Adjustment 5		(1,000)	Prepaid rent					(1,000)	Rent expense
Ending Balances	$217,000 +	$99,167		= $65,000		+	$126,000 +	$125,167	

— Income Statement   — Statement of Changes in Shareholders' Equity   — Balance Sheet   — Statement of Cash Flows

BB&B Decorating
Income Statement
For the Month Ended January 31, 2011

BB&B Decorating
Statement of Retained Earnings
For the Month Ended January 31, 2011

Revenue	$84,000
Expenses..	48,833
Net income	$35,167

Retained earnings:	
Beginning balance	$ 90,000
+ Net income...	35,167
Ending balance	$125,167

BB&B Decorating
Statement of Cash Flows
For the Month Ended January 31, 2011

BB&B Decorating
Balance Sheet
At January 31, 2011

Cash from Operating Activities	
Cash collected from customers	$ 84,000
Cash paid to suppliers..	(52,000)
Cash paid for rent...	(6,000)
Cash paid to employees..	(4,000)
Cash paid for interest...	(50)
Net cash from operating activities	$ 21,950
Cash from Investing Activities	0
Cash from Financing Activities	
Cash paid on loan principal.................................	(4,950)
Net increase in cash..	17,000
Add beginning cash balance................................	200,000
Cash balance at January 31, 2011	$217,000

Assets	
Cash..	$217,000
Supplies	5,000
Prepaid rent..	5,000
Total current assets	227,000
Equipment (net of $10,833 accumulated depreciation)...	89,167
Total assets..	$316,167
Liabilities and Shareholders' Equity	
Liabilities	
Miscellaneous payables	15,350
Salaries payable	4,600
Total current liabilities..	19,950
Long-term notes payable	45,050
Shareholders' Equity	
Common stock...	126,000
Retained earnings...	125,167
Total liabilities and shareholders' equity............	$316,167

Key Terms for Chapter 3

Accrual (p. 99)

Accumulated depreciation (p. 110)

Book value (p. 110)

Carrying value (p. 110)

Contra-asset (p. 110)

Deferral (p. 99)

Depreciation expense (p. 110)

Interest payable (p. 102)

Prepaid rent (p. 107)

Profit margin on sales (p. 121)

Realized (p. 100)

Residual value (p. 110)

Supplies (p. 108)

Timing differences (p. 99)

Unearned revenue (p. 104)

Answers to YOUR TURN Questions

Chapter 3

Your Turn 3-1

The firm has earned six months' worth of interest. The amount is $1,000 \times 0.07 \times 6/12 = \$35$. The firm would accrue the interest revenue with an increase to revenue (retained earnings column of the accounting equation) and an increase to an asset, interest receivable.

Your Turn 3-2

Yes, salary expense needs to be accrued. The expense for June would routinely be recorded on July 15 when the payment is made. To get the June salary expense on the income statement for the year ended June 30, ABC Company needs to accrue the expense. A month of salary expense for June is recorded as salary expense and salaries payable in the amount of $56,000.

Your Turn 3-3

Out of 12 months of magazines, seven months have been delivered at December 31. That means 7/12 of the $300,000 collected in advance has actually been earned by December 31. When the cash was collected, the recognition of the revenue was deferred—put off or postponed—because it had not been earned. At December 31, the company recognizes $175,000 worth of revenue. That means it will put $175,000 worth of revenue on the income statement and reduce the liability *unearned revenue* on the balance sheet.

Your Turn 3-4

When Advantage Company made the rent payment on March 1, the company recorded a decrease in cash and an increase in the asset *prepaid rent*. Now, it is 10 months later, and 10 months' worth of rent has been used. That means it should be recorded as rent expense. The March 1 payment was $3,600 for one year, which means $300 per month. Now, 10 months at $300 per month ($3,000) must be deducted from prepaid rent and added to rent expense. Then, $3,000 of rent paid on March 1 will be shown on the income statement as rent expense.

Your Turn 3-5

1. Konny started with $500 worth of supplies and then purchased an additional $650 worth, which made a total of $1,150 worth of supplies available for the company to use during the month. At the end of the month, there were $250 worth of supplies remaining. That means that the company must have used $900 worth ($1,150 − $250). Of the supplies remaining, $250 will be on the balance sheet as a current asset, *supplies*.
2. Supplies expense of $900 will be shown on the income statement for April.

Your Turn 3-6

The depreciable amount is the cost minus the residual (salvage) value, $6,500 − $500 = $6,000. The estimated life is five years. Thus, the depreciation expense per year is $6,000/5 = $1,200 per year. Because the computer was purchased on July 1, 2011, only half a year of depreciation expense, $600, will be shown on the income statement for the year ended December 31, 2011. The book value = cost less accumulated depreciation (all the depreciation that has been recorded on the asset during its life) = $6,500 − $600 (for 2011) − $1,200 (for 2012) = $4,700 at December 31, 2012.

Your Turn 3-7

For 2008: $1,165 ÷ $7,998 = 14.57%
For 2007: $854 ÷ $7,385 = 11.56%
These ratios are considerably better than the same ratios for Hormel. Additionally, the profit margin on sales ratio is growing, which is a good thing.

Questions

1. How does accrual basis accounting differ from cash basis accounting?
2. What is deferred revenue?
3. What is accrued revenue?
4. What are deferred expenses?
5. What are accrued expenses?
6. What is interest and how is it computed?
7. Explain the difference between liabilities and expenses.
8. Name two common deferred expenses.
9. What does it mean to recognize revenue?
10. How does matching relate to accruals and deferrals?
11. What is depreciation?

12. Why is depreciation necessary?
13. What is the profit margin on sales ratio and what does it indicate?
14. What risks are associated with the financial accounting records?

Multiple-Choice Questions

1. Which of the following accounts is a liability?
   a. Depreciation expense
   b. Dividends
   c. Accumulated depreciation
   d. Unearned advertising fees

2. Which of the following is an example of an accrual?
   a. Revenue collected in advance
   b. Supplies purchased for cash but not yet used
   c. Interest expense incurred but not yet paid
   d. Payment for insurance policy to be used in the next two years

3. Which of the following is an example of a deferral?
   a. Cash has not changed hands and services have not been rendered.
   b. Services have been rendered but nothing has been recorded.
   c. A business never has enough cash.
   d. Resources have been purchased for cash but not yet used.

4. The carrying (book) value of an asset is
   a. an account that increases an asset account on the balance sheet.
   b. the original cost of an asset minus the accumulated depreciation.
   c. the original cost of an asset.
   d. equivalent to accumulated depreciation.

5. Logan Company received $300 from a customer as payment for a credit sale made in a previous accounting period. Logan will record this as
   a. $300 in sales revenue.
   b. a $300 reduction in accounts payable.
   c. a $300 reduction in accounts receivable.
   d. a $300 increase in accounts receivable.

6. When a company pays cash in June to a vendor for goods purchased in May, the transaction will
   a. increase cash and decrease inventory.
   b. decrease accounts payable and decrease cash.
   c. decrease accounts receivable and decrease cash.
   d. increase accounts payable and increase inventory.

7. Z Company's accountant forgot to make an adjustment at the end of the year to record depreciation expense on the equipment. What effect did this omission have on the company's financial statements?
   a. Understated assets and liabilities
   b. Overstated assets and shareholders' equity
   c. Understated liabilities and overstated shareholders' equity
   d. Overstated assets and understated shareholders' equity

8. Phillip's Camera Store had a retained earnings balance of $1,000 on January 1, 2010. For the year 2010, sales were $10,500 and expenses were $6,500. The company declared and distributed cash dividends of $2,500 on December 31, 2010. What was the amount of retained earnings on December 31, 2010?
   a. $4,000
   b. $1,500
   c. $2,500
   d. $2,000

9. When prepaid insurance has been used, the following adjustment will be necessary:
   a. Increase insurance expense, decrease cash.
   b. Increase prepaid insurance, decrease insurance expense.
   c. Increase insurance expense, increase prepaid insurance.
   d. Increase insurance expense, decrease prepaid insurance.

10. The profit margin on sales ratio indicates how well the firm is
    a. marketing its products for sale.
    b. controlling its accounting records.
    c. managing its accruals and deferrals.
    d. controlling its costs.

Short Exercises
Set A

SE3-1A. *Analyze the effect of transactions on net income. (LO 1).* The following transactions occurred during a recent accounting period. For each, tell whether it (1) increases net income, (2) decreases net income, or (3) does not affect net income.
    a. Issued stock for cash
    b. Borrowed money from bank
    c. Provided services to customers on credit
    d. Paid rent in advance
    e. Used some supplies previously purchased
    f. Paid salaries to employees for work done this year

SE3-2A. *Calculate net income and retained earnings. (LO 1).* Capboy Company earned $5,000 of revenues and incurred $2,950 worth of expenses during the period. Capboy also declared and paid dividends of $500 to its shareholders. What was net income for the period? Assuming this is the first year of operations for Capboy, what is the ending balance in retained earnings for the period?

SE3-3A. *Account for interest expense. (LO 1, 2).* UMC Company purchased equipment on July 1, 2010, and gave a three-month, 9% note with a face value of $10,000. How much interest expense will be recognized on the income statement for the year ended December 31, 2010? What effect does the repayment of the note plus interest have on the statement of cash flows for 2010?

SE3-4A. *Account for supplies expense. (LO 1, 3).* MBI Corporation started the month with $800 worth of supplies on hand. During the month, the company purchased an additional $300 worth of supplies. At the end of the month, $150 worth of supplies was left on hand. What amount would MBI Corporation show as supplies expense on its income statement for the month? Is the needed adjustment related to an accrual or a deferral?

SE3-5A. *Account for insurance expense. (LO 1, 3).* Catrina Company was started on January 1, 2009. During its first week of business, the company paid $3,600 for 24 months' worth of fire insurance with an effective date of January 1, 2009. When Catrina Company prepares its income statement for the year ended December 31, 2009, how much prepaid insurance will be shown on the balance sheet at December 31, 2009, and how much insurance expense will be shown on the income statement? Is the needed adjustment at year end related to an accrual or a deferral?

SE3-6A. *Account for depreciation expense. (LO 1, 3).* Suppose a company purchases a piece of equipment for $30,000 at the beginning of the year. The equipment is estimated to have a useful life of three years and no residual value. Using the depreciation method you learned about in this chapter, what is the depreciation expense for the first year of the asset's life? What is the book value of the equipment at the end of the first year? What is the book value of the equipment at the end of the second year?

SE3-7A. *Account for unearned revenue. (LO 1, 3).* Able Company received $4,800 from a customer on April 1 for services to be provided in the coming year in an equal amount for each of the 12 months beginning April. In the Able information system, these cash receipts are recorded as unearned revenue. What adjustment will Able need to make when preparing the December 31 financial statements? What is the impact on the financial statements if the necessary adjustment is not made? Is this adjustment related to an accrual or a deferral?

SE3-8A. *Identify accounts. (LO 1, 2, 3).* From the following list of accounts (1) identify the assets or liabilities that commonly require an adjustment at the end of the accounting period, and (2) indicate whether the adjustment relates to a deferral or an accrual.

> Cash
> Prepaid insurance
> Inventory
> Supplies
> Accounts payable

SE3-9A. *Calculate net income. (LO 1, 4).* Suppose a company had the following accounts and balances at year end after all adjustments had been made:

Service revenue	$7,400
Interest revenue	$2,200
Unearned revenue	$3,250
Operating expenses	$1,500
Prepaid rent	$1,030

Prepare the income statement for the year.

SE3-10A. *Account for unearned revenue. (LO 1, 3).* On January 1, 2009, the law firm of Coats and Alday was formed with a contribution from each of the partners of $25,000. On February 1, 2009, the company received $24,000 from clients in advance for services to be performed monthly during the next 12 months beginning in February and recorded the full amount as unearned revenue. During the year, the firm incurred and paid expenses of $7,000. Is the adjustment to recognize the proper amount of service revenue related to an accrual or a deferral? Assuming that these were the only transactions completed in 2009, prepare the firm's income statement, statement of cash flows, statement of retained earnings for the year ended December 31, 2009, and balance sheet at December 31, 2009.

SE3-11A. *Calculate profit margin on sales ratio. (LO 5).* Suppose a firm had sales of $200,000 and net income of $7,000 for the year. What is the profit margin on sales ratio?

Set B

SE3-12B. *Analyze the effect of transactions on net income. (LO 1).* The following transactions occurred during a recent accounting period. For each, tell whether it (1) increases net income, (2) decreases net income, or (3) does not affect net income.
   a. Paid dividends
   b. Purchased inventory
   c. Made sales to customers on account
   d. Paid in advance for insurance policy
   e. Used some of the insurance purchased in item (d).
   f. Collected some cash from customers in item (c).

SE3-13B. *Calculate net income and retained earnings. (LO 1).* Petgirl Company earned $25,000 of revenues and incurred $12,950 worth of expenses during the period. Petgirl also declared and paid dividends of $1,500 to its shareholders. What was net income for the period? Assuming this is the first year of operations for Petgirl, what is the balance in retained earnings at the end of the period?

SE3-14B. *Account for interest expense. (LO 1, 2).* United Company purchased equipment on June 1, 2011, and gave a 10-month, 5% note with a face value of $20,000 with interest and principal payable at maturity. How much interest expense will be recognized on the income statement for the year ended December 31, 2011? What effect does the adjustment for interest have on the statement of cash flows for 2011? Is the adjustment to record the interest expense an accrual or a deferral?

SE3-15B. *Account for supplies expense. (LO 1, 3).* Peter's Pizza started the month with $500 worth of supplies. During the month, Peter's Pizza purchased an additional $300 worth of supplies. At the end of the month, $175 worth of supplies remained unused. Give the amount that would appear on the income statement for the month for supplies expense and the amount that would appear on the balance sheet at the end of the month as supplies on hand. Is the needed adjustment related to an accrual or a deferral?

SE3-16B. *Account for insurance expense. (LO 1, 3).* The correct amount of prepaid insurance shown on a company's December 31, 2011, balance sheet was $600. On July 1, 2012, the company paid an additional insurance premium of $1,440, recorded as more prepaid insurance. On the December 31, 2012, balance sheet, the amount of prepaid insurance was correctly shown as $720. What amount of insurance expense would appear on the company's income statement for the year ended December 31, 2012? Is the adjustment to record the insurance expense related to an accrual or a deferral?

SE3-17B. *Account for depreciation expense. (LO 1, 3).* Suppose a company purchases a piece of equipment for $80,000 at the beginning of the year. The equipment is estimated to have a useful life of five years and no residual value. Using the depreciation method you learned about in this chapter, what is the depreciation expense for the first year of the asset's life? What is the book value of the equipment at the end of the first year? What is the book value of the equipment at the end of the second year?

SE3-18B. *Account for unearned revenue. (LO 1, 3).* Kane Company received $7,200 from a customer on May 1 for services to be provided in the coming year in an equal amount for each of the 12 months beginning in May. In the Kane information system, these cash receipts are recorded as unearned revenue. What adjustment will Kane need to make when preparing the December 31 financial statements? What is the impact on the financial statements if the necessary adjustment is not made? Is this adjustment related to an accrual or a deferral?

SE3-19B. *Identify accounts. (LO 1, 2, 3).* From the following list of accounts (1) identify the assets or liabilities that commonly require an adjustment at the end of the accounting period, and (2) indicate whether the adjustment relates to a deferral or an accrual.

Cash
Accounts receivable
Building
Accumulated depreciation—building
Unearned revenue
Interest payable
Salaries payable
Common stock
Retained earnings

SE3-20B. *Calculate net income. (LO 1, 4).* Suppose a company had the following accounts and balances at year end:

Sales revenue	$5,400
Interest revenue	$1,200
Rent expense	$1,240
Other operating expenses	$3,050
Dividends paid	$1,000

Calculate net income by preparing the income statement for the year.

SE3-21B. *Account for unearned revenue. (LO 1, 3).* On January 1, 2011, the accounting firm of Klindt & Smith was formed with a contribution from each of the partners of $50,000. On March 1, 2011, the company received $36,000 from clients in advance for services to be performed monthly during the next 12 months, beginning in March, and recorded the full amount as unearned revenue. During the year, the firm incurred and paid expenses of $17,500. Is the adjustment to recognize the proper amount of service revenue related to an accrual or a deferral? Assuming that these were the only transactions completed in 2011, prepare the firm's income statement, statement of cash flows, statement of retained earnings for the year ended December 31, 2011, and balance sheet at December 31, 2011.

SE3-22B. *Calculate profit margin on sales ratio. (LO 5).* Suppose a firm had sales of $35,750 and earned a net income of $1,430. What was the profit margin on sales ratio?

Exercises
Set A

E3-23A. *Account for salaries expense. (LO 1, 2).* Matrix Accounting pays all salaried employees biweekly. Overtime pay, however, is paid in the next biweekly period. Matrix accrues salary expense only at its December 31 year end. Information about salaries earned in December 2009 is as follows:

- Last payroll was paid on December 28, 2009, for the two-week period ended December 28, 2009.
- Overtime pay earned in the two-week period ended December 28, 2009, was $7,500.
- Remaining workdays in 2009 were December 29, 30, 31; no overtime was worked on these days.
- The regular biweekly salaries total $125,000.

Using a five-day workweek, what will Matrix's balance sheet show as salaries payable on December 31, 2009?

E3-24A. *Account for unearned revenue. (LO 1, 3).* The TJ Company collects all service revenue in advance. The company showed a $12,500 liability on its December 31, 2011, balance sheet for unearned service revenue. During 2012, customers paid $50,000 for future services, and the income statement for the year ended December 31, 2012, reported service revenue of $52,700. What amount for the liability unearned service revenue will appear on the balance sheet at December 31, 2012?

E3-25A. *Account for interest expense. (LO 1, 2).* Sojourn Company purchased equipment on November 1, 2010, and gave a three-month, 9% note with a face value of $20,000. On maturity, January 31, 2011, the note plus interest will be paid to the bank. Fill in the blanks in the following chart:

	Interest expense (for the month ended)	**Cash paid for interest** (during the month ended)
November 30, 2010	_____	_____
December 31, 2010	_____	_____
January 31, 2011	_____	_____

E3-26A. *Account for insurance expense. (LO 1, 3).* Vertigo Company paid $10,000 on July 1, 2009, for a two-year insurance policy. It was recorded as prepaid insurance. Use the accounting equation to show the adjustment Vertigo will make to properly report expenses when preparing the December 31, 2009, financial statements. (Assume no previous adjustments to prepaid insurance have been made.)

E3-27A. *Account for rent expense. (LO 1, 3).* Jayne rented office space for her new business on March 1, 2010. To receive a discount, she paid $3,600 for 12 months' rent in advance, beginning with March. How will this advance payment appear on the financial statements prepared at year end, December 31? Assume no additional rent was paid in 2011. Use the following chart for your answers:

	Rent expense for the year ended December 31	**Prepaid rent at December 31**
2010	_____	_____
2011	_____	_____

E3-28A. *Account for unearned revenue. (LO 1, 3).* In July of 2009, Wizard's Corporation, a newly developed internet game company, received $1,050,000 for 2,000 three-year subscriptions to a new online game priced at $175 per year. The subscriptions do not start until November of 2009. Fill in the following chart for each of the given years to show the amount of revenue to be recognized on the income statement and the related liability reported on the year-end balance sheet. Wizard's Corp fiscal year end is December 31.

	Revenue recognized during	**Unearned revenue at December 31**
2009	_____	_____
2010	_____	_____
2011	_____	_____
2012	_____	_____

E3-29A. *Account for insurance expense. (LO 1, 3).* Yodel & Company paid $3,600 on June 1, 2010, for a two-year insurance policy beginning on that date. The company recorded the entire amount as prepaid insurance. By using the following chart, calculate how much expense and prepaid insurance will be reported on the year-end financial statements. The company's fiscal year end is December 31.

	Insurance expense	Prepaid insurance at December 31
2010		
2011		
2012		

E3-30A. *Account for depreciation expense. (LO 1, 3).* Maximus Dog Company purchased a new supply van on January 1, 2011, for $35,000. The van is estimated to last for five years and will then be sold, at which time it should be worth approximately $5,000. The company uses straight-line depreciation and has a fiscal year end of December 31.

1. How much depreciation expense will be shown on the income statement for the year ended December 31, 2011?
2. What is the book value (also called carrying value) of the van on the balance sheet for each of the five years beginning with December 31, 2011?

E3-31A. *Analyze timing of revenue recognition. (LO 1, 2, 3).* Show each of the following transactions in the accounting equation. Then, tell whether or not the original transaction as given is one that results in the recognition of revenue or expenses.
  a. Dell Inc. paid its computer service technicians $80,000 in salaries for the month ended January 31.
  b. Shell Oil used $5,000 worth of electricity in its headquarters building during March. Shell received the bill, but will not pay it until sometime in April.
  c. In 2011, Chico's, FAS had $22 million in catalogue sales. Assume all sales were recorded as credit sales.
  d. Home Depot collected $59 million in interest and investment income during 2010.

E3-32A. *Account for rent expense. (LO 1, 3).* Hobbs Company started the year with $6,000 of prepaid rent. During the year, Hobbs paid additional rent in advance amounting to $12,000. The rent expense for the year was $15,000. What was the balance in prepaid rent on the year-end balance sheet?

E3-33A. *Account for insurance expense. (LO 1, 3).* Center Corporation began the year with $9,250 prepaid insurance. During the year, Center prepaid additional insurance premiums amounting to $7,500. The company's insurance expense for the year was $6,000. What was the balance in prepaid insurance at year end?

E3-34A. *Account for rent expense and prepare financial statements. (LO 4).* On March 1, 2010, Quality Consulting, Inc., was formed when the owners contributed $35,000 cash to the business in exchange for common stock. On April 1, 2010, the company paid $24,000 cash to rent office space for the coming year. The consulting services generated $62,000 of cash revenue during 2010. Prepare an income statement, statement of changes in shareholders' equity, and statement of cash flows for the 10 months ended December 31, 2010, and a balance sheet at December 31, 2010.

E3-35A. *Account for depreciation expense and prepare financial statements. (LO 3, 4).* Southeast Pest Control, Inc., was started when its owners invested $20,000 in the business in exchange for common stock on January 1, 2011. The cash received by the company was immediately used to purchase a $15,000 heavy-duty chemical truck, which had no residual value and an expected useful life of five years. The company earned $13,000 of cash revenue during 2011 and had cash expenses of $4,500. Prepare an income statement, statement of changes in shareholders' equity, and statement of cash flows for the year ended December 31, 2011, and a balance sheet at December 31, 2011.

E3-36A. *Classify accounts. (LO 1, 4).* Tell whether each of the following items would appear on the income statement, statement of changes in shareholders' equity, balance sheet, or statement of cash flows. Some items may appear on more than one statement.

Interest receivable
Salary expense
Notes receivable
Unearned revenue
Net cash flow from investing activities
Insurance expense
Retained earnings
Prepaid insurance
Cash
Accumulated depreciation
Prepaid rent
Accounts receivable
Total shareholders' equity

Accounts payable
Common stock
Dividends
Total assets
Net income
Consulting revenue
Depreciation expense
Supplies expense
Salaries payable
Supplies
Net cash flow from financing activities
Land
Net cash flow from operating activities

E3-37A. *Analyze business transactions. (LO 1, 2, 3).* Analyze the following accounting equation worksheet for Starwood Yacht Repair Corporation and explain the transaction or event that resulted in each entry.

| Transaction | Assets | | | = Liabilities | | + | Shareholders' Equity | |
| | | | | | | | Contributed Capital | Retained Earnings |
	Cash	All other assets	(Account)	All liabilities	(Account)		Common stock	(Account)
1.	$150,000						$150,000	
2.	(125,000)	125,000	Property, plant, and equipment					
3.	100,000			100,000	Notes payable			
4.	(500)	500	Supplies					
5.	(650)	650	Prepaid insurance					
6.	15,000							15,000 Service revenue
7.		(375)	Supplies					(375) Supplies expense
8.		(325)	Prepaid insurance					(325) Insurance expense
9.				500	Salaries payable			(500) Salary expense
10.		(1,000)	Accumulated depreciation					(1,000) Depreciation expense
11.				100	Interest payable			(100) Interest expense

━ Income Statement ━ Statement of Changes in Shareholders' Equity ━ Balance Sheet ━ Statement of Cash Flows

E3-38A. *Prepare financial statements. (LO 1, 2, 3, 4).* Refer to the worksheet in E3-37A. Assume all beginning balances are zero and the information pertains to a fiscal year ended December 31. Prepare the four financial statements from the data given in the worksheet.

E3-39A. *Compute profit margin on sales ratio. (LO 5).* Use the following information to calculate the profit margin on sales ratio for the two years provided. Is the change from 2010 to 2011 positive or negative? Why?

	For the year ended December 31, 2011	For the year ended December 31, 2010
Net sales	$6,626.5	$5,567.1
Net income	$ 377.2	$ 201.4

Set B

E3-40B. *Account for salaries expense. (LO 1, 2).* Alex's Editing Company pays all salaried employees monthly on the first Monday following the end of the month. Overtime, however, is recorded as vacation time for all employees. Alex allows employees to exchange all vacation time not used during the year for pay on May 31 and actually pays it on June 15. The company accrues salary expense only at its May 31 year end. Information about salaries earned in May 2009 is as follows:

- Last payroll was paid on May 1, 2009, for the month ended April 30, 2009.
- Vacation pay exchanged at year end totaled $250,000.
- The regular yearly salaries total $3,300,000.

Using a 12-month fiscal work year, what will Alex's Editing Company's balance sheet show as salaries payable on May 31, 2009?

E3-41B. *Account for unearned revenue. (LO 1, 3).* The Einstein Cable Company collects all service revenue in advance. Einstein showed a $16,825 liability on its June 30, 2010, balance sheet for unearned service revenue. During the following fiscal year, customers paid $85,000 for future services, and the income statement for the year ended June 30, 2011, reported service revenue of $75,850. What amount for the liability unearned service revenue will appear on the balance sheet at June 30, 2011?

E3-42B. *Account for interest expense. (LO 1, 2).* The Muzby Pet Grooming Company purchased a computer on December 31, 2012, and gave a four-month, 7% note with a face value of $6,000. On maturity, April 30, 2013, the note plus interest will be paid to the bank. Fill in the blanks in the following chart:

	Interest expense (for the month ended)	Cash paid for interest (during the month ended)
January 31, 2013	_____	_____
February 29, 2013	_____	_____
March 31, 2013	_____	_____
April 30, 2013	_____	_____

E3-43B. *Account for insurance expense. (LO 1, 3).* TJ's Tavern paid $10,800 on February 1, 2010, for a three-year insurance policy. In the company's information system, this was recorded as prepaid insurance. Use the accounting equation to show the adjustment TJ's will need to make to properly report expenses when preparing the July 31, 2010, financial statements. (Assume no adjustments have been made to prepaid insurance prior to July 31.)

E3-44B. *Account for rent expense. (LO 1, 3).* Utopia Dance Clubs, Inc., rented an old warehouse for its newest club on October 1, 2010. To receive a discount, Utopia paid $11,700 for 18 months of rent in advance. How will this advance payment appear on the financial statements prepared at year end, December 31? Assume no additional rent is paid in 2011 and 2012. Use the following chart for your answers:

	Rent expense (for the year ended)	Prepaid rent at December 31
2010		
2011		
2012		

E3-45B. *Account for unearned revenue. (LO 1, 3).* In April 2010 Crummies, Inc., a newly organized style magazine, received $27,000 for 750 two-year (24-month) subscriptions to the new publication. The first issue will be delivered in August 2010. Fill in the following chart for each of the given years to show the amount of revenue to be recognized on the income statement and the related liability reported on the balance sheet. Crummies' fiscal year end is May 31.

	Revenue recognized (during the year ended May 31)	Unearned revenue at May 31
2010		
2011		
2012		

E3-46B. *Account for insurance expense. (LO 1, 3).* All Natural Medicine Corporation paid $2,178 on August 1, 2009, for an 18-month insurance policy beginning on that date. The company recorded the entire amount as prepaid insurance. By using the following chart, calculate how much expense and prepaid insurance will be reported on the year-end financial statements. The company's year end is December 31.

	Insurance expense (for the year ended December 31)	Prepaid insurance at December 31
2009		
2010		
2011		

E3-47B. *Account for depreciation expense. (LO 1, 3).* Trin's Freight purchased a new shipping truck on August 1, 2008, for $27,000. The truck is estimated to last for six years and will then be sold, at which time it should be worth nothing. The company uses straight-line depreciation and has a fiscal year end of July 31.

1. How much depreciation expense will be shown on the income statement for the year ended July 31, 2010?
2. What is the book value (also called carrying value) of the truck on the balance sheet for each of the six years beginning with July 31, 2008?

E3-48B. *Analyze timing of revenue recognition. (LO 1, 2, 3).* For each of the following transactions, tell whether or not the original transaction as shown is one that results in the recognition of revenue or expenses:

   a. On April 15, Mike's Pressure Cleaning Services, Inc., paid its employees $3,000 in salaries for services provided.
   b. Mister Hsieh Fencing Company used $1,000 worth of radio advertising during April. Mister Hsieh received the bill but will not pay it until sometime in May.

c. During the year, Tootie's Pet Training School, Inc., earned $125,000 in service revenues. Assume all services were provided on account.

d. Susan's Investment Company collected $130,000 in interest and investment income earned during the year.

E3-49B. *Account for rent expense. (LO 1, 3).* Roberto's Paper Supply started the year with $5,000 of prepaid rent. During the year, Roberto's paid $25,000 of additional rent in advance. The rent expense shown on the income statement for the year was $20,000. What was the balance in prepaid rent on the year-end balance sheet?

E3-50B. *Account for insurance expense. (LO 1, 3).* Eric's Coffee Shop began the year with $12,000 prepaid insurance. During the year, Eric's prepaid $75,000 in additional insurance premiums. According to the income statement, the company's insurance expense for the year was $62,000. What is the balance in prepaid insurance at year end?

E3-51B. *Account for rent expense and insurance expense and prepare financial statements. (LO 3, 4).* On February 1, 2010, Breeder's Choice Pet Trainers, Inc., was formed when the owners invested $25,626 cash in the business in exchange for common stock. On March 1, 2010, the company paid $22,212 cash to rent office space for the next 18 months and paid $3,414 cash for six months of prepaid insurance. The training services generated $115,725 of cash revenue during the remainder of the fiscal year. The company has chosen June 30 as the end of its fiscal year. Prepare an income statement, statement of changes in shareholders' equity, and statement of cash flows for the five months ended June 30, 2010, and a balance sheet at June 30, 2010.

E3-52B. *Account for depreciation expense and prepare financial statements. (LO 3, 4).* Northeast Termite Specialists, Inc., was started when its owners invested $32,685 in the business in exchange for common stock on July 1, 2010. Part of the cash received to start the company was immediately used to purchase a $19,875 high-pressure chemical sprayer, which had a $2,875 residual value and an expected useful life of 10 years. The company earned $68,315 of cash revenue during the year and had cash operating expenses of $27,205. Prepare an income statement, statement of changes in shareholders' equity, and statement of cash flows for the year ended June 30, 2011, and a balance sheet at June 30, 2011.

E3-53B. *Identify accounts. (LO 1, 4).* From the following list of accounts (1) identify the assets or liabilities that may require an adjustment at the end of the accounting period, and (2) indicate whether it relates to a deferral or an accrual.

Cash	Common stock
Accounts receivable	Retained earnings
Prepaid insurance	Sales revenue
Prepaid rent	Interest revenue
Supplies	Equipment
Depreciation expense	Accumulated depreciation—equipment
Insurance expense	Unearned revenue
Supplies expense	Interest payable
Utilities expense	Salaries payable
Rent expense	Accounts payable
Interest receivable	Other operating expense

E3-54B. *Analyze business transactions from the accounting equation. (LO 1, 2, 3).* Analyze the transactions for Information Resource Services, Inc., that appear in the worksheet on the following page and explain the transaction or event that resulted in each entry.

Transaction	Cash	All other assets	(Account)	All liabilities	(Account)	Common stock	(Account)
						Contributed Capital	Retained Earnings
1.	$115,000					$115,000	
2.	(112,500)	112,500	Property, plant, and equipment				
3.	85,000			85,000	Notes payable		
4.	(1,000)	1,000	Supplies				
5.	(825)	825	Prepaid rent				
6.		13,150	Accounts receivable				13,150 Service revenue
7.		(615)	Supplies				(615) Supplies expense
8.		(275)	Prepaid rent				(275) Rent expense
9.				795	Salaries payable		(795) Salary expense
10.		(1,500)	Accumulated depreciation				(1,500) Depreciation expense
11.				50	Interest payable		(50) Interest expense

Assets = Liabilities + Shareholders' Equity

—— Income Statement — — Statement of Changes in Shareholders' Equity — Balance Sheet — Statement of Cash Flows

E3-55B. *Prepare financial statements. (LO 1, 2, 3, 4).* Refer to the worksheet in E3-54B. Assume all beginning balances are zero. Prepare the four financial statements using the data provided in the worksheet.

E3-56B. *Compute profit margin on sales ratio. (LO 5).* Use the following information to calculate the profit margin on sales ratio for the two years given. Is the trend positive or negative?

	For the year ended March 31, 2010	For the year ended March 31, 2009
Net sales	$45,015	$40,023
Net income	$ 1,003	$ 1,407

MyAccountingLab

All of the A problems can be found within MyAccountingLab, an online homework and practice environment.

Problems
Set A

P3-57A. *Record adjustments and prepare income statement. (LO 1, 2, 3, 4).* Selected amounts (at December 31, 2010) from Solar Power, Inc.'s information system appear as follows:

Cash paid to employees for salaries and wages	$ 600,000
Cash collected from customers for service rendered	2,500,000
Long-term notes payable	225,000
Cash	375,000

Common stock	100,000
Equipment	750,000
Prepaid insurance	45,000
Inventory	175,000
Prepaid rent	75,000
Retained earnings	150,000
Salaries and wages expense	625,000
Service revenues	2,750,000

Requirements

1. There are five adjustments that need to be made before the financial statements can be prepared at year end. For each, show the adjustment in the accounting equation.
   a. The equipment (purchased on January 1, 2010) has a useful life of 10 years with no salvage value. (An equal amount of depreciation is taken each year.)
   b. Interest accrued on the notes payable is $2,500 as of December 31, 2010.
   c. Unexpired insurance at December 31, 2010, is $11,000.
   d. The rent payment of $75,000 covered the six months from December 1, 2010, through May 31, 2011.
   e. Employees had earned salaries and wages of $25,000 that were unpaid at December 31, 2010.
2. Prepare an income statement for the year ended December 31, 2010, for Solar Power, Inc.

P3-58A. *Record adjustments and calculate net income. (LO 1, 2, 3, 4).* The records of Poorman's, Inc., revealed the following recorded amounts at December 31, 2009, *before adjustments*:

Prepaid insurance	$ 2,700
Cleaning supplies	3,200
Unearned service fees	2,625
Notes payable	3,000
Service fees	125,000
Wages expense	90,000
Truck rent expense	6,500
Truck fuel expense	1,000
Insurance expense	0
Supplies expense	0
Interest expense	0
Interest payable	0
Wages payable	0
Prepaid rent—truck	0

Before Poorman's prepares the financial statements for the business at December 31, 2009, adjustments must be made for the following items:
   a. The prepaid insurance represents an 18-month policy purchased early in January so the policy has been in effect for the entire year.
   b. A physical count on December 31 revealed $500 of cleaning supplies on hand.
   c. On December 1, a customer paid for three months of service in advance (unearned service fees). One month's revenue has now been earned.
   d. The truck rent is $500 per month in advance. January 2010 rent was paid in late December 2009 and was included in truck rent expense for 2009.
   e. The bank loan was taken out October 1. The interest rate is 12% (1% per month) for 1 year. No interest expense has been accrued.
   f. On Wednesday, December 31, 2009, the company owed its employees for working three days. The normal workweek is five days with wages of $1,500 paid at the end of the week. No expense has been recorded for the last three days of 2009.

Requirements

1. For each item, show the adjustment in the accounting equation.
2. Prepare an income statement for the year ended December 31, 2009, for Poorman's, Inc.

P3-59A. *Account for depreciable assets. (LO 3).* Charlotte Motorcycle Repair Corporation purchased a machine on January 1, 2010, for $8,000 cash. The firm expects to use the machine for four years and thinks it will be worthless at the end of the four-year period. The company will depreciate the machine in equal annual amounts.

Requirements

1. Show the purchase of the machine and the first year's depreciation in the accounting equation.
2. Show how the machine will be presented in the asset section of the balance sheet at December 31, 2010, and December 31, 2011, after appropriate adjustments.
3. What amount of depreciation expense will be shown on the income statement for the year ended December 31, 2010? What amount will be shown for the year ended December 31, 2011?
4. Calculate the total depreciation expense for all four years of the asset's life. What do you notice about the book value of the asset at the end of its useful life?

P3-60A. *Record adjustments. (LO 1, 2, 3).* Following is a partial list of financial statement items from the records of Marshall's Company at December 31, 2010, before any adjustments have been made:

Prepaid insurance	$12,750
Prepaid rent	18,000
Interest receivable	0
Salaries payable	0
Unearned revenue	30,000
Interest revenue	10,000

Additional information includes the following:

- The insurance policy indicates that on December 31, 2010, only five months remain on the 24-month policy that originally cost $18,000 (purchased on June 1, 2009).
- Marshall's has a note receivable with $2,500 of interest due from a customer on January 1, 2011. This amount has not been recorded.
- The accounting records show that one-third of the revenue paid in advance by a customer on July 1, 2010, has now been earned.
- The company paid $18,000 for rent for nine months starting on August 1, 2010, recording the total amount as prepaid rent.
- At year end, Marshall's owed $7,000 worth of salaries to employees for work done in December 2010. The next payday is January 5, 2011. The salary expense has not been recorded.

Requirements

1. Use the accounting equation to show the adjustments that must be made prior to the preparation of the financial statements for the year ended December 31, 2010.
2. For the accounts shown, calculate the account balances that would be shown on Marshall's financial statements for the year ended December 31, 2010; balance sheet at December 31, 2010.

P3-61A. *Record adjustments. (LO 1, 2, 3).* Following is a list of financial statement items from Sugar & Spice Cookie Company as of December 31, 2010:

Prepaid insurance	$ 6,000
Prepaid rent	10,000
Wages expense	25,000
Unearned subscription revenue	70,000
Interest expense	38,000

Additional information is as follows:

- The company paid a $7,200 premium on a three-year business insurance policy on July 1, 2009. (Six months' worth was expensed on the income statement for the year ended December 31, 2009.) No expense has been recorded for the year ended December 31, 2010.

- Sugar & Spice borrowed $200,000 on January 2, 2010, and must pay 11% interest on January 2, 2011, for the entire year of 2010. The interest expense on this loan has not been recorded for 2010.
- The books show that $60,000 of the unearned subscription revenue has now been earned.
- The company paid 10 months of rent in advance on November 1, 2010. No rent expense has been booked for 2010.
- The company will pay wages of $2,000 for December 31, 2010, to employees on January 3, 2011. This amount is not included in the balance shown for wages expense.

Requirements

1. Use the accounting equation to show the adjustments that must be made prior to the preparation of the financial statements for the year ended December 31, 2010.
2. Calculate the account balances that would appear on the financial statements for the year ended December 31, 2010; balance sheet at December 31, 2010.

P3-62A. *Record adjustments. (LO 1, 2, 3).* The Gladiator Sports Company has the following account balances at the end of the year before any adjustments have been made:

Prepaid insurance	$9,000
Unearned revenue	5,300
Wages expense	7,590
Taxes payable	4,000
Interest revenue	2,000

The company also has the following information available at the end of the year:

- Of the prepaid insurance shown, $1,000 has now expired.
- Of the unearned revenue shown, $3,000 has been earned.
- The company must accrue an additional $2,250 of wages expense.
- The company has earned an additional $750 of interest revenue, not yet recorded or received.

Requirements

1. Use the accounting equation to show the adjustments needed at year end.
2. Calculate the balances in each account after the adjustments.
3. Indicate whether each adjustment is related to an accrual or a deferral.

P3-63A. *Record adjustments and prepare financial statements. (LO 1, 2, 3, 4).* The accounting records for Sony Snowboard Company, a snowboard repair company, contained the following balances as of December 31, 2008:

Sony Snowboard Company
Balance Sheet
At December 31, 2008

Assets		Liabilities and Shareholders' equity	
Cash	$40,000	Accounts payable	$17,000
Accounts receivable	16,500	Common stock	45,000
Land	20,000	Retained earnings	14,500
Totals	$76,500		$76,500

The following accounting events apply to Sony's 2009 fiscal year:

a.	January	1	The company received an additional $20,000 cash from the owners in exchange for common stock.
b.	January	1	Sony purchased a computer that cost $15,000 for cash. The computer had no salvage value and a three-year useful life.

c.	March	1	The company borrowed $10,000 by issuing a one-year note at 12%.
d.	May	1	The company paid $2,400 cash in advance for a one-year lease for office space.
e.	June	1	The company declared and paid dividends to the owners of $4,000 cash.
f.	July	1	The company purchased land that cost $17,000 cash.
g.	August	1	Cash payments on accounts payable amounted to $6,000.
h.	August	1	Sony received $9,600 cash in advance for 12 months of service to be performed monthly for the next year, beginning on receipt of payment.
i.	September	1	Sony sold a parcel of land for $13,000 cash, the amount the company originally paid for it.
j.	October	1	Sony purchased $795 of supplies on account.
k.	November	1	Sony purchased short-term investments for $18,000 cash. The investments pay a fixed rate of 6%.
l.	December	31	The company earned service revenue on account during the year that amounted to $40,000.
m.	December	31	Cash collections from accounts receivable amounted to $44,000.
n.	December	31	The company incurred other operating expenses on account during the year of $5,450.

- Salaries that had been earned by the sales staff but had not yet been paid amounted to $2,300.
- Supplies worth $180 were on hand at the end of the period.

Requirements

1. Prepare an accounting equation worksheet and record the account balances as of December 31, 2008 (beginning balances).
2. Using the worksheet, record the transactions that occurred during 2009 and the necessary adjustments needed at year end. (Based on the given transaction data, there are five additional adjustments [for a total of seven] that need to be made before the financial statements can be prepared.)
3. Prepare the income statement, statement of changes in shareholders' equity, and statement of cash flows for the year ended December 31, 2009, and the balance sheet at December 31, 2009.

P3-64A. *Record adjustments and prepare financial statements. (LO 1, 2, 3, 4).* Transactions for Pops Company for 2011 were as follows:

a. The owners started the business as a corporation by contributing $30,000 cash in exchange for common stock.
b. The company purchased office equipment for $8,000 cash and land for $15,000 cash.
c. The company earned a total of $22,000 of revenue of which $16,000 was collected in cash.
d. The company purchased $890 worth of supplies for cash.
e. The company paid $6,000 in cash for other operating expenses.
f. At the end of the year, the company owed employees $2,480 for work that the employees had done in 2011. The next payday, however, is not until January 4, 2012.
g. Only $175 worth of supplies was left at the end of the year.

The office equipment was purchased on January 1 and is expected to last for eight years (straight-line depreciation, no salvage value).

Requirements

1. Use an accounting equation worksheet to record the transactions that occurred during 2011.
2. Record any needed adjustments at year end.
3. Prepare the income statement, statement of changes in shareholders' equity, and the statement of cash flows for the year ended December 31, 2011, and the balance sheet at December 31, 2011.

P3-65A. *Record adjustments and prepare financial statements. (LO 1, 2, 3, 4).* On May 1, Matt Smith started a consulting business as a corporation. Matt started the business by contributing $20,000 in exchange for common stock. On May 1, he paid three months of rent in advance totaling

$1,500. Rent starts May 1. On May 3, Matt purchased supplies for $700 and two computers at a total cost of $3,600. Matt expects the computers to last for two years with no residual value. Matt hired an office assistant, agreeing to pay the assistant $2,000 per month to be paid $1,000 on May 15 and May 31. On May 27, Matt paid $400 for a radio advertisement to run immediately to announce the opening of the business. Matt earned $6,000 revenue in May, of which he collected $4,200 in cash. At the end of the month, Matt had $300 worth of supplies on hand.

Requirements

1. Use an accounting equation worksheet to record the transactions that occurred during the month of May and the adjustments that must be made prior to the preparation of the financial statements for the month ended May 31.
2. Prepare the income statement, statement of changes in shareholder's equity, and statement of cash flows for Matt's company for the month ended May 31 and the balance sheet at May 31.

P3-66A. *Record adjustments and prepare financial statements. (LO 1, 2, 3, 4, 5).* The following is a list of accounts and their balances for Casa Bella Interiors at May 31 before adjustments and some additional data for the fiscal year ended May 31, 2010.

Casa Bella Interiors
Accounts and balances
May 31, 2010

Cash	$ 4,300
Accounts receivable	9,300
Notes receivable	1,000
Interest receivable	—
Prepaid rent	1,700
Supplies	400
Office equipment	23,400
Accumulated depreciation (office equipment)	(1,600)
Accounts payable	500
Salaries payable	—
Interest payable	—
Unearned service revenue	2,600
Long-term notes payable	8,400
Common stock	5,000
Additional paid-in capital	2,300
Retained earnings	5,000
Service revenue	19,800
Salary expense	4,650
Rent expense	
Depreciation expense	
Advertising expense	450

Additional data follow:

- Depreciation on the office equipment for the year is $500.
- Salaries owed to employees at year end but not yet recorded or paid total $750.
- Prepaid rent that has expired at year-end amounts to $800.
- Interest due at year end on the notes receivable is $120.
- Interest owed at year end on the notes payable is $840.
- Unearned service revenue that has actually been earned by year end totals $1,500.

Requirements

1. For each account, show the adjustment needed at year end.

2. Prepare an income statement for the year ended May 31, 2010, and a balance sheet at May 31, 2010.
3. Calculate the firm's profit margin on sales ratio for the year.

P3-67A. *Analyze business transactions and prepare financial statements. (LO 1, 2, 3, 4).* Drive Fast Car Rentals generates revenue by renting high speed sports cars to tourists in the area. When a reservation is made in advance, Drive Fast collects half the week's rent to hold the reservation. However, Drive Fast does not require reservations, and sometimes customers will come in to rent a unit the same day. The accounting department for Drive Fast recorded the following transactions for 2010, the first year of business. These types of transactions require that Drive Fast's accounting department record some cash receipts as unearned revenues and others as earned revenues.

	Assets			= Liabilities		+	Shareholders' Equity	
							Contributed Capital	Retained Earnings
Transaction	Cash	All other assets	(Account)	All liabilities	(Account)		Common stock	(Account)
1.	$235,000						$235,000	
2.	(143,000)	143,000	Property, plant, and equipment					
3.	99,000			99,000	Notes payable			
4.	(3,000)	3,000	Supplies					
5.	(5,000)	5,000	Prepaid rent					
6.		17,000	Accounts receivable					17,000 Service revenue
7.		(925)	Supplies					(925) Supplies expense
8.		(800)	Prepaid rent					(800) Rent expense
9.				1,225	Salaries payable			(1,225) Salary expense
10.		(2,250)	Accumulated depreciation					(2,250) Depreciation expense
11.				225	Interest payable			(225) Interest expense

■ Income Statement   ■ Statement of Changes in Shareholders' Equity   ■ Balance Sheet   ■ Statement of Cash Flows

Requirements

1. Explain the transaction or event that resulted in each entry in the accounting equation worksheet.
2. Did Drive Fast Car Rentals generate net income or net loss for the period ended December 31, 2010? How can you tell?
3. Prepare the income statement, statement of changes in shareholders' equity, and statement of cash flows for the year ended December 31, 2010, and the balance sheet at December 31, 2010.

Set B

P3-68B. *Record adjustments and prepare income statement. (LO 1, 2, 3, 4).* Selected amounts (at December 31, 2012) from the accounting records of Dan's Billiard Supply Company are shown here. No adjustments have been made.

Cash paid to employees for salaries and wages	$ 500,000
Cash collected from customers for services rendered	2,500,000
Long-term notes payable	425,000
Cash	375,000
Common stock	50,000
Equipment	850,000
Prepaid insurance	125,000
Inventory	200,000
Prepaid rent	175,000
Retained earnings	430,000
Salaries and wages expense	600,000
Service revenue	5,250,000

Requirements

1. Five adjustments need to be made before the financial statements for the year ended December 31, 2012, can be prepared. Show each in an accounting equation worksheet.
   a. The equipment (purchased on January 1, 2012) has a useful life of 10 years with no salvage value (equal amount of depreciation each year).
   b. Interest on the notes payable needs to be accrued for the year in the amount of $60,000.
   c. Unexpired insurance at December 31, 2012, is $25,000.
   d. The rent payment of $175,000 was made on May 1. The rent payment is for 12 months beginning on the date of payment.
   e. Salaries of $65,000 were earned but unrecorded and unpaid at December 31, 2012.
2. Prepare an income statement for the year ended December 31, 2012, for Dan's Billiard Supply Company.

P3-69B. *Record adjustments and calculate net income. (LO 1, 2, 3, 4).* The records of Thinker's School Supplies showed the following amounts at December 31, 2011, before adjustments:

Prepaid insurance	$ 2,400
Supplies	2,250
Unearned service fees (unearned revenue)	5,680
Notes payable	29,000
Service fees revenue	175,000
Salary expense	95,000
Prepaid rent	6,250
Insurance expense	0
Supplies expense	0
Rent expense	0
Interest expense	0
Interest payable	0
Wages payable	0

Before Thinker's prepares the financial statements for the business at December 31, 2011, adjustments must be made for the following items:
   a. The prepaid insurance is for a 12-month policy purchased on March 1 for cash. The policy is effective from March 1, 2011, to February 28, 2012.
   b. A count of the supplies on December 31 revealed $400 worth still on hand.
   c. One customer paid for four months of service in advance on December 1. By December 31, one month of the service had been performed by Thinker's.
   d. The prepaid rent was for 10 months of rent for the company office building, beginning August 1.

e. The company took out a bank loan on October 1, 2011. The interest rate is 6% (1/2% per month) for one year.

f. As of December 31, the company owed its employees $5,000 for work done in 2011. The next payday is in January 2012.

Requirements

1. Show the adjustments in the accounting equation.
2. Prepare an income statement for the year ended December 31, 2011, for Thinker's School Supplies.

P3-70B. *Account for depreciable assets. (LO 3).* Super Clean Dry Cleaning purchased a new piece of office equipment on January 1, 2009, for $18,000 cash. The company expects to use the equipment for three years and thinks it will be worthless at the end of the three-year period. The company depreciates the equipment in equal annual amounts.

Requirements

1. Show the adjustments in an accounting equation worksheet for the first two years of depreciation.
2. Prepare the asset section of the balance sheet at December 31, 2009, and December 31, 2010, after appropriate adjustments.
3. What amount of depreciation expense will be shown on the income statement for the year ended December 31, 2009? What amount will be shown for the year ended December 31, 2010?
4. Calculate the total depreciation for the life of the asset. What do you notice about the book value of the asset at the end of its useful life?

P3-71B. *Record adjustments. (LO 1, 2, 3).* Following is a partial list of financial statement items from the records of Starnes Company at December 31, 2012, before adjustments:

Prepaid rent	$20,000
Prepaid insurance	12,000
Service revenue	35,000
Wages expense	8,000
Unearned service revenue	18,000
Interest expense	5,000

Additional information includes the following:

- The insurance policy indicates that on December 31, 2012, only five months remain on the 12-month policy that originally cost $12,000.
- Starnes has a note payable with $2,500 of interest that must be paid on January 1, 2013. No interest expense has been recorded for this note.
- The accounting records show that two-thirds of the service revenue paid in advance by a customer on March 1 has now been earned.
- On August 1, the company paid $20,000 for rent for 10 months beginning on August 1.
- At year end, Starnes Company owed $500 worth of salaries to employees for work done in December. This has not been recorded or paid. The next payday is January 3, 2013.

Requirements

1. Use an accounting equation worksheet to record the adjustments that must be made prior to the preparation of the financial statements for the year ended December 31, 2012.
2. For the accounts shown, calculate the account balances that would be shown on Starnes' financial statements for the year ended December 31, 2012; balance sheet at December 31, 2012.

P3-72B. *Record adjustments. (LO 1, 2, 3).* Following is a list of financial statement items from Chunky Candy Company as of June 30, 2010. Chunky's fiscal year is from July 1 to June 30.

Prepaid insurance	$ 3,600
Prepaid rent	5,000
Wages expense	12,000
Unearned revenue	30,000
Interest expense	0

Additional information follows:

- The company paid a $3,600 premium on a three-year insurance policy on January 1, 2010, with the insurance coverage beginning immediately.
- Chunky borrowed $100,000 on July 1, 2009, with an interest rate of 11%. No interest has been paid as of June 30, 2010.
- The books show that $10,000 of the unearned revenue has now been earned.
- The company paid 10 months of rent in advance on March 1, 2010, for rent beginning in March.
- Wages for June 30, 2010, of $1,000 will be paid to employees on July 3, 2010 (the next fiscal year).

Requirements

1. Use the accounting equation to record the adjustments that must be made prior to the preparation of the financial statements for the fiscal year ended June 30, 2010.
2. For the accounts shown, calculate the balances that would appear on the financial statements for the year ended June 30, 2010; balance sheet at June 30, 2010.

P3-73B. *Record adjustments. (LO 1, 2, 3).* Summit Climbing Tours has the following amounts in its records at the end of the fiscal year:

Prepaid insurance	$9,000
Unearned revenue	2,500
Wages expense	9,500
Accounts payable	3,575
Interest revenue	2,250

The company also has the following information available at the end of the year:

- Of the prepaid insurance, $2,000 has now expired.
- Of the unearned revenue, $2,200 has been earned.
- The company must accrue an additional $3,275 of wages expense.
- A bill for $500 from the company that provides cleaning services to Summit arrived on the last day of the year. Nothing related to this invoice has been recorded or paid.
- The company has earned an additional $750 of interest revenue, not yet received (or recorded).

Requirements

1. Use an accounting equation worksheet to show the adjustments at the end of the year.
2. Calculate the balances in each account shown after the adjustments.
3. Indicate whether each adjustment is related to an accrual or a deferral.

P3-74B. *Record adjustments and prepare financial statements. (LO 1, 2, 3, 4).* The accounting records for Beta Company contained the following balances as of December 31, 2008, as shown on the year-end balance sheet:

Beta Company
Balance Sheet
At December 31, 2008

Assets		Liabilities and Shareholders' Equity	
Cash	$50,000	Accounts payable	$17,500
Accounts receivable	26,500		
Prepaid rent	3,600	Common stock	48,600
Land	10,500	Retained earnings	24,500
Totals	$90,600		$90,600

The following accounting events apply to Beta's 2009 fiscal year:

a. January 1 Beta purchased a computer that cost $18,000 for cash. The computer had no salvage value and a three-year useful life.

b. March 1 The company borrowed $20,000 by issuing a two-year note at 12%.

c. May 1 The company paid $6,000 cash in advance for a six-month lease starting on July 1 for office space.

d. June 1 The company declared and paid dividends of $2,000 to the owners.

e. July 1 The company purchased land that cost $15,000 cash.

f. August 1 Cash payments on accounts payable amounted to $5,500.

g. August 1 Beta received $13,200 cash in advance for 12 months of service to be performed monthly for the next year, beginning on receipt of payment.

h. September 1 Beta sold a parcel of land for $13,000, its original cost of the land.

i. October 1 Beta purchased $1,300 of supplies on account.

j. November 1 Beta purchased short-term investments for $10,000 cash. The investments earn a fixed rate of 5% per year.

k. December 31 The company earned service revenue on account during the year that amounted to $50,000.

l. December 31 Cash collections from accounts receivable amounted to $46,000.

m. December 31 The company incurred other operating expenses on account during the year that amounted to $5,850.

Additional information follows:

- Salaries that had been earned by the sales staff but not yet paid amounted to $2,300.
- Supplies on hand at the end of the period totaled $200.
- The beginning balance of $3,600 in prepaid rent was completely used up by the end of the year.

Requirements

1. Set up an accounting equation worksheet and record the account balances as of December 31, 2008.
2. Record the transactions that occurred during 2009 and the necessary adjustments at year end.
3. Prepare the income statement, statement of changes in shareholders' equity, and statement of cash flows for the year ended December 31, 2009, and the balance sheet at December 31, 2009.

P3-75B. *Record adjustments and prepare financial statements. (LO 1, 2, 3, 4).* Following are transactions for Security Company for 2010:

a. The owners started the business as a corporation by contributing $50,000 cash in exchange for common stock.

b. Security Company purchased office equipment for $5,000 cash and land for $15,000 cash.

c. The company earned a total of $32,000 of revenue of which $20,000 was collected in cash.

d. The company purchased $550 worth of supplies for cash.

e. The company paid $6,000 in cash for other operating expenses.

f. At the end of the year, Security Company owed employees $3,600 for work that the employees had done in 2010. The next payday, however, is not until January 4, 2011.

g. Only $120 worth of supplies was left at the end of the year.

h. The office equipment was purchased on January 1 and is expected to last for five years. There is no expected salvage value, and the company wants equal amounts of depreciation expense each year related to this equipment.

Requirements

1. Use an accounting equation worksheet to record the transactions that occurred during 2010.
2. Record any adjustments needed at year end.
3. Prepare the income statement, statement of changes in shareholders' equity, and the statement of cash flows for the year ended December 31, 2010, and the balance sheet at December 31, 2010.

P3-76B. *Record adjustments and prepare financial statements. (LO 1, 2, 3, 4).* On October 1, Jill Jackson started Jill's Apple Farm as a corporation. Jill started the firm by contributing $50,000 in exchange for common stock. On October 1, the new firm paid six months of rent in advance totaling

$6,000 and paid eight months of insurance in advance totaling $3,000. Both rent and insurance coverage began on October 1. On October 6, the firm purchased supplies for $1,200. The firm hired one employee to help Jill and agreed to pay the worker $3,000 per month, paid on the last day of each month. Jill's Apple Farm paid $100 for a newspaper advertisement to announce the opening of the business. The farm earned revenue of $8,000 in October, of which $5,000 was in cash. At the end of the month, the firm had only $400 worth of supplies on hand.

Requirements

1. Using an accounting equation worksheet, record the transactions that occurred during the month of October and the adjustments that must be made prior to the preparation of the financial statements for the month ended October 31.
2. Prepare the income statement, statement of changes in shareholder's equity, and statement of cash flows for the month ended October 31 and the balance sheet at October 31.

P3-77B. *Record adjustments and prepare financial statements. (LO 1, 2, 3, 4, 5).* Puppy Studs, Inc., provides a stud service for serious dog breeders. The company's accountant prepared the following list of accounts with their unadjusted balances at the end of the fiscal year, March 31, 2011:

Cash	$ 52,200
Accounts receivable	47,500
Prepaid insurance	20,000
Prepaid rent	1,800
Supplies	10,350
Equipment	137,500
Accumulated depreciation	(1,700)
Accounts payable	3,500
Unearned service revenue	3,000
Long-term notes payable	35,000
Common stock	50,500
Additional paid-in capital	91,450
Retained earnings	87,120
Dividends	5,320
Service revenue	226,850
Miscellaneous operating expenses	149,450
Salary expense	75,000

Additional facts (related to adjustments that have not yet been made):
   a. The company owes its employees $2,500 for work done in this fiscal year. The next payday is not until April.
   b. $2,000 worth of the unearned service revenue has actually been earned at year end.
   c. The equipment is depreciated at the rate of $1,700 per year.
   d. At year end $600 worth of prepaid rent and $15,000 of prepaid insurance remains unexpired.
   e. Interest on the long-term note for a year at the rate of 6.5% is due on April 1.
   f. Supplies on hand at the end of the year amounted to $2,100.
   g. On the last day of the fiscal year, the firm earned $20,000. The customer paid $15,000 with cash and owed the remainder on account. However, the accountant left early that day, so the day's revenue was not recorded in the accounting records.

Requirements

1. For each account, show the adjustment needed at year end.
2. Prepare an income statement for the year ended March 31, 2011, and a balance sheet at March 31, 2011.
3. Calculate the firm's profit margin on sales ratio for the year.

P3-78B. *Analyze business transactions and prepare financial statements. (LO 1, 2, 3, 4).* The accounting department for Loud Noises Concerts (LNC) recorded the following transactions for the fiscal year ended April 30, 2009. LNC generates revenue by selling tickets for local concerts. Sometimes tickets are sold in advance and sometimes customers will purchase their tickets the same day as the event. These types of transactions require that the LNC accounting department record some cash receipts as unearned revenues and others as earned revenues.

| | | Assets | | = Liabilities | | + | Shareholders' Equity | |
| | | | | | | | Contributed Capital | Retained Earnings |
Transaction	Cash	All other assets	(Account)	All liabilities	(Account)		Common stock	(Account)
1.	$175,000						$175,000	
2.		650	Office supplies	650	Accounts (or other) payable			
3.	(22,500)	22,500	Prepaid rent					
4.		439,000	Building	439,000	Long-term notes payable			
5.	20,000			20,000	Unearned ticket revenue			
6.	(675)							(675) Miscellaneous expense
7.	(650)			(650)	Accounts (or other) payable			
8.	70,000							70,000 Ticket revenue
9.				(18,000)	Unearned ticket revenue			18,000 Ticket revenue
10.		(275)	Office supplies					(275) Office supplies expense
11.		(11,000)	Prepaid rent					(11,000) Rent expense
12.				575	Interest payable			(575) Interest expense
13.		(3,500)	Accumulated depreciation					(3,500) Depreciation expense
14.				6,250	Salaries payable			(6,250) Salaries expense
15.	(8,250)							(8,250) Dividends

▬ Income Statement ▬ Statement of Changes in Shareholders' Equity ▬ Balance Sheet ▬ Statement of Cash Flows

Requirements

1. Explain the transaction or event that resulted in each item recorded on the worksheet.
2. Did LNC generate net income or net loss for the fiscal year ended April 30, 2009? How can you tell?
3. Prepare the income statement, statement of changes in shareholders' equity, and statement of cash flows for the year ended April 30, 2009, and the balance sheet at April 30, 2009.

Financial Statement Analysis

FSA3-1. *Identify and explain accruals and deferrals. (LO 2, 3, 4, 5).* Use the selection from the annual report from Books-A-Million in Appendix A to answer these questions:

1. Does Books-A-Million have any deferred expenses? What are they, and where are they shown? (Ignore deferred taxes.)

2. Does Books-A-Million have accrued expenses? What are they, and where are they shown?
3. What is the difference between a deferred expense and an accrued expense?
4. Calculate the profit margin on sales ratio for the past two years. What information does this provide?

FSA3-2. *Identify and explain accruals and deferrals. (LO 2, 3, 4).* Use Hormel Foods' balance sheet in Exhibit 3.17 on page 120 to answer these questions:

1. The current asset section shows prepaid expenses. What might these pertain to? Have the "expenses" referred to here been recognized (i.e., included on the period's income statement)?
2. The liabilities section shows accrued expenses. What does this represent? Have the associated expenses been recognized?
3. The liabilities section shows accounts payable. Explain what this is and what Hormel Foods will do to satisfy this liability.

FSA3-3. *Identify and interpret expenses and liabilities. (LO 2, 3, 4).* Use Carnival Corporation's balance sheet to answer the questions that follow.

Carnival Corporation & PLC
Consolidated Balance Sheets
(amounts in millions, except par values)

	November 30, 2008	November 30, 2007
Assets		
Current Assets		
Cash and cash equivalents	$ 650	$ 943
Trade and other receivables, net	418	436
Inventories	315	331
Prepaid expenses and other	267	266
Total current assets	1,650	1,976
Property and Equipment, Net	26,457	26,639
Goodwill	3,266	3,610
Trademarks	1,294	1,393
Other Assets	733	563
	$33,400	$34,181
Liabilities and Shareholders' Equity		
Current Liabilities		
Short-term borrowings	$ 256	$ 115
Current portion of long-term debt	1,081	1,028
Convertible debt subject to current put options	271	1,396
Accounts payable	512	561
Accrued liabilities and other	1,142	1,353
Customer deposits	2,519	2,807
Total current liabilities	5,781	7,260
Long-Term Debt	7,735	6,313
Other Long-Term Liabilities and Deferred Income	786	645
Commitments and Contingencies (Notes 6 and 7)		
Shareholders' Equity		
Common stock of Carnival Corporation; $.01 par value; 1,960 shares authorized; 643 shares at 2008 and 2007 issued	6	6
Ordinary shares of Carnival plc; $1.66 par value; 226 shares authorized; 213 shares at 2008 and 2007 issued	354	354
Additional paid-in capital	7,677	7,599
Retained earnings	13,980	12,921
Accumulated other comprehensive (loss) income	(623)	1,296
Treasury stock; 19 shares at 2008 and 2007 of Carnival Corporation and 52 shares at 2008 and 50 shares at 2007 of Carnival plc, at cost	(2,296)	(2,213)
Total shareholders' equity	19,098	19,963
	$33,400	$34,181

1. Which current asset reflects deferred expenses? Explain what it means to defer expenses, and give the adjustment to the accounting equation that was probably made to record this asset.
2. The liabilities section shows over $2.5 billion in customer deposits at November 30, 2008. Explain why this is a liability, and give the transaction (in the accounting equation) that resulted in this liability.

Critical Thinking Problems

Risk and Controls

Is there anything in the information about Books-A-Million given in Appendix A that addresses how the firm protects its accounting data?

Ethics

DVD-Online, Inc., is in its second year of business. The company is Web-based, offering DVD rental to online customers for a fixed monthly fee. For $30 per month, a customer receives three DVDs each month, one at a time as the previous one is returned. No matter how many DVDs a customer uses (up to three), the fee is fixed at $30 per month. Customers sign a contract for a year, so DVD-Online recognizes $360 sales revenue each time a customer signs up for the service. The owner of DVD-Online, John Richards, has heard about GAAP, but he does not see any reason to follow these accounting principles. Although DVD-Online is not publicly traded, John does put the company's financial statements on the company's Web page for customers to see.

1. Explain how DVD-Online would account for its revenue if it did follow GAAP.
2. Explain to John Richards why he should use GAAP, and describe why his financial statements may now be misleading.
3. Do you see this as an ethical issue? Explain.

Group Assignment

Use the balance sheet for Carnival Corporation shown in FSA3-3. For each of the current assets and current liabilities, prepare a brief explanation of the nature of the item. For each current liability, explain how you think the company will satisfy the liability.

Internet Exercise: Darden

Please go to www.dardenrestaurants.com.

IE3-1. If you were at a Darden property, what might you be doing? List two of the Darden chains.

IE3-2. Click on Investor Relations followed by Annual Report & Financials and then select the HTML version of the most recent annual report. Find the Balance Sheets under Financials, then Financial Review, by clicking next or using the "contents" scroll bar. Does Darden use a calendar year for its fiscal year? How can you tell?

IE3-3. Refer to the asset section.

1. List the title of one asset account that includes accrued revenue—amounts earned but not yet received in cash.
2. List the title of one asset account that includes amounts that have been paid for in cash but have not yet been expensed.
3. List the title of one asset account that includes amounts that will be depreciated.
4. For each account listed in 1 through 3, identify the amount reported for the most recent year. Do these amounts still need adjusting? Explain why or why not.

IE3-4. For the two most recent years list the amounts reported for total assets, total liabilities, and total stockholders' equity. For each type of account, identify what the trend indicates. Does the accounting equation hold true both years?

Please note: Internet Web sites are constantly being updated. Therefore, if the information is not found where indicated, please explore the Web site further to find the information.

4

Payment for Goods and Services: Cash and Accounts Receivable

ETHICS Matters

Especially When It Comes to Cash

Fraud can happen anywhere. Joanna Lynn McGee, 40, who had been the CEO of a now defunct credit union in Wichita Falls, Texas, pleaded guilty in 2008 to embezzlement. She was involved in creating 129 fictitious loans and changing names and addresses of account holders who had died during her employment at the credit union. The fictitious loans totaled almost $3 million. In April 2009, she was sentenced to 71 months in prison and will have to pay back over $2.6 million in restitution.

The fraud started when Joanna helped a credit union employee cover up the employee's theft. For the next seven years, Joanna worked at covering up her own illegal activities. When a firm's product is cash, there are lots of opportunities for fraud. Experts believe that three elements—known as the fraud triangle—must be present for fraud to occur. They are pressure, rationalization, and opportunity. From an outsider's perspective, judging what pressure exists and how a person might rationalize committing fraud are difficult to identify. However, the opportunity is easily observable. This is why any firm with large amounts of cash must have sound internal controls. Joanna McGee will have almost six years in prison to think about the pressure and rationalization related to the fraud she committed, but the opportunity to steal cash can be minimized by a good system of internal controls and ethical management.

Source: TimesRecordNews, Wichita Falls Online, April 3, 2009.
http://www.timesrecordnews.com/news/2009/apr/03/woman-sentenced-in-federal-case

L.O.1
Explain how a firm controls cash and prepares a bank reconciliation.

Controlling Cash

Now that you have learned about the four basic financial statements and you know how a firm's transactions are reported on those statements, we will examine the specific kinds of transactions that make up the operating, investing, and financing activities involved in all business processes in the next several chapters. In this chapter, we'll discuss the operating activities involved in earning and collecting revenue.

Customers usually have two choices when paying for goods and services: cash or credit. A company will analyze the risks associated with a method of payment and then put controls in place to minimize those risks. For example, if a company requires a lot of cash on hand, it may keep large amounts in a locked safe. That is a control that helps protect the firm from robbery. If a company makes sales on credit, it is important that the company keep accurate records so that the customers can be properly billed for the sales. Millions of dollars of revenue are lost by businesses each year because either they miss capturing revenue they have earned or they miss collecting payment for goods and services they have delivered. By studying cash and the related controls, you will see how a company protects one of its most important assets.

Firms often keep a very significant amount of cash. For example, at the end of 2008, Yahoo! Inc. had over $2 billion in cash and cash equivalents. That is a lot of money, and Yahoo!'s management wants to make sure it is safe. Because cash is often the target of misappropriation, firms must keep tight control of this asset.

Safeguarding Cash

Cash is a valuable asset to almost anyone, and it can be used to acquire almost any other type of asset. It can easily be concealed and ownership may be hard to identify. If you found a $20 bill on the floor of your classroom, it could be difficult to identify its owner. Because of the value of cash and its characteristics, safeguarding cash is critical. One way that retail firms safeguard cash is by using cash registers. The cash is locked, and receipts are recorded for all cash collections and disbursements.

Assignment of Responsibilities for Cash

Segregation of duties means that the person who has physical custody of an asset is not the same person who has record-keeping responsibilities for that asset.

Another key control for cash is the **segregation of duties**. That means different people perform different tasks. For cash, segregation of duties means the person who has the physical custody of cash—anyone who has actual physical access to cash at any time and who can write checks and make deposits—should not be the same person who does the record keeping for cash. If the same person had responsibility for both, it would be easy for that person to keep some of the cash and alter the records to hide the theft. In general, physical control of an asset should not be given to the same person who has control of the record keeping related to that asset.

Sometimes having two people involved in the same task can help protect a firm from fraud. For example, if the firm typically receives cash and checks in the mail from its customers, having two people open the envelopes together is a common practice. Stealing money would require collusion—two or more people working together to commit fraud. At banks, you will often see two people counting cash together. Having people share this responsibility decreases both errors and fraud.

Bank Reconciliations

A bank statement is a summary of the activity in a bank account sent each month to the account holder.

A bank reconciliation is a comparison between the cash balance in the firm's accounting records and the cash balance on the bank statement to identify the reasons for any differences.

Almost all companies use banks to help them keep track of and safeguard their cash. The bank assists its customers by providing a periodic bank statement. A **bank statement** is a summary of the activity in a bank account—deposits, checks, debit card transactions—usually sent monthly to the account owner. An example is shown in Exhibit 4.1.

Someone in the firm will perform a **bank reconciliation**, sometimes called a cash reconciliation, which involves comparing the cash balance in the accounting records and the bank statement cash balance for that month. A bank reconciliation is more than simply part of the record keeping for cash. The bank reconciliation is a crucial part of controlling cash. As we all know, the bottom line in our checkbook or ATM spending records seldom agrees with the bottom line on our monthly bank statement. That is true for a business, too; the cash balance in a firm's records seldom agrees with the cash balance on its monthly bank statement. The two cash balances do not agree because there are transactions that are recorded in one place but not recorded in the other place due to timing differences. Sometimes the bank knows about a transaction that the firm has not yet recorded on

EXHIBIT 4.1

Bank Statement

AB Andover Bank
Andover, MA 01844

		Statement Date
		June 30, 2010

Account Statement

Jessica's Chocolate Shop
15 Main Street
Andover, MA 01844

356814
ACCOUNT NUMBER

Balance Last Statement	Deposits and Credits		Checks and Debits		Balance This Statement
May 31, 2010	No.	Total Amount	No.	Total Amount	June 30, 2010
19,817.02	12	20,579.05	12	12,509.93	27,886.14

DEPOSITS AND CREDITS		CHECKS AND DEBITS			DAILY BALANCE	
Date	Amount	Date	No.	Amount	Date	Amount
6-2	733.30	6-2	235	560.50	6-2	19,989.82
6-3	689.50	6-3	236	1,450.00	6-3	19,229.32
6-4	3,000.00	6-4	237	1,090.50	6-4	19,638.64
6-7	4,000.00	6-4	238	1,500.48	6-7	21,246.87
6-8	999.28	6-7	239	890.60	6-8	21,777.25
6-9 CM	1,070.00	6-7	240	1,500.87	6-9	22,847.25
6-11	1,500.72	6-8	241	468.90	6-11	22,127.12
6-14	750.25	6-11	242	2,220.85	6-14	22,877.37
6-15	1,205.50	6-25	243	1,300.08	6-15	24,082.87
6-25	1,200.00	6-29	NSF	225.65	6-25	23,982.79
6-29	3,450.80	6-29	452	875.85	6-29	26,332.09
6-30	1,979.70	6-30	DM	50.00	6-30	27,886.14
		6-30	461	375.65		

Symbols: **ATM** Automatic Teller Machine   **CM** Credit Memo   **EC** Error Correction
  NSF Not Sufficient Funds   **DM** Debit Memo   **INT** Interest Earned   **SC** Service Charge

Reconcile Your Account Promptly

its books, and sometimes the firm knows about a transaction that the bank has not yet recorded on its books. For example, a firm may make a deposit on the last day of June, but the deposit may not appear on the June bank statement due to the bank's delay in recording the deposit. Even more often, the checks a firm has written may not have reached the bank for payment—that is, the checks have not cleared the bank at the date of the bank statement. In other words, the bank does not know about those transactions on the date of the bank statement. The monthly bank statement, which contains all of the deposits, checks, ATM transactions, and other miscellaneous items, must be reconciled to the cash balance in the accounting records.

What is the purpose of a bank reconciliation? How often would a firm prepare one?

Your Turn 4-1

STEPS IN THE RECONCILIATION. Reconciling the monthly bank statement to the general ledger cash account is an important element of internal control and requires two major steps.

1. Start with the balance on the monthly bank statement, called the balance per bank, and make adjustments for all the transactions that have been recorded in the firm's books but do not appear in the bank's books because the bank did not get the transaction recorded as of the date of the bank statement.
2. Start with the firm's cash balance, called the balance per books, and make adjustments for all the transactions that the bank has recorded but have not yet been recorded on the firm's books.

After the preceding steps are complete, each section of the bank reconciliation should show the same reconciled cash balance. That balance will be the actual amount of cash the firm had on the date of the bank statement. The actual amount is called the true cash balance. A firm reconciling a bank statement divides a worksheet into two parts, as shown in Exhibit 4.2.

EXHIBIT 4.2

Format for Bank Reconciliation

To prepare a bank reconciliation, an accountant would create a worksheet divided into two parts: the Bank Statement (on the left) and the General Ledger Cash Account (on the right). Focus on the types of adjustments. We'll use the example dollar amounts later in Exhibits 4.3 and 4.4.

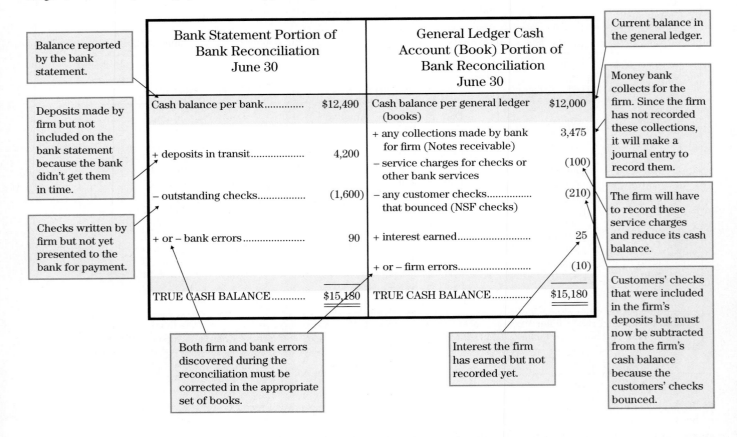

RECONCILING ITEMS. The right side of Exhibit 4.2 shows items that will need adjustments in the firm's books. Adjustments will never be required for transactions already recorded in the general ledger. The left part of Exhibit 4.2 shows **deposits in transit** and **outstanding checks**. No adjustments will be needed for these items because they have already been recorded in the firm's accounting records, and the bank will eventually receive and record those transactions in its records.

Performing a bank reconciliation enables a firm to

1. Locate any errors, whether made by the bank or by the firm.
2. Make adjustments to the cash account in the firm's books for transactions the bank has recorded but the firm has not yet recorded in its cash account.

A **deposit in transit** is a bank deposit the firm has made but is not included on the month's bank statement because the deposit did not reach the bank's record-keeping department in time to be included on the current bank statement.

The bank reconciliation begins with the balance per bank and the balance per books, one on each side of the worksheet, as of the bank statement date. Each of these balances is then adjusted to arrive at the true cash balance. A bank reconciliation has eight common adjustments. Three common adjustments may be needed to make the bank statement balance with the firm's records. Starting with the balance per bank side of the reconciliation we have the following:

> An **outstanding check** is a check the firm has written but that has not yet cleared the bank. That is, the check has not been presented to the bank for payment yet.

1. Deposits in transit are added to the balance per bank.
2. Outstanding checks are deducted from the balance per bank.
3. Errors made by the bank may require additions or deductions.

Five common adjustments may be needed to make the firm's cash record balance with the bank statement. On the balance per books side of the reconciliation we have the following:

1. Collections made by the bank on behalf of the firm are added to the balance per books.
2. Service charges by the bank, including charges for any overdraft, appear on the bank statement and are deducted from the balance per books.
3. A customer's non-sufficient-funds (NSF) check is deducted from the balance per books.
4. Interest earned on a checking account is added to the balance per books.
5. Errors made by the firm may require additions or deductions.

Exhibit 4.3 shows how each item on the bank side is treated in the bank reconciliation, and Exhibit 4.4 on the following page shows how each item on the books side is treated in the

EXHIBIT 4.3

Items Used on the Bank Side of a Bank Reconciliation

There are actually an unlimited number of adjustments that may need to be made, but these are the three most common.

Item	What happens to the item during the bank reconciliation?	What happens to the item in the firm's books?
1. Deposits in transit—deposits the firm made too late for the bank to include them on the bank statement	Adjustment is needed to add the total amount of the deposits, $4,200, to the balance per bank.	No adjustment is needed because the cash was already added when the deposits were made.
2. Outstanding checks—checks the firm has written, but they haven't cleared the bank at the time of the bank statement	Adjustment is needed to deduct the total amount of the outstanding checks, ($1,600), from the balance per bank, $12,490.	No adjustment is needed because the cash was already deducted when the checks were written.
3. Any errors the bank has made	Suppose the bank should have recorded a deposit as $980 but instead recorded it as $890. In this case, add $90 to the bank's balance.	No adjustment is needed because the bank's records are wrong. The firm had the deposit recorded correctly. The firm would call the bank to have the error corrected.

reconciliation. The dollar amounts come from the example in Exhibit 4.2. Remember that a bank reconciliation is not part of the formal records of the firm. It is just a worksheet, and any changes that the firm needs to make to its records must be done by formally recording the changes in the firm's accounting system.

EXHIBIT 4.4

Items Used on the Book Side of a Bank Reconciliation

Item	What happens to the item during the bank reconciliation?	What happens to the item in the firm's books?
1. Amounts collected by the bank on behalf of the firm; in this example, a notes receivable 	Add $3,475 to the balance per books.	Increase cash and decrease notes receivable by $3,475.
2. Service charges—amounts the bank charges for its services 	Deduct $100 from the balance per books.	Decrease cash and increase bank expenses by $100.
3. Non-sufficient-funds (NSF) checks—checks the firm received from customers and deposited that bounced 	Deduct $210 from the balance per books.	Increase (to restore) accounts receivable (specific account) and decrease cash by $210.
4. Interest earned on the bank account balance 	Add $25 to the balance per books.	Increase cash and increase interest revenue by $25.
5. Any errors the firm has made in its records 	Suppose the firm recorded a check it wrote to a vendor in payment of accounts payable for $480 when the check was actually $490. In this case, deduct $10 from the balance per books.	Decrease accounts payable and decrease cash by $10.

Exhibit 4.4 shows the information already included in the calculation of the bank's balance at the date of the bank statement but unknown to the firm until the bank statement is received.

AN EXAMPLE OF A BANK RECONCILIATION AND THE ADJUSTMENTS. We will use the relevant information from ABC Light Company to prepare a bank reconciliation. Make sure you can identify where each amount is included in the bank reconciliation.

ABC Light Company	
Information from the bank statement:	
Balance per bank statement, June 30, 2010	$4,890
Note receivable ($1,000) and interest ($30) collected by bank for ABC Light Co.	1,030
Bank service charges	10
Customer check returned and marked "NSF"	100
Information from ABC Light's accounting records:	
Company books cash balance, June 30, 2010	1,774
Checks outstanding on June 30, 2010: No. 298	1,300
304	456
306	2,358
Deposit made after bank hours by ABC Light Co. on June 30, 2010	1,750

Keep the following two additional facts in mind as you prepare the bank reconciliation:

1. The bank statement showed the bank had mistakenly charged ABC Light Company for a $150 check that was written by the ABC Chemical Company.
2. During June, ABC Light Company's bookkeeper recorded payment of an account payable incorrectly as $346. The check was paid by the bank in the correct amount of $364.

ABC Light Company Bank Reconciliation June 30, 2010	
Part I: Balance per bank statement, June 30, 2010	$ 4,890
Add: Deposits in transit*	1,750
Add: Bank error	150
Deduct: Outstanding checks (#298, #304, #306)	(4,114)
True cash balance, June 30, 2010	$ 2,676
Part 2: Balance per books, June 30, 2010	$ 1,774
Add: Note and interest collected by bank	1,030
Deduct: Bank charges	(10)
Deduct: NSF check	(100)
Deduct: Company error (+ $346 − $364 = $18)	(18)
True cash balance, June 30, 2010	$ 2,676

(*Company has made the deposit, but it was not recorded by the bank as of the date of the bank statement.)

Notice that the true cash balance—$2,676—is found on both parts of the completed bank reconciliation. As you learned earlier in the chapter, a bank reconciliation is simply a worksheet—it is not a formal part of the firm's accounting system. Nothing included on the worksheet actually corrects the accounting records. The accounting records will need to be adjusted to account for every item on the "balance per books" part of the reconciliation. Here are the adjustments that ABC Light Company would make to bring its accounting records up to date following the bank reconciliation:

Assets	=	Liabilities	+	Shareholders' equity	
				Contributed + capital	Retained earnings
1,030 cash					
(1,000) notes receivable					30 interest revenue
(10) cash					(10) bank expense
(100) cash					
100 accounts receivable					
(18) cash		(18) accounts payable			

Often a firm's bank statement will have *debit memos* and *credit memos*. The debit memos are charges to the firm's account, reducing the balance in the account. The credit memos are additions to the account, increasing its balance. The bank statement might include a debit memo for new checks that were ordered. In contrast, the bank would include a credit memo for any interest the account has earned. Accountants use debits and credits to increase and decrease account balances. Even though you may never need to know how the accounting debit-credit system works, you may actually see the terms used in business. For example, the name for your "debit" card comes from the accounting entry that a bank makes when you use money from your account. When you hear the terms debit and credit used in business, you can be sure that the meaning is derived from the accounting meanings of those terms and used from the viewpoint of that business. If you want to know more about how the accounting debit–credit system works, you can read about it in Appendix B.

Your Turn 4-2

Gifford Company's unadjusted book balance for cash amounted to $2,400. The company's bank statement included a debit memo for bank service charges of $100. There were two credit memos in the bank statement. One was for $300, which represented a collection that the bank made for Gifford. The second credit memo was for $100, which represented the amount of interest that Gifford had earned during the accounting period. Outstanding checks amounted to $250, and there were no deposits in transit. Based on this information, what is Gifford's true cash balance?

L.O.2
Describe how cash is reported on the financial statements.

Reporting Cash

Cash is an asset you will find on two financial statements: the balance sheet and the statement of cash flows. On the balance sheet, the amount of cash a firm has on the date of the balance sheet is reported. A firm often has a number of cash accounts—checking accounts and savings accounts in various banks. For example, a firm will often have a special bank account for its payroll. All of the firm's cash accounts will be combined for presentation on the balance sheet. Exhibit 4.5A shows how Yahoo! Inc. reports cash on its balance sheet.

Cash Equivalents

Cash equivalents are highly liquid investments with a maturity of three months or less that a firm can easily convert into a known amount of cash.

On the balance sheet of Yahoo! Inc. the first asset is *cash and cash equivalents*. It is the first asset listed on almost all balance sheets. **Cash equivalents** are highly liquid investments with a maturity of three months or less that a firm can easily convert into a known amount of cash. U.S. treasury bills are a common cash equivalent. The notes to the financial statements disclose how a firm defines its cash equivalents. Exhibit 4.5B shows the note defining cash equivalents from the financial statements of Yahoo! Inc. Although it is infrequent, a negative balance in cash should be listed as a current liability. This balance would indicate that a firm has had checks cleared in excess of its available cash. As you might guess, a firm does not want to have a negative cash balance.

The Statement of Cash Flows

In addition to its prominent place on the balance sheet, cash has its very own statement. As you learned in previous chapters, the statement of cash flows describes all of the cash flows for the period, which explains the change in cash from one balance sheet to the next. The

Yahoo! Inc.		
Comparative Balance Sheets (partial)		
(in thousands)		

	At December 31, 2007	At December 31, 2008
Assets		
Current assets:		
Cash and cash equivalents................................	$1,513,930	$2,292,296
Short-term marketable debt securities............	487,544	1,159,691
Accounts receivable, net of allowance		
of $46,521 and $51,600, respectively...........	1,055,532	1,060,450
Prepaid expenses and other assets..................	180,716	233,061
Total current assets.....................................	3,237,722	4,745,498

From the notes to Yahoo! Inc.:

Cash and Cash Equivalents, Short and Long-Term Marketable Debt Securities.
The Company invests its excess cash in money market funds and liquid debt instruments of the U.S. Government and its agencies, state municipalities, and in high-quality corporate issuers that are classified as marketable debt securities. All investments with an original maturity of three months or less are considered cash equivalents. Investments with effective maturities of less than 12 months from the balance sheet date are classified as current assets. Investments with effective maturities greater than 12 months from the balance sheet date are classified as long term assets.

EXHIBIT 4.5A

Current Asset Section of Yahoo! Inc. Comparative Balance Sheets
The current asset section of the balance sheet starts with cash and cash equivalents.

EXHIBIT 4.5B

Disclosure about Cash and Cash Equivalents
This note to the financial statements of Yahoo! Inc. defines "cash equivalents" as it is used by the firm.

amount of cash shown on the latest balance sheet will be the bottom line in the statement of cash flows. The statement of cash flows is an important financial statement because a business cannot survive if it does not have enough cash to pay its employees, vendors, rent, and other expenses.

Accounts Receivable and Bad Debts Expense

As you know, firms often sell goods and services on account, which means they extend credit to customers and collect the cash later. We will look at why firms extend credit and how firms record transactions in accounts receivable.

Extending Credit

When a firm makes a sale on account, the amount is recorded in **accounts receivable**, sometimes simply called *receivables*. Why would a firm make sales on account? Extending credit to customers attracts business. Whereas many retail firms use bank credit cards to satisfy customer demand to delay payment, those firms that buy and sell from other firms simply extend credit to their customers. Most firms will deal only with vendors who allow payment to be made sometime after delivery of the goods.

Exhibit 4.5A shows Yahoo's current asset section of its December 31, 2008, and December 31, 2007, balance sheets. Notice that the third asset listed is *accounts receivable (net of allowance)*. For Yahoo! Inc. these are amounts due from firms that advertise on Yahoo.

Unfortunately, a firm cannot expect to collect 100% of its accounts receivable balance. That is, not all customers will pay what they owe. For example, some customers are unable to pay as a result of a downturn in the economy or as a result of bankruptcy. If the amount a firm collects from credit sales as a percentage of total accounts receivable is low, the uncollected amounts will be costly to the firm. Every firm makes its own judgment about the percentage of uncollectible accounts it is comfortable with—there is no rule or specific amount. Having customers who do not pay is part of doing business, and a firm designs its credit policy to strike an acceptable balance between maximizing sales and minimizing the accounts receivable that are never paid.

Most companies offer credit to their customers, and they often have significant amounts of accounts receivable. Under generally accepted accounting principles (GAAP), when a firm

L.O.3
Calculate bad debts expense and explain how a firm evaluates and reports accounts receivable.

Accounts receivable is a current asset that arises from sales on credit; it is also the total amount customers owe the firm.

Net realizable value is the amount of its accounts receivable balance that the firm expects to collect.

The allowance method is a method of accounting for bad debts in which the amount of the uncollectible accounts is estimated at the end of each accounting period.

Bad debts expense is the expense to record uncollectible accounts receivable.

The allowance for uncollectible accounts is a contra-asset account, the balance of which represents the total amount the firm believes it will not collect from its total accounts receivable.

reports accounts receivable on its balance sheet, the amount must be what the firm expects to collect. The amount is called the **net realizable value (NRV)** of accounts receivable. Notice in Exhibit 4.5A that the term "net" is used in the presentation of accounts receivable. Net means Yahoo! has deducted the amount the firm believes is uncollectible from total accounts receivable. A firm generally uses a method called the **allowance method** to calculate the uncollectible amount.

A firm using GAAP applies the matching principle by putting the expense of having nonpaying customers on the same income statement as the revenue from sales made to those customers. To make this match, Yahoo will estimate and record as an expense the amount it believes it will not collect each period. Accounts receivable that a firm cannot collect are called *bad debts*, and the expense to record bad debts is called *bad debts expense*.

Recording Uncollectible Accounts

To understand how firms account for bad debts, we will start by looking at the way a firm would record bad debts in the accounting equation. Then, we will discuss how a firm arrives at the dollar amounts. To record **bad debts expense**, a firm will make an adjustment at the end of the accounting period. The adjustment starts with recording bad debts expense. This adjustment puts the expense on the income statement for the period. Now we need to balance the accounting equation. Because the accounts that will not be collected have not been identified at year end when the expense is estimated, the amount cannot be directly deducted from accounts receivable. The balance in accounts receivable is simply the total of all the individual customers' outstanding account balances, so the firm would have to know the name of the person who is not paying to deduct the amount directly from accounts receivable.

The amount that a firm estimates it will not collect—its uncollectible accounts—is put in a separate account called the **allowance for uncollectible accounts**. This account is a contra-asset and is used to hold the deductions from accounts receivable until the firm can identify specific accounts that are bad and take them off the firm's books. The balance in the allowance for uncollectible accounts is the amount that will appear on the balance sheet as a deduction from accounts receivable. Here is the adjustment a firm makes when it wants to record $5,000 as bad debts expense.

Assets	=	Liabilities	+	Shareholders' equity		
					Contributed + capital	Retained earnings
(5,000) allowance for uncollectible accounts						(5,000) bad debts expense

The amount remaining when you subtract the balance in the allowance for uncollectible accounts from the total amount of accounts receivable is called the carrying value of accounts receivable. Accountants use this terminology consistently for many different amounts on the balance sheet. Do you recall the name of the remainder when accumulated depreciation is subtracted from the cost of equipment? It is called the book value or carrying value of equipment on the balance sheet. For accounts receivable, the remainder is also called the net realizable value.

To summarize, the allowance for uncollectible accounts is a contra-asset account. The contra-asset holds the subtractions from accounts receivable, representing uncollectible accounts. Those amounts cannot be deducted directly from accounts receivable because at the time the accountant records the bad debts expense, the firm does not know exactly whose accounts will go unpaid.

Methods of Estimating Bad Debts Expense

Now that you know the terminology involved in accounting for bad debts, we will look at the procedures accountants use to estimate those bad debts. Using the allowance method, there are two ways of estimating uncollectible accounts expense: the percentage of sales method and the accounts receivable method.

ALLOWANCE METHOD—PERCENTAGE OF SALES METHOD. The percentage of sales method focuses on the income statement and the amount of the current period's credit sales for which collection is unlikely. For the purpose of putting the most meaningful amount on the income statement, the question is *How much of the credit sales will go uncollected?* The bad debts

UNDERSTANDING

Business

Managing Accounts Receivable

Accounts receivable is commonly one of a company's largest current assets. Because current assets support operations, managing the size of those assets and the timing of their use or conversion to cash is a crucial business activity.

How does a company control the size of its accounts receivable? The obvious way is to set credit policies that help achieve the desired level of credit sales and related collections. If the amount of a company's accounts receivable is larger than the company desires, it can tighten credit policies to reduce the amount of credit sales or it can increase collection efforts to speed up the collection of the related cash. If a company has a small amount of accounts receivable and is willing to increase that amount, the company may want to loosen its credit policies.

Companies often loosen their credit policies when they want to increase sales. There are other, less obvious ways for a company to manage its accounts receivable. If a company has a large amount of accounts receivable and it needs cash for operations, the company may sell its accounts receivable to a bank or finance company. This is called *factoring* accounts receivable, and the buyer is called a factor. When a company sells accounts receivable to a factor, the factor will keep a percentage of the value of the accounts receivable, similar to a credit card provider. The factor takes ownership of the accounts receivable and collects the accounts receivable as each comes due.

Managing accounts receivable is an important part of the sales and collection business process. Accounting information—the size and collection time for accounts receivable—provides crucial input for the decisions in this process.

expense is recorded as a percentage of credit sales, and the balancing amount is an addition to the allowance for uncollectible accounts. This reduces assets because it will be subtracted from accounts receivable.

Suppose you own a firm that has credit sales of $100,000 a year. To prepare your financial statements, you need to estimate the portion of those sales for which you will not collect payment. You must estimate the amount of bad debts expense based on past experience because you cannot predict exactly which customers will not pay their bills. Suppose you believed 2% of your credit sales would be uncollectible. You would record bad debts expense of $2,000 and report the net accounts receivable of $98,000—$100,000 minus the allowance for uncollectible accounts of $2,000—on the balance sheet.

ALLOWANCE METHOD—ACCOUNTS RECEIVABLE METHOD. The second method of calculating the allowance for uncollectible accounts and corresponding bad debts expense is the accounts receivable method. This method focuses on the balance sheet. A firm starts by estimating how much of the year-end balance of accounts receivable it believes it will not collect. This estimate reduces the amount of accounts receivable on the balance sheet so that a firm reports the amount it estimates it will collect, the net realizable value. To put the most meaningful amount on the balance sheet, the question is *How much of the total amount of accounts receivable will go uncollected?* (The question for the sales method is *What percentage of credit sales will not be collected?*)

Most often firms use an **aging schedule** to estimate this amount. An aging schedule is a list of the individual accounts that make up the total balance in accounts receivable categorized by how long the payment has been outstanding. Another way to estimate the amount is to take a percentage of the total balance in accounts receivable.

> An **aging schedule** is an analysis of the amounts owed to a firm by the length of time they have been outstanding.

Using the accounts receivable method of estimating the balance needed in the allowance for uncollectible accounts is sometimes called the *aging method* and sometimes called the *percent of accounts receivable method*. Both names are simply more specific names for the accounts receivable method. Using this method, the bad debts expense equals the amount needed to get the balance in the allowance for uncollectible accounts to the amount to be subtracted from accounts receivable to make it equal to the net realizable value.

Yahoo! Inc. uses the accounts receivable method (aging method) to estimate uncollectible accounts. Read how the firm describes the method in Exhibit 4.6 on the following page.

EXHIBIT 4.6

Yahoo! Inc.'s Description of Its Allowance for Uncollectible Accounts from Its 10-K for the Year Ended December 31, 2008

Yahoo! Inc. makes it clear that estimating uncollectible accounts involves a number of estimates.

Allowance for Doubtful Accounts. The Company records its allowance for doubtful accounts based upon its assessment of various factors. The Company considers historical experience, the age of the accounts receivable balances, the credit quality of its customers, current economic conditions, and other factors that may affect customers' ability to pay to determine the level of allowance required.

Notice that the firm mentions using the allowance method, assessing the collectibility of accounts, and using aging analysis to make its estimates.

How would a firm estimate bad debts expense using the balance in accounts receivable as the starting point? Suppose the balance in accounts receivable for Good Guys Co. at December 31, 2010, before any adjustments have been made, is $43,450. In this example, we have not even been told the amount of sales. To use the accounts receivable method, Good Guys Co. decides to prepare an aging schedule of accounts receivable, as shown in Exhibit 4.7. As you just learned, an aging schedule is an analysis of the amounts owed to a firm by the length of time they have been outstanding. As accounts become more overdue, they are increasingly unlikely to be collected.

EXHIBIT 4.7

Aging Schedule of Accounts Receivable

Notice that the amounts owed to the firm decrease with age. That's because most of the customers who purchased items on account pay their bills on time. Also notice that the percentages used to estimate the uncollectible portion increase as the age of the accounts increases. In this example, if an account is overdue by more than 90 days, there is a 50% chance it will never be collected.

			Number of days past due			
Customer	**Total**	**Current**	**1–30**	**31–60**	**61–90**	**Over 90**
J. Adams	$ 500	$ 300	$ 200			
K. Brown	$ 200	$ 200				
L. Cannon	$ 650		$ 300	$ 350		
M. Dibbs	$ 600				$ 200	$ 400
Other customers	$41,500	$25,000	$10,000	$3,000	$2,500	$1,000
	$43,450	$25,500	$10,500	$3,350	$2,700	$1,400
Estimated percentage uncollectible		1%	3%	8%	20%	50%
Total estimated bad debts	$ 2,078	$ 255	$ 315	$ 268	$ 540	$ 700

The amounts in this row are totals of many individual customers' accounts.

The sum of these amounts is $2,078.

Based on the aging of accounts receivable, management estimates the uncollectible amount at the end of the year to be $2,078. You can see how that total is calculated in Exhibit 4.7. So the net realizable value—the amount of accounts receivable the firm thinks it will collect—is $41,372. That is the total $43,450 minus $2,078. That amount is what Good Guys wants the balance sheet to show—the book value—at December 31, 2010. GAAP require the firm to disclose the total accounts receivable balance and its net realizable value. Some companies show the details on the balance sheet, and others include the details in the notes to the financial statements. Exhibit 4.8 shows how Good Guys might present its accounts receivable.

Balance Sheet, December 31, 2010	
Current Assets:	
Accounts receivable	$43,450
Allowance for uncollectible accounts	(2,078)
Net accounts receivable	$41,372

EXHIBIT 4.8

Balance Sheet Presentation of Accounts Receivable

In the first year of using the allowance method, with a zero balance in the allowance account, Good Guys estimated uncollectible accounts of $2,078. This is the adjustment that Good Guys will make at the end of the period.

Assets	=	Liabilities	+	Shareholders' equity	
				Contributed + capital	Retained earnings
(2,078) allowance for uncollectible accounts					(2,078) bad debts expense

Remember that rather than deducting the $2,078 directly from accounts receivable, the accountant will keep that amount in a separate allowance account, a contra-asset account, and show it on the balance sheet as a deduction from accounts receivable. Bad debts expense appears on the income statement as an operating expense.

Writing Off a Specific Account

During the following year, 2011, the firm will identify specific bad accounts and remove them from the books. That is when the firm finds out that a specific customer is not going to be able to pay his or her outstanding accounts receivable. When the firm eventually identifies the specific bad account and wants to remove it from the books, it will be done by deducting the amount from accounts receivable and also removing the amount from the allowance for uncollectible accounts. Removing the amount from accounts receivable reduces assets. Removing the amount from the allowance for uncollectible accounts *increases* assets by reducing the amount that will be deducted from accounts receivable on the balance sheet. That means there is no net effect on assets when the account is actually written off. *There is no bad debts expense recorded when the firm actually writes off a specific customer's account using the allowance method.* That is because the firm already recognized the bad debts expense when the accountant made the bad debts estimate for the adjustments at the time of the preparation of the financial statements.

When the firm writes off a specific account, the accountant is simply reclassifying an unnamed bad debt to a *named* bad debt. This is the transaction the firm would record to write off a specific account in the amount of $100.

Assets	=	Liabilities	+	Shareholders' equity	
				Contributed + capital	Retained earnings
(100) accounts receivable					
100 allowance for uncollectible accounts					

Only when you use the allowance method with accounts receivable as the basis for estimating bad debts expense do you adjust your new estimate for any over- or underestimation you made in the previous accounting period. If you write off more bad debts than you had estimated (i.e., you underestimated bad debts expense), you will end up with a shortage (negative balance) in the allowance for uncollectible accounts. However, you will adjust that balance in the allowance for uncollectible accounts when you do the end-of-period adjustments so that it will have the desired balance for the end-of-period balance sheet. If you write off fewer bad debts than you had estimated (i.e., you overestimated bad debts expense), you will end up with a bit extra (positive balance) in the allowance for uncollectible accounts. The next example will show you what to do if this happens.

Recall that Good Guys recorded $2,078 in its allowance for uncollectible accounts at December 31, 2010. This amount will be used for 2011 write-offs. Suppose the firm identifies M. Dibbs, who owes the firm $600, as an uncollectible account customer in February 2011. That means the firm's accountant or credit manager feels sure that the firm will not be able to collect his specific account. The effect on the accounting equation is a reduction in both the allowance for uncollectible accounts and accounts receivable. There is no effect on the net amount of accounts receivable. Writing off a specific account is a matter of cleaning up the firm's books. Instead of remaining an unidentified bad account, the firm can now put a name with $600 worth of bad debts. The firm already recognized the expense with the estimate it made at the end of the prior year, so no expense is recognized when a specific name is put with the uncollectible account. Here is the way the firm would write off Dibbs' account.

Assets	=	Liabilities	+	Shareholders' equity		
				Contributed capital	+	Retained earnings
(600) accounts receivable, Dibbs 600 allowance for uncollectible accounts						

Can you see what happens when you write off a specific account? With the allowance method, there is no effect on a firm's *net* accounts receivable when the firm writes off a specific account. Instead, the firm removes the account from its accounts receivable and removes an equal amount from the allowance.

	Balances on year-end balance sheet after adjustments	Effect of writing off Dibbs' account	Balances after writing off Dibbs' account
Accounts receivable	$43,450	(600)	$42,850
Allowance for uncollectible accounts	(2,078)	600	(1,478)
Net accounts receivable	$41,372		$41,372

Suppose that, by the end of the year, Good Guys has identified and written off $1,400 of accounts, in addition to Dibbs' account, for a total of $2,000 worth of specific bad accounts. This process of identifying and writing off continues throughout the year as the accounts are identified. That means the amount in the allowance account at the beginning of the year of $2,078 was $78 more than the total of the accounts actually identified and written off. The firm will ignore that difference and estimate the next year's bad debts expense in the same way as it did for the prior year. Good Guys will prepare another aging schedule and again make an estimate of uncollectible accounts. Follow along by looking at the additions and subtractions from the relevant accounts in Exhibit 4.9. Suppose credit sales for the year amounted to $100,000 and collections totaled $91,450, leaving a balance in accounts receivable of $50,000. Here is a summary of the activity in accounts receivable for the year.

- Beginning balance was $43,450 (ending 2010 balance).
- Add credit sales of $100,000.
- Deduct collections of $91,450.
- Deduct the total write-offs of $2,000.

This activity leaves an ending balance of $50,000 in accounts receivable. Suppose an aging schedule produced an estimate of uncollectible accounts of $2,500. Good Guys wants

EXHIBIT 4.9

Allowance for Uncollectible Accounts Using Accounts Receivable to Estimate Bad Debts Expense

This example begins with an accounts receivable balance of $43,450 at December 31, 2010. The allowance for uncollectible accounts is recorded along with bad debts expense for the year ended December 31, 2010, for $2,078. During 2011, the firm has credit sales of $100,000 and collections of $91,450. Both are shown in accounts receivable, along with accounts written off. During the year, $2,000 worth of bad debts are identified and written off: Dibbs for $600 and another batch totaling $1,400. Writing off these accounts reduces both accounts receivable and the allowance for uncollectible accounts. At December 31, 2011, the balance in the allowance is $78, reflecting an amount left over from the prior year. When the estimate of bad debts at December 31, 2011, of $2,500 is calculated, it is reduced by the $78 left over from the prior year. The adjustment to record bad debts expense for 2011 increases the allowance (which reduces assets) and increases bad debts expense (which reduces retained earnings).

	Accounts Receivable	Allowance for Uncollectible Accounts	Bad Debts Expense
Beginning balances from December 31, 2010, financial statements	$ 43,450	$ 2,078	$2,078 to income statement
Credit sales in 2011.................................	100,000		
Cash collections in 2011	(91,450)		
Write-offs in 2011.....................................	(600) (1,400)	(600) (1,400)	
Balance before adjustment.....................	$ 50,000	$ 78	
Desired ending balance..		$ 2,500	
Bad debts expense ($2,500 – $78) .... (amount needed to get desired balance in allowance)		$ 2,422	$2,422 to income statement

Amounts on the December 31, 2011, balance sheet

the balance sheet to use this estimate as the reduction in accounts receivable, showing the book value or carrying value of accounts receivable as $47,500. Now, Good Guys must take into consideration that it has a balance in the allowance account from last year's recording of bad debts expense. Good Guys will record bad debts expense this year of only $2,422 ($2,500 – $78). The amount carried over from last year, $78, is still in the allowance for uncollectible accounts, so the firm needs to add only $2,422 to the allowance for uncollectible accounts to get the total $2,500 needed for the balance sheet. So the firm's bad debts expense in the second year would be $2,422, and the allowance for uncollectible accounts balance at year end will be the desired $2,500. The accounts receivable balance of $50,000 will be reduced by the allowance of $2,500 to give net accounts receivable of $47,500.

Study the summary of this example in Exhibit 4.9 to make sure you understand the procedures for estimating and recording bad debts expense and the procedures for actually writing off a specific account.

When the accounts receivable method for estimating the allowance is used, the balance in the *allowance for uncollectible accounts* account and the bad debts expense are guaranteed to be equal only in the first year. After that, they would be equal only if the estimate of bad debts at the end of the previous year is exactly equal to the total amount of the accounts identified as uncollectible and written off in the subsequent year—and that rarely happens. Each year, the expense usually contains a small adjustment for the over- or underestimate from the previous year's entry.

Making the adjustment for the allowance for uncollectible accounts is part of the adjusting entries the firm records at the end of the accounting period. The amount of the bad debts estimate affects net income. To help ensure their bonuses or good salary increases, unethical managers could manipulate bad debts estimates to inflate net income. Watch for this when you read about firms' accounting problems in the news.

Exhibit 4.10 provides a summary of the allowance method for bad debts. Refer to the exhibit when you are trying to learn the differences between the methods of calculating the amounts for the allowance for uncollectible accounts and bad debts expense.

EXHIBIT 4.10

Allowance Methods of Accounting for Bad Debts

Method of Estimating Bad Debts Expense	Procedure	Effect on Income Statement	Effect on Balance Sheet
Sales method	Take a % of credit sales to record as bad debts expense	Reduces income with bad debts expense	Reduces assets with an increase in the allowance for uncollectible accounts (a contra-asset)
Accounts receivable method	Prepare an aging schedule or use a single percentage of the total balance in accounts receivable to estimate the balance needed in the allowance for uncollectible accounts	Reduces income with bad debts expense	Reduces assets with an increase in the allowance for uncollectible accounts (a contra-asset)
For both methods	Write off a specific account under both methods	No effect on income statement	No net effect on the balance sheet

Your Turn 4-3

Suppose at the end of the year Pendleton Corp.'s records showed the following:

ACCOUNT	BALANCE
Allowance for doubtful accounts	($100) (excess from prior year)
Bad debts expense*	-0-
Accounts receivable	$10,000

*Bad debts expense has a zero balance because no adjustments have been made.

Pendleton estimated the end-of-year uncollectible accounts receivable to be $500, based on an aging schedule of accounts receivable.

1. Calculate the amount of bad debts expense that should be shown on the income statement for the year.
2. What will be the net accounts receivable on the year-end balance sheet?

The Direct Write-Off Method

As you have learned, when a firm reports accounts receivable on its balance sheet, the amount must be what the firm expects to collect—that amount is the real asset. Most publicly-traded firms use the allowance method because GAAP require it when a firm has a significant amount of bad debts. There is another method called the **direct write-off method**. Using this method, a firm does not make any estimates of bad debts. The bad debts expense is recorded only when a specific account is identified as uncollectible. A firm uses the direct write-off method only when

The **direct write-off method** is a method of accounting for bad debts in which they are recorded as an expense in the period in which they are identified as uncollectible.

it has so few bad debts that almost all accounts receivable will be collected. Otherwise, the firm would be violating GAAP because it would not be matching the bad debts expense with the appropriate sales revenue, and it would not be reporting its accounts receivable at the net realizable value.

The accountant removes the "bad" account from the accounting records by deducting it from accounts receivable. The bad debts expense account is increased. Using the direct write-off method, a firm reports total accounts receivable on the balance sheet. Here is the transaction the firm records when it discovers that Jane Doe, who owes the firm $200, will not pay.

Assets	=	Liabilities	+	Shareholders' equity	
				Contributed capital	+ Retained earnings
(200) accounts receivable, J. Doe					(200) bad debts expense

Remember that the direct write-off method is not considered GAAP. Very few firms that extend credit to customers use this method if they follow GAAP because specific bad debts are written off in the period they are discovered rather than in the earlier period of the sale, which violates the matching principle. However, this is the method that firms must use for tax purposes. Remember, financial accounting and tax accounting are two very different types of accounting. Net income produced by financial accounting and taxable income produced by tax accounting are NOT the same amount. They are calculated with different rules and with very different objectives.

Exhibit 4.11 shows the relationships between the methods of accounting for bad debts that you have learned.

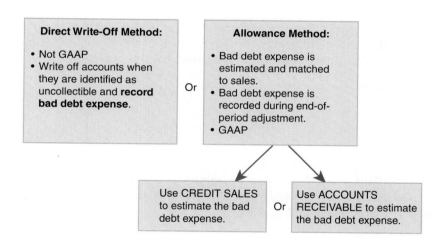

EXHIBIT 4.11

Accounting for Uncollectible Accounts

Credit Card Sales

L.O.4
Explain the difference between sales on credit and credit card sales.

One way to avoid the risk of extending credit to your customers is to accept payment with their credit cards. Banks or other financial institutions—also known as credit card companies—issue credit cards; and the users often must pay the issuer a fee to use the card. The credit card companies take the responsibility for evaluating a person's creditworthiness, and they also handle billing the customers and collecting payments. If a retailer allows customers to use a credit card to pay for their purchases, the retailer must pay the credit card company for these services. This is an important business decision, especially for small retailers. The cost of allowing customers to make purchases using credit cards must be compared with the benefits. The most significant cost is the credit card expense. Benefits may include increasing the number of customers and eliminating the risks associated with extending credit to customers. In addition, the retailer does not need to keep track of customers' credit, payments, and outstanding balances; and the retailer will not face any problems with late or uncollectible accounts.

This is how credit card sales are handled. The retailer will submit all the credit card sales receipts to the credit card company, and the credit card company will pay the retailer immediately. The amount the retailer receives will not be the gross amount of the sales. It will be a smaller amount because the credit card company will deduct a percentage of total sales as its fee for the services it provides. The retailer classifies the fees withheld by the credit card company as operating expenses.

Suppose that Wally's Tire Company accepts MasterCard®, and total credit card sales for the day were $1,000. Suppose the credit card company's fee is 5% of sales. Wally's would record the sales for the day in its accounting records as follows:

Assets	=	Liabilities	+	Shareholders' equity	
				Contributed + capital	Retained earnings
950 accounts receivable, MasterCard					1,000 sales revenue
					(50) credit card expense

When the retailer receives payment from MasterCard—typically daily or weekly, depending on the procedures for submitting credit card receipts to MasterCard—the retailer will record the increase in cash and the decrease in accounts receivable. Sometimes a firm records credit card sales as cash because the money is almost immediately deposited in the retailer's bank account by the credit card company.

NEWS FLASH Forty-one percent of college students have a credit card. Of those, about 65% pay their bills in full every month. That is higher than the general adult population.

Source: Student Monitor Annual Financial Services Study, 2008.

Your Turn 4-4

Magic Milk Company made a sale for $5,000 to a customer during December. The customer paid with MasterCard. MasterCard charges Magic Milk Company a fee of 3% of sales for its services. How much sales revenue will Magic Milk record related to this sale? How much cash will Magic Milk collect related to this sale?

L.O.5
Account for and report notes receivable.

A **promissory note** is a written promise to pay a specified amount of money at a specified time.

The **maker** of a note is the person or firm making the promise to pay.

The **payee** of a note is the person or firm receiving the money.

Notes Receivable

You have learned about the most significant receivables a firm has—accounts receivable. Another common receivable is a **promissory note**, which is a written promise to pay a specified amount of money at a specified time. The person or firm making the promise to pay is called the **maker**, and the person or firm receiving the money is called the **payee**. A promissory note is also called a *note receivable*. The main differences between accounts receivable and notes receivable related to accounting are time and interest.

First, notes receivable usually have a collection period longer than accounts receivable. A note receivable usually has a time period longer than a month associated with it, and the customer or firm who owes the money will pay interest along with the principal repayment. Frequently, a firm will renegotiate an overdue account receivable by allowing the customer to sign a promissory note giving the customer more time to pay and charging interest on the note.

Second, accounts receivable generally have no interest charges, whereas a note receivable always has interest charges. The firm calculates the interest on a note receivable in the same way it calculates interest on any debt:

$$Interest = Principal \times Rate \times Time$$

If the note is a short-term note, which the firm will classify as a current asset, the length of the note is less than a year. When calculating interest on a short-term note, be sure to keep the interest rate and the time period in the same units. Interest rates are always recorded on a note as annual rates, so the time period must be expressed as a portion of a year. A simple example will demonstrate the procedure for calculating the interest on a note.

Suppose Procter & Gamble allowed Pop's Grocery Store to renegotiate an overdue account receivable with a promissory note, dated May 1. The amount of the note is $5,000, due in three months, at an interest rate of 8%. This is how Procter & Gamble would record the note.

Assets	=	Liabilities	+	Shareholders' equity	
				Contributed capital	+ Retained earnings
(5,000) accounts receivable, Pop's Grocery					
5,000 notes receivable, Pop's Grocery					

When Pop's repays the note, it will also pay three months' worth of interest. This is the transaction as it would be recorded in Proctor & Gamble's accounting records.

Assets	=	Liabilities	+	Shareholders' equity	
				Contributed capital	+ Retained earnings
(5,000) notes receivable, Pop's Grocery					100 interest revenue*
5,100 cash					

*Interest = $5,000 \times 0.08 \times 3/12 = $100

If a note receivable is outstanding when a firm is ready to prepare financial statements, any interest that the firm has earned but not recorded must be accrued. The firm will calculate interest for the time that has passed and record interest revenue and interest receivable.

Delivery Products allowed a customer to give a note receivable in payment of a delinquent accounts receivable. The note was a six-month note for $3,000, and the interest rate was 8%. If the note was issued on September 1, how would the note and any related interest be reported on Delivery's December 31 balance sheet?

Your Turn 4-5

Team Shirts for April

When Sara began her T-shirt business, the firm's first customers were a few of Sara's friends, so collection of accounts receivable was not a problem. Now, the firm is branching out to sporting goods stores and local schools. The firm's customer base has now grown to a size that makes it

L.O.6
Prepare financial statements that include bad debts.

necessary for the firm to give serious attention to the collectibility of its accounts receivable. The April 1 balance sheet is shown in Exhibit 4.12, followed by the transactions for April (Exhibit 4.13). Make sure you understand how each transaction was posted to the accounting equation in Exhibit 4.14 before you go on to the adjustments.

EXHIBIT 4.12

Balance Sheet for Team Shirts at April 1, 2010

Team Shirts
Balance Sheet
At April 1, 2010

Assets		Liabilities and Shareholder's equity	
Current assets		Current liabilities	
Cash	$ 3,995	Interest payable	$ 30
Accounts receivable	2,000	Notes payable	3,000
Inventory	300	Total current liabilities	3,030
Prepaid insurance	75	Shareholder's equity	
Total current assets	6,370	Common stock	5,000
Computer (net of $100		Retained earnings	2,240
accumulated depreciation)	3,900	Total shareholder's equity	7,240
		Total liabilities and	
Total assets	$10,270	shareholder's equity	$10,270

EXHIBIT 4.13

Transactions for Team Shirts for April

Date	Transaction
1. April 1	Receives $2,000 from customer for payments on accounts receivable
2. April 3	Purchases 1,000 shirts for inventory at $4 each on account
3. April 15	Pays $2,400 cash for rent for a warehouse for two months, beginning on date of payment
4. April 30	During the month, sells 800 shirts at $10 each on account
5. April 30	During the month, incurs cash operating expenses $300

Adjustment 1: As part of the month-end adjustments, Team Shirts has decided to set up an allowance for uncollectible accounts. The firm will use the accounts receivable—aging method—and after consulting with some local businesses and some accountants, Sara will set up an allowance equal to 2% of ending accounts receivable (AR). Ending AR = $8,000; 2% of $8,000 = $160.

This decision is based on the matching principle. The firm wants to match the bad debts expense with the sales to which it pertains, even though the firm does not know how many or which specific customers will not pay.

Adjustment 2: Insurance for the month is $50. (Recall that the insurance policy was purchased in a prior month, so this adjustment is made to prepaid insurance.)

Adjustment 3: Rent expense for half a month is $600. (Two months' worth of rent was purchased for $2,400 on April 15.)

Adjustment 4: Depreciation for the computer needs to be recorded. It is being depreciated at $100 per month.

Adjustment 5: Interest on the short-term note payable for the computer needs to be accrued; $3,000 principal × 12% × 1/12 = $30.

After the worksheet in Exhibit 4.14 is complete, you are ready to prepare the financial statements. You will find them in Exhibit 4.15 on page 174. Make sure you can trace amounts from the financial statements back to the worksheet.

EXHIBIT 4.14

Accounting Equation Worksheet for Team Shirts for April

	Assets		=	**Liabilities**		+	**Shareholder's Equity**		
	Cash	All other assets	(Account)		All liabilities	(Account)		**Contributed Capital** Common stock	**Retained Earnings**	(Account)
Beginning Balances	$3,995	$ 2,000 300 4,000 (100) 75	Accounts receivable Inventory Computer Accumulated depreciation Prepaid insurance		$ 30 3,000	Interest payable Notes payable		$5,000	$2,240	Beginning balance in Retained earnings
Transactions										
1	2,000	(2,000)	Accounts receivable							
2		4,000	Inventory		4,000	Accounts payable				
3	(2,400)	2,400	Prepaid rent							
4		8,000 (3,200)	Accounts receivable Inventory						8,000 (3,200)	Sales Cost of goods sold
5	(300)								(300)	Operating expense
A-1		(160)	Allowance for bad debts						(160)	Bad debts expense
A-2		(50)	Prepaid insurance						(50)	Insurance expense
A-3		(600)	Prepaid rent						(600)	Rent expense
A-4		(100)	Accumulated depreciation						(100)	Depreciation expense
A-5					30	Interest payable			(30)	Interest expense
	$3,295	+ $14,565		=	$7,060		+	$5,000	+	$5,800

■ Income Statement — Statement of Changes in Shareholder's Equity — Balance Sheet — Statement of Cash Flows

Asset details:

Accounts receivable	$8,000
Allowance for bad debts	(160)
Inventory	1,100
Prepaid insurance	25
Prepaid rent	1,800
Computer	4,000
Accumulated depreciation	(200)
Total non-cash assets	$14,565

Liability details:

Account payable	$4000
Notes payable	3,000
Interest payable	60
Total liabilities	$7,060

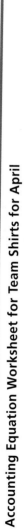

EXHIBIT 4.15

Financial Statements for Team Shirts for April 2010

Team Shirts
Income Statement
For the Month Ended April 30, 2010

Sales revenues:		$ 8,000
Expenses:		
Cost of goods sold	$3,200	
Operating expenses	300	
Bad debts expense	160	
Insurance expense	50	
Rent expense	600	
Depreciation expense	100	
Interest expense	30	
Total expenses		4,440
Net income		$3,560

Team Shirts
Statement of Changes in Shareholder's Equity
For the Month Ended April 30, 2010

Beginning common stock	$ 5,000
Common stock issued during the month	0
Ending common stock	$ 5,000
Beginning retained earnings	$ 2,240
+ Net income	3,560
– Dividends	0
Ending retained earnings	$ 5,800
Total shareholder's equity	$10,800

Team Shirts
Statement of Cash Flows
For the Month Ended April 30, 2010

Cash from operating activities:	
Cash collected from customers	$ 2,000
Cash paid for rent	(2,400)
Cash paid for operating expense	(300)
Net cash used by operating activities	(700)
Cash from investing activities:	0
Cash from financing activities:	0
Decrease in cash	(700)
Beginning cash balance	3,995
Ending cash balance	$ 3,295

Team Shirts
Balance Sheet
At April 30, 2010

Assets		
Current assets		
Cash		$ 3,295
Accounts receivable	7,840	
(net of allowance of $160)		
Inventory	1,100	
Prepaid expenses	1,825	
Total current assets		14,060
Computer (net of accumulated		
depreciation of $200)		3,800
Total assets		$17,860

Liabilities & Shareholder's Equity		
Current liabilities		
Accounts payable		$ 4,000
Interest payable		60
Notes payable		3,000
Total current liabilities		7,060
Shareholder's Equity		
Common stock		5,000
Retained earnings		5,800
Total shareholder's equity		10,800
Total liabilities and		
shareholder's equity		$17,860

Applying Your Knowledge: Ratio Analysis

Keeping control of cash through the bank reconciliation process helps ensure that the correct numbers are getting to the financial statements. The numbers for sales and accounts receivable must be accurate because managers and others use those numbers to measure the firm's ability to meet its short-term obligations. When the current ratio you learned about in Chapter 2 is computed—current assets divided by current liabilities—the numerator includes accounts receivable because it is a current asset.

Another important ratio that involves accounts receivable is the **accounts receivable (AR) turnover ratio**. This ratio—net credit sales divided by average net accounts receivable—measures how quickly a firm collects its accounts receivable. The ratio tells how many times, on average, the process of selling on account and collecting the receivables is repeated during the period. Exhibit 4.16 shows two ratios that managers can use to evaluate liquidity and receivables.

L.O.7

Analyze a firm's accounts receivable with ratio analysis.

The **accounts receivable (AR) turnover ratio** is a ratio that measures how quickly a firm collects its accounts receivable. It is defined as credit sales divided by average accounts receivable.

EXHIBIT 4.16

Two Liquidity Ratios Involving Accounts Receivable

Ratio	Description	Equation	When to Use
Current Ratio	Measure of liquidity	$\dfrac{\text{Total current assets}}{\text{Total current liabilities}}$	To evaluate a firm's ability to meet its short-term obligations
Accounts Receivable Turnover Ratio	Measure of rate of accounts receivable collections, another measure of liquidity	$\dfrac{\text{Net credit sales}}{\text{Average net accounts receivable}}$	To measure how quickly a firm is collecting its receivables; another indication of a firm's ability to meet its short-term obligations

Exhibit 4.17 shows information from the financial statements for Yahoo! Inc. and the calculation of the AR turnover ratio. The denominator of this ratio is the average of the beginning balance and ending balance of net accounts receivable. This particular ratio is useful for a firm to track over time to make sure receivables are being collected promptly.

EXHIBIT 4.17

Yahoo! Inc.: Accounts Receivable Turnover Ratio

The accounts receivable (AR) turnover ratio equals credit sales divided by average net accounts receivable. Often, however, financial statements do not provide separate amounts for cash and credit sales, so we use total sales for the numerator. It is very important to be consistent in the calculation of ratios that are compared over time and from company to company. For example, if you use total sales to compute the AR turnover ratio at the end of this year, then you must also use total sales next year to have a basis for comparison.

(dollars in thousands)	December 31, 2008	December 31, 2007	December 31, 2006
Accounts Receivable (net)	$1,060,450	$1,055,532	$930,964
Sales*	$7,208,502	$6,969,274	
Accounts Receivable Turnover Ratio	6.81 times	7.02 times	

* Accounts receivable are as of the date shown and sales amounts are for the fiscal year ended on the date shown.

The AR turnover is 6.81 times, calculated as follows:

$$\frac{\$7,208,502}{(\$1,055,532 \ + \ \$1,060,450)/2}$$

If the average turnover of accounts receivable is 6.81 times, we can calculate how long it takes for Yahoo!, on average, to collect its accounts receivable. If we divide 365—the number of days in a year—by the AR turnover ratio, we will get the number of days it takes, on average, to collect its accounts receivable. For the fiscal year ended (FYE) December 31, 2008, we will divide 365 days by 6.81 times, which equals 53.60 days. That means that it takes close to two months for Yahoo! to collect its accounts receivable. For FYE 2007, we divided 365 by 7.02, which equals 51.99 days. From FYE 2007 to 2008, Yahoo! has slightly increased its average number of days to collect its accounts receivable, which is not considered an improvement. Notice that the higher the AR turnover ratio (7.02 times versus 6.81 times), the faster the firm is collecting its accounts receivable.

If we calculate the AR turnover ratio for a retail firm, the turnover ratio will be higher and the average number of days to collect its accounts receivable will be lower than our calculations for a firm like Yahoo!. That is because a firm like Yahoo! extends credit to almost all customers and, therefore, does not have as many cash sales as a retail firm. When we use total sales as our numerator in the ratio, which include cash sales and credit card sales, we are slightly underestimating the time it takes to collect an account. For example, look at the information in Exhibit 4.18 for Books-A-Million, a retail firm.

EXHIBIT 4.18

Books-A-Million: Accounts Receivable (AR) and Sales

A retail firm will turn over its receivables very quickly. Remember that the total sales dollars include cash sales.

(dollars in thousands)	AR at February 2, 2008	AR at February 3, 2007	Sales for FYE February 2, 2008
	$6,450	$7,524	$535,128

The AR turnover ratio is 76.59, calculated as follows:

$$\frac{\$535,128}{(\$7,524 \ + \ \$6,450)/2}$$

To get the average number of days to collect its accounts receivable, we divide 365 by 76.59, which is 4.77 days. That is significantly shorter than the average 53 days it takes Yahoo! to collect its accounts receivable! Most of the sales for Books-A-Million are cash, and the amount of credit sales is not disclosed separately. Using a sales amount that includes cash and credit card sales makes the AR turnover ratio much higher because it artificially inflates the numerator.

Internally, managers will use only credit sales in the calculation of the AR turnover ratio. For external users, that information may not be available. Different industries and even different firms in the same industry may have very different AR turnover ratios. As you have learned, you must use ratio analysis carefully.

Your Turn **4-6**

Suppose a firm has beginning AR of $10,500 and ending AR of $12,500. Credit sales for the period amounted to $120,000. What is the accounts receivable turnover ratio, and how long does it take, on average, to collect an outstanding account?

Business Risk, Control, and Ethics

L.O.8
Identify the risks and controls associated with cash and receivables.

You have learned about two of the most important assets a firm has—cash and receivables. Now we are ready to resume our discussion about the way a firm makes sure the risks related to these assets are minimized. Remember that an important purpose of internal controls is to be sure a firm's assets are safeguarded and that the related financial records are accurate and reliable.

Earlier in the chapter, you learned about one of the most important controls a firm can have: segregation of duties. This control means that the person who is responsible for the record keeping related to an asset does not have physical custody or access to the asset. This is an extremely important control in safeguarding cash.

In addition to segregation of duties, there are three more key controls that help a firm safeguard its assets and enhance the accuracy and reliability of its financial records: (1) clear assignment of responsibility for physical control of the assets, (2) specific procedures for documentation related to the assets, and (3) independent internal verification of the data. We will look at each of these more closely as they relate to cash and accounts receivable.

Clear Assignment of Responsibility

The responsibility for safeguarding cash can be assigned to a variety of people in the firm. For example, in some retail stores, each cashier is responsible for safeguarding the cash in his or her own register. At the end of each shift, the money is counted and the amount is compared to the register's recorded sales. If a cashier is short by $10, it may be the cashier's responsibility to make up the $10 shortage. As shown in Exhibit 4.19, when new cashiers come on duty, they will have their own cash drawers for which they are responsible.

EXHIBIT 4.19

Clear Assignment of Responsibility

Specific Procedures for Documentation

Documentation procedures are another critical control for cash and accounts receivable. Have you ever returned an item to a department store? You may have been asked to fill out a form with your name, address, and the reason for the return. One reason for this procedure, as shown in Exhibit 4.20, is to provide documentation for the refund. Either a cash refund or a credit to your account, if your purchase was on account, must be accompanied by supporting documentation to help ensure that refunds are granted only for legitimate returns.

EXHIBIT 4.20

Documentation Procedures

Independent Internal Verification of Data

Have you ever purchased something from a store that has a sign by the cash register that reads IF YOU DO NOT GET A RECEIPT, YOUR PURCHASE IS FREE? That sign is a control to be sure that every cashier is properly recording all sales. Cashiers will not be able to take your cash and put it in their pockets without ringing it up on the cash register to produce a receipt. Why? Because if they were to do that, you would ASK for a receipt and get your purchase for free as well! You are helping the owners make sure they get their cash and that the sale is properly documented. Exhibit 4.21 gives an example of this type of control.

EXHIBIT 4.21

Independent Internal Verification of Data

Your Turn `4-7`

Explain why cashiers would not be able to pocket money from purchases if they were forced to give receipts.

Chapter Summary Points

- Cash is one of the most important assets a firm has. It is easy to steal because its ownership cannot be easily identified. Control of cash is crucial, and one of the most important controls is a bank reconciliation. That is a worksheet that reconciles the firm's cash balance with the bank statement balance at the end of each month.
- Cash is reported on the balance sheet along with very liquid investments called cash equivalents. Cash is also the focus of its own financial statement, the statement of cash flows, which gives all the sources and uses of cash during an accounting period.
- When a firm offers credit to its customers, the resulting asset is called accounts receivable. On the balance sheet, accounts receivable is a current asset and should reflect the net amount the firm expects to collect. If the firm has a significant amount of bad debts (i.e., customers who will not pay), then the firm must estimate the amount of bad debts and deduct it from gross accounts receivable to get the net realizable value of accounts receivable to report on the balance sheet. This is called the allowance method of accounting for bad debts. This means that bad debts expense will be recognized as an estimate so that the firm can match the bad debts expense with the related sales. When a specific customer is identified as one who will not pay, the account is written off but no expense is recognized at that time. (The expense was already recognized in the period of the sale.)

- Credit card sales are almost like cash to a business. The credit card company reimburses the firm and is paid a fee for the service. The risk is much less than that of extending the firm's own credit to its customers. For example, if you use a Macy's charge account, the risk is greater to Macy's than if you had used your MasterCard to make a purchase at the department store.
- Notes receivable are amounts owed to the firm, often by customers who have been slow in paying their accounts and have negotiated new payment terms that include interest.
- Firms use accounts receivable to help evaluate a firm's liquidity. The accounts receivable turnover ratio (net sales or net credit sales divided by average accounts receivable) measures how quickly the firm is collecting its accounts receivable.
- Controls are especially important with respect to cash. Three of them are (1) clear assignment of responsibility, (2) specific procedures for documentation, and (3) independent internal verification of the data.

Chapter Summary Problem

The following transactions took place during Choco Drops' fiscal year ended December 31, 2011:

a. Sold $900,000 of merchandise on account. Related cost of goods sold was $270,000.
b. Collected payment for 80% of the sales.
c. Accepted a three-month note from Nature's Grocery Store Chain for $8,000 on October 1, 2011 (due on January 1, 2012), with an interest rate of 6%, in payment of its $8,000 outstanding balance in accounts receivable.
d. Had $98,000 of cash sales. Related cost of goods sold was $29,400.
e. Wrote off a bad account for $4,000 after the bankruptcy court approved a reorganization plan for one of its struggling customers.
f. Incurred operating expenses $75,600, paid in cash.

Instructions

1. Enter each of the transactions in an accounting equation worksheet. The firm started the year with a balance of $150,000 in accounts receivable and a balance of $4,500 in the allowance for uncollectible accounts. The balance in the inventory account was $500,000. The other beginning balances are not given and not required for the problem. (These came from the December 31, 2010, balance sheet.)
2. Make the adjustment to record bad debts expense. Choco Drops uses the allowance method of accounting for uncollectible accounts, based on a percentage of the ending balance in accounts receivable. (Use the same percentage—3%—the firm used to calculate the bad debts expense for 2010. Also, be sure to accrue interest receivable on the note in Transaction (c).)
3. Prepare an income statement for the year ended December 31, 2011.

Solution

Transaction	Cash	All other assets	(Account)	All liabilities	(Account)	Contributed Capital	Retained Earnings (Account)
Assets =				**Liabilities** +		**Shareholders' Equity**	
Selected Beginning Balances		$150,000	Accounts receivable				
		(4,500)	Allowance for bad debts				
		500,000	Inventory				
a.		900,000	Accounts receivable				900,000 Sales
		(270,000)	Inventory				(270,000) Cost of goods sold
b.	720,000	(720,000)	Accounts receivable				
c.		(8,000)	Accounts receivable				
		8,000	Notes receivable				
d.	98,000						98,000 Sales
		(29,400)	Inventory				(29,400) Cost of goods sold
e.		(4,000)	Accounts receivable				
		4,000	Allowance for bad debts				
f.	(75,600)						(75,600) Operating expenses
A-1		(9,040)	Allowance for bad debts				(9,040) Bad debts expense
A-2		120	Interest receivable				120 Interest revenue

━ Income Statement   ━ Statement of Changes in Shareholders' Equity   ━ Balance Sheet   ━ Statement of Cash Flows

Calculations for bad debt expense:
1 - What is the balance in AR?

Beginning AR	$ 150,000
+ Sales	900,000
Collections	(720,000)
to Notes receivable	(8,000)
Write-offs	(4,000)
Ending AR	$ 318,000

2 - What is the balance in the allowance?

Beginning allowance	$ 4,500
Write-offs	(4,000)
+ Bad debt expense	x
Desired allowance balance	$ 9,540 (318,000 3 0.03)

Balance in allowance before adjustment: = $500

Needed to bring allowance to desired $9,540 = $9,040

Choco Drops
Income Statement
For the Year Ended December 31, 2011

Revenues		
Sales	$998,000	
Interest revenue	120	
Total revenue		$998,120
Expenses		
Costs of goods sold	$299,400	
Bad debts expense	9,040	
Operating expenses	75,600	
Total expenses		384,040
Net income		$614,080

Key Terms for Chapter 4

Accounts receivable (p. 161)	Bad debts expense (p. 162)	Maker (p. 170)
Accounts receivable (AR) turnover ratio (p. 175)	Bank reconciliation (p. 154)	Net realizable value (p. 162)
	Bank statement (p. 154)	Outstanding check (p. 157)
Aging schedule (p. 163)	Cash equivalents (p. 160)	Payee (p. 170)
Allowance for uncollectible accounts (p. 162)	Deposit in transit (p. 156)	Promissory note (p. 170)
	Direct write-off method (p. 168)	Segregation of duties (p. 154)
Allowance method (p. 162)		

Answers to YOUR TURN Questions

Chapter 4

Your Turn 4-1

The purpose of a bank reconciliation is to provide a control to protect cash. The amount of cash reported on the bank statement (an independently calculated balance) must be reconciled to the cash reported in the accounting records. A firm would prepare a bank reconciliation as often as the bank provided a statement, usually once each month.

Your Turn 4-2

To find the solution, you need to know the following information:

Balance per books	$2,400
Deduct service charges	−100
Add collection	+300
Add interest revenue	+100
True cash balance	$2,700

Outstanding checks are ignored because we are working with only the "balance per books" side of the reconciliation.

Your Turn 4-3

1. $400 ($500 desired balance − $100 remaining balance before adjustments)
2. $9,500 ($10,000 − $500)

Your Turn 4-4

Magic Milk will record revenue of $5,000. Cash collected will be 97% of $5,000 = $4,850. The remaining 3%, or $150, will be recorded as credit card expense.

Your Turn 4-5

Current assets: Notes receivable $3,000
Current assets: Interest receivable $80 [$3,000 × 0.08 × 4/12]

Your Turn 4-6

1. Sales of $120,000 divided by average AR [$11,500 = ($10,500 + $12,500) ÷ 2] = 10.43 times.
2. Days to collect: 365 days ÷ 10.43 = 35 days

Your Turn 4-7

To get the receipt to print, the transaction must be entered into the cash register or computer. If cash collected is reconciled to the records (from the register or computer), any missing amounts would be apparent.

Questions

1. What is a bank reconciliation and what does it determine?
2. What are two common adjustments made to the balance per bank on the bank reconciliation?
3. Describe two common adjustments made to the balance per books on the bank reconciliation.

4. After the bank reconciliation is complete, which adjustments are recorded in the accounting records?
5. What does true cash balance refer to?
6. Identify and explain the financial statements on which cash is reported.
7. Describe how accounts receivable arise. What does the balance in accounts receivable represent?
8. How do accounts (trade) receivables differ from other receivables?
9. Define net realizable value, book value, and carrying value as they relate to accounts receivable.
10. Explain the difference between the direct write-off method and the allowance method of accounting for bad debts. Which method is preferred and why?
11. If a company uses the allowance method of accounting for bad debts, what effect does writing off a specific account have on income?
12. Describe the two allowance methods used to estimate the amount of bad debts expense that appears on the income statement.
13. Which method of calculating the allowance for uncollectible accounts focuses on the income statement? Explain.
14. Which method of calculating the allowance for uncollectible accounts focuses on the balance sheet? Explain.
15. What are the advantages and disadvantages of allowing customers to make purchases with credit cards?
16. What is the difference between accounts receivable and notes receivable?
17. What is the formula to calculate the accounts receivable turnover ratio, and what does the formula measure?
18. How does a firm use its accounts receivable turnover ratio to determine the average number of days it takes to collect its accounts receivable?
19. Explain how the segregation of duties serves as a major control for safeguarding cash.
20. Explain why it is important to have physical control of cash.

Multiple-Choice Questions

Use the following information for questions 1–4. Fred's Supply Store just received its monthly bank statement from Local Street Bank. The bank gives a balance of $45,000. Fred's accounting clerk has calculated that outstanding checks amount to $20,000. Fred's Supply Store made a deposit of $5,000 on the last day of the month, and it was not included on the bank statement. Bank service fees, not yet recorded on the store's books, were shown on the statement as $35. The bank statement also included an NSF check returned from a new customer in the amount of $250.

1. What is the store's true cash balance at the end of the month?
   a. $25,000
   b. $30,000
   c. $29,715
   d. $29,750
2. How should outstanding checks be treated on the bank reconciliation?
   a. They should be deducted from the balance per books.
   b. They should be added to the balance per books.
   c. They should be deducted from the balance per bank.
   d. They should be added to the balance per bank.
3. Which items would need to be recorded in Fred's Supply Store's accounting records?
   a. Outstanding checks and the deposit in transit
   b. NSF check
   c. Bank service fee
   d. Both NSF check and bank service fee
4. What was the cash balance in its accounting records before Fred's Supply Store began the bank reconciliation?
   a. $30,285
   b. $30,250
   c. $45,250
   d. $25,285

Use the following information to answer multiple-choice questions 5 and 6. At the end of the year, before any adjustments are made, the accounting records for Sutton Company show a balance of $100,000 in accounts receivable. The allowance for uncollectible accounts has a remaining balance of $2,000. (This means last year's estimate was too large by $2,000.) The company uses accounts receivable to estimate bad debts expense. An analysis of accounts receivable results in an estimate of $27,000 of uncollectible accounts.

5. The bad debts expense on the income statement for the year would be
   a. $27,000.
   b. $25,000.
   c. $23,000.
   d. $29,000.

6. Net realizable value of the receivables on the year-end balance sheet would be
   a. $100,000.
   b. $75,000.
   c. $73,000.
   d. $77,000.

7. Suppose a firm uses the percentage of sales method for estimating bad debts expense. The firm has credit sales for the year of $200,000 and a balance of $80,000 in accounts receivable. The firm estimates that 2% of its credit sales will never be collected. What is the bad debts expense for the year?
   a. $1,600
   b. $2,000
   c. $4,000
   d. $3,600

8. Scott Company uses the allowance method of accounting for bad debts. During May, the company found out that one of its largest customers filed for bankruptcy. If Scott Company decides to write off the customer's account, what effect will that decision have on Scott Company's net income for the period?
   a. Bad debts expense will decrease income.
   b. Writing off the receivable will decrease income.
   c. Both a. and b. will happen.
   d. There is no effect on net income.

9. Merry Maids, Inc., sells vacuum cleaners to McKenzie-Grace Corporation for $1,000. McKenzie-Grace pays Merry Maids with the company Visa card. Visa charges Merry Maids a 3% fee for all Visa sales. What is the *net* effect of this transaction on the accounting equation for Merry Maids?
   a. Increase assets $1,000; increase retained earnings $1,000
   b. Decrease assets $1,000; decrease retained earning $1,000
   c. Increase assets $970; increase retained earnings $970
   d. Not enough information

Short Exercises
Set A

All of the A exercises can be found within MyAccountingLab, an online homework and practice environment.

SE4-1A. *Analyze bank reconciliation items. (LO 1).* For each of the following items, indicate whether or not the *balance per books* should be adjusted. For each item that affects the balance per books, indicate whether the item should be added to (+) or subtracted from (−) the balance per books.

Item	Balance per books adjusted?	+/−
Outstanding checks	No	n/a
Service charge by bank		
NSF check from customer		
Deposits in transit		
Error made by the bank		
Note receivable collected by the bank		

SE4-2A. *Calculate the true cash balance. (LO 1, 2).* At March 31, Ronca Company has the following information available about its cash account:

Cash balance per bank	$7,500
Outstanding checks	$2,500
Deposits in transit	$1,800
Bank service charge	$ 100

Determine the true cash balance per bank at March 31 and tell where it would be reported in the financial statements.

SE4-3A. *Analyze errors in a bank reconciliation. (LO 1).* Name Brand Electronics' accountant wrote a check to a supplier for inventory in the amount of $1,600 but erroneously recorded it on the company's books as $1,060. She discovered this when she saw the monthly bank statement and noticed that the check had cleared the bank for $1,600. How would this be handled on the bank reconciliation? Enter the transaction into the accounting equation Name Brand's accountant needs to make to correct its accounting records.

SE4-4A. *Determine bad debts expense using the percentage of sales method. (LO 3).* Discount Bakery has a liberal credit policy and has been experiencing a high rate of uncollectible accounts. The company estimates that 5% of credit sales become bad debts. Due to the significance of this amount, the company uses the allowance method for accounting for bad debts. During the year, credit sales amounted to $200,000. The year-end accounts receivable balance was $117,000. What was the bad debts expense for the year?

SE4-5A. *Determine bad debts expense using the accounts receivable method. (LO 3).* Don's Golf Supplies ended its first year with $50,000 of accounts receivable and estimates that 3% of that amount will never be paid. No account has been specifically identified as non-paying at the date of the year-end balance sheet. What will the income statement for the year show as the bad debts expense if Don's uses the allowance method of accounting for bad debts?

SE4-6A. *Write off uncollectible accounts. (LO 3).* Chastain's Upholstery has determined that Global Builders' accounts receivable balance of $5,500 is uncollectible. Use the accounting equation to show how Chastain's would write off the account using (a) the direct write-off method and (b) the allowance method for bad debts.

SE4-7A. *Account for credit card sales. (LO 4).* Jordan Beauty Supply accepts Discover® cards from its customers. Discover charges Jordan 3.5% of sales for its services. During the 2009–2010 fiscal year, Jordan's customers used Discover cards to purchase $65,000 worth of merchandise. How much did Jordan show as sales on the income statement for the year ended June 30, 2010? How much cash did Jordan actually receive from these sales?

SE4-8A. *Analyze notes receivable. (LO 5).* On May 1, 2011, Bob's Music renegotiated its overdue account balance of $2,500 with Spectrum Electronics by signing a two-month promissory note at an interest rate of 5%. What is the principal amount of the note? What is the due date of the note? How much will Bob's Music repay on the due date of the note?

SE4-9A. *Calculate accounts receivable turnover ratio. (LO 7).* Candid Company had the following balances:

	December 31, 2011	December 31, 2010
Receivables, net	$ 325,000	$ 285,000
Sales (all credit)	$1,757,000	$1,248,700

Calculate the accounts receivable turnover ratio for 2011. On average, how many days does it take Candid Company to collect its accounts receivable?

Set B

SE4-10B. *Analyze bank reconciliation items. (LO 1).* For each of the following items, indicate whether or not the *balance per bank* should be adjusted. For each item that affects the balance per bank, indicate whether the item should be added to (+) or subtracted from (−) the balance per bank.

Item	Balance per bank adjusted?	+/−
Outstanding checks	Yes	—
Service charge by bank		
NSF check from customer		
Deposits in transit		
Error made by the bank		
Note receivable collected by the bank		

SE4-11B. *Calculate the true cash balance. (LO 1).* Use the following information to calculate the true reconciled cash balance:

Bank statement shows interest earned for month	$50
Bank statement shows service charges for month	$10
Book shows deposits in transit	$75
Book shows outstanding checks	$25

Balance per	Books	Bank
	$100	$90
Interest earned for month	_____	_____
Service charges for month	_____	_____
Deposits in transit	_____	_____
Outstanding checks	_____	_____
Balance	_____	_____
True cash balance	_____	_____

What is the company's true cash balance at April 30?

SE4-12B. *Analyze errors in a bank reconciliation. (LO 1).* Rimes Restaurant makes large cash deposits daily. The bookkeeper recorded one of the daily deposits as $5,700 in the company's records, but the bank statement showed that deposit as $7,500. After checking the day's restaurant receipts and the original deposit slip, the bookkeeper realized the bank was correct and that he had transposed the digits when he recorded the transaction. How should this be handled on the bank reconciliation? Show what Rimes should record to correct its books.

SE4-13B. *Determine bad debts expense using the percentage of sales method. (LO 3).* Following are the 2010 year-end balances before adjustments:

Accounts receivable (AR)	$ 80,000
Allowance for uncollectible accounts	$ (2,000)
Net sales	$250,000

Using the percentage of sales method, the company estimates 3% of sales will become uncollectible. What is the bad debts expense for 2010? What will be the net realizable value of accounts receivable on the year-end balance sheet?

SE4-14B. *Determine bad debts expense using the accounts receivable method. (LO 3).* Carpet Emporium ended its first year with $300,000 of accounts receivable and estimates that 2% of that amount will never be paid. No account has been specifically identified as non-paying at the date of the year-end balance sheet. What will the income statement for the year show as the bad debts expense if Carpet Emporium uses the allowance method of accounting for bad debts?

SE4-15B. *Write off uncollectible accounts. (LO 3).* Building Supplies Corporation has determined that a customer's accounts receivable balance of $35,700 is uncollectible. Use the accounting equation to show how Building Supplies Corporation would write off the account using (a) the direct write-off method and (b) the allowance method for bad debts.

SE4-16B. *Account for credit card sales. (LO 4).* Fried Foods Corporation accepts MasterCard from its customers. MasterCard charges Fried Foods a fixed fee of $125 per month plus 4.25% of MasterCard sales. If Fried Foods had MasterCard sales of $600,000 during 2011, how much did Fried Foods pay MasterCard for its service?

SE4-17B. *Analyze notes receivable. (LO 5).* When Moss Planters Corporation was contacted by Green's Garden Center asking for a time extension on its outstanding balance of $1,000, Moss Planters Corporation offered to convert the accounts receivable into a short-term note. Green's agreed to the offer and, on June 1, signed a three-month promissory note at an interest rate of 4%. What is the principal amount of the note? What is the due date of the note? How much will Green's Garden Center repay on the due date of the note?

SE4-18B. *Calculate accounts receivable turnover ratio. (LO 7).* Ross Company had the following balances:

	December 31, 2010	December 31, 2009
Receivables, net	$ 200,000	$ 250,000
Sales (all credit)	$1,600,000	$1,000,000

Calculate the accounts receivable turnover ratio for 2010. On average, how many days does it take Ross Company to collect its accounts receivable?

All of the A exercises can be found within MyAccountingLab, an online homework and practice environment.

Exercises
Set A

E4-19A. *Prepare a bank reconciliation. (LO 1).* The bank statement for Rudy's Painting Company had an ending balance as of March 31 of $42,765.88. Also listed on the statement was a service charge for $27.50. Check 1305 that Rudy wrote to pay for equipment purchased March 25 had not cleared the bank yet—the amount was $6,725.15. Deposits in transit were $3,185.64. Rudy's bank collected a $1,100 note for him in March. After reviewing the bank statement and the canceled checks, Rudy discovered that the bank mistakenly deducted $1,185.19 from his account on a check that was written by Ruby's Landscaping.

Calculate the true cash balance as of March 31.

E4-20A. *Prepare a bank reconciliation. (LO 1).* The advertising firm Rog & Co. had the following information available concerning its cash account for the month of July:

Balance per Rog & Co. books, July 31	$24,180.55
Outstanding checks	5,440.29
NSF check from customer	800.00
Note collected by bank	1,600.00
Deposits in transit	4,960.58
Miscellaneous fees:	
Charge for collection of note	20.00
Order for checks	62.50
Interest earned on bank account	421.38

Calculate the true cash balance as of July 31.

E4-21A. *Prepare a bank reconciliation. (LO 1).* Prepare a bank reconciliation for Vartan's Coffee Shop at April 30 using the following information:

Balance per USA Bank statement at April 30	$ 9,547.21
Outstanding checks	4,815.68
NSF checks from customer	2,651.77
Deposits in transit	6,972.89
Interest revenue	305.77
Service charge	75.00
Cash balance per Vartan's records at April 30	14,125.42

Enter adjustments into the accounting equation needed to update the company's cash balance. What is the net effect on net income? Will net income be increased or decreased? By what amount?

E4-22A. *Prepare a bank reconciliation. (LO 1).* Prepare a bank reconciliation at December 31 for Sandra Warren's Smoothies using the following information:

Company's cash account balance, December 31	$6,275.34
Bank statement ending balance, December 31	4,607.51
Deposits in transit	2,504.57
Outstanding checks:	
4431	581.62
4432	246.12

Sandra found an error in the books: Check 4429 for $123.75 was correctly deducted from the bank account, but was mistakenly recorded in the books as $132.75.

E4-23A. *Identify and correct errors in a bank reconciliation. (LO 1).* Janie Johnson is having trouble with the bank reconciliation at January 31. Her reconciliation is as follows:

Cash balance per books	$4,015
Less deposits in transit	590
Add outstanding checks	730
Adjusted balance per books	$4,155
Cash balance per bank	$3,700
Add NSF check	430
Less bank service charge	25
Adjusted balance per bank	$4,105

1. Identify the errors Janie made in the preparation of the bank reconciliation.
2. What is the correct cash balance?
3. Enter adjustments into the accounting equation needed to update the company's cash balance.

E4-24A. *Determine the effects of transactions using the allowance method. (LO 3).* Health & Nutrition, Inc., uses the allowance method to account for bad debts. Indicate the effect that each of the following independent transactions will have on gross accounts receivable, the allowance for uncollectible accounts, net accounts receivable, and bad debt expense. Use (+) for increase, (−) for decrease, and (0) for no effect.

1. A customer pays his or her bill.
2. Of $400,000 in sales, 2% is estimated to be uncollectible.
3. Of $315,000 in accounts receivable, 3% is estimated to be uncollectible. Last year, an excess of $500 beyond what was expected (what had been recorded) was written off.

E4-25A. *Determine bad debts expense using the percentage of sales method. (LO 3).* Murray's Drug Supply uses the allowance method to account for bad debts. During 2010, the company recorded $425,000 in credit sales. At the end of 2010 but before adjustments, account balances were accounts receivable, $150,000 and allowance for uncollectible accounts, $(2,000).

If bad debt expense is estimated to be 2.0% of credit sales, how much bad debt expense will be on the year-end income statement?

E4-26A. *Analyze effects of accounts receivable transactions using the percentage of sales method. (LO 3).* At the beginning of 2011, Darcy's Floor Coverings had the following account balances: accounts receivable, $325,000 and allowance for uncollectible accounts, $(7,500). During the year, net credit sales were $793,250 and $10,000 of specific customer accounts were written off. Cash collections amounted to $1,000,000. At year end, Darcy's estimated that 1% of net credit sales were uncollectible.

1. Record the transactions (including beginning balances) into the accounting equation for 2011.
2. What is the net realizable value of accounts receivable at year end?
3. What amount of bad debts expense will appear on the income statement for the year ended December 31, 2011?

E4-27A. *Determine bad debts expense using the percentage of accounts receivable method. (LO 3).* A company started the year with accounts receivable of $30,000 and an allowance for uncollectible accounts of $(3,500). During the year, sales (all on account) were $90,000 and cash collections for sales amounted to $82,000. Also, $3,400 worth of uncollectible accounts were specifically identified and written off. Then, at year end, the company estimated that 2% of ending accounts receivable would be uncollectible.

1. Record the transactions (including beginning balances) into the accounting equation.
2. What amount will be shown on the year-end income statement for bad debts expense?
3. What is the balance in the allowance for uncollectible accounts after all adjustments have been made?

E4-28A. *Determine bad debts expense using the percentage of accounts receivable method. (LO 3).* Energy Less, Inc., uses the allowance method for bad debts and adjusts the allowance for uncollectible accounts to a desired amount based on an aging of accounts receivable. At the beginning of 2011, the allowance account had a balance of $(20,000). During 2011, credit sales totaled $500,000 and receivables of $18,000 were written off. The year-end aging indicated that a $21,000 allowance for uncollectible accounts was required.

1. Record the transactions (including the beginning balances) into the accounting equation.
2. What is the bad debts expense for 2011?
3. What information will be disclosed on the balance sheet at year end?
4. What information does this provide someone who is evaluating the firm's annual performance?

E4-29A. *Record credit card sales. (LO 4).* Executive Air Travel, Inc., accepts cash or credit card payment from customers. During May, Executive provided $200,000 worth of flight tickets to customers who used a Visa card to pay for their trips. Visa charges Executive 2% of ticket sales for card services. Use the accounting equation to show how Executive will record these ticket sales. Why would Executive accept Visa cards?

E4-30A. *Analyze and record notes receivable. (LO 5).* On October 1, 2009, ACME Athletic Equipment Company purchased athletic equipment on account for $10,500 from Sporting Goods Unlimited. On November 1, ACME renegotiated its debt by signing a three-month promissory note at an interest rate of 10%. Record the transactions in the accounting equation that would be recorded on October 1 and November 1 for both companies. Determine the due date of the note and prepare the transaction (using the accounting equation) to record the collection of the note on the books of both companies.

E4-31A. *Calculate accounts receivable turnover ratio. (LO 7).* Using the data from E4-26A, calculate the accounts receivable turnover ratio for 2011. On average, how many days does it take Darcy's Floor Coverings to collect its accounts receivable?

Set B

E4-32B. *Prepare a bank reconciliation. (LO 1, 2).* The bank statement for Rodney's Lawn Maintenance had an ending balance as of October 31 of $25,450.85. Also listed on the statement was a service charge for $21. Check 1825, which Rodney wrote to pay for equipment purchased October 30, had not cleared the bank yet—the amount was $5,415. Deposits in transit were $7,850.25. Rodney's bank collected a $1,275 note for him in October. After reviewing the bank statement and the canceled checks, Rodney discovered that the bank mistakenly deducted $1,875.93 from his account on a check that was written by Rogers' Lawn Maintenance.

Calculate the true cash balance as of October 31 and tell where it would be reported on the financial statements.

E4-33B. *Prepare a bank reconciliation. (LO 1).* The marketing firm Novak, Inc., had the following information available concerning its cash account for the month of May:

Balance per Novak's books, May 31	$1,375.21
Outstanding checks	420.85
NSF check from customer	50.00
Note collected by bank	650.00
Deposits in transit	215.50
Miscellaneous fees:	
Charge for collection of note	15.00
Order for checks	12.50
Interest earned on bank account	4.62

Calculate the true cash balance as of May 31.

E4-34B. *Prepare a bank reconciliation. (LO 1).* Prepare a bank reconciliation for Josey's Fresh Deli at June 30 using the following information:

Balance per USA National Bank statement at June 30	$15,398.05
Outstanding checks	3,215.83
NSF checks from customer	250.68
Deposits in transit	2,452.87
Interest revenue	251.32
Service charge	15.00
Cash balance per Josey's records at June 30	14,649.45

Enter adjustments into the accounting equation needed to update the company's cash balance. What is the net effect on net income? Will net income be increased or decreased? By what amount?

E4-35B. *Prepare a bank reconciliation. (LO 1).* Prepare a bank reconciliation at August 31 for Randy's Toy Box using the following information:

Company's cash account balance, August 31	$6,500.00
Bank statement ending balance, August 31	5,100.44
Deposits in transit	2,504.57
Outstanding checks:	
4051	1,052.15
4056	25.59

There was an error in Randy's books. Check 4052 for $825.69 was correctly deducted from the bank account, but was mistakenly recorded in the books as $852.96.

E4-36B. *Identify and correct errors in a bank reconciliation. (LO 1).* Newman Smith is having trouble with the bank reconciliation at March 31. His reconciliation is as follows:

Cash balance per bank	$7,578.65
Add NSF check	305.00
Less bank service charge	31.00
Adjusted balance per bank	$8,824.25
Cash balance per books	$9,362.65
Less deposits in transit	1,875.00
Add outstanding checks	427.00
Adjusted balance per books	$7,959.65

1. Identify the errors Newman made in the preparation of the bank reconciliation.
2. What is the correct cash balance?
3. Enter adjustments into the accounting equation needed to update the company's cash balance.

E4-37B. *Determine the effects of transactions using the allowance method. (LO 3).* Like-A-Library, Inc., uses the allowance method to account for bad debts. Indicate the effect that each of the following independent transactions will have on gross accounts receivable, the allowance for uncollectible accounts, net accounts receivable, and bad debt expense. Use (+) for increase, (−) for decrease, and (0) for no effect.
   a. A customer pays his or her bill.
   b. Of $300,000 in sales, 1.5% is estimated to be uncollectible.
   c. Of $215,000 in accounts receivable, 2% is estimated to be uncollectible. Last year, an excess of $200 beyond what was expected (what had been recorded) was written off.

E4-38B. *Determine bad debts expense using the percentage of sales method. (LO 3).* Extreme Sport, Inc., uses the allowance method to account for bad debts. During 2010, the company recorded $750,000 in credit sales. At the end of 2010 before adjustments, account balances were accounts receivable, $190,000, and allowance for uncollectible accounts, $(1,000). If bad debts expense is estimated to be 2% of credit sales, how much bad debts expense will be on the year-end income statement?

E4-39B. *Analyze effects of accounts receivable transactions using the percentage of sales method. (LO 3).* At the beginning of 2009, Runnels' Art Supply had the following account balances: accounts receivable, $285,000, and allowance for uncollectible accounts, $(8,250). During the year, net credit sales were $946,750, cash collections on accounts receivable amounted to $600,000, and $5,750 of specific customer accounts were written off. At year end, Runnels' estimated that 2.5% of net credit sales were uncollectible.

1. Record the transactions (including beginning balances) into the accounting equation for 2009.
2. What is the net realizable value of accounts receivable at year end?
3. What amount of bad debts expense will appear on the income statement for the year ended December 31, 2009?

E4-40B. *Determine bad debts expense using the percentage of accounts receivable method. (LO 3).* A company started the year with accounts receivable of $15,000 and an allowance of $(1,500). During the year, sales (all on account) were $110,000 and cash collections for sales amounted to $105,000. Also, $1,000 worth of uncollectible accounts were specifically identified and written off. Then, at year end, the company estimated that 10% of ending accounts receivable would be uncollectible.
1. Record the transactions (including beginning balances) in the accounting equation.
2. What amount will be shown on the year-end income statement for bad debts expense?
3. What is the balance in the allowance account after all adjustments have been made?

E4-41B. *Analyze effects of accounts receivable transactions using the percentage of accounts receivable method. (LO 3).* Designer Jean Industries began 2010 with accounts receivable of $650,000 and a balance in the allowance for uncollectible accounts of $(19,500). During 2010, credit sales totaled $7,290,000 and cash collected from customers totaled $7,500,000. Actual write-offs of specific accounts receivable in 2010 were $20,000. At the end of the year, an accounts receivable aging schedule indicated a required allowance of $12,600. No accounts receivable previously written off were collected.

1. Record the transactions (including the beginning balances) into the accounting equation for 2010.
2. What is the net realizable value of accounts receivable at year end?
3. What is the bad debts expense for the year 2010?

E4-42B. *Record credit card sales. (LO 4).* Quality Supplier, Inc., accepts cash or credit card payment from customers. During June, Quality provided $170,000 worth of supplies to customers who used Discover cards to pay for their purchases. Discover charges Quality Supplier 3% of sales for card services. Use the accounting equation to show how Quality Supplier will record these sales. Why would Quality Supplier accept Discover cards?

E4-43B. *Analyze and record notes receivable. (LO 5).* On April 1, 2010, Tropical Aquatics purchased aquariums and equipment on account, for $25,000 from Tanks in All Shapes & Sizes, Inc. On May 1, Tropical Aquatics renegotiated its debt by signing a promissory note for two months at an interest rate of 8%. Use the accounting equation to record the transactions on April 1 and May 1 for both companies. Determine the due date of the note and use the accounting equation to record the collection of the note on the books of both companies.

E4-44B. *Calculate accounts receivable turnover ratio. (LO 7).* Using the data from E4-39B, calculate the accounts receivable turnover ratio for 2009. On average, how many days does it take Runnels' Art Supply to collect its accounts receivable?

Problems
Set A

All of the A problems can be found within MyAccountingLab, an online homework and practice environment.

P4-45A. *Calculate the beginning book balance. (LO 1).* Consider the following information about Mile High Vintage Shop for the month of January:

- Deposits in transit as of January 31 totaled $3,425.50.
- Interest revenue earned during the month was $575.
- Bank service charges amounted to $25.
- The bank deducted from Mile High Vintage Shop's account a check for $130.25 that was written by Foot Hills Furniture Company.
- The following checks were still outstanding as of the bank statement date:
3012	$ 250.75
3008	420.82
3014	115.31
- The Mile High Vintage Shop accountant recorded a deposit of $215 as $251.
- The bank returned a check from a customer as NSF in the amount of $262.35.
- The balance per the bank at January 31 totaled $36,802.52.

Requirement
Determine the January 31 cash balance that appears on Mile High Vintage Shop's books prior to the bank reconciliation. (*Hint:* compute the true cash balance first.)

P4-46A. *Prepare a bank reconciliation. (LO 1, 2).* Anova Company began business in June and has received its first monthly bank statement. The company has also provided its cash receipts and disbursements information for the month as shown by the following:

Information from the bank statement:

Initial deposit:	June 1	$7,500.00
Deposits received:	June 5	$3,500.50
	June 8	$5,796.80
	June 15	$3,470.56
	June 20	$5,460.50
	June 23	$2,565.45
	June 28	$3,540.84
Checks cleared:	#101	$1,250.45
	#102	$ 345.82
	#103	$ 244.50
	#105	$ 150.47
	#107	$1,194.50

Other items on the bank statement:

Debit memos (reductions in account balance):

Automatic deduction for insurance payment	June 1	$ 256.00
Charges for new checks	June 10	42.30
Monthly service fee	June 30	35.00

Credit memos (additions to account balance):

Refund from insurance company for billing error	June 5	$ 4.50
BALANCE PER BANK STATEMENT	**JUNE 30**	**$28,320.11**

Information from Anova's accounting records for June:

Bank deposits:	June 1	$ 7,500.00
	June 5	$ 3,500.50
	June 8	$ 5,796.80
	June 15	$ 3,470.56
	June 20	$ 5,460.50
	June 23	$ 2,565.45
	June 28	$ 3,540.84
	June 29	$ 1,345.90
	June 30	$ 3,560.75
Checks written:	#101	$ 1,250.45
	#102	$ 345.82
	#103	$ 244.50
	#104	$ 2,500.45
	#105	$ 150.47
	#106	$ 423.50
	#107	$ 1,194.50
	#108	$ 825.80
	#109	$ 231.60
	#110	$ 2,350.00
BALANCE PER ANOVA'S BOOKS	**JUNE 30**	**$27,224.21**

Requirements

1. Prepare a bank reconciliation showing the true cash balance at June 30.
2. Prepare the necessary adjustments to the accounting equation to update the records of Anova Company.
3. On which financial statements and in which sections would Anova report its cash balance?

P4-47A. *Prepare a bank reconciliation. (LO 1).* On May 31, 2010, Sharp Company had a cash balance in its general ledger of $6,675. The company's bank statement from National Bank showed a May 31 balance of $8,240. The following facts have come to your attention:

a. Sharp's May 31 deposit of $1,000 was not included on the bank statement because it was dropped in the night depository after bank hours on May 31.

b. The bank's general service charge for the month was $100.

c. The bank collected a note receivable of $1,500 for Sharp Company along with an additional $58 for interest. The bank deducted a $30 fee for this service. Sharp Company had not accrued any interest on the note.

d. Sharp's bookkeeper erroneously recorded a payment to Williams Company for $192 as $129. The check cleared the bank for the correct amount of $192.

e. Sharp's outstanding checks at May 31 totaled $1,200.

Requirements

1. Prepare a bank reconciliation as of May 31.
2. Prepare the necessary adjustments to the accounting equation to update the records of Sharp Company.

P4-48A. *Identify and correct errors in a bank reconciliation. (LO 1).* Analyze the following errors that appeared on Black Electric's bank statement and in the accounting records:

a. The bank recorded a deposit of $30 as $300.

b. The company's bookkeeper mistakenly recorded a deposit of $250 as $520.

c. The company's bookkeeper mistakenly recorded a payment of $450 received from a customer as $540 on the bank deposit slip. The bank caught the error and made the deposit for the correct amount.

d. The bank statement shows a check that was written by the company for $392 was erroneously paid (cleared the account) as $329.

e. The bookkeeper wrote a check for $275 but erroneously wrote down $257 as the cash disbursement in the company's records.

Requirement

For each error, describe how the correction would be shown on the company's bank reconciliation.

P4-49A. *Analyze the effects of accounts receivable transactions using the percentage of sales method. (LO 3, 7).* Evaluate the following scenarios, assuming both companies use the net credit sales as the basis for estimating bad debts expense:

a. At year end, Bonnie Company has accounts receivable of $112,000. The allowance for uncollectible accounts has a balance prior to adjustment of $(400). In other words, there were fewer specific write-offs than estimated, leaving an excess in the allowance account. Net credit sales for the year were $315,000 and 3% is estimated to be uncollectible.

b. At year end, Clyde Company has accounts receivable of $220,000. The allowance for uncollectible accounts has a balance prior to adjustment of $200. In other words, more specific accounts were written off than estimated, so the allowance was short by $200. Net credit sales for the year were $1,525,000 and 1% is estimated to be uncollectible.

Requirements

For each situation, compute the following:

1. The bad debts expense for the year
2. The balance in the allowance for uncollectible accounts account at year end
3. The net realizable value of accounts receivable at year end
4. Assuming Bonnie Company had an accounts receivable (net) balance of $105,000 at the beginning of the year, what is Bonnie's accounts receivable turnover ratio for the year?
5. Assuming Clyde Company had an accounts receivable (net) balance of $226,000 at the beginning of the year, what is Clyde's accounts receivable turnover ratio for the year?

P4-50A. *Determine bad debts expense using the percentage of accounts receivable method. (LO 3).* Evaluate the following scenarios, assuming both companies use the accounts receivable method of estimating bad debts expense:

    a. At year end, Tate Company has accounts receivable of $89,000. The allowance for uncollectible accounts has a balance prior to adjustment of $(750). An aging schedule prepared on December 31 indicates that $2,100 of Tate's accounts receivable is uncollectible. Net credit sales were $325,000 for the year.

    b. At year end, Bradley Company has accounts receivable of $75,250. The allowance for uncollectible accounts has a balance prior to adjustment of $625. (The firm wrote off more than it had estimated.) An aging schedule prepared on December 31 indicates that $3,200 of Bradley's accounts receivable is uncollectible. Net credit sales were $452,000 for the year.

Requirements

For each situation, compute the following:

1. The bad debts expense for the year
2. The balance in the allowance for uncollectible accounts at year end
3. The net realizable value of accounts receivable at year end
4. Based solely on the data provided, how many days does it take each company to collect its receivables, and which company is doing a better job of collecting its receivables? Explain your answer.

P4-51A. *Account for accounts receivable, notes receivable, and credit card sales transactions. (LO 3, 4, 5).* Storkville Baby Boutique had the following transactions during the first half of 2011:

January 2	Sold merchandise on account to Tiny Tots Toys, $24,000. The cost of the merchandise sold was $18,000.
February 3	Accepted a 90-day (three month), 10% note for $24,000 from Tiny Tots Toys on account from the January 2 sale
February 4	Sold merchandise on account to Stuffed Animals Unlimited, $22,500. The cost of the merchandise sold was $17,250.
February 9	Received $10,000 of the amount due from Stuffed Animals Unlimited from the February 4 sale
March 22	Accepted a 60-day (two month), 10% note for the remaining balance on Stuffed Animals Unlimited account from the February 4 sale
March 25	Sold merchandise on account to Little Angels Boutique, $22,000. The cost of the merchandise sold was $16,500.
March 31	Storkville began accepting Visa cards on March 1 with deposits submitted monthly. The deposits for the month totaled $44,000. (Cost of merchandise sold was $25,000.) Visa charges a 2% fee.
April 30	Wrote off the Little Angels Boutique account as uncollectible after receiving news that the company declared bankruptcy. Storkville Baby Boutique uses the allowance method for accounting for uncollectible accounts.
April 30	April's Visa card sales totaled $52,000. Cost of goods sold was $27,000.
May 4	Received payments in full from Tiny Tots Toys
May 21	Received payment in full from Stuffed Animals Unlimited
May 31	May's Visa card sales totaled $65,000. Cost of goods sold was $34,000.
June 5	Sold merchandise on account to Tiny Tots Toys, $22,000. The cost of the merchandise was $16,850.
June 10	Sold merchandise on account to Stuffed Animals Unlimited, $35,000. The cost of the merchandise sold was $29,000.
June 15	Collected the amount due from Tiny Tots Toys for the June 5 sale
June 22	Collected the amount due from Stuffed Animals Unlimited for the June 10 sale
June 30	June's Visa card sales totaled $28,000. Cost of goods sold was $18,000.

June 30	Storkville Baby Boutique has $156,000 in accounts receivable and an allowance account with a negative balance of $700. That is, the firm wrote off more than its estimate. The net credit sales for the first six months of the year were $650,000, and cash sales were $115,000. Assume that Storkville Baby Boutique uses the credit sales method of accounting for uncollectible accounts. The firm's historical data indicates that approximately 2.5% of net credit sales are uncollectible.

Requirement

Use the accounting equation to record the preceding transactions. Round to the nearest dollar.

P4-52A. *Calculate accounts receivable turnover ratio. (LO 7).* Selected information from Mystic Corporation's balance sheet at December 31, 2010, and income statement for the year ended December 31, 2010 is as follows:

Cash	$ 35,000
Accounts receivable, net	73,000
Equipment, net	225,000
Interest payable	1,350
Net income	65,000
Inventory	350,000
Office supplies	5,000
Sales revenue	775,000
Interest expense	1,500
Insurance expense	5,000

Requirements

1. Calculate the corporation's accounts receivable turnover ratio. The net accounts receivable balance at December 31, 2009, was $87,000. (Round to two decimal places.) Explain what the accounts receivable turnover ratio measures.
2. On average, how many days does it take Mystic to collect its receivables?

Set B

P4-53B. *Calculate the beginning bank balance. (LO 1).* Consider the following about Computer Tech's cash account for the month of April:

- On April 30, cash per Computer Tech's records was $85,834.99.
- $16,008.13 in customer payments were received April 30 but not deposited until May 1.
- Checks totaling $22,461.87 were issued in April but had not cleared the bank as of the statement date (April 30).
- According to the bank statement, service charges for April were $54.50, and the bank collected a $4,900 note on April 19.

Requirement

Determine the April 30 cash balance that appears on Computer Tech's bank statement. (*Hint:* compute the true cash balance first.)

P4-54B. *Prepare a bank reconciliation. (LO 1, 2).* Rental Center's ending cash balance, per the general ledger, for October was $9,019.37. The owner deposited $1,000.66 on October 31 that did not appear on the bank statement. The bank collected a note with interest that totaled $500, of which $25 was interest, for Rental Center and charged the company $15 for the service. The ending balance on the bank statement for October was $8,870.83. After comparing the company's records with the bank statement, checks totaling $481.12 were found to be outstanding. Besides the collection fee, there was $45 in other service charges. Also, the statement showed that Rental Center earned $112.75 in interest revenue on the account and that checks amounting to $109.75 turned out to be NSF. Finally, an error in recording was discovered: Check 6715 for $419.63 was paid to one of Rental Center's vendors. The bank incorrectly deducted $491.63 from Rental Center's account, referencing Check 6715.

Requirements

1. Prepare a bank reconciliation at October 31.
2. Prepare the necessary adjustments to the accounting equation to update the records of Rental Center.
3. On which financial statements and in which sections would Rental Center report its true cash balance?

P4-55B. *Prepare a bank reconciliation. (LO 1).* On June 30, 2010, Roddick Company had a cash balance in its general ledger of $11,595. The company's bank statement from Bank One showed a June 30 balance of $12,540. The following facts have come to your attention:
   a. Roddick's June 30 deposit of $2,500 was not included on the bank statement because it was dropped in the night depository after bank hours on June 30.
   b. The bank's general service charge for the month was $40.
   c. The bank collected a note receivable of $2,000 for Roddick Company along with an additional $58 for interest. The bank deducted a $10 fee for this service. Roddick Company had not accrued any interest on the note.
   d. Roddick's bookkeeper erroneously recorded a payment to Federer Company for $892 as $829. The check cleared the bank for the correct amount of $892.
   e. Roddick's outstanding checks at June 30 totaled $1,500.

Requirements

1. Prepare a bank reconciliation as of June 30.
2. Prepare the necessary adjustment to the accounting equation to update the records of Roddick.

P4-56B. *Identify and correct errors in a bank reconciliation. (LO 1).* Analyze the following errors that appeared on either Pet Superstore's bank statement or in its accounting records:
   a. The bank recorded a deposit of $4,500 as $4,000.
   b. The company's bookkeeper mistakenly recorded a deposit of $750 as $570.
   c. The company's bookkeeper mistakenly recorded a payment of $175 received from a customer as $17.50 on the bank deposit slip. The bank caught the error and made the deposit for the correct amount.
   d. The bank statement shows a check that was written by the company for $970 was erroneously paid (cleared the account) as $907.
   e. The bookkeeper wrote a check for $805 but erroneously wrote down $850 as the cash disbursement in the company's records. The bank correctly cleared the check for $805.

Requirement

For each error, describe how the correction would be shown on the company's bank reconciliation.

P4-57B. *Analyze the effects of accounts receivable transactions using the percentage of sales method. (LO 3, 7).* Evaluate the following scenarios, assuming both companies use the net credit sales as the basis for estimating bad debts expense:
   a. At year end, Dash Company has accounts receivable of $184,000. The allowance for uncollectible accounts has a balance prior to adjustment of $(300). Net credit sales for the year were $450,000 and 2.5% is estimated to be uncollectible.
   b. At year end, Bridges Company has accounts receivable of $53,000. The allowance for uncollectible accounts has a negative balance prior to adjustment of $400. In other words, the firm wrote off more accounts than it had estimated. Net credit sales for the year were $250,000 and 2% is estimated to be uncollectible.

Requirements

For each preceding situation, compute the following:

1. The bad debts expense for the year
2. The balance in the allowance for uncollectible accounts account at year end
3. The net realizable value of accounts receivable at year end
4. Assuming Dash Company had an accounts receivable (net) balance of $176,000 at the beginning of the year, what is Dash's accounts receivable turnover ratio for the year?

5. Assuming Bridges Company had an accounts receivable (net) balance of $85,000 at the beginning of the year, what is Bridges' accounts receivable turnover ratio for the year?

P4-58B. *Determine bad debts expense using the percentage of accounts receivable method. (LO 3).* Evaluate the following scenarios, assuming both companies use the accounts receivable method of estimating bad debts expense:

    a. At year end, Vio Company has accounts receivable of $14,000. The allowance for uncollectible accounts has a balance prior to adjustment of $(300). An aging schedule prepared on December 31 indicates that $1,100 of Vio's accounts receivable is uncollectible. Net credit sales were $125,000 for the year.

    b. At year end, Demato Company has accounts receivable of $25,700. The allowance for uncollectible accounts has a negative balance prior to adjustment of $400. That is, the company wrote off more bad debts than it had estimated. An aging schedule prepared on December 31 indicates that $2,300 of Demato's accounts receivable is uncollectible. Net credit sales were $240,000 for the year.

Requirements

For each situation, compute the following:

1. The bad debts expense for the year
2. The balance in the allowance for uncollectible accounts at year end
3. The net realizable value of accounts receivable at year end
4. Based solely on the data provided, how many days it takes each company to collect its receivables, and which company is doing a better job of collecting its receivables. Explain your answer. (Use the ending accounts receivable balance as the denominator for the turnover ratio.)

P4-59B. *Account for accounts receivable, notes receivable, and credit card sales transactions. (LO 3, 4, 5).* Baby Trails Toys had the following transactions during the first half of 2009:

January 2	Sold merchandise on account to Thumbelina & Company, $14,000. The cost of the merchandise sold was $8,000.
February 3	Accepted a 90-day (three month), 10% note for $14,000 from Thumbelina & Company on account from the January 2 sale
February 4	Sold merchandise on account to Teddy Bears, Inc., $12,500. The cost of the merchandise sold was $7,500.
February 9	Received $1,000 of the amount due from Teddy Bears, Inc., from the February 4 sale
March 22	Accepted a 60-day (two month), 8% note for the remaining balance on Teddy Bears, Inc.'s, account from the February 4 sale
March 25	Sold merchandise on account to Tots R Us, $12,000. The cost of the merchandise sold was $6,250.
March 31	Baby Trails began accepting MasterCard on March 1 with deposits submitted monthly. The deposits for the month totaled $24,000. MasterCard charges a 3% fee. The cost of merchandise sold was $13,000.
April 30	Wrote off the Tots R Us account as uncollectible after receiving news that the company declared bankruptcy. Baby Trails Toys uses the allowance method for accounting for uncollectible accounts.
April 30	April's MasterCard sales totaled $30,000. The cost of the merchandise sold was $16,000.
May 4	Received payment in full from Thumbelina & Company
May 21	Received payment in full from Teddy Bears, Inc.
May 31	May's MasterCard sales totaled $45,000. Cost of goods sold was $18,000.
June 5	Sold merchandise on account to Thumbelina & Company for $12,000. The cost of the merchandise was $6,850.
June 10	Sold merchandise on account to Teddy Bears, Inc., $15,000. The cost of the merchandise sold was $9,000.
June 15	Collected the amount due from Thumbelina & Company for the June 5 sale
June 22	Collected the amount due from Teddy Bears, Inc. for the June 10 sale

June 30	June's MasterCard sales totaled $40,000. Cost of goods sold was $25,000.
June 30	Baby Trails Toys has $250,000 in accounts receivable and an allowance account with a negative balance of $1,500. The net credit sales for the first six months of the year were $890,000, and cash sales were $95,000. Assume that Baby Trails Toys uses the sales method of accounting for uncollectible accounts. The firm's historical data indicates that approximately 3% of net credit sales are uncollectible.

Requirement

Prepare the accounting equation entries to record the transactions. Round to the nearest dollar.

P4-60B. *Calculate accounts receivable turnover ratio. (LO 7).* Information from River Corporation's balance sheet at December 31, 2010, and income statement for the year ended December 31, 2010, is as follows:

Cash	$ 15,000
Cost of goods sold	515,000
Unearned revenue	25,000
Accounts receivable, net	115,000
Accounts payable	13,000
Net income	48,000
Inventory	212,000
Salaries payable	12,000
Sales revenue	1,825,000
Interest expense	1,350

Requirements

1. Calculate the corporation's accounts receivable turnover ratio. The accounts receivable balance (net) at December 31, 2009, was $122,000. (Round to two decimal places.) Explain what the accounts receivable turnover ratio measures.
2. On average, how many days does it take River to collect its receivables?

Financial Statement Analysis

FSA4-1. *Analyze accounts receivable and calculate accounts receivable turnover ratio. (LO 3, 7).* Use the following information from the financial statements of Hewlett-Packard Company (HP) to answer the questions:

From current assets (amounts in millions)	October 31, 2008	October 31, 2007
Cash and cash equivalents	$10,153	$11,293
Receivables, less allowance for doubtful accounts ($90 and $84, respectively)	$16,928	$13,420

1. Does HP have significant credit sales? If so, what evidence supports your opinion?
2. Sales for the fiscal year ending on October 31, 2008, were $117,994 (in millions). Compute the accounts receivable turnover ratio and comment on what it tells you about HP's credit and collection policies.
3. Can you tell what bad debts expense was for the fiscal year ending October 31, 2008? Explain.

FSA4-2. *Analyze accounts receivable and credit sales. (LO 3, 4).* An examination of the balance sheet of Family Dollar Stores, Inc., shows no allowance for bad debts.

1. Under what conditions would a company be allowed to omit this account from the balance sheet? Does this make sense for Family Dollar Stores, Inc.?
2. Many of Family Dollar Stores, Inc.'s customers pay with credit cards. How do you think those sales are reflected on the financial statements?

FSA4-3. *Analyze accounts receivable and calculate accounts receivable turnover ratio. (LO 3, 7).* The following information has been adapted from the annual financial statements of General Mills, Inc.

From the Balance Sheet:
May 25, 2008, and May 27, 2007
(in millions)

	May 25, 2008	May 27, 2007
ASSETS		
Current Assets		
Cash and cash equivalents	$ 661	$ 417.1
Trade accounts receivable, less allowance of $16.4 and $16.4, in 2008 and 2007, respectively	1,081.6	952.9
Inventories	1,366.8	1,173.4
Prepaid expenses, deferred income taxes and other current assets	$510.6	510.3
Total Current Assets	3,620.0	3,053.7
Property, plant, and equipment, net	3,108.1	3,013.9
Goodwill and intangible assets, net	6,786.1	6,835.4
Other assets	5,527.4	5,280.7
Total Assets	$19,041.6	$18,183.7

From the Income Statement:
Fiscal years ended May 25, 2008, and May 27, 2007
(dollars in millions)

	2008	2007
Net revenues (sales)	$13,652.1	$12,441.5
Cost of sales	8,778.3	7,955.1
Gross profit	$ 4,873.8	$ 4,486.4

1. What are the total amounts of accounts receivable for the two years given *before* considering the possible uncollectible accounts? That is, what are gross accounts receivable?
2. Do you think the company has a significant amount of bad debts? Why or why not?
3. Shortly after the financial statements were released, the company was notified that a major customer, who owes the company over a million dollars, had filed for bankruptcy. If the company had received that information before the financial statements were released, and recorded it, how would it have changed the financial statements for the period? Explain.
4. Calculate the accounts receivable turnover ratio for 2008 and 2007. (Net accounts receivable at the end of fiscal 2006 was $912 million.) Also, calculate the number of days it takes, on average, to collect an account receivable. Explain this information to the company's management.

Critical Thinking Problems

Risks and Controls

1. Suppose one person opens the cash receipts (checks received in the mail), makes the bank deposits, and keeps the accounts receivable records. What potential problems could arise from the lack of separation of duties?
2. Why would a store offer a free purchase to a customer who does not receive a receipt?

Ethics

You work in the billing and collections department of a small corporation. The firm offers a 2% discount if a customer pays its bill within 15 days. Over the years, you have become quite friendly with the finance manager of one of the customers. One day, he calls and asks you to change the date on your last invoice to his company to give him an extra week to pay and still be within the discount period. He offers to take you to dinner at the city's finest restaurant in exchange for this little favor.

It would be a simple change in the records, and no one would ever know. It would, you think, also create some goodwill with the customer. Would you make the change? Why or why not?

Group Assignment

The information given here was taken from Yahoo! Inc.'s recent 10-K filed with the Securities & Exchange Commission (SEC). In groups, discuss the activity in the allowance for doubtful accounts during the past three years. How is the level of write-offs associated with the annual balance in the allowance? Does Yahoo! appear to have a sufficient balance each year in its allowance account?

	Years Ended December 31, 2006, 2007, and 2008			
	Balance at Beginning of Year	Charged to Expenses	Write-Offs Net of, Recoveries	Balance at End of Year
Accounts receivable		(in thousands)		
Allowance for doubtful accounts				
2006	$41,857	$ 5,070	$ (8,731)	$38,196
2007	38,196	23,018	(14,693)	46,521
2008	46,521	24,937	(19,858)	51,600

Refer back to the balances in accounts receivable provided in Exhibit 4.5A on page 161 to help you figure out what's going on in the allowance account.

Internet Exercise: Intel Corporation

Intel, by far the world's number one maker of semiconductor chips, commands more than 80% of the PC microprocessor market. Go to www.intel.com and complete the following exercises:

IE4-1. Click on Investor Relations and then choose Financials and Filings. Use the most recent annual report to answer the following questions:

1. Identify the amounts reported for total (net sales) revenue for the three most recent years.
2. In general, who are Intel's customers? Who are Intel's two largest customers? Do you think Intel primarily has credit sales or cash sales? Why? Does Intel extend credit to its customers, or do Intel's customers use credit cards to pay the amounts owed?

IE4-2. In the annual report, use the balance sheet to answer the following questions:

1. Identify the amounts reported for trade accounts receivable, net for the two most recent year ends. Does this represent amounts owed by customers or amounts that the company estimates it will actually collect from customers?
2. Does Intel use the allowance method or the direct write-off method to record uncollectible accounts? How can you tell?

IE4-3. Again, refer to the balance sheet to answer the following questions:

1. Compute the accounts receivable turnover ratio for the two most recent years. Net accounts receivable at the end of 2006 was $2,709 million. You'll need this along with the 2007 and 2008 balances to compute the ratios. In which year did the company collect receivables the quickest? How can you tell?
2. For the most recent year, how long does it take on average for Intel to collect its accounts receivable?

Please note: Internet Web sites are constantly being updated. Therefore, if the information is not found where indicated, please explore the Web site further to find the information.

5

The Purchase and Sale of Inventory

ETHICS Matters

Watch Out for Disappearing Inventory

Firms lose billions of dollars from inventory theft. Individual firms, such as Bloomingdale's, Target, and Costco, will not talk about the numbers publicly, but the National Retail Federation gathers the data from hundreds of retailers. The bad news is that employee theft accounts for almost half of the over $30 billion annual losses from the disappearance of inventory.

What does that mean for a firm? Preston Turco, the owner of two specialty grocery stores in New York, uses elaborate security in his stores—special fraud detection software for cash registers, hidden cameras, store detectives, and an employee handprint identification device to clock his employees in and out. He has some other advice about reducing inventory theft: Hire and keep a happy and loyal staff.

We have all read about Bernie Madoff and John Sanford. They were at the center of frauds amounting to billions of dollars. But very few of us have read about the deli clerk who switched higher price tags for lower ones and tried to bribe a cashier to look the other way. That clerk is now in prison, according to Mr. Turco. It turns out that ethics matters at all levels of a business.

Acquiring and Selling Merchandise

An Operating Cycle

The operating cycle for a merchandising firm is a series of business activities that describe how a company takes cash and turns it into more cash. Exhibit 5.1 shows the operating cycle for a typical merchandising firm. For example, Target Corporation starts with cash, buys inventory, sells that inventory to customers (creating accounts receivable if a person uses credit extended by Target), and then collects the cash from the customers. Not shown is the fact that the purchase of inventory will result in an accounts payable, which will reduce cash when paid. The operating cycle is complete when Target collects the cash.

EXHIBIT 5.1

An Operating Cycle

This diagram shows a typical operating cycle of a merchandising firm. The firm begins with cash, then it purchases inventory, sells the inventory, and ends with the collection of cash. Even though it is not shown here, accounts payable result from the purchase of inventory, and a cash outflow follows for its payment.

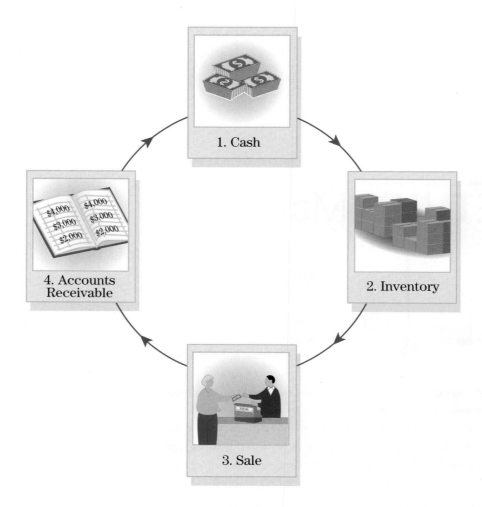

Acquiring Merchandise for Sale

Now that you know about the operating cycle of a business, we will focus on the activity of purchasing the inventory. Acquiring goods to sell is an important activity for merchandising firms. Stroll down the aisles of Staples, Inc., or OfficeMax Incorporated and imagine keeping track of all that merchandise. All goods owned and held for sale in the regular course of business are considered *merchandise* inventory. In contrast, supplies and equipment are used by most firms rather than sold by those firms. As a result, they are not considered inventory. Only the items a firm sells are considered inventory. Most large corporations have large purchasing departments dedicated exclusively to acquiring inventory. Regardless of their size, firms must keep meticulous track of their inventory purchases through their information systems. An information system refers to the way the firm records and reports its transactions, including inventory and sales.

A merchandising firm reports the inventory as a current asset until it is sold. According to the matching principle, inventory should be expensed in the period in which it is sold. So when it is sold, inventory becomes an expense—cost of goods sold. The revenue from the sales of particular goods and the cost of those goods sold during the period are matched—put on the same income statement. You can see that the value of the inventory affects both the balance sheet and the income statement. Does the value of inventory matter? On its January 31, 2009, balance sheet, Target had over $6.7 billion worth of inventory, making up over 15% of the company's total assets. That is a significant amount of the firm's assets.

We will look at the procedures for acquiring inventory and then focus on how to do the related record keeping.

Acquisition Process for Inventory

The process of acquiring inventory begins when someone in a firm decides to order merchandise for the inventory. The person requesting the purchase sends a document, called a purchase requisition, to the company's purchasing agent. For example, suppose that Office Depot, Inc., needs to order paper. The manager of the appropriate department would submit a purchase requisition in either hard copy or electronic form to the purchasing agent. The purchasing agent selects a vendor to provide the paper based on the vendor's prices, quality of goods or services needed, and the ability to deliver them in a timely manner. The purchasing agent specifies in a **purchase order**—a record of the company's request to a vendor for goods or services—what is needed, the prices, and the delivery time. A copy of the purchase order is sent to the vendor, and Office Depot keeps several copies for internal record keeping. However, no entry is made in the accounting system when a purchase order is submitted. The purchase won't be recorded until the goods are received. An example of a purchase order is shown in Exhibit 5.2.

A **purchase order** is a record of the company's request to a vendor for goods or services. It may be referred to as a P.O.

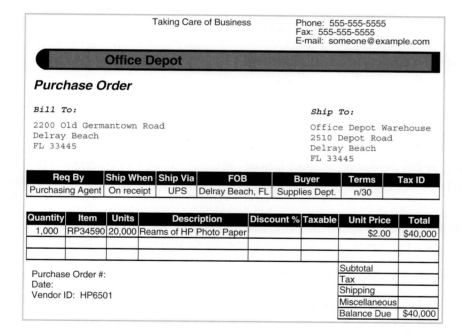

EXHIBIT 5.2

Purchase Order from Office Depot, Inc.

Office Depot's purchasing agent sends one copy of the purchase order to the receiving department and one to the accounts payable department. The receiving department will let the accounts payable department know when the goods have arrived. This is when the purchase will be recorded in the accounting records. Accounts payable will pay for the goods when it receives an invoice from the vendor to match with the purchase order. The process can be much more complicated, but it always includes cooperation between departments so that the company pays for only the goods ordered and received.

Modern technology has provided shorter and more efficient ways to manage inventory. At Wal-Mart Stores, Inc., for example, no one explicitly orders merchandise when it is needed. Using bar codes at the cash registers as each item is sold, the computerized inventory system is programmed to recognize when Wal-Mart should acquire more inventory, and the information goes directly to the vendor's computerized system. Even when the process is automated, the underlying transaction is the same: Inventory is acquired from a vendor to be available to sell to a firm's customers, and the firm wants to be sure it pays for only the merchandise it has received.

RECORDING PURCHASES. Now that you are familiar with the procedures for purchasing inventory, you are ready to learn to account for its cost. The cost of acquiring inventory includes all costs the company incurs to purchase the items and get them ready for sale. Many people in the firm need details about the cost of inventory, including the person requesting the goods, the CFO, and the CEO. This inventory information is also needed for the financial statements.

There are two ways for firms to record their inventory transactions—perpetual and periodic. These two different methods describe the timing of the firm's inventory record keeping. When a company uses a **perpetual inventory system**, the firm records every purchase of inventory directly to the inventory account at the time of the purchase. Similarly, each time an item is sold, the firm will remove the cost of the item—the cost of goods sold—from the inventory account. That is the way Team Shirts keeps track of its inventory. In the example that follows, Quality Lawn Mowers, a fictitious firm, will also use a perpetual inventory record-keeping system. We will discuss the **periodic inventory system** of record keeping—one in which the inventory account is updated only at the end of the period—later in the chapter.

We will use Quality Lawn Mowers for an example of how to account for the costs of inventory. Keep in mind that the company uses a perpetual inventory record-keeping system. Suppose that on June 1, Quality Lawn Mowers purchased 100 lawn mowers on account for $150 each from Black & Decker, a manufacturer of power tools and lawn mowers. This is how the transaction would be recorded in the accounting equation:

Assets	=	Liabilities	+	Shareholders' equity		
				Contributed capital	+	Retained earnings
15,000 inventory		15,000 accounts payable				

WHO PAYS THE FREIGHT COSTS TO OBTAIN INVENTORY? The cost a company records in its inventory account is not always the amount quoted by the vendor. One reason is shipping costs. Remember that the cost of inventory includes all the costs to obtain the merchandise and get it ready to sell. When a merchandising firm pays the transportation costs for goods purchased, the freight cost is called freight-in and is considered part of the cost of the inventory. The shipping terms are negotiated between the buyer and the vendor.

If the terms of purchase are **FOB (free on board) shipping point**, the title to the goods passes to the buyer at the shipping point (the vendor's warehouse), and the buyer is responsible for the cost of the transportation from that point on. If the terms are **FOB destination**, the vendor—Black & Decker—pays for the transportation costs until the goods reach their destination, when title passes to the buyer.

When you are the vendor and you pay the shipping costs for goods to be delivered to your customers, the expense goes on your income statement as freight-out or delivery expense. Freight-out is an operating expense, whereas freight-in is part of the cost of the inventory. Exhibit 5.3 shows the relationships among the FOB shipping point, FOB destination, buyer, and vendor.

The details of inventory purchases, such as the shipping terms, can affect the cost of the inventory. A company must pay attention to these costs because such costs can make a difference in the profitability of the company.

Suppose the shipping cost for the 100 lawn mowers purchased by Quality Lawn Mowers was $343. If the shipping terms were FOB destination, then Black & Decker paid the shipping cost; and there is no record of the shipping cost in the books of Quality Lawn Mowers. However, suppose the terms were FOB shipping point. That means title changes hands at the point of shipping—the vendor's warehouse. Because Quality Lawn Mowers then owns the goods while they are in transit, Quality Lawn Mowers will pay the shipping costs. The $343 will be

---

The **perpetual inventory system** is a method of record keeping that involves updating the inventory account at the time of every purchase, sale, and return.

The **periodic inventory system** is a method of record keeping that involves updating the inventory account only at the end of the accounting period.

FOB (free on board) shipping point means the buying firm pays the shipping costs. The amount is called freight-in and is included in the cost of the inventory.

FOB (free on board) destination means that the vendor (selling firm) pays the shipping costs, so the buyer has no freight-in cost.

EXHIBIT 5.3

Shipping Terms

Shipping terms determine who owns the goods, and at what point ownership of the goods changes. The firm that owns the goods while they are in transit must include the cost of those goods in its inventory.

Title passes here at ***FOB shipping point***…or…Title passes here at ***FOB destination***.

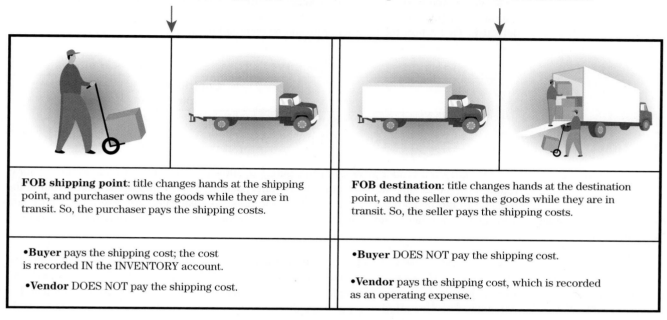

FOB shipping point: title changes hands at the shipping point, and purchaser owns the goods while they are in transit. So, the purchaser pays the shipping costs.	**FOB destination**: title changes hands at the destination point, and the seller owns the goods while they are in transit. So, the seller pays the shipping costs.
•**Buyer** pays the shipping cost; the cost is recorded IN the INVENTORY account. •**Vendor** DOES NOT pay the shipping cost.	•**Buyer** DOES NOT pay the shipping cost. •**Vendor** pays the shipping cost, which is recorded as an operating expense.

included as part of the cost of the inventory. Shipping costs are usually paid to the shipping company in cash. Here is how the transaction would be recorded in the accounting equation:

Assets	=	Liabilities	+	Shareholders' equity		
				Contributed capital	+	Retained earnings
343 inventory (343) cash						

In each separate situation, identify which company must pay the freight.

1. Company A purchased merchandise from Company X, FOB destination, for $10,000.
2. Company B purchased merchandise from Company Y, FOB shipping point, for $10,000.

Your Turn 5-1

PURCHASE RETURNS AND ALLOWANCES. Some goods may need to be returned to the vendor because the firm ordered too much inventory, ordered the wrong items, or found the goods slightly damaged. When a firm returns goods, the transaction is called a *purchase return*. In the firm's accounting system, the amount of purchase returns will be deducted from the cost of the inventory. Because the company puts the cost of the items in the inventory account, the balance in that account will be decreased when goods are returned. The details of the returns will be noted in another part of the company's information system. The firm wants to know exactly how much merchandise it is returning in any given accounting period. A firm should be sure it understands the vendor's return policy. Often, near the end of the year, a vendor will institute a very liberal return policy to make a sale. Nevertheless, the firm should buy only the amount of inventory it actually needs, not a larger amount with the idea of returning it when the next accounting period starts.

Goods damaged or defective may be kept by the purchaser with a cost reduction called a *purchase allowance*. When a company has a purchase allowance, it is like getting a discounted purchase price so the inventory account will be reduced. A purchase allowance is different from a purchase return because the goods are kept by the purchaser in the case of a purchase allowance.

When an item is returned, accounts payable, which shows the amount a firm owes its vendors, will be reduced. The inventory account will be decreased because the goods have been returned. Suppose Quality Lawn Mowers returned two of the lawn mowers because they were defective. This is how the transaction would be recorded in the accounting equation:

Assets	=	Liabilities	+	Shareholders' equity		
				Contributed capital	+	Retained earnings
(300) inventory		(300) accounts payable				

Similarly, if a vendor gives the firm a purchase allowance, the amount owed to the vendor is reduced by subtracting the amount from accounts payable. There will also be a reduction in the balance in the inventory account to reflect the reduced cost. Purchase returns and purchase allowances are often grouped together in one expression—**purchase returns and allowances**.

Purchase returns and allowances are amounts that decrease the cost of inventory due to returned or damaged merchandise.

PURCHASE DISCOUNTS. In addition to purchase returns and allowances, purchase discounts can also cause a difference between the vendor's quoted price and the actual cost to the purchasing firm. A **purchase discount** is a reduction in the purchase price in return for prompt payment. For example, a vendor offering a purchase discount for prompt payment from a customer would describe it in terms like this:

2/10, n/30

A **purchase discount** is a reduction in the price of an inventory purchase for prompt payment according to terms specified by the vendor.

This is read as "two-ten, net thirty" and means the vendor will give a 2% discount if the buyer pays for the entire purchase within 10 days of the invoice date. If not, the full amount is due within 30 days. A vendor may set any discount terms. What does 3/15, n/45 mean? The vendor will give a 3% discount if payment is made within 15 days. Otherwise, full payment must be made within 45 days. The number of days a customer has to pay an invoice starts on the day after the date of the invoice. For example, an invoice dated June 15 with the terms 2/10, n/30 gives the customer until June 25 to pay with the discount applied. The full amount is due by July 15.

A firm should take advantage of purchase discount offers from vendors whenever possible because they can amount to significant savings. If a vendor offers the terms 2/10, n/30, for example, the vendor is actually charging the firm 36% annual interest to use the money if the firm does not pay within the discount period and waits until the last day, the 30th day. Here is how we calculated the high interest rate of 36%. If the discount period expires, and the firm has not paid until the 30th day after the invoice date, the firm is "borrowing" the money from the vendor for an additional 20 days. Because the firm did not pay within the discount period, the vendor has earned 2% in 20 days. And, 2% interest on a "loan" over 20 days is the same as a 36% annual rate, determined with the help of a simple ratio:

$$2\% \div 20 \text{ days} = x \div 360$$

Solve for x and you get x = 36% annual interest—if you consider a year as having 360 days. Some companies borrow the money from the bank (at 10% or 12% annual interest) to take advantage of purchase discounts.

Suppose Black & Decker offers Quality Lawn Mowers the terms 1/10, n/30. Quality takes advantage of this discount and pays for the inventory on June 9. Recall that it purchased the inventory on June 1, so the payment is made within the discount period. Quality Lawn Mowers owes the vendor $14,700 because $300 worth of merchandise from the original purchase of $15,000 was returned. The 1% discount amounts to $147. That means that the company will pay the vendor $14,553 ($14,700 – $147). Here is the way the transaction would be recorded in the accounting equation:

Assets	=	Liabilities	+	Shareholders' equity	
				Contributed + capital	Retained earnings
(14,553) cash		(14,700) accounts			
(147) inventory		payable			

Before the payment, the balance in accounts payable was $14,700. So the entire $14,700 must be subtracted out of accounts payable. Because only $14,553 was actually paid, this is the amount deducted from the cash account. That leaves the discount amount to balance the accounting equation. This decreases the inventory account because inventory purchase was recorded at $14,700, which turned out not to be the cost of the inventory. The reduction of $147 adjusts the inventory account balance to the actual cost of the goods purchased.

If Quality Lawn Mowers did not pay within the discount period, the payment would be recorded with a reduction in accounts payable for $14,700 and a reduction in cash for $14,700.

SUMMARY OF PURCHASES FOR QUALITY LAWN MOWERS. Let us review the activity in the inventory account for Quality Lawn Mowers. First, the original purchase of the 100 lawn mowers was recorded with an increase in inventory of $15,000. Then, Quality Lawn Mowers paid the shipping costs of $343. Next, Quality returned two lawn mowers—$300 worth of inventory. Finally, the company took advantage of the purchase discount. That reduced the value of the inventory by $147. The balance in the inventory account is now $14,896 for 98 lawn mowers. That is $152 per unit. This amount is called the **cost of goods available for sale**. If Quality had started the period with a beginning inventory, cost of goods available for sale would have included the amount of the beginning inventory. A simple way to think about the calculation of cost of goods available for sale is as follows:

> **Cost of goods available for sale** is the total of beginning inventory plus the net purchases made during the period (plus any freight-in costs).

Beginning inventory	$	0
+ Net purchases (this is total purchases less returns and allowances and discounts) 15,000 − 300 −147		14,553
+ Shipping costs (freight-in)		343
= Cost of goods available for sale		$14,896

Your Turn 5-2

Jaden's Coffee Hut purchased 100 pounds of Columbian roast coffee beans to package and sell to its customers. The coffee cost $5 per pound, and Jaden's paid $100 for the bags in which to package the beans. When Jaden's received the invoice for $500 from the coffee importer, the accountant noticed that the payment terms were given as 2/10, n/30. The coffee beans were shipped FOB destination, and the shipping costs were $75. Jaden's accountant paid the coffee importer five days after the date on the invoice. The paper company that sold Jaden's the bags did not offer a discount, so Jaden's paid that firm a few weeks after receiving the invoice for $100. How much did Jaden's record in its inventory account related to these purchases?

Selling Merchandise

You now know how a company records the transactions related to the purchase of inventory. Now, we will look at what happens when the company sells the inventory.

Sales are reported net of returns, allowances, and any discounts given to customers. What you just learned about purchasing inventory also applies to selling the inventory, but everything is reversed. Instead of purchase returns and allowances, there will be *sales* returns and allowances. Instead of purchase discounts, there will be *sales* discounts.

Following are the typical business activities that take place when a firm makes a sale:

1. A customer places an order.
2. The company approves the order.
3. The warehouse packages the goods for shipment.
4. The company ships the goods.
5. The company bills the customer for the goods.
6. The company receives payment for the goods.

Computers can perform some of these steps. Whether a firm performs the steps manually or with a computer, the following objectives of those steps are the same:

- To ensure that the firm sells its goods or services to customers who will pay
- To ensure that the goods or services delivered are what the customers ordered
- To ensure that the customers are correctly billed and payment is received

SALES PROCESS. For sales, revenue is typically recognized when the goods are shipped or when they are delivered, depending on the shipping terms. For example, when Intel ships computer chips to IBM with the terms FOB shipping point, the time the shipment leaves Intel will be the point at which Intel recognizes the revenue, not when the order is placed, and not when IBM pays for the purchase. You know that the shipment of the goods is preceded by many crucial activities such as planning, marketing, and securing orders. Yet, no revenue is recognized until it is actually earned.

Exhibit 5.4 shows part of the note that IBM has included in the financial statements about its revenue recognition. Does payment need to be received before revenue is recognized at IBM? NO! Remember, GAAP (generally accepted accounting principles) are accrual accounting.

EXHIBIT 5.4

How Does IBM Recognize Revenue?

This is just a small part of IBM's note on revenue recognition.

The company recognizes revenue when it is realized or realizable and earned. The company considers revenue realized or realizable and earned when it has persuasive evidence of an arrangement, delivery has occurred, the sales price is fixed or determinable, and collectibility is reasonably assured. Delivery does not occur until products have been shipped or services have been provided to the client; the risk of loss has transferred to the client; and either client acceptance has been obtained, client acceptance provisions have lapsed, or the company has objective evidence that the criteria specified in the client acceptance provisions have been satisfied. The sale price is not considered to be fixed or determinable until all contingencies related to the sale have been resolved.

RECORDING SALES. When a sale is made, it is recorded as an increase in sales revenue, often simply called sales. Continuing our example with Quality Lawn Mowers, suppose the company sold 10 lawn mowers to Sam's Yard Service for $4,000 on account. This is the transaction in the accounting equation:

Assets	=	Liabilities	+	Shareholders' equity		
				Contributed capital	+	Retained earnings
4,000 accounts receivable						4,000 sales revenue

When a sale is made, the inventory will be reduced. Remember, this is called perpetual record keeping. Because Quality Lawn Mowers has sold 10 lawn mowers, the cost of those mowers will be deducted from the balance in the inventory account. Recall that each lawn mower had a cost of $152. Removing the 10 mowers from inventory will reduce the inventory by $1,520 ($152 × 10). Cost of goods sold, an expense account, will increase by $1,520. This is the transaction in the accounting equation:

Assets	=	Liabilities	+	Shareholders' equity		
				Contributed capital	+	Retained earnings
(1,520) inventory						(1,520) cost of goods sold

SALES RETURNS AND ALLOWANCES. A company's customers may return items, and the company may provide allowances on items it sells. These amounts will be recorded either as a reduction to sales revenue or in a separate account called **sales returns and allowances**. This account is an example of a **contra-revenue**, which will be deducted from sales revenue for the income statement. Often, you will simply see the term *net sales* on the income statement. This is gross sales minus the amount of returns and allowances. When a customer returns an item to the company, the customer's account receivable will be reduced (or cash will be reduced if the refund is made in cash). The sales returns and allowances account will be increased, and the balance in the account will eventually be deducted from sales revenue.

> **Sales returns and allowances** is an account that holds amounts that reduce sales due to customer returns or allowances for damaged merchandise.

> A **contra-revenue** is an account that is an offset to a revenue account and therefore deducted from the revenue for the financial statements.

Suppose Sam's Yard Service, the company that purchased the 10 lawn mowers, discovers that one of them is dented and missing a couple of screws. Sam's Yard Service calls Quality Lawn Mowers to complain, and the salesman for Quality Lawn Mowers offers Sam's Yard Service an allowance of $100 on the damaged lawn mower. Sam's Yard Service agrees to the allowance and will keep the lawn mower. Here is the transaction that Quality Lawn Mowers will record to adjust the amount of the sale and the amount Sam's Yard Service owes Quality Lawn Mowers:

Assets	=	Liabilities	+	Shareholders' equity		
				Contributed capital	+	Retained earnings
(100) accounts receivable						(100) sales returns and allowances

SALES DISCOUNTS AND SHIPPING TERMS. The terms of sales discounts, reductions in the sales price for prompt payment, are expressed exactly like the terms you learned for purchases. A company will offer **sales discounts** to its customers to motivate them to pay promptly.

> A **sales discount** is a reduction in the sales price of a product offered to customers for prompt payment.

Suppose Quality Lawn Mowers offers Sam's Yard Service the terms 2/10, n/30 for the sale. If Sam's Yard Service pays its account within 10 days of the invoice date, Quality Lawn Mowers will reduce the amount due by 2%. This is an offer Sam's Yard Service should not refuse. Sam's Yard Service will pay $3,822, which is 98% of the amount of the invoice of $3,900. Recall the earlier $100 sales allowance that reduced the amount from $4,000 to $3,900.

Just as with sales returns and allowances, the amount of a sales discount could be subtracted directly from the sales revenue account, reducing the balance by $78. Whether or not you use a separate account to keep track of sales discounts, the income statement will show the net amount of sales. In this example, the calculation for net sales is

Sales revenue	$4,000
Sales allowance given	(100)
Sales discount	(78)
Net sales	$3,822

Here is how the collection of cash from the customer is recorded in the accounting equation:

Assets	=	Liabilities	+	Shareholders' equity		
				Contributed capital	+	Retained earnings
3,822 cash (3,900) accounts receivable						(78) sales discounts

Notice two important things about the way the payment from Sam's Yard Service is recorded.

1. Sales discounts is a contra-revenue account like sales returns and allowances. The amount in the sales discounts account will be subtracted from sales revenue along with any sales returns and allowances to get *net sales* for the income statement.
2. Accounts receivable must be reduced by the full amount that Quality Lawn Mowers has recorded as Sam's Yard Service's accounts receivable balance. Even though the cash collected is less than this balance, Sam's Yard Service's account is paid in full with this payment, so the entire balance in Quality Lawn Mowers' accounting records for accounts receivable for Sam's Yard Service must be removed from the accounting records.

In addition to sales returns and allowances and sales discounts, a company will be concerned with shipping costs. You already learned about identifying the firm that pays for shipping by examining the shipping terms: FOB destination and FOB shipping point. When paying the shipping costs, the vendor will likely set prices high enough to cover the shipping. When the vendor pays the shipping costs, those costs are classified as operating expenses. Look back over Exhibit 5.3 on page 205. When you are working an accounting problem with shipping costs, be careful to properly identify your company as the purchaser or the vendor of the goods being shipped.

SUMMARY OF PURCHASES AND SALES FOR QUALITY LAWN MOWERS. A firm starts with beginning inventory, purchases additional inventory, and then sells some of the inventory. The following calculation shows what happened with Quality Lawn Mowers, providing a summary of the purchase and sales transactions:

Beginning inventory	$ 0
Purchases (net)	
($15,000 – 300 – 147)	14,553
Freight-in	343
Cost of goods available for sale	14,896
Cost of goods sold	1,520
Ending inventory	$13,376

SALES TAXES. In addition to collecting sales revenue, most retail firms must also collect a sales tax for the state government. A sales tax is a percentage of the sales price. Suppose that Quality Lawn Mowers sold a mower to a customer for $400 and the sales tax rate is 4%. Quality collects the sales tax on behalf of the government, so it will owe the government whatever it collects. Here is how Quality Lawn Mowers would record receipt of $416 cash from the customer:

Assets	=	Liabilities	+	Shareholders' equity		
				Contributed capital	+	Retained earnings
416 cash		16 sales taxes payable				400 sales revenue

Your Turn 5-3

Fedco sold $3,000 worth of merchandise to a customer for cash. The sales tax was 5%. How much cash did Fedco receive? How much sales revenue did Fedco earn?

Recording Inventory: Perpetual Versus Periodic Record Keeping

L.O.2
Explain the two methods of inventory record keeping.

In our examples of buying and selling inventory so far, the company used a perpetual inventory record-keeping system. With every transaction related to inventory, the inventory records were updated. As you learned earlier in the chapter, this is called a perpetual inventory system because it requires a continuous updating of the inventory records at the time of every purchase, every return, and every sale.

The other method, mentioned briefly earlier in the chapter, is called periodic inventory record keeping. When a firm uses a periodic inventory system, the firm's accountant waits until the end of an accounting period to adjust the balance in the inventory account. The accounting system uses lots of different accounts to keep track of transactions related to inventory rather than recording the transactions directly to the inventory account.

Because of technology advances, an increasing number of companies are using perpetual inventory systems. For example, when you go shopping at Target and take your cart to the check-out counter, the cashier scans each of your items. The perpetual inventory record-keeping system enables Target and stores such as Kroger, Safeway, and Macy's to do the equivalent of making the cost of goods sold adjustment at the time of sale. Of course, much more information is captured for the information system at the same time. Many companies have systems so sophisticated that the supplier of specific items will have access to the purchasing company's inventory via the Internet so that the supplying company is able to deliver goods to the purchasing company automatically. For example, Wal-Mart has many suppliers that automatically deliver goods when Wal-Mart's inventory records show that the inventory has fallen to some preset level.

Differences between Perpetual and Periodic Inventory Systems

One of the primary advantages of a perpetual system is that inventory records are always current, and a physical count can be compared to the records to see if there is any inventory shrinkage. Inventory shrinkage is a reduction in the inventory by damage, loss, or theft by either employees or customers. A perpetual system allows a company to identify shrinkage. However, a perpetual system may be too cumbersome for firms that do not have up-to-date computerized support. A company may keep the physical count of its inventory current by recording each reduction in the amount of inventory sold without actually recording the cost of goods sold. That is a way to monitor the inventory for potential shrinkage without actually using a perpetual system for the accounting records. Using a perpetual system to track physical quantities of inventory while using a periodic system to track costs is sometimes considered a hybrid system. For financial statement purposes, however, this would be considered a periodic system because accountants report the cost of the inventory, not the quantity, on the balance sheet.

When a company uses a periodic system, the accounting records for the inventory account are updated only at the end of the period. The firm must count the ending inventory and then calculate the amount for cost of goods sold. In other words, if the inventory is gone, it must have been sold. That means that any inventory shrinkage is not separately identified from the inventory sold. All missing inventory is considered inventory sold, and its cost will be included in the firm's cost of goods sold expense for the period.

Suppose a firm is very concerned about inventory theft. Which method of record keeping would be the best choice for this firm? Explain.

Your Turn 5-4

Inventory Cost Flow Assumptions

L.O.3
Define and calculate inventory using the four major inventory cost flow assumptions and explain how these methods affect the financial statements.

So far in this chapter, you have learned about the costs that must be included in the inventory account. All costs to prepare the inventory for sale become part of the cost of the inventory and then, when the goods are sold, become part of the cost of goods sold expense. That is just the beginning of the story. Inventory costing gets more complicated when the cost of the merchandise changes with different purchases.

Suppose Oakley ships 120 pairs of its new sunglasses to Sunglass Hut. The cost to Sunglass Hut is $50 per pair. Then, suppose that just a month later, Sunglass Hut needs more of the popular sunglasses and buys another 120 pairs. This time, however, Oakley charges $55 per pair. If Sunglass Hut sold 140 pairs of Oakley sunglasses during the month to its customers, which ones did it sell? The problem is how to divide the cost of the inventory between the period's cost of goods sold and the ending (unsold) inventory.

We could determine the precise cost of goods sold if we knew how many pairs costing $50 were sold and how many pairs costing $55 were sold. Suppose Sunglass Hut has no method of keeping track of that information. The store simply knows 140 pairs were sold and 100 pairs are left in inventory. There were 240 pairs available for sale at a total cost of $12,600.

$$(120 \text{ pairs at } \$50 \text{ per pair}) + (120 \text{ pairs at } \$55 \text{ per pair})$$
$$= \$12,600 \text{ cost of goods available for sale}$$

How should the store allocate that amount—$12,600—between the 140 pairs sold (cost of goods sold) and the 100 pairs not sold (ending inventory) for the month?

Sunglass Hut will make an assumption about which pairs of sunglasses flowed out of inventory to customers and which pairs remain in inventory. Did the store sell all of the $50 pairs and some of the $55 pairs? Or did the store sell all of the $55 pairs and some of the $50 pairs? The assumption the store makes is called an inventory cost flow assumption, and it is made to calculate the cost of goods sold for the income statement and the cost of ending inventory for the balance sheet. The actual physical flow of the goods does not need to be consistent with the inventory cost flow assumption. The inventory manager could actually know that all of the $50 pairs could not have been sold because of the way shipments are stored below the display counter, yet the store is still allowed to use the assumption that the $50 pairs were sold first in calculating cost of goods sold. In accounting, we are concerned with inventory cost flow—that is, the flow of the costs associated with the goods that pass through a company—rather than with the actual physical movement of goods.

GAAP allow a company to select one of several inventory cost flow assumptions. Studying several of these methods will help you understand how accounting choices can affect the amounts on the financial statements, even when the transactions are identical. There are four basic inventory cost flow assumptions used to calculate the cost of goods sold and the cost of ending inventory.

1. Specific identification
2. Weighted average cost
3. First-in, first-out (FIFO)
4. Last-in, first-out (LIFO)

Specific Identification

The **specific identification method** is one way of assigning the dollar amounts to cost of goods sold and ending inventory. A firm that uses specific identification actually keeps track of which goods were sold because the firm records the actual cost of the specific goods sold.

With the specific identification method, each item sold must be identified as coming from a specific purchase of inventory, at a specific unit cost. Specific identification can be used for determining the cost of each item of a small quantity of large, luxury items such as cars or yachts. However, this method would take too much time and money to use to determine the cost of each item of many identical items, like pairs of identical sunglasses. Companies that specialize in large, one-of-a-kind products, such as Boeing's 787 Dreamliner airplane, will definitely use specific identification. However, when you go into Foot Locker to buy a pair of Nike running shoes, the store accountant will not know exactly what the store paid Nike for that specific pair of shoes. The cost of goods sold will be determined by a method other than specific identification.

We will use a simple example to show how specific identification works. Exhibit 5.5 shows how a car dealership identifies the cost of each car sold, which is the amount the dealership paid the car manufacturer. Suppose you own a Volkswagen car dealership. You buy one Volkswagen for $22,000, a second for $23,000, and a third for $25,000. These three items for the inventory may look identical to a customer, but each car actually has its own unique VIN (vehicle identification number). By checking the VIN, you will know exactly what your dealership paid the manufacturer for each car. Suppose you sold two cars during the accounting period. What is the cost of goods sold? You will specifically identify the cars sold and their cost. If you sold the $22,000 car and the $25,000 car, then cost of goods sold would be $47,000 and ending inventory would be $23,000. However, if you sold the $23,000 car and the $25,000 car, then cost of goods sold would be $48,000 and ending inventory would be $22,000.

The **specific identification method** is the inventory cost flow method in which the actual cost of the specific goods sold is recorded as cost of goods sold.

EXHIBIT 5.5

Inventory Cost Using Specific Identification
Each car's cost to the dealership is identified as the car is sold. The cost of goods sold will reflect the cost of each specific car sold.

Weighted Average Cost

Few firms use specific identification because it is costly to keep track of each individual item in inventory. Instead, most firms use one of the other inventory cost flow assumptions: weighted average cost, FIFO, or LIFO. A firm that uses **weighted average cost** averages the cost of the items available for sale and then uses that weighted average cost to value both cost of goods sold and the ending inventory. An average unit cost is calculated by dividing the total cost of goods available for sale by the total number of units available for sale. This average unit cost is weighted because the number of units at each different price is used to weight the unit costs. The calculated average unit cost is applied to all units sold to get cost of goods sold and applied to all units remaining to get a value for ending inventory. Companies such as Best Buy, Intel, Starbucks, and Chico's use the weighted average cost method to calculate the cost of goods sold and the cost of ending inventory. Exhibit 5.6 shows how the weighted average cost method works for a shop that sells sunglasses.

Weighted average cost is the inventory cost flow method in which the weighted average cost of the goods available for sale is used to calculate the cost of goods sold and the ending inventory.

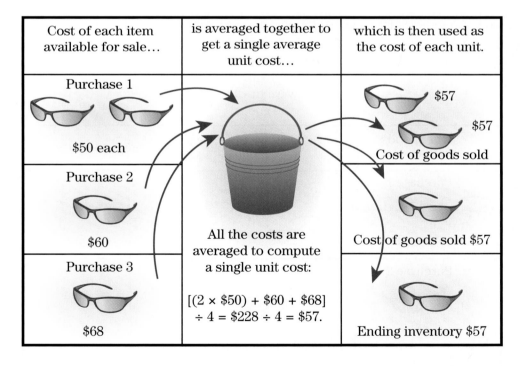

EXHIBIT 5.6

Weighted Average Inventory Costing

Consider the sunglasses shown in Exhibit 5.6. The store purchased four pairs from the manufacturer. The first two pairs cost $50, the third pair cost $60, and the fourth pair cost $68. The total cost of goods available for sale is

$$(2 \times \$50) + \$60 + \$68 = \$228$$

Averaged over four pairs, the weighted average cost per pair is $57.

$$\$228 \div 4 = \$57$$

If the store now sold three pairs to customers, the cost of goods sold would be as follows:

$$3 \times \$57 = \$171$$

The ending inventory would be $57. Notice that the cost of goods sold of $171 plus the ending inventory of $57 adds up to $228, the cost of goods available for sale.

$171 cost of goods sold
$\underline{+\ 57}$ ending inventory
$\underline{\underline{\$228}}$ cost of goods available for sale

---

Your Turn 5-5

A firm starts with 10 tea cups in its beginning inventory at a cost of $1 each. During the first day of March, the firm purchases 20 tea cups at a cost of $2 each. No other purchases were made. Between the 2nd and 31st of the month, the firm sold 15 tea cups. How much was the cost of goods sold for those 15 tea cups if the firm uses weighted average cost as its inventory cost flow assumption?

First-In, First-Out Method (FIFO)

First-in, first-out (FIFO) is the inventory cost flow method that assumes the first items purchased are the first items sold.

The **first-in, first-out (FIFO)** method is the common assumption in inventory cost flow that the first items purchased are the first ones sold. The cost of the first goods purchased is assigned to the first goods sold. The cost of the goods on hand at the end of a period is determined from the most recent purchases. Apple, Barnes & Noble, and Wendy's all use FIFO.

We will use the four pairs of sunglasses we used earlier for the weighted average method to see how FIFO works. Suppose the glasses were purchased in the order shown in Exhibit 5.7. No

EXHIBIT 5.7

FIFO Inventory Cost Flow Method

	The actual order of the items sold is not necessarily known, but the costs flow "as if" this were the flow of the goods:	
Cost of goods available for sale	Cost of goods sold	Ending inventory
Purchase 1  $50 each	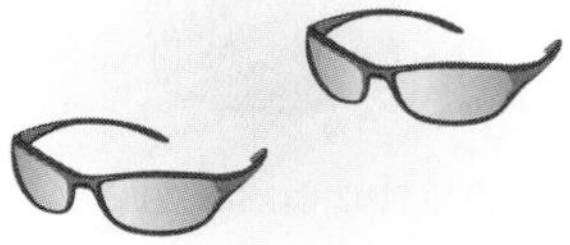	
Purchase 2  $60		
Purchase 3  $68		
$228	**$160**	**$68**

matter which ones were actually sold first, the costs of the oldest purchases will become cost of goods sold.

If the store sold three pairs, the cost of goods sold would be as follows:

$$\$50 + \$50 + \$60 = \$160$$

The ending inventory would be $68. Again notice that the cost of goods sold of $160 plus the ending inventory of $68 equals $228, the cost of goods available for sale.

$160 cost of goods sold
+ 68 ending inventory
$228 cost of goods available for sale

Last-In, First-Out Method (LIFO)

The **last-in, first-out (LIFO)** method is the inventory cost flow assumption that the most recently purchased goods are sold first. The cost of the last goods purchased is assigned to the cost of goods sold, so the cost of the ending inventory is assumed to be the cost of the goods purchased earliest. Firms from diverse industries use LIFO: Caterpillar, manufacturer of machinery and engines; Pepsico, the owner of PepsiCo Beverages North America and Frito-Lay; and McKesson Corporation, a pharmaceutical and health care company.

We will use the four pairs of sunglasses again to see how LIFO works. Suppose the glasses were purchased in the order shown in Exhibit 5.8.

Last-in, first-out (LIFO) is the inventory cost flow method that assumes the last items purchased are the first items sold.

Cost of goods available for sale	The actual order of the items sold is not necessarily known, but the costs flow "as if" this were the flow of the goods:	
	Cost of goods sold	Ending inventory
Purchase 1 $50 each		
Purchase 2 $60		
Purchase 3 $68		
$228	**$178**	**$50**

EXHIBIT 5.8

LIFO Inventory Cost Flow Method

No matter which ones were actually sold first, the costs of the most recent purchases will become cost of goods sold. If the store sold three pairs, the cost of goods sold would be as follows:

$$\$68 + \$60 + \$50 = \$178$$

The ending inventory would be $50. Again notice that the cost of goods sold of $178 plus the ending inventory of $50 equals $228, the cost of goods available for sale.

$178 cost of goods sold
+ 50 ending inventory
$228 cost of goods available for sale

Firms that use LIFO must provide extra disclosures in their financial statements. Exhibit 5.9 shows an example of the disclosure about inventory provided by Tootsie Roll Industries.

EXHIBIT 5.9

LIFO Disclosure in Notes to the Financial Statements

From Note 1 in Tootsie Roll Industries' 2008 Annual Report (dollars in millions)

Inventories:
Inventories are stated at cost, not to exceed market. The cost of substantially all of the Company's inventories ($53,557 and $54,367 at December 31, 2008 and 2007, respectively) has been determined by the last-in, first-out (LIFO) method. The excess of current cost over LIFO cost of inventories approximates $12,432 and $11,284 at December 31, 2008 and 2007, respectively.

Although Tootsie Roll uses LIFO, it discloses information about the current cost of the ending inventory. Remember that LIFO inventory will be valued at the oldest costs because the more recent costs have gone to the income statement as cost of goods sold. The old inventory is often described as old "LIFO" layers. When a LIFO firm keeps a safety stock of inventory, never selling its entire inventory, those LIFO layers may be there for a long time. LIFO is controversial because a firm can make an extra purchase of inventory at the end of the period and change its cost of goods sold without making another sale. Whether or not it is ethical to buy extra inventory for the sole purpose of changing the period's cost of goods sold is something you should think about. Even if you believe it is not ethical, you should be aware that it can be done when using LIFO.

Take a look at Exhibit 5.10 for a comparison of three methods for calculating the cost of goods sold and the cost of ending inventory—weighted average cost, FIFO, and LIFO.

EXHIBIT 5.10

A Comparison of Weighted Average Cost, FIFO, and LIFO

This exhibit compares three methods for calculating the cost of goods sold and the cost of ending inventory—weighted average cost, FIFO, and LIFO—using the example with four pairs of sunglasses. The three pairs of sunglasses sold and the pair left in ending inventory are not identifiable as to cost to emphasize that the actual physical flow of goods does not matter to the inventory cost flow method.

Purchases	Cost of goods sold	Ending inventory
$50 each $60 $68		
Weighted average cost	$57 + $57 + $57 = **$171**	**$57**
FIFO	$50 + $50 + $60 = **$160**	**$68**
LIFO	$68 + $60 + $50 = **$178**	**$50**

Jayne's Jewelry Store purchased three diamond and emerald bracelets during March. The price of diamonds has fluctuated wildly during the month, causing the supplying firm to change the price of the bracelets it sells to Jayne's Jewelry Store.

Your Turn 5-6

   a. On March 5, the first bracelet cost $4,600.
   b. On March 15, the second bracelet cost $5,100.
   c. On March 20, the third bracelet cost $3,500.

Suppose Jayne's Jewelry Store sold two of these bracelets for $7,000 each.

   1. Using FIFO, what is the cost of goods sold for these sales? What is the gross profit?
   2. Using LIFO, what is the cost of goods sold for these sales? What is the gross profit?
   3. Using weighted average cost, what is the cost of goods sold?

How Inventory Cost Flow Assumptions Affect the Financial Statements

Did you notice that the same set of facts and economic transactions in the examples you just studied resulted in different numbers on the financial statements for cost of goods sold and for ending inventory? In the following sections, you will learn how the firm's choice of inventory cost flow assumptions affects the financial statements.

DIFFERENCES IN REPORTED INVENTORY AND COST OF GOODS SOLD UNDER DIFFERENT COST FLOW ASSUMPTIONS. Exhibit 5.11 shows inventory records for Kaitlyn's Photo Shop. The shop sells a unique type of disposable camera that is relatively inexpensive. We will calculate the cost of goods sold and ending inventory for the month of January using weighted average cost, FIFO, and LIFO, first using periodic record keeping. Then, we will do each using perpetual record keeping.

January 1	Beginning Inventory	8 cameras	at $10 each
January 8	Sales	3 cameras	at $50 each
January 16	Purchase	5 cameras	at $12 each
January 20	Sales	8 cameras	at $55 each
January 30	Purchase	7 cameras	at $14 each

EXHIBIT 5.11

Inventory Records for Kaitlyn's Photo Shop

No matter which method a company selects, the cost of goods available for sale—beginning inventory plus purchases—is the same. Here is the calculation for cost of goods available for sale:

Cost of goods available for sale = Beginning inventory + purchases

For Kaitlyn's Photo Shop for January, the cost of goods available for sale is $238.

$80   + $60   + $98   = $238

(8 cameras × $10 each) + (5 cameras × $12 each) + (7 cameras × $14 each)

The inventory cost flow assumption and record-keeping method determine how that dollar amount of cost of goods available for sale is allocated between cost of goods sold and ending inventory.

Recall that a firm can update its accounting records with every sale (perpetual record keeping) or at the end of the accounting period (periodic record keeping). To keep the number of calculations to a minimum as you learn about inventory cost flow, we will start with periodic record keeping for the first examples. Then, we will repeat the examples using perpetual record keeping. No matter which record-keeping method a firm uses, the concept of cost flow differences between FIFO, LIFO, and weighted average cost is the same.

Weighted Average Cost—Periodic   When the firm chooses a periodic record-keeping system, the computations for this method of keeping track of inventory are the simplest of all methods. Kaitlyn's adds up the cost of beginning inventory and the cost of all purchases to get the cost of goods available for sale. Kaitlyn's previously calculated that amount to be $238. Then, $238 is divided by the total number of cameras available for sale—that is the number of cameras that comprised the $238—to get a weighted average cost per camera. Kaitlyn's had a total of 20 (8 + 5 + 7) cameras available for sale. Dividing $238 by 20 cameras gives $11.90 per camera. That weighted average unit cost is used to compute cost of goods sold and ending inventory:

11		$11.90		$130.90 cost of goods sold
(Number of cameras sold)	$\times$	(per unit cost)		
9	$\times$	$11.90		$107.10 ending inventory
(Number of cameras in ending inventory)		(per unit cost)		

Cost of goods sold ($130.90) and ending inventory ($107.10) add up to $238.

FIFO—Periodic   At the end of the month, Kaitlyn's knows the total number of cameras sold in January was 11. Using FIFO, Kaitlyn's counts the oldest cameras in the inventory as sold. The first items to go in the inventory are the first to go out to the income statement as cost of goods sold. So the firm counts the beginning inventory of eight cameras at $10 each as the first part of cost of goods sold. On January 16, Kaitlyn's purchased five cameras, so the firm will include three of those as part of cost of goods sold, too. That makes 11 cameras sold during the month. The income statement will show $116 as expense, or cost of goods sold.

$$8 \text{ cameras} \times \$10 \text{ per unit} = \$\ 80$$

$$3 \text{ cameras} \times \$12 \text{ per unit} = \underline{\$\ 36}$$

$$\text{Cost of goods sold} = \underline{\underline{\$116}}$$

What is left in inventory on the balance sheet?

$$2 \text{ cameras} \times \$12 \text{ per unit} = \$\ 24$$

$$7 \text{ cameras} \times \$14 \text{ per unit} = \underline{\$\ 98}$$

$$\text{Ending inventory} = \underline{\underline{\$122}}$$

Notice that the cost of goods sold plus the ending inventory equals $238—the cost of goods available for sale during January. Exhibit 5.12 shows the FIFO inventory cost flow for Kaitlyn's Photo.

LIFO—Periodic   When you use any inventory cost flow method with periodic record keeping, you start by calculating the total number of cameras sold during the month. We know that in January, Kaitlyn's Photo sold 11 cameras. Using LIFO, Kaitlyn's counts cameras from the latest purchase as those sold first. The cost of the last items put in the inventory is the first to go to the income statement as cost of goods sold. For LIFO, we start at the bottom of the list of purchases in the sequence in which the cameras were purchased.

The purchase on January 30 was seven cameras, so Kaitlyn's counts the cost of those as part of cost of goods sold first.

The purchase on January 16 was five cameras, so the firm will count four of them in the cost of goods sold to get the total of 11 cameras sold.

$$7 \text{ cameras} \times \$14 \text{ per unit} = \$\ 98$$

$$4 \text{ cameras} \times \$12 \text{ per unit} = \underline{\$\ 48}$$

$$\text{Cost of goods sold} = \underline{\underline{\$146}}$$

What is left in inventory on the balance sheet?

$$1 \text{ camera} \times \$12 \text{ per unit} = \$12$$

$$8 \text{ cameras} \times \$10 \text{ per unit} = \underline{\$80}$$

$$\text{Ending inventory} = \underline{\underline{\$92}}$$

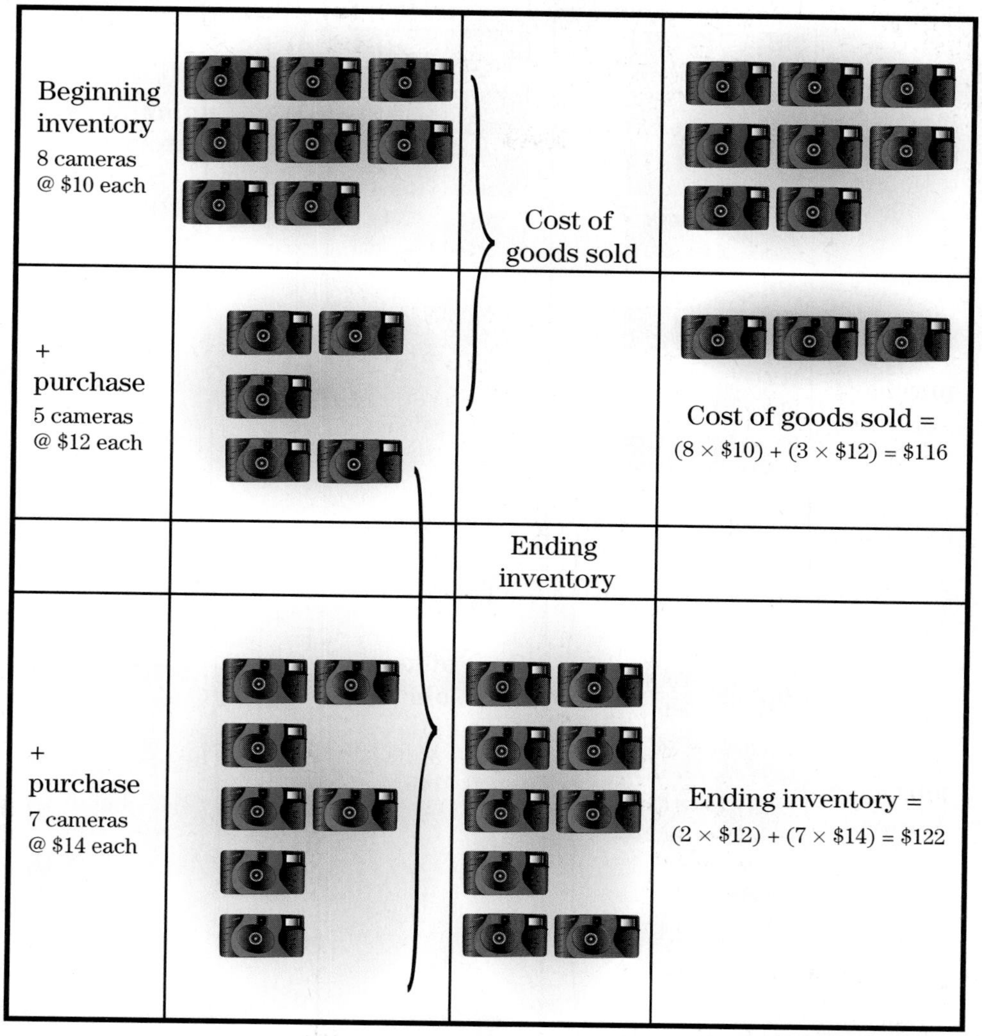

EXHIBIT 5.12

FIFO Inventory Cost Flow Assumption for Kaitlyn's Photo Shop

Even though an inventory cost flow assumption does not need to mimic the physical flow of goods, it is a useful way to visualize what is happening. In this exhibit, think of each color of camera as representing the particular cost of a camera in that purchase. The green cameras cost $10 each, the red cameras cost $12 each, and the blue cameras cost $14 each. Kaitlyn's Photo starts with 8 cameras, purchases 5 more and then 7 more, and sells 11 cameras. That leaves 9 cameras in the ending inventory—2 red and 7 blue.

Cost of goods sold = $(8 \times \$10) + (3 \times \$12) = \$116$

Ending inventory = $(2 \times \$12) + (7 \times \$14) = \$122$

Notice that the cost of goods sold ($146) plus the ending inventory ($92) equals cost of goods available for sale ($238). Exhibit 5.13 on the following page shows the LIFO inventory cost flow for Kaitlyn's Photo.

Weighted Average Cost—Perpetual   When a firm uses a perpetual inventory system, the inventory is reduced each time a sale is made. Technology makes it easy for a firm to use the perpetual system, but the calculations are a bit more complicated. Carefully trace the dates of the purchases and sales as you work through these examples.

If a company were to select perpetual record keeping with the weighted average inventory cost flow assumption, the accountant would calculate a new weighted average unit cost every time a purchase is made and every time a sale is made. The method is often called *moving* weighted average because the average changes with every transaction. A modern firm's computer system can handle this record keeping with ease. However, it can be pretty messy to use the weighted average perpetual system with only a calculator.

When Kaitlyn's Photo sells three cameras on January 8, the weighted average cost of a camera is simply the cost carried in the beginning inventory. So the cost of goods sold for the January 8 sale is $30. That leaves five cameras at a cost of $10 each in the inventory. On January 16, Kaitlyn's purchases five cameras at $12 each. The weighted average cost for a camera is now

$$\frac{(5 \times \$10) + (5 \times \$12)}{10 \text{ total}} = \$11 \text{ each}$$

On January 20, Kaitlyn's Photo sells eight cameras. The cost of goods sold is $88, and there are two cameras left in the inventory at a weighted average cost of $11 each.

EXHIBIT 5.13

LIFO Inventory Cost Flow Assumption for Kaitlyn's Photo Shop

Even though an inventory cost flow assumption does not need to mimic the physical flow of goods, it is a useful way to visualize what is happening. In this exhibit, think of each color of camera as representing the particular cost of a camera in that purchase. The green cameras cost $10 each, the red cameras cost $12 each, and the blue cameras cost $14 each. Kaitlyn's Photo starts with 8 cameras, purchases 5 more and then 7 more, and sells 11 cameras. That leaves 9 cameras in the ending inventory—8 green and 1 red.

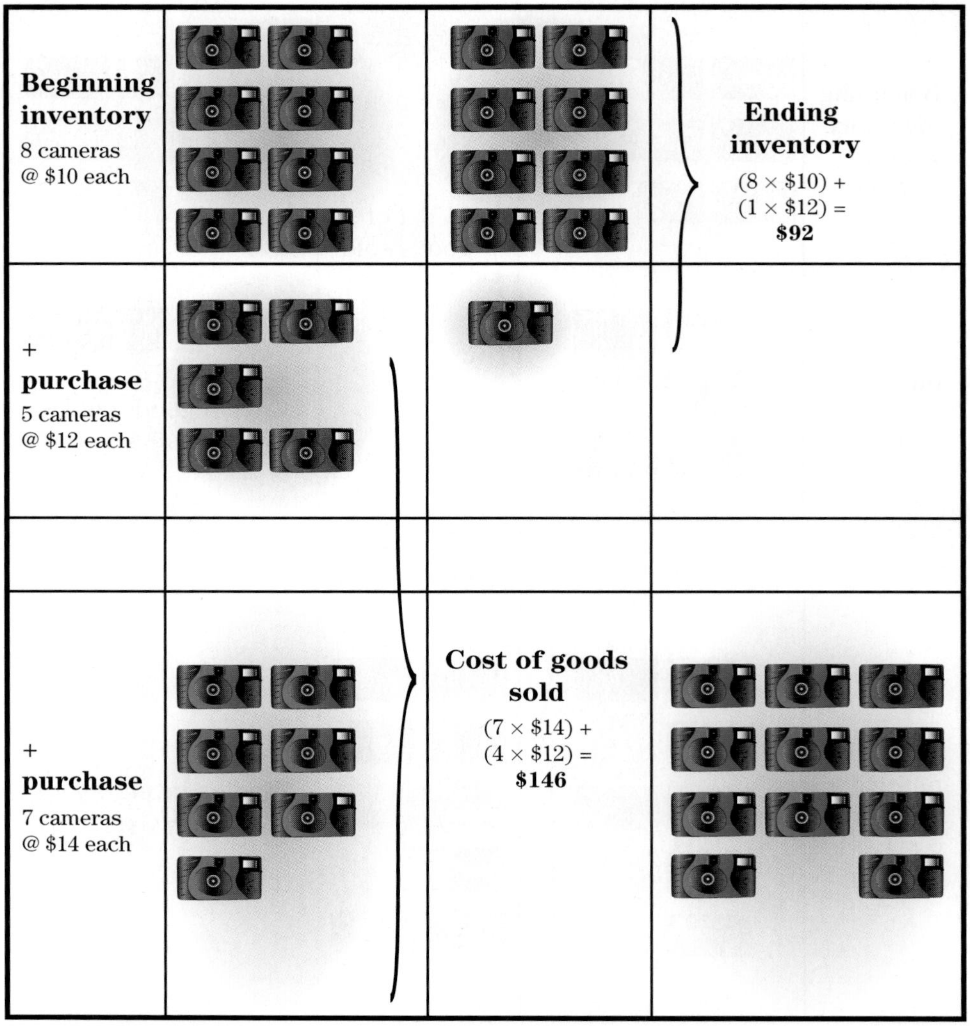

When the purchase of seven cameras at $14 each occurs on January 30, a new weighted average cost must be computed.

$$\frac{(2 \times \$11) + (7 \times \$14)}{9 \text{ total}} = \$13.33 \text{ each}$$

The cost of goods sold for the month of January is $88 + $30 = $118.

The ending inventory for the month of January is $120 (9 cameras × $13.33 each, rounded).

FIFO—Perpetual When a perpetual record-keeping system is used, the cost of goods sold for each sale must be calculated and recorded at the *time of the sale*. Only the cameras from the purchases as of the date of a sale—meaning prior and up to the date of a sale—are available to become part of the cost of goods sold. Perpetual record keeping requires you to pay attention to the dates on which goods are purchased and sold. Kaitlyn's first sale is on January 8. Only cameras from the beginning inventory are available for Kaitlyn's to use to calculate the cost of goods sold for the January 8 sale. The other purchases are in the future, and Kaitlyn's does not know anything about them on January 8.

The cost of goods sold for the January 8 sale is

$$3 \text{ cameras} \times \$10 \text{ per camera} = \$30$$

Next, eight cameras were sold on January 20. Because the inventory cost flow assumption is FIFO, Kaitlyn's uses the cameras left in the beginning inventory as part of the cost of goods sold. So the cost of goods sold for the January 20 sale must start with the five cameras remaining in the beginning inventory—that will be 5 × $10 each = $50. To get the other three needed to make the total of eight sold, Kaitlyn's will count three from the January 16 purchase. That is 3 × $12 each = $36. So, the total cost of goods sold for the January 20 sale is $86 ($50 + $36).

To summarize the cost of goods sold,

$$3 \text{ cameras} \times \$10 \text{ each} = \$ \ 30$$

$$5 \text{ cameras} \times \$10 \text{ each} = \$ \ 50$$

$$3 \text{ cameras} \times \$12 \text{ each} = \underline{\$ \ 36}$$

$$\text{Total cost of goods sold} = \underline{\underline{\$116}}$$

What is left in inventory at the end of January?

$$2 \text{ cameras} \times \$12 \text{ each} = \$ \ 24$$

$$7 \text{ cameras} \times \$14 \text{ each} = \underline{\$ \ 98}$$

$$\text{Total ending inventory} = \underline{\underline{\$122}}$$

If you refer back to the FIFO periodic example, you will notice that doing all of the work to figure out the cost of goods sold using FIFO *perpetual* gives the same amount as FIFO *periodic*, which is much easier to calculate.

Is this coincidence, or is there a predictable pattern here? Look at the particular cameras that were assumed to be sold under the two methods. You will see that it is more than coincidence. No matter how the company does the actual record keeping, either FIFO method—perpetual or periodic—will give the same dollar amount of cost of goods sold and the same dollar amount of ending inventory for the period. Unfortunately, this is *not* true for LIFO or weighted average.

LIFO—Perpetual Choosing LIFO perpetual makes life a bit more difficult for the accounting system than choosing FIFO. Each time a sale is made, the cost of goods sold is determined by using the *last* purchase as of the date of the sale. The amounts may differ slightly between LIFO periodic and LIFO perpetual because of timing differences between sales and purchases.

Kaitlyn's first sale is on January 8. Only cameras from the beginning inventory are available for Kaitlyn's to use to calculate the cost of goods sold for the January 8 sale. The other purchases are in the future, and Kaitlyn's does not know anything about them on January 8! The cost of goods sold for the January 8 sale is 3 cameras × $10 per camera = $30.

Next, eight cameras were sold on January 20. Because the inventory cost flow assumption is LIFO, Kaitlyn's uses the cameras from the most recent purchase as of January 20 to determine the cost of goods sold. So the cost of goods sold for the January 20 sale starts with the five cameras from the January 16 purchase. That is 5 × $12 each = $60. To get the remaining three cameras she needs for the total eight sold on January 20, Kaitlyn's will need to pick up three from the beginning inventory: 3 × $10 each = $30. So the total cost of goods sold for the January 20 sale is $90 ($60 + $30).

To summarize the cost of goods sold,

$$3 \text{ cameras} \times \$10 \text{ each} = \$ \ 30 \text{ Sale on January 8}$$

$$5 \text{ cameras} \times \$12 \text{ each} = \$ \ 60 \text{ Sale on January 20}$$

$$3 \text{ cameras} \times \$10 \text{ each} = \underline{\$ \ 30} \text{ Sale on January 20}$$

$$\text{Total cost of goods sold} = \underline{\underline{\$120}}$$

What is left in the inventory at the end of January?

$$2 \text{ cameras} \times \$10 \text{ each} = \$ \ 20$$

$$7 \text{ cameras} \times \$14 \text{ each} = \underline{\$ \ 98}$$

$$\text{Total ending inventory} = \underline{\underline{\$118}}$$

If you look back at the example of LIFO periodic, you will see that it resulted in a slightly higher cost of goods sold, $146. That is because, under periodic record keeping, Kaitlyn's was allowed to "pretend" to have sold the inventory purchased on January 30. That is, the inventory cost flow assumption allowed an assumed flow of goods that could not possibly have taken place.

CONCLUSIONS ABOUT INVENTORY COST FLOW ASSUMPTIONS. Firms use all of the combinations of the three inventory cost flow assumptions (weighted average, FIFO, and LIFO) and the two record-keeping methods (perpetual and periodic). Accountants and firms have modified these methods to meet the needs of specific industries. Sometimes firms keep perpetual records of inventory in units but wait until the end of the period to calculate the cost of goods sold using the periodic method. You can see from the examples we have done that the method a company selects to account for inventory can make a difference in the reported cost of goods sold, inventory, and net income.

The cost of goods sold and ending inventory for our example are shown in Exhibit 5.14 for weighted average, FIFO, and LIFO—all using periodic record keeping. In every case, notice that cost of goods sold and ending inventory together total $238, the cost of the goods available for sale. That is true for FIFO, LIFO, and weighted average using either a perpetual or a periodic system. You can read about how a firm makes this important calculation in the notes to the financial statements.

EXHIBIT 5.14

Summary of Kaitlyn's Photo Inventory Data

Inventory Cost Flow Assumption	FIFO	LIFO	Weighted Average
Cost of goods sold	$116	$146	$131
Ending inventory	$122	$ 92	$107

Note: Amounts are rounded to the nearest dollar.

Your Turn 5-7

Jones Saddle Company had the following transactions during August 2011:

- Purchased 30 units at $20 per unit on August 10, 2011
- Purchased 20 units at $21 per unit on August 15, 2011
- Purchased 20 units at $23 per unit on August 21, 2011
- Sold 35 units at $30 per unit on August 30, 2011

Calculate the cost of goods sold using each of these inventory cost flow assumptions: (1) FIFO, (2) LIFO, and (3) weighted average cost. (In this case, perpetual and periodic produce the same answers because all purchases were made before any sales.)

INCOME TAX EFFECTS OF LIFO AND FIFO. You see that the inventory cost flow assumption makes a difference in the amounts reported on the income statement for cost of goods sold and on the balance sheet for inventory. What effect do you think the inventory cost flow assumption has on the statement of cash flows? We will look at the income statement and the statement of cash flows for Kaitlyn's Photo for an explanation of what could make a company prefer one assumption over another. First, review Exhibit 5.14, which summarizes the calculation cost of goods sold under the three common methods.

Sales revenue and operating expenses are the same no matter what inventory cost flow assumption is used. Earlier we learned that sales revenue amounted to $590. Now, look at Exhibit 5.15. Notice that we have added two new numbers: Operating expenses, paid in cash, of $50 and income taxes of 30%. Exhibit 5.15 shows the income statement for each inventory cost flow assumption.

Before you decide that FIFO is best because it provides a higher net income, notice that this is true only in a period of increasing inventory costs. Additionally, we really need to look at the statement of cash flows to see what effect the inventory cost flow method has on cash flows. Exhibit 5.16 shows the statements of cash flow under each inventory cost flow assumption.

If you compare Exhibits 5.15 and 5.16, you will notice that although LIFO produces the lowest net income, it produces the largest net cash flow from operating activities. That is a direct result of the income tax savings from the lower net income. LIFO will yield the largest net cash flow in a period of rising costs of inventory. If Kaitlyn's uses LIFO instead of FIFO, it will save $9 on income taxes and have that money to spend on advertising or hiring new workers. Think of these savings in millions. Firms often save millions of dollars by using LIFO when inventory costs are rising. The disadvantage of using LIFO is that net income will be lower than it would have been with FIFO or weighted average cost.

EXHIBIT 5.15

Income Statements for Kaitlyn's Photo Using Periodic Inventory with Various Cost Flow Assumptions

Recall that the cost of the inventory has been rising. That means LIFO will yield a higher cost of goods sold and a lower taxable income. Cost of goods sold and income taxes are highlighted because those amounts are why LIFO income is lower than FIFO income.

Inventory Cost Flow Assumption	FIFO	LIFO	Weighted Average
Sales*	$590	$590	$590
Cost of goods sold	116	146	131
Operating expenses	50	50	50
Income before taxes	424	394	409
Income taxes (30%)	127	118	123
Net income	$297	$276	$286

(3 × $50) + (8 × $55) = $590

EXHIBIT 5.16

Statements of Cash Flows for Kaitlyn's Photo Using Various Inventory Cost Flow Assumptions

All inventory methods produce the same cash flows for all items except income taxes. This example assumes all transactions are cash.

Inventory Cost Flow Assumption	FIFO	LIFO	Weighted Average
Cash collected from customers	$590	$590	$590
Cash paid for inventory	(238)	(238)	(238)
Cash paid for operating expenses	(50)	(50)	(50)
Cash paid for income taxes	(127)	(118)	(123)
Net cash from operating activities	$175	$184	$179

HOW DO FIRMS CHOOSE AN INVENTORY COST FLOW METHOD? Now, think about some of the factors that might influence a firm's choice of inventory cost flow assumptions.

1. *Compatibility with similar companies.* A firm will often choose a method that other firms in the same industry use. Then, a manager can easily compare inventory levels to those of the competition. Also, investors like to compare similar companies without the complication of different inventory methods.

2. *Maximize tax savings and cash flows.* A firm may want to maximize tax savings and cash flows. As you saw in our analysis of Kaitlyn's Photo with various inventory methods, when inventory costs are rising, cost of goods sold is larger when a company uses LIFO rather than FIFO. There is a difference because the higher costs of the more recent purchases go to the income statement as cost of goods sold, and the older, lower costs are left on the balance sheet in inventory. A higher cost of goods sold expense results in a lower net income. **Although financial accounting and tax accounting are usually quite different, the IRS requires any company that uses LIFO for income taxes to also use LIFO for its financial statements. This is called the LIFO conformity rule.** So, if a firm wants to take advantage of lower income taxes when inventory costs are rising, the firm must also be willing to report a lower net income to its shareholders. Reducing income taxes is the major reason firms select LIFO. Read more about LIFO and taxes in Understanding Business on the following page.

3. *Maximize net income.* In a period of rising prices, a higher net income will come from using FIFO. That is because older, lower costs will go to the income statement as cost of goods sold. Suppose you are a CFO whose bonus depends on reaching a specific level of earnings. You may forego the tax benefits of LIFO to keep your net income higher with FIFO.

Whatever inventory cost flow method a firm uses, the method should be used consistently so that financial statements from one period can be compared to those from the previous period. A firm can change inventory cost flow methods only if the change improves the measurement of the firm's performance or financial position. Exhibit 5.17 gives an example of the type of disclosure a firm must make if it changes inventory cost flow methods.

EXHIBIT 5.17

Disclosure of a Change in Inventory Cost Flow Methods

This is just part of the inventory disclosure made by Avery Dennison Corporation in the notes to its December 29, 2007, financial statements. Notice the justification for the change in inventory methods, highlighted.

Change in Accounting Method

Beginning in the fourth quarter of 2007, the Company changed its method of accounting for inventories for the Company's U.S. operations from a combination of the use of first-in, first-out ("FIFO") and the last-in, first-out ("LIFO") methods to the FIFO method. The inventories for the Company's international operations continue to be valued using the FIFO method. The Company believes the change is preferable as the FIFO method better reflects the current value of inventories on the Consolidated Balance sheet; provides better matching of revenue and expense in the Consolidated Statement of Income; provides uniformity across the Company's operations with respect to the method of accounting for inventory accounting; and enhances comparability with peers.

If the Company had not changed its policy of accounting for inventory, pre-tax income would have been lower by $1.1 million for the year ended December 29, 2007.

UNDERSTANDING → Business

Inventory Cost Flow Assumptions and Taxes

Generally accepted accounting principles (GAAP) allow firms quite a bit of latitude in selecting a method of accounting for inventory costs. Last-in, first-out (LIFO) provides a tax benefit—lower taxes than first-in, first-out (FIFO)—in a period of rising prices. Taxes are computed based on a percentage of net income, and the cost of goods sold will be deducted in this calculation. The larger the cost of goods sold, the smaller the resulting taxable income. This is a real economic benefit that results from an accounting choice. In the past century, costs have been rising, so it would make sense for a company to take advantage of this tax savings by choosing LIFO for its inventory method. Yet, the most recent survey of accounting practices, reported in Accounting Trends & Techniques (2008), reports that only about 30% of firms use LIFO, many for only part of their inventories. What factors influence a firm's choice of inventory methods and why would a firm choose not to use LIFO?

Lower Earnings

As you just read, if a firm uses LIFO for taxes, the firm must also use LIFO for financial reporting. This is called the LIFO conformity rule. This is an exception to the general rule that a firm may use one accounting method for financial statements and a different method for taxes. With respect to

inventory, this required consistency means that choosing LIFO for taxes in a period of rising prices will result in lower reported profits for both taxes and financial statements. Why is that a problem?

Managers may worry that lower earnings will have a negative effect on the firm's stock price. Managers may have a compensation contract that is tied to earnings; so lower earnings may mean a smaller bonus.

International Financial Reporting Standards

International Financial Reporting Standards (IFRS) do not allow the use of LIFO. So if a firm has international operations, the firm will not be able to use LIFO for those operations. Many firms use LIFO for domestic inventories, but they must use FIFO or weighted average for non-domestic divisions. As we move closer to convergence between GAAP and IFRS, inventory will become an important issue to any firm using LIFO.

Most of the time, the choice of an accounting method is difficult to trace to specific economic consequences. With inventory, however, the choice of accounting method can make a significant economic difference to a firm—real dollars. That makes selecting an inventory cost flow method an important business decision.

IFRS in the *News*

One of the most well known differences between U.S. GAAP and IFRS is related to inventory. IFRS do not allow the use of LIFO. Because of GAAP's LIFO conformity rule (LIFO for taxes means you must use LIFO for financial statements), eliminating LIFO will cause some very significant tax problems for firms that have been using LIFO while the cost of their inventories has been increasing.

Explain the LIFO conformity rule. What is the usual relationship between accounting under GAAP and the Internal Revenue Service (IRS) rules?

Your Turn 5-8

Applying Inventory Assumptions to Team Shirts

Team Shirts began in January 2010 and has now completed four months of operations. As the company completes its transactions for May, inventory prices are changing. For Team Shirts, that means it must select an inventory cost flow assumption. If you look back at the first four months of transactions, you will see that inventory prices were constant at $4 per shirt. When inventory prices are constant, there is no need for a cost flow assumption. Every method produces the identical values for inventory and cost of goods sold. You will also recall that Team Shirts recorded the reduction in inventory at the same time as the related sale. You have now learned that this method is called perpetual inventory record keeping.

The balance sheet at May 1, 2010, is shown in Exhibit 5.18. As you know, it is the same as the balance sheet at April 30, 2010, from Exhibit 4.15.

L.O.4

Analyze transactions and prepare financial statements after the purchase and sale of inventory.

EXHIBIT 5.18

Balance Sheet for Team Shirts at May 1, 2010

Team Shirts
Balance Sheet
at May 1, 2010

Assets

Current Assets:	
Cash	$ 3,295
Accounts receivable (net of allowance of $160)	7,840
Inventory	1,100
Prepaid expenses	1,825
Total current assets	14,060
Computer (net of accumulated depreciation of $200)	3,800
Total assets	$17,860

Liabilities & Shareholder's Equity

Current Liabilities:	
Accounts payable	$ 4,000
Interest payable	60
Notes payable	3,000
Total current liabilities	7,060
Shareholder's Equity:	
Common stock	5,000
Retained earnings	5,800
Total shareholder's equity	10,800
Total liabilities and shareholder's equity	$17,860

The transactions for May are shown in Exhibit 5.19.

EXHIBIT 5.19

Accounting Equation Worksheet for Team Shirts for May 2010

	Cash	All other assets	(Account)	All liabilities	(Account)	Common Stock	Retained Earnings	(Account)
	Assets			**= Liabilities**		**+ Shareholder's Equity**		
						Contributed Capital	Retained Earnings	
Beginning Balances	$ 3,295	$8,000 (160) 1,100 25 1,800 4,000 (200)	Accounts receivable Allowance Inventory Prepaid insurance Prepaid rent Computer Accumulated depreciation	4,000 3,000 60	Accounts payable Notes payable Interest payable	$5,000	$5,800	
Transactions 1	(300)	300	Prepaid insurance					
2	7,900	(7,900)	Accounts receivable					
3	(4,000)			(4,000)	Accounts payable			
4		4,800	Inventory	4,800	Accounts payable			
5	9,900			9,900	Unearned revenue			
6		8,800 (3,200)	Accounts receivable Inventory				8,800 (3,200)	Sales Cost of goods sold
7	(500)	300	Prepaid Web design				(200)	Web design expense
8		(100) 100	Accounts receivable Allowance					
9		4,200	Inventory	4,200	Accounts payable			
10	(3,090)			(3,000) (60)	Notes payable Interest payable		(30)	Interest expense
11	(400)						(400)	Operating expenses
A-1		(75)	Prepaid insurance				(75)	Insurance expense
A-2		(1,200)	Prepaid rent				(1,200)	Rent expense
A-3		(50)	Prepaid Web design				(50)	Web design expense
A-4		(100)	Accumulated depreciation				(100)	Depreciation expense
A-5		(1,800)	Inventory	(4,950)	Unearned revenue		4,950 (1,800)	Sales Cost of goods sold
A-6		(116)	Allowance				(116)	Bad debts expense
	$12,805 + **$18,524**			**= $13,950**		**+ $5,000**	**+ $12,379**	

■ Income statement   ▬ Statement of changes in shareholder's equity   ▬ Balance sheet   ▬ Statement of cash flows

Assets (non cash)			Liabilities	
Accounts receivable	$ 8,800		Accounts payable	$ 9,000
Allowance	(176)		Interest payable	0
Inventory	5,100		Notes payable	0
Prepaid insurance	250		Unearned revenue	4,950
Prepaid rent	600		Total	$13,950
Prepaid Web design	250			
Computer	4,000			
Accum depreciation	(300)			
Total	$18,524			

First, we will record each transaction in the accounting equation. Then, we will review the records to identify any needed adjustments.

Transaction 1: Payment for insurance Team Shirts pays cash for insurance premium, $300 for three months; coverage starts May 15. The firm records all insurance payments to prepaid insurance. The expense will be recorded as an adjustment at the end of the month.

Assets	=	Liabilities	+	Shareholder's equity	
				Contributed capital	+ Retained earnings
(300) cash 300 prepaid insurance					

Transaction 2: Collection on accounts receivable Team Shirts collects $7,900 from customers who purchased shirts in prior months. No revenue is recognized because the revenue was already recognized when the sale was originally made. This collection simply exchanges one asset—accounts receivable—for another—cash.

Assets	=	Liabilities	+	Shareholder's equity	
				Contributed capital	+ Retained earnings
7,900 cash (7,900) accounts receivable					

Transaction 3: Payment on accounts payable Team Shirts makes a payment of $4,000 on accounts payable. This pays off the total amount of the obligation.

Assets	=	Liabilities	+	Shareholder's equity	
				Contributed capital	+ Retained earnings
(4,000) cash		(4,000) accounts payable			

Transaction 4: Purchase of inventory Team Shirts purchases 1,200 shirts at $4 each on account.

Assets	=	Liabilities	+	Shareholder's equity	
				Contributed capital	+ Retained earnings
4,800 inventory		4,800 accounts payable			

Transaction 5: Receipt of unearned revenue Team Shirts agrees to sell the local school system 900 shirts for $11 each. Team Shirts collects cash of $9,900 in advance of delivery. Half the shirts will be delivered on May 30, and the other half will be delivered in June.

Assets	=	Liabilities	+	Shareholder's equity	
				Contributed capital	+ Retained earnings
9,900 cash		9,900 unearned revenue			

Transaction 6: Sales Team Shirts sells 800 shirts at $11 each, all on account. That means the company extended credit to its customers, and Team Shirts will collect later.

Assets	=	Liabilities	+	Shareholder's equity		
				Contributed capital	+	Retained earnings
8,800 accounts receivable						8,800 sales revenue

At the same time sales revenue is recorded, Team Shirts records the reduction in inventory. As you know, the reduction in inventory is an expense called cost of goods sold. At this point, all of the items in inventory cost the same amount—$4. Team Shirts has decided to use FIFO, but there is no actual impact of that choice for this transaction. All of the shirts Team Shirts sold cost $4, so cost of goods sold is $3,200. There were 275 shirts at $4 each in the beginning inventory, so those are assumed to be sold first. The remaining 525 shirts come from the recent purchase of 1,200 shirts at $4 each.

Assets	=	Liabilities	+	Shareholder's equity		
				Contributed capital	+	Retained earnings
(3,200) inventory						(3,200) cost of goods sold

Transaction 7: Payment for Web design and for six months' worth of maintenance Team Shirts hires Web designers to start a Web page for the firm. The firm pays $200 for Web design and $300 for six months' worth of maintenance fees. A full month of maintenance will be charged for May.

Assets	=	Liabilities	+	Shareholder's equity		
				Contributed capital	+	Retained earnings
300 prepaid Web design (500) cash						(200) Web design expense

Transaction 8: Write off of a specific accounts receivable Team Shirts writes off the $100 accounts receivable balance of Ace Sports, a customer that has declared bankruptcy.

Assets	=	Liabilities	+	Shareholder's equity		
				Contributed capital	+	Retained earnings
(100) accounts receivable						
100 allowance for bad debts						

Transaction 9: Purchase of inventory Team Shirts purchases 1,000 shirts at a cost of $4.20 each, on account.

Assets	=	Liabilities	+	Shareholder's equity		
				Contributed capital	+	Retained earnings
4,200 inventory		4,200 accounts payable				

Transaction 10: Repayment of note with interest Team Shirts started the month with a short-term note payable of $3,000. It was issued on March 1, so three months' worth of interest is also paid. The interest rate on the note is 12%. Previously, at the end of March and again at the end of April, the interest for the month was accrued. That is, each month $30 of interest expense and interest payable was recorded. So the payment of interest here for three months is $90, $60 of which was interest payable and $30 will be recorded as interest expense for May. The payment of the note and the payment of the interest are shown separately because it will be easier to construct the statement of cash flows if these are separate. The repayment of the note is a financing cash outflow, whereas the interest payment is an operating cash flow. Interest payments and receipts are always classified as cash from operating activities on the statement of cash flows.

Assets	=	Liabilities	+	Shareholder's equity		
				Contributed capital	+	Retained earnings
(3,000) cash		(3,000) notes payable				
(90) cash		(60) interest payable				(30) interest expense

Transaction 11: Payment of operating expenses Team Shirts pays cash for other operating expenses of $400.

Assets	=	Liabilities	+	Shareholder's equity		
				Contributed capital	+	Retained earnings
(400) cash						(400) operating expenses

All of these routine transactions are recorded in the accounting equation worksheet in Exhibit 5.19. Now, Team Shirts must make several adjustments before it can prepare the financial statements for May. As you read about each adjustment, identify the entry in the accounting equation worksheet.

Adjustment 1: Insurance expense needs to be recorded. The total expense for May is $75. That is the total of $25 from the first half of the month (which uses up the beginning balance in prepaid insurance) and $50 for the second half of the month (from the new policy at $100 per month, beginning May 15).

Adjustment 2: Rent expense needs to be recorded. The amount is $1,200 for the month.

Adjustment 3: The Web service of $50 for May needs to be recorded.

Adjustment 4: Depreciation expense needs to be recorded on the computer, $100 per month.

Adjustment 5: Half of the 900 shirts were delivered to the schools, so half of the unearned revenue needs to be recognized. That is, $4,950 in revenue should be recorded. The reduction in inventory must also be recorded. Recall that Team Shirts is using FIFO. There are 675 shirts left that cost $4 each and a recent purchase of 1,000 shirts at $4.20 each. Using FIFO, the 450 shirts that were delivered (half of the 900 the school paid for in advance) are assumed to be from the oldest inventory, so the cost of goods sold is 450 × $4 = $1,800.

Adjustment 6: The firm must record bad debt expense based on the ending balance in accounts receivable. The ending balance is $8,800, and the firm estimates that 2% will be uncollectible. That is $176. However, the allowance account has $60 left from the prior month. The allowance balance started at $160. You can see this on the May 1 balance sheet. Then, in Transaction 8, a specific account for $100 was written off. This reduced the allowance balance to $60. Now, at the end of May, Team Shirts wants the balance to be $176 (2% of ending accounts receivable). That means that only $116 will be recorded as bad debts expense for May. The adjustment in the accounting equation will increase the allowance by $116 to an ending balance of the desired $176.

After the adjustments are made, the financial statements can be prepared. Make sure you can trace each amount on the financial statements in Exhibit 5.20 to the accounting equation worksheet in Exhibit 5.19.

EXHIBIT 5.20

Financial Statements for Team Shirts for May 2010

Team Shirts
Income Statement
For the month ended May 31, 2010

Sales revenue		$13,750
Expenses:		
Cost of goods sold	$5,000	
Operating expenses	400	
Bad debts expense	116	
Insurance expense	75	
Rent expense	1,200	
Web design expenses	250	
Depreciation expense	100	
Interest expense	30	
Total expenses		7,171
Net income		$ 6,579

Team Shirts
Statement of Changes in Shareholder's Equity
For the month ended May 31, 2010

Beginning common stock	$ 5,000
Common stock issued during the month	–
Ending common stock	$ 5,000
Beginning retained earnings	$ 5,800
Net income	6,579
Dividends	–
Ending retained earnings	$12,379
Total shareholder's equity	$17,379

Team Shirts
Statement of Cash Flows
For the month ended May 31, 2010

Cash from operating activities:	
Cash collected from customers	$17,800
Cash paid to vendors	(4,000)
Cash paid for interest	(90)
Cash paid for operating expenses	(1,200)
Net cash from operating activities	$12,510
Cash from investing activities:	0
Cash from financing activities:	
Pay off Note Payable	(3,000)
Increase in cash	9,510
Beginning cash balance	3,295
Ending cash balance	$12,805

Team Shirts
Balance Sheet
At May 31, 2010

Assets	
Current Assets:	
Cash	$12,805
Accounts receivable (net of allowance of $176)	8,624
Inventory	5,100
Prepaid expenses	1,100
Total current assets	27,629
Computer (net of accumulated depreciation of $300)	3,700
Total assets	$31,329
Liabilities and Shareholder's Equity	
Current Liabilities:	
Accounts payable	$ 9,000
Unearned revenue	4,950
Total current liabilities	13,950
Shareholder's Equity:	
Common stock	5,000
Retained earnings	12,379
Total shareholder's equity	17,379
Total liabilities and shareholder's equity	$31,329

L.O.5
Explain the lower-of-cost-or-market rule for valuing inventory.

Complications in Valuing Inventory: Lower-of-Cost-or-Market Rule

Inventory is an asset on the balance sheet, recorded at cost. As you have seen, that asset can be a significant amount. To make sure that inventory is not overstated, GAAP require companies to compare the cost of their inventory at the end of the period with the market value of that inventory, based on either individual items or total inventory. For the financial statements, the company must use the lower of either the cost or the market value of its inventory. This is called the **lower-of-cost-or-market (LCM) rule.** When you study any company's annual report, the note about inventory methods will almost always mention that the lower-of-cost-or-market valuation rule has been applied.

Estimating the market value of inventory is the difficult part of the LCM rule. The market value used is **replacement cost.** That is the cost to buy similar inventory items from the supplier to replace the inventory. A company compares the cost of the inventory, as it is recorded in the

> The **lower-of-cost-or-market (LCM) rule** is the rule that requires firms to use the lower of either the cost or the market value (replacement cost) of its inventory on the date of the balance sheet.

accounting records, to the replacement cost at the date of the financial statements and uses the lower of the two values for the balance sheet. Although there are a few more complications in applying this rule, the concept is straightforward. There is a floor (lowest possible value) and a ceiling (highest possible value), but these computations are beyond the scope of an introductory course. The main point is that inventory must not be overstated. When the inventory value is reduced, the adjustment to reduce the inventory also reduces net income.

Comparing the cost of inventory to its current replacement cost is more than a simple accounting requirement. Information about the current replacement cost of inventory is important for formulating sales strategies related to various items in inventory and for inventory-purchasing decisions.

It is common for the inventory of companies such as T-Mobile and Sony to lose value or quickly become obsolete because of new technology. These companies cannot know the value of the inventory with certainty, so they will often estimate the reduction in inventory. Sometimes this is shown on the financial statements as a "reserve for obsolescence." (Remember, a reserve like this is *not* cash.) Knowing how a company values its inventory is essential for analyzing a company's financial statements, and you will find this information in the notes to the financial statements.

> **Replacement cost** is the cost to buy similar items in inventory from the supplier to replace the inventory.

Financial Statement Analysis

Gross Profit Ratio

Each of the four financial statements is useful to investors and other users. For example, the balance sheet tells investors about a firm's financial position and its ability to meet its short-term obligations. The current ratio you studied in Chapter 2 is calculated from amounts on the balance sheet. In addition to an analysis of a firm's financial position and ability to meet its short-term obligations, investors are very interested in a firm's performance. That information comes from the income statement. An important ratio for measuring a firm's performance is the **gross profit ratio**, also called the gross margin ratio. You know that gross profit equals sales minus cost of goods sold. The gross profit ratio is defined as gross profit divided by sales. The ratio measures the portion of sales dollars a company has left after paying for the goods sold. The remaining amount must cover all other operating costs, such as salary expense and insurance expense, and be large enough to have something left over for profit.

> **L.O.6**
> Define and calculate the gross profit ratio and the inventory turnover ratio.

> **Gross profit ratio** is equal to the gross profit (sales minus cost of goods sold) divided by sales. It is a ratio for evaluating firm performance.

$$\text{Gross profit ratio} = \frac{\text{Sales} - \text{Cost of goods sold}}{\text{Sales}}$$

We will calculate the gross profit ratio for Target from its income statement shown in Exhibit 5.21 on the following page. For its fiscal year ended January 30, 2009 (fiscal year 2008), Target's gross profit was $18,727 million ($62,884 million − $44,157 million). The gross profit ratio—gross profit as a percent of sales—was 29.8%.

The gross profit ratio is very important to a retail company. As with all ratios, it is useful to compare this ratio across several years. Look at Target's income statement, and compute the gross profit ratio for its fiscal year ended February 2, 2008 (fiscal year 2007). Divide the gross profit of $18,542 million by sales of $61,471 million for a gross margin ratio of 30.2%. From 2007 to 2008, Target's gross margin ratio decreased slightly.

A retail company is particularly interested in its gross profit ratio and how it compares to that of prior years or that of competitors. When managers talk about a product's margins, they are talking about the gross profit. There is no specific amount that signifies an acceptable or good gross profit. For example, the margin on a grocery store item is usually smaller than that of a new car because a grocery store turns over its inventory more frequently than does a car dealership. When a grocery store such as Kroger or Whole Foods Market buys a grocery item, such as a gallon of milk, the sales price of that item is often not much higher than its cost. Because a grocery store sells so many different items and a large quantity of each, the gross profit on each item does not need to be very big to accumulate into a sizable gross profit for the store. However, when a company sells larger items, such as cars, televisions, or clothing, and not so many of them, it needs to have a larger gross profit on each item. For its fiscal year ended September 28, 2008, Whole Foods' gross profit ratio was 34%, whereas Guess?, Inc., with fiscal year end February 2, 2008, had a gross profit ratio of 45%. (See Exhibit 5.22 on page 233.)

EXHIBIT 5.21

Target Corporation: Consolidated Statements of Operations

Target's year end for its fiscal year 2008 was January 31, 2009. Even though only a year is given at the top, you can find the exact date of the firm's year end on the balance sheet (not shown here).

Target Corporation
Consolidated Statements of Operations
(in millions)

| | For fiscal years | | |
	2008	2007	2006
Sales	**$62,884**	$61,471	$57,878
Credit card revenues	**2,064**	1,896	1,612
Total revenues	**64,948**	63,367	59,490
Cost of sales	**44,157**	42,929	40,366
Selling, general and administrative expenses	**12,954**	12,670	11,852
Credit card expenses	**1,609**	837	707
Depreciation and amortization	**1,826**	1,659	1,496
Earnings before interest expense and income taxes	**4,402**	5,272	5,069
Net interest expense			
Nonrecourse debt collateralized by credit card receivables ..	**167**	133	98
Other interest expense	**727**	535	499
Interest income	**(28)**	(21)	(25)
Net interest expense	**866**	647	572
Earnings before income taxes	**3,536**	4,625	4,497
Provision for income taxes	**1,322**	1,776	1,710
Net earnings	**$ 2,214**	$ 2,849	$ 2,787

Inventory Turnover Ratio

Merchandising companies make a profit by selling their inventory. The faster they sell their inventory, the more profit they make. Buying inventory and then selling it makes the inventory "turn over." After a company sells its inventory, it must purchase new inventory. The more often this happens, the more profit a company makes. Financial analysts and investors are very interested in how quickly a company turns over its inventory. Inventory turnover rates vary a great deal from industry to industry. Industries with small gross margins, such as the candy industry, usually turn over their inventories more quickly than industries with large gross margins, such as the auto industry.

> The **inventory turnover ratio** is defined as cost of goods sold divided by average inventory. It is a measure of how quickly a firm sells its inventory.

The **inventory turnover ratio** is defined as cost of goods sold divided by the average inventory on hand during the year. The ratio measures how many times a firm turns over its inventory during the year—how quickly a firm is selling its inventory.

$$\text{Inventory turnover ratio} = \frac{\text{Cost of goods sold}}{(\text{Beginning inventory} + \text{ending inventory}) \div 2}$$

We will compare the inventory turnover ratio for Whole Foods Market, Inc., a large grocery chain, with that for Guess?, Inc., a smaller specialty clothing store chain. The year's cost of goods sold for each firm is found on its income statement, and average inventory can be calculated from the beginning and ending inventory amounts shown on comparative balance sheets. To get the average, we will just add the beginning and year-end inventory balances and divide by two. The data and calculations are shown in Exhibit 5.22. Notice that although Whole Foods has a lower gross profit ratio than Guess, the firm turns over its inventory many more times each year than Guess.

> The **average days in inventory** is the number of days it takes, on average, to sell an item of inventory.

Although managers want to turn over inventory rapidly, they also want enough inventory on hand to meet customer demand. Managers can monitor inventory by using the inventory turnover ratio to find out the number of days items stay in inventory. This is called the **average days in inventory**. For Whole Foods, 365 (days in a year) divided by 17.0 (inventory turnover ratio) = 21.5 days. For Guess, the average number of days in inventory is just over 77 days (365 ÷ 4.7).

(dollars in thousands) For fiscal year ended	Whole Foods Market, Inc. September 28, 2008	Guess?, Inc. February 2, 2008
(1) Sales	$7,953,912	$1,749,916
(2) Cost of goods sold	5,247,207	957,147
(3) Gross profit	2,706,705	792,769
Gross profit ratio (3) ÷ (1)	34%	45%
(4) Inventory, beginning of the year	288,112	173,668
(5) Inventory, end of the year	327,452	232,159
(6) Average inventory ((4) + (5)) ÷ 2	307,782	202,914
Inventory turnover ratio (2) ÷ (6)	17.0 times	4.7 times

Managers closely watch both the inventory turnover ratio and average days in inventory. If a manager sees the average days in inventory increasing, indicating that items are being held in inventory longer, it could indicate potential problems with old or obsolete inventory.

Your Turn 5-9

Wal-Mart reported inventory of $35,159 and $34,511 on its balance sheets at the end of the fiscal years 2007 and 2008, respectively. During the 2008 fiscal year (ended on January 31, 2009), the company's cost of goods sold was $306,158. (All dollars are in millions.) What was Wal-Mart's inventory turnover ratio for the year? How many days, on average, did merchandise remain in the inventory?

Business Risk, Control, and Ethics

L.O.7
Describe the risks associated with inventory and the controls that minimize those risks.

Inventory is a very important asset and ties up a large percentage of a firm's cash. Managing inventory is important to a successful business. Making sure there is enough inventory on hand to meet demand, without having too much inventory because it is costly to store and maintain, is key for merchandising and manufacturing firms. Wal-Mart, for example, has spent millions of dollars to establish and maintain its state-of-the-art inventory system.

In addition to the routine management of inventory, however, the firm must also evaluate and control the risk of losing inventory. Have you ever read how much money retail companies lose from shoplifting? The 20th Annual Retail Theft Survey reported that over $6.7 billion was lost from shoplifting and employee theft in just 24 U.S. retail companies in 2007. It is no surprise that retail firms such as Macy's and Target are very concerned about inventory theft. All consumers pay for that loss in higher merchandise prices; therefore, good controls on inventory are important to both the company and the consumer.

Like any company asset, the inventory must be protected from damage and theft. The policies and procedures we have discussed can help reduce the risks associated with the actual purchase of the inventory—selecting a reliable vendor and making sure the items received are the ones ordered. To safeguard inventory from theft, companies can use controls such as locking storage rooms and limiting access to the inventory. When you buy clothes from Abercrombie & Fitch or The Gap, you might notice a sensor attached to the clothing that the salesclerk must remove before you leave the store. You may have experienced the unpleasant beeping of a sensor if a store clerk forgets to remove the device.

Segregation of duties is a control that helps companies minimize the risk of losing inventory to error or theft. The person who keeps the inventory records should not be the same person who has physical control of the inventory. This separation of record keeping and physical control of assets makes it impossible for a single individual to steal the inventory and cover it up with false record keeping. When this control is in place and functioning properly, it would take collusion—two or more people getting together on the plan—to lose inventory in this way.

Large retail firms such as Target have extensive inventory controls. There are many places—from the receiving dock to the front door of the store—where Target must keep an eye on its inventory. When goods arrive at the receiving dock, a clerk will make a record of the type and amount of merchandise that has arrived on a copy of the original purchase order without any quantities listed. The firm wants the receiving clerk to independently check the type and amount of goods that have been received. This record will be sent to the accounts payable department where a clerk in that department will compare the record of the goods received with the original purchase order, which was sent over earlier from the purchasing department. Do you see the controls in place to safeguard the incoming shipments of merchandise? Several different departments are keeping a record of the goods ordered and received. The receiving clerk sends the merchandise to the inventory department where physical custody of the goods is separate from the record keeping, which we have seen is verified by several departments.

Obsolescence

Inventory is such an important asset to a firm that financial analysts and investors are very concerned that it is properly reported on the financial statements. In addition to protecting inventory from damage and theft, firms risk losing inventory as a result of obsolescence. If you were the manager of Best Buy, you would hate to have a warehouse full of VHS tapes when DVDs are available.

Firms that deal with cutting-edge technologies are at most risk for having obsolete inventory. Sprint PCS or T-Mobile would not want to have a huge inventory of analog-only phones now that digital phones are the better choice. With the new Bluetooth technology, the cell phone business is at risk with its old inventories. Each year, a company's inventory is evaluated for obsolescence at the same time the lower-of-cost-or-market rule is applied. Inventory must be written off, which will increase the cost of goods sold, when it is deemed to be obsolete. For example, in the notes to its financial statements, shown in Exhibit 5.23, SanDisk Corporation, the manufacturer of flash storage, has a note about inventory obsolescence.

EXHIBIT 5.23

SanDisk Corporation's Note about the Risk of Inventory Obsolescence

SanDisk is in the technology business, so the company is especially concerned about inventory obsolescence.

The Company reduces the carrying value of its inventory to a new basis for estimated obsolescence or unmarketable inventory by an amount equal to the difference between the cost of the inventory and the estimated market value based upon assumptions about future demand and market conditions, including assumptions about changes in average selling prices. If actual market conditions are less favorable than those projected by management additional reductions in inventory valuation may be required.

The Ethics of Inventory Losses

Inventory losses have an ethical component. The obvious one is that unethical people may steal a firm's inventory. Less obvious is the opportunity that inventory provides for misstating the value of the firm's assets. Failure to write down inventory that has lost value means that earnings will be overstated by the amount of the decline in inventory. As you know by now, managers rarely want to recognize expenses that do not produce any revenue, and they often look for ways to boost earnings. Inventory valuation is an area where the flexibility of accounting standards can lead to manipulation of earnings. When you study a firm's financial statements, be sure to read the notes to the financial statements about the firm's policy on writing down its obsolete inventory.

Chapter Summary Points

- A firm records the purchase of inventory at cost. That includes all costs to get the inventory ready for sale. Shipping costs, purchase discounts, and purchase returns and allowances all must be considered in calculating the cost of inventory.
- When a firm sells the inventory, the firm must consider sales discounts and sales returns and allowances when calculating net sales revenue.
- Inventory record keeping can be done at the time of each sale (perpetual inventory system), or the record keeping can be done at the end of the period (periodic inventory system).
- If a firm does not specifically identify the inventory item sold at the time of the sale, the firm will select one of three common cost flow assumptions to value inventory sold. Making a cost flow assumption is necessary when inventory costs are not constant and the specific identification of inventory units sold is too costly. The three methods are weighted average cost;

first-in, first-out (FIFO); and last-in, first-out (LIFO). When costs of inventory are changing, these methods most often will produce different amounts for cost of goods sold.

- To avoid overvaluing inventory, firms must compare the cost of their inventory to the market value of the inventory and value the inventory at the lower of the two. This is called the lower-of-cost-or-market rule for valuing inventory.
- The gross profit ratio and the inventory turnover ratio are both useful in evaluating a firm's performance with respect to inventory. Gross profit ratio is equal to the gross profit divided by sales. The inventory turnover ratio is equal to cost of goods sold divided by average inventory.
- Firms face the risk of inventory being lost, damaged, and stolen. Controls include physically guarding the inventory (security services, locks, and alarms) and regular record keeping to identify potential problems. Many firms, high-tech firms in particular, run the risk of having obsolete inventory. Again, regular monitoring of purchases and sales will help control this risk.

Chapter Summary Problem

To compare the inventory methods for TV Heaven, a retail firm that specializes in high-end televisions, we will look at a single item to keep the analysis simple. Our results will apply to the other items in the inventory as well. Suppose TV Heaven started March with an inventory of 50 plasma TVs that cost $2,010 each, for a total beginning inventory of $100,500. During March, the firm made the following purchases:

March 2	200 TVs for $2,000 each
March 10	150 TVs for $1,800 each
March 20	100 TVs for $1,500 each
March 29	50 TVs for $1,000 each

During March, the firm made the following sales:

March 5	110 TVs for $4,000 each
March 12	160 TVs for $4,000 each
March 25	150 TVs for $4,000 each

Instructions

1. Using *periodic inventory record keeping*, calculate the cost of goods sold for the month and the inventory at the end of the month. Do these calculations using three methods: weighted average cost, FIFO, and LIFO. All other operating expenses amounted to $250,000. Assume these are the only transactions for the period. Calculate net income using each of the three methods. Which method provides the highest net income? What is causing this method to produce the highest net income?

2. Using *perpetual inventory record keeping*, calculate the cost of goods sold for the month and the inventory at the end of the month. Do these calculations using three methods: weighted average cost, FIFO, and LIFO. All other operating expenses amounted to $250,000. Assume these are the only transactions for the period. Calculate net income using each of the three methods. Which method provides the highest net income? Explain why weighted average cost and LIFO produce different amounts under perpetual than they do under periodic.

Solution

1. Periodic Inventory

Cost of Goods Sold			
	No. of Units	**Unit Cost**	**Total Cost**
Beginning inventory	50	$2,010	$100,500
Purchases March 2	200	$2,000	$400,000
March 10	150	$1,800	$270,000
March 20	100	$1,500	$150,000
March 29	50	$1,000	$ 50,000
Goods available for sale	550		$970,500
Units sold	420		

Weighted average cost $970,500 ÷ 550   = $ 1,765 per unit (rounded)

Cost of goods sold =   420 units × $1,765 = $741,300   Ending inventory
                                                130 units × $1,765 = $229,450

FIFO				
	50 × $2,010 =	$100,500		
	200 × $2,000 =	$400,000		
	150 × $1,800 =	$270,000	80 × $1,500 =	$120,000
	20 × $1,500 =	$ 30,000	50 × $1,000 =	$ 50,000
Cost of goods sold	420 units	$800,500	Ending inventory	$170,000
LIFO				
	50 × $1,000 =	$ 50,000		
	100 × $1,500 =	$150,000		
	150 × $1,800 =	$270,000	80 × $2,000 =	$160,000
	120 × $2,000 =	$240,000	50 × $2,010 =	$100,500
Cost of goods sold	420 units	$710,000	Ending inventory	$260,500

TV Heaven
Income Statement
For the Month Ended March 31

	Weighted Average Cost	FIFO	LIFO
Sales revenue	$1,680,000	$1,680,000	$1,680,000
Cost of goods sold	741,300	800,500	710,000
Gross profit	938,700	879,500	970,000
Other operating expenses	250,000	250,000	250,000
Net income	$ 688,700	$ 629,500	$ 720,000

Net income is highest using LIFO because the cost of the inventory is going down. More often, costs go up so companies use LIFO to minimize net income. In this case, the technology advances are likely driving down the cost of plasma TVs.

2. Perpetual Inventory

Cost of Goods Sold

	No. of Units	Unit Cost	Total Cost
Beginning inventory	50	$2,010	$100,500
Purchases March 2	200	$2,000	$400,000
March 10	150	$1,800	$270,000
March 20	100	$1,500	$150,000
March 29	50	$1,000	$ 50,000
Goods available for sale	550		$970,500
Units sold March 5	110		
March 12	160		
March 25	150		
Ending inventory	130		

Weighted average (WA) cost		Average unit cost	Cost of goods sold
WA cost on March 5	50 at $2,010 ⎱ 200 at $2,000 ⎰ =	$500,500 ÷ 250 = $2,002 avg. cost	110 units × $2,002 = $220,220
WA cost on March 12	140 at $2,002 ⎱ 150 at $1,800 ⎰ =	$550,280 ÷ 290 = $1,898 average cost (rounded)	160 units × $1,898 = $303,680

		Average unit cost	Cost of goods sold
WA cost on March 25	130 at $1,898 100 at $1,500 } =	$396,740 ÷ 230 = $1,725 average cost (rounded)	150 units × $1,725 = $258,750
Total cost of goods sold			$782,650
(Ending inventory)	80 at $1,725 50 at $1,000 } =	$188,000 ÷ 130 = $1,446 per unit (rounded)	$188,000

Note: Under WA perpetual, the ending inventory plus cost of goods sold is $150 more than goods available for sale. This differential is due to rounding. If you carry out the calculations to several decimal places, you will eliminate this rounding error. This type of calculation is typically done in a computer program that will not round as we have done here.

FIFO

		Cost of goods sold
Sale on March 5 (110 units)	50 at $2,010 60 at $2,000 } =	$220,500
Sale on March 12 (160 units)	140 at $2,000 20 at $1,800 } =	$316,000
Sale on March 25 (150 units)	130 at $1,800 20 at $1,500 } =	$264,000
Cost of goods sold		$800,500
FIFO ending inventory	80 at $1,500 50 at $1,000 } =	$170,000

LIFO

		Cost of goods sold
Sale on March 5 (110 units)	110 at $2,000	$220,000
Sale on March 12 (160 units)	150 at $1,800 10 at $2,000 } =	$290,000
Sale on March 25 (150 units)	100 at $1,500 50 at $2,000 } =	$250,000
Cost of goods sold		$760,000
LIFO ending inventory	50 at $1,000 30 at $2,000 50 at $2,010 } =	$210,500

TV Heaven
Income Statement
For the Month Ended March 31

	Weighted Average Cost	FIFO	LIFO
Sales revenue	$1,680,000	$1,680,000	$1,680,000
Cost of goods sold	782,650	800,500	760,000
Gross profit	897,350	879,500	920,000
Other operating expenses	250,000	250,000	250,000
Net income	$ 647,350	$ 629,500	$ 670,000

Net income is highest under LIFO because the cost of the inventory is going down.

When a firm uses perpetual record keeping, it cannot assume to have sold units that were not purchased by the date of the sale. On the other hand, when a firm uses periodic record keeping, every purchase made during the period—no matter how the purchase dates match up to the sales dates—is part of the calculation of cost of goods sold. For weighted average cost, the average is different because the late purchase is included in the average cost calculation under periodic but not perpetual record keeping. For LIFO periodic, that last and cheapest purchase can be counted in the cost of goods sold. (Under perpetual, it could not be used because it had not been purchased at the time of the last sale.)

Key Terms for Chapter 5

Average days in inventory (p. 232)
Contra-revenue (p. 209)
Cost of goods available for sale (p. 207)
First-in, first-out (FIFO) (p. 214)
FOB destination (p. 204)
FOB shipping point (p. 204)
Gross profit ratio (p. 231)
Inventory turnover ratio (p. 232)

Last-in, first-out (LIFO) (p. 215)
Lower-of-cost-or-market (LCM) rule (p. 230)
Periodic inventory system (p. 204)
Perpetual inventory system (p. 204)
Purchase discount (p. 206)
Purchase order (p. 203)

Purchase returns and allowances (p. 206)
Replacement cost (p. 231)
Sales discount (p. 209)
Sales returns and allowances (p. 209)
Specific identification method (p. 212)
Weighted average cost (p. 213)

Answers to YOUR TURN Questions

Chapter 5

Your Turn 5-1

1. Company X pays the freight.
2. Company B pays the freight.

Your Turn 5-2

Coffee	98% of $500 =	$490
Bags		100
Total inventory cost		$590

Note: Shipping costs are not included because the purchase was FOB destination.

Your Turn 5-3

Cash collected: $3,150 ($3,000 + 5% of $3,000)
Revenue: $3,000

Your Turn 5-4

The firm should use perpetual. At the time of each sale, the inventory account will be reduced. When the period is over and the inventory is counted, any difference between the inventory amount shown in the records and the inventory amount identified by a physical count of the inventory will be the amount of inventory shrinkage. If the firm used a periodic system, all inventory not present at the end of the period is assumed to be part of cost of goods sold.

Your Turn 5-5

The weighted average cost of a unit is $[((\$10 \times 1) + (\$20 \times 2))/30] = \$1.66667$ per unit
Cost of goods sold = 15 units $\times$ $1.66667 = **$25**

Your Turn 5-6

1. Cost of goods sold is $4,600 + $5,100 = $9,700; and the gross profit is $14,000 − $9,700 = $4,300.
2. Cost of goods sold is $3,500 + $5,100 = $8,600; and the gross profit is $14,000 − $8,600 = $5,400.
3. Weighted average cost of the bracelets is $13,200/3 = $4,400. The cost of goods sold for the sale of two bracelets would be 2 $\times$ $4,400 = $8,800.

Your Turn 5-7

1. FIFO: $705 [(30 × $20) + (5 × $21)]
2. LIFO: $775 [(20 × $23) + (15 × $21)]
3. [(30 × $20) + (20 × $21) + (20 × $23)] ÷ 70 units = $21.143 (rounded)
   $21.143 × 35 = $740

Your Turn 5-8

The LIFO conformity rule says that if a firm uses LIFO for tax purposes, it must also use LIFO for accounting (GAAP) purposes. It is unusual for accounting and tax rules to overlap. Usually accounting rules (GAAP) do not follow tax law.

Your Turn 5-9

Inventory turnover ratio = $306,158 ÷ [(35,159 + 34,511) ÷ 2] = 8.79
Average days in inventory = 365 ÷ 8.79 = 41.5 days

Questions

1. Explain the terms *FOB shipping point* and *FOB destination.* What are the accounting and business implications of the shipping terms? Why is it important to know who owns goods during shipping?
2. What is the difference between freight-in and freight-out?
3. What is the difference between a purchase return and a purchase allowance? What is the effect of purchase returns and allowances on the overall cost of inventory to the buyer?
4. What is a purchase discount? What is the effect of a purchase discount on the overall cost of inventory to the buyer?
5. Explain the terms of a purchase described as *2/15, n/30.* Would you take advantage of this offer? Why or why not?
6. What is a contra-revenue account? Give two examples of contra-revenue accounts.
7. What is a sales discount? What is the effect of a sales discount on the total sales revenue of the seller?
8. What is the difference between a periodic and perpetual inventory system?
9. What is inventory shrinkage?
10. What is the difference between the physical flow of inventory and the inventory cost flow?
11. What are the common cost flow methods for accounting for inventory? Describe the differences.
12. If inventory costs are rising, which method (FIFO, LIFO, or weighted average cost) results in the highest net income? Explain your answer.
13. If inventory costs are rising, which method (FIFO, LIFO, or weighted average cost) results in the lowest net income? Explain your answer.
14. Does LIFO or FIFO give the best—most current—balance sheet value for the ending inventory? Why?
15. How do taxes affect the choice between LIFO and FIFO?
16. Does the periodic or perpetual choice affect the choice of a cost flow (LIFO versus FIFO) method? Explain.
17. What is the *lower-of-cost-or-market* rule and why is it necessary?
18. What does the gross profit percentage measure? How is it calculated?
19. What does the inventory turnover ratio measure? What does *average-days-in-inventory* mean?
20. What are some of the risks associated with inventory? How do managers minimize these risks?

Multiple-Choice Questions

1. When inventory is purchased, it is recorded as a(n) ——————— and when sold it becomes a(n) ———————.
   a. liability; withdrawal
   b. asset; expense
   c. liability; asset
   d. asset; contra-asset

Use the following information to answer questions 2–5:

Inventory data for Newman & Frith Merchandisers, Inc., is provided here. Sales for the period were 2,800 units. Each sold for $8. The company maintains a periodic inventory system.

Date		Number of Units	Unit Cost	Total Cost
January	Beginning inventory	1,000	$3.00	$ 3,000
February	Purchases	600	$3.50	$ 2,100
March	Purchases	800	$4.00	$ 3,200
April	Purchases	1,200	$4.25	$ 5,100
Totals		3,600		$13,400

2. Determine the ending inventory assuming the company uses the FIFO cost flow method.
   a. $3,400
   b. $2,400
   c. $9,200
   d. $10,000

3. Determine the cost of goods sold assuming the company uses the FIFO cost flow method.
   a. $3,400
   b. $10,000
   c. $10,200
   d. $2,400

4. Determine the ending inventory assuming the company uses the weighted average cost flow method. (Round average cost to two decimal places.)
   a. $2,300
   b. $3,300
   c. $9,800
   d. $2,976

5. Determine the gross profit assuming the company uses the LIFO cost flow method.
   a. $11,400
   b. $14,400
   c. $22,400
   d. $19,700

6. Using LIFO will produce a lower net income than using FIFO under which of the following conditions?
   a. Inventory costs are decreasing.
   b. Inventory costs are increasing.
   c. Inventory costs are not changing.
   d. Sales prices are decreasing.

Use the following information to answer questions 7–10:

Sales revenue	$480,000
Cost of goods sold	300,000
Sales discounts	20,000
Sales returns and allowances	15,000
Operating expenses	85,000
Interest revenue	5,000

7. What is the net sales revenue?
   a. $400,000
   b. $445,000
   c. $415,000
   d. $455,000

8. What is the gross profit?
   a. $145,000
   b. $105,000
   c. $140,000
   d. $90,000

9. What is the net income?
   a. $60,000
   b. $65,000
   c. $55,000
   d. $180,000
10. What is the gross profit percentage?
   a. 13.54%
   b. 14.61%
   c. 32.58%
   d. 21.67%

Short Exercises
Set A

SE5-1A. *Calculate cost of inventory. (LO 1).* Invoice price of goods is $5,000. Purchase terms are 2/10, n/30 and the invoice is paid in the week of receipt. The shipping terms are FOB shipping point, and the shipping costs amount to $200. What is the total cost of the inventory?

SE5-2A. *Record sale of merchandise inventory: perpetual inventory system. (LO 1, 2).* Brenda Bailey's Textiles, Inc., uses a perpetual inventory system. Enter the following transaction into the accounting equation:

In February, Brenda Bailey's sold $500,000 of merchandise on account with terms 2/10, n/30. The cost of the merchandise sold was $230,000.

SE5-3A. *Calculate gross profit and the gross profit ratio. (LO 1, 6).* Using the information in SE5-2A, calculate the gross profit from the sale and the gross profit ratio. Assume that the customer does not pay within the discount period.

SE5-4A. *Calculate cost of goods sold and ending inventory: weighted average cost. (LO 3).* Calculate the cost of goods sold and the cost of the ending inventory using the weighted average cost flow assumption. Assume periodic record keeping.

Sales	100 units at $15 per unit
Beginning inventory	90 units at $6 per unit
Purchases	60 units at $9 per unit

SE5-5A. *Calculate cost of goods sold and ending inventory: FIFO. (LO 3).* Using the data from SE5-4A, calculate the cost of goods sold and the cost of the ending inventory using the FIFO periodic cost flow assumption.

SE5-6A. *Calculate cost of goods sold and ending inventory: LIFO. (LO 3).* Using the data from SE5-4A, calculate the cost of goods sold and the cost of the ending inventory using the LIFO periodic cost flow assumption.

SE5-7A. *Analyze the effect of the cost flow method on net income. (LO 3).* Given the following information, calculate the amount by which net income would differ between FIFO and LIFO. Assume the periodic system.

Beginning inventory	3,000 units at $100 per unit
Purchases	8,000 units at $130 per unit
Units sold	6,000 units at $225 per unit

SE5-8A. *Analyze the effect of the cost flow method on gross profit. (LO 3, 4).* Given the following information, calculate the amount by which gross profit would differ between FIFO and LIFO. Assume the periodic system.

Beginning inventory	1,500 units at $55 per unit
Purchases	2,750 units at $58 per unit
Units sold	2,250 units at $99 per unit

SE5-9A. *Apply the lower-of-cost-or-market rule. (LO 5).* The following information pertains to item #007SS of inventory of Marine Aquatic Sales, Inc.:

	Per unit
Cost	$180
Replacement cost	181
Selling price	195

The physical inventory indicates 2,000 units of item #007SS on hand. What amount will be reported on the Marine Aquatic Sales, Inc.'s balance sheet for this inventory item?

SE5-10A. *Calculate the gross profit ratio, inventory turnover ratio, and average days in inventory. (LO 6).* Using the following information, calculate inventory turnover ratio, the average days in inventory, and the gross profit ratio for Barkley Company for the year ended December 31, 2012. (Round to two decimal places.)

Sales	$125,000
Cost of goods sold	75,000
Ending inventory, December 31, 2011	15,275
Ending inventory, December 31, 2012	18,750
Net income	26,500

Set B

SE5-11B. *Calculate cost of inventory. (LO 1).* Invoice price of goods is $1,000. Purchase terms are 1/10, n/30 and the invoice is paid in the week of receipt. The shipping terms are FOB shipping point, and the shipping costs amount to $200. What is the total cost of the inventory?

SE5-12B. *Record sale of merchandise inventory: perpetual inventory system. (LO 1, 2).* Sam's Supply, Inc., uses a perpetual inventory system. Enter the following transaction into the accounting equation:

In February, Sam's sold $320,000 of merchandise on account with terms 3/10, n/30. The cost of the merchandise sold was $100,000.

SE5-13B. *Calculate gross profit and the gross profit ratio. (LO 1, 6).* Using the information in SE5-12B, calculate the gross profit from the sale and the gross profit ratio. Assume the customer does not pay within the discount period.

SE5-14B. *Calculate cost of goods sold and ending inventory: weighted average cost. (LO 3).* Calculate the cost of goods sold and the cost of the ending inventory using the weighted average cost flow assumption. Assume periodic record keeping.

Sales	150 units at $5 per unit
Beginning inventory	100 units at $2 per unit
Purchases	60 units at $3 per unit

SE5-15B. *Calculate cost of goods sold and ending inventory: FIFO. (LO 3).* Using the data from SE5-14B, calculate the cost of goods sold and the cost of the ending inventory using the FIFO periodic cost flow assumption.

SE5-16B. *Calculate cost of goods sold and ending inventory: LIFO. (LO 3).* Using the data from SE5-14B, calculate the cost of goods sold and the cost of the ending inventory using the LIFO periodic cost flow assumption.

SE5-17B. *Analyze the effect of the cost flow method on net income. (LO 3).* Given the following information, calculate the amount by which net income would differ between FIFO and LIFO. Assume the periodic system.

Beginning inventory	2,000 units at $10 per unit
Purchases	5,000 units at $12 per unit
Units sold	6,500 units at $25 per unit

SE5-18B. *Analyze the effect of the cost flow method on gross profit. (LO 3, 4).* Given the following information, calculate the amount by which gross profit would differ between FIFO and LIFO. Assume the periodic system.

Beginning inventory	500 units at $50 per unit
Purchases	1,200 units at $48 per unit
Units sold	900 units at $60 per unit

SE5-19B. *Apply the lower-of-cost-or-market rule. (LO 5).* The following information pertains to item #3801B of inventory of Parts-A-Plenty:

	Per unit
Cost	$180
Replacement cost	170
Selling price	195

The physical inventory indicates 1,000 units of item #3801B on hand. What amount will be reported on Parts-A-Plenty's balance sheet for this inventory item?

SE5-20B. *Calculate the gross profit ratio, inventory turnover ratio, and average days in inventory. (LO 6).* Using the following information, calculate inventory turnover ratio, the average days in inventory, and the gross profit ratio for Howard Company for the year ended December 31, 2011. (Round to two decimal places.)

Sales	$225,000
Cost of goods sold	175,000
Ending inventory, December 31, 2011	15,275
Ending inventory, December 31, 2010	18,750
Net income	36,500

Exercises
Set A

MyAccountingLab

All of the A exercises can be found within MyAccountingLab, an online homework and practice environment.

E5-21A. *Record merchandising transactions: perpetual inventory system. (LO 1, 2).* Assume the following transactions for Clark's Appliances, Inc., took place during May. Clark's Appliances uses a perpetual inventory system. Enter each of the transactions into the accounting equation.

May 2	Purchased refrigerators on account at a total cost of $500,000; terms 1/10, n/30
May 9	Paid freight of $800 on refrigerators purchased from GE
May 16	Returned refrigerators to GE because they were damaged; received a credit of $5,000 from GE
May 22	Sold refrigerators costing $100,000 for $180,000 to Pizzeria Number 1 on account, terms n/30
May 24	Gave a credit of $3,000 to Pizzeria Number 1 for the return of a refrigerator not ordered. Clark's cost was $1,200.

E5-22A. *Record merchandising transactions: perpetual inventory system. (LO 1, 2).* The Fedora Company had a beginning inventory balance of $25,750 and engaged in the following transactions during the month of June:

June 2	Purchased $4,000 of merchandise inventory on account from Plumes, Inc., with terms 2/10, n/30 and FOB destination. Freight costs associated with this purchase were $225.
June 4	Returned $400 of damaged merchandise to Plumes, Inc.
June 6	Sold $7,000 of merchandise to Fancy Caps on account, terms 1/15, n/30 and FOB shipping point. Freight costs were $125. The cost of the inventory sold was $3,500.
June 9	Paid the amount owed to Plumes, Inc.
June 10	Granted Fancy Caps an allowance on the June 6 sale of $300 for minor damage found on several pieces of merchandise

June 22	Received total payment owed from Fancy Caps
June 24	Paid sales salaries of $1,850
June 25	Paid the rent on the showroom of $1,200

Enter each of the transactions for the Fedora Company into the accounting equation, assuming it uses a perpetual inventory system.

Use the following data to answer the questions in E5-23A through E5-26A:

Box Office Projectors began the month of August with three movie projectors in inventory, each unit costing $350. During August, eight additional projectors of the same model were purchased.

August 11	Purchased four units at $400 each
August 13	Sold five units at $425 each
August 14	Purchased three units at $375
August 18	Sold two units at $425 each
August 21	Sold three units at $425 each
August 26	Purchased one unit at $380

E5-23A. *Calculate cost of goods sold and ending inventory: periodic FIFO. (LO 3, 4).* Assume Box Office uses a periodic record-keeping system and the FIFO cost flow method.

1. Calculate the cost of goods sold that will appear on the income statement for the month of August.
2. Determine the cost of inventory that will appear on the balance sheet at the end of August.

E5-24A. *Calculate cost of goods sold and ending inventory: periodic LIFO. (LO 3, 4).* Assume Box Office uses a periodic record-keeping system and the LIFO cost flow method.

1. Calculate the cost of goods sold that will appear on the income statement for the month of August.
2. Determine the cost of inventory that will appear on the balance sheet at the end of August.

E5-25A. *Calculate cost of goods sold and ending inventory: perpetual FIFO. (LO 3, 4).* Assume Box Office uses a perpetual record-keeping system and the FIFO cost flow method.

1. Calculate the cost of goods sold that will appear on the income statement for the month of August.
2. Determine the cost of inventory that will appear on the balance sheet at the end of August.

E5-26A. *Calculate cost of goods sold and ending inventory: perpetual LIFO. (LO 3, 4).* Assume Box Office uses a perpetual record-keeping system and the LIFO cost flow method.

1. Calculate the cost of goods sold that will appear on the income statement for the month of August.
2. Determine the cost of inventory that will appear on the balance sheet at the end of August.

E5-27A. *Calculate cost of goods sold and ending inventory: periodic weighted average cost. (LO 3, 4).* The Fancy Phones Company sells phones to business customers. The company began 2009 with 2,000 units of inventory on hand. These units cost $200 each. The following transactions related to the company's merchandise inventory occurred during the first quarter of 2009:

January 14	Purchased 750 units for $225 each
February 13	Purchased 500 units for $175 each
March 30	Purchased <u>200</u> units for $205 each
Total purchases	1,450 units

All unit costs include the purchase price and freight charges paid by Fancy Phones. During the quarter ending March 31, 2009, sales totaled 2,500 units, leaving 950 units in ending inventory.

Assume Fancy Phones uses a periodic record-keeping system and the weighted average cost flow method.

1. Calculate the cost of goods sold that will appear on Fancy Phone's income statement for the quarter ending March 31.
2. Determine the cost of inventory that will appear on Fancy Phone's balance sheet at the end of March.

E5-28A. *Calculate cost of goods sold and ending inventory: perpetual weighted average cost.* *(LO 3, 4).* Speedy Wireless, Inc., sells netbooks. The company began the fourth quarter of the year on October 1, 2009, with 500 units of inventory on hand. These units cost $250 each. The following transactions related to the company's merchandise inventory occurred during the fourth quarter of 2009:

October 3	Sold 400 units for $400 each
November 5	Purchased 600 units for $275 each
November 29	Sold 500 units for $425 each
December 1	Purchased 700 units for $260 each
December 24	Sold 600 units for $450 each

All unit costs include the purchase price and freight charges paid by Speedy Wireless.

Assume the company uses a perpetual record-keeping system and the weighted average cost flow method.

1. Calculate the cost of goods sold that will appear on the income statement for the quarter ending December 31, 2009.
2. Determine the cost of inventory that will appear on the balance sheet at December 31, 2009.

E5-29A. *Apply the lower-of-cost-or-market rule. (LO 5).* Use the data provided to answer the question that follows:

Ending inventory at cost, December 31, 2011	$ 17,095
Ending inventory at replacement cost, December 31, 2011	16,545
Cost of goods sold, balance at December 31, 2011	250,765
Sales revenue, balance at December 31, 2011	535,780
Cash, balance at December 31, 2011	165,340

What inventory amount will this firm report on its balance sheet at December 31, 2011?

E5-30A. *Apply the lower-of-cost-or-market rule. (LO 5).* In each case, indicate the correct amount to be reported for the inventory on the year-end balance sheet.

1. Ending inventory at cost $125,000
   Ending inventory at market $121,750
2. Ending inventory at cost $117,500
   Ending inventory at market $120,250

E5-31A. *Calculate gross profit and gross profit percentage: FIFO and LIFO. (LO 6).* Given the following information, calculate the gross profit and gross profit ratio under (a) FIFO periodic and under (b) LIFO periodic:

Sales	250 units at $100 per unit
Beginning inventory	75 units at $75 per unit
Purchases	300 units at $60 per unit

Set B

E5-32B. *Record merchandising transactions: perpetual inventory system. (LO 1, 2).* Assume the following transactions for Jennifer's Fix-It-Up, Inc., took place during March. Jennifer's uses a perpetual inventory system. Enter each of the transactions into the accounting equation.

March 3	Purchased televisions from Sanyo on account at a total cost of $650,000, terms 2/10, n/25
March 8	Paid freight of $1,000 on televisions purchased from Sanyo
March 16	Returned televisions to Sanyo because they were damaged. Received a credit of $15,000 from Sanyo.

| March 22 | Sold televisions costing $125,000 for $225,000 to Joe's Sports Bar & Grille on account, terms n/15 |
| March 28 | Gave a credit of $2,800 to Joe's Sports Bar & Grille for the return of a television not ordered. Jennifer's cost was $1,600. |

E5-33B. *Record merchandising transactions: perpetual inventory system. (LO 1, 2).* Discount Wines, Inc., had a beginning inventory balance of $85,450 and engaged in the following transactions during the month of October:

October 2	Purchased $15,000 of merchandise inventory on account from Joe's Winery with terms 2/10, n/30 and FOB destination. Freight costs for this purchase were $750.
October 5	Returned $100 of damaged merchandise to Joe's
October 6	Sold $18,000 of merchandise to Tasty Catering Service on account, terms 2/15, n/30 and FOB shipping point. Freight costs were $155. The cost of the inventory sold was $10,500.
October 10	Paid the amount owed to Joe's
October 10	Granted Tasty an allowance on the October 6 sale of $200 for some soured wine
October 23	Received total payment owed from Tasty
October 29	Paid sales salaries of $1,500
October 31	Paid the rent on the warehouse of $1,450

Enter each of the transactions for Discount Wines, Inc., into the accounting equation, assuming it uses a perpetual inventory system.

E5-34B. *Calculate cost of goods sold and ending inventory: periodic weighted average cost. (LO 3, 4).* Tom's Trampoline Company sells commercial-size trampolines. The company's most recent fiscal year began on August 1, 2009, and ended July 31, 2010. The company began the year with 500 units of inventory on hand. These units cost $500 each. The following transactions related to the company's merchandise inventory occurred during the first quarter of the year:

August 14	Purchased 200 units for $525 each
September 12	Purchased 175 units for $490 each
October 20	Purchased <u>100</u> units for $510 each
Total purchases	475 units

During the quarter ending October 31, sales totaled 625 units.

Assume the company uses a periodic record-keeping system and the weighted average cost flow method.

1. Calculate the cost of goods sold that will appear on the company's income statement for the quarter ending October 31.
2. Determine the cost of inventory that will appear on the company's balance sheet at the end of October.

E5-35B. *Calculate cost of goods sold and ending inventory: perpetual weighted average cost. (LO 3, 4).* Bob's Barber Supplies sells hair clippers to local businesses. The company began the first quarter of the year January 1, 2009, with 1,000 units of inventory on hand. These units cost $50 each. The following transactions related to the company's merchandise inventory occurred during the first quarter of 2009:

January 12	Sold 800 units for $75 each
January 20	Purchased 500 units for $45 each
February 8	Sold 400 units for $75 each
March 5	Purchased 600 units for $60 each
March 19	Sold 500 units for $75 each

Assume the company uses a perpetual record-keeping system and the weighted average cost flow method.

1. Calculate the cost of goods sold that will appear on the income statement for the quarter ending March 31, 2009.
2. Determine the cost of inventory that will appear on the balance sheet at the end of March.

Use the following data to answer E5-36B through E5-39B:

Radio Tech Sales & Service, Inc., began the month of April with three top-of-the-line radios in inventory, Model # RD58V6Q; each unit cost $235. During April, nine additional radios of the same model were purchased.

April 9	Purchased three units at $230 each
April 11	Sold five units at $350 each
April 17	Purchased two units at $195 each
April 18	Sold one unit at $350
April 20	Sold two units at $350 each
April 28	Purchased four units at $180 each

E5-36B. *Calculate cost of goods sold and ending inventory: periodic FIFO. (LO 3, 4).* Assume Radio Tech uses a periodic inventory system and the FIFO cost flow method.

1. Calculate the cost of goods sold that will appear on Radio Tech's income statement for the month of April.
2. Determine the cost of inventory that will appear on Radio Tech's balance sheet at the end of April.

E5-37B. *Calculate cost of goods sold and ending inventory: periodic LIFO. (LO 3, 4).* Assume Radio Tech uses a periodic inventory system and the LIFO cost flow method.

1. Calculate the cost of goods sold that will appear on Radio Tech's income statement for the month of April.
2. Determine the cost of inventory that will appear on Radio Tech's balance sheet at the end of April.

E5-38B. *Calculate cost of goods sold and ending inventory: perpetual FIFO. (LO 3, 4).* Assume Radio Tech uses a perpetual inventory system and the FIFO cost flow method.

1. Calculate the cost of goods sold that will appear on Radio Tech's income statement for the month of April.
2. Determine the cost of inventory that will appear on Radio Tech's balance sheet at the end of April.

E5-39B. *Calculate cost of goods sold and ending inventory: perpetual LIFO. (LO 3, 4).* Assume Radio Tech uses a perpetual inventory system and the LIFO cost flow method.

1. Calculate the cost of goods sold that will appear on Radio Tech's income statement for the month of April.
2. Determine the cost of inventory that will appear on Radio Tech's balance sheet at the end of April.

E5-40B. *Apply the lower-of-cost-or-market rule. (LO 5).* Use the data provided to answer the question that follows:

Ending inventory at cost, June 30, 2010	$ 25,180
Ending inventory at replacement cost, June 30, 2010	25,130
Cost of goods sold, balance at June 30, 2010	150,550
Sales revenue, balance at June 30, 2010	275,625
Cash, balance at June 30, 2010	285,515

ASB Hardware, Inc., uses a perpetual inventory system and the FIFO cost flow method to account for its inventory. What inventory amount will ASB Hardware report on its balance sheet at June 30, 2010?

E5-41B. *Apply the lower-of-cost-or-market rule. (LO 5).* In each case, indicate the correct amount to be reported for the inventory on the year-end balance sheet.

1. Ending inventory at cost $275,000
   Ending inventory at market $271,250
2. Ending inventory at cost $185,250
   Ending inventory at market $187,550

E5-42B. *Calculate gross profit and gross profit ratio: FIFO and LIFO. (LO 6).* Given the following information, calculate the gross profit and gross profit ratio under (a) FIFO periodic and under (b) LIFO periodic:

Sales	300 units at $75 per unit
Beginning inventory	425 units at $40 per unit
Purchases	100 units at $50 per unit

All of the A problems can be found within MyAccountingLab, an online homework and practice environment.

Problems
Set A

P5-43A. *Analyze purchases of merchandise inventory. (LO 1).* Rondo's Sports Wear made the following purchases in June of the current year:

June 7	Purchased $5,000 of merchandise, terms 5/15, n/60, FOB shipping point
June 15	Purchased $2,500 of merchandise, terms 3/10, n/30, FOB shipping point
June 25	Purchased $7,500 of merchandise, terms 2/10, n/30, FOB destination

Requirements

1. For each of the purchases listed, how many days does the company have to take advantage of the purchase discount?
2. What is the amount of the cash discount allowed in each case?
3. Assume the freight charges are 10% of the gross sales price. What is the amount of freight that Rondo's must pay for each purchase?
4. What is the total cost of inventory for Rondo's for the month of June, assuming that all discounts were taken?

P5-44A. *Analyze purchases of merchandise inventory. (LO 1)* Carrie & Runnels Bikes Plus, Inc., made the following purchases in December of the current year:

December 5	Purchased $2,600 of merchandise, terms 3/10, n/30, FOB destination
December 14	Purchased $6,150 of merchandise, terms 1/10, n/60, FOB shipping point
December 24	Purchased $8,375 of merchandise, terms 2/05, n/20, FOB destination

Requirements

1. For each purchase, by what date is the payment due, assuming the company takes advantage of the discount?
2. For each purchase, when is the payment due if the company does not take advantage of the discount?
3. In each case, what is the amount of the cash discount allowed?
4. Assume the freight charges are $365 on each purchase. For which purchase(s) is Bikes Plus responsible for the freight charges?
5. What is the total cost of inventory for Bikes Plus for the month of December, assuming that all discounts were taken?

P5-45A. *Record merchandising transactions, prepare financial statements, and calculate gross profit ratio: perpetual inventory system. (LO 1, 2, 4, 6).* At the beginning of February, Ace Distribution Company, Inc., started with a contribution of $10,000 cash in exchange for common stock from its shareholders. The company engaged in the following transactions during the month of February:

February 2	Purchased merchandise on account from Enter Supply Co. for $7,100, terms 2/10, n/45
February 5	Sold merchandise on account to Exit Company for $6,000, terms 2/10, n/30 and FOB destination. The cost of the merchandise sold was $4,500.
February 6	Paid $100 freight on the sale to Exit Company
February 8	Received credit from Enter Supply Co. for merchandise returned for $500
February 10	Paid Enter Supply Co. in full
February 12	Received payment from Exit Company for sale made on February 5
February 14	Purchased merchandise for cash for $5,200
February 16	Received refund from supplier for returned merchandise on February 14 cash purchase of $350
February 17	Purchased merchandise on account from Inware Distributors for $3,800, terms 1/10, n/30
February 18	Paid $250 freight on February 17 purchase
February 21	Sold merchandise for cash for $10,350. The cost of the merchandise sold was $8,200.
February 24	Purchased merchandise for cash for $2,300
February 25	Paid Inware Distributors for purchase on February 17
February 27	Gave refund of $200 to customer from February 21. The cost of the returned merchandise was $135.
February 28	Sold merchandise of $3,000 on account with the terms 2/10, n/30. The merchandise cost $2,300.

Requirements

1. Enter each transaction into the accounting equation, assuming Ace Distribution Company uses a perpetual inventory system. Start with the opening balances in cash and common stock described at the beginning of the problem.
2. Calculate the balance in the inventory account at the end of February.
3. Prepare a multistep income statement, the statement of changes in shareholders' equity, and the statement of cash flows for the month of February. Prepare a balance sheet at February 28.
4. Calculate the gross profit ratio.

P5-46A. *Record merchandising transactions, prepare financial statements, and calculate gross profit ratio: perpetual inventory system. (LO 1, 2, 4, 6).* The following transactions occurred during July 2010 at Tiny's Sports Shop:

July 2	Purchased weights on credit from Barbells Company for $900, with terms 3/10, n/30
July 4	Paid freight of $75 on the July 2 purchase
July 8	Sold merchandise to members on credit for $500, terms n/45. The merchandise sold cost $425.
July 9	Received credit of $50 from Barbells for damaged goods that were returned
July 11	Purchased workout equipment from Spinners for cash for $2,000
July 13	Paid Barbells Company in full
July 15	Purchased gloves and workout belts from Get Pumped on credit for $1,000, terms 5/15, n/60
July 17	Received credit of $25 from Get Pumped for damaged merchandise
July 19	Sold merchandise to members on account, $750, terms n/15. The cost of the merchandise sold was $250.
July 20	Received $700 in cash payment on account from members
July 23	Paid Get Pumped in full
July 27	Granted an allowance of $50 to members for gear that didn't work properly
July 29	Received $400 in cash payments on account from members
July 31	Paid cash operating expenses of $500 for the month

Requirements

1. Suppose Tiny's Sports Shop started the month with cash of $8,000, merchandise inventory of $2,000, and common stock of $10,000. Enter each transaction into the accounting equation, assuming Tiny's Sports Shop uses a perpetual inventory system.
2. Calculate the cost of goods sold for July and the ending balance in inventory.
3. Prepare the multistep income statement, and the statement of changes in shareholders' equity for the month of July, and the balance sheet at July 31.
4. Calculate the gross profit ratio for Tiny's Sports Shop for July. Explain what the ratio measures.

P5-47A. *Analyze accounting methods and prepare corrected income statement. (LO 1, 2, 4).* You are the accountant for Baldwin Company, and your assistant has prepared the following income statement for the year ended September 30, 2010:

Baldwin Company
Income Statement
For the Year Ended September 30, 2010

Sales revenue		$850,000
Sales returns and allowances	$ 22,500	
Freight costs	14,300	(36,800)
Net sales		813,200
Expenses		
Cost of goods sold	$540,000	
Selling expenses	150,000	
Insurance expense	20,000	
Administrative expenses	40,000	
Dividends	8,000	
Total expenses		758,000
Net income		$ 55,200

You have uncovered the following errors:
   a. Sales revenue includes $5,000 of items that have been back-ordered. (The items have not been delivered to the customers, and the customers have not been billed for the items.)
   b. Selling expenses include $250 of allowances that were given to customers who received damaged products.
   c. Insurance expense includes $100 worth of insurance that applies to 2011.
   d. Administrative expenses include a loan made to worker who had some serious financial trouble and needed $500 to pay a hospital bill. The worker plans to repay the money by the end of December.

Requirements

1. Prepare a corrected multistep income statement for the year. Baldwin shows sales as the net amount only on its income statement.
2. Write a memo to your assistant explaining why each error you found is incorrect and what the correct accounting treatment should be.

P5-48A. *Calculate cost of goods sold and ending inventory and analyze effect of each method on financial statements. (LO 3, 4).* Jefferson Company had the following sales and purchases during 2011, its first year of business:

January 5	Purchased 40 units at $100 each
February 15	Sold 15 units at $150 each
April 10	Sold 10 units at $150 each
June 30	Purchased 30 units at $105 each

| August 15 | Sold 25 units at $150 each |
| November 28 | Purchased 30 units at $110 each |

Requirements

1. Calculate the ending inventory, the cost of goods sold, and the gross profit for the December 31, 2011, financial statements under each of the following assumptions:
   a. FIFO periodic
   b. LIFO periodic
   c. Weighted average cost periodic
2. How will the differences between the methods affect the income statement for the year and balance sheet at December 31, 2011?

P5-49A. *Calculate cost of goods sold and ending inventory; analyze effects of each method on financial statements; apply lower-of-cost-or-market rule; calculate inventory turnover ratio. (LO 3, 4, 5, 6).* The following series of transactions occurred during 2009:

January 1	Beginning inventory was 70 units at $10 each
January 15	Purchased 100 units at $11 each
February 4	Sold 60 units at $20 each
March 10	Purchased 50 units at $12 each
April 15	Sold 70 units at $20 each
June 30	Purchased 100 units at $13 each
August 4	Sold 110 units at $20 each
October 1	Purchased 80 units at $14 each
December 5	Sold 50 units at $21 each

Requirements

1. Calculate the value of the ending inventory and cost of goods sold, assuming the company uses a periodic inventory system and the FIFO cost flow assumption.
2. Calculate the value of the ending inventory and cost of goods sold, assuming the company uses a periodic inventory system and the LIFO cost flow assumption.
3. Calculate the value of the ending inventory and cost of goods sold, assuming the company uses a periodic record-keeping system and the weighted average cost flow assumption.
4. Which of the three methods will result in the highest cost of goods sold for the year ended December 31, 2009?
5. Which of the three methods will provide the most current ending inventory value for the balance sheet at December 31, 2009?
6. How will the differences between the methods affect the income statement for the year and the balance sheet at year end?
7. Calculate the company's inventory turnover ratio and average days in inventory for the year for each method in items 1, 2, and 3.
8. At the end of the year, the current replacement cost of the inventory is $1,100. Indicate at what amount the company's inventory will be reported using the lower-of-cost-or-market rule for each method (FIFO, LIFO, and weighted average cost).

P5-50A. *Calculate cost of goods sold, ending inventory, and inventory turnover ratio. (LO 3, 6).* The following merchandise inventory transactions occurred during the month of May for the Super Stars, Inc.:

May 1	Inventory on hand was 2,000 units at $10 each
May 9	Sold 1,000 units at $15 each
May 15	Purchased 1,500 units at $11 each
May 21	Sold 1,250 units at $14 each
May 29	Purchased 3,000 units at $9 each

Requirements

1. Assume Super Stars uses a periodic record-keeping system and compute the cost of goods sold for the month ended May 31 and ending inventory at May 31 using each of the following cost flow methods:
   a. FIFO

      b. LIFO

      c. Weighted average cost

2. Using the information for item (1), calculate the inventory turnover ratio and average days in inventory for the month of May for each method.

3. Assume Super Stars uses the perpetual inventory system and compute the cost of goods sold for the month ended May 31 and ending inventory at May 31 using each of the following cost flow methods:

      a. FIFO

      b. LIFO

P5-51A. *Analyze effect of cost flow method on financial statements and inventory turnover ratio. (LO 2, 4, 6).* Green Bay Cheese Company is considering changing inventory cost flow methods. Green Bay's primary objective is to maximize profits. Currently, the firm uses weighted average cost. Data for 2011 are provided.

Beginning inventory (10,000 units)	$ 14,500
Purchases	
60,000 units at $1.50 each	$ 90,000
50,000 units at $1.60 each	80,000
70,000 units at $1.70 each	119,000
Sales	
130,000 units at $3.00 each	

Operating expenses were $120,000 and the company's tax rate is 30%.

Requirements

1. Prepare the multistep income statement for 2011 using each of the following methods:

      a. FIFO periodic

      b. LIFO periodic

2. Which method provides the more current balance sheet inventory balance at December 31, 2011? Explain your answer.

3. Which method provides the more current cost of goods sold for the year ended December 31, 2011? Explain your answer.

4. Which method provides the better inventory turnover ratio for the year? Explain your answer.

5. In order to meet its goal, what is your recommendation to Green Bay Cheese Company? Explain your answer.

P5-52A. *Calculate cost of goods sold and ending inventory; analyze effects of each method on financial statements; apply lower-of-cost-or-market rule; calculate inventory turnover ratio. (LO 3, 4, 5, 6).* The following information is for Leo's Solar Supplies for the year ending December 31, 2010.

At January 1, 2010:

- Cash amounted to $15,550.
- Beginning inventory was $20,000 (100 units at $200 each).
- Contributed capital was $19,000.
- Retained earnings was $16,550.

Transactions during 2010:

- Purchased 250 units for cash at $225 each
- Purchased 100 more units for cash at $250 each
- Cash sales of 300 units at $400 each
- Paid $11,500 cash for operating expenses
- Paid cash for income tax at a rate of 30% of net income

Requirements

1. Compute the cost of goods sold for the year and ending inventory at December 31, 2010, using each of the following cost flow methods:
   a. FIFO periodic
   b. LIFO periodic
   c. Weighted average cost periodic

2. For each method, prepare the balance sheet at December 31, 2010, a multistep income statement, statement of cash flows, and statement of changes in shareholders' equity for Leo's for the year ended December 31, 2010.

3. What is income before taxes and net income after taxes under each of the three inventory cost flow assumptions? What observations can you make about net income from the analysis of the three methods?

4. For each method, calculate the inventory turnover ratio and average days in inventory for the year ended December 31, 2010.

5. At the end of the year, the current replacement cost of the inventory is $35,000. Indicate at what amount the company's inventory will be reported using the lower-of-cost-or-market rule for each method (FIFO, LIFO, and weighted average cost).

P5-53A. *Calculate the gross profit ratio and inventory turnover ratio. (LO 6).* The following information is from the financial statements of Abby's International Pasta Corporation:

For year ended (amounts in thousands)	June 30, 2011	June 30, 2010	June 30, 2009
Sales	$416,049	$429,813	$445,849
Cost of sales	92,488	98,717	110,632
Inventory	17,030	16,341	12,659

Requirements

1. Calculate the gross profit ratio for the last two years shown.
2. Calculate the inventory turnover ratio for the last two years shown.
3. What information do these comparisons provide?

Set B

P5-54B. *Analyze purchases of merchandise inventory. (LO 1).* Deborah Hart's Professional Costumers, Inc., made the following purchases in November of the current year:

November 7	Purchased $2,500 of merchandise, terms 3/15, n/20, FOB shipping point
November 12	Purchased $4,300 of merchandise, terms 1/05, n/25, FOB destination
November 16	Purchased $6,200 of merchandise, terms 2/10, n/40, FOB shipping point

Requirements

1. For each of the listed purchases, how many days does the company have to take advantage of the purchase discount?
2. What is the amount of the cash discount allowed in each case?
3. Assume the freight charges are $115 on each purchase. What is the amount of freight that Professional Costumers must pay for each purchase?
4. What is the total cost of inventory for Professional Costumers for the month of November, assuming that all discounts were taken?

P5-55B. *Analyze purchases of merchandise inventory. (LO 1).* Cynthia's Pet Supplies, Inc., made the following purchases in March of the current year:

March 6	Purchased $3,500 of merchandise, terms 2/10, n/30, FOB shipping point
March 11	Purchased $5,250 of merchandise, terms 3/10, n/30, FOB destination
March 12	Purchased $4,000 of merchandise, terms 3/15, n/60, FOB shipping point

Requirements

1. For each purchase, by what date is the payment due, assuming the company takes advantage of the discount?
2. For each purchase, when is the payment due if the company does not take advantage of the discount?
3. In each case, what is the amount of the cash discount allowed?
4. Assume the freight charges are $100 on each purchase. For which purchase(s) is Cynthia's responsible for the freight charges?
5. What is the total amount of inventory costs for the month of March, assuming that all discounts were taken?

P5-56B. *Record merchandising transactions, prepare financial statements, and calculate gross profit ratio: perpetual inventory system. (LO 1, 2, 4, 6).* At the beginning of April, Morgan Parts Company, Inc., started with a contribution of $20,000 cash in exchange for common stock from its shareholders. The company engaged in the following transactions during the month of April:

April 3	Purchased merchandise on account from Thompson Supply Co. for $5,000, terms 1/10, n/30
April 4	Sold merchandise on account to Brown Company for $3,500, terms 2/10, n/30. The cost of the merchandise sold was $1,500.
April 7	Paid $100 freight on the sale to Brown Company
April 8	Received credit from Thompson Supply Co. for merchandise returned for $500
April 10	Paid Thompson Supply Co. in full
April 15	Received payment from Brown Company for sale made on April 4
April 16	Purchased merchandise for cash for $3,200
April 17	Received refund from supplier for returned merchandise on April 16 cash purchase of $350
April 19	Purchased merchandise on account from Kelsey Distributors for $4,100, terms 2/10, n/30
April 20	Paid $350 freight on April 19 purchase
April 21	Sold merchandise for cash for $12,170. The cost of the merchandise sold was $9,500.
April 24	Purchased merchandise for cash for $5,300
April 25	Paid Kelsey Distributors for purchase on April 19
April 27	Gave refund of $800 to customer from April 21. The cost of the returned merchandise was $535.
April 30	Sold merchandise of $2,000 on account with the terms 2/10, n/30. The merchandise cost $1,200.

Requirements

1. Enter each transaction into the accounting equation, assuming Morgan Parts Company, Inc., uses a perpetual inventory system. Start with the opening balances in cash and common stock described at the beginning of the problem.
2. Calculate the balance in the inventory account at the end of April.
3. Prepare a multistep income statement for the month of April and a balance sheet at April 30.
4. Calculate the gross profit ratio.

P5-57B. *Record merchandising transactions, prepare financial statements, and calculate gross profit ratio: perpetual inventory system. (LO 1, 2, 4, 6).* Wood Chuck Lumber Supplies is a finished wood provider for several local businesses. At the beginning of January, Wood Chuck had a $25,000 balance in cash and $25,000 in common stock. During the month of January, the following transactions took place:

January 2	Purchased $5,000 worth of lumber on account from a local lumberjack. The terms were 2/15, n/30, FOB shipping point. Freight costs were $100.
January 6	Sold $2,000 of lumber to Locked Up Fencing on account, with terms 1/05, n/25, FOB destination. Freight costs were $25. The cost of the inventory sold was $750.

January 12	Paid for the January 2 purchase
January 15	Received payment in full from Locked Up Fencing
January 18	Sold $3,000 worth of wood to Extreme Cabinet Makers on account, with terms 5/10, n/45, FOB shipping point. Freight costs were $75. The cost of the inventory sold was $2,000.
January 19	Returned a small amount of poor quality lumber to the lumberjack and received cash payment of $75
January 22	Purchased $7,000 of lumber from Tree Choppers on account. Terms were n/45, FOB destination. Freight costs were $100.
January 25	Sold $5,000 worth of lumber to Cabin Fever for cash. Cabin Fever picked up the order, so there were no shipping costs. The cost of the inventory sold was $2,750.
January 31	Paid for the purchase made on January 22.
January 31	Declared and paid cash dividends of $400

Requirements

1. Enter each transaction into the accounting equation, assuming Wood Chuck Lumber Supplies uses a perpetual inventory system. Start with the opening balances in cash and common stock described at the beginning of the problem.
2. Calculate the cost of goods sold for January and the ending balance in inventory.
3. Prepare the multistep income statement and the statement of changes in shareholders' equity for the month of January, and the balance sheet at January 31.
4. Calculate the gross profit ratio for Wood Chuck Lumber Supplies for the month of January. Explain what the ratio measures.

P5-58B. *Analyze accounting methods and prepare corrected income statement. (LO 1, 2, 4).* You are the accountant for Celebration Company, and your assistant has prepared the following income statement for the year ended December 31, 2010:

Celebration Company
Income Statement
For the Year Ended December 31, 2010

Sales revenue		$650,000
Sales returns and allowances	$ 18,100	
Freight expenses	2,000	
Selling expenses	48,300	(68,400)
Net sales		581,600
Expenses		
Cost of goods sold	350,000	
Salary expenses	82,000	
Rent expense	10,000	
Administrative expenses	23,500	
Dividends	4,000	
Total expenses		469,500
Net income		$112,100

You have uncovered the following facts:
  a. Sales revenue includes $6,000 of items that have been back-ordered. (The items have not been delivered to the customers, although the customers have paid for the items.)
  b. Selling expenses include $4,000 of allowances that were given to customers who received damaged products.
  c. Rent expense includes $400 worth of rent that applies to 2011.
  d. Salary expenses include $10,000 loaned to one of the executives for a boat.

Requirements

1. Prepare a corrected multistep income statement for the year. Celebration shows sales as the net amount only on its income statement.
2. Write a memo to your assistant explaining why each error you found is incorrect and what the correct accounting treatment should be.

P5-59B. *Calculate cost of goods sold and ending inventory and analyze effect of each method on the financial statements. (LO 3, 4).* Washington Company had the following sales and purchases during 2009, its first year of business:

January 8	Purchased 125 units at $100 each
February 20	Sold 75 units at $150 each
April 13	Sold 35 units at $150 each
June 28	Purchased 235 units at $105 each
August 2	Sold 175 units at $150 each
November 24	Purchased 140 units at $110 each

Requirements

1. Calculate the ending inventory, the cost of goods sold, and the gross profit for the December 31, 2009, financial statements under each of the following assumptions:
   a. FIFO periodic
   b. LIFO periodic
   c. Weighted average cost periodic
2. How will the differences between the methods affect the income statement for the year and balance sheet at December 31, 2009?

P5-60B. *Calculate cost of goods sold and ending inventory; analyze effects of each method on financial statements; apply lower-of-cost-or-market rule; calculate inventory turnover ratio. (LO 3, 4, 5, 6).* Kami's Pink Purses buys and then resells a special type of pink purse. Here is some information concerning Kami's inventory activity during the month of August 2010:

August 2	860 units on hand at a total cost of $51,600
August 6	Sold 400 units at $120 per unit
August 8	Purchased 640 units at $55 per unit
August 12	Purchased 425 units at $50 per unit
August 15	Sold 600 units at $120 per unit
August 21	Purchased 300 units at $50 per unit
August 24	Sold 800 units at $115 per unit
August 31	Purchased 100 units at $45 per unit

Requirements

1. Calculate the value of the ending inventory and cost of goods sold, assuming the company uses a periodic inventory system and the FIFO cost flow assumption.
2. Calculate the value of the ending inventory and cost of goods sold, assuming the company uses a periodic inventory system and the LIFO cost flow assumption.
3. Calculate the value of the ending inventory and cost of goods sold, assuming the company uses a periodic inventory system and the weighted average cost flow assumption.
4. Which of the three methods will result in the highest cost of goods sold for August?
5. Which of the three methods will provide the most current ending inventory value for Kami's balance sheet at August 31, 2010?
6. How would the differences between the methods affect Kami's income statement for August and balance sheet at August 31, 2010?

7. Calculate the company's inventory turnover ratio and average days in inventory for the month for each method in items (1), (2), and (3).
8. At the end of the month, the current replacement cost of the inventory is $32,000. Indicate at what amount the company's inventory will be reported using the lower-of-cost-or-market rule for each method (FIFO, LIFO, and weighted average cost).

P5-61B. *Calculate cost of goods sold, ending inventory, and inventory turnover ratio. (LO 3, 6).* The following merchandise inventory transactions occurred during the month of June for Heavy Metal Guitars (HMG):

June 6	Inventory on hand was 500 units at a cost of $100 each
June 11	Sold 100 units for $200 each
June 15	Purchased 200 units at $125 each
June 21	Sold 300 units for $225 each
June 27	Purchased 100 units for $75 each

Requirements

1. Assume HMG uses a periodic inventory system and compute the cost of goods sold for the month ended June 30 and ending inventory at June 30 using each of the following cost flow methods:
   a. FIFO
   b. LIFO
   c. Weighted average cost
2. Using the information for item (1), calculate the inventory turnover ratio and average days in inventory for the month of June for each method.
3. Assume HMG uses the perpetual inventory system and compute the cost of goods sold for the month ended June 30 and ending inventory at June 30 using each of the following cost flow methods:
   a. FIFO
   b. LIFO

P5-62B. *Analyze effect of cost flow method on financial statements and inventory turnover ratio. (LO 2, 4, 6).* Castana Company is considering changing inventory cost flow methods. Castana's primary objective is to minimize its tax liability. Currently, the firm uses weighted average cost. Data for 2012 are provided.

Beginning inventory (2,000 units)	$ 10,000
Purchases	
5,000 units at $6 each	$ 30,000
4,000 units at $6.50 each	26,000
6,000 units at $7 each	42,000
Sales	
15,000 units at $10 each	$150,000

Operating expenses were $12,000 and the company's tax rate is 25%.

Requirements

1. Prepare the income statement for 2012 using each of the following methods:
   a. FIFO periodic
   b. LIFO periodic
2. Which method provides the more current balance sheet inventory balance at December 31, 2012? Explain your answer.

3. Which method provides the more current cost of goods sold for the year ended December 31, 2012? Explain your answer.
4. Which method provides the better inventory turnover ratio for the year? Explain your answer.
5. In order to meet its goal, what is your recommendation to Castana Company? Explain your answer.

P5-63B. *Calculate cost of goods sold and ending inventory; analyze effects of each method on financial statements; apply lower-of-cost-or-market rule; calculate inventory turnover ratio. (LO 3, 4, 5, 6).* The following information is for Falling Numbers Computers for the year ended December 31, 2010.

At January 1, 2010:

- Cash amounted to $20,000.
- Beginning inventory was $35,000 (1,400 units at $25 each).
- Contributed capital was $25,000.
- Retained earnings was $45,000.

Transactions during 2010:

- Purchased 1,250 units for cash at $30 each
- Purchased 750 more units for cash at $20 each
- Cash sales of 2,400 units at $50 each
- Paid $10,000 cash for operating expenses
- Paid cash for income taxes at a rate of 40% of net income

Requirements

1. Compute the cost of goods sold and ending inventory at December 31, 2010, using each of the following cost flow methods:
   a. FIFO periodic
   b. LIFO periodic
   c. Weighted average cost periodic
2. For each method, prepare the balance sheet at December 31, 2010, a multistep income statement, and statement of cash flows for the fiscal year ended December 31, 2010.
3. What is income before taxes and net income after taxes under each of the three inventory cost flow assumptions? What observations can you make about net income from the analysis of the three methods?
4. For each method, calculate the inventory turnover ratio and average days in inventory for the fiscal year ended December 31, 2010.
5. At the end of the year, the current replacement cost of the inventory is $33,000. Indicate at what amount the company's inventory will be reported using the lower-of-cost-or-market rule for each method (FIFO, LIFO, and weighted average cost).

P5-64B. *Calculate the gross profit ratio and inventory turnover ratio. (LO 6).* The following information is from the financial statements of Toys for Toddlers Company:

For year ended (amounts in thousands)	December 31, 2012	December 31, 2011	December 31, 2010
Sales	$2,534,135	$2,187,438	$1,925,319
Cost of goods sold	1,634,562	1,383,665	1,229,277
Inventory	54,353	47,433	45,334

Requirements

1. Calculate the gross profit ratio for the last two years shown.
2. Calculate the inventory turnover ratio for the last two years shown.
3. What information do these comparisons provide?

Financial Statement Analysis

FSA5-1. *Analyze income statement. (LO 6).* The income statements for Williams-Sonoma, Inc., for the fiscal years ended February 1, 2009, and February 3, 2008, are shown here. Compare the company's performance for the two years. Is the company controlling its cost of inventory? Is the company controlling its other expenses well? Be able to support your answers.

Williams-Sonoma, Inc.
Consolidated Statements of Earnings

	Fiscal Year Ended	
(Dollars in thousands)	Feb. 1, 2009 (52 Weeks)	Feb. 3, 2008 (53 Weeks)
Net revenues	$3,361,472	$3,944,934
Cost of goods sold	2,226,300	2,408,963
Gross margin	1,135,172	1,535,971
Selling, general and administrative expenses	1,093,019	1,222,573
Interest income	(1,280)	(5,041)
Interest expense	1,480	2,099
Earnings before income taxes	41,953	316,340
Income taxes	11,929	120,583
Net earnings	$ 30,024	$ 195,757

FSA5-2. *Analyze inventory management. (LO 6).* Use the following information from The Wet Seal, Inc., to analyze the firm's inventory management. Calculate the gross profit ratio and the inventory turnover ratio for each year. How do you think Wet Seal is managing its inventory? What other information would be useful in answering this question?

The Wet Seal, Inc.
Consolidated Statements of Operations
(In thousands)

	Fiscal Years Ended		
	January 31, 2009	February 2, 2008	February 3, 2007
Net sales	$592,960	$611,163	$564,324
Cost of sales	400,521	408,892	370,888
Gross margin	192,439	202,271	193,436
Selling, general, and administrative expenses	154,671	177,468	178,703
Store-closure costs	—	—	(730)
Asset impairment	5,611	5,546	425
Operating income	32,157	19,257	15,038
Interest income	2,182	5,489	4,387
Interest expense	(2,863)	(1,136)	(31,955)
Interest (expense) income, net	(681)	4,353	(27,568)
Income (loss) before provision for income taxes	31,476	23,610	(12,530)
Provision for income taxes	1,322	378	308
Net income (loss)	$ 30,154	$ 23,232	$(12,838)

From the balance sheet at January 31, 2009
Inventory $25,529 (in thousands)
From the balance sheet at February 2, 2008
Inventory $31,590
From the balance sheet at February 3, 2007
Inventory $34,231
From the balance sheet at January 28, 2006
Inventory $25,475

FSA5-3. *Analyze inventory management. (LO 6).* Use the following information to analyze the inventory management of Amazon.com, Inc.:

(in millions)	For the year ended December 31, 2008	For the year ended December 31, 2007	At December 31, 2006
Sales	$19,166	$14,835	
Cost of sales	$14,896	$11,482	
Net income	$ 645	$ 476	
Inventory (at year end)	$ 1,399	$ 1,200	$877

Write a short report for Amazon.com's shareholders with your comments about its inventory management.

Critical Thinking Problems

Risks and Controls

In this chapter, you learned that retail firms are at risk that their inventory will become obsolete. What can a firm do to minimize this risk? What types of firms are most at risk? Least at risk?

Ethics

Jim's Music Company uses LIFO for inventory, and the company's profits are quite high this year. The cost of the inventory has been steadily rising all year, and Jim is worried about his taxes. His accountant has suggested that the company make a large purchase of inventory to be received during the last week in December. The accountant has explained to Jim that this would reduce his income significantly.

1. Jim does not understand the logic of the accountant's suggestion. Explain how the purchase would affect taxable income.
2. Is this ethical? Jim is uncertain about the appropriateness of this action from a legal and an ethical standpoint.

Group Assignment

Select a retail firm that you think might be concerned about obsolete inventory and another that you believe would not be very concerned. Then, find the financial statements and calculate the inventory turnover ratio of these two firms for the past two fiscal years. Are your results what you expected? Explain what you expected to find and your results.

Internet Exercise: Gap

The Gap, Inc., was founded in 1969 by Donald and Doris Fisher in San Francisco, California, with a single store and a handful of employees. Today, the company is one of the world's largest specialty retailers with three of the most recognized brands in the apparel industry (Gap, Banana Republic, and Old Navy). The Gap, Inc., has more than 134,000 employees supporting about 3,100 stores in the United States, United Kingdom, Canada, France, and Japan.

   Go to www.gapinc.com.

IE5-1. Click on Investors, followed by Financials, and then Annual Reports and Proxy. Download the latest annual report.

1. Which inventory cost flow assumption is used to measure the cost of inventory? Does The Gap, Inc., value inventory at the lower-of-cost-or-market value? If so, how is market value determined? Does this policy comply with GAAP?
2. For the three most recent years, list the amounts reported for net sales and gross profit. Is net sales increasing or decreasing? Is gross profit increasing or decreasing? Are these trends favorable or unfavorable? Explain your answer.
3. Using the financial statements, calculate the inventory turnover ratio for the three most recent years. (You will need inventory values from the 2007 and 2006 10Ks or annual reports, available on the Web site.) Did the inventory turnover ratio increase or decrease? What does this measure? What does The Gap, Inc., do to identify inventory that is slow moving and how is this inventory treated?
4. For cost of goods sold, The Gap, Inc., uses Cost of Goods Sold and Occupancy Expenses. What is included in this amount?

IE5-2. Go back to The Gap, Inc., homepage and click on Social Responsibility.

1. Does The Gap, Inc., do anything to ensure its garment workers are treated fairly? If so, why is this important for the company to do?
   Go back to About Gap Inc.
2. Click on How Our Clothes Are Made. List and briefly describe The Gap, Inc.'s five steps of its product life cycle.

Please note: Internet Web sites are constantly being updated. Therefore, if the information is not found where indicated, please explore the annual report further to find the information.

Appendix 5A

Inventory Errors

L.O.8
Describe and calculate the effect of inventory errors on the financial statements.

You know that the cost of the beginning inventory plus the cost of purchases equals the cost of goods available for sale. The cost of goods available for sale is then allocated between the cost of goods sold and the ending inventory. That is,

$$
\begin{aligned}
&\text{Beginning inventory} \\
&\underline{+ \ \text{Purchases}} \\
&= \text{Cost of goods available for sale} \\
&\underline{- \ \text{Ending inventory}} \\
&= \text{Cost of goods sold}
\end{aligned}
$$

Because inventory directly affects cost of goods sold, a major expense, errors in the calculation of beginning inventory or ending inventory will affect net income. Tracing the effects of errors requires slow, focused deliberation. To show how inventory errors can affect income, here is a simple numerical example that shows an ending inventory error and a beginning inventory error. Read each description and study the related examples.

Ending Inventory Errors

Suppose a firm has the correct amount for beginning inventory and the correct amount for purchases. Then, cost of goods available for sale is correct. If the ending inventory is overstated, cost of goods sold must be understated. Why? Because ending inventory and cost of goods sold are the two parts of cost of goods available for sale. Cost of goods sold is an expense. If the expense deducted from sales is too small, the result is that net income will be too large. Suppose you have correctly calculated the cost of goods available for sale (beginning inventory + purchases) to be $10. Those goods will either be sold and become part of cost of goods sold, or they will not be sold and will still be part of the inventory.

So, the cost of goods available for sale consists of two parts—cost of goods sold and ending inventory. Suppose the correct ending inventory is $2, but you erroneously give it a value of $3. If ending inventory is incorrectly valued at $3, then cost of goods sold will be valued at $7. Remember, the ending inventory and cost of goods sold must add up to $10 in this example. What is wrong with cost of goods sold? If ending inventory is actually $2, then cost of goods sold should be $8. See what happens? You understate cost of goods sold when you overstate the ending inventory. Anytime you understate an expense, you will overstate net income.

If ending inventory is too small (understated), cost of goods sold must be too large (overstated). The result is that net income will be understated. Let us use the same example, in which the cost of goods available for sale was correctly computed at $10. If ending inventory is actually $2 but you erroneously understate it as $1, then cost of goods sold will be valued as $9. It should be $8. So, an understatement in ending inventory has caused an overstatement of cost of goods sold. If you overstate an expense, then you will understate net income.

Beginning Inventory Errors

If ending inventory is overstated in 2009, then beginning inventory in 2010 will be overstated. After all, it is the same number. Errors in the ending inventory will, therefore, affect two consecutive years—ending inventory one year and beginning inventory the following year. If beginning inventory is overstated, then the cost of goods available for sale is overstated. If ending inventory is counted correctly, then cost of goods sold will be overstated. So, net income will be understated. Let us continue the previous example. If you value beginning inventory at $3 (and the correct value is $2) and you correctly add the purchases for the second year—say, $15 worth—then, the cost of goods available for sale will be $18. Keep in mind, the correct amount is $17. At year end, you count the ending inventory correctly at $6. The calculated cost of goods sold would be $12. Ending inventory and cost of goods sold must total $18. However, we know that the true cost of goods available for sale is $17. If the correct ending inventory is $6, then the correct cost of goods sold is $11. The calculated cost of goods sold was overstated by $1. When an expense is overstated, then net income will be understated.

If beginning inventory is understated, then the cost of goods available for sale is understated. If ending inventory is counted correctly, then cost of goods sold will be understated. So, net income will be overstated. Try thinking about the example in the format given in Exhibit 5A.1. As you can see, when you understate the beginning inventory, you will naturally understate cost of goods sold. This understated expense will result in an overstatement of net income.

	Calculated Amounts	Correct Amounts
Beginning inventory	$ 1 (understated from prior year error)	$ 2
+ Purchases	+ $15	+ $15
Cost of goods available for sale	$16	$17
− Ending inventory	$ 6	$ 6
Cost of goods sold	$10	$11

EXHIBIT 5A.1

Error in the Beginning Inventory

Note that over a period of two years the errors will counterbalance—they will cancel each other out. However, it is important that the financial statements be correct each year, not every other year, so a company will correct inventory errors if they are discovered, rather than wait for the errors to cancel each other out.

Berry Corporation miscounted the ending inventory at December 31, 2010. The balance sheet reported inventory of $360,000, but $25,000 worth of items were omitted from that amount. Berry reported net income of $742,640 for the year. What effect did this inventory error have on Berry's cost of goods sold for the year? What is the correct net income for the year ended December 31, 2010?

Your Turn 5A-1

Answer: Ending inventory was understated, so cost of goods sold was overstated. Too much expense was deducted, so net income should have been higher by $25,000 for a correct net income of $767,640.

Short Exercises

SE5A-1A. *Calculate inventory errors. (LO 8).* How would each of the following inventory errors affect net income for the year? Assume each is the only error during the year.
1. Ending inventory is overstated by $3,000.
2. Ending inventory is understated by $1,500.
3. Beginning inventory is understated by $3,000.
4. Beginning inventory is overstated by $1,550.

SE5A-2B. *Calculate inventory errors. (LO 8).* How would each of the following inventory errors affect net income for the year? Assume each is the only error during the year.
1. Ending inventory is overstated by $1,000.
2. Ending inventory is understated by $2,500.
3. Beginning inventory is understated by $4,000.
4. Beginning inventory is overstated by $2,500.

All of the A exercises can be found within MyAccountingLab, an online homework and practice environment.

Exercises

E5A-3A. *Calculate inventory errors. (LO 8).* Ian's Small Appliances reported cost of goods sold as follows:

All of the A exercises can be found within MyAccountingLab, an online homework and practice environment.

	2009	2010
Beginning inventory	$130,000	$ 50,000
Purchases	275,000	240,000
Cost of goods available for sale	405,000	290,000
Ending inventory	50,000	40,000
Cost of goods sold	$355,000	$250,000

Ian's made two errors:

1. 2009 ending inventory was understated by $5,000.
2. 2010 ending inventory was overstated by $2,000.

Calculate the correct cost of goods sold for 2009 and 2010.

E5A-4B. *Calculate inventory errors. (LO 8).* Tire Pro Company's records reported the following at the end of the fiscal year:

Beginning inventory	$ 80,000
Ending inventory	85,000
Cost of goods sold	295,000

A physical inventory count showed that the ending inventory was actually $78,000. If this error is not corrected, what effect would it have on the income statement for this fiscal year and the following fiscal year?

Problems

P5A-5A. *Analyze results of physical count of inventory and calculate cost of goods sold. (LO 8).* Matrix Company uses a periodic, weighted average inventory system. The company's accounting records showed the following related to November 2010 transactions:

	Units	Cost
Beginning inventory, November 1	400	$ 900
Purchases during November	1,250	4,275
Goods available for sale	1,650	$5,175
Cost of goods sold	1,300	4,077
Ending inventory, November 30	350	$1,098

On November 30, 2010, Matrix conducted a physical count of its inventory and discovered there were only 300 units of inventory actually on hand.

Requirements

1. Using the information from the physical count, correct the company's cost of goods sold for November.
2. How would this correction change the financial statements for this month?
3. What are some possible causes of the difference between the inventory amounts in the accounting records and the inventory amount from the physical count?

P5A-6B. *Analyze results of physical count of inventory and calculate cost of goods sold. (LO 8).* Paige's Office Paper Company uses a perpetual inventory system, so the cost of goods sold is recorded and the inventory records are updated at the time of every sale. The company's accounting records showed the following related to September 2009 transactions:

	Units	Total Cost
Beginning inventory, September 1	500	$ 1,500
Purchases during September	3,750	11,250
Goods available for sale	4,250	$12,750
Cost of goods sold	2,200	6,600
Ending inventory, September 30	2,050	$ 6,150

On September 30, 2009, Paige conducted a physical count of its inventory and discovered there were actually 1,900 units of inventory on hand.

Requirements

1. Using the information from the physical count, correct Paige's Office Paper's cost of goods sold for September.
2. How would this correction change the financial statements for the month?
3. What are some possible causes of the difference between the inventory amounts in the company's accounting records and the inventory amount from the physical count?

Appendix 5B

Gross Profit Method of Estimating Ending Inventory

L.O.9
Estimate inventory using the gross profit method.

There are times when a company might want to *estimate* the cost of the ending inventory rather than count the units to calculate the cost. For example, if a company prepares monthly or quarterly financial statements, GAAP allow ending inventory to be estimated for reporting on those financial statements. This saves a company the trouble of counting the inventory every quarter. Also, if the inventory is destroyed or stolen, the company will have a reliable estimate of the cost of the destroyed inventory for the insurance claim.

First, you must know the usual gross profit percentage—the gross profit ratio you learned about in Chapter 5—for the company. Gross profit percentage is gross profit divided by sales. You can calculate the gross profit ratio using prior years' sales and cost data. Then, you multiply that percentage by the sales for the period, which gives the estimated gross profit. You then subtract the estimated gross profit from sales to get the estimated cost of goods sold. Because you know (a) beginning inventory (from the last period's financial statements), (b) purchases (from your records), and (c) an estimate for cost of goods sold, you can estimate ending inventory.

For example, suppose Super Soap Company lost its entire inventory in a flood on April 16. Super Soap had prepared a set of financial statements on March 31, when the inventory on hand was valued at $2,500. During the first part of April, purchases amounted to $3,500. The usual gross profit percentage in this business is 40%. If Super Soap had sales of $8,200 during the first 16 days of April, how much inventory was lost?

1. If sales were $8,200 and the usual gross profit percentage is 40%, then the gross profit would be $3,280.
2. If sales were $8,200 and gross profit is $3,280, then cost of goods sold would be $4,920. In other words, if the gross profit percentage is 40%, then the other 60% must be the cost of goods sold. So 60% of $8,200 = cost of goods sold = $4,920.
3. Beginning inventory + purchases − cost of goods sold = ending inventory. $2,500 + $3,500 − $4,920 = $1,080. This is our best estimate of the lost inventory.

Suppose Base Company began May with inventory of $2,000 and purchased $8,000 worth of inventory during the first half of May. Sales for the first half of May amounted to $12,000.

Then, a fire destroyed the remaining inventory. Base Company has had a gross profit ratio of approximately 30% for the first four months of the year. Approximately how much inventory did Base Company lose in the fire?

Answer: $12,000 × 0.7 + Cost of goods sold, so $8,400 worth of inventory has been sold. $10,000 − $8,400 = $1,600 worth of inventory must have been lost in the fire.

Your Turn 5B-1

Short Exercise

MyAccountingLab

All of the A exercises can be found within MyAccountingLab, an online homework and practice environment.

SE5B-1A. *Estimate inventory. (LO 9).* Fantasy Games, Inc., wants to estimate its ending inventory balance for its quarterly financial statements for the first quarter of the year. Given the following, what is your best estimate?

Beginning inventory	$75,800
Net sales	$92,500
Net purchases	$50,500
Gross profit ratio	20%

SE5B-2B. *(Estimate inventory. (LO 9).* Knick-Knacks wants to estimate its ending inventory balance for its quarterly financial statements for the first quarter of the year. Given the following, what is your best estimate?

Beginning inventory	$3,800
Net sales	$9,500
Net purchases	$5,500
Gross profit ratio	20%

Exercises

E5B-3A. *Estimate inventory. (LO 9).* The following information is available for the Arizona Chemical Supply Company:

Inventory, January 1, 2009	$240,000
Net purchases for the month of January	750,000
Net sales for the month of January	950,000
Gross profit ratio (historical)	40%

Estimate the cost of goods sold for January and the ending inventory at January 31, 2009.

E5B-4B. *Estimate inventory. (LO 9).* The records of Florida Tool Shop revealed the following information related to inventory destroyed in Hurricane Frances:

Inventory, beginning of period	$300,000
Purchases to date of hurricane	140,000
Net sales to date of hurricane	885,000
Gross profit ratio	55%

The company needs to file a claim for lost inventory with its insurance company. What is the estimated value of the lost inventory?

Problems

P5B-5A. *Estimate inventory. (LO 9).* Hines Fruit Corp. sells fresh fruit to tourists on Interstate 75 in Florida. A tornado destroyed the entire inventory in late June. In order to file an insurance claim, Hazel and Gene, the owners of the company, must estimate the value of the lost inventory. Records from January 1 through the date of the tornado in June indicated that Hines Fruit Corp. started the year with $4,000 worth of inventory on hand. Purchases for the year amounted to $9,000, and sales up to the date of the tornado were $16,000. Gross profit percentage has traditionally been 30%.

Requirements

1. How much should Hazel and Gene request from the insurance company?
2. Suppose that one case of fruit was spared by the tornado. The cost of that case was $700. How much was the inventory loss under these conditions?

P5B-6B. *Estimate inventory. (LO 9).* Carrie's Cotton Candy Company sells cotton candy to visitors at a traveling county fair. During a drought a fire destroyed the entire inventory in late July. In order to file an insurance claim, Carrie, the owner of the company, must estimate the value of the lost inventory. Records from January 1 through the date of the fire in July indicated that Carrie's Cotton Candy Company started the year with $4,250 worth of inventory on hand. Purchases for the year amounted to $8,000, and sales up to the date of the fire were $17,500. Gross profit percentage has traditionally been 35%.

Requirements

1. How much should Carrie request from the insurance company?
2. Suppose that one bag of cotton candy mix was spared by the fire. The cost of that bag was $50. How much was the inventory loss under these conditions?

Acquisition and Use of Long-Term Assets

LEARNING OBJECTIVES

When you are finished studying Chapter 6, you should be able to:

1. Explain how long-term assets are classified and how their costs are computed.

2. Explain and compute how tangible assets are written off over their useful lives and reported on the financial statements.

3. Explain and compute how intangible assets are written off over their useful lives and reported on the financial statements.

4. Explain how decreases in value, repairs, changes in productive capacity, and changes in estimates of useful life and salvage value of long-term assets affect the financial statements.

5. Explain how the disposal of a long-term asset is reflected in the financial statements.

6. Recognize and explain how long-term assets are reported on the financial statements, and prepare financial statements that include long-term assets.

7. Use return on assets (ROA) and the asset turnover ratio to help evaluate a firm's performance.

8. Identify and describe the business risks associated with long-term assets and the controls that can minimize those risks.

9. (Appendix 6) Explain how depreciation for financial statements differs from depreciation for taxes.

ETHICS Matters

Anyone Need a Forklift?

Most thieves prefer cash; some may even prefer jewelry. However, very few prefer forklifts. Large, expensive assets that a firm uses over a period of years are often difficult to steal. It's impossible to sneak out of the factory building with a forklift in your briefcase. These assets, however, can be stolen. The challenge with these types of assets is to make sure that the people who have access to them have the appropriate authorization.

In June 2009, three contract employees for the Metropolitan Transportation Authority (New York's MTA) were charged with stealing eight forklifts and other equipment from a warehouse in Queens. The employees who were in charge of the warehouse thought that the three contract workers were authorized to dispose of the equipment. Why? Because the three wore the uniforms of the firm that has the maintenance contract with the MTA. The accused thieves sold the forklifts to a scrap yard for a little over $7,000. The cost to replace the stolen property was more than $250,000.

According to the Association of Certified Fraud Examiners' 2008 Report to the Nation on Occupational Fraud & Abuse, 16.3% of all occupational fraud is due to misappropriation of noncash assets. Some of those assets were obviously taken in broad daylight. The lesson is that all assets, no matter how unlikely to be stolen, need appropriate safeguarding.

Acquiring Long-Term Assets

So far, you have learned how a firm provides goods and services to its customers and the related collection of the payments. In this chapter, we will look at the purchase of long-term assets, also called long-lived assets or fixed assets, which are used in the operation of a business.

All businesses purchase long-term operational assets, such as computers, copy machines, and furniture, as well as short-term assets, such as folders, paper, and pens. Acquiring long-term assets is usually more complicated than acquiring short-term assets. Purchasing long-term assets is complex for several reasons. With long-term assets, a firm must put a great deal of care in selecting the vendor because the relationship could last for a significant amount of time. In addition, the monetary investment in long-term assets is typically much greater than the investment in short-term assets and it is more difficult to dispose of long-term assets if the company makes a bad decision. For example, a new computer system for tracking inventory would cost a firm like Staples thousands of dollars more than the purchase of a new telephone for the employee lounge. If the Staples manager did not like the kind of phone that was purchased, he or she would simply give the phone away or donate it to the local Goodwill and buy another. What happens if the manager decides that the company purchased the wrong computerized inventory system? It is significantly harder to get rid of the long-term asset, and it could reflect poorly on the manager who made the decision to purchase the system in the first place.

Before a firm purchases a long-term asset, it must determine how much revenue that asset will generate and how much the asset will cost. The cost of a long-term asset must include all of the costs to get the asset ready for use. Long-term assets often require extensive setup and preparation before they become operational, and employees need to be trained to use them. If Staples purchases a new computerized inventory system, it may require new hardware and software, and employees will need to be trained to use the new system. All of these costs will be recorded as part of the cost of the asset.

Considering all of these costs is part of the business process of acquiring a long-term asset. Accountants then use these costs to account for the purchase and use of the asset. What assets to buy and how to pay for them are decisions that do not affect the income statement at the time of the purchase. Recording the purchase of a long-term asset affects the balance sheet and potentially the statement of cash flows. As you saw in Chapter 3, a business defers recognizing the expense of a long-term asset until the asset is actually used in the business. When the asset is used and the expense is recognized, the expense is called depreciation expense. This deferral is an example of a timing difference. We have purchased a long-term asset at one point in time in the past, and we will use that asset over a subsequent period of time.

Types of Long-Lived Assets: Tangible and Intangible

Tangible assets are assets with physical substance; they can be seen and touched.

There are two categories of long-term assets used in a business: **tangible assets** and **intangible assets**. Exhibit 6.1 shows the long-term asset section of Staples' balance sheet, where you will see both types of long-term assets.

Common tangible assets are property, plant, and equipment (PPE). Common intangible assets are trademarks, patents, and copyrights. We will discuss these in detail later in the chapter.

Intangible assets are rights, privileges, or benefits that result from owning long-lived assets that do not have physical substance.

Acquisition Costs

Consider the purchase of a long-term asset. The historical cost principle requires a company to record an asset at the amount paid for the asset—its cost. The cost for property, plant, and equipment includes all expenditures that are reasonable and necessary to get an asset in place and ready for use. The reason for reporting all of these costs on the balance sheet, as part of the cost of the asset, is to defer recognition of the expense until the asset is actually used to generate revenue. This is, as you know, the matching principle, which provides the foundation for accrual basis accounting. The assets are put on the balance sheet and then written off as expenses over the accounting periods in which they are used to generate revenue. Following are some common components of the cost of property, plant, and equipment:

1. When a firm purchases land to use as the location of a building or factory, the acquisition cost includes the following:
   a. Price paid for the land
   b. Real estate commissions

EXHIBIT 6.1

From the Balance Sheet of Staples

You won't know the meaning of some terms Staples has used, but you will learn about many of them in this chapter.

```
From the Balance Sheet of Staples, Inc.
                (in thousands)
```

	January 31, 2009	February 2, 2008
Property and equipment:		
Land and buildings	$1,040,754	$ 859,751
Leasehold improvements	1,183,879	1,135,132
Equipment	1,949,646	1,819,381
Furniture and fixtures	926,702	871,361
Total property and equipment	5,100,981	4,685,625
Less accumulated depreciation and amortization	2,810,355	2,524,486
Net property and equipment	2,290,626	2,161,139
Lease acquisition costs net of accumulated amortization	26,931	31,399
Intangible assets net of accumulated amortization	701,918	231,310
Goodwill	3,780,169	1,764,928
Other assets	476,153	292,186
Total long-term assets	$7,275,797	$4,480,962

These are *tangible* assets: Land and buildings, Leasehold improvements, Equipment, Furniture and fixtures

These are *intangible* assets: Lease acquisition costs net of accumulated amortization, Intangible assets net of accumulated amortization, Goodwill

c. Attorneys' fees
d. Costs of preparing the land for use, such as clearing or draining
e. Costs of tearing down existing structures

In general, land is not depreciated. Because land typically retains its usefulness and is not consumed to produce revenue, its cost remains unchanged on the balance sheet as a long-term asset. Even if the land's value increases, financial statements prepared under U.S. GAAP will show the land at cost.

2. When a firm purchases a physical plant, the acquisition cost includes the following:
   a. Purchase cost of buildings or factories
   b. Costs to update or remodel the facilities
   c. Any other costs to get the plant operational
3. When a firm purchases equipment, the acquisition cost includes the following:
   a. Purchase cost
   b. Freight-in—cost to have the equipment delivered
   c. Insurance while in transit
   d. Installation costs, including test runs
   e. Cost of training employees to use the new equipment
4. When a firm constructs or renovates a building, the acquisition cost includes the following:
   a. Architects' or contractors' fees
   b. Construction costs
   c. Cost of renovating the building

In contrast to the accounting treatment of land, even if a firm expects a building to increase in value, the asset will be depreciated. In practice, most assets used in a business to generate revenues will decrease in value as they are used. Recall that depreciation is not meant to value an asset at its market value. Rather, it is the systematic allocation of the cost of an asset to the periods in which the asset is used by the firm to generate revenue.

Your Turn 6-1

For each of the following costs, indicate whether it should be recorded as an asset or recorded as an expense at the time of the transaction:

1. Payment for employee salaries
2. Purchase of new delivery truck
3. Rent paid in advance
4. Rent paid in arrears (after use of the building)

Basket Purchase Allocation

Calculating the acquisition cost of certain assets can be difficult. Buying a building with the land it occupies is an example of a "basket purchase" because two assets are acquired for a single price. For the accounting records, the firm must calculate a separate cost for each asset. Why? The firm will depreciate the building but it will not depreciate the land. The firm divides the purchase price between the building and land by using the **relative fair market value method**. Suppose a company purchased a building and its land together for one price of $100,000. The company would obtain a market price, usually in the form of an appraisal, for each item separately. Then, the company uses the relative amounts of the individual appraisals to allocate the purchase price of $100,000 between the two assets. Suppose the building was appraised at $90,000 and the land was appraised at $30,000. The total appraised value is $120,000 ($90,000 + $30,000).

The building accounts for three-quarters of the total appraised value.

$$\$90,000 \div \$120,000 = 3/4$$

So, the accountant records the building at three-fourths of the total cost of the basket purchase.

$$3/4 \times \$100,000 = \$75,000$$

The cost assigned to the land will be the remaining $25,000.

$$\$100,000 - \$75,000 = \$25,000$$

Or if you want to calculate it,

$$1/4 \times \$100,000 = \$25,000$$

This same method—using an asset's proportion of the total appraised value of a group of assets—can be used for any number of assets purchased together for a single price.

Relative fair market value method is a way to allocate the total cost for several assets purchased together to each of the individual assets. This method is based on the assets' individual market values.

Your Turn 6-2

Bargain Company paid $480,000 for a building and the land on which it is located. Independent appraisals valued the building at $400,000 and the land at $100,000. How much should Bargain Company record as the cost of the building and how much as the cost of the land? Why does the company need to record the costs separately?

L.O.2
Explain and compute how tangible assets are written off over their useful lives and reported on the financial statements.

Using Long-Term Tangible Assets: Depreciation and Depletion

Now that you are familiar with the types of assets a firm may have and the costs associated with their acquisition, we are ready to talk about using the assets. Until property, plant, and equipment are put into use, their costs remain as assets on the balance sheet. As soon as the firm uses the asset to help generate revenue, the financial statements will show some amount of expense on the income statement. Recording a cost as an asset, rather than recording it as an expense, is called **capitalizing** the cost. That cost will be recognized as an expense during the periods in which the asset is used. Recall from Chapter 3 that depreciation is a systematic and rational allocation process to recognize the expense of long-term assets over the periods in which the assets are used. Depreciation is an example of the matching principle—matching the cost of an asset with the revenue it helps generate. For each year a company plans to use an asset, the company will recognize depreciation expense on the income statement.

To **capitalize** is to record a cost as an asset rather than to record it as an expense.

If you hear or read, "The asset is worth $10,000 on our books," that does not mean the asset is actually worth that amount if it were sold. Instead, it means that $10,000 is the carrying value or book value of the asset in the accounting records—it is the amount not yet depreciated. It is called the carrying value because that is the amount at which we carry our assets on the balance sheet. The amount not yet depreciated is also known as the book value because it is the value of the asset in the accounting records. As you read about the specific methods of depreciating assets, refer to the vocabulary of depreciation in Exhibit 6.2.

Amortization means to write off the cost of a long-term asset over more than one accounting period.

Accountants primarily use three terms to describe how a cost is written off over several accounting periods. **Amortization** is the most general expression for writing off the cost of a

EXHIBIT 6.2

Depreciation Terminology

Term	Definition	Example	
Cost or **acquisition cost**	The amount paid for the asset, including all amounts necessary to get the asset up and running	Staples purchases computer cash registers for its new store for $21,000.	
Estimated useful life	How long the company plans to use the asset; may be measured in years or in units that the asset will produce	Staples plans to use these cash registers for 10 years.	
Salvage value or **residual value**	Estimated value the asset will have when the company is done with it—the salvage value is the estimated market value on the anticipated disposal date	When Staples is done using the cash registers, the company plans to sell them for $1,000.	
Depreciable base	*Cost* minus *salvage value*	The depreciable base is $21,000 − $1,000 = $20,000.	
Book value or **carrying value**	*Cost* less accumulated *depreciation*	If Staples uses the straight-line method, the company's depreciation expense will be $2,000 per year. After the first year, the book value will be $19,000 (= $21,000 − $2,000).	

long-term asset. **Depreciation** is the specific word that describes the amortization of certain kinds of property, plant, or equipment. **Depletion** is the specific term that describes the amortization of a natural resource. There is no specific term for writing off intangible assets, so accountants use the general term *amortization* to describe writing off the cost of intangible assets.

All of these terms—amortization, depreciation, and depletion—refer to allocating the cost of an asset to more than one accounting period.

Accountants use several methods of depreciation for the financial statements. We will discuss three of the most common methods:

1. Straight-line depreciation
2. Activity (units-of-production) depreciation
3. Declining balance depreciation

> **Depreciation** is a systematic and rational allocation process to recognize the expense of long-term assets over the periods in which the assets are used.
>
> **Depletion** is the amortization of a natural resource.

For each of the following, give the term for writing off the cost of the asset:

Your Turn 6-3

1. Equipment
2. Building
3. Oil well

Straight-Line Depreciation

Straight-line depreciation is a depreciation method in which the depreciation expense is the same each period.

Straight-line depreciation is the simplest way to allocate the cost of an asset to the periods in which the asset is used. This is the method we used in Chapter 3. Using this method, the depreciation expense is the same every period. To calculate the appropriate amount of depreciation expense for each accounting period, you follow several steps.

1. Estimate the useful life of the asset. The firm should consider this estimate when purchasing an asset and use the estimate after the purchase to properly account for the cost of that asset.

Salvage value (also known as *residual value*) is the estimated value of an asset at the end of its useful life.

2. Estimate the **salvage value**, the amount you believe the asset will be worth when the company is finished using it. Salvage value is the amount you think someone will pay you for the used asset. Someone who knows a lot about the asset and the relationship between the use of the asset and its market value will estimate the salvage value. Salvage value is an estimate that you may need to revise more than once during the life of the asset. The useful life and the salvage value are related, and the firm should have made these estimates as part of the acquisition decision.
3. Calculate the depreciable base—the amount you want to depreciate—by deducting the salvage value from the acquisition cost of the asset.
4. Divide the depreciable base—the difference between the asset's cost and its estimated salvage value—by the estimate of the number of years of the asset's useful life. This gives you the annual depreciation expense.

$$[\text{Acquisition cost} - \text{Salvage value}] \div \text{Estimated useful life in years}$$
$$= \text{Annual depreciation expense}$$

We will use an orange juice machine purchased by Holiday Hotels to demonstrate all of the depreciation methods. Exhibit 6.3 summarizes the information we need for all three depreciation methods.

EXHIBIT 6.3

Holiday Hotels' Orange Juice Machine

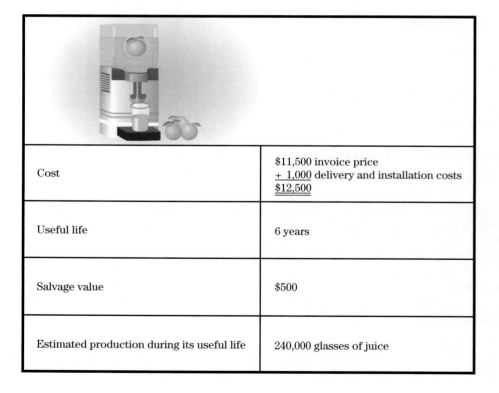

Cost	$11,500 invoice price + 1,000 delivery and installation costs $12,500
Useful life	6 years
Salvage value	$500
Estimated production during its useful life	240,000 glasses of juice

Suppose Holiday Hotels purchases a new squeeze-your-own orange juice machine for its self-service breakfast bar. Such a machine is expensive and requires large supplies of fresh oranges. After considering the risks and rewards of purchasing the machine and evaluating the effect such a purchase would have on the financial statements, Holiday Hotels decides to purchase an $11,500 machine with an estimated useful life of six years. In addition to the invoice price of $11,500, delivery and installation costs amount to $1,000. Holiday will capitalize these costs as part of the acquisition cost of the asset. Holiday estimates that the machine will have a salvage value of $500 at the end of six years. After someone in the firm who is knowledgeable about the characteristics of the asset reviews and confirms the judgments about useful life and salvage value, Holiday will calculate the yearly depreciation expense.

First, Holiday calculates the depreciable base by subtracting the salvage value from the cost.

$$\text{Cost} = \$11,500 + \$1,000 = \$12,500$$
$$\text{Salvage value} = \$500$$
$$\text{Depreciable base} = \$12,500 - \$500 = \$12,000$$

Then, Holiday divides the depreciable base by the number of years of useful life.

$$\text{Annual depreciation expense} = \$12,000/6 \text{ years} = \$2,000 \text{ per year}$$

Each year the income statement will include depreciation expense of $2,000, and each year the carrying value of the asset will be reduced by $2,000. This reduction in carrying value is accumulated over the life of the asset. A company's accounting records always preserve the acquisition cost of the asset and disclose the cost on the balance sheet or in the notes, so Holiday will keep the total accumulated depreciation in a separate account and subtract it from the acquisition cost of the asset on the balance sheet. If Holiday bought the machine on January 1, 2010, and the company's fiscal year ends on December 31, then the income statement for the year ended December 31, 2010, would include depreciation expense of $2,000. The balance sheet would show the acquisition cost of $12,500 and the accumulated depreciation at December 31, 2010 of $2,000. This is how the adjustment for depreciation expense would look in the accounting equation:

Assets	=	Liabilities	+	Shareholders' equity		
				Contributed capital	+	**Retained earnings**
Accumulated depreciation— Equipment (2,000)						Depreciation expense (2,000)

The equipment account will have a balance of $12,500 during the entire life of the asset. The accumulated depreciation account, a contra-asset, will have a balance of $2,000 after the 2010 depreciation is recorded. Here is how the asset is reported on the balance sheet at December 31, 2010:

	December 31, 2010
Equipment	$12,500
Less: accumulated depreciation	(2,000)
Net book value	$10,500

In the following year, 2011, the income statement for the year would again include $2,000 depreciation expense. The straight-line method gets its name from the fact that the same amount is depreciated each year, so the depreciation expense could be graphed as a straight horizontal line across the life of the asset. The adjustment at the end of 2011 will be identical to the adjustment at the end of 2010. It will add $2,000 to the accumulated depreciation account, so the new balance is $4,000. Because the income statement is only for a single year, the depreciation expense will again be $2,000. The balance sheet at December 31, 2011, would show how the carrying value of our asset is declining, because on that date Holiday has used it for two years.

	December 31, 2011
Equipment	$12,500
Less: accumulated depreciation	(4,000)
Net book value	$ 8,500

Exhibit 6.4 shows the depreciation expense and accumulated depreciation amounts for the year-end financial statements during the entire life of the asset. At the end of the useful life of the

asset, the carrying value will equal the salvage value. Holiday has previously estimated that it could sell the asset at the end of its useful life for a price equal to its carrying value—$500.

EXHIBIT 6.4

Straight-Line Depreciation

The depreciation expense each year is always $2,000, as shown in the table and accompanying graph. The carrying value decreases over time, from $10,500 at December 31, 2010, to $500 at December 31, 2015.

Year	Depreciation Expense for the Year on the Income Statement	Accumulated Depreciation on Year-End Balance Sheet	Carrying or Book Value on the Year-End Balance Sheet
2010	$2,000	$ 2,000	$10,500
2011	$2,000	$ 4,000	$ 8,500
2012	$2,000	$ 6,000	$ 6,500
2013	$2,000	$ 8,000	$ 4,500
2014	$2,000	$10,000	$ 2,500
2015	$2,000	$12,000	$ 500

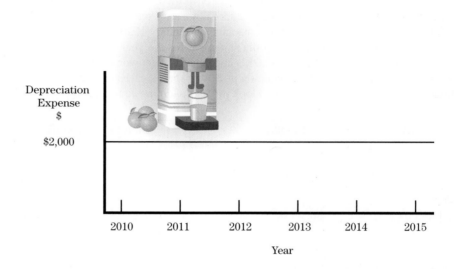

Your Turn 6-4

On January 1, 2010, Access Company purchased a new computer system for $15,000. The estimated useful life of the computer system was five years, with an estimated salvage value of $3,000. Using straight-line depreciation, how much depreciation expense will Access Company include on the income statement for the year ended December 31, 2011? Determine the book value of the asset on December 31, 2011.

Activity (Units-of-Production) Depreciation

Another way a firm determines depreciation expense is by estimating the productivity of the asset—how much the asset will produce during its useful life. How many units will the asset produce or how much work will the asset do during its useful life? This way of determining depreciation expense is called the **activity method of depreciation**, also known as the units-of-production method. Examples of activities are miles driven or units produced. If a company buys a car, it may decide to use it for 100,000 miles before trading it in. The activity method is similar to the straight-line method. The difference is that an estimate of the number of units of activity over the asset's life is used as the allocation base instead of an estimate of the number of years of useful life.

Activity method of depreciation is the method of depreciation in which useful life is expressed in terms of the total units of activity or production expected from the asset, and the asset is written off in proportion to its activity during the accounting period.

$$\frac{\text{Acquisition cost} - \text{Salvage value}}{\text{Estimated useful life in activity units}} = \text{Rate per activity unit}$$

$$\text{Rate} \times \text{Actual activity level for the year} = \text{Annual depreciation expense}$$

To use the activity method of depreciation, Holiday needs to estimate how many units the machine will be able to produce during its useful life. Suppose Holiday estimates the machine will be able to produce 240,000 glasses of juice during its useful life. You calculate the depreciable base in exactly the same way when using the activity method of depreciation as when using straight-line depreciation—subtract the expected salvage value from the cost. In this example, the depreciable base is $12,000 ($12,500 – $500). You then divide the depreciable base by the total number of units you expect to produce with the machine during its useful life.

Here is how the activity method of depreciation can be applied to Holiday's orange juice machine. Start by dividing the depreciable base—$12,000—by the estimated number of glasses of orange juice the machine will produce. That gives the depreciation rate.

$$\$12,000 \div 240,000 \text{ glasses} = \$0.05 \text{ per glass}$$

Holiday will use this rate of $0.05 per glass to depreciate the machine for each glass of juice it produces. Suppose the machine has a built-in counter that showed 36,000 glasses of juice were squeezed during the first year. The depreciation expense shown on the income statement for that year would be $1,800.

$$36,000 \text{ glasses} \times \$0.05 \text{ per glass} = \$1,800 \text{ depreciation expense}$$

That is the depreciation expense for the year, and the book value of the asset would decline by that amount when the year-end adjustment is made. It is important to keep a record of the book value of the asset so that Holiday Hotels does not depreciate the asset lower than its $500 estimated salvage value. The salvage value will equal the carrying value when the asset has reached the end of Holiday's estimate of the useful life.

Exhibit 6.5 shows the depreciation schedule for the orange juice machine, given the production levels for each year as shown.

EXHIBIT 6.5

Activity Method of Depreciation

Year	Production Each Year— Number of Glasses of Orange Juice	Depreciation Rate × Number of Glasses of Juice *Rate: $0.05 per Glass	Depreciation Expense for the Year (Income Statment)	Accumulated Depreciation (Balance Sheet at the End of the Year)	Book Value of the Asset (Balance Sheet at the End of the Year)
2010	36,000	$0.05 × 36,000	$1,800	$ 1,800	$10,700
2011	41,000	$0.05 × 41,000	$2,050	$ 3,850	$ 8,650
2012	39,000	$0.05 × 39,000	$1,950	$ 5,800	$ 6,700
2013	46,000	$0.05 × 46,000	$2,300	$ 8,100	$ 4,400
2014	43,000	$0.05 × 43,000	$2,150	$10,250	$ 2,250
2015	35,000	$0.05 × 35,000	$1,750	$12,000	$ 500

Cost of machine of $12,500 minus salvage value of $500, gives a depreciable base of $12,000. Total estimated production is 240,000 glasses. *Rate = $12,000 ÷ 240,000 = $0.05 per glass.

With the activity depreciation method, the depreciation expense each year depends on how many units the asset produces each year. This method matches the expense to the amount of work performed by the asset. Although the book value is decreasing each year, the amount of depreciation expense will likely vary from year-to-year, as shown in both the table and graph. As always, accumulated depreciation is working its way up until it reaches the depreciable base—cost minus salvage value. That means the book value will be equal to the estimated salvage value at the end of its useful life.

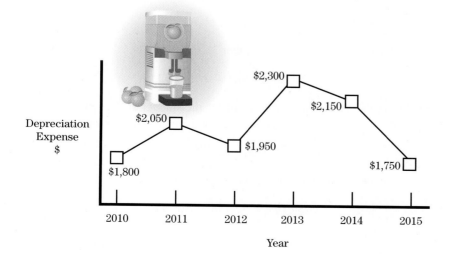

Your Turn 6-5

Hopper Company purchased a weaving machine on January 1, 2009, for $44,000. The expected useful life is 10 years or production of 100,000 rugs, and its salvage value is estimated at $4,000. In 2009, 13,000 rugs were made, and in 2010, 14,000 rugs were made. Calculate the depreciation expense for 2009 and 2010 using activity depreciation.

Declining Balance Depreciation

Declining balance depreciation is an accelerated depreciation method in which depreciation expense is based on the declining book value of the asset.

Accelerated depreciation is a depreciation method in which more depreciation expense is taken in the early years of the asset's life and less in the later years.

You have learned about the straight-line depreciation method and the activity method of depreciation. The third method is **declining balance depreciation**. This method is considered an **accelerated depreciation** method, one that allows more depreciation in the early years of an asset's life and less in the later years. The higher depreciation charges will occur in the early, more productive years when the equipment is generating more revenue. Depreciating more of the asset in the first few years also helps even out the total expenses related to an asset. In later years, the depreciation expense is lower but repair expenses are likely to increase.

The declining balance method speeds up an asset's depreciation by applying a constant rate to the declining book value of an asset. Frequently, firms use a version of the declining balance method called double-declining balance. The firm takes 200% of the straight-line rate to use as the annual depreciation rate. For example, if the useful life of an asset were five years, the straight-line rate would be one-fifth, or 20%. That is because 20% of the asset would be depreciated each year for five years using straight-line depreciation. The rate used for double-declining balance depreciation would be 40%, which is 200%, or twice the straight-line rate. Here is how this method works and why it is called double-declining balance. Every year, the accountant depreciates the carrying value, or book value, of the asset by an amount equal to twice the straight-line rate.

$$\text{Book value} \times (2 \times \text{Straight-line rate}) = \text{Yearly expense}$$

An example will help you see how this method works. Suppose the useful life of an asset is four years. The double-declining rate would be 50%:

$$100\% \div 4 \text{ years} = 25\% \text{ per year} = \text{Straight-line rate}$$

$$\text{Double it: } 50\% = \text{Double-declining balance rate}$$

Using this depreciation method for Holiday Hotels' orange juice machine, the book value at the beginning of the first year is $12,500—its acquisition cost. Notice that the calculation of the annual depreciation expense when using double-declining balance ignores any salvage value. Remember that book value equals cost minus accumulated depreciation. Recall that the useful life of the juice machine is six years. So the depreciation rate is $2 \times (1/6)$, which is 1/3.

The depreciation expense for the first year is

$$1/3 \times \$12,500 = \$4,167$$

The book value on the balance sheet at December 31, 2010, will be

$$\$12,500 - \$4,167 = \$8,333$$

For the second year, the accountant again calculates the amount of depreciation as one-third of the *book value* (not the *cost*). For the second year, the depreciation expense is

$$1/3 \times \$8,333 = \$2,778 \text{ (rounded)}$$

The accumulated depreciation at the end of the second year is

$$\$4,167 + \$2,778 = \$6,945$$

The book value on the December 31, 2011, balance sheet is

$$\$12{,}500 - \$6{,}945 = \$5{,}555$$

Although salvage value is ignored in the calculation of each year's expense, you must always keep the salvage value in mind so that the book value of the asset is never lower than its salvage value. Exhibit 6.6 shows how Holiday Hotels' orange juice machine would be depreciated using double-declining balance depreciation.

EXHIBIT 6.6

Double-Declining Balance Depreciation

Year	Depreciation Rate = 1/3 or 33.333%	Book Value before Depreciating the Asset for the Year	Depreciation Expense for the Year	Accumulated Depreciation (At the End of the Year)	Book Value at the End of the Year: $12,500– Accumulated Depreciation
2010	0.33333	$12,500	$4,167	$ 4,167	$8,333
2011	0.33333	$ 8,333	$2,778	$ 6,945	$5,555
2012	0.33333	$ 5,555	$1,852	$ 8,797	$3,703
2013	0.33333	$ 3,703	$1,234	$10,031	$2,469
2014	0.33333	$ 2,469	$ 823	$10,854	$1,646
2015	0.33333	$ 1,646	$1,146*	$12,000	$ 500**

*The calculation of (0.33333 × $1,646) indicates depreciation expense of $549. Because this is the last year of its useful life and the book value after this year's depreciation should be $500, the depreciation expense must be $1,146 to bring the total accumulated depreciation to $12,000.
**The depreciation expense for 2015 must be calculated to make this the book value at the end of the useful life—because the book value should be the estimated salvage value.

With double-declining depreciation, depreciation expense is larger in the early years of the asset's life and smaller in the later years. The book value is decreasing at a decreasing rate. Still, the balance in Accumulated Depreciation is working its way up until it reaches the cost minus salvage value. A firm always wants the book value of the asset to be equal to the estimated salvage value at the end of its useful life.

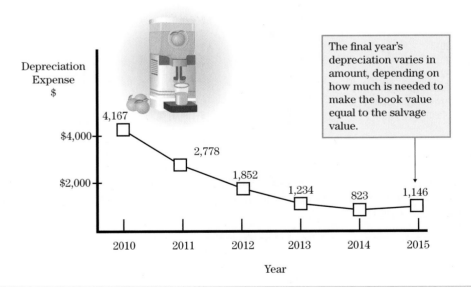

The final year's depreciation varies in amount, depending on how much is needed to make the book value equal to the salvage value.

Sometimes depreciation expense for the last year of the asset's useful life is more than the amount calculated by multiplying the book value by the double-declining rate, and sometimes it is less. When the asset has a large salvage value, the depreciation expense in the last year of the asset's life will be less than the amount calculated using the double-declining depreciation rate and the carrying value. When the asset has no salvage value, the depreciation expense in the last year will be more than the calculated amount. The last year's depreciation expense will be the amount needed to get the book value of the asset equal to the salvage value.

Exhibit 6.7 summarizes the calculations for the three depreciation methods.

EXHIBIT 6.7

Depreciation Methods

Method	Formula for Depreciation Expense
Straight-line	$\dfrac{\text{Acquisition cost} - \text{Salvage value}}{\text{Estimated useful life in years}} = \text{Yearly depreciation expense}$
Activity	$\dfrac{\text{Acquisition cost} - \text{Salvage value}}{\text{Estimated useful life in activity units}} = \text{Unit depreciation rate}$ Rate × Actual activity level for the year = Yearly depreciation expense
Double-declining balance	Beginning-of-the-year book value × (2/Estimated useful life in years) = Yearly depreciation expense

Over the useful life of the asset, the same total depreciation expense will be recognized no matter which method is used. Exhibit 6.8 compares the depreciation expense of the orange juice machine with the three different depreciation methods.

EXHIBIT 6.8

Comparison of Depreciation Expense by Year over the Life of the Orange Juice Machine for Holiday Hotels

Notice that the annual depreciation expense differs among the three methods, but the total depreciation expense taken over the life of the asset is the same for all methods.

Year	Straight-Line	Activity	Double-Declining Balance
2010	$ 2,000	$ 1,800	$ 4,167
2011	$ 2,000	$ 2,050	$ 2,778
2012	$ 2,000	$ 1,950	$ 1,852
2013	$ 2,000	$ 2,300	$ 1,234
2014	$ 2,000	$ 2,150	$ 823
2015	$ 2,000	$ 1,750	$ 1,146
Total depreciation expense during the life of the asset	$12,000	$12,000	$12,000

Your Turn 6-6

An asset costs $50,000, has an estimated salvage value of $5,000, and has a useful life of five years. Calculate the amount of depreciation expense for the second year using the double-declining balance method.

Depletion

Now that you know how equipment and similar kinds of fixed assets are written off using various depreciation methods, we turn our attention to the way natural resources are written off. When a company uses a natural resource to obtain benefits for the operation of its business, the write-off of the asset is called *depletion*. Often, all amounts of accumulated depreciation, accumulated depletion, and accumulated amortization are captured in a single total on the balance sheet.

Depletion is similar to the activity method of depreciation, but it applies only to writing off the cost of natural resources. Examples of such natural resources are land being used for oil wells and mines. A depletion cost per unit is calculated by dividing the cost of the natural resource less any salvage value by the estimated units of activity or output available from that natural resource.

The depletion cost per unit is then multiplied by the units pumped, mined, or cut per period to determine the total depletion related to the activity during the period.

Suppose that, on January 1, 2011, a company purchases the rights to an oil well in Texas for $100,000, estimating that the well will produce 200,000 barrels of oil during its life. The depletion rate per barrel is

$$\$100,000 \div 200,000 \text{ barrels} = \$0.50 \text{ per barrel}$$

If 50,000 barrels are produced in the year 2011, then the depletion related to the 50,000 barrels produced in 2011 will be

$$\$0.50 \text{ per barrel} \times 50,000 \text{ barrels} = \$25,000$$

On the December 31, 2011, balance sheet, the book value of the oil rights will be

$$\$100,000 - \$25,000 = \$75,000$$

Using Intangible Assets: Amortization

In addition to tangible assets, most firms have intangible assets, which are rights, privileges, or benefits that result from owning long-lived assets. Intangible assets have long-term value to the firm, but they are not visible or touchable. Their value resides in the rights and privileges given to the owners of the asset. These rights are often represented by contracts. Like tangible assets, they are recorded at cost, which includes all of the costs a firm incurs to obtain the asset.

If an intangible asset has an indefinite useful life, the asset is not amortized. However, the firm will periodically evaluate the asset for any permanent decline in value and then write it down if necessary. The idea here is that the balance sheet should include any asset that has future value to produce revenue for the firm, but the asset should never be valued at more than its fair value. Writing down an asset due to a permanent decline in value means reducing the amount of the asset and recording an expense on the income statement.

Intangible assets that have a limited life are written off over their useful or legal lives, whichever is shorter, using straight-line amortization. That means an equal amount is expensed each year. Accumulated depreciation and accumulated amortization are often added together for the balance sheet presentation.

L.O.3
Explain and compute how intangible assets are written off over their useful lives and reported on the financial statements.

Copyrights

Copyright is a form of legal protection for authors of "original works of authorship," provided by U.S. law. When you hear the term copyright, you probably think of written works such as books and magazine articles. Copyright protection extends beyond written works to musical and artistic works and is available to both published and unpublished works. According to the 1976 Copyright Act, the owner of the copyright can

A **copyright** is a form of legal protection for authors of "original works of authorship," provided by U.S. law.

- copy the work.
- use the work to prepare related material.
- distribute copies of the work to the public by selling, renting, or lending it.
- perform the work publicly, in the case of literary, musical, dramatic, and choreographic works.
- perform the work publicly by means of a digital audio transmission, in the case of sound recordings.

All costs to obtain and defend copyrights are part of the cost of the asset. Copyrights are amortized using straight-line amortization over their legal or useful lives, whichever is shorter.

Patents

A **patent** is a property right that the U.S. government grants to an inventor "to exclude others from making, using, offering for sale, or selling the invention throughout the United States or importing the invention into the United States for a specified period of time in exchange for public disclosure of the invention when the patent is granted." In 2009, IBM announced that it shattered the 2008 record for the number of patents granted in a single year—4,186. This was more than the number issued to Microsoft, Hewlett Packard, Oracle, Apple, and Google combined.

A **patent** is a property right that the U.S. government grants to an inventor "to exclude others from making, using, offering for sale, or selling the invention throughout the United States or importing the invention into the United States for a specified period of time."

As with copyrights, costs to defend patents are *capitalized* as part of the cost of the asset. Patents are amortized using straight-line amortization over their useful or legal lives, whichever is shorter. For example, most patents have a legal life of 20 years. However, a company may believe the useful life of a patent is less than that. If the company believes the patent will provide value for only 10 years, the company should use the shorter time period for amortizing the asset.

Trademarks

A **trademark** is a symbol, word, phrase, or logo that legally distinguishes one company's product from any others.

A **trademark** is a symbol, word, phrase, or logo that legally distinguishes one company's product from any others. One of the most recognized trademarks is Nike's swoosh symbol. In many cases, trademarks are not amortized because their useful lives are indefinite. Registering a trademark with the U.S. Patent and Trademark Office provides 10 years of protection, renewable as long as the trademark is in use.

Franchises

A **franchise** is an agreement that authorizes someone to sell or distribute a company's goods or services in a certain area.

A **franchise** is an agreement that authorizes someone to sell or distribute a company's goods or services in a certain area. The initial cost of buying a franchise is the franchise fee, and this is the intangible asset that is capitalized. It is amortized over the life of the franchise if there is a limited life. If the life of the franchise is indefinite, it will not be amortized. In addition to the initial fee, franchise owners pay an ongoing fee to the company that is usually a percentage of sales. You might be surprised at some of the top franchises for 2009. Number 1 was Subway; others include McDonald's and Pizza Hut.

Goodwill

Goodwill is the excess of cost over market value of the net assets when one company purchases another company.

Goodwill is the excess of cost over market value of the net assets when one company purchases another company. When the term *goodwill* is used in everyday conversation, it refers to favorable qualities. However, when you see goodwill on a company's balance sheet you know that it is a result of purchasing another company for more than the fair market value of its net assets. Goodwill is an advanced topic for intermediate or advanced accounting courses. However, you should have a general understanding of goodwill because it appears on the balance sheet of many firms.

Suppose that The Home Depot purchased Pop's Hardware store for $950,000 cash. The inventory and building—all of Pop's assets—were appraised at $750,000; and the small hardware store had no debt. Why would The Home Depot pay more than the market value for the net tangible assets of Pop's Hardware? Pop's Hardware store had been in business for many years, and the store had a terrific location and a loyal customer base. All of this is goodwill that Pop's had developed over years of business. GAAP do not allow a company to recognize its internally developed goodwill, so Pop's financial statements do not include goodwill. Now that The Home Depot has decided to purchase Pop's Hardware, however, the goodwill will be recorded. Here is how the transaction affects the accounting equation for The Home Depot:

Assets	=	Liabilities	+	Shareholders' equity		
				Contributed capital	+	Retained earnings
(950,000) Cash						
750,000 Various assets						
200,000 Goodwill						

What happens to the intangible asset goodwill? Goodwill is not amortized because it is assumed to have an indefinite life. Even though goodwill is not amortized, companies must evaluate goodwill to make sure it is not overvalued on the balance sheet. This is called evaluating it for impairment, and we will come back to this topic later in the chapter. Goodwill that has lost some of its value must be written down—that is, the asset is reduced and an expense is recorded. You can read about a firm's goodwill in the notes to the financial statements.

Research and Development Costs

Research and development (R&D) costs have benefits to the firm—at least that is the goal of R&D. However, R&D costs are expensed and are not capitalized as part of the cost of an asset because it is not clear that these costs represent something of value. Software development costs are considered research costs until they result in a product that is technologically feasible, so these costs must also be expensed as they are incurred. However, once the software is considered technologically feasible, the costs incurred from that point on are capitalized as part of the cost of the software. Deciding when a piece of software is technologically feasible is another example of how firms need to use judgment when making accounting decisions. The firm's developers and computer experts would make this judgment.

Changes after the Purchase of the Asset

We started the chapter with a discussion of the types and costs of long-term assets. Then, we discussed how the accounting records show the firm's use of those assets. Now we discuss how to adjust financial statements to record three things that may take place after an asset has been in use. First, the asset may lose value due to circumstances outside the firm's control. Second, the firm may make expenditures to maintain or improve the asset during its useful life. And third, the firm may need to revise its prior estimates of an asset's estimated life and salvage value.

L.O.4
Explain how decreases in value, repairs, changes in productive capacity, and changes in estimates of useful life and salvage value of long-term assets affect the financial statements.

Asset Impairment

By now you know that accountants want to avoid overstating assets on the balance sheet or revenue on the income statement. A firm that is getting ready to prepare its financial statements must evaluate its long-term assets, including goodwill and other intangible assets, for **impairment**—a permanent reduction in the fair market value of an asset below its book value—if certain changes have occurred. Such changes include

Impairment is a permanent decline in the fair market value of an asset such that its book value exceeds its fair market value.

1. a downturn in the economy that causes a significant decrease in the market value of a long-lived asset.
2. a change in how the company uses an asset.
3. a change in the business climate that could affect the asset's value.

An asset is considered impaired when the book value of the asset or group of assets is greater than its fair market value. Impairment is not easy to measure, but you will read about it in the notes to almost every set of financial statements. Because testing an asset for impairment can be quite difficult, it is a topic reserved for more advanced courses. However, you should be familiar with the terminology because you will see it in almost every annual report.

Exhibit 6.9 shows a portion of the disclosure made by Darden Restaurants, Inc., regarding its reported asset impairment charges (losses) in 2007 and 2008. A company must disclose in the notes to the financial statements a description of the impaired asset and the facts and circumstances leading to the impairment.

EXHIBIT 6.9

Disclosure about Asset Impairment in Darden Restaurants' Notes to the Financial Statements

The Notes to the Financial Statements provide important information about the amounts in the financial statements.

> From the Notes to the Financial Statements
> of Darden Restaurants, Inc.

During fiscal 2008 we recorded less than $0.1 million of long-lived asset impairment charges. During fiscal 2007, we recorded $2.6 million of long-lived asset impairment charges primarily related to the permanent closure of one Red Lobster and one Olive Garden restaurant.

Expenditures to Improve an Asset or Extend Its Useful Life

Another change in the value of an asset may be the result of the firm spending money to improve its assets. Any expenditure that will benefit more than one accounting period is called a **capital expenditure**. A capital expenditure is recorded as an asset when it is incurred, and it is expensed or amortized over the accounting periods in which it is used.

A **capital expenditure** is a cost that is recorded as an asset, not an expense, at the time it is incurred. This is also called *capitalizing* a cost.

Just the opposite of a capital expenditure is an expenditure that does *not* extend the useful life or improve the quality of the asset. Any expenditure that will benefit only the current accounting period is expensed in the period in which it is incurred. It is sometimes called a *revenue expenditure*, although *expense* really captures its meaning in a more logical way.

Many companies establish policies that categorize purchased items as capital expenditures or revenue expenditures—expenses, often based on dollar amounts. The accounting constraint of materiality applies here so that small dollar amounts can simply be expensed.

Remodeling and improvement projects are capital expenditures because they will offer firms benefits over a number of years. An example of remodeling would be a new wiring system to increase the efficiency of the electrical system of a building. Improvements might include items such as a more energy-efficient air-conditioning system.

Ordinary repairs are recognized as current expenses because they are routine and do not increase the useful life of the asset or its efficiency. Ordinary repairs, such as painting, tune-ups for vehicles, or cleaning and lubricating equipment, are expenditures that are necessary to maintain an asset in good operating condition and are expensed as incurred.

Suppose the computer terminals at Staples' corporate offices need a monthly tune-up and cleaning. The cost of this maintenance would be an expense—recognized in the period the work was done. But suppose Staples upgraded its computer hardware to expand its capacity or its useful life. This cost would be considered a capital expenditure and capitalized—recorded as part of the cost of the asset and depreciated along with the asset over its remaining useful life.

Revising Estimates of Useful Life and Salvage Value

Sometimes after an asset has been used for a period of time, managers realize that they need to revise their estimates of the useful life or the salvage value of the asset. Evaluating estimates related to fixed assets is an ongoing part of accounting for those assets. In accounting for long-term assets, revising an estimate is not treated like an error—you do not go back and correct any previous records or financial statements. Those amounts were correct at the time—because the best estimates at that time were used for the calculation. Suppose managers believe that a smoothly running machine will offer a useful life beyond the original estimate. The undepreciated balance—the book value of the asset—reduced by the estimated salvage value would be spread over the new estimated remaining useful life. Similarly, if managers come to believe that the salvage value of the machine will be greater than their earlier estimate, the depreciation expense in the future will be recalculated with the new salvage value. This approach is similar to treating the undepreciated balance like the cost of the asset at the time of the revised estimates and using the new estimates of useful life and salvage value to calculate the depreciation expense for the remaining years of the asset's life.

Suppose Staples purchased a copy machine that cost $50,000, with an estimated useful life of four years and an estimated salvage value of $2,000. Using straight-line depreciation, a single year's depreciation is

$$\frac{\$50,000 - \$2,000}{4 \text{ years}} = \frac{\$48,000}{4 \text{ years}} = \$12,000 \text{ per year}$$

Suppose Staples has depreciated the machine for two years. That would make the book value $26,000.

$$\$50,000 - \$12,000 - \$12,000 = \$26,000$$

$$\text{Cost} - \underset{\text{year 1}}{\text{Depreciation}} - \underset{\text{year 2}}{\text{Depreciation}} = \text{Book value}$$

As Staples begins the third year of the asset's life, the manager realizes that Staples will be able to use it for *three* more years (rather than two more years as originally estimated), but now believes that the salvage value at the end of that time will be $1,000 (not $2,000 as originally estimated).

The depreciation expense for the first two years will not be changed. For the next three years, however, the depreciation expense will be different than it was for the first two years. The acquisition cost of $50,000 less $24,000 of accumulated depreciation gives us the undepreciated balance of $26,000. This amount is treated as if it were now the cost of the asset. The estimated salvage value is $1,000, and the estimated remaining useful life is three years. The calculation is

$$\frac{\$26,000 - 1,000}{3 \text{ years}} = \frac{\$25,000}{3 \text{ years}} = \$8,333.33 \text{ per year}$$

The asset will now be depreciated for three years at $8,333.33 per year. At the end of that time the book value of the asset will be $1,000 [$26,000 − ($8,333.33 per year × 3 years)].

Your Turn 6-7

At the beginning of 2010, White Company hired a mechanic to perform a major overhaul of its main piece of equipment at a cost of $2,400. The equipment originally cost $10,000 at the beginning of 2006, and the book value of the equipment on the December 31, 2009, balance sheet was $6,000. At the time of the purchase, White Company estimated that the equipment would have a useful life of 10 years and no salvage value. The overhaul at the beginning of 2010 extended the useful life of the equipment. White Company's new estimate is that the equipment will now last until the end of 2017—eight years from the date of the overhaul. Expected salvage value is still zero. White uses straight-line depreciation for all of its assets. Calculate the depreciation expense for White's income statement for the year ended December 31, 2011.

Selling Long-Term Assets

L.O.5
Explain how the disposal of a long-term asset is reflected in the financial statements.

We have bought the long-term asset and used it—depreciating, depleting, or amortizing it over its useful life. Now, we deal with getting rid of an asset. Disposing of an asset means to sell it, trade it in, or simply toss it in the trash (please recycle!). When would a company sell an asset? Sometimes an asset is sold because it is no longer useful to the company. Other times an asset is replaced with a newer model, even though there is remaining productive capacity in the current asset. You calculate the gain or loss on the disposal of an asset by comparing the cash received for the sale of the asset—also known as cash proceeds—and the asset's book value at the time of disposal. One of three situations will exist:

1. Cash proceeds are greater than the book value. There will be a gain.
2. Cash proceeds are less than the book value. There will be a loss.
3. Cash proceeds are equal to the book value. There will be no gain or loss.

Suppose you decide to sell equipment that was purchased seven years ago. At the time of the purchase, you estimated it would last 10 years. The asset cost $25,000, and you used straight-line depreciation with an estimated salvage value of zero. The depreciation expense each year was $2,500. Now, seven years later, you sell the asset for $8,000. Is there a gain or loss on the sale? First, calculate the book value on the date you sold the asset:

$$\text{Book value} = \text{Cost} - \text{Accumulated depreciation}$$
$$\text{Book value} = \$25,000 - (7 \text{ years} \times \$2,500 \text{ per year})$$
$$\text{Book value} = \$25,000 - \$17,500 = \$7,500$$

Then, subtract the book value from the cash proceeds to calculate the gain or loss on the sale.

$$\$8,000 - \$7,500 = \$500$$

Because the proceeds of $8,000 are larger than the book value of $7,500, there is a gain on the sale. The gain from the sale will be shown on the income statement as revenue. A gain has this special name because it is not a normal part of business operations. You are not in business to buy and sell the equipment you use in your business, so the income from such a transaction is called a gain rather than simply called revenue.

Another way to calculate the gain or loss on the sale of an asset is to record the three amounts you know.

1. Record the receipt of cash.
2. Remove the asset and its accumulated depreciation.

3. Balance the transaction in the accounting equation with a gain or loss.

Assets	=	Liabilities	+	Shareholders' equity	
				Contributed capital	+	Retained earnings

Assets	=	Liabilities	+	Contributed capital	+	Retained earnings
8,000 Cash						
(25,000) Equipment						500
17,500						Gain on sale
Accumulated depreciation						of equipment

Now suppose instead that you sell the asset after seven years for $5,000 rather than $8,000. Is there a gain or loss on the sale? You already know the book value is $7,500 at the date of the sale. Subtract the book value from the cash proceeds.

$$\$5,000 - \$7,500 = -\$2,500$$

Because the proceeds are less than the book value, there is a loss on the sale. A loss is an expense, and it is shown on the income statement.

Suppose you sold the asset for exactly the book value, $7,500. There would be no gain or loss on the sale. Look at the following accounting equation to see the effect of selling an asset for its book value.

Assets	=	Liabilities	+	Shareholders' equity	
				Contributed capital	+	Retained earnings

Assets	=	Liabilities	+	Contributed capital	+	Retained earnings
7,500 Cash						
(25,000) Equipment						
17,500						
Accumulated depreciation						

There is no gain or loss. Selling an asset for its book value, therefore, does not affect the income statement.

UNDERSTANDING Business

Selling Assets to Raise Cash

Firms invest in long-term assets to use them for generating revenue for a significant amount of time, often decades. For example, the average age of an airplane in Delta's fleet is 13.8 years. Buildings and equipment can have useful lives of 40 years or longer. Firms sell assets when newer, more productive assets become available or when the assets wear out and need to be replaced. However, it's very uncommon for a firm to sell its long-term assets simply to raise money.

During a serious recession, that could change. In a recent survey of 1,275 chief financial officers of firms in the United States, Asia, and Europe, researchers from Duke University and the University of Illinois found that 59% of U.S. firms reported that the tight credit market had directly affected their firms' plans for investing in new projects. Of those firms, 70% reported that they were selling more corporate assets in order to raise cash than they did before the start of the credit crisis that began in 2008.

State governments are also looking at the possibility of selling assets to help meet budget deficits predicted for 2009 and beyond. For example, the governor of Arizona announced a plan that includes selling state office buildings and prisons to investors. The state would then lease them back from the investors.

When you examine a firm's financial statements, be sure to look at what is happening with its long-term assets. Failing to invest in new projects as well as selling off productive assets could be a sign of bad times ahead.

Source: "Firms Take Drastic Actions in Response to Credit Crisis," News Release, Duke University, Fuqua School of Business, February 3, 2009. www.fuqua.duke.edu/news_events/releases/credit_crisis_cash

Perry Plants Company owned an asset that originally cost $24,000. The company sold the asset on January 1, 2010, for $8,000 cash. Accumulated depreciation on the day of sale was $18,000. Determine whether Perry should recognize a gain or a loss on the sale. If so, how much?

Presentation of Long-Term Assets on the Financial Statements

L.O.6
Recognize and explain how long-term assets are reported on the financial statements, and prepare financial statements that include long-term assets.

Reporting Long-Term Assets

In this chapter you have seen that both tangible and intangible long-term assets are recorded at the amount the firm paid for them. The assets are shown on the balance sheet in the last half of the asset section, after current assets. Because the carrying value of property, plant, and equipment (PPE) is the difference between the cost of the asset and its accumulated depreciation, accountants say that PPE is reported at its *amortized cost* or its *depreciated cost*. The notes to the financial statements are a good place to learn the types of assets, approximate age of the assets, and depreciation method(s) used.

The use of long-term assets is shown on the income statement with depreciation, depletion, and amortization expense. Often, the amount is included in the total of several accounts for presentation on the income statement, so you may not see it as a separate line item.

The statement of cash flows will indicate any cash expenditures for PPE as cash used for investing activities. Any cash received from the sale of long-term assets will be shown as an inflow in the same section—cash from investing activities—of the statement. Remember that the gain or loss on the sale of a long-term asset, reported on the income statement, is *not* the cash related to the sale. The cash collected from the sale will appear on the statement of cash flows (investing activities).

Exhibit 6.10 shows the asset section of Best Buy's balance sheet. The firm shows the various categories of fixed assets at their cost and then shows the deduction for accumulated depreciation. This is all the depreciation that the firm has taken on its property, plant, and

EXHIBIT 6.10

Presentation of Long-Term Assets

This shows how Best Buy presents information about its fixed assets on the balance sheet.

Best Buy Co., Inc.
Consolidated Balance Sheets (partial)

($ in millions)	February 28, 2009	March 1, 2008
Assets		
Current assets		
Cash and cash equivalents	$ 498	$ 1,438
Short-term investments	11	64
Receivables	1,868	549
Merchandise inventories	4,753	4,708
Other current assets	1,062	583
Total current assets	8,192	7,342
Property and Equipment		
Land and buildings	755	732
Leasehold improvements	2,013	1,752
Fixtures and equipment	4,060	3,057
Property under capital lease	112	67
	6,940	5,608
Less accumulated depreciation	2,766	2,302
Net property and equipment	4,174	3,306
Goodwill	2,203	1,088
Tradenames	173	97
Other Assets	1,084	925
Total Assets	$15,826	$12,758

equipment since the purchase of the items. Some firms show only the net amount, leaving the details for the notes to the financial statements. In any case, you should be able to find or calculate the cost of a firm's long-term assets.

IFRS and Long-Lived Assets

U.S. GAAP value long-term assets at historical cost less accumulated depreciation. International Financial Reporting Standards (IFRS) allow revaluation of assets to their fair value if fair value can be measured reliably. Then, accumulated depreciation would be deducted. Notice that IFRS do not *require* revaluation.

Another significant difference between IFRS and U.S. GAAP relates to impairment. Under GAAP, when assets are written down due to impairment, the impairment losses cannot be reversed even if conditions change. However, under IFRS, impairment losses can be reversed (except those related to goodwill) if circumstances change.

There are many other differences in accounting for long-lived assets between IFRS and U.S. GAAP, but they are quite technical. If you major in accounting, you'll learn more about these in an advanced accounting course.

Preparing Statements for Team Shirts

Since beginning in January 2010, Team Shirts has now finished five months of business. Refresh your memory by reviewing the June 1 balance sheet in Exhibit 6.11, before Team Shirts begins the month of June.

EXHIBIT 6.11

Balance Sheet for Team Shirts at June 1, 2010

Team Shirts
Balance Sheet
At June 1, 2010

Assets		Liabilities and Shareholder's Equity	
Current assets		Current liabilities	
Cash	$12,805	Accounts payable	$ 9,000
Accounts receivable		Unearned revenue	4,950
(net of allowance of $176) ..	8,624	Total current liabilities	13,950
Inventory	5,100	Shareholder's equity	
Prepaid expenses	1,100	Common stock	5,000
Total current assets	27,629	Retained earnings	12,379
Computer (net of $300		Total shareholder's equity ..	17,379
accumulated			
depreciation)	3,700	Total liabilities and	
		shareholder's equity	$31,329
Total assets	$31,329		

The company has been struggling along, but Sara believes that she can make a big profit breakthrough if she can expand the business. Her research indicates a large demand for her T-shirts, so she plans a major expansion in June. Read through each of the transactions and study how they have been entered in the accounting equation worksheet in Exhibit 6.12. Then, we will make the end-of-the-month adjustments and prepare the four financial statements.

Transaction 1: On June 1, Team Shirts purchased a van for $25,000. The company paid an additional $5,000 to have it equipped with the racks for T-shirts. Team Shirts financed the $30,000 with a note payable at 6% per year for five years with a local bank. On May 31 of each year beginning in 2011, Team Shirts will pay the bank the interest it owes for the year plus $6,000 of the $30,000 with a note payable principal. Team Shirts expects the van to be driven for approximately 200,000 miles and have a residual value of $1,000 at the end of its useful life. The company decided to depreciate the van using the activity method, based on miles.

Transaction 2: Team Shirts received cash payments on accounts receivable of $8,000.

Transaction 3: Team Shirts found several big sporting goods stores to buy its shirts, so the firm must increase the inventory. Team Shirts purchases 3,000 T-shirts at $4.20 each on account.

Transaction 4: Team Shirts paid $9,000 on accounts payable.

Transaction 5: Team Shirts paid rent in advance on the warehouse. On June 1, the company still had half a month of prepaid rent ($600). In June, the company paid in advance for six more months of rent, from June 15 to December 15, in the amount of $7,200 ($1,200 × 6 months).

Transaction 6: Team Shirts sold and delivered 2,000 shirts for $10 each to several different sports shops on June 15 on account.

Transaction 7: Team Shirts paid cash for $2,300 worth of general operating expenses.

Transaction 8: Team Shirts found out that one of its customers, B&B Sports, had declared bankruptcy, so the firm wrote off B&B's outstanding balance of $150.

After you understand each of the transactions shown in Exhibit 6.12, you are ready to make the needed adjustments before the June financial statements can be prepared. As you read each of the explanations for the adjustments, follow along on the bottom part of the worksheet in Exhibit 6.12.

Adjustment 1: Team Shirts needs to adjust prepaid insurance. On June 1, there was $250 worth of prepaid insurance on the balance sheet. Recall, Team Shirts purchased three months of insurance in May for a total cost of $300, which is $100 per month. (Only half a month's worth expired in May.)

Adjustment 2: Another item that needs to be adjusted is prepaid rent. Team Shirts monthly rent is $1,200.

Adjustment 3: Prepaid Web costs must be adjusted for the June expense of $50.

Adjustment 4: Unearned revenue at the beginning of the month has now been earned. The sales revenue of $4,950 must be recognized and the cost of goods sold of $1,890 (450 shirts at $4.20 each) must be recorded.

Adjustment 5: Depreciation expense for the computer needs to be recorded. Recall, it is being depreciated at $100 per month.

Adjustment 6: Depreciation expense for the new van needs to be recorded. It cost $30,000 and has an estimated residual value of $1,000. It is being depreciated using the activity method based on an estimated 200,000 miles. During June, the van was driven 5,000 miles. The rate is $0.145 per mile ($29,000 depreciable base divided by 200,000 miles). The depreciation expense for June is $0.145 per mile × 5,000 miles = $725.

Adjustment 7: Interest expense on the note for the van needs to be accrued. The $30,000 note at 6% was signed on June 1. Interest for June will be $150 ($30,000 × 0.06 × 1/12).

Adjustment 8: The allowance for bad debts must be recorded. The current balance in accounts receivable (AR) is $20,650, and Team Shirts wants an allowance of 2% of ending AR. That would be $413. However, the allowance has a current balance of $26 (beginning balance $176 minus $150 write off). That means the firm must record bad debts expense (and an increase to the allowance) of $387 ($413 − $26).

Using the accounting equation worksheet in Exhibit 6.12, you can see how the financial statements are derived. Study each of them by tracing the numbers from the worksheet to the appropriate financial statement, shown in Exhibit 6.13.

EXHIBIT 6.12

Accounting Equation Worksheet for Team Shirts for June

All of the transactions for June and adjustments needed at the end of the month are shown in this accounting equation worksheet.

	Assets			=	Liabilities		+	Shareholder's Equity		
								Contributed Capital	Retained Earnings	
	Cash	All other assets	(Account)		All liabilities	(Account)		Common Stock	(Account)	
Beginning Balances	$12,805	$8,800	Accounts receivable		$9,000	Accounts payable		$5,000	$12,379	
		(176)	Allowance for bad debts		4,950	Unearned revenue				
		5,100	Inventory							
		250	Prepaid insurance							
		600	Prepaid rent							
		250	Prepaid Web design							
		4,000	Computer							
		(300)	Accumulated depreciation							
Transactions 1		30,000	Truck		30,000	Notes payable				
2	8,000	(8,000)	Accounts receivable							
3		12,600	Inventory		12,600	Accounts payable				
4	(9,000)				(9,000)	Accounts payable				
5	(7,200)	7,200	Prepaid rent							
6		20,000	Accounts receivable						20,000	Sales
		(8,355)	Inventory						(8,355)	Cost of goods sold*
7	(2,300)								(2,300)	Operating expenses
8		(150)	Accounts receivable							
		150	Allowance for bad debts							
A-1		(100)	Prepaid insurance						(100)	Insurance expense
A-2		(1,200)	Prepaid rent						(1,200)	Rent expense
A-3		(50)	Prepaid Web design						(50)	Web design expense
A-4		(1,890)	Inventory		(4,950)	Unearned revenue			4,950	Sales
									(1,890)	Cost of goods sold
A-5		(100)	Accumulated depreciation computer						(100)	Depreciation expense
A-6		(725)	Accumulated depreciation truck						(725)	Depreciation expense
A-7					150	Interest payable			(150)	Interest expense
A-8		(387)	Allowance for bad debts						(387)	Bad debts expense
	$2,305 + $67,517			=	$42,750		+	$5,000 +	$22,072	

▬ Income statement   ▬ Statement of changes in shareholder's equity   ▬ Balance sheet   ▬ Statement of cash flows

*Cost of goods sold: (225 shirts × $4.00) + (1,775 shirts × $4.20)

Assets (non cash)			Liabilities	
Accounts receivable	$20,650		Accounts payable	$12,600
Allowance for bad debts	(413)		Interest payable	150
Inventory	7,455		Notes payable	30,000
Prepaid insurance	150			
Prepaid rent	6,600		Total	$42,750
Prepaid Web design	200			
Computer	4000			
Accumulated depreciation	(400)			
Truck	30,000			
Accumulated depreciation	(725)			
Total	$67,517			

EXHIBIT 6.13

Financial Statements for Team Shirts for June 2010

The arrows should help you see the relationships among the financial statements.

Team Shirts
Income Statement
For the Month Ended June 30, 2010

Sales revenue		$24,950
Expenses:		
Cost of goods sold	$10,245	
Operating expenses	2,300	
Bad debts expense	387	
Insurance expense	100	
Rent expense	1,200	
Web design expenses	50	
Depreciation expense	825	
Interest expense	150	
Total expenses		15,257
Net income		$ 9,693

Team Shirts
Statement of Changes in Shareholder's Equity
For the Month Ended June 30, 2010

Beginning common stock	$ 5,000
Common stock issued during month	0
Ending common stock	$ 5,000
Beginning retained earnings	$12,379
Net income	9,693
Dividends	0
Ending retained earnings	$22,072
Total shareholder's equity	$27,072

Team Shirts
Statement of Cash Flows
For the Month Ended June 30, 2010

Cash from operating activities	
Cash collected from customers	$ 8,000
Cash paid to vendors	(9,000)
Cash paid for operating expenses	(9,500)
Net cash used by operating activities	$(10,500)
Cash from investing activities*	0
Cash from financing activities	0
Decrease in cash	(10,500)
Beginning cash balance	12,805
Ending cash balance	$ 2,305

*Note: The firm purchased a $30,000 truck by issuing a $30,000 note payable.

Team Shirts
Balance Sheet
At June 30, 2010

Assets

Current Assets		
Cash		$ 2,305
Accounts receivable (net of allowance of $413)		20,237
Inventory		7,455
Prepaid expenses		6,950
Total current assets		36,947
Property and equipment		
Computer	$ 4,000	
Truck	30,000	
Accumulated depreciation		(1,125)
Net property and equipment		32,875
Total assets		$69,822

Liabilities and Shareholder's Equity

Current Liabilities	
Accounts payable	$12,600
Notes payable (due 5/31/11)	6,000
Interest payable	150
Total current liabilities	18,750
Notes payable	24,000
Total Liabilities	42,750
Shareholder's Equity	
Common stock	5,000
Retained earnings	22,072
Total shareholder's equity	27,072
Total liabilities and shareholder's equity	$69,822

Applying Your Knowledge—Ratio Analysis

At this point, you have learned how a firm records the purchase of long-term assets and how it accounts for the use of those assets. Now we will look at how you can use the information about long-term assets to help evaluate the performance of the firm.

Return on Assets

A company purchases assets to help generate future revenue. Recall the definition of an asset—something of value used by a business to generate revenue. A ratio that measures how well a company is using its assets to generate income is **return on assets** (ROA). ROA is an overall measure of a company's profitability. Like much of the terminology in accounting, the name of this ratio is descriptive. A company's return is what the company is getting back. We want to measure that return as a percentage of assets. So return on assets is literally *return*—net income—divided by *assets*.

$$\text{Return on assets} = \frac{\text{Net income}}{\text{Average total assets}}$$

L.O.7
Use return on assets (ROA) and the asset turnover ratio to help evaluate a firm's performance.

Return on assets is a ratio that measures how well a company is using its assets to generate income. It is defined as net income divided by average total assets.

This ratio measures a company's success in using its assets to earn income for investors. This is a simplified version of ROA, so you may encounter the more complex version of ROA that adds back interest expense, net of tax, to net income in the numerator. Because interest expense is part of what has been earned to pay creditors, adding it back to net income makes the ratio a more specific measure of return to all investors, both shareholders and creditors, before either is paid. Because it is not always straightforward to calculate the tax effect of the interest payment, however, we will use the simpler version of the ratio with net income by itself as the numerator. The denominator is average total assets.

Using a ratio such as ROA gives financial statement users a way to standardize net income across companies. Exhibit 6.14 provides an example. For the fiscal year ended September 27, 2008, Apple Inc. had a net income of $4,834 million and average assets of $32,460 million. For the fiscal year ended January 30, 2009, Dell Inc. had net income of $2,478 million and average assets of $27,031 million. It appears that Apple is outperforming Dell. But that comparison does not tell us how well each company is using its assets to make that net income. If we divide net income by average total assets, we will get the return on assets for the year, which enables us to better compare the performance of the two companies.

EXHIBIT 6.14

Return on Assets for Apple and Dell

	Apple Inc. For the Year Ended September 27, 2008	Dell Inc. For the Year Ended January 30, 2009
(dollars in millions)		
Net income	$ 4,834	$ 2,478
Average assets	$32,460	$27,031
Return on assets	14.89%	9.17%

This comparison shows that Apple is earning a better return with its total assets than Dell is earning with its assets. The industry average for firms in this industry for return on assets is 12.6%. Apple's ROA is 14.89% and Dell's ROA is 9.17% using the results from the fiscal years shown in Exhibit 6.14. You can find up-to-date information on the firms' ROA at www.moneycentral.msn.com.

Asset Turnover Ratio

Asset turnover ratio measures how efficiently a company is using its assets to generate sales. It is defined as net sales divided by average total assets.

Another ratio that helps us evaluate a firm's use of its assets is the **asset turnover ratio**. This ratio indicates how efficiently a company is using its assets to generate sales. The ratio is defined as net sales divided by average total assets. The ratio answers the question: *How many dollars of sales are generated by each dollar invested in assets?*

$$\text{Asset turnover ratio} = \frac{\text{Net sales}}{\text{Average total assets}}$$

Look at Apple and Dell again. Sales for Apple for the fiscal year ended September 27, 2008, were $32,479 million; sales for Dell for the fiscal year ended January 30, 2009, totaled almost twice that at $61,101 million. The asset turnover ratio for each is as follows:

(dollars in millions)	Apple	Dell
Sales	$32,479	$61,101
Average assets	$32,460	$27,031
Asset turnover ratio	1.00	2.26

Asset turnover ratios vary significantly from industry to industry, so it is important to compare firms only in the same industry. Dell's use of its assets to generate revenue was quite a bit better than that of Apple during this time period. It is interesting to note, however, that Apple's net income for the year was $4,834 million, while Dell's was only $2,478 million.

Remember that all ratios have this in common: To be meaningful, ratios must be compared to the ratios from other years with the same company or with other companies. Industry standards are also often available for common ratios to help investors and analysts evaluate a company's performance using ratio analysis. Also, one or two ratios will not give you a clear picture of any firm's performance. Ratio analysis is just one tool among many needed to understand a firm's financial statements.

Business Risk, Control, and Ethics

A firm risks losing long-term assets due to theft. This risk is not a problem with some large assets, such as a factory, but it is a very serious problem with smaller, mobile, fixed assets—such as cars, computers, and furniture and fixtures. Even large assets, such as buildings and factories, are at risk for damage due to vandalism, hurricanes, or terrorist activities. One of the major functions of any company's internal control system is to safeguard all assets from theft and damage—whether intentional or unintentional. The cost of safeguarding assets can be tremendous, as can the cost of replacing them if they are destroyed.

Physical controls to safeguard assets may be as simple as a lock on a warehouse door, a video camera in a retail store, or a security guard who remains in an office complex overnight. Even when assets are protected in a secure facility with guards, fences, or alarms, the company must be sure that only the appropriate people have access to the assets. As you learned in the story about the forklifts at the beginning of the chapter, the proper authorization for access to assets is crucial.

Complete and reliable record keeping for the assets is also part of safeguarding assets. With assets such as cash and inventory, the people who are responsible for the record keeping for long-term assets should be different than the people who have physical custody of the assets. As you learned in earlier chapters, this is called segregation of duties and is a very common control.

Monitoring is another control to safeguard assets. This means that someone needs to make sure the other controls—physical controls, segregation of duties, and any other policies and procedures related to protecting assets—are operating properly. Often, firms have internal auditors—their own employees—who perform this function as part of their job responsibilities. You may recall that it was an internal auditor who first blew the whistle on the WorldCom fraud.

> **L.O.8**
> Identify and describe the business risks associated with long-term assets and the controls that can minimize those risks.

Chapter Summary Points

- Assets that last longer than a year are classified as noncurrent (or long-term) on the balance sheet. They are recorded at cost, including all of the costs necessary to get the asset ready for use.
- Long-term assets are written off over their useful lives. For plant and equipment, an asset may be written off using either straight-line, activity, or double-declining balance depreciation methods. Intangible assets with a definite life are written off, or amortized, using the straight-line method.
- Routine repair and maintenance costs are expensed as incurred, whereas improvements to the productive capacity or the useful life of an asset are capitalized as part of the cost of the asset.
- Any revisions in the useful life or the estimated salvage value of an asset are implemented at the time of the revision and in future periods. Any past depreciation expense is *not* revised.
- When an asset is sold, the gain or loss is calculated as the difference between the proceeds (sales amount) and the book value (cost − accumulated depreciation) of the asset.

Chapter Summary Problems

Suppose Pencils Office Supply started the fiscal year with the following balance sheet:

Pencils Office Supply
Balance Sheet
At January 1, 2008

Assets

Cash	$390,000
Accounts receivable	136,000
Inventory	106,350
Prepaid insurance	3,000
Equipment	261,000
Accumulated depreciation—equipment	(75,800)
Total assets	$820,550

Liabilities & Shareholders' Equity

Accounts payable	26,700
Salaries payable	13,500
Unearned revenue	35,000
Long-term note payable	130,000
Other long-term liabilities	85,000
Common stock	250,000
Retained earnings	280,350
Total liabilities and shareholders' equity	$820,550

Suppose the company engaged in the following transactions during its fiscal year ended December 31, 2008:

a. The company purchased new equipment at the beginning of the fiscal year. The invoice price was $158,500, but the manufacturer of the equipment gave Pencils a 3% discount for paying cash for the equipment on delivery. Pencils paid shipping costs of $1,500 and paid $700 for a special insurance policy to cover the equipment while in transit. The installation cost was $3,000, and Pencils spent $6,000 training employees to use the new equipment. Additionally, Pencils hired a new supervisor at an annual salary of $40,000 to be responsible for the printing services area where the new equipment will be used. All payments were made in cash as the costs were incurred.

b. The company sold some old equipment with an original cost of $12,300 and related accumulated depreciation of $11,100. Proceeds from the sale amounted to $1,500.

c. The company collected cash of $134,200 on accounts receivable.

d. The company purchased $365,500 worth of inventory during the year, paying $200,000 cash, with the remainder purchased on account.

e. The company paid insurance premiums of $12,000.

f. The company paid $170,000 on accounts payable.

g. The company paid employees total cash for salaries of $72,250. (This includes the amount owed at the beginning of the year and the salary expense for the new supervisor.)

h. The company made sales to customers in the amount of $354,570. They collected $200,000 in cash, and the remainder was on account. (Inventory sold cost $110,000.) The company uses only one revenue account: sales and service revenue.

i. The company paid $50,000 to reduce principal of the long-term note and paid interest of $10,400.

j. The company paid operating expenses in the amount of $30,000 in cash.

Other Information

- The company owed salaries of $10,250 to employees at year end (earned but not paid).
- Insurance left unused at year end amounted to $2,000.
- The company estimates that the new equipment will last for 20 years and have a salvage value of $2,945 at the end of its useful life. The company uses the straight-line depreciation method.
- Previously purchased fixed assets are being depreciated at a rate of 10% per year.
- Unearned service revenue of $21,000 has been earned at year end.

Requirement

Set up an accounting equation worksheet. Enter the beginning balances, the transactions, and any needed adjustments at year end. Then, prepare an income statement, statement of changes in shareholders' equity, the statement of cash flows (all for the fiscal year), and the balance sheet at December 31, 2008.

Solution

	Assets			=	Liabilities		+	Shareholders' Equity		
								Contributed Capital	Retained Earnings	
	Cash	All other assets	(Account)		All liabilities	(Account)		Common stock		(Account)
Beginning Balances	$ 390,000	$136,000 106,350 3,000 261,000 (75,800)	Accounts receivable Inventory Prepaid insurance Equipment Accumulated depreciation		$ 26,700 13,500 35,000 130,000 85,000	Accounts payable Salaries payable Unearned revenue Long-term notes payable Other long-term liabilities		$250,000		$280,350
Transaction a.	(164,945)	164,945	Equipment							
b.	1,500	(12,300) 11,100	Equipment Accumulated depreciation						300	Gain on sale of property, plant, and equipment
c.	134,200	(134,200)	Accounts receivable							
d.	(200,000)	365,500	Inventory		165,500	Accounts payable				
e.	(12,000)	12,000	Prepaid insurance							
f.	(170,000)				(170,000)	Accounts payable				
g.	(72,250)				(13,500)	Salaries payable			(58,750)	Salaries expense
h.	 200,000	154,570 (110,000)	Accounts receivable Inventory						354,570 (110,000)	Sales and service revenue Cost of goods sold
i.	(50,000) (10,400)				(50,000)	Long-term notes payable			(10,400)	Interest expense
j.	(30,000)								(30,000)	Operating expenses
Adjustment 1					10,250	Salaries payable			(10,250)	Salary expense
Adjustment 2		(13,000)	Prepaid insurance						(13,000)	Insurance expense
Adjustment 3		(8,100)	Accumulated depreciation						(8,100)	Depreciation expense
Adjustment 4		(24,870)	Accumulated depreciation						(24,870)	Depreciation expense
Adjustment 5					(21,000)	Unearned revenue			21,000	Sales
	$ 16,105 + $836,195			=	$211,450		+	$250,000 + $390,850		

■ Income statement   ■ Statement of changes in shareholders' equity   ■ Balance sheet   ■ Statement of cash flows

Pencils Office Supply
Income Statement
For the Year Ended December 31, 2008

Sales and service revenue		$ 375,570
Cost of goods sold		110,000
Gross profit		265,570
Gain on sale of asset		300
Other expenses		
Insurance expense	$13,000	
Salaries expense	69,000	
Depreciation expense	32,970	
Interest expense	10,400	
Other operating expense	30,000	(155,370)
Net income		$ 110,500

Pencils Office Supply
Statement of Changes in Shareholders' Equity
For the Year Ended December 31, 2008

Common stock			
Beginning balance	$250,000		
+ New contributions	−		
Ending balance			$250,000
Retained earnings			
Beginning balance	$280,350		
+ Net income	110,500		
– Dividends	−		
Ending balance			$390,850
Total shareholders' equity			$ 640,850

Pencils Office Supply
Statement of Cash Flows
For the Year Ended December 31, 2008

Cash from operating activities	
Cash collected from customers	$ 334,200
Cash paid to vendors	(370,000)
Cash paid for insurance	(12,000)
Cash paid to employees	(72,250)
Cash paid for interest	(10,400)
Cash paid for other operating expenses	(30,000)
Net cash from (used for) operating activities	(160,450)
Cash from investing activities	
Proceeds from sale of equipment	1,500
Cash paid for purchase of equipment	(164,945)
Net cash from (used for) investing activities	(163,445)
Cash from financing activities	
Cash paid on long-term note payable	(50,000)
Increase (decrease) in cash during the year	(373,895)
Add beginning cash balance	390,000
Cash balance at December 31, 2008	$ 16,105

Pencils Office Supply
Balance Sheet
At December 31, 2008

Assets	
Cash	$16,105
Accounts receivable	156,370
Inventory	361,850
Prepaid insurance	2,000
Total current assets	536,325
Equipment (net of $97,670 accumulated depreciation)	315,975
Total assets	$852,300
Liabilities and Shareholders' Equity	
Liabilities	
Accounts payable	22,200
Salaries payable	10,250
Unearned revenue	14,000
Total current liabilities	46,450
Long-term notes payable	80,000
Other long-term liabilities	85,000
Shareholders' Equity	
Common stock	250,000
Retained earnings	390,850
Total liabilities and shareholders' equity	$852,300

Key Terms for Chapter 6

Accelerated depreciation (p. 276)

Activity method of depreciation (p. 274)

Amortization (p. 270)

Asset turnover ratio (p. 290)

Capital expenditure (p. 281)

Capitalize (p. 270)

Copyright (p. 279)

Declining balance depreciation (p. 276)

Depletion (p. 271)

Depreciation (p. 271)

Franchise (p. 280)

Goodwill (p. 280)

Impairment (p. 281)

Intangible assets (p. 268)

Modified accelerated cost recovery system (MACRS) (p. 316)

Patent (p. 279)

Relative fair market value
  method (p. 270)
Return on assets ratio
  (p. 289)

Salvage value (p. 272)
Straight-line depreciation
  (p. 272)

Tangible assets (p. 268)
Trademark (p. 280)

Answers to YOUR TURN Questions

Chapter 6

Your Turn 6-1

1. Expense
2. Asset
3. Asset
4. Expense

Your Turn 6-2

Four-fifths of the costs [(400,000/500,000) × $480,000 = $384,000] should be recorded as the cost of the building, and one-fifth of the cost [(100,000/500,000) × $480,000 = $96,000] should be recorded as the cost of the land. These two costs need to be separated because the company will depreciate the building but not the land.

Your Turn 6-3

1. Depreciation
2. Depreciation
3. Depletion

Your Turn 6-4

Each year's depreciation is $2,400 [($15,000 − $3,000)/5 years] per year, so that amount will be on the income statement for the year ended December 31, 2011. At December 31, 2011, the company will have taken two years' worth of depreciation, so the book value will be $10,200 ($15,000 − $4,800).

Your Turn 6-5

Rate = ($44,000 − $4,000) ÷ 100,000 = $0.40 per unit
2009: 13,000 units × $0.40 = $5,200
2010: 14,000 units × $0.40 = $5,600

Your Turn 6-6

$50,000 × 2/5 = $20,000 for the first year
New book value = $50,000 − $20,000 = $30,000
$30,000 × 2/5 = $12,000 for the second year

Your Turn 6-7

$6,000 + $2,400 = $8,400 new depreciable amount
$8,400/8 years remaining life = $1,050 per year for each remaining year

Your Turn 6-8

There is a $2,000 gain on the sale. The proceeds of $8,000 are greater than the book value of $6,000.

Questions

1. Describe the difference between tangible and intangible assets.
2. What is the difference between capitalizing and expensing a cost?
3. What is depreciation?
4. What does amortization mean?
5. Explain the difference between depreciation and depletion.
6. How do firms determine the cost of property, plant, and equipment?

7. What is a basket purchase? What accounting problem does this type of purchase create, and how do firms deal with the accounting problem?
8. What is the carrying value, or book value, of an asset? Is this value equal to the market value of the asset? Explain your answer.
9. What is the residual value, or salvage value, of an asset?
10. What is the difference between depreciation expense and accumulated depreciation? On which financial statement(s) do depreciation expense and accumulated depreciation appear?
11. How does the matching principle apply to depreciation?
12. Explain the difference between the three depreciation methods allowed by GAAP.
13. What is a copyright and how is it accounted for?
14. What is a patent and how is it accounted for?
15. What does it mean for an asset to be impaired?
16. What types of costs related to long-term operational assets are capitalized and what types are expensed?
17. How is a gain or loss on the disposal of an asset calculated? On which financial statement(s) would the gain or loss appear?
18. How does goodwill arise?
19. How do you calculate the return on assets (ROA) ratio and what does this ratio measure?
20. How do you calculate the asset turnover ratio and what does this ratio measure?
21. List two types of controls that safeguard assets.

Multiple-Choice Questions

1. Which of the following is an intangible asset?
   a. Franchise
   b. Oil reserves
   c. Land
   d. Repairs
2. Depreciation is the systematic allocation of the cost of an asset
   a. over the periods during which the asset is paid for.
   b. over the periods during which the market value of the asset decreases.
   c. over the periods during which the company uses the asset.
   d. over the life of the company.
3. Writing off a cost means
   a. putting the cost on the balance sheet as an asset.
   b. evaluating the useful life of the asset.
   c. recording the cost as an expense.
   d. deferring the expense.
4. Suppose a firm purchases a new building for $500,000 and spends an additional $50,000 making alterations to it before it can be used. How much will the firm record as the cost of the asset?
   a. $500,000
   b. $550,000
   c. $450,000
   d. It depends on who performed the alterations.
5. Suppose a firm buys a piece of land with a building for $100,000. The firm's accountant wants to divide the cost between the land and building for the firm's financial records. Why?
   a. Land is always more expensive than buildings.
   b. Land will not be depreciated but the building will be depreciated, so the accountant needs two different amounts.
   c. Land will appreciate and its recorded cost will increase over time, whereas the building will be depreciated.
   d. Depreciation expense will be separated from accumulated depreciation after the first year.
6. When an expenditure to repair an existing asset extends the useful life of the asset, the cost should be
   a. classified as a revenue expenditure because it will result in increased revenue.
   b. capitalized and written off over the remaining life of the asset.

   c. expensed in the period of the repair.

   d. presented on the income statement or in the notes.

7. When goodwill is determined to be impaired, a firm will

   a. increase its book value to market value.

   b. sell it immediately.

   c. reduce the value of the goodwill with a charge against income (impairment loss).

   d. reduce the value of the goodwill with a charge to paid-in capital (reduce paid-in capital).

8. When a company's balance sheet shows goodwill for $300,000, what does that mean?

   a. The company has developed a strong reputation valued at $300,000 if the company were to be sold.

   b. The company is worth $300,000 more than the balance sheet indicates.

   c. The company purchased another company and paid $300,000 more than the fair market value of the company's net assets.

   d. The company has invested $300,000 in new equipment during the period.

9. Suppose a firm purchased an asset for $100,000 and estimated its useful life as 10 years with no salvage value on the date of the purchase. The firm uses straight-line depreciation. After using the asset for five years, the firm changes its estimate of the remaining useful life to four years (a total of nine years rather than the original 10 years). How much depreciation expense will the firm recognize in the sixth year of the asset's life?

   a. $12,500

   b. $10,000

   c. $11,111

   d. $31,111

10. Suppose a firm purchased an asset for $50,000 and depreciated it using straight-line depreciation for its 10-year useful life, with no salvage value. At the end of the seventh year of use, the firm decided to sell the asset. Proceeds from the sale were $17,500. What was the gain or loss from the sale of the asset? How did the sale affect the statement of cash flows?

   a. $2,500 loss; $2,500 cash outflow from investing activities

   b. $32,500 loss; $17,500 cash inflow from investing activities

   c. $17,500 gain; $17,500 cash inflow from investing activities

   d. $2,500 gain; $17,500 cash inflow from investing activities

Short Exercises
Set A

All of the A exercises can be found within MyAccountingLab, an online homework and practice environment.

SE6-1A. *Calculate the cost of an asset. (LO 1).* Susan's Bake Shop bought a new air-conditioning system when the old one stopped working. The invoice price of the system was $45,000. Susan's also had the following expenses associated with the purchase:

Delivery charge	$1,925
Installation	3,250
Power to run the system for the first year	1,275

What amount should Susan's record on the books for this air-conditioning system?

SE6-2A. *Account for basket purchase. (LO 1).* Marketing Consultants Corporation obtained a building, its surrounding land, and a computer system in a lump-sum purchase for $375,000. An appraisal set the value of land at $189,000, the building at $126,000, and the computer system at $105,000. At what amount should Marketing Consultants record each new asset on its books?

SE6-3A. *Account for basket purchase. (LO 1).* Wrecker Specialist Corporation purchased three new pieces of equipment at a total cost of $415,000. The appraised values of the individual pieces of equipment were as follows:

Equipment 1	$162,750
Equipment 2	116,250
Equipment 3	186,000

What amounts should be recorded as the cost for each of the pieces of equipment in Wrecker Specialist's accounts?

SE6-4A. *Calculate depreciation expense: straight-line. (LO 2).* Calculate the annual straight-line depreciation expense for an asset that cost $20,000, has a useful life of four years, and has an estimated salvage value of $4,000.

SE4-5A. *Calculate depreciation expense: activity method. (LO 2).* Using the activity method, calculate the first two years of depreciation expense for a vehicle that cost $32,000, has an estimated useful life of five years or 125,000 miles, and has an estimated salvage value of $2,500. The number of miles driven each year is as follows:

Year 1	25,000
Year 2	35,000
Year 3	15,000
Year 4	45,000
Year 5	5,000

SE6-6A. *Calculate depreciation expense: double-declining balance. (LO 2).* Using the double-declining balance method, calculate the annual depreciation expense that will be recorded each year for an asset that cost $18,500, has a useful life of four years, and has an estimated salvage value of $3,500. Explain what accounting issue arises, if any, in the third and fourth years.

SE6-7A. *Determine the cost of an asset. (LO 1, 2).* If an asset with a salvage value of $1,500 is being depreciated at a rate of $1,500 per year using the straight-line method over a useful life of four years, how much did the asset cost?

SE6-8A. *Determine the useful life of an asset. (LO 2).* Suppose an asset cost $28,500 and has an estimated salvage value of $3,500. At the end of two years, the carrying value of the asset is $18,500. What is the useful life of the asset? Assume straight-line depreciation.

SE6-9A. *Calculate depletion. (LO 2).* Mining Expedition Company purchased a coal mine on January 1, 2010, for $8,400,000 and expects the mine to produce 3,500,000 pounds of coal over its useful life. In 2010, 1,100,000 pounds of coal were recovered. In 2011, 900,000 pounds of coal were recovered. What is the depletion for each of these years?

SE6-10A. *Amortization of intangible assets. (LO 3).* Unique Quality Recourses purchased a patent for $150,000 on July 1, 2009. The estimated useful life is 20 years. The legal life is 15 years. What is the amortization expense for the fiscal year ended June 30, 2010?

SE6-11A. *Analyze revenue and capital expenditures. (LO 4).* Categorize each of the following as a capital expenditure or a revenue expenditure (expensed) for Dalton & Sons and explain why:

1. In accordance with the long-term maintenance plan, paid for a newly reshingled roof (replacing similar old shingles)
2. Built an annex to the building for the executive offices
3. Improved the ventilation system to increase energy efficiency in the building
4. Replaced parts in major equipment as needed

SE6-12A. *Calculate depreciation expense with change in estimate of salvage value. (LO 4).* On January 1, 2010, the Premium Beer Corporation purchased equipment at a cost of $110,000. It was expected to have a useful life of eight years and no salvage value. The straight-line depreciation method was used. In January 2012, the estimate of salvage value was revised from $0 to $7,500. How much depreciation should Premium Beer Corporation record for 2012?

SE6-13A. *Account for asset impairment. (LO 4, 6).* Delta Airlines has determined that several of its planes are impaired. The book value of the planes is $10 million, but the fair market value of the planes is $9 million. How would this impairment affect the income statement in the period it is recorded?

SE6-14A. *Account for disposal of an asset. (LO 5).* A machine is purchased on July 1, 2009, for $170,000. It has an expected useful life of 10 years and no salvage value. After eight years, the machine is sold for $36,000 cash. What is the gain or loss on the sale?

Set B

SE6-15B. *Calculate the cost of an asset. (LO 1).* Bargain Basement Shopping Corporation purchased new credit card equipment. The invoice price of the equipment was $25,000. Bargain also had the following expenses associated with purchasing this equipment:

Shipping and delivery insurance	$1,750
Staff training to use new equipment	3,175
Electricity costs the first year	125

What amount should Bargain record on the books for this equipment?

SE6-16B. *Account for basket purchase. (LO 1).* Warehouse Supply Corporation obtained land, a factory, and manufacturing equipment in a lump-sum purchase for $495,000. An appraisal set the value of land at $296,400, the factory at $210,900, and the equipment at $62,700. At what amount should Warehouse Supply record each new asset on its books?

SE6-17B. *Account for basket purchase. (LO 1).* Dependable Courier purchased four vehicles at a total cost of $55,500. The appraised values of the individual vehicles were as follows:

Vehicle 1	$12,390
Vehicle 2	13,570
Vehicle 3	15,930
Vehicle 4	17,110

What amounts should be recorded as the cost for each of the vehicles in Dependable Courier's accounts?

SE6-18B. *Calculate depreciation expense: straight-line. (LO 2).* Calculate the annual straight-line depreciation expense for an asset that cost $45,000, has a useful life of eight years, and has an estimated salvage value of $5,000.

SE6-19B. *Calculate depreciation expense: activity method. (LO 2).* Using the activity method, calculate the first two years of depreciation expense for a piece of equipment that cost $85,000, has an estimated useful life of 5,000,000 hours, and has an estimated salvage value of $5,000. The number of hours used each year is as follows:

Year 1	1,250,000
Year 2	1,000,000
Year 3	650,000
Year 4	850,000
Year 5	1,250,000

SE6-20B. *Calculate depreciation expense: double-declining balance. (LO 2).* Using the double-declining balance method, calculate the annual depreciation expense that will be recorded each year for an asset that cost $23,000, has a useful life of eight years, and has an estimated salvage value of $3,500. Explain what accounting issue arises, if any, in the seventh and eighth years.

SE6-21B. *Determine the cost of an asset. (LO 1, 2).* If an asset with a salvage value of $1,000 is being depreciated at a rate of $1,250 per year using the straight-line method over a useful life of eight years, how much did the asset cost?

SE6-22B. *Determine the useful life of an asset. (LO 2).* Suppose an asset cost $28,000 and has an estimated salvage value of $1,000. At the end of four years, the carrying value of the asset is $16,000. What is the useful life of the asset? Assume straight-line depreciation.

SE6-23B. *Calculate depletion. (LO 2).* CNA Enterprises purchases an oil field and expects it to produce 1,000,000 barrels of oil. The oil field, acquired in January 2008, cost CNA $1.5 million. In 2008, the oil field produced 280,000 barrels. In 2009, the oil field produced 350,000 barrels. What is the depletion for each of these years?

SE6-24B. *Amortization of intangible assets. (LO 3).* STAT Research purchased a patent for $120,000 on January 1, 2010. The estimated useful life is five years. The legal life is 10 years. What is the amortization expense for the fiscal year ended December 31, 2010?

SE6-25B. *Analyze revenue and capital expenditures. (LO 4).* Categorize each of the following as a capital expenditure or a revenue expenditure (expense) for Service Enterprises and explain why:

1. In accordance with the long-term maintenance plan, painted the building
2. Purchased land next to the building to expand parking
3. Remodeled building increasing its useful life
4. Performed routine maintenance on the copier machines

SE6-26B. *Calculate depreciation expense with change in estimate of salvage value. (LO 4).* On January 1, 2010, Arbuckle's Carpet Cleaners purchased a machine at a cost of $42,000. The machine was expected to have a useful life of six years and no salvage value. The straight-line depreciation method was used. In January 2013, the estimate of salvage value was revised from $0 to $3,000. How much depreciation should Arbuckle's record for 2013?

SE6-27B. *Account for asset impairment. (LO 4, 6).* Similar Motors has determined that several of its plants are impaired. The book value of the plants is $8.34 billion, but the fair market value of the plants is just $7.56 billion. How would Similar Motors record this decline in the accounting equation worksheet?

SE6-28B. *Account for disposal of an asset. (LO 5).* A machine is purchased on May 10, for $45,000. It has an expected useful life of nine years and no salvage value. After seven years, the machine is sold for $10,000 cash. What is the gain or loss on the sale?

Exercises
Set A

E6-29A. *Account for basket purchase. (LO 1, 2).* Connor's Tasty Vegan Restaurant purchased an oven and a delivery vehicle from a "going out of business" sale for a combined total of $32,000. An independent appraiser provides the following market values: oven—$15,000; delivery vehicle—$35,000.

1. How much of the purchase price should Connor's allocate to each of the assets?
2. If the oven has a useful life of four years and an estimated salvage value of $1,600, how much depreciation expense should Connor's record each year using the straight-line method?
3. If the delivery vehicle has a useful life of eight years and an estimated salvage value of $2,000, what would the book value of the vehicle be at the end of three years using the double-declining balance method?

E6-30A. *Calculate the cost of an asset and depreciation expense. (LO 1, 2).* True Light Electricity Company purchased land for $180,000 cash and a building for $420,000 cash. The company paid attorney fees of $22,000 associated with the purchase and allocated that cost to the building and the land based on the purchase price. Redesign costs on the building were $52,000.

Use the accounting equation to record the purchase of the property, including all related expenditures. Assume that all transactions were for cash and that all purchases occurred at the beginning of the year.

1. Compute the annual straight-line depreciation, assuming a 25-year estimated useful life and a $17,400 estimated salvage value for the building.
2. What would the book value of the building be at the end of the third year?
3. What would the book value of the land be at the end of the third year?

E6-31A. *Calculate depreciation expense: straight-line and activity methods. (LO 2).* Paper Printing Company purchased a copy machine for $65,000 on January 1, 2010. The copy machine had an estimated useful life of five years or 1,000,000 copies. Paper Printing estimated the copy machine's salvage value to be $5,000. The company made 250,000 copies in 2010 and 190,000 copies in 2011.

1. Compute the depreciation expense for 2010 and 2011, first using the straight-line method, then the activity method.
2. Which method portrays the actual use of this asset more accurately? Explain your answer.

E6-32A. *Calculate depreciation expense: straight-line and double-declining balance methods. (LO 2).* On July 1, 2010, Seminole Construction Corporation purchased equipment for $62,000. Seminole also paid $2,500 to train employees how to use it. The equipment is expected to have a useful life of eight years and a salvage value of $500.

1. Compute the depreciation expense for years ended June 30, 2011–2013, using the straight-line method.
2. Compute the depreciation expense for the years ended June 30, 2011–2013, using the double-declining balance method. (Round your answers to the nearest dollar.)
3. What is the book value of the equipment at the year ended June 30, 2013, under each method?

E6-33A. *Calculate depreciation under alternative methods. (LO 2).* Burgers to Go purchased a new delivery car at the beginning of the year at a cost of $25,700. The estimated useful life of the car is five years, and its estimated productivity is 80,000 miles. Its salvage value is estimated to be $1,700. Miles used yearly are as follows: Year 1, 16,000 miles; Year 2, 20,000 miles; Year 3, 13,000 miles; Year 4, 15,000 miles; and Year 5, 16,000 miles. Complete a separate depreciation schedule for each of the three methods given for all five years. (Round your answers to the nearest dollar.)

1. Straight-line method
2. Activity method
3. Double-declining balance method

E6-34A. *Calculate depreciation under alternative methods. (LO 2).* Soda Pop Bottling Company bought equipment for $75,500 cash at the beginning of 2009. The estimated useful life is four years and the estimated salvage value is $3,500. The estimated productivity is 150,000 units. Units actually produced were 37,500 in 2009 and 40,000 in 2010. Calculate the depreciation expense for 2009 and 2010 under each of the three methods given. (Round your answers to the nearest dollar.)

1. Straight-line method
2. Activity method
3. Double-declining balance method

E6-35A. *Calculate depletion. (LO 2).* On January 1, 2010, USA Oil Corporation purchased the rights to an offshore oil well for $55,000,000. The company expects the oil well to produce 10,000,000 barrels of oil during its life. During 2010, USA Oil removed 675,000 barrels of oil.

1. How much depletion should USA Oil Corporation record for 2010?
2. What is the book value of the oil rights at December 31, 2010, the end of the fiscal year?

E6-36A. *Amortize intangible assets. (LO 3).* Carterette Research Corporation registered a patent with the U.S. Patent and Trademark Office. The total cost of obtaining the patent was $195,000. Although the firm believes the patent will be useful for only 10 years, it has a legal life of 20 years. What will Carterette Research Corporation record for its annual amortization expense? Show how it would be recorded in the accounting equation.

E6-37A. *Calculate goodwill. (LO 3).* International Manufacturing decides to acquire a small local manufacturing company called Township Manufacturing. Township Manufacturing has assets with a market value of $120,000 and no liabilities, but International Manufacturing pays $135,000. Use the accounting equation to record the purchase.

E6-38A. *Evaluate asset impairment. (LO 4).* During its most recent fiscal year, Bargain Airlines grounded 10 of its 747s due to a potential problem with the wing flaps. Although the planes had been repaired by the end of the fiscal year, the company believed the problems indicated the need for an evaluation of potential impairment of these planes. The results of the analysis indicated that the planes had permanently declined in fair value by $120 million below their book value. What effect would this decline in value have on Bargain Airlines' net income for the year?

E6-39A. *Distinguish between capital and revenue expenditures (expenses). (LO 1, 4).* Classify the following items as either a capital expenditure or a revenue expenditure (an expense):

1. Changed oil in the delivery truck
2. Replaced the engine in the delivery truck
3. Paid sales tax on the new delivery truck
4. Installed a new, similar roof on the office building
5. Paid freight and installation charges for a new computer system
6. Repainted the administrative offices
7. Purchased and installed a new toner cartridge in the laser printer
8. Replaced several missing shingles on the roof
9. Trained an employee prior to using the new computer system
10. Replaced the brake pads on the delivery truck

E6-40A. *Account for capital and revenue expenditures (expenses) and calculate depreciation expense. (LO 2, 4).* Pet Food Enterprises has had a machine for five years. At the beginning of the sixth year, the machine was not performing as well as expected. First, Pet Food performed regularly scheduled maintenance on the machine, which cost $170. Then, the company replaced some worn-out parts, which cost $575. Finally, at the beginning of the sixth year, the company completed a major overhaul of the machine that not only fixed the machine but also added new functionality and extended its useful life by four years (to a total of 10 years) with no salvage value. The overhaul cost $25,000. (Originally, the machine cost $100,000, had a salvage value of $7,000, and had an estimated useful life of six years.)

1. Which of these costs are capital expenditures? How would these amounts appear on the financial statements?
2. Which are revenue expenditures? How would these amounts appear on the financial statements?
3. Assuming Pet Food Enterprises uses the straight-line method of depreciation, how much depreciation expense will be reported on the income statements for years 6–10?

E6-41A. *Account for capital and revenue expenditures (expenses) and calculate depreciation expense. (LO 2, 4).* Reengineering Corporation operates a small repair facility for its products. At the beginning of 2009, the accounting records for the company showed the following balances for its only piece of equipment, purchased at the beginning of 2006:

Equipment	$135,000
Accumulated depreciation	45,000

During 2009, the following costs were incurred for repairs and maintenance on the equipment:

Routine maintenance and repairs	$ 815
Major overhaul of the equipment that improved efficiency	32,000

The company uses the straight-line method, and it now estimates the equipment will last for a total of 12 years with $500 estimated salvage value. The company's fiscal year ends on December 31.

1. How much depreciation did Reengineering Corporation record on the equipment at the end of 2008?
2. After the overhaul at the beginning of 2009, what is the remaining estimated life of the equipment?
3. What is the amount of depreciation expense the company will record for 2009?

E6-42A. *Account for disposal of an asset. (LO 5).* Erickson Electricity bought a utility truck for $70,000. The utility truck is expected to have an eight-year useful life and a salvage value of $6,000.

1. If Erickson sells the utility truck after four years for $40,000, would the company realize a gain or loss? How much? (Assume straight-line depreciation.)
2. What would the gain or loss be if the company sold the utility truck for $17,000 after six years?

E6-43A. *Account for disposal of an asset. (LO 5).* Uptown Bakery purchased a grain grinding machine five years ago for $21,000. The machinery was expected to have a salvage value of $1,000 after a 10-year useful life. Assuming straight-line depreciation is used, calculate the gain or loss realized if the machinery was sold after five years for

1. $13,500
2. $8,400

E6-44A. *Account for disposal of an asset. (LO 5).* Gourmet Pizza's Delivery disposed of a delivery car after using it three years. The records of the company provide the following information:

Delivery car	$25,000
Accumulated depreciation	15,000

Calculate the gain or loss on the disposal of the car for each of the following independent situations:

1. Gourmet Pizza's sold the car to Desserts on Wheels for $13,500.
2. Gourmet Pizza's sold the car to Premium Beer Corporation for $10,000.
3. Gourmet Pizza's sold the car to Organic Food Market for $8,250.
4. The car was stolen out of Gourmet Pizza's parking lot, and the company had no insurance.

E6-45A. *Account for disposal of an asset. (LO 5).* Paper Printing Company disposed of a copy machine after using it for two years. The copy machine originally cost $65,000 and had associated accumulated depreciation of $32,500. Calculate the gain or loss on the disposal of the copy machine for each of the following situations:

1. The company sold the copy machine to a church for $27,500.
2. The company sold the copy machine to a local bank for $33,000.
3. The company gave the copy machine to a hauling company in return for hauling it to the local dump. The copy machine was considered worthless.

E6-46A. *Calculate gain or loss and cash flow. (LO 5, 6).* Big Peach Athletics sold assets with an original cost of $21,000 and accumulated depreciation of $11,500. If the cash proceeds from the sale were $10,250, what was the gain or loss on the sale? On which financial statement would that amount be shown? How much would be shown on the statement of cash flows and in which section?

E6-47A. *Identify items on financial statements. (LO 6).* For each of the following, give the financial statement on which it would appear:

1. Book value of fixed assets of $56,900
2. Proceeds from sale of fixed assets of $20,000
3. Loss on sale of fixed assets of $12,500
4. Accumulated depreciation on equipment of $10,000
5. Depreciation expense on equipment of $2,000
6. Impairment write off on assets of $45,000

E6-48A. *Calculate return on assets and asset turnover ratios. (LO 7).* Using the selection from Books-A-Million's annual report in Appendix A at the back of the book, calculate the following ratios for the most recent fiscal year:

1. Return on assets (ROA)
2. Asset turnover ratio

Set B

E6-49B. *Account for basket purchase. (LO 1, 2).* Runnels' Doggie Daycare purchased a building and land for a total cash price of $150,000. An independent appraiser provides the following market values: building, $59,500; land, $110,500.

1. How much of the purchase price should the company allocate to each of the assets?
2. If the building has a useful life of eight years and an estimated salvage value of $10,500, how much depreciation expense should Runnels record each year using the straight-line method?
3. Using the double-declining balance method, what would the book value of the building be at the end of four years?

E6-50B. *Calculate the cost of an asset and depreciation expense. (LO 1, 2).* Top Dollar Realty purchased a building for $157,500 cash and the land for $192,500 cash. The company paid real estate closing costs of $8,000 and allocated that cost to the building and the land based on the purchase price. Renovation costs on the building were $52,500.

Use the accounting equation to record the purchase of the property, including all related expenditures. Assume that all transactions were for cash and that all purchases occurred at the beginning of the year.

1. Compute the annual straight-line depreciation, assuming a 25-year estimated useful life and a $12,600 estimated salvage value for the building.
2. What would the book value of the building be at the end of the seventh year?
3. What would the book value of the land be at the end of the thirteenth year?

E6-51B. *Calculate depreciation expense: straight-line and activity methods. (LO 2).* Treadmill Repair Masters purchased equipment for $34,000 on January 1, 2010. The equipment had an estimated useful life of five years or 400,000 units of production. Treadmill Repair Masters estimated the equipment's salvage value to be $2,000. The equipment was used to produce 80,000 units in the year ended December 31, 2010, and 97,500 units in the year ended December 31, 2011.

1. Compute the depreciation expense for 2010 and 2011, first using the straight-line method, then the activity method.
2. Which method portrays more accurately the actual use of this asset? Explain your answer.

E6-52B. *Calculate depreciation expense: straight-line and double-declining balance methods. (LO 2).* On January 1, 2010, Ocean's Front Restaurant purchased new meat slicing equipment for $37,500. Ocean's Front also paid $1,000 for shipping and $3,500 to train employees to use the new equipment. The equipment is expected to have a useful life of five years and a salvage value of $2,000.

1. Compute the depreciation expense for the years 2010–2012, using the straight-line method. (December 31 is the fiscal year end.)
2. Compute the depreciation expense for the years 2010–2012, using the double-declining balance method. (Round your answers to the nearest dollar.)
3. What is the book value of the equipment at the end of 2010 under each method?

E6-53B. *Calculate depreciation under alternative methods. (LO 2).* Books Unlimited Corporation purchased a new copy machine at the beginning of the year at a cost of $36,500. The estimated useful life of the machine is five years, and its estimated productivity is 250,000 copies. Its salvage value is estimated to be $1,500. Yearly production for Year 1 was 50,000 copies; Year 2 was 45,000 copies; Year 3 was 55,000 copies; Year 4 was 40,500 copies; and Year 5 was 59,500 copies. Complete a separate depreciation schedule for each of the three methods given for all five years. (Round your answers to the nearest dollar.)

1. Straight-line method
2. Activity method
3. Double-declining balance method

E6-54B. *Calculate depreciation under alternative methods. (LO 2).* Pristine Carpet Cleaner bought a new steamer for $137,000 cash at the beginning of 2010. The estimated useful life is eight years and the estimated salvage value is $2,000. The estimated productivity is 225,000 hours. Hours actually used were 30,000 in 2010 and 28,125 in 2011. Calculate the depreciation expense for 2010 and 2011 under each of the three methods given. (Round your answers to the nearest dollar.)

1. Straight-line method
2. Activity method
3. Double-declining balance method

E6-55B. *Calculate depletion. (LO 2).* On July 1, 2010, Premier Paper Company purchased 1,000 acres of timberland for $22,427,500. The land without the timber is valued at $2,427,500. The land contained 5,494,505 board feet of timber. During the year ended June 30, 2011, Premier Paper Company logged and sold 525,000 board feet of timber.

1. How much depletion should Premier Paper Company record for the year ended June 30, 2011?
2. What is the book value of the timber at June 30, 2011, the end of the fiscal year?

E6-56B. *Amortize intangible assets. (LO 3).* Microtech registered a trademark with the U.S. Patent and Trademark Office. The total cost of obtaining the trademark was $55,000. Although the trademark has a legal life of 10 years, the firm believes it will be renewed indefinitely. What will Microtech record for its annual amortization expense?

E6-57B. *Calculate goodwill. (LO 3).* Big Apple Realty has decided to acquire a competing realty firm. The competitor firm has assets with a market value of $375,000 and liabilities with a market value of $110,000, and Big Apple pays $285,000. Use the accounting equation to record the purchase.

E6-58B. *Evaluate asset impairment. (LO 4).* During its fiscal year ended June 30, Super Shippers Delivery Service had to decommission 1,500 delivery trucks due to a potential problem with the fuel tank. Although the trucks had been repaired by the end of the fiscal year, the company determined that the problems required an evaluation of potential impairment of these trucks. The results of the analysis indicated that the trucks had permanently declined in fair value by $7.5 million below their book value. What effect would this decline have on Super Shippers' net income for the year?

E6-59B. *Distinguish between capital and revenue expenditures (expenses). (LO 1, 4).* Classify the following items as either a capital expenditure or a revenue expenditure (expense):

1. Changed the filter in the moving van
2. Painted the moving van
3. Paid sales tax on the new moving van
4. Installed a new energy-efficient air-conditioning system for the office building
5. Cleaned and lubricated sewing equipment
6. Performed routine yearly maintenance on copy machine
7. Purchased and installed a new set of energy-efficient deep fryers
8. Replaced several cracked tiles in company bathroom floor
9. Trained an employee prior to using the new energy-efficient deep fryers
10. Replaced the tires on the moving van

E6-60B. *Account for capital and revenue expenditures (expenses) and calculate depreciation expense. (LO 2, 4).* McKinney Library Services has had a file server (computer) for seven years. At the beginning of the eighth year, it wasn't performing as well as it should have been. First, McKinney had the server cleaned, which cost $125. Then, the company had the annual maintenance performed, which cost $275. Finally, at the beginning of the eighth year, McKinney completed a major upgrade of the server that not only fixed it, but also added new functionality to it and extended the useful life by four years (to a total of 12 years) with no salvage value. The overhaul cost $25,000. (Originally, the server cost $45,000, had a salvage value of $5,000, and an estimated useful life of eight years.)

1. Which of these costs are capital expenditures? How would these amounts appear on the financial statements?
2. Which are revenue expenditures? How would these amounts appear on the financial statements?
3. Assuming McKinney uses the straight-line method of depreciation, how much depreciation expense will be reported on the income statements for years 8–12?

E6-61B. *Account for capital and revenue expenditures (expenses) and calculate depreciation expense. (LO 2, 4).* At the beginning of 2010, the accounting records for Bright Tans showed the following balances for its deluxe high-pressure tanning bed, purchased at the beginning of 2007:

Deluxe high-pressure tanning bed	$65,000
Accumulated depreciation	30,000

During 2010, the following cash costs were incurred for repairs and maintenance on the tanning bed:

Routine maintenance and repairs	$ 350
Major overhaul of the tanning bed that improved efficiency	18,000

The company uses straight-line depreciation and it now estimates the tanning bed will last for a total of 10 years with $150 estimated salvage value. The company's fiscal year ends on December 31.

1. How much did the company record for depreciation on the tanning bed at the end of 2009?
2. After the overhaul, at the beginning of 2010, what is the remaining estimated life?
3. What is the amount of depreciation expense the company will record for 2010?

E6-62B. *Account for disposal of an asset. (LO 5).* Cupcake Factory purchased an industrial oven for $8,000. The company expects the oven to have a six-year useful life and a salvage value of $500. (Assume straight-line depreciation.)

1. If Cupcake sells the oven after three years for $3,500, would it realize a gain or loss? How much?
2. What would the gain or loss be if the oven were sold for $2,500 after five years?

E6-63B. *Account for disposal of an asset. (LO 5).* Industry Leading Manufacturers purchased equipment five years ago for $78,000. The company expects the equipment to have a salvage value of $3,000 after an eight-year useful life. Assuming the company uses straight-line depreciation; calculate the gain or loss realized if the company sells the equipment after four years for

1. $ 42,050.
2. $ 39,875.

E6-64B. *Account for disposal of an asset. (LO 5).* Fast Pizza Delivery disposed of a delivery vehicle that had been used in the business for four years. The records of the company provide the following information:

Delivery vehicle	$35,000
Accumulated depreciation	20,000

Calculate the gain or loss on the disposal of the delivery vehicle for each of the following independent situations:

1. Fast Pizza sold the delivery vehicle to the business manager for $15,000.

2. Fast Pizza sold the delivery vehicle to a homeless shelter for $10,000.
3. Fast Pizza sold the delivery vehicle to a customer for $17,000.
4. Fast Pizza caught on fire and the delivery vehicle was destroyed; Fast Pizza had no insurance.

E6-65B. *Account for disposal of an asset. (LO 5).* Sylvan Manufacturing disposed of equipment that had been used in the business for six years. The equipment originally cost $65,000 and had associated accumulated depreciation of $45,000. Calculate the gain or loss on the disposal of the equipment for each of the following situations:

1. The company sold the equipment to a scrap yard for $10,000.
2. The company sold the equipment to a competitor for $23,525.
3. The company called the city trash collectors to pick up the equipment because it was totally worthless.

E6-66B. *Calculate gain or loss and cash flow. (LO 5, 6).* Vintage Records sold assets with an original cost of $45,000 and accumulated depreciation of $30,000. If the cash proceeds from the sale were $13,500, what was the gain or loss on the sale? On which financial statement would that amount be shown? How much would be shown on the statement of cash flows and in which section?

E6-67B. *Identify items for financial statements. (LO 6).* For each of the following, give the financial statement on which it would appear:

1. Cost of fixed assets of $100,000
2. Proceeds from sale of land of $120,000
3. Gain on sale of fixed assets of $12,500
4. Accumulated depreciation on equipment of $50,000
5. Depreciation expense on equipment of $7,000
6. Impairment write off on assets of $65,000

E6-68B. *Calculate return on assets and asset turnover ratios. (LO 7).* Use the information from the 2008 annual report of Barnes & Noble to calculate the following ratios for the two most recent fiscal years:

(dollars in thousands)	2008	2007	2006
Sales (net)	$5,121,804	$5,286,674	$5,139,618
Net income	$ 75,920	$ 135,799	$ 150,527
Total assets	$2,993,888	$3,249,826	$3,196,798*

*From the 2007 annual report

1. Return on assets (ROA)
2. Asset turnover ratio

Problems
Set A

All of the A problems can be found within MyAccountingLab, an online homework and practice environment.

P6-69A. *Calculate capitalized cost and depreciation expense. (LO 1, 2).* Auto Mechanics, Inc., purchased a new piece of equipment for one of the company's repair shops on January 1, 2010. The invoice price was $64,700, but the salesperson gave Auto a 5% discount for paying cash for the equipment. Delivery costs amounted to $2,500, and Auto paid $300 for a special insurance policy to cover the equipment while in transit. The installation cost was $1,250, and Auto spent $2,500 training the employees to use the new equipment. Additionally, Auto had to spend $7,500 to customize the equipment to fit the shop's needs and hired a special mechanic at an annual salary of $55,000 who had several years experience with this type of equipment.

Requirements

1. What amount should be capitalized for this new asset?
2. To calculate the depreciation expense for 2010, what other information do you need? Do you think the company should gather this information before purchasing the asset? Why or why not?

P6-70A. *Calculate and analyze depreciation under alternative methods. (LO 2).* On January 1, 2010, the Super Fast Subs Company purchased a delivery automobile for $31,000. The estimated useful life of the vehicle is five years, and the estimated salvage value is $1,000. The company expects the automobile to be driven 200,000 miles during its service life. Actual miles driven were:

Year	Miles
2010	35,000
2011	40,000
2012	45,000
2013	39,000
2014	41,000

Requirements

1. Calculate the depreciation expense for each year of the five-year life of the automobile using the following methods. (Round your answers to the nearest dollar.)
   a. Straight-line method
   b. Double-declining balance method
   c. Activity method
2. How does the choice of depreciation methods affect net income in each of the years? How does the choice of depreciation methods affect the balance sheet in each of the years?

P6-71A. *Calculate and analyze depreciation under alternative methods. (LO 2).* Marshall's Dry Cleaning purchased new equipment on January 1, 2010, at a cost of $125,000. The estimated useful life is eight years with a salvage value of $15,000.

Requirements

1. Prepare two different depreciation schedules for the equipment—one using the straight-line method, and the other using the double-declining balance method. (Round to the nearest dollar.)
2. Determine which method would result in the greatest net income for the year 2010.

P6-72A. *Calculate and analyze depreciation under alternative methods. (LO 2).* Schillig & Gray Industries purchased a new machine at the beginning of 2011 for $9,500. The company expected the machine to last for four years and have a salvage value of $500. The productive life of the machine was estimated to be 180,000 units. Yearly production was as follows: in 2011 it produced 50,000 units; in 2012 it produced 45,000 units; in 2013 it produced 30,000 units; and in 2014 it produced 55,000 units.

Requirements

1. Calculate the depreciation expense for each year of the four-year life of the machine using the following methods. (Round to the nearest dollar.)
   a. Straight-line method
   b. Double-declining balance method
   c. Activity method using units
2. For each method, give the amount of accumulated depreciation that would be shown on the balance sheet at the end of each year.
3. Calculate the book value of the machine at the end of each year for each method.

P6-73A. *Account for intangible assets. (LO 3, 6).* Scientific Genius Company had the following balances in its intangible assets accounts at the beginning of the year. The trademarks have a remaining useful life of 15 years, and the copyright has a remaining useful life of nine years.

Trademarks	$45,000
Copyrights	36,000
Goodwill	50,000

Transactions during the year are as follows:

    a. At the beginning of the year, Scientific Genius filed for a new trademark. The costs totaled $30,000. Its useful life is estimated at 15 years.

    b. Scientific Genius incurred R&D costs of $75,000 related to new product development. No new products have been identified.

    c. Scientific Genius evaluated the goodwill for impairment and reduced its book value by $5,000.

    d. Scientific Genius successfully defended one of its copyrights in court. Fees totaled $18,000.

Requirements

1. Show each of the transactions in the accounting equation, including any adjustments that would need to be made for the year-end financial statements.
2. Prepare the intangible assets section of the balance sheet at year end.

P6-74A. *Account for change in estimates for depreciation. (LO 4).* In January 2009, Flooring Installation & Repair, Inc., purchased a van that cost $45,000. The firm estimated that the van would last for six years and have a salvage value of $3,000 at the end of 2014. The company uses the straight-line method of depreciation. Analyze each of the following independent scenarios:

    a. Before the depreciation expense is recorded for the year 2012, the mechanic tells Flooring that the van can be used until the end of 2014 as planned, but that it will be worth only $750.

    b. Before depreciation expense is recorded for the year 2012, Flooring decides that the van will last only until the end of 2013. The company anticipates the value of the van at that time will still be $1,500.

    c. Before depreciation expense is recorded for the year 2012, Flooring decides that the van will last until the end of 2015, but that it will be worth nothing at that time.

    d. Before the depreciation expense is recorded for the year 2012, the mechanic tells Flooring that the van can be used until the end of 2017 if the company spends $5,000 on a major overhaul. However, the estimated salvage value at that time (end of 2017) would be $100. Flooring decides to follow the mechanic's advice and has the van overhauled.

Requirement

Calculate the amount of depreciation expense related to the van that Flooring Installation & Repair, Inc., would report on its income statement for the year ended December 31, 2012, for each scenario.

P6-75A. *Account for disposal of an asset. (LO 5).* Analyze each of the following independent scenarios:

    a. A machine that cost $22,000 had an estimated useful life of three years with salvage value of $1,000. After two years of using straight-line depreciation, the company sold the machine for $8,000.

    b. A van that cost $40,000 had an estimated useful life of 10 years and a salvage value of $4,000. After 10 years of using straight-line depreciation, the company sold the completely worn-out van for $1,000 as scrap.

    c. Equipment that cost $45,000 had an estimated useful life of eight years and a salvage value of $3,000. After four years of using double-declining balance depreciation, the company sold the equipment for $14,750. (Round to the nearest dollar.)

    d. An asset that cost $21,000 had an estimated useful life of seven years and no salvage value. After six years of using straight-line depreciation, the company deemed the asset worthless and hauled it to the dump.

Requirement

For each scenario, calculate the gain or loss, if any, that would result upon disposal.

P6-76A. *Calculate depreciation under alternative methods and account for disposal of an asset. (LO 2, 5).* Hope Construction purchased new equipment on January 1, 2011, for $55,000. The company expects the equipment to have a useful life of five years and no salvage value. The company's fiscal year ends on December 31.

Requirements

1. Calculate the depreciation expense for the fiscal years 2011 and 2012 using each of the following methods:
   a. Straight-line method
   b. Double-declining balance method
2. Hope Construction sold the equipment on January 1, 2013, for $33,000. What was the gain or loss on the sale using each of the depreciation methods? On which financial statement would the gain or loss appear?

P6-77A. *Calculate depreciation under alternative methods and account for disposal of an asset. (LO 2, 5).* Book Printing Company bought a machine four years ago for $60,000. The company expects the machine to have a useful life of five years with no salvage value. The company has taken four full years of depreciation expense.

Requirements

1. Assume that the company uses straight-line depreciation. If the machine is sold for $11,000, will there be a gain or loss on the sale? If so, how much will that gain or loss be? How will the sale affect the financial statements for the year?
2. Assume that the company uses double-declining balance depreciation. If the machine is sold for $9,000, will there be a gain or loss on the sale? If so, how much will that gain or loss be? How will the sale affect the financial statements for the year?
3. Assume the company uses straight-line depreciation and sells the machine for $13,000. Would there be a gain or loss on the sale? How would that change if the company had been using double-declining balance depreciation?

P6-78A. *Analyze and correct accounting errors related to long-term assets. (LO 4, 6).* Due to an umpire strike early in 2011, Umpire's Empire had some trouble with its information processing and some errors were made in accounting for certain transactions. Evaluate the following independent situations that occurred during the year:
   a. At the beginning of 2011, a building and land were purchased together for $100,000. Even though the appraisers determined that 90% of the price should be allocated to the building, Umpire's decided to allocate the entire purchase price to the building. The building is being depreciated using the straight-line method over 40 years, with an estimated salvage value of $10,000.
   b. During the year, Umpire's did some R&D on a new gadget to keep track of balls and strikes. The R&D cost $20,000, and Umpire's capitalized it. The company intends to write it off over five years, using straight-line depreciation with no salvage value.
   c. Near the beginning of the year, Umpire spent $10,000 on routine maintenance for its equipment, and the accountant decided to capitalize these costs as part of the equipment. (Equipment is depreciated over five years with no salvage value.)
   d. Umpire spent $5,000 to extend the useful life of some of its equipment. The accountant capitalized the cost.

Requirements

1. For each situation, describe the error made and list the effect, if any, that the uncorrected error would have on the following items for Umpire's 2011 financial statements: net income, long-term assets, and retained earnings. If there is no error, simply write N/A next to the item.
2. Describe the adjustments that would correct the company's accounting records and make the 2011 financial statements accurate. If there is no error, write N/A next to the item.

Set B

P6-79B. *Calculate capitalized cost and depreciation expense. (LO 1, 2).* The executives for Paradise Island resorts bought a piece of property adjacent to the resort with an old medical facility to build a golf course on July 1, 2009. The land with the old medical facility was $1,750,000. Real estate commissions and fees including the title search were $250,750. Paradise paid $45,500 for the medical facility to be demolished and an additional $21,000 for medical and hazard waste cleanup. The company paid $60,000 for vegetation and sand for the new area. Paradise paid $550,000 to an architectural landscaper and contractor to design and build the golf course. Paradise hired two new employees at a salary of $40,000 a year each to maintain the landscaping for the new area.

Requirements

1. What amount should be capitalized for this new asset?
2. Would there be any depreciation expense for land for the year ended June 30, 2010? Explain your answer.

P6-80B. *Calculate and analyze depreciation under alternative methods. (LO 2).* Daniel's Cement Company purchased new cement pouring equipment at a cost of $22,500 at the beginning of July 2009. The equipment was estimated to have a salvage value of $2,500 at the end of its useful life of five years. Equipment like this is supposed to deliver 250,000 hours of service. The actual number of hours that the equipment was used per year is as follows:

Year Ended	Hours
June 30, 2010	44,000
June 30, 2011	50,000
June 30, 2012	39,000
June 30, 2013	57,000
June 30, 2014	60,000

Requirements

1. Calculate the depreciation expense for each year of the five-year life of the cement pouring equipment using the following methods:
   a. Straight-line method
   b. Activity method
   c. Double-declining balance method
2. How does the choice of depreciation method affect net income in each of the years?
3. How does the choice of depreciation method affect the balance sheet in each of the years?

P6-81B. *Calculate and analyze depreciation under alternative methods. (LO 2).* Stanley Lawn Service purchased new equipment on January 1, 2012, at a cost of $45,000. The company estimates the equipment has a useful life of four years with a salvage value of $6,000.

Requirements

1. Prepare two different depreciation schedules for the equipment—one using the straight-line method and the other using the double-declining balance method. (Round to the nearest dollar.)
2. Determine which method would result in the greater net income for the year 2014.

P6-82B. *Calculate and analyze depreciation under alternative methods. (LO 2).* Soft Fabrics Manufacturing purchased new textile machinery at the beginning of 2010 for $150,000. It was expected to last for 10 years and have a salvage value of $10,000. The estimated productive life of the machine was 250,000 units. Yearly production was as follows: in 2010 it produced 25,000 units; in 2011 it produced 28,000 units; in 2012 it produced 18,000 units; in 2013 it produced 29,000 units; in 2014 it produced 23,000 units; in 2015 it produced 15,000 units; in 2016 it produced 40,000 units; in 2017 it produced 25,000 units; in 2018 it produced 21,000 units; and in 2019 it produced 26,000 units.

Requirements

1. Calculate the depreciation for each year using each of these depreciation methods. (Round to the nearest dollar.)
   a. Straight-line method
   b. Activity method based on units
   c. Double-declining balance method
2. For each method, give the amount of accumulated depreciation that would be shown on the balance sheet at the end of each year.
3. Calculate the book value of the textile machinery at the end of each year for each method.

P6-83B. *Account for intangible assets. (LO 3, 6).* Hargrove Dynamics, Inc., had the following balances in its intangible asset accounts at the beginning of the year:

Patents	$65,000
Copyrights	42,000
Goodwill	67,500

The patents have a remaining useful life of 10 years, and the copyright has a remaining useful life of 12 years.

Transactions during the year were as follows:
   a. At the beginning of the year, Hargrove filed for a new patent. The costs totaled $35,000. Its useful life is estimated at 10 years.
   b. Hargrove incurred R&D costs of $45,000, related to new product development. No new products have been identified.
   c. Hargrove evaluated the goodwill for impairment and reduced its book value by $2,500.
   d. Hargrove successfully defended its patents in court. Fees totaled $13,500.

Requirement

Show each of the transactions in the accounting equation, including any adjustments that would need to be made for the year-end financial statements. Then prepare the intangible assets section of the balance sheet at year end.

P6-84B. *Account for change in estimates for depreciation. (LO 4).* In July 2009, Bottling Company purchased equipment that cost $55,000. The company estimates that the equipment will last for four years and will have a salvage value of $5,000. The company uses the straight-line method of depreciation and has a June 30 fiscal year end. Analyze each of the following independent scenarios:
   a. Before depreciation expense is recorded for the fiscal year ended June 30, 2011, Bottling decides that the equipment will last until June 30, 2013, but that it will be worth only $500 at that time.
   b. Before depreciation expense is recorded for the fiscal year ended June 30, 2011, Bottling decides that the equipment will last only until June 30, 2012. The company anticipates the value of the equipment at that time will still be $5,000.
   c. Before depreciation expense is recorded for the fiscal year ended June 30, 2011, Bottling decides that the equipment will last until June 30, 2013, but that it will be worth only $50 at that time.
   d. Before depreciation expense is recorded for the fiscal year ended June 30, 2011, Bottling is told by the manufacturer that with an upgrade, the equipment's estimated life will be extended to June 30, 2016; however, the estimated salvage value at that time would be zero. The company spends $10,000 on upgrades.

Requirement

Calculate the amount of depreciation expense related to the equipment Bottling will report on its income statement for the fiscal year ended June 30, 2011, for each scenario.

P6-85B. *Account for disposal of an asset. (LO 5).* Analyze each of the following independent scenarios:
   a. Equipment that cost $44,000 had an estimated useful life of six years and a salvage value of $2,000. After five years of using straight-line depreciation, the company sold the equipment for $9,500.
   b. A computer system that cost $95,000 had an estimated useful life of four years and no salvage value. After two years of using double-declining balance depreciation, the company sold the computer system for $40,000.
   c. A company truck that cost $32,000 had an estimated useful life of six years and a salvage value of $2,000. After five years of using straight-line depreciation and driving the truck many miles on tough terrain, the company sold the completely worn-out truck for $750 for spare parts.

d. An asset that cost $35,000 had an estimated useful life of five years and a salvage value of $2,500. After three years of using double-declining balance depreciation, the company sold the asset for $7,500.

Requirement

For each scenario, calculate the gain or loss, if any, that would result upon disposal.

P6-86B. *Calculate depreciation under alternative methods and account for disposal of an asset. (LO 2, 5).* Elite Cleaners bought a new machine on January 1, 2010, for $75,000. The company expects the machine to have a useful life of 10 years and a salvage value of $10,000. The company's fiscal year ends on December 31.

Requirements

1. Calculate the depreciation expense for the fiscal years 2010 and 2011 using each of the following methods:
   a. Straight-line method
   b. Double-declining balance method
2. Elite Cleaners sold the machine on January 1, 2012, for $59,000. What was the gain or loss on the sale using each of the depreciation methods? (Round your answers.) On which financial statement would the gain or loss appear?

P6-87B. *Calculate depreciation under alternative methods and account for disposal of an asset. (LO 2, 5).* Whitehouse Air-Conditioning purchased a machine two years ago for $84,000. The company expects the machine to have a useful life of eight years and a $4,000 salvage value. Whitehouse Air has taken two full years of depreciation expense.

Requirements

1. Assume that Whitehouse Air uses straight-line depreciation. If the machine is sold for $70,000, will there be a gain or loss on the sale? If so, how much will the gain or loss be? How will it affect Whitehouse Air's financial statements for the year?
2. Assume that Whitehouse Air uses double-declining balance depreciation. If the machine is sold for $45,000 will there be a gain or loss on the sale? If so, how much will the gain or loss be? How will it affect Whitehouse Air's financial statements for the year?
3. Assume Whitehouse Air uses double-declining balance depreciation and sells the machine for $60,000. Would there be a gain or loss on the sale? How would that change if Whitehouse Air had been using straight-line depreciation?

P6-88B. *Analyze and correct accounting errors related to long-term assets. (LO 4, 6).* During 2009, Jule's Gym had some trouble with its information processing due to several hurricanes, and some errors were made in accounting for certain transactions. The firm uses straight-line depreciation for all of its long-term assets. Evaluate the following independent situations that occurred during the year:
   a. At the beginning of the year, a basket purchase of a building and land was made for $350,000. The appraisers indicated that the market value of the land was $135,000 and the market value of the building was $250,000. So, Jule's Gym allocated $135,000 of the purchase price to the land and the remainder of the purchase price to the building. The building has an estimated useful life of 20 years and an estimated salvage value of $25,000.
   b. The plumber spent a great deal of time repairing broken toilets in one of the gym's buildings this year. Total cost, which Jule's Gym capitalized, was $5,000. Jule's Gym decided it was best to leave it on the books as an asset and not write it off, because the toilets will be used for quite a few more years. (Use 20 years as the estimated remaining useful life of the toilets.)
   c. Jule's Gym purchased a new van. It cost $20,000 and is expected to last three years. It has a salvage value of $2,000. To properly equip it for transporting gym equipment between locations, the inside was customized at a cost of $6,000. The cost of the van was capitalized, and the cost of the customization was expensed.
   d. Jule's Gym spent $5,500 on routine maintenance of its exercise equipment. The cost was expensed.

Requirements

1. For each situation, describe the error made and list the effect, if any, that the uncorrected error would have on the following items for Jule's Gym's 2009 financial statements: net income, long-term assets, and retained earnings. If there is no error, simply write N/A next to the item.
2. Use the accounting equation to show the adjustments that would correct the company's accounting records and make the 2009 financial statements accurate.

Financial Statement Analysis

FSA6-1. *Analyze long-term assets on the balance sheet. (LO 6).* The following information comes from The Home Depot Annual Report:

Information from the Balance Sheet of The Home Depot:

(dollars in millions)	At February 1, 2009	At February 3, 2008
Property and Equipment		
Land	$ 8,301	$ 8,398
Buildings	16,961	16,642
Furniture, fixtures, and equipment	8,741	8,050
Leasehold improvements	1,359	1,390
Construction in progress	625	1,435
Other	490	497
	36,477	36,412
Less: accumulated depreciation and amortization	10,243	8,936
Net property and equipment	$26,234	$27,476

Requirements

1. Can you tell how much The Home Depot paid for the buildings it owns? If so, how do you know?
2. Can you tell how much the buildings are worth (the market value)?
3. Explain what you think is included in each category of Property and Equipment.
4. The Home Depot says it spent less for capital expenditures in fiscal 2008 (FYE February 1, 2009) than it did in fiscal 2007 (FYE February 3, 2008). Is this supported by any of the information given here?

FSA6-2. *Analyze long-term assets on the balance sheet. (LO 2, 3, 5, 6).* Use the selection from Books-A-Million's annual report in Appendix A at the back of the book to help you answer the following questions:

1. What type of depreciable assets does Books-A-Million have? What methods does the company use to depreciate these assets?
2. Does Books-A-Million have any intangible assets? What are they and how does the company account for them?
3. What can you tell about the age and/or condition of Books-A-Million's property and equipment? Is the company continuing to invest in property, plant, and equipment?
4. Is the company making good use of its assets? How can you evaluate this?

Critical Thinking Problems

Risk and Control

What kinds of risks does a firm like Barnes & Noble face with respect to safeguarding its assets? What types of controls do you think it already has in place to minimize these risks? Go to the firm's Web site at www.barnesandnobleinc.com and click on For Investors. You'll be able to find the firm's annual report to help you answer these questions. Are any specific controls mentioned in the annual report?

Ethics

Rachel works in a real estate office that is equipped with up-to-date copiers, scanners, and printers. She is frequently the only employee working in the office in the evenings and often has spare time to do personal work. She has begun to use the office equipment for her children's school reports and for her husband's business. Do you think Rachel's use of the office equipment is harmless, or is she behaving unethically? Why? If you believe her behavior is unethical, what controls could be in place to prevent it? Have you ever used office resources for personal tasks? Under what conditions could such use of office resources be justified?

Group Assignment

Select one of the three depreciation methods presented in the chapter. Discuss reasons why the method should be used and reasons why the method is not a good choice. Determine the method you think is most consistent with the objectives of financial reporting.

Internet Exercise: Best Buy

Best Buy is the number-one specialty retailer of consumer electronics, personal computers, entertainment software, and appliances. Best Buy operates in the United States, Canada, Mexico, Europe, and China, employing over 155,000 people worldwide (at the end of fiscal 2008). Go to www.bestbuy.com and complete the following exercises:

IE6-1. Select For Our Investors near the bottom of the page. Then, select Best Buy's most recent annual report in the PDF format. Use the consolidated balance sheets to answer the following questions. At the most recent year end, examine Property and Equipment.

1. What is the acquisition cost of these assets?
2. What is the book value (carrying value)?
3. What amount of the acquisition cost has already been expensed?
4. Are any of the assets listed not being depreciated?

IE6-2. Use the notes to financial statements to answer the following questions (the information can usually be found in note 1):

1. Find the heading Property and Equipment. What depreciation method does Best Buy use for property and equipment? What is the range of useful lives for buildings and for fixtures and equipment? Do these useful lives make sense?
2. Find the heading Goodwill. What type of an asset is goodwill? Does Best Buy write off this asset? Explain what the company does.

IE6-3. On page 27 of Best Buy's annual report for its fiscal year ended February 28, 2009, there is a five-year summary of financial highlights. (If you have trouble finding this page, you can look on the financial statements for this information.)

1. Identify the amounts reported for total assets at the four most recent year ends.
2. Identify the amounts reported for revenues and net earnings (net income) for the three most recent years.
3. Compute the asset turnover ratio for the two most recent fiscal years. In which fiscal year did the company make best use of its assets? How can you tell?

Appendix 6

Depreciation and Taxes

The accounting information a company presents on its financial statements is not the same information the company reports to the IRS on its federal income tax return. The company follows GAAP reporting standards when preparing financial statements because those statements are provided to shareholders, who are the owners of the company. The information for taxes is determined by the legal rules of the Internal Revenue Code. GAAP and the IRS require different information to be reported, so companies will use an information system that can produce two sets of data.

> **Modified accelerated cost recovery system (MACRS)** is the method that the IRS requires firms to use to depreciate its assets for tax purposes.

For depreciating fixed assets, corporations use a method called the **Modified Accelerated Cost Recovery System (MACRS)** to calculate the deduction for their tax returns. MACRS is allowed for tax purposes but not GAAP. The goal of MACRS is to give companies incentive to invest in new property, plant, and equipment. If an asset can be written off quickly—large depreciation deductions over a small number of years—the tax benefit from the depreciation deductions leaves the company more cash to invest in new assets.

How does more depreciation expense result in lower taxes? Suppose a company's income before depreciation and before taxes is $10,000. If depreciation expense for taxes is $2,000, then the company has taxable income of $8,000. Suppose the company's tax rate is 25%. Then, the company must pay $2,000 (= $8,000 × 0.25) in taxes. (Net income will be $6,000.)

Now, suppose the company can depreciate the assets using a more accelerated depreciation method that results in $4,000 worth of depreciation expense. Income before depreciation and taxes is $10,000, so income before taxes will be $6,000 (= $10,000 − $4,000). With a tax rate of 25%, the company will have to pay $1,500 in taxes. (Net income will be $4,500.)

When depreciation expense is larger, the amount of taxes a company must pay is smaller. A smaller tax bill means less cash has to be paid to the IRS, so the company's net cash flow for the year will be greater. However, as we have seen from comparing straight-line depreciation and double-declining balance depreciation, *over the life of an asset*, the total depreciation expense is the same no matter what method the company uses. The difference between the methods is reflected in the way the total depreciation is allocated to the years the asset is used. The reason a company wants to use an accelerated method like MACRS for tax purposes is so that the largest deductions are taken as soon as possible. Saving tax dollars *this* year is preferred to saving them *next* year because it is cash the company can use to buy assets that can increase production and therefore profits.

7

Accounting for Liabilities

LEARNING OBJECTIVES

When you are finished studying Chapter 7, you should be able to:

1. Define definitely determinable liability and explain how payroll is recorded.

2. Define estimated liability and explain how warranties are recorded.

3. Explain how long-term notes and mortgages work.

4. Record the issue of bonds and payment of interest to bondholders.

5. Prepare financial statements that include long-term debt.

6. Explain capital structure and compute the debt-to-equity ratio.

7. Identify the major risk associated with long-term debt and the related controls.

8. (Appendix 7) Compute present value and proceeds from a bond issue.

ETHICS Matters

What's in a Rating?

When a company wants to borrow large sums of money, it often issues bonds. Similar to issuing stock, issuing bonds is a way to finance a business with money from investors. However, a bond is a debt instrument and doesn't represent ownership like stock does. A bondholder—an investor buying a bond—is loaning money to the company that issues the bond. To help investors evaluate the risk associated with corporate bonds, rating agencies provide credit ratings for bonds. Standard & Poor's, Moody's, and Fitch are the three most well-known. These agencies played a major role in the financial crisis of 2008.

As financial firms were putting together complicated debt securities (related to subprime mortgages), the rating agencies were hired by the firms to rate the securities. The best rating is AAA and indicates very little risk with an investment. (After that, the ratings go to AA, A, BBB, BB, B, CCC, CC, and C. Bonds rated BB and below are sometimes called junk bonds.) For months, the rating firms were giving AAA ratings to complicated debt securities without actually being able to assess the riskiness of those securities. The ratings agencies admit now that they just didn't have the data to make the ratings. But they were getting paid to do the ratings. The more AAA ratings they gave, the more business they got.

Frank Raiter, a former managing director at Standard & Poor's, believes the credit rating agencies could have stopped the financial meltdown that came to a crisis point in 2008. Simply stated, greed got the best of the agencies. Joseph Stiglitz, a Nobel prize-winning economist, called the ratings "hocus pocus." Raiter, once demoted for his unwillingness to go along with the deceit, resigned rather than giving in to the pressure to compromise his standards.

The question of ethics isn't always a legal issue. Hundreds of people in these agencies focused on the deal rather than the credit quality of the securities they were rating. In this case, the goal of profit maximization came face-to-face with ethical decision making and the consequences involved the most serious financial crisis since the Great Depression of the 1930s. If you'd like to learn more about the issue, do some research on the role of the credit rating agencies in the 2008 financial crisis. The resulting discussion continues, as Congress and the SEC continue to grapple with changes to this industry in an effort to make sure this doesn't happen again.

Source: NOW on PBS Video, Credit and Credibility (12-26-08).

Types of Liabilities

L.O.1
Define a definitely determinable liability and explain how payroll is recorded.

You have learned how a firm acquires and accounts for many of its assets—inventory, property, and equipment—and operating items, such as insurance and supplies. Now we will see that a firm pays for those assets with current liabilities and long-term liabilities. You will recall from earlier chapters that liabilities are a firm's obligations that arise during the course of business. They are settled by the transfer of economic benefits—cash, goods, or services. A liability is recognized—recorded in the accounting records so that it will appear on the balance sheet—when an obligation is incurred. For example, when The Home Depot, Inc., receives merchandise from The Black & Decker Corporation, it records the asset in its inventory account and the liability in accounts payable. Liabilities are based on past transactions and are generally recognized when incurred.

Liabilities can be definitely determinable (that is, the company can determine the amount), or a liability may be estimated. A definitely determinable liability is a liability with an exact amount the firm owes a creditor. **Estimated liabilities**, on the other hand, involve judgment in arriving at the amount to record for the obligation. In this chapter, we discuss both types of liabilities. Exhibit 7.1 shows the liability section of The Home Depot's balance sheet. As we discuss various liabilities, you may want to refer back to this exhibit.

Estimated liabilities are obligations that have some uncertainty in the amount, such as the cost to honor a warranty.

Definitely Determinable Liabilities

Definitely determinable **liabilities** are obligations that can be measured exactly.

Definitely determinable liabilities are liabilities that can be measured exactly. When Walgreens purchases drugs from pharmaceutical supplier McKesson Corporation, Walgreens knows the cost of the drugs and will record the liability at its exact amount. The company will record the amount of the obligation and an increase in inventory. Examples of liability accounts with amounts that are definitely determinable are accounts payable, bank loans or lines of credit, and notes payable.

In Exhibit 7.1, The Home Depot's balance sheet at February 1, 2009, shows accounts payable of $4,822 million. That is the amount The Home Depot owes its suppliers, and it is a definitely determinable liability. When The Home Depot buys drills from Black & Decker on account, its accountant will increase the balance in its inventory account, increasing an asset, and will increase the balance in accounts payable. Some accrued liabilities, such as salaries payable and interest payable, are usually definitely determinable.

Payroll

Payroll is an example of a common business expense that results in a definitely determinable, current liability. The government requires firms to supply them with the amounts of federal, state, and social security taxes each worker pays, so firms have to record more information about payroll than other accounts on the balance sheet. Accounting for payroll can take significant company resources, so frequently a company will hire another company such as Automatic Data Processing (ADP) to manage its payroll. Learning a little about payroll will help you understand your next check from your employer and will help you see how liabilities are recorded.

Suppose The Home Depot hires a former police officer to guard the company's headquarters building for a salary of $500 per week. That amount is the employee's gross pay. As you may know from your work experience, gross pay is not the amount the employee takes home. Exhibit 7.2 on page 320 shows where each piece of a paycheck goes.

EXHIBIT 7.1

Balance Sheet from The Home Depot, Inc.

Focus on the liability section of The Home Depot's balance sheet. You may want to refer to it as you study the chapter.

The Home Depot, Inc., and Subsidiaries
Consolidated Balance Sheets

amounts in millions, except share and per share data	February 1, 2009	February 3, 2008
Assets		
Current assets:		
Cash and cash equivalents	$ 519	$ 445
Short-term investments	6	12
Receivables, net	972	1,259
Merchandise inventories	10,673	11,731
Other current assets	1,192	1,227
Total current assets	13,362	14,674
Property and equipment, at cost:		
Land	8,301	8,398
Buildings	16,961	16,642
Furniture, fixtures and equipment	8,741	8,050
Leasehold improvements	1,359	1,390
Construction in progress	625	1,435
Capital leases	490	497
	36,477	36,412
Less accumulated depreciation and amortization	10,243	8,936
Net property and equipment	26,234	27,476
Notes receivable	36	342
Goodwill	1,134	1,209
Other assets	398	623
Total assets	**$41,164**	$44,324
Liabilities and Stockholders' Equity		
Current liabilities:		
Short-term debt	$ —	$ 1,747
Accounts payable	4,822	5,732
Accrued salaries and related expenses	1,129	1,094
Sales taxes payable	337	445
Deferred revenue	1,165	1,474
Income taxes payable	289	60
Current installments of long-term debt	1,767	300
Other accrued expenses	1,644	1,854
Total current liabilities	11,153	12,706
Long-term debt, excluding current installments	9,667	11,383
Other long-term liabilities	2,198	1,833
Deferred income taxes	369	688
Total liabilities	23,387	26,610
Stockholders' equity:		
Common stock, par value $0.05; authorized: 10 billion shares; issued 1.707 billion shares at February 1, 2009 and 1.698 billion shares at February 3, 2008; outstanding 1.696 billion shares at February 1, 2009 and 1.690 billion shares at February 3, 2008	85	85
Paid-in capital	6,048	5,800
Retained earnings	12,093	11,388
Accumulated other comprehensive income (loss)	(77)	755
Treasury stock, at cost, 11 million shares at February 1, 2009 and 8 million shares at February 3, 2008	(372)	(314)
Total stockholder's equity	17,777	17,714
Total liabilities and stockholder's equity	**$41,164**	$44,324

See accompanying Notes to Consolidated Financial Statements.

EXHIBIT 7.2

Where Does Your Paycheck Go?

Everybody wants a piece of the payroll pie. The amounts that are withheld in this example don't include health insurance premiums, state income taxes, or retirement contributions. Most people take home even less than 72% of their gross pay.

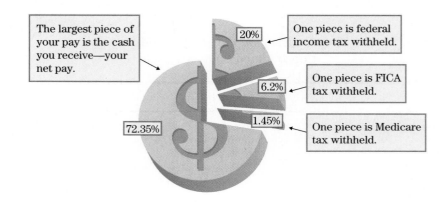

From the gross pay amount, the company makes several deductions. First, the company withholds income taxes. To withhold taxes means that the employer, The Home Depot, deducts money from the employee's pay and sends it to the U.S. government. In doing so, The Home Depot is acting as an *agent* for the government. Second, the U.S. government requires the company to deduct social security taxes at the current legal rate (6.2% as this book was going to press) and Medicare taxes at the current legal rate (1.45% as this book was going to press). These two amounts must be "matched" by the employer. That means in addition to being an agent for the government, the company must also make its own payment. The company's payment is classified as payroll tax expense.

We will calculate the various amounts that The Home Depot must withhold from the $500 gross pay of the security guard. Let's assume that only 10% is withheld for federal income taxes (FIT) in this case, The Home Depot would deduct $50. We will use social security taxes (FICA) at 6.2%, which amount to $31.00, and Medicare taxes at 1.45%, which amount to $7.25. So the amount The Home Depot will pay the employee is

$$\$500.00 - \$50.00 - \$31.00 - \$7.25 = \$411.75$$

Gross pay − FIT − FICA − Medicare = Net pay

The $411.75 cash that The Home Depot pays the employee is called net pay or net wages. The withheld amounts are payable to the various governmental agencies designated. Here is how the company's accountant would record the disbursement to the employee.

Assets	=	Liabilities	+	Shareholders' equity	
				Contributed capital	+ Retained earnings
(411.75) cash		50.00 FIT payable 31.00 FICA taxes payable 7.25 Medicare taxes payable			(500) salary expense

When The Home Depot makes a payment to the government for social security and Medicare, the company will "match" those amounts. Often, these payments are made through the firm's bank. A company "deposits" its payroll taxes, which actually means the bank forwards the payment to the government for the company. Here is how The Home Depot would record the payment to the government, including the company's portion of payroll taxes.

Assets	=	Liabilities	+	Shareholders' equity	
				Contributed capital	+ Retained earnings
(126.50) cash		(50.00) FIT payable (31.00) FICA taxes payable (7.25) Medicare taxes payable			(38.25) payroll tax expense

There are other taxes the employer must pay to state and federal agencies, such as state and federal unemployment taxes. These are part of the employer's payroll tax expense.

Sandy earned $1,500 at her job at Paula's Bookstore during February. Sandy has 20% of her gross pay withheld for federal income taxes, 6.2% withheld for social security (FICA) taxes, and 1.45% withheld for Medicare taxes. What will be the net amount of Sandy's February paycheck? How will Paula's Bookstore record the payment to Sandy in the accounting equation?

Your Turn `7-1`

Other Short-Term Liabilities: Using a Line of Credit

Almost every company will need to borrow money during its life—sometimes to maintain a positive cash flow for regular operations and sometimes to expand or make other major changes to the business. Selecting the type of financing to obtain is a major business decision. Later in the chapter, we'll discuss long-term financing options. Before that, you should be aware of one common way to help a company manage its cash flow without long-term borrowing—a line of credit. This is an excellent choice for financing the regular operations of a business.

What is a line of credit? It is an arrangement between a company and its bank in which the bank allows the company to borrow money for routine operating expenses up to the maximum amount of the credit line. The interest rate charged by the bank for this type of loan is usually much lower than the interest rate for credit card purchases, but it may be a bit higher than a typical bank loan for a specific amount and term. There is typically a short repayment "window" for a line of credit—60 to 90 days.

What kind of business should use a line of credit? First, the business must be a profitable, established business. Second, the business should have predictable cash flows. A line of credit works best when there is a predictable, temporary, short-term shortage of cash. The amount used—the amount borrowed—needs to be repaid in a short time to make a line of credit a cost-effective financing choice. Having a line of credit is also a good choice for a company that does not have a current cash flow problem but would like a backup in case of a cash flow problem.

When is a line of credit a poor financing choice? If your company needs to make large purchases of major long-term assets, then a loan with a longer term and a lower interest rate would be a better type of financing. If the cash shortage is more than temporary, the company should make a long-term plan for a solution. It is also not a good idea to use a line of credit to pay employees. Payroll is an expense that should be a priority for a company's regular cash inflow. In most cases, a company that must borrow money to meet its payroll needs to rethink its financial situation.

What does a business need to provide to get a line of credit? One of the most important items a company should have is a set of financial statements, particularly a balance sheet and an income statement. In addition to the basic financial statements, a company should have a detailed schedule of projected cash inflows and outflows. Other important items are several years of tax returns, a list of current bank accounts, a current business plan, and appraisals of any assets that might be used as collateral.

Check out the financial statements of some well-known companies. You will find information about their lines of credit in the notes to the financial statements.

Estimated Liabilities

There are times when a company must estimate an expense so that it can be put on the income statement with the revenue it matches. If, at the end of the accounting period, the company has incurred an expense but doesn't yet know the specific amount, that expense will have to be estimated. In Chapter 4, you learned about one such expense—bad debts expense. It had to be estimated so that it could be properly matched with the sales revenue to which it pertained. In that case, the company recorded a contra-asset, the allowance for bad debts, along with the bad debt expense.

L.O.2
Define estimated liability and explain how warranties are recorded.

Warranties

Now we are going to discuss another expense that the company must estimate, but this time it will be recorded with a liability. When a company provides a warranty with a product it sells, the costs associated with that warranty should be recognized (shown on the income statement) in the same period as the sale. Let's see how that would be done. (The warranties discussed here are the ones that accompany a product without any additional charge. Extended warranties that are purchased have a very different accounting treatment.)

Why would a company provide a warranty on a product or service? Just like the decision to offer credit sales, providing a warranty is a sales and marketing tool; and whether or not to provide a warranty is one of the strategic decisions a company must make. For financial statement purposes, a company wants to recognize warranty expense at the time of the sale of the product. Why? The matching principle applies to this situation. Revenues and expenses that go together should be on the same income statement. The company does not know exactly how much it will cost to honor the warranty, so the cost must be estimated. Because the company is not actually disbursing the cash to fix or replace the warranted item yet—at the time of the sale—a liability is recorded along with the warranty expense. It is an adjustment made either at the time of the sale or when it is time to prepare financial statements. Liabilities are increased by the same amount as warranty expense. The liability is sometimes called a reserve for warranties. Notice that this type of reserve is NOT a cash reserve. It is simply a liability recorded because the firm had to record an estimated expense.

The accounting treatment that requires estimates of future warranty costs reflects the underlying business process. It is crucial for a company to consider and estimate such costs to make sound business decisions. These future costs may be significant, and the accounting rules force companies to record these costs when the sale is made instead of when the warranty is honored. What happens when the cash is actually paid to fix a product with a warranty? No expense is recorded. Instead, the liability previously set up is reduced. So actual expenditures result in a reduction in cash or some other asset (used to fix the item) and an equal reduction in the amount of the liability. It's sometimes called "writing off the cost against the reserve" rather than against income. Let's look at an example.

Suppose Brooke's Bike Company sold 100 bicycles during June and provided a one-year warranty. The accountant estimated that future repairs and replacement related to the June sales would be approximately $30 per bicycle. (No expenditures were made related to the warranties during the month of June.) What amount of warranty expense would appear on the income statement for the month ended June 30? Brooke's Bike Company would want to show the entire amount, $3,000, as an expense for the month. What is the amount of the June 30 liability (warranty payable or estimated warranty liability)? The total $3,000 would be shown as a liability on the balance sheet.

Assets	=	Liabilities	+	Shareholders' equity	
				Contributed + capital	Retained earnings
		3,000 estimated warranty liability			(3,000) warranty expense

Suppose July was a slow month, and Brooke's Bike Company did not sell any bicycles. However, there were several bicycles from sales in June that were repaired in July. The repairs cost Brooke's Bike Company $250. What amount of warranty expense would appear on the income statement for the month ended July 31? None. Brooke's Bike Company recognized the expense when the sale was made, so no expense is recognized when the repairs are made. The cost of the repairs is deducted from the amount "owed" to the customers. So the amount of the July 31 liability (warranty payable or estimated warranty liability) is $2,750 ($3,000 – $250). This is called writing off the cost against the reserve.

Assets	=	Liabilities	+	Shareholders' equity	
				Contributed + capital	Retained earnings
(250) cash		(250) estimated warranty liability			

Your Turn 7-2

Suppose that August was another slow month for bicycle sales (none were made), but again Brooke's Bike Company did some repairs related to the warranties on previous sales. The total spent was $500. What amount of warranty expense would appear on Brooke's Bike Company's income statement for the month ended August 31? What is the amount of the August 31 liability (warranty payable or estimated warranty liability)?

Long-Term Notes Payable and Mortgages

L.O.3
Explain how long-term notes and mortgages work.

You have learned how companies record current liabilities. In this section, you will learn how companies record long-term liabilities. When a company borrows money for longer than one year, that obligation is usually called a long-term note payable. Long-term notes differ from short-term notes in several ways. Recall from Chapter 3 that short-term notes are debt obligations that a company will repay in one year or sooner. A company may repay long-term notes in a lump sum at the note's maturity or with a series of equal payments over the life of the note. A loan to buy a home is an example of a loan with payments made over the life of the loan. The monthly payments are a combination of interest and principal. With each monthly payment, the borrower is paying that month's interest on the loan as well as paying back a small part of the principal balance due. Each month when the bank calculates the interest on the outstanding principal balance, the interest amount becomes a smaller portion of the payment. Why? Because the total amount of each payment stays the same, but the outstanding principal balance decreases. A larger part of each monthly payment is, therefore, available to reduce the outstanding principal.

Exhibit 7.3 shows why the interest amount on a loan becomes smaller over time for a loan of $100,000 with a 15-year term and an interest rate of 10% per year. The annual payment is the same every year, but the portion of the payment that is interest expense decreases, while the portion of the payment that reduces the outstanding principal balance increases.

EXHIBIT 7.3

Payments Comprised of Interest and Principal

This graph shows the payment schedule for a $100,000 loan for 15 years at 10% annual interest. There will be 15 annual payments of approximately $13,147 each, due at the end of each year. With each payment, the principal balance is reduced, so there is less interest expense each year. Because the payment stays the same, more of the payment goes toward reducing the principal each year. The graph shows how the proportion of interest in each payment decreases over time, while the proportion of principal in each payment increases over time.

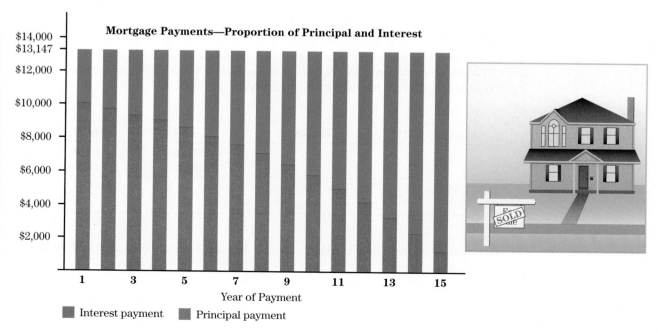

Mortgage Payments—Proportion of Principal and Interest

Year of Payment

■ Interest payment   ■ Principal payment

A mortgage loan is a note payable that gives the lender a claim against that property if the borrower does not make payments. Like most long-term notes, mortgage loans are debt obligations commonly repaid in periodic installments—each payment is part principal and part interest.

Suppose you sign, on January 1, a $100,000, three-year mortgage with SunTrust with an 8% annual interest rate to buy a piece of land. Payments are to be made annually on December 31 of each year in the amount of $38,803.35. How did SunTrust figure out that annual payment for the $100,000 loan for three years at 8% annual interest? The bank calculates what it would receive if it invested the $100,000 for three years at an interest rate of 8%. That is the amount the bank expects to receive from you. Appendix 7 discusses the details of this type of calculation.

In this example, payments are annual, and the first payment will be made at the end of the first year of the loan. After the three payments, both the principal and the interest will be repaid. Exhibit 7.4 shows how each payment reduces the outstanding principal. This is called an **amortization schedule** for this loan.

Amortization schedule is a chart that shows the amount of principal and the amount of interest that make up each payment of a loan.

EXHIBIT 7.4

Amortization Schedule for a Mortgage

Mortgage Balance		Annual Payment	Interest Portion of Payment (8% × mortgage balance)	Amount of Mortgage Reduction (annual payment — interest portion)
Beginning balance $100,000.00	1st	$38,803.35	$8,000.00	$30,803.35
After 1st payment $ 69,196.65	2nd	$38,803.35	$5,535.73	$33,267.62
After 2nd payment $ 35,929.03	3rd	$38,803.35	$2,874.32	$35,929.03
After 3rd payment -0-				

How much of the first payment is interest expense and how much goes toward paying back the principal? Remember, interest is the cost of using someone else's money. The interest is based on the amount of the principal, the interest rate, and the amount of time for which the money is borrowed.

$$\text{Interest} = \text{Principal} \times \text{Rate} \times \text{Time}$$

The bank lends you $100,000 on Day 1 of the note. On Day 365, you make a $38,803.35 payment to the bank. The interest on the $100,000 for the year that has just passed is

$$\textbf{\$100,000 principal} \times \textbf{0.08 annual interest} \times \textbf{1 year} = \textbf{\$8,000}$$

You borrowed the entire $100,000 for a full year, so you multiply the principal by the annual rate and by the one-year duration to get the interest expense for the year. Of the $38,803.35 payment, $8,000 is interest, so the remaining portion of the payment—$30,803.35—is repayment of principal. Here is how the first payment would be recorded.

Assets	=	Liabilities	+	Shareholders' equity		
				Contributed capital	+	Retained earnings
(38,803.35) cash		(30,803.35) mortgage payable				(8,000) interest expense

The principal of the mortgage has been reduced. In other words, the outstanding balance is lower—meaning you have less of the bank's money at the end of the first year.

Therefore, the interest owed to the bank for the second year will be smaller than the interest paid for the first year. That is because the interest rate will be applied to a smaller principal—that is, a smaller outstanding balance. Again, we use the interest formula to calculate the portion of the payment that is interest for the second year, and then subtract the interest from the total payment to calculate the amount of the payment that reduces the principal.

- Outstanding balance due at the start of the second year: $69,196.65 ($100,000 original principal − $30,803.35 reduction in principal from the first payment)
- Interest expense for year 2: $69,196.65 principal for year 2 × 0.08 interest rate × 1 year = $5,535.73

The amount of interest you owe the bank is smaller each year because the outstanding balance of the note is smaller each year. At the end of year 2, the bank receives the second payment of $38,803.35. As the preceding calculation shows, $5,535.73 of that payment is interest expense. The rest of the payment—$33,267.62 ($38,803.35 − $5,535.73)—reduces the outstanding balance. After the second payment, the outstanding balance is $35,929.03. For the third payment of $38,803.35

$$\text{New principal} = \$35,929.03$$
$$\text{Interest expense for year 3} = \$35,929.03 \times 0.08 \times 1 = \$2,874.32$$

When you subtract the interest of $2,874.32 from the third payment of $38,803.35, the remaining $35,929.03 reduces the principal—in this case, to zero. Is it just a coincidence that the remaining outstanding balance is exactly that amount? No, the bank did the calculations with the principal, interest rate, and length of the loan so that it would come out to exactly that amount at the end of the third year.

Tompkins Corporation purchased a building on January 1 by signing a long-term $600,000 mortgage with monthly payments of $5,500. The mortgage carries an interest rate of 9% per year. How much of the first payment due January 31 is interest and how much is principal?

Your Turn 7-3

Long-Term Liabilities: Raising Money by Issuing Bonds

L.O.4
Record the issue of bonds and payment of interest to bondholders.

Long-term notes and mortgages are one way to borrow money with repayment over an extended period of time. Often, companies want to raise large amounts of money to build new stores or warehouses. One way to borrow this money is to issue bonds to the general public.

What Is a Bond?

A **bond** is an interest-bearing, long-term note payable issued by corporations, universities, and governmental agencies. Issuing bonds means a company is borrowing money from individual investors as well as other companies that want to invest. A bond certificate is a written agreement that specifies the company's responsibility to pay interest and repay the principal to the bondholders at the end of the term of the bond. The bond certificate will show the interest rate, the face amount of the bond, and the term of the bond. Exhibit 7.5 on the next page shows an actual bond certificate.

A **bond** is an interest-bearing, long-term note payable issued by corporations, universities, and governmental agencies.

There are three main reasons why a company would borrow money by issuing bonds rather than going to a bank for a loan.

1. Firms can borrow more money from issuing bonds than a bank may be willing to lend.
2. Bondholders are typically willing to lend money for a longer time. Many bonds are 15-, 20-, or 30-year bonds. Some banks will not lend businesses money for such long periods of time. Bondholders are willing to lend money for a long time because they can convert bonds into cash at any time by selling the bond to another investor in the bond market.
3. The rate of interest on a bond—the rate the borrower pays the bondholder—is commonly lower than the rate on loans charged by banks. Banks pay one rate of interest to people who deposit their money in saving accounts—the savings rate of interest—but charge a higher interest rate to lend money—the borrowing rate of interest.

A disadvantage to a firm of borrowing money by issuing bonds is that the firm may be restricted from borrowing additional money from other sources, or the firm may be required to

EXHIBIT 7.5

Bond Certificate

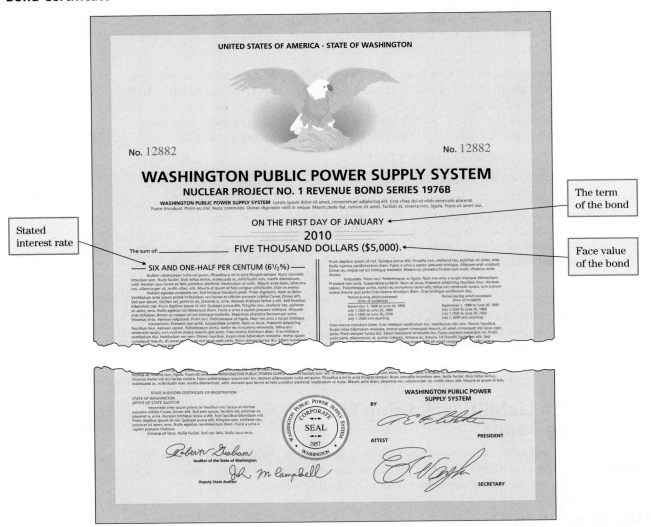

maintain a certain debt-to-equity ratio—the ratio of liabilities to shareholders' equity. These restrictions, called bond covenants, are specified in the bond agreement to protect the interests of the bondholders. Recall that creditors, including bondholders, have priority over the claims of owners.

Issuing Bonds Payable: Getting the Money

Corporations issue bonds to raise money. Most bonds issued in the United States pay the bondholders annual or semiannual interest payments during the life of the bonds. The interest rate is given on the face of the bond. At a specific future date, called the maturity date, bondholders also receive a lump sum payment equal to the face amount of the bond. The face amount is also referred to as the stated value or the par value of the bond. Most bonds are issued with a face value in multiples of $1,000. The company borrowing the money is selling—or issuing—a legally binding promise to repay the buyer. The initial buyer is not really "buying" but rather lending the price paid for the bond. Bondholders are creditors of the company; they are not owners of the company.

The rate stated on the bonds determines the interest payments to the bondholders. The calculation of the interest payments to the bondholders is completely independent of the market interest rate at the date of the bond issue. The interest payments are calculated by multiplying the face or par value of the bond by the interest rate stated on the bond.

However, the **market rate of interest** at the time the bonds are issued determines the amount of money the bondholders are willing to lend—which is really the amount they are willing to pay for the bonds—to get the fixed payments at specified times in the future. *The demand from the bond market will set the price of the bond so that it will earn exactly the market rate of return.* The market rate of return is considered to be the interest rate that could be earned from a similar investment with the same amount of risk. To make the business decision to issue bonds, a company must understand this fact and estimate the cash proceeds when planning the bond issue. So the face of the bond may have a principal amount—its face—that is different than the amount of money the company collects from the bondholder when it issues the bond.

The price of a bond when it is issued—the amount of money the company will collect from the bondholder—is calculated by the bond market and is stated in terms of a percentage of the face value. The cash the company receives when issuing a bond is call the **proceeds**. If a bond is stated as selling for 98.375, that means it is selling for 98.375% of $1,000 or $983.75. Bonds issued at exactly the face amount are called **bonds issued at par**. Bonds issued for less than the face value are called **bonds issued at a discount**. Bonds issued for more than the face value are called **bonds issued at a premium**.

- A bond that is selling at 100 is selling at par—100% of its face value.
- A bond selling below 100 is selling at a discount.
- A bond selling above 100 is selling at a premium.

There are many types of bonds. The most common types are shown in Exhibit 7.6.

> The **market rate of interest** is the interest rate that an investor could earn in an equally risky investment.

> **Proceeds** are the amount of cash the bond issuer collects from the bondholders when the bonds are issued.

> **Bonds issued at par** are bonds issued for the face value of the bond. This happens when the market rate of interest is equal to the bond's stated rate of interest.

> **Bonds issued at a discount** are bonds issued for an amount less than the face value of the bond. This happens when the market rate of interest is greater than the bond's stated rate of interest.

> **Bonds issued at a premium** are bonds issued for an amount more than the face value of the bond. This happens when the market rate of interest is less than the bond's stated rate of interest.

EXHIBIT 7.6

Types of Bonds

Type of Bond	Feature of the Bond or Description of the Bond
Secured	Give the bondholders a claim to a specific asset of the company in case of default
Unsecured (also known as debenture)	Are not linked to specific assets and are issued on the general credit of the company
Term	All mature on the same date
Serial	Mature periodically over a period of several years
Convertible	Give the bondholder the option of exchanging the bond for common stock
Callable	May be retired—called—prior to maturity at the option of the issuer for a specified amount of money
Zero interest (also known as zero coupon)	Pay no interest over the life of the bonds. (Interest is paid at the end of the life of the bond at the same time the principal is repaid.)
Junk	Have been downgraded by a bond-rating agency to below investment grade. (Ratings range from AAA—low risk bonds—to C or D. When a bond is rated BB or below, it is called a junk bond.)

If a $1,000 bond is selling for 95.5, how much cash does the bondholder pay for the bond? If a $1,000 bond is selling for 102, how much cash does the bondholder pay for the bond?

Your Turn 7-4

Recording the Bond Issue

Suppose Muzby Minerals issued a $1,000 bond for six years with interest paid annually and a stated interest rate of 5%. Exhibit 7.7 on the following page shows the cash flows associated with this bond.

If the market rate of interest and the stated rate of interest on the bond are the same, investors will pay exactly the face value for the bonds. As you read in the last section, bonds issued with a stated rate equal to the market rate are said to be issued at par. The cash flows associated with the bond will be annual interest payments of $50 at the end of each of the next six years and a lump

EXHIBIT 7.7

Cash Flows Defined by a Six-Year, $1,000, 5% Bond

It may be helpful to think of a bond as a series of cash payments. When a firm issues a bond, it is selling the bondholder a series of future payments. How much the bondholder will pay for those cash payments depends on the market rate of interest at the time the bonds are issued.

Year	0	1	2	3	4	5	6
Cash flow to bondholder		$50	$50	$50	$50	$50	$50 $1,000

sum principal payment of $1,000 at the end of the sixth year. This is how Muzby Minerals would record the issue of a $1,000 bond at par.

Assets	=	Liabilities	+	Shareholders' equity	
				Contributed capital	+ Retained earnings
1,000 cash		1,000 bonds payable			

BONDS ISSUED AT A DISCOUNT. However, if the market rate were more than 5%, investors would pay less for the bond than the face value. The reason this would be the case is that no one would pay the face amount to earn a return of 5% if that money could be invested somewhere else and earn the higher market rate. The market will set a lower price for the bond, a price that will earn the investor exactly the market rate on the bond. When bonds are issued with a stated rate less than the market rate, the bonds are issued at a discount.

Suppose the market rate of interest was approximately 6% when the bond was issued. Because investors would require this return, the bonds must sell for less than $1,000. The bond market would calculate the selling price of the bond. In other words, the market will determine how much the bondholders will pay to receive $50 at the end of each of the next six years along with $1,000 at the end of year six. This particular bond will be issued at 95.1. That means bondholders will pay 95.1% of the face, or $951.

This is how the transaction would affect the accounting equation:

Assets	=	Liabilities	+	Shareholders' equity	
				Contributed capital	+ Retained earnings
951 cash		951 bonds payable (net)			

Discount on bonds payable is a contra-liability that is deducted from bonds payable on the balance sheet; it is the difference between the face value of the bond and its selling price when the selling price is less than the face (par) value.

The carrying value of a bond is the amount that the balance sheet shows as the net value of the bond, similar in meaning to the carrying value of a fixed asset. It is equal to the face value of the bond minus any discount or plus any premium.

While the net effect on liabilities is $951, firms actually record the face value of the bonds payable ($1,000) along with the discount to be deducted in an account called **discount on bonds payable**, a contra-liability account. You learned about contra-accounts in Chapter 3. Every contra-account has a partner account. For example, the contra-account *accumulated depreciation* is partnered with a fixed asset account such as *equipment*. Discount on bonds payable is deducted from its partner account, bonds payable, and the result is the net value of the liability. Contra-accounts are considered valuation accounts. They are used to value the associated asset or liability. In the long-term liabilities portion of the balance sheet, the bond would be reported net of the balance in its discount account. The net value of bonds payable is also called the **carrying value** of the bonds.

BONDS ISSUED AT A PREMIUM. If, on the other hand, the bond with a 5% stated rate of interest is issued when market rate of interest is less than 5%, investors will have to pay *more* for the bond than the face value. The bond, with its higher interest rate, is so appealing that the market demand will bid up the price, until the price the market settles on is the one that makes the investment in the bond earn exactly the market rate of return. The bonds will sell for more than par value. When bonds are issued with a stated rate higher than the market rate, the bonds are issued at a premium. The amount of the proceeds in excess of par is called the **premium on bonds payable**.

Suppose the market rate of interest was approximately 4% when the bond with a stated rate of 5% was issued. The market would price the bonds to yield the market rate of return. The bonds would be issued for 105.2. In other words, the proceeds will be 105.2% of the face value, or $1,052. This is how the transaction would be recorded in the accounting equation:

Assets	=	Liabilities	+	Shareholders' equity	
				Contributed capital	+ Retained earnings
1,052 cash		1,052 bonds payable (net)			

> **Premium on bonds payable** is an adjunct-liability that is added to bonds payable on the balance sheet; it is the difference between the face value of the bond and its selling price, when the selling price is more than the face (par) value.

The amount of the face value of the bond (bonds payable at $1,000) and the premium on bonds payable (at $52) are both liabilities, and the firm keeps the amounts in separate accounts in its accounting system. Premium on bonds payable is called an adjunct liability. Adjunct means an add-on and describes the relationship between bonds payable and premium on bonds payable. The premium on bonds payable is a partner of the bonds payable liability it is paired with, and they are added together on the balance sheet. The bond will be shown at its net value, the sum of the face value of the bonds and the premium.

Paying the Bondholders

Remember, no matter how much the bondholder pays for the bond—whether the issue price is above or below the price stated on the bond—the series of payments is established by what is printed on the face of the bond. That series of cash flows is what the bondholder is buying. In this example with a single bond issued by Muzby Minerals, the cash flows are set at $50 interest annually and a lump sum of $1,000 at maturity.

However, there are some complications related to the accounting records of the firm that issued the bonds. Now we will turn to the accounting for bonds issued for more or less than the face value.

AMORTIZING BOND DISCOUNTS AND PREMIUMS: EFFECTIVE INTEREST METHOD. Bond discounts and bond premiums are written off over the life of the bonds. The carrying value of the bond—the net amount shown as the liability—on the date of maturity needs to be its face value because that is exactly the amount of the liability on the date of maturity. Over the life of the bond, the book value of the bond will change just a little each time the firm makes a payment to the bondholder, until the book value equals the face value at maturity. This is called amortizing the bond discount or premium. The amortization of bond premiums or discounts is a natural result of calculating the correct amount of interest expense, using the effective interest method, for the period when the company makes an interest payment to the bondholder. Remember, the amount of the cash payments to the bondholders is established before the bond is issued. **But when bonds are issued at a discount or at a premium, the cash payment and the interest expense are not equal.**

Amortizing a Discount   To show how a bond's book value changes as the discount is amortized, we will continue the example of the $1,000 bond issued for $951. The stated rate of interest on the bond is 5% and the market rate of interest is 6%. When the bonds are issued, the carrying value of the liability is $951. Each time the firm makes an interest payment to the bondholder, the carrying value of the bond goes up a little bit. The amount of the increase is the difference between the interest expense and the cash interest payment to the bondholders.

Suppose the bond is issued on January 1. The first interest payment to the bondholders, on December 31, will be $50 ($1,000 × 0.05 × 1 year). Remember that this is established by what is printed on the face of the bond, no matter how much the bond was issued for. However, the interest expense—shown on the income statement—is not equal to the cash interest payment to the bondholders. The interest expense is calculated using the usual interest rate formula.

$$\textbf{Interest} = \textbf{Principal} \times \textbf{Rate} \times \textbf{Time}$$

In this case, the principal amount borrowed is $951. That is the amount the bondholders actually loaned the company on the date of the bond issue. The interest rate the firm must pay to borrow the money is 6%— the market rate at the date of issue, and the time period is one year.

$$\$951 \times 6\% \times 1 \text{ year} = \$57.06$$

The difference between the cash interest payment of $50 and the interest expense of $57.06 is the amount that will increase the carrying value of the bond. The same thing happens each time an interest payment is made. The difference between the interest payment and the interest expense will increase the carrying value of the bond. The accounting terminology for that process is called *amortizing* the discount, and this method is called the effective interest method of amortization. Over the life of the bonds, the discount is amortized, so that the carrying value of the bonds at the date of maturity is exactly the face value.

When the firm makes the $50 payment to the bondholders on the first interest payment date, the firm actually owes the bondholder an additional $7.06. Because the payment to the bondholder is fixed, the extra $7.06 will be added to the outstanding principal balance of $951. After the first interest payment, the new principal balance is $958.06 ($951 + $7.06). The $7.06—the difference between the interest expense and the interest payment—is sometimes called the amortization of the discount. The payment to the bondholder of $50 and the discount amortization affects the accounting equation as follows:

Assets	=	Liabilities	+	Shareholders' equity	
				Contributed + capital	Retained earnings
(50) cash		7.06 net bonds payable			(57.06) interest expense

The amortization schedule for this bond is shown in Exhibit 7.8. Notice what happens over the life of the bond. The interest payment is exactly the same each year. However, the difference between the interest expense and the interest payment—the part the firm owes but does not pay in the periodic interest payment—must be added to the outstanding principal, therefore increasing the carrying value of the bonds. At maturity, the carrying value will equal the face value.

EXHIBIT 7.8

Amortization Schedule for a Bond Issued at a Discount

In this case, a $1,000 bond with a stated interest rate of 5% has been issued at a discount because the market rate of interest is 6%. To sell the bond, the firm must offer it at a discount. The actual return to the bondholder will be 6%.

	(1) Beginning carrying value	(2) Cash payment $1,000 × 0.05	(3) Interest expense (1) × 0.06	(4) Amortization of discount (3) − (2)	(5) Ending carrying value (1) + (4)
Year 1	$951.00	$50.00	$57.06	$7.06	$ 958.06
Year 2	958.06	50.00	57.48	7.48	965.54
Year 3	965.54	50.00	57.93	7.93	973.47
Year 4	973.47	50.00	58.41	8.41	981.88
Year 5	981.88	50.00	58.91	8.91	990.79
Year 6	990.79	50.00	59.21	9.21	1,000.00*

*This is rounded to make it equal the face value at maturity. The interest rate was approximately 6%, but we used exactly 6% in our calculations.

Your Turn 7-5

Try this example with semiannual interest payments. Just divide the annual interest rate by two and count the periods as the number of six-month periods.

Knollwood Corp. issued $200,000 of 6% per year, 20-year bonds at 98 on January 1, 2010. The market rate of interest was approximately 6.5%. Interest is paid on June 30 and on December 31. The company uses the effective interest method of amortization. How much interest expense will Knollwood show on the income statement for the year ending December 31, 2010? What is the carrying value of the bonds on the balance sheet at December 31, 2010?

Amortizing a Premium We will now use the same bond but assume it was issued at a premium. Recall, the market rate of interest of 4% is lower than the stated rate on the bond of 5%, so the bondholder will pay a premium for the bond's series of payments. In this example, the amount the bondholder pays—which we should not forget is actually a loan to the firm—is $1,052 for the bond. Just as it is calculated for a bond issued at a discount, the interest expense for bonds issued at a premium is calculated using the market rate interest. For the first year, the interest expense is

$$\textbf{Interest} = \textbf{Principal} \times \textbf{Rate} \times \textbf{Time}$$
$$\text{Interest} = \$1,052 \times 4\% \times 1 \text{ year} = \$42.08$$

When the bond issuer makes the cash payment of $50, that amount pays the bondholder the interest for the first year *plus* a small amount of the principal. The amount of principal paid off is the difference between the cash interest payment and the interest expense.

$$\$50 \text{ payment} - \$42.08 \text{ interest expense} = \$7.92$$

This $7.92 is the amortization of the premium on bonds payable. The carrying value of the bond will be reduced a little bit each time the bond issuer makes an interest payment to the bond-holder, until the carrying value equals the face value at maturity. At maturity, the bond issuer pays the bondholder the $1,000 face amount. The following shows how the interest payment to the bondholder affects the accounting equation.

Assets	=	Liabilities	+	Shareholders' equity	
				Contributed capital	+ Retained earnings
(50) cash		(7.92) net bonds payable			(42.08) interest expense

Issuing a bond at a premium results in interest expense (to the bond issuer) that is less than the actual cash payment of interest to the bondholder because the 4% interest rate in the market is lower than the 5% interest rate specified on the bond. Each time the bond issuer makes a cash payment for interest, a little of the original principal of the "loan" is paid off. How much? The difference between the cash interest payment and the interest expense will be the amount of the reduction in the carrying value of the bond. At maturity, the carrying value will equal the face value.

The amortization schedule for this bond is shown in Exhibit 7.9. Notice what happens over the life of the bond. The interest payment is exactly the same each year. However, all of the payment is not really interest due to the bondholder (although it's still called the interest payment). Some of the payment is going toward reducing the principal. At maturity, the total amount that has been paid to the bondholders in addition to the interest they have been due is the premium. So the carrying value will equal the face value at maturity.

EXHIBIT 7.9

Amortization Schedule for a Bond Issued at a Premium

	(1) Beginning carrying value	(2) Cash payment $1,000 × 0.05	(3) Interest expense (1) × 0.04	(4) Amortization of premium (3) – (2)	(5) Ending carrying value (1) + (4)
Year 1	$1,052.00	$50.00	$42.08	$(7.92)	$1,044.08
Year 2	1,044.08	50.00	41.76	(8.24)	1,035.84
Year 3	1,035.84	50.00	41.43	(8.57)	1,027.27
Year 4	1,027.27	50.00	41.09	(8.91)	1,018.36
Year 5	1,018.36	50.00	40.73	(9.27)	1,009.09
Year 6	1,009.09	50.00	40.91	(9.09)	1,000.00*

* This number is rounded to equal the face value of the bond.

In this case, a $1,000 bond with a stated interest rate of 5% has been issued at a premium because the market rate of interest is 4%. The bondholder must pay more than the face value to buy the bond. The actual return to the bondholder will be 4%.

Your Turn 7-6

On January 1, 2011, Wood Corp. issued $200,000 of 20-year, 10% interest bonds when the market rate of interest was 9%. The proceeds were $218,257. Interest is paid annually on December 31. The company uses the effective interest method of amortization. How much interest expense will Wood show on the income statement for the year ending December 31, 2011? What is the carrying value of the bonds on the balance sheet at December 31, 2011?

STRAIGHT-LINE AMORTIZATION OF BOND DISCOUNTS AND PREMIUMS. In addition to the effective interest method of amortizing a bond discount or premium, firms sometimes use another method called the straight-line method. Straight-line amortization simply divides the amount of the premium or discount equally over the number of interest payment periods. The effective interest method makes logical sense with respect to interest expense being calculated on the outstanding principal, but there is no particular logic to the straight-line method. It is a simple calculation, much easier than the effective interest method, and this simplicity is its only attractive feature. Straight-line amortization often does a poor job of matching and is not part of generally accepted accounting principles (GAAP). However, if the straight-line method and the effective interest method produce similar amounts for interest expense and for net bonds payable—if the differences are not material—then the accounting standards allow the use of the straight-line method of amortization. This is an application of the materiality constraint you read about in Chapter 2.

We will look at the last example—6-year bonds, 5% stated rate, $1,000 face value, market rate of 4% at issue—and see how straight-line amortization works. Recall, the bond will be issued at a premium, and we calculated the issue price to be $1,052. The difference between the face value of $1,000 and the issue price of $1,052 is a premium. We have already seen how the premium of $52 would be amortized using the effective interest method, shown in Exhibit 7.9. Now we will amortize the premium using the straight-line method. First, divide the premium by the number of interest payments to the bondholders. That means the same amount will be amortized each time an interest payment is made. In this example, in which the premium is $52, the

UNDERSTANDING → Business

How to Read a Bond Quote

After a firm issues bonds, the bonds can be bought and sold in a secondary market. Just like stock, after the corporation completes the original issue, buyers and sellers get together via the bond market to trade bonds. The price of a bond on the secondary market will be different from the original bond price, depending on whether interest rates have increased or decreased since the date of the original bond issue. Bond prices have an inverse relationship with interest rates: When interest rates increase, bond prices decrease, and vice versa. The bond market will price the bond to yield the market rate for investments with similar risk. Because interest payments on a bond are fixed, when the market rate of interest goes down, those fixed rates look better.

For example, suppose a $1,000 bond pays 9% interest per year. If the market rate of interest is 9%, the bond would sell for $1,000. If the market rate of interest goes up to 10%, this 9% bond of $1,000 is not as attractive as other investments. Thus, the price of this bond will go down. That is the inverse relationship: Market interest rate goes up, and the bond price goes down. If the market rate of interest goes down to 8%, then the 9% bond of $1,000 is a very attractive investment; and the price of the bond will go up.

Prices of bonds trading in the secondary market fluctuate with changes in interest rates, the economy, and the risks associated with particular firms' bonds. Newspapers and financial Web sites typically report data about corporate bonds. This is an example of what you might find.

Company	Price (% of face)	Coupon %	Maturity	Current Yield (%)	Fitch Ratings
IBM	109.62	5.050	22-Oct-2012	4.607	A
Ford MTR	58.00	7.700	15-May-2097	13.276	CCC

The IBM bond is trading (selling) for 109.62% of its face or par value. IBM is paying the bondholder 5.05% of the face (annually), and the bonds mature on October 22, 2012. The current yield is the true return that the current buyer will earn on the investment in the bond. It's the interest payment (coupon) divided by the price of the bond. The coupon of 5.050 divided by the price of 109.62 gives a yield of 4.607. Notice the difference between the bond rating of IBM and that of Ford Motor. Due to the current economic conditions in the American auto industry, loaning money to Ford as a bondholder is pretty risky. Just ask the bondholders of the former General Motors (GM). When GM filed for bankruptcy protection in 2009, bondholders lost millions of dollars.

amount of premium amortized will be $8.67 (rounded) per year. The amortization schedule using straight-line amortization is shown in Exhibit 7.10.

	(1) Beginning carrying value	(2) Cash payment $1,000 × 0.05	(3) Amortization of premium $52.00 ÷ 6	(4) Interest expense (2) − (3)	(5) Ending carrying value
Year 1	$1,052.00	$50.00	$8.67	$41.33	$1,043.33
Year 2	1,043.33	50.00	8.67	41.33	1,034.66
Year 3	1,034.66	50.00	8.67	41.33	1,025.99
Year 4	1,025.99	50.00	8.67	41.33	1,017.32
Year 5	1,017.32	50.00	8.67	41.33	1,008.65
Year 6	1,008.65	50.00	8.65*	41.35*	1,000.00

*adjusted for rounding

EXHIBIT 7.10

Straight-Line Amortization of a Bond Issued at a Premium

The premium of $52 is simply divided evenly over the life of the bond when straight-line amortization is used.

To use the straight-line method of amortization, you do not need to know the market interest rate to calculate the interest expense. Each period the interest expense is the same; the amortization of the discount or premium is the same; and, of course, the interest payment is the same. You can see how that makes the calculations easy. However, remember that it is only permissible to use the straight-line method when the interest expense calculated with this method is not significantly different than the interest expense calculated using the effective interest method. The numbers in this example are small, and the difference does not seem to be significant. When a company has hundreds of thousands or even millions of dollars of bonds outstanding, the two methods can produce significantly different amounts of interest expense.

Team Shirts for July

When Sara started her T-shirt business in January, she borrowed a small amount of money from her sister. Now that she has the business up and running, Sara decides she needs more space for inventory and for the actual business operations. This is crucial if she wants to take advantage of the demand for her shirts. Sara finds an excellent deal on a small office complex; so she goes to her local bank and secures a mortgage loan for $85,000, the cost of the office complex. The transactions for July are shown in Exhibit 7.11 on the following page, and the balance sheet at July 1 is shown in Exhibit 7.12 on the following page. Remember that this is the same as the June 30 balance sheet from Chapter 6, Exhibit 6.13.

L.O.5
Prepare financial statements that include long-term debt.

Following is some additional information needed to make the month-end adjustments:

1. The van was driven 3,000 miles this month.
2. Bad debts expense is calculated based on the same percentages as Team Shirts used in June: 2% of the ending balance in accounts receivable should be in the allowance account.

First, we will use an accounting equation worksheet to record the transactions and the necessary adjustments. Then, we will prepare the four basic financial statements for Team Shirts for the month of July. As usual, we will simply ignore income taxes.

Trace each transaction in Exhibit 7.11 to the accounting equation worksheet in Exhibit 7.13 on page 335.

To the right of the worksheet, you can find some details of the beginning and ending balances of the assets and liabilities. Notice that Transaction 9 is the very last one on the worksheet, shown after the adjustments. It is really recorded before the adjustments, but remember that dividends are not included in net income. So, the dividends cannot be in the red box. After you study the transactions, look at the adjustments, A-1 through A-9. Identifying the needed adjustments is often the job of a firm's accounting staff. Exhibit 7.14 on page 336 provides some detailed computations that will help you understand the amounts calculated for the adjustments. The exhibit also explains how Team Shirts computed the current portion of its long-term mortgage.

EXHIBIT 7.11

Transactions for Team Shirts for July

1	July 1	Purchased building and land for $85,000. Ninety percent of the purchase price is allocated to the building. Estimated salvage value is $1,500 and estimated useful life is 25 years. (For this example, we are recording monthly depreciation.)
		The mortgage for $85,000 is for 10 years, with monthly payments of $900 each beginning August 1. The stated rate of interest is 5%.
2	July 10	Cash collected on accounts receivable, $18,000
3	July 12	Cash paid on accounts payable, $12,600
4	July 15	Purchased 10,000 shirts at $3.60 each on account
5	July 20	Sold 9,000 shirts at $11 each, on account
6	July 22	Additional collections on accounts receivable, $45,000
7	July 24	Paid cash operating expenses of $6,000
8	July 28	Specific account recognized as uncollectible and written off, total $400
9	July 30	Declared and paid cash dividends of $2,000

EXHIBIT 7.12

Balance Sheet for Team Shirts at July 1, 2010

Team Shirts
Balance Sheet
At July 1, 2010

Assets

Current assets		
Cash		$ 2,305
Accounts receivable (net of allowance of $413)		20,237
Inventory		7,455
Prepaid expenses		6,950
Total current assets		36,947
Property and equipment		
Computer	$ 4,000	
Truck	30,000	34,000
Accumulated depreciation		(1,125)
Net property and equipment		32,875
Total assets		$69,822

Liabilities and Shareholder's Equity

Current liabilities	
Accounts payable	$12,600
Notes payable (current portion)	6,000
Interest payable	150
Total current liabilities	18,750
Notes payable (long-term)	24,000
Total liabilities	42,750
Shareholder's equity	
Common stock	5,000
Retained earnings	22,072
Total shareholder's equity	27,072
Total liabilities and shareholder's equity	$69,822

EXHIBIT 7.13

Accounting Equation Worksheet for Team Shirts for July

Detail of Assets and Liabilities

Assets (except cash)	Beginning	Ending
Accounts receivable	$20,650	$ 56,250
Allowance for bad debts	(413)	(1,125)
Inventory	7,455	9,990
Prepaid insurance	150	50
Prepaid rent	6,600	5,400
Prepaid Web design	200	150
Computer	4,000	4,000
Accumulated depreciation	(400)	(500)
Truck	30,000	30,000
Accumulated depreciation	(725)	(1,160)
Land		8,500
Building		76,500
Accumulated depreciation		(250)
	$67,517	$187,805

Liabilities	Beginning	Ending
Accounts payable	$12,600	$ 36,000
Interest payable		654
Notes payable (truck)	30,000	30,000
Mortgage payable		85,000
	$42,750	$151,654

Worksheet

	Assets: Cash	All other assets	(Account)	= Liabilities: All liabilities	(Account)	+ Contributed Capital	Retained Earnings	(Account)
Beginning Balances	$ 2,305	$ 67,517	See details to the right of the worksheet	$42,750	See details to the right of the worksheet	$5,000	$22,072	
Transaction 1		8,500 / 76,500	Land / Building	85,000	Mortgage payable			
2	18,000	(18,000)	Accounts receivable					
3	(12,600)			(12,600)	Accounts payable			
4		36,000	Inventory	36,000	Accounts payable			
5		99,000 / (33,465)	Accounts receivable / Inventory				99,000 / (33,465)	Sales / Cost of goods sold
6	45,000	(45,000)	Accounts receivable					
7	(6,000)						(6,000)	Operating expenses
8		(400) / 400	Accounts receivable / Allowance for bad debts					
A-1		(100)	Accumulated depreciation, computer				(100)	Depreciation expense
A-2		(435)	Accumulated depreciation, truck				(435)	Depreciation expense
A-3		(250)	Accumulated depreciation, building				(250)	Depreciation expense
A-4		(100)	Prepaid insurance				(100)	Insurance expense
A-5		(1,200)	Prepaid rent				(1,200)	Rent expense
A-6		(50)	Prepaid Web design				(50)	Web design expense
A-7				150	Interest payable		(150)	Interest expense
A-8				354	Interest payable		(354)	Interest expense
A-9		(1,112)	Allowance for bad debts				(1,112)	Bad debts expense
9	(2,000)						(2,000)	Dividends
	$ 44,705	+$187,805		= $151,654		+ $5,000	+ $75,856	

Shareholder's Equity includes columns: Contributed Capital, Retained Earnings, (Account)

— Income statement   — Statement of changes in shareholder's equity   — Balance sheet   — Statement of cash flows

EXHIBIT 7.14

Details of Team Shirts' Computations for July Financial Statements

Depreciation

Computer	$100	
Truck	$435	$0.145 per mile × 3,000 miles
Building	$250	$ 76,500 Cost (90% of purchase)
		(1,500) Salvage value
	$785	$ 75,000 Depreciable base
		÷ 300 25 years × 12 months
		$ 250.00 Monthly depreciation

Cost of goods sold

Beginning inventory	1,775 shirts at $4.20 each	$ 7,455
Purchases	10,000 at $3.60	36,000
Goods available for sale		$ 43,455
Sale of 9,000 shirts:		
Cost of goods sold	1,775 at $4.20 ⎤	$ 33,465
	7,225 at $3.60 ⎦	
Ending inventory	2,775 at $3.60	9,990
		$ 43,455

Bad Debts expense

Beginning allowance for bad debts	$ 413
Write-offs during the month	(400)
Balance before adjustment	$ 13
Desired balance	
2% of ending accounts receivable =	
2% of $56,250	$ 1,125
Needed adjustment = bad debts expense	$ 1,112

Interest expense and current portion of long-term mortgage

This is the amortization schedule for the first 12 months of the mortgage. The annual interest rate of 5% is divided by 12 to get a monthly rate. The difference between the monthly payment and the interest expense will reduce the principal balance. The total principal reduction for the 12 months will be the current portion of the long-term debt. It is the amount of the principal that will be due in the next year. Remember that the interest won't be recorded as a liability until the time has passed. At the end of the first month of the mortgage, July, Team Shirts accrued the first month's interest of $354.

Beginning balance (monthly)	Interest expense (monthly) 5% / 12	Monthly payment given	Reduction in principal	Ending balance
$85,000	$354**	$900	$ 546	$84,454
84,454	352	900	548	83,906
83,906	350	900	550	83,356
83,356	347	900	553	82,803
82,803	345	900	555	82,248
82,248	343	900	557	81,691
81,691	340	900	560	81,131
81,131	338	900	562	80,569
80,569	336	900	564	80,005
80,005	333	900	567	79,438
79,438	331	900	569	78,869
78,869	329	900	571	78,298
			$ 6,702	

▢ The amounts can be found on the financial statements.

**0.00417 × $85,000 = $354

From the accounting equation worksheet, you can prepare the financial statements. Exhibit 7.15 shows the four basic financial statements. You should be able to see where the amounts on the financial statements have come from on the accounting equation worksheet and from the details in Exhibit 7.14.

EXHIBIT 7.15

Financial Statements for Team Shirts for July 2010

Team Shirts
Income Statement
For the Month Ended July 31, 2010

Sales revenue:		$99,000
Expenses:		
Cost of goods sold	$33,465	
Operating expenses	6,000	
Bad debts expense	1,112	
Insurance expense	100	
Rent expense	1,200	
Web design expense	50	
Depreciation expense	785	
Interest expense	504	
Total expenses		43,216
Net income		$55,784

Team Shirts
Statement of Changes in Shareholder's Equity
For the Month Ended July 31, 2010

Beginning common stock	$ 5,000
Common stock issued during month	0
Ending common stock	$ 5,000
Beginning retained earnings	$22,072
Net income	55,784
Dividends	(2,000)
Ending retained earnings	$75,856
Total shareholder's equity	$80,856

Team Shirts
Statement of Cash Flows
For the Month Ended July 31, 2010

Cash from operating activities	
Cash collected from customers	$ 63,000
Cash paid to vendors	(12,600)
Cash paid for operating expense	(6,000)
Net cash from operating activities	$ 44,400
Cash from investing activities*	0
Cash from financing activities	
Dividends paid	(2,000)
Increase in cash	42,400
Beginning cash balance	2,305
Ending cash balance	$44,705

*Note: The firm purchased land and a building in exchange for a $85,000 mortgage payable.

Team Shirts
Balance Sheet
At July 31, 2010

Assets

Current assets		
Cash		$44,705
Accounts receivable (net of allowance of $1,125)		55,125
Inventory		9,990
Prepaid expenses		5,600
Total current assets		115,420
Property and equipment		
Land		$ 8,500
Computer	4,000	
Truck	30,000	
Building	76,500	$110,500
Accumulated depreciation		(1,910)
Net property and equipment		117,090
Total assets		$232,510

Liabilities and Shareholder's Equity

Current liabilities	
Accounts payable	$ 36,000
Interest payable	654
Current portion of note payable	6,000
Current portion of mortgage payable	6,702
Total current liabilities	49,356
Notes payable	24,000
Mortgage payable	78,298
Total liabilities	151,654
Shareholder's equity	
Common stock	$ 5,000
Retained earnings	75,856
Total shareholder's equity	80,856
Total liabilities and shareholder's equity	$232,510

L.O.6
Explain capital structure
and compute the debt-to-
equity ratio.

Capital structure is the
combination of debt and equity that
a firm uses to finance its business.

Financial leverage is the
use of borrowed funds to
increase earnings.

Debt-to-equity ratio compares
the amount of a firm's liabilities to
the amount of its equity, an
indication of solvency.

Applying Your Knowledge: Financial Statement Analysis

You know that the two ways to finance a business are debt and equity. The combination of debt and equity that a company chooses is called its **capital structure**. That is because debt and equity are the two sources of capital, and every company can choose the proportion of each that makes up its total capital.

When should a company borrow money? A very simplistic cost-benefit analysis would suggest that when the benefit of borrowing the money (what it can earn for the business) exceeds the cost of borrowing the money (interest expense) then borrowing money is a good idea. Look back at The Home Depot's balance sheet in Exhibit 7.1 on page 319. The Home Depot's total debt is $23,387 million at February 1, 2009. That is almost 57% of its financing (debt + shareholders' equity = $41,164 million at February 1, 2009). How does the company's percentage of total debt compare with other firms in related industries? At January 30, 2009, Lowe's had total liabilities of $14,631 million and total debt plus shareholders' equity of $32,686 million. Debt is almost 45% of Lowe's capital structure. There is no rule about how much debt a firm should have. If you take a finance course, you will study the topic of optimal capital structure and find there is no simple answer.

Closely related is the concept of **financial leverage**, which means using borrowed funds to increase earnings. If a company earns more with the money it borrows than it must pay to borrow that money, it is called positive financial leverage. Suppose Anna Chase has invested $50,000 in her new business and has no debt. If the business earns $5,000 net income during the year, then she has earned a return on her investment of 10%. Suppose Anna wants to expand her business. She might earn an additional $5,000 the next year if she borrows an additional $50,000. If the after-tax cost of borrowing the money is 8% ($4,000), then Anna would be taking advantage of financial leverage if she borrows the money. That is because earnings could increase by more than the cost of borrowing the money. The new total income for the second year ($5,000 + $5,000 − $4,000 interest) would be $6,000. Anna's return on equity for the second year is $6,000 ÷ $50,000 = 12%.

Debt ratios measure a company's debt position and its ability to meet its interest payments. The most common is the **debt-to-equity ratio**.

$$\text{Debt-to-equity ratio} = \frac{\text{Total liabilities}}{\text{Total shareholders' equity}}$$

This ratio compares the amount of creditors' claims to the assets of the firm with owners' claims to the assets of the firm. Sometimes the numerator will include only long-term debt rather than total liabilities. Just be sure you are consistent when you are comparing two firms or are comparing various times across a single firm. A firm with a high debt-to-equity ratio is often referred to as a highly leveraged firm. A debt-to-equity ratio around 100% (half debt and half equity) is quite common. Exhibit 7.16 shows the debt-to-equity ratios for The Home Depot and Lowe's. Notice that it gives us the same type of information that we got when we determined what percentage of debt each company had in its capital structure in the prior section. There are many ratios that address the same basic comparison of how much debt and how much equity make up a firm's capital structure.

EXHIBIT 7.16

Debt-to-Equity Ratios for The Home Depot, Inc., and Lowe's Companies, Inc.

	The Home Depot At February 1, 2009	Lowe's At January 30, 2009
($ in millions)		
Total debt	$23,387	$14,631
Total shareholders' equity	$17,777	$18,055
Debt-to-equity ratio	131.6%	81.0%

The details of a company's long-term debt are often found in the notes to the financial statements, rather than on the face of the balance sheet, so it is important to study these notes. For example, the liabilities section of The Sherwin-Williams Company's balance sheet, shown in Exhibit 7.17, shows only the basic amounts of long-term obligations, whereas the notes give the details.

EXHIBIT 7.17

Details of Long-Term Debt from the Financial Statements of The Sherwin-Williams Company

This shows both the liabilities from the balance sheet and the notes that provide the related details.

From the Financial Statements
of The Sherwin-Williams Company
(thousands of dollars)

From Liabilities and Shareholders' Equity Section

	At December 31,		
	2008	2007	2006
Total current liabilities	$1,936,736	$2,141,385	$2,074,815
Long-term debt	303,727	293,454	291,876
Postretirement benefits other than pensions	248,603	262,720	301,408
Other long-term liabilities	321,045	372,054	334,628
Total shareholders' equity	1,605,648	1,785,727	1,992,360
Total Liabilities and Shareholders' Equity	$4,415,759	$4,855,340	$4,995,087

Note 7 - Debt

Long-term debt

		Amounts Outstanding		
	Due Date	2008	2007	2006
7.375% Debentures	2027	$137,047	$137,044	$137,041
7.45% Debentures	2097	146,967	146,960	146,954
1.0% to 13.5% Promissory Notes	Through 2007	19,713	9,450	7,881
		$303,727	$293,454	$291,876

Calculate the debt-to-equity ratio for Sherwin-Williams for each of the years shown in Exhibit 7.17. What trend do you see, and how might an investor interpret it?

Your Turn 7-7

Business Risk, Control, and Ethics

The primary risk for a company associated with long-term debt is the risk of not being able to make the debt payments. The more debt a business has, the more risk there is that the company will not be able to pay the debt as it becomes due. That would result in serious financial trouble, possibly even bankruptcy. For The Home Depot, this does not seem to be an immediate problem. As you just read, the firm's debt is approximately 57% of its capital structure, a much lower percentage than many firms. However, just four years ago, debt was only 40% of The Home Depot's capital structure. Financial analysts who follow The Home Depot are definitely watching this ratio. The inability of a firm to pay its debt is a significant risk for the creditors and investors, too. If a company has trouble making its debt payments, you would not like to be one of its creditors or an investor.

There are two major things a company can do to minimize the risk associated with long-term debt.

L.O.7
Identify the major risk associated with long-term debt and the related controls.

1. Be sure a thorough business analysis accompanies any decision to borrow money. This is where the concept of positive financial leverage comes in. The company must make sure there is a high probability of earning a higher return with the borrowed funds than the interest costs associated with borrowing the funds. How high the probability should be is an individual business decision. The more money involved, the higher the probability should be.

2. Study the characteristics of various types of debt—terms, interest rates, ease of obtaining the money—and evaluate their attractiveness in your specific circumstances, given the purpose of the loan and the financial situation of the company. For example, bonds are more flexible than a bank loan because the terms and cash flows can be varied, but a bank loan can be arranged more quickly than a company can issue bonds. As you know, debt shows up on a firm's balance sheet. When a firm structures a transaction to keep debt off of its balance sheet, it is called off-balance-sheet financing. The topic is a bit complicated for an introductory course, but you should be familiar with the expression and its general meaning. Off-balance-sheet financing is not always illegal or a violation of GAAP, but there are well-known cases where GAAP were violated to keep debt off a firm's balance sheet. This was the major fraud at Enron. The firm used creative bookkeeping to keep debt off the balance sheet that actually should have been shown there. The well-known Enron bankruptcy in 2002 shows that ethics touches every aspect of accounting, even how debt is recorded.

Chapter Summary Points

- A definitely determinable liability is one whose amount is known, and it is recorded when incurred. A typical example is payroll. The firm knows how much to record for salary expense. The firm serves as an agent for the government to collect social security, Medicare, and income taxes from the employee.
- An estimated liability is one that must be estimated for the financial statements. It is necessary so that the firm can record an expense prior to knowing the precise amount of the expense. A typical example is warranty liability. Warranties provided with a product require a firm to estimate future expenditures so that the warranty expense can be recorded in the same period as the sale. With the expense, the firm records a liability, often called a reserve. It's not cash! It's an account that the firm will use when the expenditures are actually made related to the warranty. At that time, no expense will be recorded, and the cost will be written off against the reserve.
- Long-term mortgages usually have payments that include both principal and interest. To calculate the portion of the payment that is interest expense, multiply the interest rate (adjusted for the appropriate time period; e.g., a monthly rate for a monthly payment) by the outstanding principal balance at the beginning of the period. Then, subtract that amount of interest from the payment to find the amount of principal reduction.
- Bonds are debt instruments issued by a firm to borrow money from the capital markets (general public). They may be issued at par, at a discount, or at a premium. The issue price of a bond—which is the proceeds to the firm—is stated as a percentage of the bond's face value and is determined by the market at the time the bonds are issued. The bonds are shown on the balance sheet—the carrying value—at a "net" amount. Any applicable discount (or premium) has been deducted from (or added to) the face value of the bonds.
- Capital structure refers to the proportion of debt and equity a firm has. Debt-to-equity ratio is, as it sounds, the firm's total debt divided by the firm's equity. It tells investors and creditors how much of the firm's capital structure is debt compared to equity.
- The major risk for the firm is that it will not be able to make its debt payments. The best controls for this risk are sound financial planning and the profitable operation of the firm.

Chapter Summary Problems

The following transactions took place during HPC Company's most recent fiscal year:

1. On February 1, the first day of the fiscal year, HPC Company issued $5,000,000 worth of 10-year, 8% bonds at 98. At the time, the market rate was approximately 8.3%. Interest is payable annually on February 1. The discount will be amortized using the effective interest method.

2. HPC Company borrowed $10,000,000. The loan is for 20 years at 6.5% with quarterly payments of $224,260. HPC borrowed the money on the last day of the third quarter of the fiscal year and made the first payment on the last day of the fiscal year.
3. HPC spent $55,780 to honor warranties on products sold previously.
4. HPC purchased $675,000 worth of inventory on account. The firm uses a perpetual record-keeping inventory system.
5. HPC paid vendors $563,000 for part of the merchandise purchased in item (4).
6. Of the beginning amount of unearned service revenue, HPC earned $57,000 during the year.
7. HPC received $25,990 in advance from customers for products to be delivered next year.
8. HPC estimated it will spend $50,000 in the next two years honoring warranties related to this year's sales. (Two-year warranties are given for all products.)
9. HPC made the payment on the loan from transaction 2. above.

Suppose HPC started the year with the following liability accounts and balances:

Accounts payable	$75,500
Unearned service revenue	$57,960
Warranty payable	$68,950

Instructions

1. Show each of the transactions in the accounting equation.
2. Give the adjustments that HPC needs to make as the result of these transactions at year end.
3. Prepare the liability section of HPC's balance sheet at the end of the fiscal year.

Solution

	Assets				= Liabilities		+	Shareholders' Equity	
								Contributed Capital	Retained Earnings
	Cash	All other assets	(Account)		All liabilities	(Account)			
Selected Beginning Balances				$	75,500 57,960 68,905	Accounts payable Unearned revenue Warranties payable			(Account)
Transaction 1	$ 4,900,000				4,900,000	Bonds payable			
2	10,000,000				10,000,000	Long-term notes payable			
3	(55,780)				(55,780)	Warranty payable			
4		675,000	Inventory		675,000	Accounts payable			
5	(563,000)				(563,000)	Accounts payable			
6					(57,000)	Unearned revenue			57,000 Revenue
7	25,990				25,990	Unearned revenue			
8					50,000	Warranty payable			(50,000) Warranty expense
9	(224,260)				(61,760)	Long-term notes payable			(162,500) Interest expense
Adjustment 1					400,000 6,700	Interest payable Bonds payable			(406,700) Interest expense

— Income statement   — Statement of changes in shareholders' equity   — Balance sheet   — Statement of cash flows

Supporting Computations

Bonds:

Interest expense for bonds:

$$\$4,900,000 \times 0.083 = \$406,700$$

Interest payment:

$$\$5,000,000 \times 0.08 = \$400,000$$

Discount amortization:

$$\$406,700 - \$400,000 = \$\ 6,700$$

Liabilities Section of the Year-End Balance Sheet:

Current Liabilities:	
Accounts payable	$ 187,500
Interest payable	400,000
Unearned revenue	26,950
Warranty payable	63,170
**Current portion of long-term debt	257,241
Total current liabilities	934,861
Long-Term Liabilities:	
**Notes payable	9,680,999
Bonds payable (net of a discount of $93,300)	4,906,700
Total liabilities	$15,522,560

** A partial amortization schedule for the long-term loan with quarterly payments is shown. In the next fiscal year, four of those payments will be due. Only the principal portion is recorded as a current liability because the interest has not yet been incurred at the end of the year. The total current portion is the sum of the highlighted values in the Principal Reduction column. The remaining amount of the note payable, highlighted in the Beginning Principal column, is shown as a long-term liability.

	Beginning Principal	Quarterly Interest (6.5 ÷ 4) 0.01625	Payment	Principal Reduction	
Q1, Y1	$10,000,000	$162,500	$224,260	$61,760	Payment made
Q2, Y1	9,938,240	161,496	224,260	62,764	Next year's
Q3, Y1	9,875,476	160,476	224,260	63,784	payment of
Q4, Y1	9,811,692	159,440	224,260	64,820	principal
Q1, Y2	9,746,872	158,387	224,260	65,873	$257,241
Q2, Y2	9,680,999				
	Long-term portion				

Key Terms for Chapter 7

Amortization schedule (p. 324)
Annuity (p. 363)
Bond (p. 325)
Bonds issued at a discount (p. 327)
Bonds issued at a premium (p. 327)
Bonds issued at par (p. 327)
Capital structure (p. 338)

Carrying value (p. 328)
Debt-to-equity ratio (p. 338)
Definitely determinable liabilities (p. 318)
Discount on bonds payable (p. 328)
Discount rate (p. 363)
Discounting (p. 363)
Estimated liabilities (p. 318)

Financial leverage (p. 328)
Market rate of interest (p. 327)
Ordinary annuity (p. 363)
Premium on bonds payable (p. 329)
Present value (p. 361)
Proceeds (p. 327)

Answers to YOUR TURN Questions

Chapter 7

Your Turn 7-1

Sandy's paycheck will be in the amount of $1,085.25.
The transaction would be recorded as follows:

Assets	=	Liabilities	+	Shareholders' equity	
				Contributed + capital	Retained earnings
(1,085.25) cash		300.00 FIT payable 93.00 FICA taxes payable 21.75 Medicare taxes payable			(1,500) salary expense

Your Turn 7-2

1. No warranty expense would be on the August income statement.
2. The liability would be $2,250 ($2,750 – $500).

Your Turn 7-3

The interest is $600,000 × 9% × 1/12 = $4,500. The total payment is $5,500, so the principal reduction is the remaining $1,000.

Your Turn 7-4

A $1,000 bond issued at 95.5 will sell for $955.
A $1,000 bond issued at 102 will sell for $1,020.

Your Turn 7-5

Interest expense (as opposed to interest payment) is calculated by multiplying the bond's carrying value (the bonds) by the market rate of interest. The amount of proceeds (selling price of the bonds) equals the carrying value of the bonds on the date of the first interest payment.

Proceeds = 98% of $200,000 = $196,000
Interest expense = $196,000 × 0.065 × 1/2 = $6,370 (for the first six months)
Interest payment = $200,000 × 6% × 1/2 = $6,000
Difference between expense and payment = $370

This amount ($370) will be added to the carrying value of the bonds (which is the same as subtracting it from the discount on bonds payable).
Carrying value of the bonds to $196,370 after the first interest payment:
Beginning book value of $196,000 + amortization of discount of $370
At December 31, 2010, Knollwood will record interest expense for the last half of the year as follows:

Interest expense = $196,370 × 0.065 × 1/2 year = $6,382
Interest payment = $6,000
Difference between expense and payment = $382
This amount will be added to the carrying value of the bonds (subtracted from the discount).
Carrying value of the bonds on December 31, 2010 = $196,752.
The total interest expense for the year is $6,370 + $6,382 = $12,752.

Your Turn 7-6

On the first interest payment, the interest expense, which will be shown on the income statement, is $19,643.13 (9% × $218,257).
The cash payment to the bondholders is $20,000.00.
The difference of $356.87 is the amortization of the premium.
The carrying value, shown on the December 31 balance sheet, is $217,900.13 ($218,257.00 – $356.87).

Your Turn 7-7

2008: $2,810,111 (total liabilities) ÷ $1,605,648 (total equity) = 175%
2007: $3,069,613 (total liabilities) ÷ $1,785,727 (total equity) = 172%
2006: $3,002,727 (total liabilities) ÷ $1,992,360 (total equity) = 151%
The ratio is increasing, but we would need some industry comparisons for a meaningful analysis.

Questions

1. What are the two main sources of financing for a business?
2. What is the difference between a definitely determinable liability and an estimated liability? Give an example of each.
3. What is a mortgage?
4. When installment loan payments on a mortgage are made, the amount paid reduces cash. What other two items on the financial statements are affected?
5. What is the difference between how bonds are repaid compared to other forms of financing that require installment payments?
6. What advantage is there to obtaining financing using bonds compared to getting a loan from a bank?
7. How are the interest payments associated with a bond calculated?
8. Explain the difference between the stated rate and the effective rate of interest on a bond.
9. What is another name for the face value of a bond?
10. When is a bond issued at a discount? When is a bond issued at a premium?
11. How is the debt-to-equity ratio calculated, and what does this ratio measure?
12. To what does the term *capital structure* refer?
13. Explain *financial leverage*.

Multiple-Choice Questions

1. Partco hired a secretary for $900 a week. The secretary's first paycheck had 20% withheld for income taxes, 6.2% for social security, and 1.45% for Medicare taxes. What is Partco's total expense (including payroll tax expense) related to this payment?
   a. $68.85
   b. $968.85
   c. $651.15
   d. $720.00
2. All of the following are current liabilities except
   a. salaries payable.
   b. mortgage payable.
   c. unearned revenue.
   d. accounts payable.
3. The amount a company owes its employees for current work done is
   a. shown on the balance sheet as pension liability.
   b. shown as a current liability.
   c. called postretirement benefits on the balance sheet.
   d. not shown on the balance sheet.
4. Liabilities are often estimated because
   a. the related expense needs to be recorded to match the appropriate revenues.
   b. it gives managers a way to manage assets.
   c. they are usually not disclosed until they are settled.
   d. the related assets are already recorded.
5. Advanced Music Technology, Inc., estimated that its warranty costs would be $900 for items sold during the current year, an amount it considers significant. During the year Advanced paid $750 to repair merchandise that was returned by customers. What is the amount of warranty expense for the current year?
   a. $750
   b. $900

    c. $150

    d. Cannot be determined

6. On January 1, Sonata Company issued 10-year bonds with a face value of $400,000 and a stated rate of 10%. The cash proceeds from the bond issue amounted to $354,120. Sonata Company will pay interest to the bondholders annually. How much cash will Sonata pay the bondholders on the first payment date?

    a. $40,000

    b. $48,000

    c. $35,412

    d. $42,494

7. Refer to the information in multiple-choice question 6. How did the market interest rate compare to the stated rate on the date the bonds were issued?

    a. The market rate is higher than the stated rate.

    b. The market rate is lower than the stated rate.

    c. Both rates are the same.

    d. It cannot be determined.

8. Bonds issued with a stated interest rate that is higher than the prevailing market rate are issued at

    a. a premium.

    b. a discount.

    c. par.

    d. It cannot be determined.

9. A $1,000 bond with a stated rate of 8% is issued when the market rate is 10%. How much interest will the bondholders receive each year for the annual interest payments?

    a. $100

    b. $80

    c. $20

    d. $800

10. Positive financial leverage means that a company

    a. has more debt than equity.

    b. earns more with borrowed money than the cost of borrowing it.

    c. has the correct amount of debt.

    d. has more equity than debt.

Short Exercises
Set A

All of the A exercises can be found within MyAccountingLab, an online homework and practice environment.

SE7-1A. *Classify liabilities. (LO 1, 2).* Tell whether each of the following liabilities is definitely determinable or an estimate: accounts payable, unearned revenue, and warranty liability.

SE7-2A. *Classify liabilities. (LO 1).* Taylor Company has the following obligations at December 31: (a) a note payable for $10,000 due in six months; (b) unearned revenue of $12,500; (c) interest payable of $15,000; (d) accounts payable of $60,000; and (e) note payable due in two years. For each obligation, indicate whether or not it should be classified as a current liability.

SE7-3A. *Account for payroll. (LO 1).* Jimmy Paycheck earned $1,500 per month as the manager of a recording studio. Jimmy has 25% of his earnings withheld for federal income taxes. There are no other amounts withheld except for those required by the federal government. What are the other amounts that must be deducted from Jimmy's earnings? Calculate the net amount Jimmy will receive on his next paycheck.

SE7-4A. *Account for warranties. (LO 2).* Key Company offers a three-year warranty on its premium door locks. During the year, the company had sales of $100,000. Related to the sales, warranty costs should be approximately $3,000 per year. How much warranty expense related to these sales will Key Company's income statement show in the year of the sales? How much warranty expense related to these sales will Key Company have in the two years after the sales?

SE7-5A. *Account for mortgages. (LO 3).* Nunez Company has arranged to borrow $25,000 for five years at an interest rate of 8%. The annual payments will be $6,261.41. When Nunez makes its first payment at the end of the first year of the loan, how much of the payment will be interest?

SE7-6A. *Account for mortgages. (LO 3).* Feathers and Furs borrowed $75,000 to buy a new faux fur storage facility. The company borrowed the money for 10 years at 12%, and the monthly payments are $1,076.03. When the company makes the first monthly payment at the end of the first month of the loan, by how much will the payment reduce the principal of the loan?

SE7-7A. *Account for bonds. (LO 4).* If a $1,000 bond is selling at 95, how much cash will the issuing company receive? If a $1,000 bond is selling at par, how much cash will the issuing company receive? If a $1,000 bond is selling at 101, how much cash will the issuing company receive?

SE7-8A. *Account for bonds. (LO 4).* For each of the following situations, tell whether the bond described will be issued at a premium, at a discount, or at par:

1. Colson Company issued $200,000 worth of bonds with a stated interest rate of 10%. At the time of issue, the market rate of interest for similar investments was 9%.
2. Dean Company issued $100,000 worth of callable bonds with a stated rate of 12%. At the time of issue, the market rate of interest for similar investments was 9%.
3. Liddy Company issued $200,000 worth of bonds with a stated rate of 8%. At the time of issue, the market rate of interest for similar investments was 9%.

SE7-9A. *Account for bonds. (LO 4).* For each of the following situations, compute the proceeds from the bond issue:

1. Haldeman Hair Systems issued $20,000 worth of bonds at 106.
2. Erlichman Egg Company issued $100,000 worth of bonds at 99.
3. Carl's Cutlery Company issued $500,000 worth of bonds at 96.5.

SE7-10A. *Account for bonds. (LO 4).* Altoona Company was able to issue (sell) $200,000 of 9% bonds for $220,000 because its credit rating is excellent and market interest rates have fallen. How much interest will be paid in cash during the first year? Will the interest expense be higher or lower than the interest payment?

SE7-11A. *Calculate the debt-to-equity ratio. (LO 6).* Suppose that for 2010 Axel Company's current assets totaled $57,855; total assets totaled $449,999; current liabilities totaled $71,264; and total liabilities totaled $424,424. Calculate the debt-to-equity ratio for Axel for 2010.

Set B

SE7-12B. *Classify liabilities. (LO 1).* Tell whether each of the following liabilities is definitely determinable or an estimate: salaries payable, warranty liability, and notes payable.

SE7-13B. *Classify liabilities. (LO 1, 2).* Swift Company has the following obligations at December 31: (a) a note payable for $10,000 due in 18 months; (b) unearned revenue of $12,500; (c) interest payable of $15,000; (d) accounts payable of $60,000; and (e) note payable due in three months. For each obligation, indicate whether or not it should be classified as a current liability.

SE7-14B. *Account for payroll. (LO 1).* Johnny Worker earns $2,500 per month as the manager of a grocery store. Johnny has 20% of his earnings withheld for federal income taxes. There are no other amounts withheld except for those required by the federal government. What are the other amounts that must be deducted from Johnny's earnings? Calculate the net amount Johnny will receive on his next paycheck.

SE7-15B. *Account for warranties. (LO 2).* Tom's Toasters, Inc., began the year with $30,000 in its warranty liability. During the year, the firm spent $20,000 to honor past warranties. Will the $20,000 be the warranty expense for the year? Why or why not?

SE7-16B. *Account for mortgages. (LO 3).* Curtain Company borrowed $10,000 at 9% for seven years. The loan requires annual payments of $1,986.91. When Curtain Company makes the first annual payment at the end of the first year of the loan, how much of the payment will be interest and how much will reduce the principal of the loan?

SE7-17B. *Account for mortgages. (LO 3).* On July 1, 2006, Maxine's Equipment Company signed a long-term note with the local bank for $50,000. The term of the note was 10 years, at an annual interest rate of 8%. If Maxine's makes annual payments of $7,451.47, beginning on June 30, 2007, how much of the first payment will be interest?

SE7-18B. *Account for bonds. (LO 4).* If $100,000 of 8% bonds are issued (sold) for $95,000, was the market rate of interest at the time of issue higher or lower than 8%? What is the amount of the annual interest payments to be received by the bondholders?

SE7-19B. *Account for bonds. (LO 4).* For each of the following situations, tell whether the bond described will be issued at a premium, at a discount, or at par:

1. Kami Company issued $100,000 worth of bonds with a stated interest rate of 9%. At the time of issue, the market rate of interest for similar investments was 10%.
2. Fun Company issued $300,000 worth of callable bonds with a stated rate of 4.5%. At the time of issue, the market rate of interest for similar investments was 4%.
3. Rider Company issued $500,000 worth of bonds with a stated rate of 5%. At the time of issue, the market rate of interest for similar investments was 5.2%.

SE7-20B. *Account for bonds. (LO 4).* For each of the following situations, compute the proceeds from the bond issue:

1. Quality Bank issued $100,000 worth of bonds at 104.
2. Tool & Dye Company issued $50,000 worth of bonds at 98.
3. Connie's Can Company issued $400,000 worth of bonds at 97.5.

SE7-21B. *Account for bonds. (LO 4).* Data Company was able to issue (sell) $100,000 of 6% bonds for $110,000 because its credit rating is excellent and market interest rates have fallen. How much interest will be paid in cash during the first year? Will the interest expense be higher or lower than the interest payment?

SE7-22B. *Calculate the debt-to-equity ratio. (LO 6).* Suppose that for 2011 Rod Company's current assets totaled $35,600; total assets totaled $70,000; current liabilities totaled $16,000; and total liabilities totaled $25,600. Calculate the debt-to-equity ratio for Rod Company for 2011.

Exercises
Set A

MyAccountingLab

All of the A exercises can be found within MyAccountingLab, an online homework and practice environment.

E7-23A. *Classify liabilities. (LO 1).* For each item in the following list, tell whether it is a definitely determinable liability, an estimated liability, or neither:

1. Amount owed to vendor for purchase of inventory
2. Potential proceeds from pending lawsuit
3. Amount of warranty obligations
4. Amount of loan payment due next year
5. Amount of vacation pay to accrue for employees for next year

E7-24A. *Account for payroll. (LO 1).* A company has gross payroll of $30,000; federal income tax withheld of $6,000; FICA (social security) taxes withheld of $1,860; and Medicare taxes withheld of $435.

1. How much will the balance sheet show for salaries payable (to employees)?
2. How much will the income statement show for salary expense?
3. What type of liability is salaries payable?

E7-25A. *Account for payroll. (LO 1).* During February, Winter Company's employees earned wages of $50,000. Social security (FICA) withheld was $2,500; federal income taxes withheld were $3,500; and employees' contributions to United Way withheld totaled $500. Use the accounting equation to record wages expense and wages payable at the end of February. Winter Company will pay employees their February wages and pay the payroll taxes to the government during the first week in March.

E7-26A. *Account for warranties. (LO 2).* When Park Avenue Pet Shop sells a puppy, it provides a health warranty for the little critter. If a puppy becomes ill in the first two years after the sale, Park Avenue Pet Shop will pay the vet bill up to $300. Because this is normally a significant expense for the shop, the accountant insists that Park Avenue Pet Shop record an estimated warranty liability at the end of every year before the financial statements are prepared. On December 31, 2010, the accountant estimated that the warranty costs for puppies sold in 2010 would be $2,000 and made the appropriate entry to record that liability. On March 30, 2011, the store received a $50 vet bill from one of its customers, who had bought a puppy in 2010. Park Avenue Pet Shop wrote a check for $50 to reimburse the puppy's owner.

1. Enter the transaction into the accounting equation to record the estimated warranty liability at December 31, 2010.
2. Enter the transaction into the accounting equation to record the payment of the vet bill on March 30, 2011. What effect did this payment have on the 2011 financial statements of Park Avenue Pet Shop?

E7-27A. *Account for long-term liabilities. (LO 3, 5).* Larry the Locksmith needed some long-term financing and arranged for a $200,000, 20-year mortgage loan on December 31, 2009. The interest rate is 7% per year, with $20,000 (rounded) payments made at the end of each year, starting December 31, 2010.

1. What is the amount of interest expense related to this loan for 2010?
2. What amount of liability should appear on the December 31, 2010, balance sheet?
3. What is the amount of interest expense related to this loan for 2011?
4. What amount of liability should appear on the December 31, 2011, balance sheet?

E7-28A. *Account for long-term liabilities. (LO 3, 5).* Grace's Gems purchased some property on December 31, 2011, for $100,000, paying $20,000 in cash and obtaining a mortgage loan for the other $80,000. The interest rate is 8% per year, with $2,925 payments made at the end of March, June, September, and December 2012.

1. What amounts should appear as interest expense on the quarterly income statements and as liabilities on the quarterly balance sheets during 2012?
2. What amount of interest expense should appear on the income statement for the year ended December 31, 2012?

E7-29A. *Account for long-term liabilities. (LO 3, 5).* Suppose MegaStore, Inc., signed a $750,000, 15-year, 10% note payable to finance the expansion of its business on January 1, 2010. The terms provide for semiannual payments of $49,000 on June 30 and December 31, 2010. On the December 31, 2010, balance sheet, how much will MegaStore show as the principal of this note payable?

E7-30A. *Account for long-term liabilities. (LO 3).* On April 1, Mark Hamm borrowed $15,000 on an eight-month, 6% note from State Bank of New York to open a business, Gymnastics World. The debt was in the company's name. The note and interest will be repaid on November 30.

1. Use the accounting equation to show how Gymnastics World would record the receipt of the funds.
2. Suppose Gymnastics World wants to prepare an income statement for the month of April. Use the accounting equation to show how the firm will accrue interest for the month.
3. Assume that Gymnastics World accrues the interest expense related to this note at the end of each month. What is the balance in the interest payable account on September 30?
4. Use the accounting equation to show how the firm would record the transaction on November 30, when the loan is repaid with the interest. (Assume 3. above was completed.)

E7-31A. *Account for bonds. (LO 4).* On December 31, 2009, Alejandro Enterprises issued $25,000 worth of 5% bonds at 99. These are 10-year bonds with interest paid annually on December 31.

1. What are the interest payments for the first two years?
2. Was the market interest rate higher or lower than 5% at the date of issue?
3. Will the interest expense be higher or lower than the interest payment?

E7-32A. *Account for bonds. (LO 4).* On December 31, 2010, Carl's Cartons, Inc., issued $100,000 worth of 9% bonds at 104. The interest on these bonds is paid annually on December 31.

1. What are the interest payments for the first two years?
2. Was the market interest rate higher or lower than 9% at the date of issue?
3. Will the interest expense be higher or lower than the interest payment?

E7-33A. *Account for bonds. (LO 4).* On January 1, 2010, Conway Computers issued $500,000, 15%, 10-year bonds at face value. Interest is payable on January 1. Use the accounting equation to record the following:

1. The bond issue
2. The accrual of interest on December 31, 2010
3. The payment of interest on January 1, 2011

E7-34A. *Account for bonds. (LO 4).* On December 31, 2012, Dave's Delivery Service issued $10,000 worth of 10% bonds at approximately 89. These are 10-year bonds with interest paid semiannually on June 30 and December 31.

1. What are the interest payments for the first two years?
2. Was the market interest rate higher or lower than 10% at the date of issue?
3. Will the interest expense be higher or lower than the interest payment?

E7-35A. *Account for bonds. (LO 4).* On June 30, 2009, Sam's Office Supplies issued $50,000 face value of 8% bonds at 106. They were five-year bonds with interest paid semiannually, on December 31 and June 30.

1. What are the interest payments for the first two years?
2. Was the market interest rate higher or lower than 8% at the date of issue?
3. Will the interest expense be higher or lower than the interest payment?

E7-36A. *Account for bonds. (LO 4).* On June 30, 2011, Sugar Fudge Co. issued $50,000 worth of 10% bonds for $50,000. The interest is paid annually on June 30.

1. What are the interest payments for the first two years?
2. Was the market interest rate higher or lower than 10% at the date of issue?
3. Will the interest expense be higher or lower than the interest payment?

E7-37A. *Calculate interest expense using the effective interest method. (LO 4, 5).* On June 30, 2010, Mako Company issued $50,000 worth of five-year, 10% bonds when the market rate was 9%. Proceeds were $51,945. The interest is paid annually on June 30.

1. What is the annual interest payment?
2. What is the amount of interest expense on the date of the first interest payment?
3. How would the bonds payable and the interest expense be shown on the year-end financial statements (June 30, 2011)?

E7-38A. *Calculate interest expense using the effective interest method. (LO 4, 5).* On June 30, 2010, Superfast Shoes issued $200,000 worth of 15-year, 9% bonds when the market rate was 10%. Proceeds were $184,788. The interest is paid annually on June 30.

1. What is the annual interest payment?
2. What is the amount of interest expense on the date of the first interest payment?
3. How would the bonds payable and the interest expense be shown on the year-end financial statements (June 30, 2011)?

E7-39A. *Prepare an amortization schedule for a bond issued at a discount. (LO 4).* Jamison Corporation issued $100,000, 8%, 10-year bonds on January 1, 2012, when the market rate of interest was 10%. Proceeds were $87,710.87. Interest is payable annually on January 1. Jamison uses the effective interest method to amortize bond premiums and discounts. Prepare an amortization schedule for the life of the bonds.

E7-40A. *Prepare an amortization schedule for a bond issued at a premium. (LO 4).* Old School Vacations issued $100,000, 10%, 10-year bonds on January 1, 2010, when the market rate of interest was 8%. Proceeds were $113,420.16. Interest is payable annually on January 1. Old School uses the effective interest method to amortize bond premiums and discounts. Prepare an amortization schedule for the life of the bonds.

Use the following financial data for eBay to answer E7-41A:

> ### From the Consolidated Balance Sheet of eBay Inc.

	December 31, 2007	December 31, 2008
	(dollars in thousands)	
Assets		
Total current assets	$ 7,122,505	$ 6,286,590
Total assets	$15,366,037	$15,592,439
Liabilities and stockholders' equity		
Total current liabilities	$ 3,099,579	$ 3,705,087
Total liabilities	3,661,435	4,508,581
Total stockholders' equity	11,704,602	11,083,858
Total liabilities and stockholders' equity	$15,366,037	$15,592,439

E7-41A. *Calculate the debt-to-equity ratio. (LO 6).* Using the information provided for eBay, calculate the debt-to-equity ratio at December 31, 2007, and December 31, 2008. (Notice that eBay puts the most recent year in the right column rather than the usual left column.) Provide an explanation of what this ratio measures and whether the ratio has improved from 2007 to 2008.

Set B

E7-42B. *Classify liabilities. (LO 1, 2).* For each item in the following list, tell whether it is a definitely determinable liability, an estimated liability, or neither:

1. Amount of cash revenue received from customer that is unearned
2. Corporate income tax for the year
3. Coupons unredeemed at the end of the year (some percentage expected to be redeemed)
4. Amount of salaries payable to accrue at the end of the year
5. Account payable owed to vendor for purchase on credit

E7-43B. *Account for payroll. (LO 1).* A company has gross payroll of $30,000; federal income tax withheld of $6,000; and FICA (social security) taxes and Medicare taxes withheld of $2,295.

1. How much will the balance sheet show for salaries payable (to employees)?
2. How much will the income statement show for salary expense?
3. What type of liability is salaries payable?

E7-44B. *Account for payroll. (LO 1).* During March, the Wessue Coffee Emporium's employees earned wages of $18,000. Social security (FICA) withheld was $1,377; federal income taxes withheld were $3,600; and employees' contributions to the American Red Cross withheld totaled $175. Use the accounting equation to record wages expense and wages payable at the end of March. Wessue will pay employees their March wages and will pay the withholding taxes during the first week in April.

E7-45B. *Account for warranties. (LO 2).* When Boyd Pools installs a pool, it provides a three-year warranty (from the date of the sale) for any repairs needed that are not considered general maintenance. If a pool should need to be repaired in the first three years after the sale, Boyd will repair the pool for a cost of up to $1,000. Because this is normally a significant expense, the accountant insists that Boyd record an estimated warranty liability at the end of every year before the financial statements are prepared. On average, Boyd spends $400 per pool to fulfill its warranty obligations over the life of the warranty. For the year ended June 30, 2011, the accountant made the appropriate entry to record that liability based on sales and installations for the year of 360 pools. On January 4, 2012, Boyd paid $750 to an independent contractor to repair a pool for one of its customers, who had purchased the pool on March 15, 2011.

1. Enter the transaction into the accounting equation to record the estimated warranty liability at June 30, 2011.
2. Enter the transaction into the accounting equation to record the payment of the repair bill on January 4, 2012. For the year ended June 30, 2012, what effect did this payment have on the financial statements of Boyd Pools?

E7-46B. *Account for long-term liabilities. (LO 3, 5).* Mark's Martial Arts Academy needed some long-term financing and arranged for a $200,000, 20-year mortgage loan on December 31, 2009. The interest rate is 7.5% per year, with $19,620 (rounded) payments made at the end of each year, starting December 31, 2010.

1. What is the amount of interest expense related to this loan for 2010?
2. What amount of liability should appear on the December 31, 2010, balance sheet?
3. What is the amount of interest expense related to this loan for 2011?
4. What amount of liability should appear on the December 31, 2011, balance sheet?

E7-47B. *Account for long-term liabilities. (LO 3, 5).* Molly Merry's Accounting Firm purchased some property on December 31, 2010, for $150,000, paying $30,000 in cash and obtaining a mortgage loan for the other $120,000. The interest rate is 12% per year, with $8,065 payments made at the end of March, June, September, and December 2011.

1. What amounts should appear as interest expense on the quarterly income statements and as liabilities on the quarterly balance sheets during 2011?
2. What amount of interest expense should appear on the 2011 year-end income statement?

E7-48B. *Account for long-term liabilities. (LO 3).* The Decadent Ice Cream Company signed a $250,000, 15-year, 9% note payable to finance the expansion of its business on January 1. The terms provide for semiannual payments of $15,350 on June 30 and December 31. Use the accounting equation to record the receipt of the proceeds of the loan and the first two payments.

E7-49B. *Account for long-term liabilities. (LO 3, 5).* On March 1, Delvis Cromartie borrowed $7,500 on a five-month, 8% note from Florida First Bank & Trust to open a business, Orchids & Such Nursery. The debt was in the company's name. The note and interest will be repaid on July 31.

1. Use the accounting equation to record the receipt of the funds.
2. Suppose Orchids & Such Nursery wants to prepare an income statement for the month of March. Use the accounting equation to accrue interest for the month.
3. Assume that Orchids & Such Nursery accrues the interest expense related to this note at the end of each month. What is the balance in the interest payable account on May 31?
4. Use the accounting equation to record the transaction on July 31, when the loan is repaid with the interest. (Assume 3. above was completed.)

E7-50B. *Account for bonds. (LO 4).* On June 30, 2010, Kenneth's Watch Co. issued $50,000 worth of 6% bonds at 110. These are 10-year bonds with interest paid annually on June 30.

1. What are the interest payments for the first two years?
2. Was the market interest rate higher or lower than 6% at the date of issue?
3. Will the interest expense be higher or lower than the interest payment?

E7-51B. *Account for bonds. (LO 4).* On February 28, 2011, Newman & Spears Enterprises, Inc., issued $150,000 worth of 7% bonds at 92. The interest on these bonds is paid annually on February 28.

1. What are the interest payments for the first two years?
2. Was the market interest rate higher or lower than 7% at the date of issue?
3. Will the interest expense be higher or lower than the interest payment?

E7-52B. *Account for bonds. (LO 4).* On January 1, 2011, Allied Robotics issued $500,000, 4%, five-year bonds at par. Interest is payable on January 1. Use the accounting equation to record the following:

1. The bond issue
2. The accrual of interest on December 31, 2011
3. The payment of interest on January 1, 2012

E7-53B. *Account for bonds. (LO 4).* On June 30, 2010, McCorvey's Lawn Service issued $7,500 worth of 6% bonds at approximately 102. These are five-year bonds with interest paid semi-annually on December 31 and June 30.

1. What are the interest payments for the first two years?
2. Was the market interest rate higher or lower than 6% at the date of issue?
3. Will the interest expense be higher or lower than the interest payment?

E7-54B. *Account for bonds. (LO 4).* On December 31, 2012, Advanced Defense Contractors issued $25,000 face value of 10% bonds at 95. They were five-year bonds with interest paid semi-annually, on June 30 and December 31.

1. What are the interest payments for the first two years?
2. Was the market interest rate higher or lower than 10% at the date of issue?
3. Will the interest expense be higher or lower than the interest payment?

E7-55B. *Account for bonds. (LO 4).* On June 30, 2010, Nikki C. Records, Inc., issued $35,000 worth of 8% bonds for $35,000. The interest is paid annually on June 30.

1. What are the interest payments for the first two years?
2. Was the market interest rate higher or lower than 8% at the date of issue?
3. Will the interest expense be higher or lower than the interest payment?

E7-56B. *Calculate interest expense using the effective interest method. (LO 4, 5).* On March 30, 2009, Canine Company issued $80,000 worth of 10-year, 6% bonds when the market rate was 5%. Proceeds were $86,177. The interest is paid annually on March 30.

1. What is the annual interest payment?
2. What is the amount of interest expense on the date of the first interest payment?
3. How would the bonds payable and the interest expense be shown on the year-end (March 30, 2010) financial statements?

E7-57B. *Calculate interest expense using the effective interest method. (LO 4, 5).* On June 30, 2010, Dogs & Cats Pet Store issued $250,000 worth of 10-year, 9% bonds when the market rate was 6%. Proceeds from the bond issue were approximately $305,200. The interest is paid annually on June 30.

1. What is the annual interest payment?
2. What is the amount of interest expense on the date of the first interest payment?
3. How would the bonds payable and the interest expense be shown on the year-end (June 30, 2011) financial statements?

E7-58B. *Prepare an amortization schedule for a bond issued at a premium. (LO 4).* Designer Clothes, Inc., issued $200,000, 10%, 10-year bonds on July 1, 2011, when the market rate of interest was 8%. Interest is payable annually on July 1. Proceeds from the bond issue were approximately $226,840.33. Designer uses the effective interest method to amortize bond premiums and discounts. Prepare an amortization schedule for the life of the bonds.

E7-59B. *Prepare an amortization schedule for a bond issued at a discount. (LO 4).* Golden Coast Beach Resorts issued $1,000,000, 11%, 10-year bonds on June 30, 2009, when the market rate of interest was 10%. Proceeds from the bond issue were approximately $1,061,445.67. Interest is payable annually on June 30. Golden Coast uses the effective interest method to amortize bond premiums and discounts. Prepare an amortization schedule for the life of the bonds.

Use the following financial data for Netflix, Inc., to answer E7-60B.

	Netflix, Inc. Consolidated Balance Sheet (adapted)	

	December 31, 2007	December 31, 2008
	(dollars in thousands)	
Assets		
Total current assets	$432,423	$361,447
Total assets	$678,998	$617,946
Liabilities and Shareholders' Equity		
Total current liabilities	$208,905	$216,017
Total liabilities	249,186	270,791
Total shareholders' equity	429,812	347,155
Total liabilities and shareholders' equity	$678,998	$617,946

E7-60B. *Calculate the debt-to-equity ratio. (LO 6).* Using the information provided for Netflix, Inc., calculate the debt-to-equity ratio at December 31, 2007, and December 31, 2008. Provide an explanation of what this ratio measures and whether the ratio has improved from 2007 to 2008.

Problems
Set A

All of the A problems can be found within MyAccountingLab, an online homework and practice environment.

P7-61A. *Account for current liabilities. (LO 1, 5).* On March 1, 2011, the accounting records of Stein Company showed the following liability accounts and balances:

Accounts payable	$21,600
Short-term notes payable	10,000
Interest payable	800
Unearned service revenue	12,500

a. On March 1, 2011, Stein Company signed a three-month note for $12,000 at 7.5%.

b. During March, Stein Company paid off the $10,000 short-term note and the interest payable shown on the March 1 balance sheet.

c. Stein paid off the beginning accounts payable.

d. During the month, Stein purchased $25,000 of merchandise on account.

e. Also during March, Stein's employees earned salaries of $36,000. Withholdings related to these wages were $2,232 for social security (FICA), $3,800 for federal income tax, and $1,140 for state income tax. The company will pay March salaries and taxes withheld on April 1. No entry had been recorded for salaries or payroll tax expense as of March 31.

Requirements

1. Use the accounting equation to show each of the transactions.
2. Use the accounting equation to show the adjustments needed for interest on the notes payable for the month of March and for salary expense and payroll tax expense.
3. Prepare the current liabilities section of the balance sheet at March 31, 2011.

P7-62A. *Account for warranties. (LO 2).* In 2012, Best Stuff, Inc., had sales of $90,000 of its new video recorders. The company gives a two-year warranty with the purchase of a video recorder. When Best Stuff recorded the sales, the company also estimated that it would spend $8,400 to honor those warranties. When the company prepared its annual financial statements for 2012, no video recorders had been brought in for repair. In January 2013, however, 20 people brought in their broken video recorders, and Best Stuff spent a total of $750 repairing them (at no charge to the customers, because the video recorders were under warranty). Assume no additional sales were made in January 2013 (i.e., no new warranties were given in January).

Requirements

1. How much warranty expense related to the sales of video recorders would Best Stuff show on an income statement for the year 2012?
2. Would Best Stuff have a warranty liability on the balance sheet at the end of 2012? If so, how much?
3. How much warranty expense would Best Stuff show on an income statement for the month of January 2013 related to these video recorders?
4. Would Best Stuff have a warranty liability on the balance sheet at January 31, 2013? If so, how much?

P7-63A. *Account for notes payable with periodic payments of principal and interest. (LO 3).* Ultra Power, Inc., engaged in the following transactions related to long-term liabilities during 2011:

    a. On March 1, the company borrowed $50,000 for a machine. The loan is to be repaid in equal annual payments of $6,793 at the end of each of the next 10 years (beginning February 28, 2012); the interest rate is 6%.

    b. On October 1, the company borrowed $100,000 from the local credit union at an interest rate of 8%. The loan is for seven years, and Ultra Power will make annual payments of $19,207 on September 30 of each year.

Requirements

1. For each loan, prepare an amortization schedule for the first four payments. Show the reduction in principal and the interest expense for each payment.
2. What total interest expense related to these two loans would Ultra Power, Inc., show on its income statement for the year ended December 31, 2011?
3. How much interest payable would Ultra Power, Inc., show on its balance sheet at December 31, 2011?

P7-64A. *Account for notes payable with periodic payments of principal and interest. (LO 3).* Joe Brinks is making plans to finance the following projects:

    a. Purchase a truck for $30,000 to be repaid in equal monthly payments of $601 over the next five years. The bank has quoted an interest rate of 7.5%.

    b. Purchase a piece of land, whose owner is offering to sell it to Joe for $25,000. The seller would accept five annual payments of $6,595 at 10%.

    c. Sell some old equipment for $4,000. Joe is willing to accept quarterly payments of $546 for the next two years at an interest rate of 8%.

    d. Purchase land and building for $50,000, with a down payment of $5,000, and semiannual payments of $3,095 for the next 10 years at an interest rate of 6.5%.

Requirement

For each independent scenario, show the transactions in the accounting equation for the first two payments.

P7-65A. *Account for bonds payable. (LO 4).* Julie's Cleaning Service issued $25,000 worth of 10-year bonds at 105. The bonds have a stated rate of 9%.

Requirements

1. Was the market interest rate at the time of issue higher or lower than 9%? How do you know?
2. What were the proceeds from the bond issue?
3. Will the interest expense each period be higher or lower than the interest payment?
4. Will the book value of the bonds be higher or lower than $25,000 after five years?

P7-66A. *Account for bonds payable. (LO 4).* Adam Ship Builders issued $5 million of its 7% bonds on February 8, 2010, at 96. The bonds mature on June 30, 2020. Interest is payable semi-annually on June 30 and December 31.

Requirements

1. What were the proceeds from the bond issue?
2. Was the market interest rate at the time of issue higher or lower than 7%?
3. Will interest expense each period be higher or lower than the interest payment?
4. What will the book value of the bonds be at maturity?

Set B

P7-67B. *Account for current liabilities. (LO 1, 5).* On May 1, 2010, the accounting records of Sea Salt Company showed the following liability accounts and balances:

Accounts payable	$35,600
Short-term notes payable	15,000
Interest payable	950
Unearned service revenue	6,000

a. On May 1, 2010, Sea Salt Company signed a six-month note for $20,000 at 6%.
b. During May, Sea Salt Company paid off the $15,000 short-term note and the interest payable shown on the May 1 balance sheet.
c. The company also paid off the beginning balance in accounts payable.
d. During the month, Sea Salt purchased $40,000 of merchandise on account.
e. Also during May, Sea Salt's employees earned salaries of $25,000. Withholdings related to these wages were $1,550 for social security (FICA), $5,000 for federal income tax, and $2,500 for state income tax. The company will pay May salaries and taxes withheld on June 1. No entry had been recorded for salaries or payroll tax expense as of May 31.

Requirements

1. Use the accounting equation to record the transactions described.
2. Show how Sea Salt Company would record the interest on the notes payable for the month of May and the salary expense and payroll tax expense.
3. Prepare the current liabilities section of the balance sheet at May 31, 2010.

P7-68B. *Account for warranties. (LO 2).* Fancy Frames prepares monthly financial statements. The following took place during the months of April and May at Fancy Frames:

a. In April, $15,000 worth of frames was sold. Each is guaranteed for 12 months. Any defective frame will be repaired or replaced free of charge during that period.
b. Fancy Frames estimated that it would cost $500 during the next year to honor the warranties on the April sales.
c. During May, Fancy Frames spent $150 dollars to honor warranties related to April sales.

Requirements

1. What amount of warranty expense would be shown on the income statement for April?
2. What amount of warranty liability would be shown on the April 30 balance sheet?
3. What effect did recording the warranty expense have on owner's equity?

4. What amount of warranty expense related to these frames would be shown on the income statement for May?
5. What effect did spending the $150 in May have on owner's equity?

P7-69B. *Account for notes payable with periodic payments of principal and interest. (LO 3, 5).* Zelda's Diamond Emporium engaged in the following transactions related to long-term liabilities during 2009:

a. On July 1, 2009, the company borrowed $150,000 for a new piece of office equipment. The loan is to be repaid in equal annual payments of $15,444 at the end of each of the next 15 years (beginning June 30, 2010); and the interest rate Zelda's is paying for this loan is 6%.
b. On October 1, the company borrowed $250,000 from the local credit union at an interest rate of 8%. The loan is for 15 years, and Zelda's will make annual payments of $29,207 on September 30 of each year.

Requirements

1. For each loan, prepare an amortization schedule for the first four payments. Show the reduction in principal and the interest expense for each payment.
2. What total interest expense related to these two loans would Zelda's show on its income statement for the year ended December 31, 2009?
3. How much interest payable would Zelda's show on its balance sheet at December 31, 2009?

P7-70B. *Account for notes payable with periodic payments of principal and interest. (LO 3).* Black Company is making plans to finance the following projects:

a. Purchase a boat for $50,000 to be repaid in equal monthly payments of $977.51 over the next six years. The bank has quoted an interest rate of 12%.
b. Purchase a property for $125,000. The seller would accept 10 semiannual payments of $15,411.37 at 8% (annual rate).
c. Sell some old equipment for $8,000. Black Company is willing to accept quarterly payments of $1,092 for the next two years at an interest rate of 8% (annual rate).
d. Purchase land and building for $250,000, with a down payment of $50,000, and semiannual payments of $16,048.52 for the next 10 years at an interest rate of 10% (annual rate).

Requirement

For each situation, use the accounting equation to show how the firm would record the first two payments.

P7-71B. *Account for bonds payable. (LO 4).* Hard Top Patios issued $225,000 worth of five-year bonds with a stated interest rate of 9.5% and interest payable annually on December 31. The bonds were issued at 95. The bonds were issued on January 1, 2012. The fiscal year end is December 31.

Requirements

1. Was the market interest rate at the time of issue higher or lower than 9.5%? Explain.
2. Will the interest payment be more or less than the interest expense each year?
3. Will the carrying value be more or less than $225,000 after three years? After four years? At maturity?

P7-72B. *Account for bonds payable. (LO 4).* Fischer's Fishing Gear issued $100,000 worth of 15-year bonds at 105. The bonds have a stated rate of 6%.

Requirements

1. What were the proceeds from the bond issue?
2. Describe the change in carrying value of the bonds over the 15-year life.
3. Will interest expense be larger or smaller than the interest payment each year?

Financial Statement Analysis

FSA7-1. *Calculate debt-to-equity ratio and analyze financial data. (LO 5, 6, 7).* The following information comes from the balance sheet of Nordstrom, Inc.:

Nordstrom, Inc.
Consolidated Balance Sheets (partial)
(in millions)

	January 31, 2009	February 2, 2008
Liabilities and Shareholders' Equity		
Current liabilities:		
Commercial paper	$ 275	–
Accounts payable	563	$ 556
Accrued salaries, wages and related benefits	214	268
Other current liabilities	525	550
Current portion of long-term debt	24	261
Total current liabilities	1,601	1,635
Long-term debt, net	2,214	2,236
Deferred property incentives, net	435	369
Other liabilities	201	245
Commitments and contingencies		
Shareholders' equity:		
Common stock, no par value: 1,000 shares authorized; 215.4 and 220.9 shares issued and outstanding	997	936
Retained earnings	223	201
Accumulated other comprehensive loss	(10)	(22)
Total shareholders' equity	1,210	1,115
Total liabilities and shareholders' equity	$5,661	$5,600

1. Calculate the debt-to-equity ratio for the years shown.
2. Who would be interested in this information and why?
3. Suppose you were considering investing in some stock. What do you think of the change in this ratio from one year to the next?
4. If Nordstrom, Inc., has bonds payable, where do you think they might be included on the balance sheet?
5. What risks are associated with the long-term debt on Nordstrom's balance sheet?

FSA7-2. *Calculate debt-to-equity ratio and analyze financial data. (LO 5, 6, 7).* The following information comes from the balance sheet of Micros Systems, Inc.:

Micros Systems, Inc., and Subsidiaries
Consolidated Balance Sheets

	June 30,	
(in thousands, except par value data)	2008	2007
Assets		
Current Assets:		
Cash and cash equivalents	$ 381,964	$242,702
Short-term investments	—	86,950
Accounts receivable, net of allowance for doubtful accounts of $28,348 at June 30, 2008, and $23,110 at June 30, 2007	192,445	180,203
Inventory, net	64,575	47,790
Deferred income taxes	18,724	16,683
Prepaid expenses and other current assets	29,737	27,650
Total current assets	687,445	601,978
Investments, non-current	65,216	—
Property, plant, and equipment, net	29,165	27,955
Deferred income taxes, non-current	7,108	23,145
Goodwill	159,722	138,332
Intangible assets, net	16,168	14,509
Purchased and internally developed software costs, net of accumulated amortization of $61,691 at June 30, 2008, and $54,708 at June 30, 2007	30,846	36,296
Other assets	7,336	4,541
Total assets	$1,003,006	$846,756
Liabilities and shareholders' equity		
Current Liabilities:		
Bank lines of credit	$ 989	$ 2,308
Accounts payable	46,843	43,126
Accrued expenses and other current liabilities	124,913	117,142
Income taxes payable	6,363	8,094
Deferred revenue	115,398	86,742
Total current liabilities	294,506	257,412
Income taxes payable, non-current	18,302	—
Deferred income taxes, non-current	2,181	15,934
Other non-current liabilities	8,103	17,554
Total liabilities	323,092	290,900
Minority interests and minority ownership put arrangement	6,898	4,723
Commitments and contingencies (Note 12)		
Shareholders' equity:		
Common stock, $0.00625 par value; authorized 120,000 shares; issued and outstanding 80,898 at June 30, 2008 and 81,096 at June 30, 2007	506	507
Capital in excess of par	131,517	149,089
Retained earnings	480,777	382,785
Accumulated other comprehensive income	60,216	18,752
Total shareholders' equity	673,016	551,133
Total liabilities and shareholders' equity	$1,003,006	$846,756

The accompanying notes are an integral part of the consolidated financial statements.

1. Calculate the debt-to-equity ratio for the years shown.
2. Who would be interested in this information and why?
3. Suppose you were considering investing in some of this firm's stock. What do you think of the change in this ratio from one year to the next?
4. If Micros Systems has bonds payable, where do you think they might be included on the balance sheet?
5. What risks are associated with the long-term debt on the balance sheet of Micros Systems, Inc.?

FSA7-3. *Calculate the debt-to-equity ratio and analyze financial data. (LO 6, 7).* Use Books-A-Million's financial statements, which can be found in Appendix A at the back of the book, to answer the following questions:

1. What types of debt does Books-A-Million have? Where did you find this information?
2. Compute the debt-to-equity ratio for at least two consecutive years. What information do these ratios provide?
3. Does Books-A-Million mention any risks associated with its long-term debt? If so, where does it mention them?

Critical Thinking Problems

Risks and Controls

One of the risks of borrowing money is changing interest rates. For example, if a company issues bonds when the market rate is 7%, what happens if the market rate goes down while the bonds are outstanding? Name some actions a company could take to control this risk. For several companies that have outstanding long-term debt, read the notes to the financial statements that address this interest rate risk.

Ethics

Lucy Shafer wants to borrow $100,000 to expand her dog-breeding business. She is preparing a set of financial statements to take to the local bank with her loan application. She currently has an outstanding loan from her uncle for $50,000. Lucy's uncle is letting her borrow the money at a very low interest rate, and she does not need to make any principal payments for five years. Due to the favorable terms of the loan from her uncle, Lucy has decided that it is not significant enough to disclose on her financial statements. Instead, Lucy has classified the $50,000 as contributed capital, and the interest payments are included in miscellaneous expenses on Lucy's income statement.

1. What are the effects of Lucy's classifications of her uncle's loan and the related interest payments on the financial statements?
2. Are there any ratios that might be of interest to the local bank that will be misstated by Lucy's actions?
3. Do you think Lucy's actions are unethical? Suppose Lucy's uncle agrees to be a partner in the company until Lucy can afford to buy his share by repaying the $50,000 with interest. Does that change your opinion?

Group Assignment

With the class divided into groups, assign one of the following companies to each group:

Southwest Airlines
Delta Airlines
United Airlines
AirTran
Continental Airlines

For your company, analyze the liability section of the balance sheet. For each liability, write a short description. Use information from the notes to help you. Then, calculate the debt-to-equity ratio for the years with available information. What tentative conclusions can you draw about the debt position of your airline?

Internet Exercise: Starbucks

Starbucks is the number one specialty coffee retailer, operating more than 16,000 coffee shops around the world. The company also sells coffee beans to restaurants, businesses, airlines, and hotels and offers mail-order and online shopping. Go to CNN Money, at http://money.com or http://finance.yahoo.com and enter the company symbol SBUX, the stock symbol of the Starbucks Corporation, and then find the financial statements.

IE7-1. Use the annual balance sheet. Identify amounts reported for total liabilities and total shareholders' equity at the three most recent year ends.

IE7-2. Calculate the debt-to-equity ratio (total liabilities to total shareholders' equity) for each year end.

IE7-3. Do owners or creditors have more claims on the Starbucks' assets? How can you tell?

IE7-4. What types of financial risks apply to Starbucks?

Appendix 7

Time Value of Money

L.O.8
Compute present value and proceeds from a bond issue.

If you ever used a credit card or borrowed money for longer than one year, you have experience with the time value of money. The term means that money has value over time. That's because money that you invest can earn interest. A person would prefer to receive a dollar today rather than receive a dollar a year from now because the dollar received today can earn interest during the year. Then, it will be worth *more* than a dollar a year from now.

Simple versus Compound Interest

We have calculated the interest on the principal of a loan in several chapters. When interest is computed on the principal only, it is called *simple interest*. Simple interest usually applies to short-term loans, which are loans with terms of one year or less.

When interest is computed on the principal of a loan *plus* any interest that has been earned but not collected or paid, it is called *compound interest*. The interest earned during a year is added to the original principal, and that new larger amount is used to calculate the interest earned during the next year. Each year, the interest is calculated on a larger amount. The larger amount comes from adding each successive year's earned interest to the prior year's interest plus the initial principal.

Exhibit 7A.1 on the following page shows what happens to $1,000 if you invest it today and watch it grow over 10 years. You can easily see that compound interest makes your money grow much faster than simple interest.

You can use the concept of compound interest to calculate the amount of money you will have at some point in the future with a deposit made today. Let's work through an example.

How much money will you have in 10 years if you deposit $1,000 today and it earns 10% interest per year?

- If the money earns simple interest, you'll have $2,000 at the end of 10 years. Each year, the principal of $1,000 will earn $100.
- If the money earns compound interest, you'll have $2,594 at the end of 10 years. Each year, the principal *plus the previously earned interest* will earn interest.

Present Value

Sometimes we want to know how much a future amount is worth today. That is, we want to know the **present value** of a future cash flow.

PRESENT VALUE OF A SINGLE AMOUNT. The present value of a sum of money to be received in the future is the value in *today's dollars*. If you are promised a payment of $100 one year from today, how much is it worth today? In other words, how much would you have to deposit today to have it grow to be $100 in a year? Here's the formula for calculating present value:

The **present value** is the value today of a given amount to be invested or received in the future, assuming compound interest.

$$PV = FV_n \left(\frac{1}{(1 + i)^n} \right)$$

where PV = present value
  FV = future value
  n = number of periods
  i = interest rate

EXHIBIT 7A.1

Simple versus Compound Interest

Deposit today at 10% annual interest	You'll have this much at the end of **Year 1**	...at the end of **Year 2**	...at the end of **Year 3**	...at the end of **Year 4**	...at the end of **Year 5**	...at the end of **Year 6**	...at the end of **Year 7**	...at the end of **Year 8**	...at the end of **Year 9**	You'll have this much at the end of **Year 10**
Simple interest										
$1,000	$1,100	$1,200	$1,300	$1,400	$1,500	$1,600	$1,700	$1,800	$1,900	$2,000
Compound interest										
$1,000	$1,100	$1,210	$1,331	$1,464	$1,610	$1,772	$1,949	$2,144	$2,358	$2,594

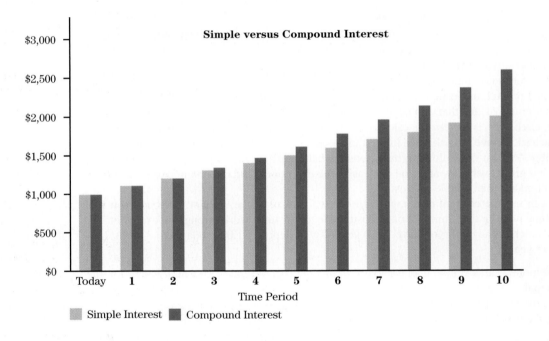

Let's compute the present value of $100 one year from now at an annual interest rate of 10%.

$$PV = \$100\ (1/(1 + 0.10)^1)$$
$$PV = \$100\ (0.90909)$$
$$PV = \$90.91$$

This calculation shows that having $90.91 today is equivalent to having $100 in one year, when the annual interest rate is 10%. We can check it out logically: If we deposit $90.91 today and it earns 10% interest per year, at the end of the year we will have $100 ($90.91 × 1.10 = $100.001).

Let's figure out the present value of $100 two years from now at an annual interest rate of 10%:

$$PV = \$100\ (1/(1 + 0.10)^2)$$
$$PV = \$100\ (0.82644628)$$
$$PV = \$82.6446$$

This calculation shows that having $82.6446 today is equivalent to having $100 in two years, when the interest rate is 10%. We can check it out logically: If we deposit $82.6446 today and earn 10% interest, we will have $90.909 [= 82.6446 (1 + 0.10)] after one year. Then, our

$90.909 has a year to earn 10% interest, so at the end of the second year we will have $99.9999—which rounds to $100.

Fortunately, we do not have to use the formula to calculate the present value of a future amount. We can use a present value table, a financial calculator, or Excel. Let's see how a present value table works.

The present value table is based on $1. A full table is provided at the end of this appendix, Exhibit 7A.5. To solve this problem, you can simply look at a small portion of that table, shown in Exhibit 7A.2. Find the 10% column and the 2-year row. The factor from the table is 0.82645. Multiply that factor by $100, and the present value is $82.645.

(n) periods	8%	9%	10%	11%
1	0.92593	0.91743	0.90909	0.90090
2	0.85734	0.84168	**0.82645**	0.81162
3	0.79383	0.77218	0.75131	0.73119
4	0.73503	0.70843	0.68301	0.65873

EXHIBIT 7A.2

From the Present Value of $1 Table

You can also compute present value on your financial calculator (some calculators may differ slightly):

- Enter $100 for the future value (*FV* key).
- Enter 10 for the interest rate (*i%* key, sometimes the I/Y key).
- Enter 2 for the number of periods (*n* key).
- Press **CPT** and then **PV** to compute the present value.

You should see $82.645 in the display.

Finding the present value of a future amount is called **discounting** the cash flow, and when discounting a cash flow, the interest rate is called the **discount rate**. Discounting a cash flow strips the amounts of the interest built in for the passage of time, bringing the cash flow back to equivalent dollars today.

PRESENT VALUE OF AN ANNUITY. In addition to discounting a single amount—often referred to as a lump sum—we may need to calculate the present value of a *series* of payments. A stream of deposits or payments that are the same and made periodically over equally spaced intervals is called an **annuity**. Its name comes from the idea of *annual* payments, because most annuities are annual. The present value of an annuity has many practical applications. Most present value problems involving annuities have payments at the end of the period, and they are called **ordinary annuities**. First, try a simple example to see how the formulas work (Your Turn 7A-1). Then, we'll look at some examples that may be familiar to you—buying a motorcycle or a car by borrowing money and making payments to repay the loan.

Discounting means to compute the present value of future cash flows.

The **discount rate** is the interest rate used to compute the present value of future cash flows.

An **annuity** is a series of equal cash receipts or cash payments over equally spaced intervals of time.

An **ordinary annuity** is an annuity whose payments are made at the end of each interval or period.

John wants to have $5,000 in five years. How much should he deposit today to have $5,000 in five years if the annual interest rate is 10%? In other words, what is the present value of $5,000 in five years? Try using the formula, the present value table, and your financial calculator (if you have one).

Your Turn 7A-1

Suppose you are selling your old motorcycle and a friend offers you a series of four payments of $500 each at the end of each of the next four years. How much is your friend actually offering for your motorcycle? It's *not* simply 4 × $500, or $2,000, because of the time value of money. Getting $500 a year from now is *not* the same as getting $500 today. To find out how much a series of four payments of $500 over the next four years is worth today, you need to use an appropriate interest rate and discount the payments to get the present value of each payment. Suppose the interest rate is 5% per year.

The first payment, made at the end of one year, will be discounted back one year. The second payment, made at the end of two years, will be discounted back two years. And so on, for the third and fourth payments. The present value of the series of payments will be the sum of the individual present value amounts. Here's how it looks in the formula:

$$PV = FV_n\left(\frac{1}{(1+i)^n}\right)$$

$$PV = \$500(1/(1+.05)^1) = 500(0.95238) = \$476.19$$

$$PV = \$500(1/(1+.05)^2) = 500(0.90703) = \$453.51$$

$$PV = \$500(1/(1+.05)^3) = 500(0.86384) = \$431.92$$

$$PV = \$500(1/(1+.05)^4) = 500(0.82270) = \underline{\$411.35}$$

$$\text{Total } PV = \underline{\$1{,}772.97}$$

This calculation shows that, if you could deposit $1,772.97 today to earn 5%, you would be indifferent between receiving $1,772.97 today and receiving four payments of $500 each at the end of each of the next four years. Another way to express the same idea is that your friend is paying you $1,772.97 for your motorcycle by offering you the four $500 annual payments. The difference between the total payments of $2,000 and the $1,772.97 price of the motorcycle is interest.

The present value of an annuity table compiles the individual factors from the present value of $1 table. A full present value of an annuity table is provided at the end of this appendix in Exhibit 7A.6. Rather than using the present value table four times, we can use the present value of an annuity table, which provides a single factor to solve the same problem. Find the column for 5% and the row for 4 (periods), and you'll see the factor of 3.54595. If you multiply the payment of $500 by the factor 3.54595 you'll get **$1,772.98**. (It's off by a cent due to rounding the factors.)

EXHIBIT 7A.3

From the Present Value of an Annuity Table

(n) periods	4%	5%	6%	7%
3	2.77509	2.72325	2.67301	2.62432
4	3.62990	**3.54595**	3.46511	3.38721
5	4.45182	4.32948	4.21236	4.10020
6	5.24214	5.07569	4.91732	4.76654

You may want to compute present value of an annuity on your financial calculator.

- Enter $500 as the payment (**PMT** key);
- enter 4 as the number of periods (**n** key);
- enter 5 as the interest rate (**i%** or the I/Y key); then
- press the **CPT** key, followed by the **PV** key.

You'll see $1,772.98 in the display. That's the present value of the series of payments.

Let's look at buying a car as an example. Suppose you find a car that you want to buy for $23,000. You have $1,000 for a down payment, and you'll have to borrow $22,000. If you borrow the money for three years at an annual interest rate of 6%, how much will your monthly payments be? Pay special attention to the timing of the payments in this situation. Rather than making annual payments, you'll be making monthly payments. To accommodate this payment plan, you'll need to make sure your time periods, n, and your interest rate, $i\%$, are both expressed with the same time frame. If the period is a month, the annual interest rate must be changed to a monthly interest rate. You are borrowing money for 36 periods (= 3 years × 12 months per year) at a rate of 1/2% (= 0.50% or .005) per month (that's an annual rate of 6%).

In this case, you have the present value—that's the amount you are borrowing for the car. We need to find the payment, which is actually a *series of payments,* when we already know the present value. Exhibit 7A.4 shows a portion of the present value of an annuity table with the factors we need. (The factors for 36 periods have been added because we need it for this problem.)

PV (annuity) = Payment x (factor for 36 periods, 0.5%)
$22,000 = Payment x (32.87102)
Payment = $669.28

So, your monthly car payment would be $669.28, to be paid at the end of each of the next 36 months.

(n) periods	0.50%	1%	2%	3%
35	32.03537	29.40858	24.99862	21.48722
36 →	**32.87102**	30.10751	25.48884	21.83225
37	33.70250	30.79951	25.96945	22.16724
38	34.52985	31.48466	26.44064	22.49246

EXHIBIT 7A.4

From the Present Value of an Annuity Table

Calculating the Proceeds from the Issue of Bonds

Earlier in this chapter you read that the market sets the price of a bond based on the market rate of interest and the cash flows that the bond represents. The market does this by discounting the cash flows to their present value, using the market rate of interest. Let's use the example from the chapter to see how the market sets the price for a bond. Recall that Muzby Minerals issued a $1,000 bond for six years with interest paid annually and a stated interest rate of 5%.

BONDS ISSUED AT PAR. If the market rate of interest and the stated rate of interest on the bond are the same, investors will pay exactly the face value for the bonds. The cash flows associated with the bond are the annual interest payments of $50 at the end of each of the next six years and a lump sum principal payment of $1,000 at the end of the sixth year. If this series of cash flows is sold for $1,000, then that means the buyers of the bond believe that is the present value—today's value—of those future cash flows. Let's check it out:

PV of $50 payments for 6 years using a discount rate of 5% =

50 payments	×	5.07569 PV of an annuity 5%, 6 years	=	$253.78 PV of the interest payments

plus the PV of $1,000 in 6 years =

$1,000 payment	×	0.74622 PV of $1 5%, 6 years	=	$746.22 PV of the principal payment

$1,000

BONDS ISSUED AT A DISCOUNT. However, if the market rate were more than 5%, investors would pay less for the bond than the face value because it would not take an amount as large as $1,000 today to cover the future 5% interest payments and the principal payment at the end of the life of the bonds. The present value of the cash flows would be less than $1,000, so the bonds would sell at less than par. As you learned earlier in this chapter, when bonds are issued with a stated rate less than the market rate, the bonds are issued at a discount.

Suppose the market rate of interest was 6% when the bond was issued. Because investors would require this return, the bonds must sell for less than $1,000. To calculate the issue price, you take the present value of the future cash flows associated with the bond. In other words, how much will the bondholders pay to receive $50 at the end of each of the next 6 years along with $1,000 at the end of year 6?

There are several ways to calculate the present value of these cash flows—using tables, financial calculators, and even Excel. In this example, we will use values from present value tables such as those found at the end of this appendix.

PV of $50 payments for 6 years using a discount rate of 6% =

50 payments	×	4.91732 PV of an annuity 6%, 6 years	=	$245.87 PV of the interest payments

plus the PV of $1,000 in 6 years =

$1,000 payment	×	0.70496 PV of $1 6%, 6 years	=	$704.96 PV of the principal payment

$950.83

The issue price of this bond would be $950.83.

Your Turn `7A-2` Suppose Action Company issues a $1,000, 10-year, 11.5% bond with interest payable annually at a time when the market interest rate is 12%. What are the proceeds—cash received by Action Company—from this bond issue?

BONDS ISSUED AT A PREMIUM. If, on the other hand, the bond with a 5% stated rate of interest is issued when the market rate of interest is less than 5%, investors will have to pay more for the bond than the face value because it will take more than $1,000 today to cover the future 5% interest payments and the principal payment at the end of the life of the bonds. The present value of the cash flows will be greater than $1,000, so the bonds will sell for more than par value. When bonds are issued with a stated rate higher than the market rate, the bonds are issued at a premium. The amount of the proceeds in excess of par is called the premium on bonds payable.

Suppose the market rate of interest was 4% when the bond with a stated rate of 5% was issued. Because the market would price the bonds to yield the market rate of return, the bonds would sell for more than $1,000. Think of the extra amount as the amount needed to help the company meet interest payments of 5%, the face rate. Just as with a discount situation, the issue price is equal to the present value of the future cash flows associated with the bond. In other words, how much will the bondholders pay to receive $50 at the end of each of the next 6 years along with $1,000 at the end of year 6?

The present value of the future cash flows is calculated as follows.

> PV of $50 payments for 6 years using a discount rate of 4% =
> 50 × 5.24214 = $262.11
> plus the PV of $1,000 in 6 years =   } $1,052.42
> 1,000 × 0.79031= $790.31

The issue price of this bond would be $1,052.42.

Your Turn `7A-3` Suppose HPS Company issues a $1,000 face value, 10-year, 11.5% bond, with interest payable annually. At the time of issue, the market interest rate is 10%. How much money will HPS get for the bond?

Solutions to YOUR TURN Questions

Your Turn 7A-1

$5,000 × 0.62092 = $3,104.60

Your Turn 7A-2

The PV of the interest payments = $115 × 5.65022 =	$649.78
The PV of the principal payment = $1,000 × 0.32197 =	$321.97
The proceeds—cash received for the bond =	$971.75

Your Turn 7A-3

The PV of the interest payments = $115 × 6.14457 =	$ 706.63
The PV of the principal payment = $1,000 × 0.38554 =	$ 385.54
The proceeds—cash received for the bond =	$1,092.17

Short Exercises

MyAccountingLab

The A exercises can be found within MyAccountingLab, an online homework and practice environment.

SE7A-1A. *Present value. (LO 8).* Suppose you want to have $5,000 saved at the end of five years. The bank will pay 2% interest on your money. How much would you have to deposit today to have the $5,000 you want at the end of five years?

SE7A-2B. *Present value. (LO 8).* Able Company has offered to sell Cane Company some used office equipment. Able wants Cane to pay $100 per quarter (three-month period) for the next three years, with the payment due at the end of each quarter. Suppose the appropriate discount rate is 4. What is the actual sale price of the office equipment?

Exercises

E7A-3A. *Calculate payments using time value of money concepts. (LO 8).* For each of the following, calculate the payment each loan would require. Assume the payments are made at the end of the period in each case. Interest rates are annual rates.
1. Principal = $30,000; interest rate = 5%; term = 5 years; payments = annual
2. Principal = $30,000; interest rate = 8%; term = 5 years; payments = annual
3. Principal = $30,000; interest rate = 8%; term = 10 years; payments = annual
4. Principal = $30,000; interest rate = 8%; term = 10 years; payments = semi-annual
5. Principal = $30,000; interest rate = 12%; term = 2 years; payments = monthly

E7A-4B. *Calculate payments using time value of money concepts. (LO 8).* For each of the following, calculate the payment each loan would require. Assume the payments are made at the end of the period in each case. Interest rates are annual rates.
1. Principal = $25,000; interest rate = 6%; term = 5 years; payments = annual
2. Principal = $25,000; interest rate = 9%; term = 5 years; payments = annual
3. Principal = $35,000; interest rate = 7%; term = 8 years; payments = annual
4. Principal = $35,000; interest rate = 7%; term = 8 years; payments = semiannual
5. Principal = $40,000; interest rate = 12%; term = 2 years; payments = monthly

Problems

MyAccountingLab

The A problem can be found within MyAccountingLab, an online homework and practice environment.

P7A-5A. *Account for bonds using time value of money concepts. (LO 8).* Andre's Imports issued $150,000 of bonds on January 1, 2009. The bonds mature on January 1, 2019. Interest is payable annually on December 31. The stated rate of interest is 10%, and the market rate of interest was 13% at the time of issue.

Requirements
1. Calculate the proceeds for the bond issue. How would issuing the bonds affect the financial statements for Andre's (on the date of issue)?
2. Prepare an amortization schedule for the first three years of the life of the bonds, showing the interest expense and the carrying value at the end of each interest period. Andre's uses the effective interest method for amortizing discounts and premiums.
3. How much interest expense related to these bonds would Andre's show on its income statement for the year ended December 31, 2010? (Assume effective interest method.)
4. Calculate the interest expense for the year ended December 31, 2010, using the straight-line method of amortization. Then, compare that amount to the amount calculated using the effective interest method. Which method do you think Andre's should use and why?

P7A-6B. *Account for bonds using time value of money concepts. (LO 8).* Gordon's Gadgets issued $2,000,000 of bonds on January 1, 2010. The bonds mature on January 1, 2018. Interest is payable annually each December 31. The stated rate of interest is 3%, and the market rate of interest was 2% at the time of issue.

Requirements

1. Calculate the proceeds for the bond issue. How would issuing the bonds affect the financial statements for Gordon's (on the date of issue)?
2. Prepare an amortization schedule for the first four years of the life of the bonds, showing the interest expense and the carrying value at the end of each interest period. Gordon's uses the effective interest method for amortizing discounts and premiums.
3. How much interest expense related to these bonds would Gordon's show on its income statement for the year ended December 31, 2015? (Assume effective interest method.)
4. Calculate the interest expense for the year ended December 31, 2015, using the straight-line method of amortization. Then, compare that amount to the amount calculated using the effective interest method. Which method do you think Gordon's should use and why?

EXHIBIT 7A.5

Present Value of a $1 Table

The Present Value of a Single Amount ($1)

$$PV = \frac{1}{(1+i)^n}$$

Periods	0.50%	1%	2%	3%	4%	5%	6%	7%	8%	9%	10%	11%	12%	13%	14%	15%
1	0.99502	0.99010	0.98039	0.97087	0.96154	0.95238	0.94340	0.93458	0.92593	0.91743	0.90909	0.90090	0.89286	0.88496	0.87719	0.86957
2	0.99007	0.98030	0.96117	0.94260	0.92456	0.90703	0.89000	0.87344	0.85734	0.84168	0.82645	0.81162	0.79719	0.78315	0.76947	0.75614
3	0.98515	0.97059	0.94232	0.91514	0.88900	0.86384	0.83962	0.81630	0.79383	0.77218	0.75131	0.73119	0.71178	0.69305	0.67497	0.65752
4	0.98025	0.96098	0.92385	0.88849	0.85480	0.82270	0.79209	0.76290	0.73503	0.70842	0.68301	0.65873	0.63552	0.61332	0.59208	0.57175
5	0.97537	0.95147	0.90573	0.86261	0.82193	0.78353	0.74726	0.71299	0.68058	0.64993	0.62092	0.59345	0.56743	0.54276	0.51937	0.49718
6	0.97052	0.94205	0.88797	0.83748	0.79031	0.74622	0.70496	0.66634	0.63017	0.59627	0.56447	0.53464	0.50663	0.48032	0.45559	0.43233
7	0.96569	0.93272	0.87056	0.81309	0.75992	0.71068	0.66506	0.62275	0.58349	0.54703	0.51316	0.48166	0.45235	0.42506	0.39964	0.37594
8	0.96089	0.92348	0.85349	0.78941	0.73069	0.67684	0.62741	0.58201	0.54027	0.50187	0.46651	0.43393	0.40388	0.37616	0.35056	0.32690
9	0.95610	0.91434	0.83676	0.76642	0.70259	0.64461	0.59190	0.54393	0.50025	0.46043	0.42410	0.39092	0.36061	0.33288	0.30751	0.28426
10	0.95135	0.90529	0.82035	0.74409	0.67556	0.61391	0.55839	0.50835	0.46319	0.42241	0.38554	0.35218	0.32197	0.29459	0.26974	0.24718
11	0.94661	0.89632	0.80426	0.72242	0.64958	0.58468	0.52679	0.47509	0.42888	0.38753	0.35049	0.31728	0.28748	0.26070	0.23662	0.21494
12	0.94191	0.88745	0.78849	0.70138	0.62460	0.55684	0.49697	0.44401	0.39711	0.35553	0.31863	0.28584	0.25668	0.23071	0.20756	0.18691
13	0.93722	0.87866	0.77303	0.68095	0.60057	0.53032	0.46884	0.41496	0.36770	0.32618	0.28966	0.25751	0.22917	0.20416	0.18207	0.16253
14	0.93256	0.86995	0.75788	0.66112	0.57748	0.50507	0.44230	0.38782	0.34046	0.29925	0.26333	0.23199	0.20462	0.18068	0.15971	0.14133
15	0.92792	0.86135	0.74301	0.64186	0.55526	0.48102	0.41727	0.36245	0.31524	0.27454	0.23939	0.20900	0.18270	0.15989	0.14010	0.12289
16	0.92330	0.85282	0.72845	0.62317	0.53391	0.45811	0.39365	0.33873	0.29189	0.25187	0.21763	0.18829	0.16312	0.14150	0.12289	0.10686
17	0.91874	0.84438	0.71416	0.60502	0.51337	0.43630	0.37136	0.31657	0.27027	0.23107	0.19784	0.16963	0.14564	0.12522	0.10780	0.09293
18	0.91414	0.83602	0.70016	0.58739	0.49363	0.41552	0.35034	0.29586	0.25025	0.21199	0.17986	0.15282	0.13004	0.11081	0.09456	0.08081
19	0.90959	0.82774	0.68643	0.57029	0.47464	0.39573	0.33051	0.27651	0.23171	0.19449	0.16351	0.13768	0.11611	0.09806	0.08295	0.07027
20	0.90506	0.81954	0.67297	0.55368	0.45639	0.37689	0.31180	0.25842	0.21455	0.17843	0.14864	0.12403	0.10367	0.08678	0.07276	0.06110
21	0.90056	0.81143	0.65978	0.53755	0.43883	0.35894	0.29416	0.24151	0.19866	0.16370	0.13513	0.11174	0.09256	0.07680	0.06383	0.05313
22	0.89608	0.80340	0.64684	0.52189	0.42196	0.34185	0.27751	0.22571	0.18394	0.15018	0.12285	0.10067	0.08264	0.06796	0.05599	0.04620
23	0.89162	0.79544	0.63416	0.50669	0.40573	0.32557	0.26180	0.21095	0.17032	0.13778	0.11168	0.09069	0.07379	0.06014	0.04911	0.04017
24	0.88719	0.78757	0.62172	0.49193	0.39012	0.31007	0.24698	0.19715	0.15770	0.12640	0.10153	0.08170	0.06588	0.05323	0.04308	0.03493
25	0.88277	0.77977	0.60953	0.47761	0.37512	0.29530	0.23300	0.18425	0.14602	0.11597	0.09230	0.07361	0.05882	0.04710	0.03779	0.03038
30	0.86103	0.74192	0.55207	0.41199	0.30832	0.23138	0.17411	0.13137	0.09938	0.07537	0.05731	0.04368	0.03338	0.02557	0.01963	0.01510
35	0.83982	0.70591	0.50003	0.35538	0.25342	0.18129	0.13011	0.09366	0.06763	0.04899	0.03558	0.02592	0.01894	0.01388	0.01019	0.00751
40	0.81914	0.67165	0.45289	0.30656	0.20829	0.14205	0.09722	0.06678	0.04603	0.03184	0.02209	0.01538	0.01075	0.00753	0.00529	0.00373

(PV = present value, i = interest rate per period in decimal form, n = number of periods)

EXHIBIT 7A.6

Present Value of an Annuity Table

The Present Value of Annuity $1.00 in Arrears*

$$PV_a = \frac{1}{i}\left[1 - \frac{1}{(1+i)^n}\right]$$

Periods	0.50%	1%	2%	3%	4%	5%	6%	7%	8%	9%	10%	11%	12%	13%	14%	15%
1	0.99502	0.99010	0.98039	0.97087	0.96154	0.95328	0.94340	0.93458	0.92593	0.91743	0.90909	0.90090	0.89286	0.88496	0.87719	0.86957
2	1.98510	1.97040	1.94156	1.91347	1.86609	1.85941	1.83339	1.80802	1.78326	1.75911	1.73554	1.71252	1.69005	1.66810	1.64666	1.62571
3	2.97025	2.94099	2.88388	2.82861	2.77509	2.72325	2.67301	2.62432	2.57710	2.53129	2.48685	2.44371	2.40183	2.36115	2.32163	2.28323
4	3.95050	3.90197	3.80773	3.71710	3.62990	3.54595	3.46511	3.38721	3.31213	3.23972	3.16987	3.10245	3.03735	2.97447	2.91371	2.85498
5	4.92587	4.85343	4.71346	4.57971	4.45182	4.32948	4.21236	4.10020	3.99271	3.88965	3.79079	3.69590	3.60478	3.51723	3.43308	3.35216
6	5.89638	5.79548	5.60143	5.41719	5.24214	5.07569	4.91732	4.76654	4.62288	4.48592	4.35526	4.23054	4.11141	3.99755	3.88867	3.78448
7	6.86207	6.72819	6.47199	6.23028	6.00205	5.78637	5.58238	5.38929	5.20637	5.03295	4.86842	4.71220	4.56376	4.42261	4.28830	4.16042
8	7.82296	7.65168	7.32548	7.01969	6.73274	6.46321	6.20979	5.97130	5.74664	5.53482	5.33493	5.14612	4.96764	4.79877	4.63886	4.48732
9	8.77906	8.56602	8.16224	7.78611	7.43533	7.10782	6.80169	6.51523	6.24689	5.99525	5.75902	5.53705	5.32825	5.13166	4.94637	4.77158
10	9.73041	9.47130	8.98259	8.53020	8.11090	7.72173	7.36009	7.02358	6.71008	6.41766	6.14457	5.88923	5.65022	5.42624	5.21612	5.01877
11	10.67703	10.36763	9.78685	9.25262	8.76048	8.30641	7.88687	7.49867	7.13896	6.80519	6.49506	6.20652	5.93770	5.68694	5.45273	5.23371
12	11.61893	11.25508	10.57534	9.95400	9.38507	8.86325	8.38384	7.94269	7.53608	7.16073	6.81369	6.49236	6.19437	5.91765	5.66029	5.42062
13	12.55615	12.13374	11.34837	10.63496	9.98565	9.39357	8.85268	8.35765	7.90378	7.48690	7.10336	6.74987	6.42355	6.12181	5.84236	5.58315
14	13.48871	13.00370	12.10625	11.29607	10.56312	9.89864	9.29498	8.74547	8.24424	7.78615	7.36669	6.98187	6.62817	6.30249	6.00207	5.72448
15	14.41662	13.86505	12.84926	11.93794	11.11839	10.37966	9.71225	9.10791	8.55948	8.06069	7.60608	7.19087	6.81086	6.46238	6.14217	5.84737
16	15.33993	14.71787	13.57771	12.56110	11.65230	10.83777	10.10590	9.44665	8.85137	8.31256	7.82371	7.37916	6.97399	6.60388	6.26506	5.95423
17	16.25863	15.56225	14.29187	13.16612	12.16567	11.27407	10.47726	9.73622	9.12164	8.54363	8.02155	7.54879	7.11963	6.72909	6.37286	6.04716
18	17.17277	16.39827	14.99203	13.75351	12.65930	11.68959	10.82760	10.05909	9.37189	8.75563	8.20141	7.70162	7.24967	6.83991	6.46742	6.12797
19	18.08236	17.22601	15.67846	14.32380	13.13394	12.08532	11.15812	10.33560	9.60360	8.95011	8.36492	7.83929	7.36578	6.91797	6.55037	6.19823
20	18.98742	18.04555	16.35143	14.87747	13.59033	12.46221	11.46992	10.59401	9.81815	9.12855	8.51356	7.96333	7.46944	7.02475	6.62313	6.25933
21	19.88798	18.85698	17.01121	15.41502	14.02916	12.82115	11.76408	10.83553	10.01680	9.29224	8.64869	8.07507	7.56200	7.10155	6.68696	6.31246
22	20.78406	19.66038	17.65805	15.93692	14.45112	13.16300	12.04158	11.06124	10.20074	9.44243	8.77154	8.17574	7.64465	7.16951	6.74294	6.35866
23	21.67568	20.45582	18.29220	16.44361	14.85684	13.48857	12.30338	11.27219	10.37106	9.58021	8.88322	8.26643	7.71843	7.22966	6.79206	6.39844
24	22.56287	21.24339	18.91393	16.93554	15.24696	13.79864	12.55036	11.46933	10.52876	9.70661	8.98474	8.34814	7.78432	7.28288	6.83514	6.43377
25	23.44564	22.02316	19.52346	17.41315	15.62208	14.09394	12.78336	11.65358	10.67478	9.82258	9.07704	8.42174	7.84314	7.32998	6.87293	6.46415
30	27.79405	25.80771	22.39646	19.60044	17.29203	15.37245	13.76483	12.40904	11.25778	10.27365	9.42691	8.69379	8.05518	7.49565	7.00266	6.56598
35	32.03537	29.40858	24.99862	21.48722	18.66461	16.37419	14.49825	12.94767	11.65457	10.56682	9.64416	8.85524	8.17550	7.58557	7.07005	6.61661
40	36.17223	32.83469	27.35548	23.11477	19.79277	17.15909	15.04620	13.33171	11.92461	10.75736	9.77908	8.95105	8.24378	7.63438	7.10504	6.64178

*Payments (or receipts) at the end of each period.

(PV_a = present value of an annuity, i = interest rate per period in decimal form, n = number of periods in which a payment is made or received)

Accounting for Shareholders' Equity

LEARNING OBJECTIVES

When you are finished studying Chapter 8, you should be able to:

1. Explain how a company finances its business with equity.

2. Account for the payment of cash dividends and calculate the allocation of dividends between common and preferred shareholders.

3. Define treasury stock, explain why a company would purchase treasury stock, and account for its purchase.

4. Explain stock dividends and stock splits.

5. Define retained earnings and account for its increases and decreases.

6. Prepare financial statements that contain equity transactions.

7. Compute return on equity and earnings per share, and explain what these ratios mean.

8. Recognize the business risks associated with shareholders' equity and the related controls.

ETHICS Matters

Buy Low, Sell High

Imagine that you owned quite a bit of a certain company's stock, and you were getting ready to sell it. You would certainly want to sell it for as high a price as possible. Perhaps you've heard the investment advice "buy low, sell high." Hopefully, you would not be willing to commit a crime to influence the price of the stock. This was not the case for a Seattle attorney and three others who were charged with fraud by the SEC in July 2009. These people were involved in a scheme that attempted to boost the price of a stock through recommendations based on false, misleading, or greatly exaggerated statements. This type of scheme is called "pump and dump." Pump up the stock price with false information and then dump (sell) your stock at the new, higher price. It generally happens with small, publicly-traded firms in which the perpetrator has a significant investment in the firm's stock and can influence others to buy it. The firm has to be small enough for its stock price to be influenced by a small number of buyers.

David Otto and three others have been accused of providing false and misleading press releases and information on Web sites about anti-aging, nutritional supplements that never existed. The chief executive of MitoPharm, the company said to be producing these supplements, was also charged in the crime. After they drove up the stock price with false information, the accused perpetrators sold their own stock in MitoPharm for more than a million dollars.

Source: "SEC Charges Four With Fraud," by Kathy Shwiff, *Wall Street Journal*, July 14, 2009, p. C8.

L.O.1
Explain how a company finances its business with equity.

Components of Shareholders' Equity in a Corporation—Contributed Capital

Every business has owners. As you learned in Chapter 1, there are three general forms of business organizations.

1. Sole proprietorships
2. Partnerships
3. Corporations

No matter which form a business takes, it needs money—contributions—from the owners to operate. With sole proprietorships and partnerships, individual owners use their own money or borrow money from family, friends, or banks. Corporations have access to more money because they sell stock to investors. In this chapter, we will focus on how a firm acquires and accounts for money from owners.

The claims of the owners to the assets of the firm are called shareholders' equity or stockholders' equity. Recall that there are two major parts to stockholders' equity—contributed capital and retained earnings. Each part is recorded and reported on the balance sheet as a separate amount. Contributed capital is the amount owners have invested in the corporation. Contributed capital is generally subdivided into two parts: capital stock and additional paid-in capital.

Stock—Authorized, Issued, and Outstanding

In return for their contributions, the owners receive shares of stock, representing units of ownership in the corporation. A corporation may have a variety of different ownership levels, usually known as classes of stock. All shares in the same class of stock have the same rights as every other share in that class. Rights of the shareholders, however, are different for different classes of stock. Every corporation has to have a class of stock that represents the basic ownership interest in the corporation, and that is called **common stock**.

When a corporation is formed, the state in which the firm incorporates requires an agreement called a charter that specifies the characteristics of the firm. For example, the charter sets a maximum number of shares of stock it can issue, called **authorized shares**.

Issued shares are shares offered and sold to shareholders in batches, during times when a company needs capital.

Exhibit 8.1 shows the shareholders' equity section of PetSmart, Inc., at February 1, 2009, and February 3, 2008. Notice that the number of shares of common stock authorized is 625 million and the number of shares issued is 159,770,000 at February 1, 2009. An issued share of

Common stock is the most widespread form of ownership in a corporation; common shareholders have a vote in the election of the firm's board of directors.

Authorized shares are shares of stock that are available for a firm to issue per its corporate charter.

Issued shares are shares of stock that have been offered and sold to shareholders.

EXHIBIT 8.1

Shareholders' Equity Section of the Balance Sheet of PetSmart, Inc.

As you read about the different parts of shareholders' equity, refer to this information from the balance sheet of PetSmart, Inc.

PetSmart, Inc.
Consolidated Balance Sheets (partial)
(in thousands, except par value)

	February 1, 2009	February 3, 2008
Stockholders' equity:		
Preferred stock; $.0001 par value; 10,000 shares authorized, none issued and outstanding	–	–
Common stock; $.0001 par value; 625,000 shares authorized; 159,770 and 158,104 shares issued	16	16
Additional paid-in capital	1,117,557	1,079,190
Retained earnings	936,100	758,674
Accumulated other comprehensive (loss) income	(2,714)	5,585
Less: treasury stock, at cost, 32,408 and 30,066 shares	(906,823)	(856,868)
Total stockholders' equity	1,144,136	986,597
Total liabilities and stockholders' equity	$2,357,653	$2,167,257

stock does not need to remain outstanding. Because firms can purchase their own stock in the stock market, all issued shares may not be outstanding. **Outstanding shares** are owned by stockholders rather than by the corporation.

When a company buys back its stock, those shares of stock are called **treasury stock**. Any stock that has been issued by a company may be either outstanding, which is owned by investors, or treasury stock, which is held in the company's treasury. Notice in Exhibit 8.1 that PetSmart has a significant amount of treasury stock (32,408,000 shares at February 1, 2009), shown at the end of the shareholders' equity section where it is subtracted from total shareholders' equity.

Exhibit 8.2 shows the relationships among authorized shares, issued shares, outstanding shares, and treasury shares.

> **Outstanding shares** are shares of stock that are owned by stockholders.

> **Treasury stock** is stock that has been repurchased by the issuing firm.

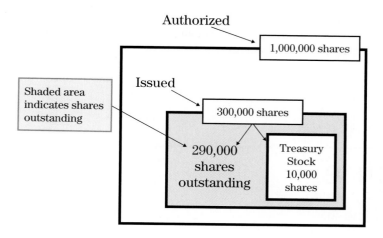

EXHIBIT 8.2

Authorized, Issued, and Outstanding Stock

In this example, 1,000,000 shares are authorized, but only 300,000 are issued. Of the issued shares, 290,000 are outstanding, and 10,000 are treasury shares.

Common Stock

Common stock, as the name suggests, is the most common type of capital stock representing ownership of a corporation. All corporations must have common stock. The owners of common stock generally have the right to

1. vote for members of the board of directors.
2. share in the corporation's profits.
3. share in any assets left if the corporation must dissolve (for example, if the company goes out of business due to bankruptcy).
4. acquire more shares when the corporation issues new stock, often referred to as a pre-emptive right (although this right is often given up by the shareholders).

The corporate charter often provides a fixed per-share amount called the **par value** of the stock. Par value is an arbitrary amount and has no real meaning in today's business environment, and most states do not require a par value. The corporation must maintain a specific amount of capital, as determined by the state or contained in the corporate charter. That amount could be the total par value of the outstanding stock. Frequently, however, other means are used to determine the legal capital to protect creditors. Some firms actually issue no-par stock. Exhibit 8.1 shows that PetSmart common stock has a par value of $0.0001 per share. If you know the par value per share of the common stock and you know the dollar amount in the common stock account, you can calculate the number of shares that have been issued. Use the balance sheet in Exhibit 8.1 to see how that can be done. At February 1, 2009, the common stock account has a balance of $16,000, and the par value of the stock is $0.0001 per share. To calculate the number of shares issued, divide the common stock balance by the par value per share to see how many shares are represented by the balance in the common stock account.

> **Par value** is the monetary amount assigned to a share of stock in the corporate charter. It has little meaning in today's business environment.

$$\frac{\$16,000}{\$0.0001} = 160,000,000 \text{ shares}$$

Because the common stock account balance was rounded to $16,000, the number of shares from the calculation will also be rounded. The actual number of shares issued is 159,770,000. Our rounded calculation shows 160,000,000 shares.

Stock is usually sold for more than its par value. In some states, it is a legal requirement that stock sell for at least par value. Suppose the par value of a company's stock is $2 per share, the market price of the stock on the date the stock is issued is $10 per share, and the company issues 100 shares. Here is how to calculate the dollar amount that will be recorded as common stock.

$$\$2 \text{ par value per share} \times 100 \text{ shares} = \$200$$

The amount of $200 will be shown on the balance sheet in an account separate from any contributions in excess of the par value. The remaining $8 per share will be shown in another account called additional paid-in capital.

$$\$8 \text{ excess over par (per share)} \times 100 \text{ shares} = \$800$$

The total par value amount—$200—is called common or capital stock, and the excess contributions amount—$800—is called additional paid-in capital. Both amounts are reported on the balance sheet. Exhibit 8.3 shows how the amount of cash from the issue of stock is divided between the two paid-in capital accounts when the stock has a par value. For no-par stock, the full amount will be recorded in the common stock account. Remember that paid-in capital designates both capital stock and additional paid-in capital. All amounts of contributed capital are called paid-in capital.

UNDERSTANDING Business

Corporate Bankruptcy: Dividing the Spoils

In the United States, there are two ways a firm can file for bankruptcy. The first is called Chapter 7 (for its location in the U.S. Bankruptcy Code), and it signals the end of the business. Operations are stopped, and a trustee is appointed to sell the company's assets and pay off the company's debt. This is called liquidation. There is rarely enough money to repay all of the creditors and also pay the owners their investment or their share of the company's retained earnings. The creditors are first in line for payment. Bondholders will get their share before any of the stockholders. And among the stockholders, the preferred shareholders are first in line. The common shareholders are last.

The second form of bankruptcy is called Chapter 11. This type of bankruptcy signals a reorganization of the business. A firm in Chapter 11 expects to continue in business and return to sound financial condition at some point in the future. Often, a firm files for Chapter 11 when it can no longer pay its debt holders. The debt is restructured—perhaps with a lower interest rate and a longer time horizon—according to the reorganization plan. This plan must be approved by the bankruptcy court and includes a committee to represent the interests of creditors and stockholders. The interests of the creditors continue to have priority over the interests of the stockholders.

Most publicly-traded firms prefer Chapter 11 to Chapter 7 bankruptcy because they want to continue their operations and return to profitable operations in the future.

Here's what the SEC says about investors of a company in bankruptcy:

"During Chapter 11 bankruptcy, bondholders stop receiving interest and principal payments, and stockholders stop receiving dividends. If you are a bondholder, you may receive new stock in exchange for your bonds, new bonds or a combination of stock and bonds. If you are a stockholder, the trustee may ask you to send back your stock in exchange for shares in the reorganized company. The new shares may be fewer in number and worth less. The reorganization plan spells out your rights as an investor and what you can expect to receive, if anything, from the company." (www.sec.gov/investor/pubs/bankrupt.htm)

In the summer of 2009, General Motors became the second largest industrial bankruptcy in history. Bondholders agreed to exchange their portion of the company's $27.1 billion unsecured debts for 10% of the equity of the new GM. The U.S. government is now a common shareholder of GM, owning 60% of the new company. You may want to read about this historic bankruptcy and see how the structure of GM changes when it emerges from Chapter 11. (Start your search for information at www.nytimes.com.)

Cash ($10 per share)	Common Stock at Par ($2 per share)	Additional Paid-In Capital ($8 per share)
Company receives cash from issuing stock	The amount, $10, is divided between two accounts: common stock and additional paid-in capital	
Amount received by the company: 100 × $10 per share = $1,000	Common Stock: 100 × $2 per share = $200 + Additional Paid-In Capital: 100 × ($10 − $2) per share = $800	

EXHIBIT 8.3

Recording the Issue of Stock

One hundred shares of stock are issued for $10 each. Par value is $2 per share. The proceeds from the stock issue, $1,000, are divided between two accounts: common stock and additional paid-in capital.

Suppose the corporate charter of Miles Barkery authorizes 50 shares of common stock at par value $1 per share. Suppose the company issues 30 shares at $15 per share. Here is how the firm would record the transaction.

Assets	=	Liabilities	+	Shareholders' equity	
				Contributed capital	+ Retained earnings
450 cash				30 common stock	
				420 additional paid-in capital	

How would this transaction be shown on Miles Barkery's financial statements? Suppose the company is issuing the stock for the first time. The shareholders' equity section of the balance sheet would show this information in the part of the statement that shows contributed capital.

Contributed capital	
Common stock (par value $1 per share; 50 shares authorized; 30 shares issued and outstanding)	$ 30
Additional paid-in capital	420

Suppose General Mills issued 10,000 shares of $1 par value per share common stock for $20 per share. How would the company record this transaction?

Your Turn 8-1

Preferred Stock

As you read earlier in the chapter, corporations may have other classes of stock in addition to common stock. Many firms have a class of stock called **preferred stock**. Owners of preferred stock must receive their dividends before the common shareholders and also have a preferred claim on assets. If a firm goes out of business, the preferred shareholders have the right to receive assets that remain after the creditors have been paid. The common shareholders then get any remaining assets. However, the owners of preferred stock usually do not have voting rights.

Cash Dividends

People buy stock in a corporation because they expect the value of the corporation to increase. Selling stock for more than its cost is one way a shareholder can make money on the investment. The other way is by receiving distributions from the firm. The distributions shareholders receive from the earnings of the corporation are called **dividends**. The board of directors decides the amount of dividends to be paid and when they will be paid to the shareholders. Remember that if the corporation has any preferred shareholders, those owners will get their dividends first. The directors are also free not to pay dividends any time they believe it is in the best interest of the corporation. The board of directors may want to reinvest the available cash in the business by buying more equipment or inventory.

Microsoft Corporation, for example, was started in 1975 and did not pay a dividend until 2003. Some firms traditionally pay a dividend, and others have never paid a dividend. Exhibit 8.4 shows how General Electric Company and Papa John's International, Inc., explain their dividend policies. Notice that General Electric pays a dividend and Papa John's does not. Often new companies do not pay any dividends because they want to reinvest all of their earnings in the business. Established companies, on the other hand, often do not have the growth potential of new firms and can use regular dividend payments to attract investors.

EXHIBIT 8.4

Dividend Policies: General Electric Corporation and Papa John's International, Inc.

Some firms, like General Electric, consistently pay a dividend. Other firms, like Papa John's, do not pay dividends. Compare the dividend policy for General Electric (left) and Papa John's (right).

General Electric Corporation	Papa John's International, Inc.
WE DECLARED $12.6 BILLION IN DIVIDENDS IN 2008. Common per-share dividends of $1.24 were up 8% from 2007, following a 12% increase from the preceding year. On February 6, 2009, our Board of Directors approved a regular quarterly dividend of $0.31 per share of common stock, which is payable April 27, 2009, to share owners of record at close of business on February 23, 2009. The Board will continue to evaluate the Company's dividend level for the second half of 2009 in light of the growing uncertainty in the economy, including U.S. government actions, rising unemployment, and the recent announcements by the rating agencies. In 2008, we declared $0.1 billion in preferred stock dividends.	*Since our initial public offering of common stock in 1993, we have not paid dividends on our common stock, and have no current plans to do so.*

Important Dates Related to Dividends

When the board of directors decides that a cash dividend will be paid, there are three important dates: the declaration date, the date of record, and the payment date.

DECLARATION DATE. The dividend declaration date is the date on which the board of directors decides a dividend will be paid and announces it to shareholders. On this date, a legal liability called dividends payable is created. The amount of this liability is balanced in the accounting equation with a reduction from retained earnings. Dividends are not deducted from the contributed capital accounts because they are a distribution of earnings, not a distribution of the shareholders' original paid-in capital. Here is how a firm would record the declaration of $50,000 dividends to be divided among its shareholders.

Assets	=	Liabilities	+	Shareholders' equity	
				Contributed capital +	Retained earnings
		50,000 dividends payable			(50,000) dividends

Remember, dividends are not included as an expense on the income statement because they are not related to generating revenue. Rather than a deduction from a company's earnings, dividends are considered a distribution of a company's earnings to owners in proportion to their share of ownership.

DATE OF RECORD. The date of record is used to determine exactly who will receive the dividends. Anyone owning the stock on this date is entitled to the dividend. After a corporation originally sells stock to investors, they are free to trade—sell and buy—shares of stock with other people. Whoever owns the stock on the date of record will receive the dividend. A stockholder may own the stock for only one day and receive the full dividend amount. After this date, stock is said to be ex-dividend. That is, if it is traded after the date of record, the new owner will not get the dividend. The firm does not record anything in its accounting records on the date of record. Notice GE's reference to this date in its dividend note in Exhibit 8.4.

PAYMENT DATE. The payment date is when the cash is actually paid to the shareholders. This payment has the same effect on the accounting equation as the payment of any liability: Assets (cash) are reduced and liabilities (dividends payable) are reduced.

Assets	=	Liabilities	+	Shareholders' equity	
				Contributed capital +	Retained earnings
(50,000) cash		(50,000) dividends payable			

Distribution of Dividends between Common and Preferred Shareholders

As you have read, the corporation must give holders of preferred stock a certain amount of dividends before common stockholders can receive any dividends. (Note, however, that bondholders must have received any interest payments due to them before dividends of any kind can be distributed.) Dividends on preferred stock are usually fixed at a percentage of the par value of the stock. For example, preferred stock characterized as 10% preferred ($100 par) will receive a dividend of $10 in any year the corporation's board of directors declares a dividend. The preferred shareholders must get their $10 per preferred share before the common shareholders receive any dividends. The board of directors has discretion about whether or not to pay dividends to the preferred shareholders, but the board does not decide on the amount of the dividend for the preferred shareholders. The dividend for preferred shareholders is typically shown on the face of the preferred stock certificate. There are two types of preferred stock—cumulative and noncumulative.

- Cumulative preferred stock means the fixed dividend amount accumulates from year to year, and the entire amount of all past unpaid dividends must be paid to the preferred shareholders before any dividends can be paid to the common shareholders. Any dividends that are owed to holders of cumulative preferred stock from past years, but are undeclared are called dividends in arrears. The corporation does not consider such dividends liabilities but does disclose them in the notes to the financial statements. Only after a dividend is actually declared is it considered a liability. Most preferred stock is cumulative preferred stock.
- With noncumulative preferred stock, the board determines whether or not to make up any missed dividends to the preferred shareholders.

An Example of a Dividend Payment

Suppose JG Company has the following stock outstanding:

- 1,000 shares of 9%, $100 par, cumulative preferred stock
- 50,000 shares of $0.50 per share par common stock

The company last paid dividends in December 2009. With the 2009 payment, JG paid all dividends through December 31, 2009. There were no dividends in arrears prior to 2010. No dividends were paid in 2010. On October 1, 2011, the board of directors declares a total of $30,000 in dividends for its shareholders to be paid on December 15, 2011, to all shareholders of record on November 1, 2011. How much of the dividend will go to the preferred shareholders, and how much will go to the common shareholders?

First, calculate the annual dividend for the preferred shareholders.

$$1,000 \text{ shares} \times \$100 \text{ par value} \times 0.09 = \$9,000$$

Because the preferred stock is cumulative and no dividends were paid to the preferred shareholders in 2010, JG must first pay the 2010 dividend of $9,000 to the preferred shareholders. Then, JG must pay the current year's (2011) $9,000 dividend to the preferred shareholders. The company pays a total of $18,000 to the preferred shareholders, and the remaining $12,000 goes to the common shareholders. On the date of declaration, October 1, the company incurs the legal liability for the dividend payment. Following is how the company records the transaction:

Assets	=	Liabilities	+	Shareholders' equity		
				Contributed capital	+	Retained earnings
		18,000 dividends payable, preferred shareholders 12,000 dividends payable, common shareholders				(30,000) dividends

On the declaration date, the company records the liability. If JG were to prepare its balance sheet, it would show a current liability called dividends payable. This liability is a debt owed to the shareholders for dividends. A corporation may list the liability to common shareholders separately from the liability to preferred shareholders, as shown in the preceding example, or the corporation may combine the preferred and common dividends into one amount for total dividends payable.

On December 15, when JG actually pays the cash to the shareholders to fulfill the obligation, cash is reduced and the liability—dividends payable—is removed from the records. Following is how the company records the transaction:

Assets	=	Liabilities	+	Shareholders' equity		
				Contributed capital	+	Retained earnings
(30,000) cash		(18,000) dividends payable, preferred shareholders (12,000) dividends payable, common shareholders				

Suppose the preferred stock was noncumulative. Then, JG would pay only the current year's dividend of $9,000 to the preferred shareholders, and the remaining $21,000 would go to the common shareholders.

Your Turn 8-2

A corporation has 10,000 shares of 8% cumulative preferred stock and 20,000 shares of common stock outstanding. Par value for each is $100. No dividends were paid last year, but this year $200,000 in dividends is paid to stockholders. How much of this $200,000 goes to the holders of preferred stock?

Treasury Stock

L.O.3
Define treasury stock, explain why a company would purchase treasury stock, and account for its purchase.

Companies can trade—buy and sell—their own stock on the open market. (The timing of these transactions is controlled by Securities and Exchange Commission (SEC) rules.) Treasury stock refers to common stock that has been issued and subsequently purchased by the company that issued it. Once it is purchased by the company, the stock is considered treasury stock until it is resold or retired—taken completely out of circulation.

Why Do Firms Buy Their Own Stock?

There are many reasons companies purchase shares of their own stock. Here are a few of the most common ones:

1. ***To have stock to distribute to employees for compensation plans.*** When a firm wants to give employees or corporate executives shares of stock, the firm will often use treasury shares. Issuing new shares is a costly and time-consuming project, with many requirements set by the SEC, so firms typically issue new shares only to raise a significant amount of money.
2. ***To return cash to the shareholders using a way that is more flexible for both the firm and the shareholder than paying cash dividends.*** Firms that have a great deal of cash will often buy their own stock as a way to get the cash to the shareholders. The firm has complete flexibility over when to buy the stock and how much to buy, and the individual shareholders have complete flexibility over whether or not they sell their shares back to the company. This flexibility benefits the firm and the shareholder. The firm can control the mix of debt and equity in its capital structure. For example, it can reduce equity by buying back stock. The shareholders can decide when to take cash out of their investment in the firm by deciding whether or not to sell back their stock.
3. ***To increase the company's earnings per share.*** When a firm decreases the number of shares outstanding, earnings per share will increase with no change in net income due to the mathematics of the EPS calculation. However, a firm must consider that the cash used to buy back the stock would have earned some return—at least interest revenue—that would increase the numerator by some amount.
4. ***To reduce the cash needed to pay future dividends.*** When a firm reduces the number of shares outstanding, the total cash needed for future dividends decreases. Treasury shares do not receive dividends.
5. ***To reduce chances of a hostile takeover.*** Top management or the board of directors may help the firm resist a takeover by making sure the treasury stock is distributed or sold to the right people—those who would resist the takeover. Buying stock also reduces cash reserves, which are a popular attraction for takeover attempts.

The board of directors of a firm decides if and when that firm will pursue a strategy to buy back its shares. This has become quite common, and you can read about it in the firm's notes to the financial statements. Exhibit 8.5 shows an excerpt from the notes to the financial statements of PetSmart for the fiscal year ended February 1, 2009. Notice that PetSmart has a very active stock repurchase program. Over half of the firms that trade on the New York Stock Exchange regularly purchase their own stock.

EXHIBIT 8.5

PetSmart, Inc., Purchases Its Own Common Stock

Share Purchase Programs—excerpts from the Notes to the Financial Statements

In August 2007, the Board of Directors approved a new share purchase program authorizing the purchase of up to $300.0 million of our common stock through August 2, 2009.

During 2008, we purchased 2.3 million shares of our common stock for $50.0 million. As of February 1, 2009, the amount remaining under the August 2007 share purchase authorization was $25.0 million.

Accounting for the Purchase

The purchase of treasury stock reduces a company's assets (cash) and reduces shareholders' equity. Suppose Papa John's decided to buy back some of the stock it had previously issued. Treasury stock is most often recorded at cost. Here is what the company will record if it buys back 100 shares at $16 per share.

Assets	=	Liabilities	+	Shareholders' equity		
				Contributed capital	+	Retained earnings
(1,600) cash				(1,600) treasury stock		

The par value and the price at which the stock was previously issued do not matter. Using this method, called the cost method, treasury stock is simply recorded at the amount the firm pays to repurchase it. Under the cost method, the following procedures are used:

- Treasury stock holdings for the company are shown as a reduction in the total of shareholders' equity on the balance sheet. Therefore, treasury stock is a type of shareholders' equity. Unlike other equity accounts, however, the cost of treasury stock reduces shareholders' equity. Due to its presence in the shareholders' equity section of the balance sheet and its negative effect on total equity, the treasury stock account is called a contra-equity account and is subtracted from total shareholders' equity.
- No gains or losses are recorded in the company's financial records when a company purchases treasury stock or later resells it. Even if a company acquired one of its own shares for $4 and later sold it for $6, the company would not show a gain of $2. Instead, the company would have more money from the sale of stock—which is contributed capital.

Your Turn 8-3

Suppose a company originally issued 100,000 shares of $1 par common stock for $15 per share. Several years later, the company decides to buy back 1,000 shares of common stock. The stock is selling for $50 per share at the time of the stock repurchase. (a) How would the transaction be recorded in the accounting equation? (b) After the transaction, how many shares are issued and how many shares are outstanding?

Selling Treasury Stock

If treasury stock is sold, the shares sold will be removed from the treasury stock account at the amount the firm paid for the stock when it was repurchased. If the treasury stock is sold at a price higher than its cost, the excess will be classified as paid-in capital from treasury stock transactions.

Suppose a firm purchased 1,000 treasury shares at $50 per share. A year later, the firm sells half of the shares for $60 each. Removing 500 shares of treasury stock at $50 cost will increase total shareholders' equity by reducing the balance in the treasury stock account, a contra-equity account, and will increase additional paid-in capital. Here is how the firm would record selling 500 shares of stock that cost $50 per share for $60 per share:

Assets	=	Liabilities	+	Shareholders' equity		
				Contributed capital	+	Retained earnings
30,000 cash				25,000 treasury stock		
				5,000 paid-in capital from treasury stock transactions		

There would be 500 shares remaining in the treasury stock account, each at a cost of $50. Suppose the firm sold those shares for $48 per share. As in the previous example, the treasury stock must be removed from the total amount of treasury stock at its cost. In this example, instead of having additional paid-in capital, the firm would reduce a paid-in capital account to balance the accounting equation. The difference between the cost and the reissue price—$2 per share × 500 shares = $1,000—would be deducted from paid-in capital from treasury stock transactions. Here is how a firm would record selling 500 treasury shares—originally costing the company $50 per share—for a reissue price of $48:

Assets	=	Liabilities	+	Shareholders' equity	
				Contributed capital	+	**Retained earnings**
24,000 cash				25,000 treasury stock (1,000) paid-in capital from treasury stock transactions	

If the amount in the account paid-in capital from treasury stock transactions were insufficient to cover the $2 per share decrease in stock price, then retained earnings would be reduced by the amount needed to balance the accounting equation.

Reporting Treasury Stock

Treasury stock is most often reported as a deduction from shareholders' equity on the balance sheet. As noted previously, this is called the cost method of accounting for treasury stock. Exhibit 8.6 shows how the shares Abercrombie & Fitch Co. has repurchased are reported on its balance sheet.

EXHIBIT 8.6

From the Balance Sheet of Abercrombie & Fitch Co.

> ### Abercrombie & Fitch Co.
> ### Consolidated Balance Sheets (partial)

(dollars in thousands except per share amounts)	January 31, 2009	February 2, 2008
Class A common stock—$0.01 par value: 150,000,000 shares authorized and 103,300,000 shares issued at January 31, 2009 and February 2, 2008, respectively	1,033	1,033
Paid-in capital	328,488	319,451
Retained earnings	2,244,936	2,051,463
Accumulated other Comprehensive (Loss) Income, net of tax	(22,681)	7,118
Treasury stock, at Average cost 15,573,789 and 17,141,116 shares at January 31, 2009 and February 2, 2008, respectively	(706,198)	(760,752)
Total Shareholders' Equity	1,845,578	1,618,313
Total liabilities and Shareholders' Equity	$2,848,181	$2,567,598

From the 10-K:
During Fiscal 2008, A&F repurchased approximately 0.7 million shares of A&F Common Stock with a value of approximately $50.0 million. During Fiscal 2007, A&F repurchased approximately 3.6 million shares of A&F Common Stock with a value of approximately $287.9 million. A&F did not repurchase any shares of A&F Common Stock during Fiscal 2006. Both the Fiscal 2008 and the Fiscal 2007 repurchases were pursuant to A&F Board of Directors' authorizations.

Your Turn 8-4

Surety Corporation started the year 2010 with 125,000 shares of common stock with par value of $1 issued and outstanding. The issue price of these shares averaged $6 per share. During 2010, Surety purchased 1,000 shares of its own stock at an average price of $7 per share. How would Surety report its treasury stock on the balance sheet at December 31, 2010?

L.O.4
Explain stock dividends and
stock splits.

Stock Dividends and Stock Splits

You have learned about issuing stock and buying back stock. There are two other transactions that a company may have with stock: a stock dividend and a stock split.

Stock Dividends

A corporation may want to pay a dividend to shareholders but not have sufficient cash on hand. Instead of giving the shareholders cash, the corporation may give the shareholders additional shares of stock in the company. This is called a **stock dividend**. Recording the stock dividend simply reclassifies amounts in the shareholders' equity accounts. The corporation that issues a stock dividend converts retained earnings to contributed capital, thereby giving the stockholders a more direct claim to that portion of equity. A stock dividend is not income to the shareholder. As a matter of fact, theoretically there is no value to the shareholder from receiving a stock dividend. The shareholder still owns the same relative percentage of the company.

> **Stock dividends** are new shares of stock that are distributed to the company's current shareholders.

Generally accepted accounting principles (GAAP) distinguish between a small stock dividend (usually considered less than 25% of a company's outstanding stock) and a large stock dividend (greater than 25% of a company's outstanding stock). For a small stock dividend, the company uses the market value of the stock to record the transaction because a small stock dividend has a negligible effect on a stock's market price. For a large stock dividend, the company uses the par value of the stock to record the transaction because a large stock dividend puts so much new stock in the market that the market price per share adjusts to the increased number of shares.

Suppose a company declares and issues a 10% stock dividend to its current shareholders. The stock has a par value of $1 per share, and the current market price is $18 per share. The company will record the stock dividend at its market value. Before the stock dividend, the company has 150,000 shares outstanding. Therefore, the company will issue 15,000 new shares (150,000 × 10%) to shareholders. The total amount of retained earnings that will be converted in to contributed capital will be $270,000 (15,000 × $18). Here is how this company will record the stock dividend:

Assets	=	Liabilities	+	Shareholders' equity		
				Contributed capital	+	Retained earnings
				15,000 common stock		(270,000) retained earnings
				255,000 additional paid-in capital		

This is sometimes called capitalizing retained earnings. Exhibit 8.7 shows how the equity section of the balance sheet is affected by a stock dividend. When considering stock dividends, remember that stock dividends do not increase any shareholder's percentage of ownership in the company. If you owned 5% of the company before the stock dividend, you own 5% of the company after the stock dividend. After the dividend, your 5% includes more shares—but every shareholder's portion of ownership remains the same.

EXHIBIT 8.7

Shareholders' Equity before and after a Stock Dividend

A stock dividend does not change total shareholders' equity. It simply takes a small portion of retained earnings and reclassifies it as paid-in capital.

Shareholders' Equity

Shareholders' Equity	Before Stock Dividend	After Stock Dividend
Common stock, $1 par	$ 150,000	$ 165,000
Additional paid-in capital	600,000	855,000
Total paid-in capital	750,000	1,020,000
Retained earnings	950,000	680,000
Total shareholders' equity	$1,700,000	$1,700,000

Stock Splits

Stock splits occur when a corporation increases the number of shares outstanding and proportionately decreases the par value per share. The outstanding shares are "split" into two or more shares with a corresponding division of the par value. Sometimes a firm will call in all the old shares and reissue new shares. Other times, the firm will issue additional split shares with a notice to the shareholders of a change in par value of all shares.

Suppose you own 100 shares of Target stock. It has a par value of $1 a share and a market value of $24 a share. Suppose Target's board of directors votes to split the stock 2 for 1. After the split, instead of having 100 shares with a par value of $1 per share, you have 200 shares with a par value of $0.50 per share. Theoretically, a stock split should not affect the stock price beyond splitting the price in the same proportions as the stock split. For example, if a share was trading for $24 before a 2-for-1 split, a new share should trade for $12. Companies record the details of the stock split parenthetically in the shareholders' equity part of the financial statements. There is nothing formally recorded in the accounting records.

> A **stock split** is the division of the current shares of stock by a specific number to increase the number of shares outstanding.

Your Turn 8-5

1. Compare a stock split and a stock dividend.
2. Suppose you own 1,500 shares, which is 3%, of ABC Company's outstanding stock. If ABC declares a 2-for-1 stock split, how many shares will you own? What percentage ownership will your shares now represent?

Retained Earnings

Retained earnings is the amount of all the earnings of the firm—since its beginning—that have not been distributed to the stockholders. Retained earnings may also be called earned capital. As you know, retained earnings are not cash!

Retained earnings includes

1. net incomes since the day the company began, minus
2. any net losses since the day the company began, minus
3. any dividends declared since the company began.

Because retained earnings is a part of shareholders' equity, the change in retained earnings during the period is contained in the statement of changes in shareholders' equity. Sometimes the part of the shareholders' equity statement that provides the details of the changes in retained earnings is shown separately and is called a statement of retained earnings.

In a firm's accounting system, the retained earnings account does not directly receive additions for revenue earned or deductions for expenses incurred during the normal course of business. Technically, those amounts are kept in separate revenue and expense accounts. Then, at the end of the accounting period, when it is time to prepare the financial statements, the income statement is prepared using those balances in the revenue and expense accounts. At that time, those income statement accounts are added to (revenue accounts) and subtracted from (expense accounts) the actual retained earnings account. Remember this important computation:

> **L.O.5**
> Define retained earnings and account for its increases and decreases.

> **Retained earnings** is the total earnings of a firm since its inception—all of its net incomes, reduced by any net losses, that have not been distributed to shareholders.

Beginning retained earnings

+ Net income for the period (or − net loss)

− Dividends

= Ending retained earnings

Suppose B&B Company started the year with retained earnings of $84,500. During the year, B&B had net income of $25,600 and declared cash dividends of $12,200. What was the ending balance in retained earnings?

Your Turn 8-6

L.O.6
Prepare financial
statements that contain
equity transactions.

Team Shirts Issues New Stock

When a privately-owned company decides it wants to offer ownership to the public in order to raise a significant amount of capital, the form of the business organization must be a corporation. (A sole proprietorship or a partnership wanting to offer ownership to the public must first change its form to a corporation.) The first public offering of stock on one of the stock exchanges is called an initial public offering (IPO). Much like the work done before a company issues bonds, a company must do a great deal of work to prepare for an IPO. The SEC requires the company to provide many reports, including a set of financial statements contained in a report called a prospectus. Remember, the job of the SEC is to protect the public.

In August, Sara decides her company could raise a great deal of capital by "going public." Sara decides it would be a good long-term strategy to increase the company's equity to provide more funds for expansion without increasing the company's debt. As you know, a company's creditors and owners have claim to the company's assets, and the relationship between the amount of debt and the amount of equity in a company is called the company's capital structure. To increase the company's equity, Team Shirts will offer the opportunity to the general public to become part owners in the company.

Exhibit 8.8 shows the balance sheet for Team Shirts at the beginning of August. This is the July 31 balance sheet you saw in Chapter 7 (Exhibit 7.15). The first transaction for August is the Team Shirts IPO. Although the form of the company has been a corporation, Team Shirts has a lot of work to do to prepare to go public. The SEC requirements for this IPO are extensive, and we will let the investment bankers do the work behind the scenes. These are finance, accounting,

EXHIBIT 8.8

**Balance Sheet for Team
Shirts at August 1, 2010**

Team Shirts
Balance Sheet
At August 1, 2010

Assets

Current assets		
Cash		$ 44,705
Accounts receivable (net of allowance of $1,125)		55,125
Inventory		9,990
Prepaid expenses		5,600
Total current assets		115,420
Property and equipment		
Land	$ 8,500	
Computer	4,000	
Truck	30,000	
Building	76,500	$119,000
Accumulated depreciation		(1,910)
Net property and equipment		117,090
Total assets		$232,510

Liabilities & Shareholder's Equity

Current liabilities	
Accounts payable	$ 36,000
Interest payable	654
Current portion of note payable	6,000
Current portion of mortgage payable	6,702
Total current liabilities	49,356
Notes payable	24,000
Mortgage payable	78,298
Total liabilities	151,654
Shareholder's equity	
Common stock	$ 5,000
Retained earnings	75,856
Total shareholder's equity	80,856
Total liabilities and shareholder's equity	$232,510

and legal experts in the area of IPOs. The accounting changes in the balance sheet depend on the characteristics of the debt and equity of the company and the agreements the creditors and owners make. We will make it very simple for Team Shirts, but in a real-world IPO, transactions could be much more complicated.

Sara works with an investment banking firm and an accounting firm to prepare the stock offering—the IPO. The investment bankers do the legal work and essentially buy the stock and then offer it to the public. (For simplicity, we will assume that all of their fees have been deducted from the issue price of the stock.) Team Shirts' corporate charter has 100,000 shares of common stock authorized with a par value of $0.01. Sara's personal ownership has been assigned 30,000 shares. Remember that she is the only shareholder at this time, so all of shareholder's equity belongs to her. Sara wants to retain a majority of the stock so that she can retain control of the company, so Team Shirts decides to issue 25,000 additional common shares in this initial offering. The $0.01 par value shares are issued at $3 per share.

Assets	=	Liabilities	+	Shareholders' equity		
				Contributed capital	+	Retained earnings
75,000 cash				250 common stock 74,750 additional paid-in capital		

The remaining August transactions for Team Shirts are given in Exhibit 8.9. Trace each one to the accounting equation worksheet in Exhibit 8.10 on the following page. Then, study the list of adjustments.

1   Issued 25,000 shares of common stock for $75,000, $0.01 par value

2   Paid $30,000 on accounts payable

3   Collected $40,000 on accounts receivable

4   Purchased inventory on account: 25,000 shirts at $3.50 each

5   Found out that Play Ball Sports, one of its customers with an outstanding balance of $1,000, has filed for bankruptcy, so wrote off the account balance

6   Sold 26,119 shirts at $10 each on account

7   Collected $25,000 on accounts receivable

8   Incurred cash operating expenses of $12,000

9   Renewed insurance policy for 12 months for $2,400 cash. The new policy takes effect on August 15, when the old policy expires.

10   Made first mortgage payment of $900. (See amortization schedule in Exhibit 8.11 on page 387 for breakdown of interest and principal. Remember, the interest was accrued at the end of July.)

EXHIBIT 8.9

Transactions for Team Shirts for August

To make the following necessary adjustments, you'll find some additional information included in the descriptions.

1. Depreciation on computer ($100 per month)
2. Team Shirts drove the truck 4,000 miles in August. So the depreciation on the truck is $580 (4,000 miles × 0.145 per mile).
3. Depreciation on building ($250 per month)
4. Insurance—$150 ($50 + $100) for August
5. Rent—$1,200 for August
6. Web design expense—$50 for August

7. Interest on truck loan ($30,000 × 0.06 = $1,800 per year; $150 per month)
8. Interest on mortgage. (See amortization schedule in Exhibit 8.11.)
9. Allowance for uncollectible accounts will remain at 2% of the ending accounts receivable balance.

EXHIBIT 8.10

Accounting Equation Worksheet for Team Shirts for August

	Cash	All other assets	(Account)	All liabilities	(Account)	Contributed Capital	Retained Earnings	(Account)
		Assets	**=**	**Liabilities**	**+**	**Shareholders' Equity**		
Beginning Balances	$ 44,705	$187,805	See details below	$151,654	See details below	$ 5,000	$ 75,856	
Transactions 1	75,000					250 / 74,750		
2	(30,000)			(30,000)	Accounts payable			
3	40,000	(40,000)	Accounts receivable					
4		87,500	Inventory	87,500	Accounts payable			
5		(1,000) / 1,000	Accounts receivable / Allowance for bad debts					
6		261,190 / (91,694)	Accounts receivable / Inventory				261,190 / (91,694)	Sales / Cost of goods sold
7	25,000	(25,000)	Accounts receivable					
8	(12,000)						(12,000)	Operating expenses
9	(2,400)	2,400	Prepaid insurance					
10	(900)			(546) / (354)	Mortgage payable / Interest payable			
A-1		(100)	Accumulated depreciation, computer				(100)	Depreciation expense
A-2		(580)	Accumulated depreciation, truck				(580)	Depreciation expense
A-3		(250)	Accumulated depreciation, building				(250)	Depreciation expense
A-4		(150)	Prepaid insurance				(150)	Insurance expense
A-5		(1,200)	Prepaid rent				(1,200)	Rent expense
A-6		(50)	Prepaid web design				(50)	Web design expense
A-7				150	Interest payable		(150)	Interest expense
A-8				352	Interest payable		(352)	Interest expense
A-9		(4,904)	Allowance for bad debts				(4,904)	Bad debts expense
	$139,405 + $374,967			**= $208,756**		**+**	**$80,000 + $225,616**	

Check 514,372 = 514,372

━ Income statement ━ Statement of changes in shareholders' equity ━ Balance sheet ━ Statement of cash flows

Assets (except cash)	Beginning	Ending
Accounts receivable	$ 56,250	$251,440
Allowance for bad debts	(1,125)	(5,029)
Inventory	9,990	5,796
Prepaid insurance	50	2,300
Prepaid rent	5,400	4,200
Prepaid web design	150	100
Computer	4,000	4,000
Accumulated depreciation	(500)	(600)
Truck	30,000	30,000
Accumulated depreciation	(1,160)	(1,740)
Land	8,500	8,500
Building	76,500	76,500
Accumulated depreciation	(250)	(500)
	$187,805	$374,967
Liabilities		
Accounts payable	$ 36,000	$ 93,500
Interest payable	654	802
Notes payable (truck)	30,000	30,000
Mortgage payable	85,000	84,454
	$151,654	$208,756

Depreciation

Computer	$100	
Truck	$580	$0.145 per mile × 4,000 miles
Building	$250	

$76,500	Cost (90% of purchase)
(1,500)	Salvage value
$75,000	Depreciable base
÷ 300	25 years × 12 months
$250.00	Monthly depreciation

Cost of goods sold (FIFO)

Beginning inventory	2,775 shirts at $3.60 each	$ 9,990
Purchases	25,000 at $3.50	87,500
Goods available for sale		$97,490
Sale of 26,119 shirts:	2,775 at $3.60	$ 9,990
	23,344 at $3.50	81,704
Cost of goods sold		91,694
Ending inventory	1,656 at $3.50	5,796
		$97,490

Bad debts expense

Beginning allowance for bad debts	$ 1,125
Write-offs during the month	(1,000)
Balance before adjustment	$ 125
Desired balance	
2% of ending AR =	
2% of $251,440	5,029
Needed adjustment = bad debts expense	$ 4,904

Interest expense and current portion of long-term mortgage

This is the amortization schedule for the first 13 months of the mortgage. The annual interest rate of 5% is divided by 12 to get a monthly rate. The difference between the monthly payment and the interest expense will reduce the principal balance. The total principal reduction for the next 12 months will be the current portion of the long-term debt. It is the amount of the principal that will be due in the next year. Remember that the interest won't be recorded as a liability until the time has passed. At the end of the second month of the mortgage, August, Team Shirts accrued the second month's interest of $352.

Beginning balance (monthly)	Interest expense (monthly) 5%/12	Monthly payment given	Reduction in principal	Ending balance
$85,000	$354	$900	$546	$84,454
84,454	352	900	548	83,906
83,906	350	900	550	83,356
83,356	347	900	553	82,803
82,803	345	900	555	82,248
82,248	343	900	557	81,691
81,691	340	900	560	81,131
81,131	338	900	562	80,569
80,569	336	900	564	80,005
80,005	333	900	567	79,438
79,438	331	900	569	78,869
78,869	329	900	571	78,298
78,298	326	900	574	77,724
			$6,730	

▢ The amounts can be found on the financial statements.

Mortgage payable before the second payment	$84,454
Current portion	6,730
Remaining long-term mortgage payable	$77,724

All of the adjustments are shown on the accounting equation worksheet in Exhibit 8.10.

Details of the depreciation, inventory, bad debts expense, and long-term mortgage are shown in Exhibit 8.11.

After you understand all of the entries on the worksheet, trace the numbers to the financial statements shown in Exhibit 8.12.

EXHIBIT 8.12

Financial Statements for Team Shirts for August 2010

Team Shirts
Income Statement
For the Month Ended August 31, 2010

Sales revenue	$261,190
Expenses:	
Cost of goods sold	$91,694
Operating expenses	12,000
Bad debts expense	4,904
Insurance expense	150
Rent expense	1,200
Web design expense	50
Depreciation expense	930
Interest expense	502
Total expenses	111,430
Net income	$149,760

Team Shirts
Statement of Changes in Shareholders' Equity
For the Month Ended August 31, 2010

Beginning common stock	$ 5,000
Common stock issued during month	250
Additional paid-in capital from common stock issue	74,750
Ending contributed capital	$ 80,000
Beginning retained earnings	$ 75,856
Net income	149,760
Dividends	0
Ending retained earnings	$225,616
Total shareholders' equity	$305,616

Team Shirts
Statement of Cash Flows
For the Month Ended August 31, 2010

Cash from operating activities	
Cash collected from customers	$ 65,000
Cash paid to vendors	(30,000)
Cash paid for operating expenses	(14,400)
Cash paid for interest	(354)
Net cash from operating activities	$ 20,246
Cash from investing activities	0
Cash from financing activities	
Cash paid on mortgage	$ (546)
Cash from issue of common stock	75,000
Net cash from financing activities	74,454
Increase in cash	94,700
Beginning cash balance	44,705
Ending cash balance	$139,405

Team Shirts
Balance Sheet
At August 31, 2010

Assets		
Current assets		
Cash		$139,405
Account receivable (net of allowance of $5,029)		246,411
Inventory		5,796
Prepaid expenses		6,600
Total current assets		398,212
Property and equipment		
Land	$ 8,500	
Computer	4,000	
Truck	30,000	
Building	76,500	$119,000
Accumulated depreciation		(2,840)
Net property and equipment		116,160
Total assets		$514,372

Liabilities and Shareholders' Equity	
Current liabilities	
Accounts payable	$ 93,500
Interest payable	802
Current portion of note payable	6,000
Current portion of mortgage payable	6,730
Total current liabilities	107,032
Notes payable	24,000
Mortgage payable	77,724
Total liabilities	208,756
Shareholders' equity	
Common stock	$ 5,250
Additional paid-in capital	74,750
Retained earnings	225,616
Total shareholders' equity	305,616
Total liabilities and shareholders' equity	$514,372

L.O.7
Compute return on equity and earnings per share, and explain what these ratios mean.

Applying Your Knowledge: Ratio Analysis

The shareholders' equity of a firm can provide information useful for financial statement analysis. There are two ratios that help us evaluate the return to shareholders.

1. Return on equity
2. Earnings per share

Return on Equity

Return on equity (ROE) measures the amount of income earned with each dollar of common shareholders' investment in the firm. To calculate ROE, we need the amount of common shareholders' equity at the beginning and at the end of the accounting period. Common shareholders' equity is all the equity except the preferred shareholders' equity. The ratio uses common shareholders' equity because common shareholders are considered to be the true owners of the firm. Then, we use the net income, reduced by the amount of preferred dividends declared, for the numerator. The reason for deducting preferred dividends from net income is that we are calculating the return to the common shareholder. The ratio takes preferred shareholders out of both the numerator and denominator. Recall that common shareholders are entitled to the earnings of the firm only after preferred dividends are paid. Return on equity tells us how well the company is using the common shareholders' contributions and earnings retained in the business.

> **Return on equity (ROE)** measures the amount of income earned with each dollar of common shareholders' investment in the firm. To calculate ROE, take net income minus preferred dividends divided by average common shareholders' equity.

$$\text{Return on equity} = \frac{\text{Net income} - \text{preferred dividends}}{\text{Average common shareholders' equity}}$$

Exhibit 8.13 shows the information needed to calculate Papa John's return on equity for two consecutive years. The size of the return needs to be compared to other similar companies or to industry standards for a meaningful analysis of a firm's performance. Notice that Papa John's ROE has increased from about 23.9% to about 28.6%. Any analyst would want to get more information about an increase this large. Remember that when we calculate the ratios, we use a simple average of beginning and ending common shareholders' equity for the denominator.

EXHIBIT 8.13

Return on Equity for Papa John's International, Inc.

(dollars in thousands)	For the Year Ended December 28, 2008	For the Year Ended December 30, 2007
Net income	$36,796	$32,735
Average common equity	($129,986 + 126,903)/2 = $128,445	($126,903 + 146,782)/2 = $136,843
Return on equity	28.6%	23.9%

Earnings Per Share

Earnings per share (EPS) is perhaps the most well-known and most commonly used ratio because analysts and investors use current earnings to predict future dividends and stock prices. This ratio is the per-share portion of net income of each common shareholder.

> **Earnings per share (EPS)** is a commonly used measure of firm performance, defined as net income minus preferred dividends divided by the weighted average number of common shares outstanding.

$$\text{Earnings per share} = \frac{\text{Net income} - \text{Preferred dividends}}{\text{Weighted average number of common shares outstanding}}$$

The "earnings" in the numerator of this ratio begins with net income. Because EPS is designated as the earnings for the common shareholders, preferred dividends must be deducted from net income. An investor, who saw the corporation's net income increase year after year, might be fooled into thinking that he or she was doing better each year. The investor might be worse off, however, if the amount of common stock outstanding has been increasing, because those increases could dilute the investor's portion of the earnings. Even though net income went up, it must be shared among many more owners. The denominator is the weighted average number of common shares outstanding. For example, suppose a firm began the year, January 1, with 100,000 common shares outstanding and issued an additional 10,000 common shares on April 1. The weighted average number of common shares outstanding for the year would be

$$(100,000 \times 3/12) + (110,000 \times 9/12) = 107,500 \text{ shares}$$

The fractions, 3/12 and 9/12, represent the fraction of the year in which that particular number of shares was outstanding. In other words, the number of shares outstanding is weighted by the amount of time those shares were outstanding.

Suppose the firm had net income of $129,000 for the year and did not have any preferred stock. Then, EPS would be

$$\frac{\$129,000}{107,500} = \$1.20 \text{ per share}$$

EPS helps an investor predict stock prices, which is why it is a popular ratio. All publicly-traded firms' financial statements provide EPS (on the income statement) because it is required by GAAP. EPS is the most common indicator of a company's overall performance. EPS is forecast by financial analysts, anticipated by investors, managed by business executives, and announced with great anticipation by major corporations.

Dollar Tree Stores, Inc.'s income statement in Exhibit 8.14 shows two amounts for earnings per share. The first is called basic net income per share. This is a straightforward calculation of net income divided by the weighted average number of common shares outstanding. The second is called diluted net income per share. This is a "what-if" calculation: What if all of the potential securities that could have been converted into common stock actually had been converted to common stock at year end? Those securities could be securities such as convertible bonds or exercised stock options, both of which could be exchanged for shares of common stock. If you were a shareholder, you might want to know the worst-case scenario for your EPS. That is referred to as the diluted EPS. Calculations for diluted EPS can be complicated and are done by a company's accountant when the annual financial statements are prepared. Fortunately, a firm's income statement will always show the firm's EPS because it is a requirement of GAAP. That means we won't have to compute this ratio when we analyze a publicly-traded firm's financial statements. However, should you decide to become an accountant, you will spend lots of time learning the intricacies of the EPS computation.

EXHIBIT 8.14

Presentation of Earnings per Share on an Income Statement (Statement of Operations)

Dollar Tree Stores, Inc., and Subsidiaries
Consolidated Statements of Operations

(In millions, except per share data)	Year Ended January 31, 2009	Year Ended February 2, 2008	Year Ended February 3, 2007
Net sales	$4,644.9	$4,242.6	$3,969.4
Cost of sales	3,052.7	2,781.5	2,612.2
Gross profit	1,592.2	1,461.1	1,357.2
Selling, general and administrative expenses	1,226.4	1,130.8	1,046.4
Operating income	365.8	330.3	310.8
Interest income	2.6	6.7	8.6
Interest expense	(9.3)	(17.2)	(16.5)
Income before income taxes	359.1	319.8	302.9
Provision for income taxes	129.6	118.5	110.9
Net income	$ 229.5	$ 201.3	$ 192.0
Basic net income per share	$ 2.54	$ 2.10	$ 1.86
Diluted net income per share	$ 2.53	$ 2.09	$ 1.85

See accompanying Notes to Consolidated Financial Statements.

By now you should be getting used to the variety of terms accountants have for the same thing. Dollar Tree Stores doesn't have anything labeled earnings per share. Instead, the firm calls it net income per share.

Business Risk, Control, and Ethics

Generally, we have been looking at the risks faced by the firm. We will now look at the risks associated with shareholders' equity from an owner's point of view.

L.O.8
Recognize the business risks associated with shareholders' equity and the related controls.

Risks Faced by Owners

Anyone who purchases a share of stock in a company risks losing that money. At the same time, however, there is the potential of earning a corresponding significant return. In the first few months of 2000, technology stocks were booming. It was called the dot-com boom because so many of the new firms were Internet-based. In March 2000, the NASDAQ (National Association of Securities Dealers Automated Quotation system) closed at a peak of 5,048.62, more than double its value just 14 months before. Many investors reaped the rewards of the stock price increases. Then, prices began to fall. One day after reaching its peak, the NASDAQ lost almost 3% of its value. By October 2002, it had dropped to 1,114.11, a loss of 78% of its peak value. The dot-com boom had become the dot-com bust.

Many investors made money in the dot-com boom, and some technology firms did not lose their value. For example, if you bought a share of stock in eBay in July 2002, you paid approximately $14 for that share of stock. You could have sold it in January of 2005 for over $57. This is the reward side of the risk associated with equity ownership for an individual investor.

In 2008, we saw this phenomenon again as the stock market lost over 20% of its value in a single week in October. According to Urban Institute, a nonpartisan economic and social policy research center, the S&P 500 fell by over a third between year end 2007 and year end 2008. This drop has had a negative effect on the economy and on the retirement funds of millions of people. The long-term effects of the 2008 crash will depend on how the market recovers. Anyone near retirement age has much more to be concerned about than those who have many years to restore their lost wealth. What has become quite clear, however, is that there is significant risk in stock ownership.

How can the risk of stock ownership be controlled? The best way to minimize the risks of stock ownership is to diversify your investments. If you own stock in many different types of firms, the stock prices of some should go up when others are going down. For example, if you own stock in a firm in the retail grocery business, such as Kroger, it might be wise to balance that investment with stock in a restaurant, such as Darden, the parent company of Olive Garden and Red Lobster. Then, if the popular trend is to eat at home, the grocery store stock might increase in value. If eating out becomes more popular, then the restaurant stock might become more valuable. This example is quite simplistic, and finance experts have a much more complicated concept of diversification. The bottom line, however, is quite straightforward. Do not put all your eggs in one basket.

Other risks of stock ownership result from the problems associated with the separation of ownership and management that is common in today's corporation. Considering the potential damage that can result from the actions of unethical management, investors considering ownership in a large corporation must take this risk seriously. Controls that monitor the behavior and decisions of management—such as boards of directors and independent audits—will help minimize these risks. Many of these risks are addressed by the Sarbanes-Oxley Act of 2002, which you can read more about in Chapter 11.

Chapter Summary Points

- Corporations raise money by issuing preferred stock and common stock. The number of shares of stock can be classified as authorized, issued, and outstanding.
- Preferred shareholders get their dividends before the common shareholders. The amount of the dividend is fixed by the par value and the percentage given on the stock certificate. The remaining dividends, out of the total declared by the board of directors, go to the common shareholders. Remember, a firm is not required to pay dividends. Some, like Papa John's, have never paid a cash dividend.
- Treasury stock is stock a firm has issued and later repurchased on the open market. A firm might buy its own stock to have shares available for employees and managers as part of compensation packages.

- A stock dividend is a dividend consisting of shares of stock rather than cash. Each shareholder receives an amount of stock that will maintain the pre-dividend proportion of ownership. A stock split is when the company reduces the par value per share and increases the number of shares proportionately. For example, if you own 5 shares of $3 par stock and the company enacts a 3-for-1 split, the new par value of the stock is $1 per share and you will now own 15 shares. This reduces the market price of the stock. (No entry is made in the formal accounting records for stock splits.)
- The balance in retained earnings is the sum of all the net incomes minus any net losses and minus any dividends declared over the entire life of the company. It is the company's earnings that have been kept in the company.
- Return on equity is defined as net income for the common shareholders divided by average common shareholders' equity. It measures a company's profitability. Earnings per share is defined as net income divided by the weighted average number of shares outstanding (again, common shareholders only). This measures each common shareholder's proportionate share of net income.
- The biggest risk related to stock ownership is the potential for a decrease in the value of your stock. Because owners and managers are often different, the owners may have a problem monitoring the decisions of the managers. For firms, the risk of being publicly traded relates to the complicated requirements set forth by the SEC and the Sarbanes-Oxley Act.

Chapter Summary Problems

Suppose that Pia's Pizza engaged in the following transactions in the fiscal year ended December 28, 2011:

Pia's Pizza
Shareholders' Equity Section of the Balance Sheet
(dollars in thousands)

	At 12/28/11	12/28/10
Shareholders' Equity:		
Preferred stock ($0.01 par value per share; authorized 5,000,000 shares; no shares issued)		
Common stock ($0.01 par value per share; authorized 50,000,000 shares; xxxxxx shares issued at December 28, 2011, and 31,716,105 shares issued at December 28, 2010)		$ 317
Additional paid-in capital-common stock		219,584
Accumulated other comprehensive income (loss)	(3,116)	(3,116)
Retained earnings		293,921
Treasury stock (xxxxxx shares at December 28, 2011, and 13,603,587 shares at December 28, 2010, at cost)		(351,434)
Total shareholders' equity		$ 159,272

1. The company issued 100,000 shares of common stock, par value of $0.01 per share, for $24 per share.
2. Cash revenues for the year amounted to $100,690,000, and cash expenses amounted to $50,010,000.
3. The company declared cash dividends of $300,000.
4. The company repurchased 25,000 shares of its own stock (treasury stock) for an average cost of $22 per share.

Instructions

Use the accounting equation to show how Pia's Pizza would record each of the transactions. Then, update the shareholders' equity section of Pia's Pizza's balance sheet by filling in the shaded areas.

Solution

Assets	=	Liabilities	+	Shareholders' equity	
				Contributed capital +	**Retained earnings**
1. 2,400,000 cash				1,000 common stock 2,399,000 additional paid-in capital	
2. 100,690,000 cash (50,010,000) cash					100,690,000 revenues (50,010,000) expenses
3.		300,000 dividends payable			(300,000) dividends
4. (550,000) cash				(550,000) treasury stock	

Pia's Pizza
Shareholders' Equity Section of the Balance Sheet
(dollars in thousands)

	At 12/28/11	12/28/10
Shareholders' Equity:		
Preferred stock ($0.01 par value per share; authorized 5,000,000 shares; no shares issued)		
Common stock ($0.01 par value per share; authorized 50,000,000 shares; 31,816,105 shares issued at December 28, 2011, and 31,716,105 shares issued at December 28, 2010)	$ 318	$ 317
Additional paid-in capital-common stock	221,983	219,584
Accumulated other comprehensive income (loss)	(3,116)	(3,116)
Retained earnings	344,301	293,921
Treasury stock (13,628,587 shares at December 28, 2011, and 13,603,587 shares at December 28, 2010, at cost)	(351,984)	(351,434)
Total shareholders' equity	$ 211,502	$ 159,272

Key Terms for Chapter 8

Answers to YOUR TURN Questions

Chapter 8

Your Turn 8-1

Assets	=	Liabilities	+	Shareholders' equity		
				Contributed capital	+	Retained earnings
200,000 cash				10,000 common stock		
				190,000 additional paid-in capital		

Your Turn 8-2

($100 × 10,000 × 0.08) = $80,000 for last year and $80,000 for this year for a total of $160,000 to the preferred shareholders. The remaining $40,000 goes to the common shareholders.

Your Turn 8-3

a.

Assets	=	Liabilities	+	Shareholders' equity		
				Contributed capital	+	Retained earnings
(50,000) cash				(50,000) treasury stock		

b. One hundred thousand shares are issued and 99,000 shares are outstanding.

Your Turn 8-4

Treasury stock would be deducted from shareholders' equity. The amount would be $7,000, the cost of repurchasing the shares of stock.

Your Turn 8-5

1. A stock split is a division of the par value of the stock and an increase in the number of shares owned by each shareholder, proportionate to the presplit ownership distribution. A stock dividend is a distribution of stock to the current shareholders as a dividend, similarly maintaining the pre-dividend distribution of ownership.
2. You will own 3,000 shares, which will still be 3% of the outstanding stock.

Your Turn 8-6

$84,500 + $25,600 − $12,200 = $97,900

Questions

1. What are the two primary ways for a company to finance its business?
2. What is the difference between common stock and preferred stock?
3. Explain how par value affects the issuance of common stock and preferred stock.
4. What is the difference between paid-in capital in general and additional paid-in capital on the balance sheet?
5. What are the two ways that shareholders can make money on an investment in a corporation's stock?
6. Are dividends expenses of a corporation? Explain why or why not.
7. What are the three dates corporations consider when issuing a dividend?

8. What is the difference between cumulative and noncumulative preferred stock?
9. What are dividends in arrears?
10. What is treasury stock and why might a company acquire it?
11. What effect does the purchase of treasury stock have on a company's financial statements?
12. Would treasury stock be considered authorized, issued, or outstanding? Explain your answer.
13. Explain the difference between stock dividends and cash dividends.
14. What is the effect of a stock dividend on a company's financial statements?
15. What is a stock split and what effect does it have on a company's shareholders' equity?
16. What are the two sections of the shareholders' equity section of the balance sheet? Explain what each section reports.
17. How is return on equity calculated? What does this ratio measure?
18. Explain how earnings per share (EPS) is calculated. What does this ratio measure?
19. Of all the financial ratios you have studied, which is the only one that is required by U.S. GAAP to be reported in the financial statements? On which financial statement will it appear?

Multiple-Choice Questions

1. Which of the following *does not* affect retained earnings?
   a. Net income for the period
   b. Dividends declared for common shareholders
   c. Repayment of the principal of a loan
   d. All of the above affect retained earnings.
2. Preferred stock is stock that is
   a. traded above the price of common stock.
   b. issued and later repurchased.
   c. bought and sold to smooth a company's earnings.
   d. given priority over common stock for dividends.
3. Treasury stock is
   a. a company's own stock that it has repurchased and added to its short-term trading securities (current assets) as an investment.
   b. a company's own stock that is considered issued but not outstanding.
   c. a company's own stock that may be used to "manage" earnings—it could be sold for a gain when the price of the stock increases to help a company meet its earnings forecast.
   d. booked as an increase to assets and a decrease to shareholders' equity when it is purchased.
4. The two major components of shareholders' equity are
   a. preferred stock and common stock.
   b. contributed capital and paid-in capital.
   c. contributed capital and retained earnings.
   d. common stock and treasury stock.
5. The purchase of treasury stock will
   a. increase assets and shareholders' equity.
   b. decrease assets and shareholders' equity.
   c. have no effect on assets or shareholders' equity.
   d. decrease assets but have no effect on shareholders' equity.
6. If a company purchased 50 shares of its own stock for $10 per share and later sold it for $12 per share, the company would
   a. record a gain of $2 per share.
   b. record an increase to retained earnings of $100.
   c. show a gain on the sale.
   d. show an increase of $100 of paid-in capital.
7. The number of shares of stock designated as *issued* on the year-end balance sheet are those shares that
   a. were issued during the year.
   b. have been issued during the firm's life.
   c. are authorized to be issued.
   d. have been repurchased during the year.

8. When treasury stock is reissued for more than the company paid to buy it, the difference is
   a. a gain that will increase the firm's income.
   b. included in sales revenue for the period.
   c. added to an additional paid-in capital account.
   d. given to the current shareholders as a dividend.
9. The payment of dividends is
   a. required by corporate law.
   b. determined by the firm's board of directors.
   c. related in amount to the firm's earnings per share.
   d. determined by the Securities and Exchange Commission.
10. Return on equity measures how well a firm is using
   a. owners' original contributions to the firm.
   b. creditors' investment in the firm.
   c. shareholders' total investment in the firm, both contributed and earned.
   d. its assets.

MyAccountingLab

All of the A exercises can be found within MyAccountingLab, an online homework and practice environment.

Short Exercises
Set A

SE8-1A. *Classify stock. (LO 1).* Delta Corporation's corporate charter authorizes the company to sell 450,000,000 shares of $1.50 par common stock. As of December 31, 2011, the company had issued 180,915,000 shares of common stock for an average price of $4 each. Delta has 57,000,000 shares of treasury stock. How many shares of common stock will be disclosed as authorized, issued, and outstanding on the December 31, 2011, balance sheet?

SE8-2A. *Record issuance of common stock. (LO 1).* Vest Corporation sells and issues 100 shares of its $10 par value common stock at $11 per share. Show how this transaction would be recorded in the accounting equation.

SE8-3A. *Analyze effect of issuance of common stock on financial statements. (LO 1).* Ice Video Corporation issued 5,000 shares of $0.01 par value common stock for $32.50 per share. How much cash did Ice Video Corporation receive from the stock issue? How will the transaction be shown in the shareholders' equity section of the balance sheet?

SE8-4A. *Analyze effect of dividends on financial statements. (LO 2).* On December 15, 2010, the board of directors of Seat Corporation declared a cash dividend, payable January 8, 2011, of $1.50 per share on the 100,000 common shares outstanding. The accounting period ends December 31. How will this be reflected on the balance sheet at December 31, 2010?

SE8-5A. *Distribute dividend between preferred and common shareholders. (LO 2).* In 2012, the board of directors of Tasty Bakery Corporation declared total dividends of $40,000. The company has 2,000 shares of 6%, $100 par, preferred stock. There are no dividends in arrears. How much of the $40,000 will be paid to the preferred shareholders? How much will be paid to the common shareholders?

SE8-6A. *Record sale of treasury stock. (LO 3).* Suppose Fitness and Fashion Corporation paid $20 per share for 690 shares of its own common stock on August 30, 2011, and then resold these treasury shares for $22.50 per share on September 25, 2011. Show the transaction on September 25, 2011, in the accounting equation. What effect do these transactions have on the shareholders' equity section of the balance sheet at September 30, 2011?

SE8-7A. *Analyze effect of stock dividend on financial statements. (LO 4).* Zorro Company declared and issued a 10% stock dividend on June 1, 2010. Before this dividend was declared and issued, there were 220,000 shares of $0.10 par common stock outstanding. After the stock dividend, how many shares are outstanding? What is the par value of each share?

SE8-8A. *Analyze effect of stock split on financial statements. (LO 4).* Romax Company announced a 2-for-1 stock split on its common stock. Before the announcement, there were

200,000 shares of $1 par common stock outstanding. Determine how many shares of common stock will be outstanding after the stock split. What will be the par value of each share? What effect does the stock split have on total shareholders' equity?

SE8-9A. *Calculate retained earnings balance. (LO 5).* On January 1, 2011, Green Corporation started the year with a $520,000 balance in retained earnings. During 2011, the company earned net income of $89,500 and declared and paid dividends of $10,000. Also, the company received cash of $150,000 from a new issue of common stock. What is the balance in retained earnings on December 31, 2011?

SE8-10A. *Calculate retained earnings balance. (LO 5).* Suppose Hillard Company started the year with a balance of $450,000 in retained earnings. During the year, the company declared and paid dividends of $20,000. If the ending balance in retained earnings was $495,500, how much was net income (or net loss) for the year?

SE8-11A. *Calculate return on equity. (LO 7).* Use the following data to calculate the return on equity for Mighty Motors (MM), Inc. At the beginning of 2010, MM's current assets totaled $57,855; total assets totaled $449,999; and total liabilities totaled $424,424. For the year ended December 31, 2010, net income was $3,822. At the end of 2010, the current assets were $62,397; total assets were $369,053; and total liabilities were $361,960. Mighty Motors has no preferred stock. Calculate the return on equity (ROE) for MM for 2010. Make sure you use *average* shareholders' equity in your calculation.

Set B

SE8-12B. *Classify stock. (LO 1).* Sunshine Corporation began operations on July 1, 2009. When Sunshine's first fiscal year ended on June 30, 2010, the balance sheet showed 200,000 shares of common stock issued and 195,000 shares of common stock outstanding. During the second year, Sunshine repurchased 10,000 shares for the treasury. No new shares were issued in the second year. On the balance sheet at June 30, 2011, how many shares would be classified as issued? How many shares are outstanding?

SE8-13B. *Record issuance of common stock. (LO 1).* Nugget Corporation issues 300 shares of its $1 par value common stock at $3.50 per share. Show how this transaction would be recorded in the accounting equation.

SE8-14B. *Analyze effect of issuance of common stock on financial statements. (LO 1).* If a company issues 10,000 shares of $1 par common stock for $8.50 per share, what is the effect on total paid-in capital? What is the effect on additional paid-in capital (also known as paid-in capital in excess of par)?

SE8-15B. *Analyze effect of dividends on financial statements. (LO 2).* On March 15, 2011, the board of directors of Everyman Corporation declared a cash dividend, payable July 10, 2011, of $0.30 per share on the 120,000 common shares outstanding. The accounting period ends June 30. How will this be reflected on the balance sheet at June 30, 2011?

SE8-16B. *Distribute dividend between preferred and common shareholders. (LO 2).* Bates Corporation has 7,000 shares of 5%, $100 par, cumulative preferred stock outstanding and 50,000 shares of $1 par common stock outstanding. If the board of directors declares $80,000 of total dividends and the company did not pay dividends the previous year, how much will the preferred and common shareholders receive?

SE8-17B. *Record purchase of treasury stock. (LO 3).* If Fitness and Fashion Corporation paid $10 per share for 590 shares of its own stock, how would the transaction be shown in the accounting equation? How would the transaction be reflected in the shareholders' equity section of the balance sheet?

SE8-18B. *Analyze effect of stock dividend on financial statements. (LO 4).* Inter Company declared and issued a 5% stock dividend on May 1, 2011. Before this dividend was declared and issued, there were 120,000 shares of $0.50 par common stock outstanding. After the stock dividend, how many shares are outstanding? What is the par value of each share?

SE8-19B. *Analyze effect of stock split on financial statements. (LO 4).* Rail Company announced a 2-for-1 stock split on its common stock. Before the announcement, there were 300,000 shares of $0.50 par common stock outstanding. Determine how many shares of common stock will be outstanding after the stock split. What will be the par value of each share? What effect does the stock split have on total shareholders' equity?

SE8-20B. *Calculate retained earnings balance. (LO 5).* On January 1, 2010, Harrison Corporation started the year with a $422,000 balance in retained earnings. During 2010, the company earned net income of $130,000 and declared and paid dividends of $20,000. Also, the company received cash of $450,000 from a new issue of common stock. What is the balance in retained earnings on December 31, 2010?

SE8-21B. *Calculate retained earnings balance. (LO 5).* Baltimore Manufacturing, Inc., had net income for 2010 of $58,280. During the fiscal year, which began on January 1, 2010, the company declared and paid dividends of $5,500. On the balance sheet at December 31, 2010, the balance in retained earnings was $295,880. What was the December 31, 2009, balance (i.e., the beginning balance) in retained earnings?

SE8-22B. *Calculate net income amount using return on equity ratio. (LO 7).* Octevo Corporation had a return on shareholders' equity (ROE) of 12% in 2012. If total average shareholders' equity for Octevo Corporation was $500,000 and the company has no preferred stock, what was net income for 2012?

MyAccountingLab

All of the A exercises can be found within MyAccountingLab, an online homework and practice environment.

Exercises
Set A

E8-23A. *Analyze equity section of balance sheet. (LO 1, 5).* Super Retail Corporation reported the following information on the financial statements included with its 2010 annual report:

(dollars in thousands)	March 31, 2010	March 31, 2009
Common stock, par value $0.0005		
Authorized: 370,000,000 shares;		
Issued and outstanding 74,758,500 shares at March 31, 2010	37	
72,406,500 shares at March 31, 2009		36
Paid-in capital	396,200	352,633
Retained earnings	143,190	66,272

Were any new shares of common stock issued between March 31, 2009, and March 31, 2010? Did the company report net income for the year ended March 31, 2010? Explain how you know.

E8-24A. *Classify stock and prepare shareholders' equity section of balance sheet. (LO 1, 6).* Royal Knight Printing Company's corporate charter allows it to sell 400,000 shares of $3 par value common stock. To date, the company has issued 75,000 shares for a total of $337,500. Last month, Royal Knight repurchased 5,000 shares for $4.75 per share.

1. If Royal Knight were to prepare a balance sheet, how many shares would it show as authorized, issued, and outstanding?
2. In addition to the shareholders' equity given previously, Royal Knight also has $295,000 in retained earnings. Using this information, prepare the shareholders' equity section of Royal Knight's balance sheet.

E8-25A. *Record stock transactions. (LO 1, 3).* Show how each of the following transactions affects the accounting equation:

March 1	Issued 75,000 shares of $0.02 par value common stock for cash of $99,750
April 1	Issued 1,000 shares of $95 par value preferred stock for cash at $115 per share
June 30	Purchased 1,000 shares of treasury stock for $3 per share (i.e., the company bought its own common stock in the stock market)

E8-26A. *Analyze effects of stock transactions on financial statements. (LO 1, 3).* Refer to the information in E8-25A. How many shares of common stock will be classified as issued at June 30? How many shares will be classified as outstanding at June 30?

E8-27A. *Analyze effects of dividends on financial statements. (LO 2).* Burlon Printing Company had net income of $175,000 for the year ended June 30, 2009. On July 15, 2009, the board of directors met and declared a dividend of $0.35 per share for each of the 150,000 outstanding shares of common stock. The board voted to make the actual distribution on September 1 to all shareholders of record as of August 1. What is (a) the date of declaration, (b) the date of record, and (c) the date of payment? If Burlon Printing Company were to prepare a balance sheet on July 31, 2009, how would it report the dividends (if at all)?

E8-28A. *Distribute dividend between preferred and common shareholders. (LO 2).* Holly Brown Architectural Company has 5,000 shares of 8%, $70 par, cumulative preferred stock outstanding and 7,500 shares of $2.50 par value common stock outstanding. The company began operations on July 1, 2009. The cash dividends declared and paid during each of the first three years of Holly Brown's operations are shown. Calculate the amounts that went to the preferred and the common shareholders (SHs) each year.

Year Ended	Total Dividends Paid	Dividends to Preferred SHs	Dividends to Common SHs
June 30, 2010	$20,000		
June 30, 2011	36,000		
June 30, 2012	40,000		

E8-29A. *Analyze equity section of balance sheet. (LO 1, 2).* Athletic Endurance Company had the following stockholders' equity section on the December 31, 2010, balance sheet:

Preferred stock, 6%, $120 par, cumulative	$1,170,000
Common stock, $1.50 par value	300,000
Paid-in capital in excess of par, common stock	1,200,000
Retained earnings	2,500,000
Total	$5,170,000

1. How many shares of common stock are classified as issued?
2. How many shares of common stock are outstanding?
3. How many shares of preferred stock are outstanding?
4. What was the average selling price of a share of common stock?
5. If $115,000 of dividends was declared and there were no dividends in arrears, how much of the total would go to the common shareholders?

E8-30A. *Record stock transactions. (LO 1, 2, 3).* Surfing Dewd Corporation is authorized to issue both preferred and common stock. Surfing Dewd's preferred stock is $105 par, 6% preferred stock. During the first month of operations, the company engaged in the following transactions related to its stock. Show each of the following transactions in the accounting equation:

March 1	Issued 16,000 shares of $0.50 par value common stock for cash at $5 per share
March 11	Issued 1,500 shares of preferred stock at par
March 16	Purchased 3,000 shares of common stock to be held in the treasury for $7 per share

March 18	Issued 32,000 shares $0.50 par value common stock for cash at $10 per share
March 20	Sold 2,900 shares of the treasury stock purchased on the 16th for $12 per share
March 31	Declared a $10,000 dividend

E8-31A. *Prepare equity section of the balance sheet. (LO 1, 2, 3, 6).* Use the data from E8-30A to prepare the shareholders' equity section of the balance sheet at March 31. Retained earnings at month end are $75,000.

E8-32A. *Analyze equity accounts. (LO 1, 2, 3, 5).* The following balances were shown on the year-end balance sheets for 2009 and 2010 for Columbia Company. For each item, give the most likely reason for the change from one year to the next.

	December 31, 2009	December 31, 2010	Explanation
Common stock	$ 45,000	$ 50,000	
Paid-in capital	$200,000	$230,000	
Retained earnings	$182,500	*$200,000	
Treasury stock	$ (3,450)	$ (5,450)	

*Net income for the year was $20,000.

E8-33A. *Analyze equity section of balance sheet. (LO 1, 2, 3).* Answer the following questions using the shareholders' equity section of Enthusiastic Learning Corporation's balance sheet at June 30:

Shareholders' equity	
Preferred stock, cumulative, 15,000 shares authorized, 5,000 shares issued and outstanding	$ 525,000
Additional paid-in capital, preferred stock	75,000
Common stock, $1.00 par, 500,000 shares authorized, 375,000 shares issued	375,000
Additional paid-in capital, common stock	750,000
Retained earnings	855,000
	2,580,000
Less: treasury stock (5,000 common shares)	(25,000)
Total shareholders' equity	$2,555,000

1. How many shares of common stock are outstanding?
2. On average, what was the issue price of the common shares issued?
3. What is the par value of the preferred stock?
4. If the total annual dividend on preferred stock is $31,500, what is the dividend rate on preferred stock?
5. On average, how much per share did the company pay for the treasury stock?

E8-34A. *Record stock transactions. (LO 1, 2, 3, 4).* On the first day of the fiscal year, Music Productions Corporation had 210,000 shares of $2 par common stock issued (at par) and outstanding, and the retained earnings balance was $900,000. Show how each of the following transactions would affect the accounting equation:

1. Issued 5,000 additional shares of common stock for $10 per share
2. Declared and distributed a 5% stock dividend when the market price was $10 per share
3. Issued 15,000 additional shares of common stock for $12 per share
4. Declared a cash dividend on outstanding shares of $1.30 per share
5. Paid the dividend declared in item (4)
6. Purchased 5,000 shares of treasury stock for $14 per share
7. Sold 2,000 shares of treasury stock for $16 per share

8. Sold 2,500 shares of treasury stock for $15 per share
9. Declared 2-for-1 stock split

E8-35A. *Prepare equity section of the balance sheet. (LO 1, 2, 3, 4, 6).* Use the data from E8-34A to prepare the shareholders' equity section of the balance sheet at year end. Net income for the year was $150,000.

E8-36A. *Prepare equity section of the balance sheet. (LO 1, 3, 5, 6).* The following account balances can be found in the general ledger of Zebra Enterprises at year end. Prepare the shareholders' equity section of the balance sheet.

Retained earnings	$ 650,000
Treasury stock (10,000 common shares at cost)	85,000
Common stock ($2 par, 500,000 shares authorized, 220,000 shares issued)	440,000
Additional paid-in capital, common stock	1,100,000
Preferred stock ($12 par value, 8%, 75,000 shares authorized, 25,000 shares issued)	300,000
Additional paid-in capital, preferred stock	50,000

E8-37A. *Calculate return on equity and earnings per share. (LO 7).* The following financial information is available for High-Speed Internet Company at the end of its two most recent fiscal years. The company has no preferred stock. Calculate (1) return on equity and (2) earnings per share for 2009 and 2010. What do the ratios indicate about the company's performance during the year?

(amounts in thousands)	2010	2009
Average common shareholders' equity	$3,984	$3,450
Dividends declared for common shareholders	1,500	1,455
Net income	6,045	4,266
Weighted average number of common shares outstanding during the year	6,558	5,850

E8-38A. *Analyze effects of equity transactions on financial statements. (LO 1, 2, 3, 4, 5).* Analyze the following transactions and indicate the dollar increase (+) or decrease (−) each has on the balance sheet. If there is an overall change in shareholders' equity, also indicate whether contributed capital, retained earnings, or treasury stock is affected. If the transaction has no effect on the balance sheet, enter NA for that item. The first row is filled in for you as an example.

	Assets	Liabilities	Shareholders' Equity	Equity Section Affected
Issued 1,000 shares of $1 par common stock at par	+1,000		+1,000	Contributed capital
Issued 1,500 shares of $1 par common stock for $14				
Declared a cash dividend of $0.25 per share				
Paid the $0.25 cash dividend				
Purchased 200 shares of treasury stock for $17 per share				
Sold 100 shares of treasury stock for $17 per share				
Declared and distributed a 10% common stock dividend (when the market price was $17 per share)				
Announced a 2-for-1 stock split				
Issued 2,000 shares of $100 par, 4% noncumulative preferred stock				

Set B

E8-39B. *Analyze equity section of balance sheet. (LO 1, 5).* Shipping Unlimited, Inc., reported the following information on the financial statements included with its 2011 annual report:

(dollars in thousands)		June 30, 2011	June 30, 2010
Common stock, par value $0.02			
Authorized:	200,000 shares;		
Issued:	95,000 shares at June 30, 2011;		
	95,000 shares at June 30, 2010	$2	$2
Outstanding:	85,000 shares at June 30, 2011;		
	75,000 shares at June 30, 2010		
Additional paid-in capital		205,015	195,820
Retained earnings		835,880	705,970

Were any new shares of common stock issued during the year ended June 30, 2011? Did the company report net income for the year ended June 30, 2011? Explain how you know.

E8-40B. *Classify stock and prepare shareholders' equity section of balance sheet. (LO 1, 6).* Soper Classic Music, Inc.'s corporate charter allows it to sell 250,000 shares of $1 par value common stock. To date, the company has issued 150,000 shares for a total of $225,000. Last month, Soper Classic repurchased 1,000 shares for $2.00 per share.

1. If Soper Classic were to prepare a balance sheet, how many shares would it show as authorized, issued, and outstanding?
2. In addition to the shareholders' equity given previously, Soper Classic also has $285,000 in retained earnings. Using this information, prepare the shareholders' equity section of Soper Classic Music, Inc.'s balance sheet.

E8-41B. *Record stock transactions. (LO 1, 3).* Show how each of the following transactions would be recorded in the accounting equation:

August 1	Issued 75,000 shares of $0.05 par value common stock for cash of $750,000
November 1	Issued 2,500 shares of $100 par value preferred stock for cash at $160 per share
December 31	Purchased 5,000 shares of treasury stock (i.e., the company bought its own common stock in the stock market) for $11.00 per share

E8-42B. *Analyze effects of stock transactions on financial statements. (LO 1, 3).* Refer to the information in E8-41B. How many shares of common stock will be classified as issued at December 31? How many shares of common stock will be classified as outstanding at December 31?

E8-43B. *Analyze effects of dividends on financial statements. (LO 2).* Steverson Air Conditioning, Inc., had net income of $210,000 for the year ended December 31, 2009. On January 15, 2010, the board of directors met and declared a dividend of $0.15 per share for each of the 200,000 outstanding shares of common stock. The board voted to make the actual distribution on April 1 to all shareholders of record as of March 1. What is (a) the date of declaration, (b) the date of record, and (c) the date of payment? If Steverson Air were to prepare a balance sheet on January 31, 2010, how would the dividends be reported (if at all)?

E8-44B. *Distribute dividend between preferred and common shareholders. (LO 2).* State of Grace Publishing, Inc., has 6,000 shares of $120 par, 10% cumulative preferred stock outstanding and 10,000 shares of $1.50 par value common stock outstanding. The company began operations on January 1, 2010. The cash dividends declared and paid during each of the first three years of State of Grace's operations are shown next. Calculate the amounts that went to the preferred shareholders and the common shareholders (SHs) each year.

Year	Total Dividends Paid	Dividends to Preferred SHs	Dividends to Common SHs
2010	$100,000		
2011	70,000		
2012	98,000		

E8-45B. *Analyze equity section of balance sheet. (LO 1, 2).* Frozen Entrée Corporation had the following stockholders' equity section on the June 30, 2011, balance sheet:

Preferred stock, $125 par, 8% cumulative	$1,112,500
Common stock, $3 par value	900,000
Paid-in capital in excess of par, common stock	1,500,000
Retained earnings	3,115,000
Total	$6,627,500

1. How many shares of common stock are classified as issued?
2. How many shares of common stock are outstanding?
3. How many shares of preferred stock are outstanding?
4. What was the average selling price of a share of common stock?
5. If $145,000 of dividends was declared and there were $15,000 dividends in arrears at that time, how much of the dividend would go to the common shareholders?

E8-46B. *Record stock transactions. (LO 1, 2, 3).* Minute Magazine Publications, Inc., is authorized to issue both preferred and common stock. Minute Magazine's preferred stock is $155 par, 10% preferred stock. During the first month of operations, the company engaged in the following transactions related to its stock. For each of the following transactions, show how it would be recorded in the accounting equation:

May 1	Issued 50,000 shares of $1.00 par value common stock for cash at $12 per share
May 9	Issued 2,000 shares of preferred stock at par
May 17	Purchased 2,500 shares of common stock to be held in the treasury for $15 per share
May 21	Issued 35,000 shares $1.00 par value common stock for cash at $18 per share
May 28	Sold 2,000 shares of the treasury stock purchased on the 17th for $20 per share
May 31	Declared a $39,000 dividend

E8-47B. *Prepare equity section of the balance sheet. (LO 1, 2, 3, 6).* Use the data from E8-46B to prepare the shareholders' equity section of the balance sheet at May 31. Retained earnings at month-end are $105,000.

E8-48B. *Analyze equity accounts. (LO 1, 2, 3, 5).* The following balances were shown on the year-end balance sheets for 2010 and 2011 for High Note Publishing Company. For each item, give the most likely reason for the change from one year to the next.

	December 31, 2010	December 21, 2011	Explanation
Common stock	$ 35,000	$ 43,000	
Paid-in capital	$115,000	155,000	
Retained earnings	$142,000	*$160,500	
Treasury stock	$ (2,125)	$ (2,625)	

*Net income for the year was $22,750.

E8-49B. *Analyze equity section of balance sheet. (LO 1, 2, 3).* Answer the following questions using the shareholders' equity section of Technical Data Corporation's balance sheet at June 30:

Shareholders' equity	
Preferred stock, cumulative, 20,000 shares authorized, 5,000 shares issued and outstanding	$ 550,000
Additional paid-in capital, preferred stock	50,000
Common stock, $1.25 par, 650,000 shares authorized, 350,000 shares issued	437,500
Additional paid-in capital, common stock	2,012,500
Retained earnings	1,425,000
	4,475,000
Less: treasury stock (6,500 common shares)	(52,000)
Total shareholders' equity	$4,423,000

1. How many shares of common stock are outstanding?
2. On average, what was the issue price of the common shares issued?
3. What is the par value of the preferred stock?
4. If the total annual dividend on preferred stock is $49,500, what is the dividend rate on preferred stock?
5. On average, how much per share did the company pay for the treasury stock?

E8-50B. *Record stock transactions. (LO 1, 2, 3, 4).* On the first day of the fiscal year, TH Construction, Inc., had 150,000 shares of $1.00 par common stock issued (at par) and outstanding, and the retained earnings balance was $275,000. Show each of the following transactions in the accounting equation:

1. Issued 10,000 additional shares of common stock for $5 per share
2. Declared and distributed a 10% stock dividend when the market price was $5 per share
3. Issued 20,000 additional shares of common stock for $7 per share
4. Declared a cash dividend on outstanding shares of $0.75 per share
5. Paid the dividend declared in item (4)
6. Purchased 8,000 shares of treasury stock for $9 per share
7. Sold 6,500 shares of treasury stock for $10 per share
8. Sold 1,400 shares of treasury stock for $8 per share
9. Declared 2-for-1 stock split

E8-51B. *Prepare equity section of the balance sheet. (LO 1, 2, 3, 4, 6).* Use the data from E8-50B to prepare the shareholders' equity section of the balance sheet at year end. Net income for the year was $90,000.

E8-52B. *Prepare equity section of the balance sheet. (LO 1, 3, 5, 6).* The following account balances can be found in the general ledger of McKinney de Garcia Energy Products Corporation at year end. Prepare the shareholders' equity section of the balance sheet.

Retained earnings	$ 320,000
Treasury stock (5,000 common shares at cost)	45,000
Common stock ($1 par, 600,000 shares authorized, 275,000 shares issued)	275,000
Additional paid-in capital, common stock	1,787,500
Preferred stock ($6 par value, 10%, 80,000 shares authorized, 25,000 shares issued)	150,000
Additional paid-in capital, preferred stock	25,000

E8-53B. *Calculate return on equity and earnings per share. (LO 7).* The following financial information is available for Book Publishing Company at the end of its two most recent fiscal years.

The company has no preferred stock. Calculate (1) return on equity and (2) earnings per share for 2010 and 2011. What do the ratios indicate about the company's performance during the year?

(amounts in thousands)	2011	2010
Average common stockholders' equity	$3,120	$2,470
Dividends declared for common stockholders	600	530
Net income	6,020	3,130
Weighted average number of common shares outstanding during the year	4,100	3,270

E8-54B. *Analyze effects of equity transactions on financial statements. (LO 1, 2, 3, 4, 5).* Analyze the following transactions and indicate the dollar increase (+) or decrease (−) each has on the balance sheet. If there is an overall change in shareholders' equity, also indicate whether contributed capital, retained earnings, or treasury stock is affected. If the transaction has no effect on the balance sheet, enter NA for that item. The first row is filled in for you as an example.

	Assets	Liabilities	Shareholders' Equity	Equity Section Affected
Issued 1,000 shares of $0.50 par common stock at par	+500		+500	Contributed capital
Issued 2,500 shares of $0.50 par common stock for $6.50				
Declared a cash dividend of $0.50 per share				
Paid the $0.50 cash dividend				
Purchased 175 shares of treasury stock for $9 per share				
Sold 65 shares of treasury stock for $9 per share				
Declared and distributed a 5% common stock dividend (when the market price was $9 per share)				
Announced a 2-for-1 stock split				
Issued 5,000 shares of $75 par, 6% noncumulative preferred stock at par				

Problems
Set A

All of the A problems can be found within MyAccountingLab, an online homework and practice environment.

P8-55A. *Account for stock transactions. (LO 1, 6).* Runnels Geometric Designs Company was started on January 1, 2009. The company is authorized to issue 50,000 shares of 8%, $105 par value preferred stock and 600,000 shares of common stock with a par value of $2 per share. The following stock transactions took place during 2009:

January 15	Issued 5,000 shares of common stock for cash at $3 per share
March 1	Issued 10,000 shares of preferred stock for cash at $110 per share
July 12	Issued 30,000 shares of common stock for cash at $5 per share
October 10	Issued 5,000 shares of preferred stock for cash at $108 per share
December 1	Issued 20,000 shares of common stock for cash at $7 per share

Requirements

1. Show each transaction in the accounting equation.
2. Prepare the contributed capital portion of the stockholders' equity section of the balance sheet at December 31, 2009.

P8-56A. *Analyze and record stock dividend transactions. (LO 4).* As of December 31, 2010, Hargrove Dynamics, Inc., had 75,000 shares of $5 par value common stock issued and outstanding. The retained earnings balance was $265,000. On January 15, 2011, Hargrove Dynamics declared and issued an 8% stock dividend to its common shareholders. At the time of the dividend, the market value of the stock was $25 per share.

Requirements

1. Show how the stock dividend would affect the accounting equation.
2. How many shares of stock are outstanding after the stock dividend?
3. If you owned 7% of the outstanding common stock of Hargrove Dynamics, Inc., before the stock dividend, what is your percentage ownership after the stock dividend?

P8-57A. *Analyze and record stock transactions and prepare equity section of balance sheet. (LO 1, 2, 3, 4, 5, 6).* The following information pertains to the equity accounts of Bottling Company:

    a. Contributed capital on January 1, 2010, consisted of 80,000 issued and outstanding shares of common stock with par value of $1; additional paid-in capital in excess of par of $480,000; and retained earnings of $560,000.

    b. During the first quarter of 2010, Bottling Company issued an additional 5,000 shares of common stock for $7 per share.

    c. On July 15, the company declared a 3-for-1 stock split.

    d. On October 15, the company declared and distributed a 5% stock dividend. The market price of the stock on that date was $8 per share.

    e. On November 1, the company declared a dividend of $0.90 per share to be paid on November 15.

    f. Near the end of the year, the company's CEO decided the company should buy 1,000 shares of its own stock. At that time, the stock was trading for $9 per share in the stock market.

    g. Net income for 2010 was $75,500.

Requirements

1. Show how each of the transactions would affect the accounting equation.
2. Prepare the shareholders' equity section of the balance sheet at December 31, 2010.

P8-58A. *Record stock transactions, prepare equity section of balance sheet, and calculate ratios. (LO 1, 2, 3, 5, 6, 7).* On January 1, 2011, Classic Clothing Corporation's shareholders' equity account balances were as follows:

Preferred stock (5%, $80 par noncumulative, 35,000 shares authorized)	$ 800,000
Common stock ($1 par value, 750,000 shares authorized)	500,000
Additional paid-in capital, preferred stock	30,000
Additional paid-in capital, common stock	2,000,000
Retained earnings	1,650,000
Treasury stock—common (10,000 shares, at cost)	60,000

During 2011, Classic Clothing Corporation engaged in the following transactions:

January 1	Issued 10,000 shares of common stock for $6 per share
April 1	Purchased 10,000 additional shares of common treasury stock at $8 per share
June 1	Declared the annual cash dividend on preferred stock, payable June 30
December 1	Declared a $0.55 per share cash dividend to common stockholders payable December 31, 2011

Net income for the year was $940,000.

Requirements

1. Show each of the transactions in the accounting equation.
2. Prepare the shareholders' equity section of the balance sheet at December 31, 2011.
3. Calculate return on common stockholders' equity for the year ended December 31, 2011.

P8-59A. *Prepare equity section of balance sheet. (LO 1, 2, 5, 6).* On November 1, 2009, Dazzling Desserts Corporation had 300,000 shares of $1 par common stock issued and outstanding. The shareholders' equity accounts at November 1, 2009, had the following balances:

Common stock	$ 300,000
Additional paid-in capital	2,700,000
Retained earnings	3,500,000

The following transactions occurred during the fiscal year ended October 31, 2010:
   a. On November 30, issued 30,000 shares of 7%, $95 par, cumulative preferred stock at $100.
   b. On December 31, reacquired 5,000 shares of common stock for $12 per share.
   c. On January 1, declared a cash dividend of $0.75 per share on the common stock outstanding, payable on January 31, 2010, to shareholders of record on December 15.
   d. Declared and paid dividends to preferred shareholders on March 1, 2010.
   e. Net income for the year ended October 31, 2010, was $675,000.

Requirement

Prepare the shareholders' equity section of Dazzling Desserts' balance sheet at October 31, 2010.

P8-60A. *Analyze equity section of balance sheet. (LO 1, 2, 3, 5).* The following information is from the equity sections of the comparative balance sheets for Freedman Cosmetics Company:

	December 31, 2010	December 31, 2009
Common stock ($20 par)	$ 600,000	$500,000
Additional paid-in-capital	800,000	400,000
Retained earnings	105,000	55,000
Total shareholders' equity	$1,505,000	$955,000

Net income for the year ended December 31, 2010, was $250,000.

Requirements

1. How many new shares of common stock were issued during 2010?
2. What was the average issue price of the stock issued during 2010?
3. What was the amount of dividends declared during 2010?
4. Did the company have any treasury shares at the end of 2010?

P8-61A. *Analyze equity section of balance sheet. (LO 1, 2, 5).* At June 30, 2011, Vision Specialty Company reported the following on its comparative balance sheets:

	June 30, 2011	June 30, 2010
Common stock		
Authorized: 1,200 shares		
Issued: 1,000 shares at June 30, 2011	$20,000	
800 shares at June 30, 2010		$16,000
Paid-in capital in excess of par	22,000	16,000
Retained earnings	40,000	29,500

Requirements

1. What is the par value of the company's common stock?
2. Did the company issue any new shares during the fiscal year ended June 30, 2011?
3. What was the approximate (average) issue price of the stock issued during the year ended June 30, 2011?
4. Did Vision Specialty Company earn net income (loss) during the year ended June 30, 2011? Assuming no dividends were declared and paid, how much was net income (loss)?

P8-62A. *Analyze equity section of balance sheet. (LO 1, 2, 3, 4).* The following information is from the equity section of the comparative balance sheets of Veridian Dynamic, Inc.:

Veridian Dynamics, Inc.
From the **Consolidated Balance Sheets**

Shareholders' equity:	June 30, 2010	June 30, 2009
Common stock, $1.00 par value; 500,000 shares issued and _____ shares outstanding at June 30, 2010; and 320,000 shares issued and _____ shares outstanding at June 30, 2009.	$ 500,000	$ 320,000
Additional paid-in-capital	3,180,000	1,920,000
Retained earnings	1,050,000	975,000
Treasury stock, at cost, 15,000 shares at June 30, 2010, and 9,000 shares at June 30, 2009	(105,000)	(54,000)

Requirements

1. What was the average issue price per share of the 500,000 shares classified as "issued" at June 30, 2010? (Round the answer to the nearest cent.)
2. What was the average issue price of the 180,000 shares of common stock issued during the fiscal year ended June 30, 2010?
3. How many shares were outstanding at June 30, 2010? How many shares were outstanding at June 30, 2009?
4. How many shares did the company buy back during the year? What was the average cost of a share of the treasury shares purchased during the year? (Assume no treasury stock was sold during the year.)
5. If no dividends were declared and paid, what was net income for the year ended June 30, 2010?

Set B

P8-63B. *Account for stock transactions. (LO 1, 6).* Clarkson Chivas, Inc., was started on July 1, 2010. The company is authorized to issue 200,000 shares of 6%, $110 par value preferred stock, and 1,500,000 shares of common stock with a par value of $1 per share. The following stock transactions took place during the fiscal year ended June 30, 2011:

July 15	Issued 10,000 shares of common stock for cash at $2 per share
October 1	Issued 5,000 shares of preferred stock for cash at $115 per share
January 12	Issued 15,000 shares of common stock for cash at $4 per share
March 10	Issued 7,500 shares of preferred stock for cash at $120 per share
June 1	Issued 25,000 shares of common stock for cash at $6 per share

Requirements

1. Show each transaction in the accounting equation.
2. Prepare the contributed capital portion of the shareholders' equity section of the balance sheet at June 30, 2011.

P8-64B. *Analyze and record stock dividend transactions. (LO 4).* At June 30, 2010, Soft Fabrics Manufacturing had 150,000 shares of $7 par common stock issued and outstanding. The retained earnings balance was $190,000. On July 15, 2010, Soft Fabrics declared and issued a 5% stock dividend to its common shareholders. At the time of the dividend, the market value of the stock was $15 per share.

Requirements

1. How would the stock dividend be shown in the accounting equation?
2. How many shares of stock are outstanding after the stock dividend?
3. If you owned 10% of the outstanding common stock of Soft Fabrics Manufacturing before the stock dividend, what is your percentage ownership after the stock dividend?

P8-65B. *Analyze and record stock transactions and prepare equity section of balance sheet.* (LO 1, 2, 3, 4, 5, 6). The following information pertains to Books & Calendars, Inc.:

a. Contributed capital on November 1, 2009, consisted of 75,000 issued and outstanding shares of common stock with par value of $2; additional paid-in capital in excess of par of $375,000; and retained earnings of $525,000.

b. During the first quarter of the fiscal year, Books & Calendars issued an additional 10,000 shares of common stock for $6 per share.

c. On April 15, the company declared a 2-for-1 stock split.

d. On May 31, the company declared and distributed a 10% stock dividend. The market price of the stock on that date was $8 per share.

e. On June 30, the company declared a dividend of $0.25 per share to be paid on July 15.

f. During October 2010, Books & Calendars' CEO decided the company should buy 2,000 shares of its own stock. At that time, the stock was trading for $9 per share.

g. Net income for the year ended October 31, 2010, was $67,500.

Requirements

1. Show each of the transactions in the accounting equation.
2. Prepare the shareholders' equity section of the balance sheet at October 31, 2010.

P8-66B. *Record stock transactions, prepare equity section of balance sheet, and calculate ratios.* (LO 1, 2, 3, 5, 6, 7). On January 1, 2010, the Manny's Make-up Corporation shareholders' equity account balances were as follows:

Preferred stock (7.5%, $110 par noncumulative, 20,000 shares authorized)	$ 550,000
Common stock ($2 par value, 3,000,000 shares authorized)	800,000
Additional paid-in capital, preferred stock	50,000
Additional paid-in capital, common stock	1,600,000
Retained earnings	1,890,000
Treasury stock—common (1,000 shares, at cost)	9,000

During 2010, Manny's Make-up Corporation engaged in the following transactions:

January 1	Issued 10,000 shares of common stock for $10 per share
March 1	Purchased 1,000 additional shares of common treasury stock at $12 per share
June 1	Declared the annual cash dividend on preferred stock, payable June 30
December 1	Declared a $0.50 per share cash dividend to common stockholders payable December 31, 2010

Net income for the year was $641,250.

Requirements

1. Show the transactions in the accounting equation.
2. Prepare the shareholders' equity section of the balance sheet at December 31, 2010.
3. Compute earnings per share and return on common shareholders' equity for the year ended December 31, 2010.

P8-67B. *Prepare equity section of balance sheet.* (LO 1, 2, 5, 6). On July 1, 2009, Pet Supplies Company had 600,000 shares of $0.50 par common stock issued and outstanding. The shareholders' equity accounts at July 1, 2009, had the following balances:

Common stock	$ 300,000
Additional paid-in capital	1,500,000
Retained earnings	2,650,000

The following transactions occurred during the fiscal year ended June 30, 2010:

a. On July 30, issued 40,000 shares of $75 par value, 5% cumulative preferred stock at $85.

b. On October 1, reacquired 10,000 shares of common stock for $4 per share.

c. On December 1, declared a cash dividend of $1.00 per share on the common stock outstanding, payable on December 31, 2009, to shareholders of record on November 15.
d. Declared and paid dividends to preferred shareholders on December 31, 2009.
e. Net income for the year ended June 30, 2010, was $925,000.

Requirement

Prepare the shareholders' equity section of Pet Supplies Company's balance sheet at June 30, 2010.

P8-68B. *Analyze equity section of balance sheet. (LO 1, 2, 3, 5).* The following information was shown on the recent comparative balance sheets for Snipes Couriers, Inc.:

	June 30, 2011	June 30, 2010
Common stock ($5 par)	$250,000	$100,000
Additional paid-in-capital	300,000	60,000
Retained earnings	89,000	68,000
Total shareholders' equity	$639,000	$228,000

Net income for the year ended June 3, 2011, was $42,000.

Requirements

1. How many shares of common stock were issued to new shareholders during the year ended June 30, 2011?
2. What was the average issue price of the stock issued during the year ended June 30, 2011?
3. What was the amount of dividends declared during the year ended June 30, 2011?
4. Can you tell if the company had any treasury shares at June 30, 2011?

P8-69B. *Analyze equity section of balance sheet. (LO 1, 2, 5).* At December 31, 2009, Orange Cleaning Supplies Company reported the following on its comparative balance sheet, which included 2008 amounts for comparison:

	December 31	
	2009	2008
Common stock		
Authorized: 5,000 shares		
Issued: 2,900 shares in 2009	$29,000	
2,800 shares in 2008		$28,000
Paid-in capital in excess of par	8,700	5,780
Retained earnings	30,100	28,600

Requirements

1. What is the par value of the company's common stock?
2. Did the company issue any new shares during the fiscal year ended December 31, 2009?
3. What was the approximate (average) issue price of the stock issued during the year ended December 31, 2009?
4. Did Orange Cleaning Supplies Company earn net income (loss) during the year ended December 31, 2009? Assuming no dividends were paid this year, what was net income (loss)?

P8-70B. *Analyze equity section of balance sheet. (LO 1, 2, 3, 4).* The following information is from the equity section of the comparative balance sheets of Shelby Electronics, Inc.:

Shelby Electronics, Inc.
From the Consolidated Balance Sheets

	November 30, 2010	November 30, 2009
Common stock, $2.00 par value; 250,000 shares issued and _____ shares outstanding at November 30, 2010; and 175,000 shares issued and _____ shares outstanding at November 30, 2009	500,000	350,000
Additional paid-in capital	2,175,000	1,050,000
Retained earnings	675,000	580,000
Treasury stock at cost, 20,000 shares at November 30, 2010, and 16,000 shares at November 30, 2009	(140,000)	(96,000)

Requirements

1. What was the average issue price per share of the 250,000 shares classified as "issued" at November 30, 2010? (Round the answer to the nearest cent.)
2. What was the average issue price of the 75,000 shares of common stock issued during the fiscal year ended November 30, 2010?
3. How many shares were outstanding at November 30, 2010? How many shares were outstanding at November 30, 2009?
4. How many shares did the company buy back during the year? What was the average cost of a share of the treasury shares purchased during the year? (Assume no treasury stock was sold during the year.)
5. If no dividends were declared and paid, what was net income for the year ended November 30, 2010?

Financial Statement Analysis

FSA8-1. *Analyze equity section of balance sheet. (LO 1, 2, 5).* ConAgra Foods reported the following information on its comparative balance sheet at May 25, 2008 (dollars in millions):

	May 25, 2008	May 27, 2007
Common stock, par value _____		
Authorized: 1.2 billion shares		
Issued: 566,653,605 shares in 2008	$2,833.4	
566,410,152 shares in 2007		$2,832.2
Additional paid-in capital	866.9	816.8
Retained earnings	3,409.5	2,856.0
Accumulated other comprehensive income	286.5	(5.9)
Treasury stock, at cost 82,282,300 and 76,631,063 shares, respectively	(2,058.9)	(1,916.2)

1. Explain what Additional paid-in capital and retained earnings each represent.
2. What is the approximate par value of ConAgra's common stock?
3. How many new shares of common stock did the company issue during the fiscal year ended May 25, 2008?
4. What was the approximate (average) issue price of the stock issued during the year?
5. Did ConAgra earn a net income during the year?
6. If ConAgra paid dividends of $377.1 (million) total, what would you estimate net income for the year to be?

FSA8-2. *Analyze equity section of balance sheet. (LO 1, 3, 5).* The following information is from the comparative balance sheets of Ameristar Casinos, Inc.:

Adapted from Ameristar Casinos, Inc.
From the **Consolidated Balance Sheets**
(*amounts in thousands, except share data*)

Shareholders' equity:	December 31, 2008	December 31, 2007
Preferred stock, $0.01 par value, 30,000,000 shares authorized; none issued and outstanding	–	–
Common stock, $0.01 par value; 120,000,000 shares authorized; 58,093,041 shares issued and _____ shares outstanding at December 31, 2008; and 57,946,167 shares issued and _____ shares outstanding at December 31, 2007	$ 581	$ 579
Additional paid-in-capital	246,662	234,983
Retained earnings	136,551	285,238
Other comprehensive gain (loss)	(27,295)	
Treasury stock, at cost, 792,322 shares at December 31, 2008, and 787,236 shares at December 31, 2007	(17,719)	(17,674)
Total shareholders' equity	$338,780	$503,126

1. How many shares of common stock were outstanding at December 31, 2008?
2. How many shares of common stock were outstanding at December 31, 2007?
3. What was the average issue price per share of the 58,093,041 shares classified as "issued" at December 31, 2008? (Round the answer to the nearest cent.)
4. The company paid cash dividends of $18,015 (in thousands) during the year ended December 31, 2008. What was the company's net income or net loss for the year ended December 31, 2008?

FSA8-3. *Analyze equity section of balance sheet. (LO 3, 7).* Use the annual report of Barnes & Noble, Inc., found on the firm's Web site, www.barnesandnobleinc.com/for_investors/for_investors.html, to answer the following:

1. Does Barnes & Noble buy back its own stock? Where, in the financial statements, is this disclosed? Explain the treasury stock transaction(s) that took place during the most recent fiscal year.
2. Compute the return on equity for the two most recent consecutive years. What information do these ratios provide?

Critical Thinking Problems

Business Risk

When the stock market is going up over a long period of time, investors can become complacent about the risks of being a stockholder. After the significant decline of the stock market in 2008, people have begun to rethink the risk involved in owning stock. What kinds of risks do the owners of publicly-traded companies face? What could you do, as an investor, to continue to invest in the market but minimize your risk?

Ethics

AVX Electronics is very close to bringing a revolutionary new computer chip to the market. The company fears that it could soon be the target of a takeover by a giant telecommunications company if this news were to leak before the product is introduced. The current AVX management intends to redistribute the company's stock holdings so its managers will have a larger share of ownership. So, management has decided to buy back 20% of the company's common stock while the price is still quite low and distribute it to the managers—including themselves—as part of the company's bonus plan. Are the actions of AVX management ethical? Explain why this strategy would reduce the risk of a hostile takeover. Was any group hurt by this strategy?

Group Assignment

In groups, select two companies that you would invest in if you had the money. Find their financial statements on the Internet and examine the shareholders' equity section of their balance sheets. What does your analysis tell you about each firm? Is this a good investment? Explain your findings and conclusion.

Internet Exercise: Hershey Foods Corporation

Hershey is the market leader, ahead of Mars, Incorporated, in the U.S. candy market. The company makes such well-known chocolate and candy brands as Hershey's Kisses, Reese's peanut butter cups, Twizzlers licorice, Jolly Rancher, Mounds, Super Bubble gum, and Kit Kat (licensed from Nestlé). Its products are sold throughout North America and exported to over 90 countries.
    Go to www.hersheys.com.

IE8-1. Explore Investor's Relations. In what city is the Hershey factory located? The current stock quote (market price) of Hershey's stock is how much per share? Is this market price reflected on the Hershey balance sheet? If it is, where is it found?

Use the most recent annual report and find the consolidated balance sheets to answer the following questions.

IE8-2. How many types of stock have been authorized and issued? For the most recent year, how many shares are issued and are outstanding?

IE8-3. For the most recent year end, identify total stockholders' equity. Of this total, how much was contributed by shareholders for issued shares? On average, how much did shareholders pay per issued share? Is the average issue price more or less than the current market price? Give an explanation for this difference.

IE8-4. For the most recent year end, what amount of stockholders' equity is earned capital? What is the name of the earned capital account? Did earned capital increase or decrease compared with the previous year? What might cause this change?

IE8-5. Has the company reacquired any of its common stock? How you can tell? What is reacquired stock called? When a company reacquires stock does total stockholders' equity increase or decrease? Why might a company want to reacquire issued shares?

9

Preparing and Analyzing the Statement of Cash Flows

LEARNING OBJECTIVES

When you are finished studying Chapter 9, you should be able to:

1. Explain the importance of the statement of cash flows and the three classifications of cash included on it.

2. Explain the difference between the direct method and the indirect method of preparing the statement of cash flows.

3. Convert accrual amounts to cash amounts.

4. Prepare the *cash flows from operating activities* section of the statement of cash flows using the direct method.

5. Prepare the *cash flows from operating activities* section of the statement of cash flows using the indirect method.

6. Prepare the *cash flows from investing activities* section and the *cash flows from financing activities* section of the statement of cash flows.

7. Perform general analysis of the statement of cash flows and calculate free cash flow.

8. Use the statement of cash flows and the related controls to evaluate the risk of investing in a firm.

ETHICS Matters

Follow the Cash

In May 2008, a *Wall Street Journal (WSJ)* article emphasized the importance of cash flows in evaluating stocks. Because earnings can be affected by accounting choices, cash flows may be a better gauge than net income of a firm's financial health.

Headline earnings numbers—typically net income— can be massaged by perfectly legal tricks, such as changing a depreciation schedule or the way revenue is recognized. Cash flows—how much actual money a company spits out—are by no means immune from shenanigans, but many analysts consider them a cleaner way to assess a company's health.

In the *WSJ* article, Richard Sloan of Barclays Global Investors used General Electric Co. as an example of a company with a growing gap between net income and cash flow. He was quoted as saying that this "suggested the company had been stretching to meet its numbers."

In August 2009, GE agreed to pay a $50 million fine to the Securities and Exchange Commission (SEC) to settle civil fraud and other charges that GE's financial statements in 2002 and 2003 mislead investors. According to the director of the SEC's Division of Enforcement, "GE bent the accounting rules beyond the breaking point. Overly aggressive accounting can distort a company's true financial condition and mislead investors." In the settlement of these charges, GE did not admit or deny the allegations.

Did the gap between GE's cash flows and net income, as observed by Sloan, provide some hint about the accounting problems at GE that were yet to be uncovered? Never underestimate the insights to be gained by following the cash. Start by understanding the statement of cash flows, the topic of this chapter.

Sources: "Cash Flow Reigns Once Again," by Tom Lauricella. *Wall Street Journal*, May 12, 2008, p. C1 and "GE Settles Civil-Fraud Charges," by Paul Glader and Kara Scannell. *Wall Street Journal*, August 5, 2009, p. B2.

L.O.1

Explain the importance of the statement of cash flows and the three classifications of cash included on it.

The Importance of the Statement of Cash Flows

The statement of cash flows—one of the four financial statements a company must prepare as part of generally accepted accounting principles (GAAP) and International Financial Reporting Standards (IFRS)—shows all the cash the company has received and all the cash the company has disbursed during a specific accounting period. Each cash flow relates to one of three business activities—operating, investing, or financing activities. Exhibit 9.1 shows a summary of the information presented on the statement of cash flows.

EXHIBIT 9.1

The Statement of Cash Flows

A firm's statement of cash flows will include every cash inflow and outflow for a specific period of time or for a specific accounting period. The cash flows are divided into three categories: operating, investing, and financing.

	Operating	**Investing**	**Financing**
Types of transactions	Cash related to the day-to-day activities of running the business—revenue and expense transactions	Cash related to buying and selling assets that the firm plans to use for longer than one year	Cash receipts and disbursements related to loans (principal only); cash contributions from and distributions to owners
Examples **Inflows**	Cash collections from customers	Cash proceeds from the sale of land or building	Cash proceeds from a new stock issue
Outflows	Cash paid to vendors for inventory	Cash paid for new land or building	Cash dividends paid to shareholders
Cash flows are generally related to these balance sheet accounts	Current assets and current liabilities	Long-term assets	Long-term liabilities and shareholders' equity

Thousands of companies go bankrupt each year because they fail to plan their cash flows effectively. When the time comes to pay their bills, they do not have enough cash on hand. Preparing a cash budget is a crucial activity for all companies. It is more complicated than just estimating cash inflows and outflows for the accounting period. The sources of cash and the uses of cash must be estimated in detail—both the amounts of cash and when cash is needed. Each month, projected cash inflows and outflows must be budgeted by source and use. With this level of detail, a company can plan ahead for any cash shortage by (1) securing a line of credit from a local bank, (2) borrowing the money, or (3) altering the timing of its receipts (tightening up credit policies) or disbursements (postponing purchases).

A cash budget is a detailed plan of a company's estimated cash receipts and estimated cash disbursements, with very specific forecasts of the sources, uses, and the timing of the cash flows. The budgeted cash flows in the cash budget can then be compared with actual cash flows, and the comparison is the basis for planning and evaluating performance. To compare the actual cash flows for an accounting period with the period's cash budget, a company must produce details about the actual sources of cash and actual uses of cash from the company's records. Comparing actual cash flows with budgeted cash flows gets a company ready to prepare the next period's budgeted cash flows. Even though the focus of financial reporting is financial statements for shareholders and investors, the information about cash flows is equally useful to managers of a company.

Since Sara started her T-shirt business in January 2010, we have prepared the four basic financial statements for her business every month, including the statement of cash flows. The way we have prepared the statement of cash flows has been to do the following:

1. Identify every cash transaction on our accounting equation worksheet, and then
2. classify each cash amount as one of three types: operating, investing, or financing.

When we use a separate column in the accounting equation worksheet for cash transactions, we simply take each addition of cash and each subtraction of cash; then we classify each cash flow as cash from operating activities, cash from investing activities, or cash from financing activities. Because a real company has a much more complex accounting system, needed to handle thousands or millions of transactions, examining each transaction is not a feasible way for a company to prepare the statement of cash flows. In this chapter, we will discuss how the statement is actually prepared.

Two Methods of Preparing and Presenting the Statement of Cash Flows

L.O.2
Explain the difference between the direct method and the indirect method of preparing the statement of cash flows.

Both GAAP and IFRS describe two ways of preparing the statement of cash flows: the **direct method** and the **indirect method**. These two methods are named for the way in which the operating section of the statement of cash flows (cash from operating activities) is prepared, either directly by presenting major classes of inflows and outflows of cash, or indirectly by starting with net income and adjusting it until you have the net cash from operating activities. For the other two sections, investing and financing, there is only one way to compute the cash flows: The transactions are directly identified. Thus, in any discussion about different methods of preparing a statement of cash flows, the difference between the direct method and the indirect method applies only to cash from operating activities.

Before we discuss the two different methods in detail, we will look at a simple example of the difference between these methods of preparing the statement of cash flows. We will start with the first month of business for a simple company with the following transactions:

The **direct method** shows every cash inflow and outflow to prepare the statement of cash flows.

The **indirect method** starts with net income and makes adjustments for items that are not cash to prepare the statement of cash flows.

1. Purchase of inventory for $250—paid cash of $200 to vendor with the remaining $50 on account (accounts payable)
2. Sales of all inventory for $600—$500 for cash and $100 on account (accounts receivable)
3. Purchase of supplies for cash of $30—used $20 worth of them, with $10 worth remaining for next month

Net income is calculated as follows:

$600	–	$250	–	$20	=	$330
Sales		Cost of goods sold		Supplies expense		Net income

Cash collected and disbursed is calculated next:

$500	–	$200	–	$30	=	$270
Cash sales		Inventory purchases		Supplies purchase		Net cash flow

This change from accrual basis numbers to cash basis numbers can be done in the two ways shown in Exhibit 9.2 on the following page—directly or indirectly. To use the direct method we will examine each item on the income statement, one by one. In contrast, the indirect method is more mechanical: Net income is adjusted for noncash items from the income statement and for all the changes in current assets and current liabilities, excluding cash. Exactly how this is done will be discussed later in the chapter. You may want to study the transactions and the exhibit again after you learn more about how to prepare the statements. Notice that the only cash flows in this example are cash flows from operating activities, and that both methods produce the same amount of net cash from operating activities.

Both methods of preparing the operating section of the statement of cash flows require information about the underlying transactions so the cash can be separated from the accrual accounting numbers. For example, the amount of sales must be examined to get the actual cash collected from making those sales. Supplies expense must be examined to get the actual cash paid for supplies. Doing this converts accrual-basis amounts to cash-basis amounts.

EXHIBIT 9.2

Comparison of the Direct and Indirect Methods for the Statement of Cash Flows

Both methods result in the same net cash from operating activities.

Statement of Cash Flows

(cash from operating activities only)

Direct Method		**Indirect Method**	
Cash from operating activities:		Cash from operating activities:	
Cash collected from customers	$500	Net income	$330
Cash paid for supplies	(30)	– increase in accounts receivable	(100)
Cash paid to vendors for inventory	(200)	– increase in supplies	(10)
Net cash from operating activities	$270	+ increase in accounts payable	50
		Net cash from operating activities	$270

Your Turn 9-1

What is the major difference between the direct and indirect methods of presenting the statement of cash flows? What are the similarities?

L.O.3
Convert accrual amounts to cash amounts.

Accrual Accounting versus Cash Basis Accounting

As you know, companies that follow GAAP maintain their accounting records using the accrual basis. Preparing the statement of cash flows actually involves converting the records of the business to cash basis. That is what you see in Exhibit 9.2. There are many reasons why accrual basis accounting and cash basis accounting are not generally the same.

Sales versus Cash Collected from Customers

For example, a company will record a sale and recognize the revenue on the income statement when the merchandise is shipped or delivered. Does the company always receive the cash at that time? No. Thus, the amount of revenue earned from sales for an accounting period may not be the same as the amount of cash collected during the period. At the end of the accounting period, when the company is preparing its financial statements, customers may still owe the company some money—there may be outstanding accounts receivable. That is one reason the cash collected from sales might not equal the amount of the sales for a specific accounting period.

Also, the company may have collected cash during the current period from sales made during the prior accounting period—accounts receivable from the prior year may have been collected in the current year. Thus, to calculate the cash collected from customers for the statement of cash flows, we must make an adjustment for the change in accounts receivable.

Suppose a company began 2011 with accounts receivable of $500. These accounts receivable were recorded during 2010 when the revenue from the sales was recognized. All sales are made on credit; and during 2011 the company had sales of $3,000. At the end of 2011, the balance in accounts receivable was $600. How much cash was collected from customers during 2011? Because accounts receivable started with a balance of $500 and ended with a balance of $600, the increase represents sales that have not been collected from the customers. Therefore, although sales amounted to $3,000, only $2,900 worth of those sales must have been collected in cash.

Beginning accounts receivable	$ 500
+ Sales	+3,000
− Cash collected from customers	− x
= Ending accounts receivable	$ 600

Simply solve this equation for x: $500 + 3,000 - x = 600$

$$x = \$2,900$$

Another way to think about it is first to suppose that customers paid off their old accounts of $500. If total sales were $3,000 and if an ending accounts receivable balance was $600, then $2,400 of the current sales must have been collected. The beginning balance of $500 was collected plus current sales of $2,400 have been collected—making the total cash collected from customers during the period equal to $2,900. This is the sort of reasoning that must be applied to each item on the income statement to prepare the statement of cash flows using the *direct* method.

Salary Expense versus Cash Paid to Employees

The amount for every item on the income statement is potentially different from the cash paid or received for it. As we just discussed, the dollar amount of sales is potentially different from cash collected from customers. For instance, cost of goods sold is potentially different from cash paid for inventory; insurance expense is potentially different from the cash paid to the insurance company; and so on, for all items on the income statement.

The change in a current asset or a current liability will reflect the difference between the accrual-based income statement amount and the cash amount. Consider an expense on the income statement. Suppose salary expense is shown on the year's income statement as $75,000. For the statement of cash flows, we want to show cash paid to employees as an operating cash outflow. What could make salary expense different from cash paid to employees?

First, we could have paid some employees cash that we owed them from last year. The cash payment would reduce the liability salaries payable. If we did pay some salaries we owed at the beginning of the year, that cash paid would be in addition to any current year's salary paid to employees. What else could make *cash paid to employees* different from salary expense? We could have incurred salary expense that will not be paid until next year. In other words, we recognized some salary expense that did not get paid to the employees. We must have recorded it as salaries payable. In both cases, the difference between salary expense and *cash paid to employees* is reflected in the change in salaries payable from the beginning of the year to the end of the year. This is the sort of reasoning that must be applied to each current asset and each current liability (excluding cash) on the balance sheet to prepare the statement of cash flows.

Suppose we started the year with salaries payable of $690. Our salary expense for the year, as shown on the income statement, is $75,000. If the balance in salaries payable is $500 at year end, how much cash was actually paid to employees? First, we must have paid off the amount we owed at the beginning of the year, $690. Then, because the ending balance in salaries payable is $500, we must have paid only $74,500 ($75,000 − $500) of the current year's salary expense. Thus, the total cash paid to employees is $75,190 ($690 + $74,500).

Another way to interpret what happened is to say that we paid the full $75,000 of this year's expense in cash and we paid down our salaries payable by $190 ($690 down to $500). That total is $75,190. It's really just an analysis of the balance sheet account(s) related to the income statement account, where the cash amount is the unknown value we want to find:

Beginning balance in salaries payable	$ 690
Increased by salary expense	+75,000
Decreased by cash paid to employees	− x
Ending balance in salaries payable	$ 500

Solving for x gives $75,190, the cash amount we need for the statement of cash flows.

Your Turn 9-2

Robo Company began the year with $25,000 in accounts receivable. During the year, Robo's sales totaled $50,000. At year end, Robo had an accounts receivable balance of $15,000. How much cash did Robo collect from customers during the year? How is that amount of cash classified on the statement of cash flows?

L.O.4

Prepare the *cash flows from operating activities* section of the statement of cash flows using the direct method.

Preparing the Statement of Cash Flows: Direct Method

Now you are ready to learn the procedures for preparing a statement of cash flows. First, the cash from operating activities section of the statement of cash flows is prepared using one of the following two methods we have already discussed.

1. Direct method: Each item on the accrual-based income statement is converted to cash.
2. Indirect method: Net income is the starting point, and adjustments are made by adding and subtracting amounts necessary to convert net income into net cash from operating activities.

After you have determined the cash flows from operating activities, you determine the cash flows from investing activities and cash flows from financing activities. You will learn about them later in the chapter.

To use the direct method of computing cash flows from operating activities, we will begin with an analysis of the income statement. Item by item, we will analyze every amount on the statement to determine how much cash was actually collected or disbursed related to that item. (Exactly how a firm's accounting system would prepare the data may be different than our method here.)

Revenue → Cash Collected from Customers

The first item on the income statement is usually revenue. What makes revenue on the income statement different from cash collected from customers? Any cash collected for sales in previous periods—that is, accounts receivable—must be counted as cash collected even though it is not included as revenue. Conversely, any sales for the period for which cash has not been collected must be excluded from cash collections. Both cash collected but not counted as revenue and cash not collected but included in revenue can be identified by looking at the change in accounts receivable during the period.

We will use Team Shirts' third month of business—March—to see how this works. We start at the beginning of the income statement, shown in Exhibit 9.3 (first seen as Exhibit 3.13), for the month and analyze each amount to change it from accrual to cash.

EXHIBIT 9.3

Income Statement for Team Shirts for the Month Ended March 31

Team Shirts		
Income Statement		
For the Month Ended March 31, 2010		

Sales revenue		$2,000
Expenses		
Cost of goods sold	$800	
Depreciation expense	100	
Insurance expense	50	
Interest expense	30	(980)
Net income		$1,020

Sales on the income statement for March amounted to $2,000. What we need to know for the statement of cash flows is how much cash was collected from customers during March. We need to see how accounts receivable changed during the month. On March 1, Team Shirts had $150 worth of accounts receivable, and on March 31 the firm had $2,000 worth of accounts receivable.

By comparing the balance sheet at the beginning of the month with the balance sheet at the end of the month, both shown in Exhibit 9.4, we can see accounts receivable increased by $1,850. The amount of the change in accounts receivable came from the current period's sales for which the cash was not collected.

EXHIBIT 9.4

Comparative Balance Sheets for Team Shirts

Team Shirts Comparative Balance Sheets At March 1 and March 31, 2010					
	March 31	March 1		March 31	March 1
Cash	$ 3,995	$6,695	Accounts payable	$ 0	$ 800
Accounts receivable ...	2,000	150	Other payables	0	50
Inventory	300	100	Interest payable	30	0
Prepaid insurance	75	125	Notes payable	3,000	0
Prepaid rent	0	0	Total liabilities	3,030	850
Computer (net of $100 accumulated depreciation)	3,900	0	Common stock	5,000	5,000
			Retained earnings	2,240	1,220
Total assets	$10,270	$7,070	Total liabilities and shareholder's equity	$10,270	$7,070

Analyze what happened to accounts receivable. It started with $150. Then during the month, credit sales of $2,000 were made (sales on the income statement). The ending balance in accounts receivable is $2,000. Thus, the cash collected from customers must have been $150 ($2,000 − $1,850). If you go back and look at the transactions for Team Shirts during March (in Chapter 3), you will find $150 was exactly the amount of cash the company collected from customers.

Beginning accounts receivable	$ 150
+ Credit sales	+2,000
− Cash collected	− x
= Ending accounts receivable	$ 2,000

Solving for x gives $150, the amount of cash collected from customers.

Cost of Goods Sold → Cash Paid to Vendors

Continuing down the March income statement, the next item is cost of goods sold of $800. This is the cost of the merchandise sold during the month. How does that compare with the amount of cash paid to vendors during the month? Did Team Shirts sell anything it bought the previous month from the beginning inventory, or did the company buy more goods in March than it actually sold in March? We need to look at what happened to the amount of inventory during the month. The beginning inventory balance was $100. The ending inventory balance was $300. That means Team Shirts bought enough inventory to sell $800 worth and to build up the inventory by an additional $200. Thus, purchases of inventory must have been $1,000. Did Team Shirts pay cash for these purchases of inventory?

To see how the purchases of $1,000 worth of inventory compare with the cash paid to vendors, we look at the change in accounts payable (to vendors). The beginning balance in accounts payable was $800, and the ending balance was zero. That means Team Shirts must have paid $1,000 to vendors for the month's purchases and the $800 owed from February. Thus, the total paid to vendors was $1,800.

Beginning inventory	$ 100
+ Purchases	+ x
− Cost of goods sold	−800
= Ending inventory	$ 300

When we solve for x, we find that Team Shirts purchases were $1,000. Now, to see how much cash we paid to vendors, we have to analyze accounts payable:

Beginning accounts payable	$ 800
+ Purchases (on account)	+1,000 (= x from above)
− Cash paid to vendors	− y
= Ending accounts payable	-0-

Solving for y, we find that $1,800 was the amount of cash paid to vendors.

Other Expenses → Cash Paid for Other Expenses

The next expense on the March 31 income statement is depreciation expense. Depreciation expense is a noncash expense. That means we do not have any cash outflow when we record depreciation expense. The cash we spend to buy equipment is considered an investing cash flow, and the periodic depreciation does not involve cash. Depreciation is one expense we can skip when we are calculating cash from operating activities using the direct method.

Insurance expense of $50 is shown on the March 31 income statement. How much cash was actually paid for insurance? When a company pays for insurance, the payment is generally recorded as prepaid insurance. Examining the change in the prepaid insurance account will help us figure out how much cash was paid for insurance during the month. Prepaid insurance started with a balance of $125 and ended with a balance of $75. Because the decrease in prepaid insurance is exactly the same as the insurance expense, Team Shirts did not pay for any insurance this month. All the expense came from insurance that was paid for in a previous period.

The last expense we need to consider is interest expense. On the income statement for March, we see interest expense of $30. Did Team Shirts pay that in cash? On the balance sheet, the company began the month with no interest payable and ended the month with $30 interest payable. If it started the month without owing any interest and ended the month owing $30, how much of the $30 interest expense did the company pay for with cash? None. Team Shirts must not have paid any cash for interest because it owes the entire amount of the expense at year end.

Team Shirts paid out one more amount of cash related to operating activities during the month. Can you find it? On the March 1 balance sheet, there is $50 that Team Shirts owed; it is called *other payables*. By the end of March, that payable has been reduced to zero. Only one thing could have caused that reduction: a cash payment to settle the obligation related to advertising. Thus, we will also put the cash outflow of $50 on the statement of cash flows.

Summary of Direct Method

To summarize, we have "translated" the accrual amounts found on the income statement to cash amounts for the statement of cash flows. The cash collected from customers was $150. Team Shirts paid its vendors cash of $1,800. It also paid $50 of other payables. Net cash flow from operating activities was $(1,700). The operating section of the statement of cash flows using the direct method is shown in Exhibit 9.5.

EXHIBIT 9.5

Cash from Operating Activities—Direct Method

Team Shirts
Partial Statement of Cash Flows
For the Month Ended March 31, 2010

Cash from operating activities	
Cash collected from customers	$ 150
Cash paid to vendors	(1,800)
Cash paid for advertising	(50)
Net cash from operating activities	**$(1,700)**

Remember, Exhibit 9.5 shows only the cash flows from operating activities. To explain the entire change in cash from March 1 to March 31, the investing and financing cash flows must be included.

Your Turn 9-3

Flex Company began the year 2010 with $350 of prepaid insurance. For 2010, the company's income statement showed insurance expense of $400. If Flex Company ended the year with $250 of prepaid insurance, how much cash was paid for insurance during 2010? On the statement of cash flows, how would that cash be classified?

Preparing the Statement of Cash Flows: Indirect Method

L.O.5
Prepare the *cash flows from operating activities* section of the statement of cash flows using the indirect method.

Even though the Financial Accounting Standards Board (FASB) and the International Accounting Standards Board (IASB) have encouraged companies to use the direct method of preparing the statement of cash flows, more than 90% of companies use the indirect method. That is because most accountants think it is easier to prepare the statement of cash flows using the indirect method. Also, the requirement that a company using the direct method provide a reconciliation of net income to net cash from operating activities means more work for the company using the direct method. Some companies even suggest that their accounting systems do not produce the information needed to prepare the statement using the direct method.

Start with Net Income

Preparing the statement of cash flows using the indirect method—applied just to the operating section of the statement of cash flows—starts with net income. Following net income, any amounts on the income statement that are completely noncash must be added or subtracted to undo their original effect on net income. Typical noncash items are depreciation and amortization expenses and any gains or losses on the sale of assets. Remember that a gain or loss on the sale of a long-term asset is not cash; it is the difference between the book value of the asset and the proceeds from the sale. (We will include the proceeds from the sale in the cash from investing activities section of the statement of cash flows.)

We will start with net income for Team Shirts for March. Exhibits 9.3 and 9.4 show the numbers we need to prepare the statement of cash flows using the indirect method.

The net income for March was $1,020. The first adjustment we make is to add back any noncash expenses such as depreciation. For Team Shirts, we must add back to net income the $100 depreciation expense. When we calculated the net income of $1,020, we subtracted $100 that was not a cash outflow. So, we must add it back to net income in our task of changing net income to a cash number.

Next, we will adjust net income for other amounts on the income statement that are not cash flows. Recall that in the direct method, we use changes in accounts receivable to convert sales revenue into cash collected from customers, and we use changes in inventory and accounts payable to convert cost of goods sold to cash paid to vendors. For the indirect method, if we adjust net income for every change in each current asset—with the exception of cash—and every change in each current liability, we will make every adjustment we need to convert net income into net cash from operating activities.

We will continue preparing the statement of cash flows using the indirect method with Team Shirts for March. We start with net income of $1,020 and add back any noncash expenses. Depreciation expense of $100 is added back. Then, using Exhibit 9.4, we examine each current asset account and each current liability account for changes during the month.

Examine Current Asset and Current Liability Accounts

Accounts receivable increased by $1,850. That increase represents sales for which we did not collect any cash yet. Thus, we need to subtract this increase in accounts receivable from net income to convert net income into a cash number.

The next change in a current asset is the increase in inventory of $200. This $200 represents purchases made that have not yet been reported as part of cost of goods sold on the income statement because the items have not been sold. Still, Team Shirts did buy them (we will take into account any purchases for which the firm did not yet pay when we examine accounts payable), so the amount needs to be deducted from net income because it was a cash outflow.

Prepaid insurance decreased from $125 to $75. This decrease of $50 was deducted as insurance expense on the income statement, but it was not a cash outflow this period. This amount must be added back to net income because it was not a cash outflow.

The last changes in current assets and current liabilities are the changes in payables. Team Shirts started the month with $800 of accounts payable and $50 of other payables. Team Shirts ended the month with a zero amount of each of these. That means $850 was the cash outflow related to these two amounts. The other current liability is interest payable. It started the month with no interest payable but ended the month with $30 of interest payable. That is $30 Team Shirts did not pay out, so $30 must be added back.

Look at the operating section of the statement of cash flows for Team Shirts for March in Exhibit 9.6. The statement starts with net income and makes all the adjustments we discussed. Compare the cash from operating activities section of this statement of cash flows prepared using the indirect method with the same section using the direct method shown in Exhibit 9.5. The net cash flow from operating activities is the same no matter how we prepare it—when we prepare the statement by examining every cash transaction, as we did in Chapter 3; when we prepare it using the direct method, as we did earlier in this chapter; and when we prepare it using the indirect method, as we just did.

EXHIBIT 9.6

Cash from Operating Activities—Indirect Method

Team Shirts Partial Statement of Cash Flows For the Month Ended March 31, 2010	
Net income	$ 1,020
+ Depreciation expense	100
– Increase in accounts receivable	(1,850)
– Increase in inventory	(200)
+ Decrease in prepaid insurance	50
– Decrease accounts payable	(800)
– Decrease other payables	(50)
+ Increase interest payable	30
Net cash from operating activities	$(1,700)

Exhibit 9.7 provides a summary of how to adjust net income into cash from operating activities. Although these "rules" always hold for the indirect method, be sure you understand the reasons for either adding or subtracting the change in the current asset or current liability account balance.

EXHIBIT 9.7

Indirect Method: Changing Net Income to Cash from Operations

What to Do	Example
Start with net income	net income
Add any noncash expenses	+ depreciation expense
Subtract any gains	– gain on sale of equipment
Add back any losses	+ loss on the sale of equipment
Deduct an increase in a current asset	– increase in accounts receivable
	– increase in prepaid rent
Add a decrease in a current asset	+ decrease in inventory
	+ decrease in prepaid insurance
Add an increase in a current liability	+ increase in accounts payable
	+ increase in salaries payable
Deduct a decrease in a current liability	– decrease in income taxes payable
	– decrease in accrued liabilities

Comparing the Direct and Indirect Methods

Which method is easier to understand? The presentation produced by the direct method—the presentation shown in Exhibit 9.5—gives details about cash that are often considered easier to understand than the details provided by the indirect method. Still, most companies today use the indirect method, which provides information not found on the statement prepared using the direct method. A change in this practice could be a real benefit to users of financial statements. A recent discussion paper (2008) released jointly by the FASB and the IASB has proposed that only the direct method be used in the future. Stay tuned for developments on this issue. It is not likely to be resolved easily or quickly.

Suppose a company had net income of $50,000 for the year. Depreciation expense, the only noncash item on the income statement, was $7,000. The only current asset that changed during the year was accounts receivable, which began the year at $6,500 and ended the year at $8,500. The only current liability that changed was salaries payable, which began the year at $2,500 and ended the year at $3,000. Assume this is all the relevant information. Calculate net cash from operating activities using the indirect method.

Your Turn 9-4

Cash from Investing and Financing Activities

In addition to cash from operating activities, there are two other classifications of cash flows found on the statement of cash flows: cash from investing activities and cash from financing activities. No matter which method you use to prepare the statement of cash flows, direct or indirect, the cash from investing activities and cash from financing activities sections are prepared the same way—by reviewing noncurrent balance sheet accounts. The primary amounts on the balance sheet to review are property, plant, and equipment; notes payable; bonds payable; common stock; and retained earnings.

L.O.6

Prepare the *cash flows from investing activities* section and the *cash flows from financing activities* section of the statement of cash flows.

Investing Activities

Information about cash flows related to investing activities will be found by analyzing the long-term asset section of the balance sheet. For Team Shirts the balance sheet at March 31 shows a computer with a cost of $4,000. The carrying value is $3,900 and the accumulated depreciation is $100, for a total cost of $4,000. The asset representing this computer was not on the March 1 balance sheet, so Team Shirts must have purchased a $4,000 computer during March. The purchase of a computer is an investing cash flow.

When we see that a company purchased a long-term asset, we must investigate how the company paid for the asset. In this case, we find that Team Shirts paid cash of $1,000 and signed a note for $3,000. We include only the $1,000 cash outflow in the statement of cash flows, but we must add a note disclosing the amount of the computer purchase financed by the note payable. All investing and financing activities must be disclosed, even if there was no cash involved.

Financing Activities

Information about cash flows related to financing activities will be found by analyzing the long-term liability section and the equity section of the balance sheet. Notice that on the balance sheet at March 1, Team Shirts shows no notes payable. On the balance sheet at March 31, notes payable shows a balance of $3,000. That means that Team Shirts borrowed $3,000 during March. Again, when we discover such a change, we must find out the details of the transaction before we can decide how the transaction affects the statement of cash flows. Generally, borrowing money using a note would result in a financing cash inflow. However, in this case, the note was given in exchange for a computer. Notice that the loan is disclosed, even though the amount is not included on the statement of cash flows. Whenever a company engages in a financing or investing activity, it must be disclosed on the statement of cash flows, even though the company never actually received or paid out any cash. The cash is considered implicit in the transaction. It is as if Team Shirts received the cash from the loan and immediately turned around and purchased the computer with it.

Other transactions we should look for when preparing the financing section of the statement of cash flows include any principal payments on loans and any new capital contributions—such as stock issued. We should also look for any dividends paid to the stockholders. For Team Shirts for March 2010, none of these transactions took place.

Putting It All Together

When we put the information about investing activities and financing activities with the cash from operating activities we have already prepared, we have all the information we need to complete the statement of cash flows. Look at the two statements in Exhibit 9.8. We used different methods to prepare the statements, but they are similar in form and amounts.

EXHIBIT 9.8A

Statement of Cash Flows (Direct)

Team Shirts
Statement of Cash Flows
For the Month Ended March 31, 2010

Cash from operating activities		
Cash collected from customers	$ 150	
Cash paid to vendors	(1,800)	
Cash paid for advertising	(50)	
Net cash from operating activities		$(1,700)
Cash from investing activities		
Purchase of computer	$(1,000)[a]	
Net cash from investing activities		(1,000)
Cash from financing activities		0
Net increase (decrease) in cash		$(2,700)
Beginning cash balance		6,695
Ending cash balance		$ 3,995

[a]A computer was purchased for $4,000. A note was signed for $3,000 and cash paid was $1,000.

EXHIBIT 9.8B

Statement of Cash Flows (Indirect)

Team Shirts
Statement of Cash Flows
For the Month Ended March 31, 2010

Cash from operating activities		
Net income	$ 1,020	
+ Depreciation expense	100	
− Increase in accounts receivable	(1,850)	
− Increase in inventory	(200)	
+ Decrease in prepaid insurance	50	
− Decrease in accounts payable	(800)	
− Decrease in other payables	(50)	
+ Increase in interest payable	30	
Net cash from operating activities		$(1,700)
Cash from investing activities		
Purchase of computer	(1,000)[a]	
Net cash from investing activities		(1,000)
Cash from financing activities		0
Net increase (decrease) in cash		$(2,700)
Beginning cash balance		6,695
Ending cash balance		$ 3,995

[a]A computer was purchased for $4,000. A note was signed for $3,000 and cash paid was $1,000.

Check it out. The balance sheets in Exhibit 9.4 show that cash went from $6,695 on March 1 to $3,995 on March 31. The difference is a $2,700 decrease in cash. Explaining that change in the cash balance is the purpose of the statement of cash flows.

Summary of Direct and Indirect Methods

As you have seen, there are two ways, both acceptable using GAAP, to prepare and present the statement of cash flows: the direct method and the indirect method. The direct method provides more straightforward details about cash from operating activities, because it shows the individual operating cash flows. When a company uses the direct method, GAAP requires that the company also show a reconciliation of net income to net cash from operating activities in a supplemental schedule. That reconciliation looks exactly like the operating section of the statement of cash flows using the indirect method.

The indirect presentation of the statement of cash flows is easier to prepare from the income statement and the beginning and ending balance sheets for the period, but the presentation of the information may not be as easy to understand. A company that uses the indirect method must make separate disclosures for cash paid for interest and cash paid for taxes somewhere in the financial statements. This is required by GAAP. Keep in mind that the investing activities and the financing activities sections for the two methods are identical; and the total change in cash is the same for both methods.

Applying Your Knowledge: Financial Statement Analysis

L.O.7
Perform general analysis of the statement of cash flows and calculate free cash flow.

Look at the statement of cash flows for AutoZone, Inc., shown in Exhibit 9.9 on the following page. First, notice the organization of the statement. The statement has the three required parts: (1) cash flows from operating activities; (2) cash flows from investing activities; and (3) cash flows from financing activities. Second, notice that the first section—cash provided by operating activities—is prepared using the indirect method.

Cash from Operating Activities—AutoZone

The statement starts with the amount for net income and makes several adjustments to that amount. Look at the adjustments and see if you understand what information they provide. For example, depreciation and amortization are added back to net income to work toward net cash from operating activities because the amounts for depreciation and amortization were subtracted in the original computation of net income but they were not cash expenditures. That subtraction is undone by adding the amounts back to net income. There are many other adjustments that are beyond the scope of an introductory accounting course, but you should understand why these adjustments are being made. The adjustments are "undoing" the effect of the noncash amounts that were included in the calculation of net income. Investors are looking for a positive net cash flow from operating activities. In the long run, this is crucial to the continuing success of any business.

Cash from Investing Activities—AutoZone

The cash flows from investing activities section of the statement shows capital expenditures as the first entry. Those are items such as property, plant, and equipment. Recall the discussion in Chapter 6 about capital versus revenue expenditures—capitalizing a cost versus expensing a cost. These are costs that have been capitalized by AutoZone. Other entries in the cash flows from investing activities section include cash inflows and outflows related to the purchase and sale of long-term assets not related to the normal operations of AutoZone. (When AutoZone buys the items that it resells in the normal course of business, the cash flows are included in the first section—cash provided from operating activities.)

The cash flows from investing activities section of the statement of cash flows gives information about the company's plans for the future. Investments in property, plant, and equipment may indicate an expansion or, at the very least, a concern about keeping the company's infrastructure up to date. Over time, a company's failure to invest in the infrastructure may indicate a problem.

EXHIBIT 9.9

AutoZone's Statement of Cash Flows

This statement of cash flows has been prepared using the indirect method.

AutoZone, Inc.
Statement of Cash Flows

(in thousands)	Year Ended		
	August 30, 2008 (53 Weeks)	August 25, 2007 (52 Weeks)	August 26, 2006 (52 Weeks)
Cash flows from operating activities:			
Net income	$ 641,606	$ 595,672	$ 569,275
Adjustments to reconcile net income to net cash provided by operating activities:			
Depreciation and amortization of property and equipment	169,509	159,411	139,465
Amortization of debt origination fees	1,837	1,719	1,559
Income tax benefit from exercise of stock options	(10,142)	(16,523)	(10,608)
Deferred income taxes	67,474	24,844	36,306
Share-based compensation expense	18,388	18,462	17,370
Changes in operating assets and liabilities:			
Accounts receivable	(11,145)	20,487	37,900
Merchandise inventories	(137,841)	(160,780)	(182,790)
Accounts payable and accrued expenses	175,733	186,228	184,986
Income taxes payable	(3,861)	17,587	28,676
Other, net	9,542	(1,913)	608
Net cash provided by operating activities	921,100	845,194	822,747
Cash flows from investing activities:			
Capital expenditures	(243,594)	(224,474)	(263,580)
Purchase of marketable securities	(54,282)	(94,615)	(159,957)
Proceeds from sale of investments	50,712	86,921	145,369
Disposal of capital assets	4,014	3,453	9,845
Net cash used in investing activities	(243,150)	(228,715)	(268,323)
Cash flows from financing activities:			
Net (repayments of) proceeds from commercial paper	(206,700)	84,300	(51,993)
Proceeds from issuance of debt	750,000	—	200,000
Repayment of debt	(229,827)	(5,839)	(152,700)
Net proceeds from sale of common stock	27,065	58,952	38,253
Purchase of treasury stock	(849,196)	(761,887)	(578,066)
Income tax benefit from exercise of stock options	10,142	16,523	10,608
Payments of capital lease obligations	(15,880)	(11,360)	—
Other	(8,286)	(2,072)	(3,778)
Net cash used in financing activities	(522,682)	(621,383)	(537,676)
Effect of exchange rate changes on cash	539	—	—
Net increase (decrease) in cash and cash equivalents	155,807	(4,904)	16,748
Cash and cash equivalents at beginning of year	86,654	91,558	74,810
Cash and cash equivalents at end of year	$ 242,461	$ 86,654	$ 91,558
Supplemental cash flow information:			
Interest paid, net of interest cost capitalized	$ 107,477	$ 116,580	$ 104,929
Income taxes paid	$ 313,875	$ 299,566	$ 267,913
Assets acquired through capital lease	$ 61,572	$ 69,325	$ —

Cash from Financing Activities—AutoZone

The cash flows from financing activities section of the statement of cash flows shows the cash flows related to the way the company is financed. Some of the items should be recognizable—proceeds from issuance of debt and proceeds from the sale of common stock. Notice the large amount that AutoZone spent to repurchase its own stock. All of the items in this section relate to AutoZone's financing. This information, when combined with the information on the balance sheet, gives the financial statement user a complete picture of the way the company is financing the business.

Other Characteristics of the Statement of Cash Flows

We should consider two more characteristics of the statement. First, following the calculation of the net increase or decrease in cash for the year, the statement includes the reconciliation from the year's beginning cash balance to the year's ending cash balance. Second, it also discloses supplementary information concerning the cash paid for interest and the cash paid for taxes during the year. This is required by GAAP. The information is not always on the face of the statement of cash flows, but, if not, it will be included in the notes.

Free Cash Flow

When analyzing the statement of cash flows, managers and analysts often calculate an amount called **free cash flow**. Free cash flow is defined as net cash from operating activities minus dividends and capital expenditures. This gives a measure of a firm's ability to engage in long-term investment opportunities. It is sometimes seen as a measure of a company's financial flexibility. For fiscal year ended August 30, 2008, AutoZone's free cash flow is quite adequate: $921.1 million − $243.6 million = $677.5 million. Looking over the capital expenditures for the past two years, you can see that $677.5 million should be enough for new investment opportunities.

> **Free cash flow** is equal to net cash from operating activities minus dividends and minus capital expenditures.

DRP Company reported net cash from operating activities of $45,600. Suppose the firm purchased $25,000 worth of new long-term assets for cash and did not pay any dividends during the year. The firm's average current liabilities for the year were $40,000. What was the firm's free cash flow during the year?

Your Turn 9-5

UNDERSTANDING → # Business

Cash Burn Rate

General Motors had a cash problem. For the third quarter of 2008, the company had a net loss of $4.2 billion and was spending cash at a rate of approximately $6.9 billion per quarter. For the first quarter of 2009, the company reported a net loss of $6 billion and was spending cash at a rate of $10.2 billion per quarter.

The rate at which a firm spends its cash is called the cash burn rate. GM's cash burn rate was alarming in 2008 and early 2009. On June 1, 2009, GM filed for Chapter 11 bankruptcy protection.

Having enough cash is crucial for survival. When a business runs out of cash and cannot borrow any more money, then bankruptcy is a likely outcome. However, there are steps that any business can take to minimize the risk of running out of cash.

First, planning is essential. A cash budget is a crucial component of any budget. Know your cash burn rate! When preparing a cash budget, a firm estimates when it will collect cash and when it will disburse cash. In this process, the potential for experiencing a cash shortfall can be identified. Knowing the timing of cash flows enables a company to secure a line of credit or other short-term borrowing to navigate the business through a shortfall and plan how to repay the short-term debt when the cash flow is adequate.

Second, managing cash flows is important. A key management function is to make sure that a company's receivables and inventories are being managed efficiently. Making sure there is an adequate level of product availability and appropriate credit polices are part of this function. A company does not want to tie up too much cash in receivables and inventory, so there is a balance that must be achieved. Collecting receivables in a timely manner is a crucial component of managing cash flows.

GM's problems have been complicated and extensive, but the company collapsed when it ran out of cash. Even billions of dollars from the U.S. government wasn't enough cash to keep the company from bankruptcy.

Even though Wall Street puts significant emphasis on a firm's earnings—net income—cash flows are also important. In some ways, managing cash is even more crucial than managing earnings. There is truth to the old adage that "cash is king."

Sources: "GM's Crippling Burn Rate," *BusinessWeek*, November 7, 2008, and "Time To Cut Our Losses? GM's Cash Burn Rate Increases To An Alarming $113 MILLION A Day!" AutoSpies.com, May 7, 2009.

The statement of cash flows provides important information for managers, creditors, and investors. In corporate annual reports, the statement of cash flows is presented with the other three basic financial statements—the income statement, the balance sheet, and the statement of changes in shareholders' equity—to provide information needed to evaluate a company's performance and to provide a basis for predicting a company's future potential.

L.O.8

Use the statement of cash flows and the related controls to evaluate the risk of investing in a firm.

Business Risk, Control, and Ethics

In Chapter 4, you learned about the controls a company should have to minimize the risks associated with cash. Now we will talk about investors' risks associated with the statement of cash flows. The misleading financial statements that have been at the heart of such failures as Enron and WorldCom have been the income statement and the balance sheet. Managers can rarely falsify cash inflows and outflows, so few people think of the statement of cash flows as a place where the ethics of a firm's management could be tested. However, managers can manipulate the classification of the cash flows. Because analysts are often looking for positive net cash flows from operating activities, especially in established companies, a firm's managers may feel some pressure to make sure that this part of the statement of cash flows is positive. There is an opportunity to engage in the same type of manipulation as WorldCom did when it classified expenses that belonged on the income statement as long-term assets on the balance sheet. Someone could misclassify cash outflows from operating activities as investing cash outflows. This changes the whole nature of such expenditures. Operating expenses are the costs of doing business, so investors want to see a low number. Investing cash outflows are often interpreted as a positive signal for future growth of the firm, so investors want to see a high number.

There is a great deal of information in the statement of cash flows, and it deserves careful consideration when you are analyzing a firm's financial statements. As with the information provided by the other financial statements, the statement of cash flows provides reliable information only when the firm's management is ethical.

Chapter Summary Points

- The statement of cash flows explains the change in cash from the beginning of the accounting period to the end of the accounting period—the amount on one balance sheet and the amount on the subsequent balance sheet.
- Cash flows can be categorized as cash from operating activities, cash from investing activities, or cash from financing activities. The statement of cash flows has a section for each of these categories.
- There are two methods—direct and indirect—for preparing and presenting the statement of cash flows. The direct method simply provides all operating cash inflows and outflows in a straightforward manner. The indirect method starts with net income and adjusts it for all noncash items—depreciation expense and gains or losses on the sale of long-term assets are typical noncash items. It also adjusts for changes in the current assets (excluding cash) and the current liabilities. These two methods describe the cash from the operating activities section of the statement. The other two sections—cash from investing activities and cash from financing activities—are the same on both types of statements of cash flows.
- Free cash flow is the amount of cash left after cash spent on investments in long-term assets and cash paid for dividends are subtracted from net cash from operating activities. It measures how much cash a firm has available for long-term investment opportunities.
- Before you invest in a firm, look at its statement of cash flows. A growing or established firm should be generating positive net cash flows from operating activities. Investing cash flows may provide insights into the firm's plans for the future. Be sure to look at the firm's cash situation over several years and also compare the firm's sources and uses of cash to those of its competitors.

Chapter Summary Problems

Suppose Attic Treasures, a retail store, provided you with the following comparative balance sheets and the related income statement. (Notice the most recent year is in the right column. It is always important to pay attention to the way the years are ordered on a set of comparative financial statements.) Assume the firm did not purchase any property, plant, and equipment (PPE) during the year.

Attic Treasures
Comparative Balance Sheets

At	January 30, 2008	January 30, 2009
Assets		
Cash	$ 23,000	$ 39,200
Accounts receivable	12,000	23,450
Merchandise inventory	25,200	28,100
Prepaid rent	6,000	5,500
Property, plant, and equipment (PP&E)	79,500	70,000
Accumulated depreciation	(24,000)	(29,000)
Total assets	$121,700	$137,250
Liabilities and Shareholders' Equity		
Accounts payable	$ 12,300	$ 26,200
Income taxes payable	10,000	8,100
Long-term notes payable	39,700	25,800
Common stock and additional paid-in capital	18,500	20,000
Retained earnings	41,200	57,150
Total liabilities and shareholders' equity	$121,700	$137,250

Attic Treasures
Income Statement
For the Year Ended January 29, 2009

Sales		$234,900
Cost of goods sold		178,850
Gross margin		56,050
Selling expenses	$24,000	
General expense*	8,500	32,500
Income from operations		23,550
Interest expense		1,200
Income before income taxes		22,350
Income tax expense		3,400
Net income		$ 18,950

* includes rent expense of $2,000 and depreciation expense of $6,000

Instructions

Prepare a statement of cash flows. Your instructor will tell you whether to use the indirect method or the direct method (or both). Solutions for each are provided.

Solution

Direct Method

To prepare the cash from operating activities section using the direct method, go down the income statement and convert the accrual amounts to cash amounts by referring to the related current asset or current liability account.

1. Convert *sales* to *cash collected from customers*.

    Sales = $234,900.

    Increase in accounts receivable (AR) from $12,000 to $23,450 = $11,450.

    The increase in AR is the amount of sales Attic Treasures did NOT collect in cash, so the cash collected from customers is $234,900 − $11,450 = **$223,450**.

2. Convert *cost of goods sold* to *cash paid to vendors*. This takes two steps. First, convert cost of goods sold to total purchases.

    Cost of goods sold = $178,850.

    Increase in inventory from $25,200 to $28,100 = $2,900 of additional purchases.

    The increase in inventory is added to the cost of goods sold to get total purchases = $178,850 + $2,900 = $181,750. Then, convert total purchases to cash paid to vendors.

    Total purchases = $181,750.

    Increase in accounts payable of $12,300 to $26,200 = $13,900 represents purchases that did not get paid for, so cash paid to vendors = $181,750 − $13,900 = **$167,850**.

3. Convert *selling expenses* to *cash paid for selling expenses*. Because there are no current assets or current liabilities related to selling expenses (such as accrued selling expenses), Attic Treasures must have paid cash for this entire amount. So cash paid for selling expenses = **$24,000**.

4. Convert *general expenses* to *cash paid for general expenses*.

    General expenses = $8,500. This includes $2,000 rent expense and $6,000 depreciation expense. So we could break down the general expenses as follows:

Rent expense	$2,000
Depreciation expenses	$6,000
Other expenses	$ 500

    First, rent expense is related to prepaid rent on the balance sheet. Prepaid rent decreased from $6,000 to $5,500. This means the company used rent it had already (last year) paid for, so the decrease in prepaid rent reduces the rent expense by $500 to get cash paid for rent = $2,000 − $500 = $1,500.

    Depreciation expense is a noncash expense, so there is no cash flow associated with it. Other expenses of $500 must have been all cash because there are no associated current assets or current liabilities on the balance sheet. So the total cash paid for general expenses = $1,500 + $500 = **$2,000**.

5. Change *interest expense* to *cash paid for interest*.

    Interest expense = $1,200.

    This must have been all cash because there were no current assets or current liabilities associated with it. Cash paid for interest = **$1,200**.

6. Change *income tax expense* to *cash paid for taxes*:

    Income tax expense = $3,400.

    Decrease in income taxes payable from $10,000 to $8,100 = $1,900, which represents additional taxes the company paid beyond the income tax expense on the income statement. Cash paid for income taxes = $3,400 + $1,900 = **$5,300**.

You have now converted all the income statement items to cash inflows and outflows and are ready to prepare the first part of the statement of cash flows.

Cash from operating activities:	
Cash collected from customers	$223,450
Cash paid to vendors	(167,850)
Cash paid for selling expenses	(24,000)
Cash paid for general expenses	(2,000)
Cash paid for interest	(1,200)
Cash paid for income taxes	(5,300)
Net cash provided by operating activities	$ 23,100

7. Next, calculate cash from investing activities. An analysis of long-term assets shows that property, plant, and equipment decreased by $9,500. A decrease is caused by disposing of assets. Because the income statement showed no gain or loss from disposal of long-term assets, the assets must have been sold for book value. The property, plant, and equipment account decreased by $9,500 (the cost of the PPE sold) and the accumulated depreciation account increased by $5,000. Recall from the income statement that depreciation expense for the year was $6,000. If accumulated depreciation only increased by $5,000, then $1,000 must have been subtracted. That means the PPE sold had a book value of $8,500 ($9,500 − $1,000). Because there was no gain or loss on the disposal, the company must have received proceeds equal to the book value. So the cash inflow—proceeds—from disposal of PPE was an investing cash inflow of **$8,500**.

8. To calculate the cash flows from financing activities, analyze what happened in the long-term liability accounts and the shareholders' equity accounts. Long-term notes payable decreased from $39,700 to $25,800. That must have been a cash outflow of **$13,900**. Common stock and additional paid-in capital increased by **$1,500**. That must have been a cash inflow from the issue of stock of $1,500. Lastly, see if the company declared any dividends during the year. Retained earnings increased from $41,200 to $57,150 = $15,950. How does that compare to net income? Net income was $18,950 but retained earnings only increased by $15,950, so **$3,000** must have been declared as dividends. The absence of dividends payable indicates that the dividends were paid. You are now ready to put the whole statement together using the direct method.

Attic Treasures
Statement of Cash Flows—Direct Method
For the Year Ended January 29, 2009

Cash from operating activities	
Cash collected from customers	$ 223,450
Cash paid to vendors	(167,850)
Cash paid for selling expenses	(24,000)
Cash paid for general expenses	(2,000)
Cash paid for interest	(1,200)
Cash paid for income taxes	(5,300)
Net cash provided by operating activities	$ 23,100
Cash from investing activities	
Cash proceeds from sale of property, plant, and equipment	$ 8,500
Cash from financing activities	
Cash paid on loan principal	(13,900)
Cash proceeds from stock issue	1,500
Cash paid for dividends	(3,000)
Net cash used for financing activities	$ (15,400)
Net increase in cash during the year	16,200
Cash balance, beginning of the year	23,000
Ending cash balance	$ 39,200

Indirect Method

To prepare the statement using the indirect method, start with net income. Adjust it for any non-cash expenses and the change in every current asset (excluding cash) and every current liability. The other two sections—cash from investing activities and cash from financing activities—are the same as for the direct method.

Attic Treasures
Statement of Cash Flows—Indirect Method
For the Year Ended January 29, 2009

Cash from operating activities	
Net income	$ 18,950
Add depreciation expense	6,000
Deduct increase in accounts receivable	(11,450)
Deduct increase in inventory	(2,900)
Add decrease in prepaid rent	500
Add increase in accounts payable	13,900
Deduct decrease in income taxes payable	(1,900)
Net cash provided by operating activities	$ 23,100
Cash from investing activities	
Cash proceeds from sale of property, plant, and equipment	$ 8,500
Cash from financing activities	
Cash paid on loan principal	$(13,900)
Cash proceeds from stock issue	1,500
Cash paid for dividends	(3,000)
Net cash used for financing activities	$(15,400)
Net increase in cash during the year	$ 16,200
Cash balance, beginning of the year	23,000
Ending cash balance	$ 39,200

Key Terms for Chapter 9

Direct method (p. 417)   Free cash flow (p. 429)   Indirect method (p. 417)

Answers to YOUR TURN Questions

Chapter 9

Your Turn 9-1

The difference is in the section that examines cash flows from operating activities. The direct method identifies each cash flow, whereas the indirect method starts with net income and adjusts it to a cash amount. The net cash flow from operating activities is the same no matter which method is used. The other two sections—cash from investing activities and cash from financing activities—are identical with both methods.

Your Turn 9-2

$50,000 + ($25,000 − $15,000) = $60,000.
This is a cash flow from operating activities.

Your Turn 9-3

$400 − ($350 − $250) = $300.
This is a cash flow from operating activities.

Your Turn 9-4

Begin with net income and add back depreciation expense: $50,000 + $7,000 = $57,000. Then, subtract the $2,000 increase in accounts receivable. Sales on account were included in net income but should be deducted if the cash has not been collected. Next, add the $500 increase in salaries payable. Some of the salaries expense, which was deducted on the income statement, was not paid at the balance sheet date.
$50,000 + $7,000 − $2,000 + $500 =
$55,500 net cash from operating activities.

Your Turn 9-5

Free cash flow = Net cash from operations − Purchase of long-term assets − Dividends =
$45,600 − $25,000 − $0 = $20,600.

Questions

1. What is the purpose of the statement of cash flows?
2. Which two financial statements are used to prepare the statement of cash flows?
3. Describe the three categories of cash flows that explain the total change in cash for the year.
4. Why is the statement of cash flows so important?
5. What are the two traditional approaches for preparing and presenting the statement of cash flows? What is the difference between these two approaches?
6. Which types of business transactions would result in cash from operating activities? Give three examples of transactions that would be classified as cash flows from operating activities.
7. Which types of business transactions would result in cash flows from investing activities? Give three examples of transactions that would be classified as cash flows from investing activities.
8. Which types of business transactions would result in cash flows from financing activities? Give three examples of transactions that would be classified as cash flows from financing activities.
9. How is depreciation expense treated when using the direct method of preparing the statement of cash flows? When using the indirect method?
10. Which account(s) must be analyzed to determine the cash collected from customers? How is this cash flow classified?
11. Which account(s) must be analyzed to determine the proceeds from the sale of a building? How is this cash flow classified?
12. Which account(s) must be analyzed to determine the cash paid to vendors? How is this cash flow classified?
13. Which account(s) must be analyzed to determine the cash paid for dividends? How is this cash flow classified?
14. How is interest collected or interest paid classified on the statement of cash flows?
15. Define free cash flow and explain what this amount indicates about a firm.
16. How might a firm misuse the statement of cash flows to give investors a better impression of the firm's operations?

Multiple-Choice Questions

Use the following information to answer questions 1–3.
Quality Products engaged in the following **cash** transactions during May:

Purchase of inventory	$ 5,000
Cash proceeds from loan	$ 7,000
Cash paid for interest	$ 400
Cash collected from sales	$26,500
New stock issued	$25,000
Salaries paid to employees	$ 4,600
Purchase of new delivery van	$20,000

(Note: Answers in parentheses indicate net cash outflows.)

1. How much is net cash from financing activities?
    a. $ 7,000
    b. $25,000
    c. $31,600
    d. $32,000
2. How much is net cash from investing activities?
    a. $(20,000)
    b. $(25,000)
    c. $ 25,000
    d. $ 32,000
3. How much is net cash from operating activities?
    a. $26,500
    b. $ (3,500)
    c. $16,500
    d. $16,900
4. Cash from the sale of treasury stock
    a. would not be included in the statement of cash flows.
    b. would be classified as a contra-equity cash flow.
    c. would be classified as an investing cash flow.
    d. would be classified as a financing cash flow.
5. The cash proceeds from the sale of a building will be
    a. the cost of the building.
    b. the book value of the building.
    c. the book value plus any gain or minus any loss.
    d. shown on the financing portion of the appropriate financial statement.
6. If a firm has net investing cash inflows of $5,000; net financing cash inflows of $24,000; and a net increase in cash for the year of $12,000, how much is net cash from operating activities?
    a. Net cash inflow of $17,000
    b. Net cash inflow of $29,000
    c. Net cash outflow of $17,000
    d. Net cash outflow of $19,000
7. Depreciation for the year was $50,000 and net income was $139,500. If the company's transactions were all cash except those related to long-term assets, how much was net cash from operating activities?
    a. $139,500
    b. $189,500
    c. $ 89,500
    d. It cannot be determined from the given information.

Use the following information to answer questions 8–10.
The income statement and additional data for Frances Company for the year ended December 31, 2011, follow:

Frances Company
Income Statement
For the Year Ended December 31, 2011

Sales revenue		$400,000
Expenses:		
Cost of goods sold	$165,000	
Salary expense	70,000	
Depreciation expense	55,000	
Insurance expense	20,000	
Interest expense	10,000	
Income tax expense	18,000	338,000
Net income		$ 62,000

Accounts receivable decreased by $12,000. Inventories increased by $6,000 and accounts payable decreased by $2,000. Salaries payable increased by $8,000. Prepaid insurance increased by $4,000. Interest expense and income tax expense equal their cash amounts. Frances Company uses the direct method for its statement of cash flows.

8. How much cash did Frances Company collect from customers during 2011?
   a. $400,000
   b. $412,000
   c. $406,000
   d. $388,000

9. How much cash did Frances Company pay its vendors during 2011?
   a. $173,000
   b. $165,000
   c. $167,000
   d. $163,000

10. How much cash did Frances Company pay for insurance during the year?
   a. $20,000
   b. $24,000
   c. $16,000
   d. $48,000

Short Exercises
Set A

All of the A exercises can be found within MyAccountingLab, an online homework and practice environment.

SE9-1A. *Identify cash flows. (LO 1).* Given the following cash transactions, classify each as a cash flow from (1) operating activities, (2) investing activities, or (3) financing activities.
   a. Payment to employees for work done
   b. Dividends paid to shareholders
   c. Payment for new equipment
   d. Payment to supplier for inventory
   e. Interest payment to the bank related to a loan

SE9-2A. *Calculate and identify cash flows. (LO 1, 3, 4).* College Television Company had supplies on its balance sheet at December 31, 2010, of $20,000. The income statement for 2011 showed supplies expense of $50,000. The balance sheet at December 31, 2011, showed supplies of $25,000. If no supplies were purchased on account (all were cash purchases), how much cash did College Television Company spend on supplies during 2011? How would that cash outflow be classified on the statement of cash flows?

SE9-3A. *Calculate and identify cash flows. (LO 3, 6).* A building cost $55,000 and had accumulated depreciation of $15,000 when it was sold for a gain of $5,000. It was a cash sale. How much cash was collected from this transaction and how would it be classified on the statement of cash flows?

SE9-4A. *Calculate and identify cash flows. (LO 1, 3, 4).* Sales for 2010 were $50,000; cost of goods sold was $35,000. If accounts receivable increased by $2,000; inventory decreased by $1,300; accounts payable decreased by $2,000; and other accrued liabilities decreased by $1,000, how much cash was paid to vendors and suppliers during the year? How would the cash from this transaction be classified on the statement of cash flows?

SE9-5A. *Evaluate adjustments to net income using the indirect method. (LO 5).* The income statement for Lilly's Company for the year ended June 30, 2010, showed sales of $50,000. During the year, the balance in accounts receivable increased by $7,500. What adjustment to net income would be shown in the operating section of the statement of cash flows prepared using the indirect method related to this information? How much cash was collected from customers during the fiscal year ended June 30, 2010?

SE9-6A. *Evaluate adjustments to net income using the indirect method. (LO 5).* During 2011, Mail Direct, Inc., incurred salary expense of $67,500, as shown on the income statement. The

January 1, 2011, balance sheet showed salaries payable of $10,450; and the December 31, 2011, balance sheet showed salaries payable of $13,200. What adjustment to net income would be shown in the operating section of the statement of cash flows prepared using the indirect method related to this information? How much cash was paid to employees (for salary) during 2011?

SE9-7A. *Calculate and identify cash flows using the indirect method. (LO 5).* Beta Company spent $40,000 for a new delivery truck during the year. Depreciation expense of $2,000 related to the truck was shown on the income statement. How are the purchase of the truck and the related depreciation reflected on the statement of cash flows prepared using the indirect method?

SE9-8A. *Evaluate adjustments to net income under the indirect method. (LO 1, 5).* In 2012, Jewels Company had net income of $350,000. The depreciation on plant assets during 2012 was $73,000, and the company incurred a loss on the sale of plant assets of $20,000. All other transactions were cash. Compute net cash provided by operating activities under the indirect method.

SE9-9A. *Calculate and identify cash flows. (LO 5).* C&S Supply, Inc., had $125,000 of retained earnings at the beginning of the year and a balance of $150,000 at the end of the year. Net income for the year was $80,000. What caused the change in the retained earnings balance? Other than net income, how would any change in retained earnings be shown on the statement of cash flows?

Set B

SE9-10B. *Identify cash flows. (LO 1).* Given the following cash transactions, classify each as a cash flow from (1) operating activities, (2) investing activities, or (3) financing activities.
  a. Principal payment to the bank for a loan
  b. Collection from customers to whom sales were previously made on account
  c. Collection from customers for cash sales
  d. Collection for sale of land that had been purchased as a possible factory site
  e. Petty cash used to pay for doughnuts for staff

SE9-11B. *Calculate and identify cash flows. (LO 1, 3, 4).* Col Corporation reported credit sales of $150,000 for 2010. Col's accounts receivable from sales were $25,000 at the beginning of 2010 and $38,000 at the end of 2010. What was the amount of cash collected from sales in 2010? How would this cash be classified on the statement of cash flows?

SE9-12B. *Calculate and identify cash flows. (LO 3, 6).* A machine cost $235,000 and had accumulated depreciation of $200,000 when it was sold for a loss of $10,000. It was a cash sale. How much cash did the company collect for the sale and how would it be classified on the statement of cash flows?

SE9-13B. *Calculate and identify cash flow. (LO 1, 3, 4).* During 2011, Cameron Company had $300,000 in cash sales and $3,500,000 in credit sales. The accounts receivable balances were $450,000 and $530,000 at December 31, 2010 and 2011, respectively. What was the total cash collected from all customers during 2011? How should this cash be classified on the statement of cash flows?

SE9-14B. *Evaluate adjustments to net income using the indirect method. (LO 5).* The income statement for Sharp, Inc., for the month of May showed insurance expense of $250. The beginning and ending balance sheets for the month showed an increase of $50 in prepaid insurance. There were no payables related to insurance on the balance sheet. What adjustment to net income, related to this information, would be shown in the operating section of the statement of cash flows prepared using the indirect method? How much cash was paid for insurance during the month?

SE9-15B. *Evaluate adjustments to net income using the indirect method. (LO 5).* Havelen's Road Paving Company had depreciation expense of $43,000 on the income statement for the year. How would this expense be shown on the statement of cash flows prepared using the indirect method? Why?

SE9-16B. *Evaluate adjustments to net income under the indirect method. (LO 5).* B&W, Inc., reported net income of $1.2 million in 2011. Depreciation for the year was $120,000; accounts receivable increased $728,000; and accounts payable decreased $420,000. Compute net cash provided by operating activities using the indirect method.

SE9-17B. *Evaluate adjustments to net income under the indirect method. (LO 5).* The comparative balance sheets for JayCee Company showed the following changes in current asset accounts: accounts receivable decreased by $50,000, prepaid expenses decreased by $23,000, and merchandise inventory increased by $17,000. These were all the changes in the current assets and current liability accounts (except cash). Net income for the year was $275,500. Compute net cash provided by or used by operating activities using the indirect method.

SE9-18B. *Calculate and identify cash flows. (LO 5).* Idea, Inc., had $375,000 of retained earnings at the beginning of the year and a balance of $590,000 at the end of the year. Net income for the year was $320,000. What caused the change in the retained earnings balance? Other than net income, how would any change in retained earnings be shown on the statement of cash flows?

Exercises
Set A

MyAccountingLab

All of the A exercises can be found within MyAccountingLab, an online homework and practice environment.

E9-19A. *Identify cash flows. (LO 1).* For each of the following items, tell whether it is a cash inflow or cash outflow and the section of the statement of cash flows in which the item would appear. (Assume the direct method is used.)

Item	Inflow or Outflow	Section of the Statement
a. Cash collected from customers		
b. Proceeds from issue of stock		
c. Interest payment on loan		
d. Principal repayment on loan		
e. Cash paid for advertising		
f. Proceeds from sale of treasury stock		
g. Money borrowed from the local bank		
h. Cash paid to employees (salaries)		
i. Purchase of equipment for cash		
j. Cash paid to vendors for inventory		
k. Taxes paid		

E9-20A. *Identify cash flows. (LO 1, 4, 6).* For each transaction, indicate the amount of the cash flow, indicate whether each results in an inflow or outflow of cash, and give the section of the statement in which each cash flow would appear. Assume the statement of cash flows is prepared using the direct method.

Transaction	Amount	Inflow or Outflow	Section of the Statement
a. Issued 1,000 shares of $1 par common stock for $8 per share			
b. Purchased $800 of supplies for $650 cash and the balance on account			
c. Borrowed $9,500 from a local bank to expand the business			
d. Purchased some office equipment for $5,200 cash			
e. Earned revenue of $16,000, receiving $8,500 cash and the balance on account			
f. Repaid $6,000 of the bank loan along with $500 interest			
g. Hired an office assistant and paid her $750 cash			
h. Declared and paid cash dividends of $875			

E9-21A. *Prepare cash from operating activities section of statement of cash flows using the direct method. (LO 4).* Use the income statement for Hargrove Dynamics, Inc., for the past year ended December 31, 2011, and the information from the comparative balance sheets shown for the beginning and the end of the year to prepare the cash from operating activities section of the statement of cash flows using the direct method.

Hargrove Dynamics, Inc.
Income Statement
For the Year Ended December 31, 2011

Sales		$120,000
Cost of goods sold		40,000
Gross margin		80,000
Operating expenses		
Wages	$ 7,500	
Rent	10,200	
Utilities	4,800	
Insurance	1,500	24,000
Net income		$ 56,000

Selected accounts from the balance sheet:

Account	Beginning of the Year	End of the Year
Accounts receivable	$ 5,000	$15,000
Inventory	32,000	12,500
Prepaid insurance	1,500	500
Accounts payable	12,000	17,500
Wages payable	1,850	1,600
Utilities payable	500	-0-

E9-22A. *Prepare cash from operating activities section of statement of cash flows using the indirect method. (LO 5).* Use the information from E9-21A to prepare the cash from operating activities section of the statement of cash flows using the indirect method. Then, compare it with the statement you prepared for E9-21A. What are the similarities? What are the differences? Which statement do you find most informative?

E9-23A. *Calculate change in cash. (LO 1, 4, 6).* Given the following information, calculate the change in cash for the year:

Cash sales collected from customers	$31,000
Cash received from sale of vehicle	5,000
Goodwill amortization expense for the year	3,200
Cash received from issuance of stock	75,000
Cash paid for salaries	19,800
Cash received from sale of land	21,200
Cash paid for other operating expenses	14,000
Cash paid to vendor for inventory	10,550

E9-24A. *Calculate cash from operating activities. (LO 3, 4).* Use the information given for Very Heavenly Desserts, Inc., to calculate the following:
   a. Cash paid for salaries
   b. Cash paid for income taxes
   c. Cash paid for inventory items

d. Cash collected from customers

e. Cash proceeds from stock issue

From the Financial Statements for Very Heavenly Desserts, Inc.

	Income Statement Amount for the Year	Balance Sheet Beginning of the Year	End of the Year
Sales revenue	$67,000		
Accounts receivable		$ 8,800	$ 3,500
Salary expense	18,750		
Salaries payable		3,000	3,250
Cost of goods sold	31,200		
Inventory		11,600	9,500
Accounts payable		1,500	1,750
Income tax expense	7,500		
Income taxes payable		1,500	1,600
Common stock and additional paid-in capital		500,000	750,000

E9-25A. *Prepare the cash from operating activities section of the statement of cash flows and determine the method used. (LO 2, 4, 6).* Use the information from E9-24A to calculate the cash flow from operations for Very Heavenly Desserts, Inc. Based on the information provided, which method of preparing the statement of cash flows does the company use?

E9-26A. *Calculate cash flows from investing and financing activities. (LO 1, 6).* The following events occurred at Voich Plumbing, Inc., during 2011:

January 10	Issued common stock for $160,000
February 27	Signed a note with Last Local Bank for $15,000
May 12	Sold old service truck for $4,500 resulting in a $500 gain
May 30	Purchased a new service truck for $42,000
August 15	Paid cash dividends of $5,400
October 30	Purchased a new computer server for $25,000 cash
December 31	Paid interest expense with $1,500 cash to Last Local Bank

Compute Voich Plumbing, Inc.'s net cash flow from (1) investing activities and from (2) financing activities for 2011.

E9-27A. *Calculate cash from operating activities using the direct method. (LO 1, 4).* The following information applies to Quality Tech, Inc.:

> Quality Tech, Inc.
> Income Statement
> For the Year Ended June 30, 2009

Sales	$ 75,000
Cost of goods sold	(25,000)
Gross margin	50,000
Insurance expense	(5,000)
Net income	$ 45,000

1. Accounts receivable started the year with a balance of $2,500 and ended the year with a balance of $500.
2. The beginning balance in accounts payable (to vendors) was $5,000, and the ending balance for the year was $3,000. Inventory at the end of the year was $1,000 more than at the beginning of the year.
3. The company started the year with $5,000 of prepaid insurance and ended the year with $5,750 of prepaid insurance.

Determine the following cash flows:
    a. Cash collected from customers for sales during the year
    b. Cash paid to vendors for inventory during the year
    c. Cash paid for insurance during the year

E9-28A. *Calculate cash from operating activities using the indirect method. (LO 5, 6).* Brenda Textiles, Inc., reported net income of $120,000 for 2011. The company also reported depreciation expense of $35,000 and a loss of $2,500 on the sale of sewing equipment. The comparative balance sheet shows a decrease in accounts receivable of $5,000 for the year, a $2,500 decrease in accounts payable, and a $1,980 increase in prepaid expenses. Prepare the cash from operating activities section of the statement of cash flows for 2011 using the indirect method.

E9-29A. *Calculate cash from operating activities using the indirect method. (LO 5).* The following information was taken from Artist, Inc.'s balance sheets at December 31, 2009 and 2010:

	2010	2009
Current assets		
Cash	$ 65,000	$ 60,000
Accounts receivable	10,000	30,000
Inventory	66,000	59,000
Prepaid expenses	50,000	23,500
Total current assets	$191,000	$172,500
Current liabilities		
Accrued expenses payable	$ 8,500	$ 4,500
Accounts payable	30,000	42,000
Total current liabilities	$ 38,500	$ 46,500

Net income for 2010 was $21,000. Depreciation expense was $11,000.

Prepare the cash provided by operating activities section of the company's statement of cash flows for the year ended December 31, 2010, using the indirect method.

E9-30A. *Calculate cash from operating activities using the direct method. (LO 4).* Stackhouse International, Inc., completed its first year of operations on June 30, 2010. The firm's income statement for the year showed revenues of $250,000 and operating expenses of $75,000. Accounts receivable was $71,000 at year end and payables related to operating expense were $35,000 at year end. Compute net cash from operating activities using the direct method.

E9-31A. *Calculate cash from operating activities using the direct method. (LO 1, 4).* During the fiscal year ended March 31, 2009, Fins & Feathers Pet Company engaged in the following transactions:
    a. Collected $125,000 on accounts receivable
    b. Paid interest of $5,000
    c. Made cash sales of $225,000
    d. Paid salaries of $45,000
    e. Paid income taxes of $15,000
    f. Recorded amortization expense of $35,000
    g. Sold vehicle for cash of $12,000
    h. Made payments to vendors of $85,200
    i. Issued bonds for $375,000

j. Purchased new vehicle for cash of $37,000
k. Purchased land for cash of $350,000
l. Paid operating expenses of $29,800

Using the relevant transactions, prepare the cash from operating activities section of the statement of cash flows using the direct method.

E9-32A. *Prepare the statement of cash flows using the indirect method. (LO 5, 6).* Use the following information for Eriksen Sporting Goods, Inc., to prepare a statement of cash flows using the indirect method:

<table>
<tr><td colspan="3">**Eriksen Sporting Goods, Inc.**
Comparative Balance Sheets</td></tr>
<tr><td></td><td>December 31, 2010</td><td>December 31, 2009</td></tr>
<tr><td>**Assets**</td><td></td><td></td></tr>
<tr><td>Cash ....</td><td>$ 386,000</td><td>$ 241,000</td></tr>
<tr><td>Accounts receivable ....</td><td>128,000</td><td>120,000</td></tr>
<tr><td>Inventories ....</td><td>240,000</td><td>350,000</td></tr>
<tr><td>Land ....</td><td>190,000</td><td>240,000</td></tr>
<tr><td>Equipment ....</td><td>500,000</td><td>360,000</td></tr>
<tr><td>Accumulated depreciation ....</td><td>(150,000)</td><td>(90,000)</td></tr>
<tr><td>Total assets ....</td><td>$1,294,000</td><td>$1,221,000</td></tr>
<tr><td>**Liabilities and Shareholders' Equity**</td><td></td><td></td></tr>
<tr><td>Accounts payable ....</td><td>$ 84,000</td><td>$ 100,000</td></tr>
<tr><td>Bonds payable ....</td><td>320,000</td><td>440,000</td></tr>
<tr><td>Common stock and additional paid-in capital ..</td><td>400,000</td><td>360,000</td></tr>
<tr><td>Retained earnings ....</td><td>490,000</td><td>321,000</td></tr>
<tr><td>Total liabilities and shareholders' equity ....</td><td>$1,294,000</td><td>$1,221,000</td></tr>
</table>

Additional information follows:
a. Net income for the fiscal year ended December 31, 2010, was $190,000.
b. The company declared and paid cash dividends.
c. The company redeemed bonds payable amounting to $120,000 for cash of $120,000.
d. The company issued common stock for $40,000 cash.

E9-33A. *Analyze a statement of cash flows. (LO 7).* The following information has been taken from the most recent statement of cash flows of Expansion Company:

Net cash used by operating activities	$ (932,000)
Net cash provided by investing activities	$1,180,500
Net cash provided by financing activities	$2,107,000

1. What information do these subtotals from the statement of cash flows tell you about Expansion Company?
2. What additional information would you want to see before you analyze Expansion Company's ability to generate positive operating cash flows in the future?
3. Did Expansion have a positive net income for the period? What information would you like to see to help you predict next year's net income?

Set B

E9-34B. *Identify cash flows. (LO 1).* For each of the following items, tell whether it is a cash inflow or cash outflow and the section of the statement of cash flows in which the item would appear. (Assume the direct method is used.)

Item	Inflow or Outflow	Section of the Statement
a. Cash paid to vendor for supplies		
b. Purchase of treasury stock		
c. Principal repayment on bonds		
d. Interest payment on bonds		
e. Cash paid for salaries		
f. Cash from issuance of common stock		
g. Cash dividends paid		
h. Cash paid for rent and utilities		
i. Purchase of computer for cash		
j. Cash paid for company vehicle		
k. Income taxes paid		

E9-35B. *Identify cash flows. (LO 1, 4).* For each transaction, indicate the amount of the cash flow, indicate whether each results in an inflow or outflow of cash, and give the section of the statement in which each cash flow would appear. Assume the statement of cash flows is prepared using the direct method.

Transaction	Amount	Inflow or Outflow	Section of the Statement
a. Issued 5,000 shares of $0.50 par common stock for $25 per share			
b. Paid $15,000 cash for office renovations			
c. Sold $32,000 of inventory, received $27,000 in cash and remaining $5,000 on account			
d. Paid $6,500 for security services			
e. Repaid a $8,000 short-term note along with $800 interest			
f. Purchased a delivery truck for $42,000			
g. Paid salary expenses totaling $7,950			
h. Purchased $8,000 of treasury stock			

E9-36B. *Prepare cash from operating activities using the direct method. (LO 4).* Use the income statement for Arbuckle's Anti-Aging, Inc., for the year ended December 31, 2011, and the information from the comparative balance sheets shown for the beginning and the end of the year to prepare the operating section of the statement of cash flows using the direct method.

<table>
<tr><td colspan="3" align="center">Arbuckle's Anti-Aging, Inc.
Income Statement
For the Year Ended December 31, 2011</td></tr>
<tr><td>Sales</td><td></td><td>$250,000</td></tr>
<tr><td>Cost of goods sold</td><td></td><td>50,000</td></tr>
<tr><td>Gross margin</td><td></td><td>200,000</td></tr>
<tr><td>Operating Expenses:</td><td></td><td></td></tr>
<tr><td>Wages</td><td>$4,750</td><td></td></tr>
<tr><td>Rent</td><td>2,050</td><td></td></tr>
<tr><td>Utilities</td><td>1,000</td><td></td></tr>
<tr><td>Insurance</td><td>2,400</td><td>10,200</td></tr>
<tr><td>Net income</td><td></td><td>$189,800</td></tr>
</table>

Account	Beginning of the Year	End of the Year
Accounts receivable	$15,000	$18,000
Inventory	5,000	30,000
Prepaid insurance	100	1,000
Accounts payable	4,000	8,500
Wages payable	375	400
Utilities payable	0	85

E9-37B. *Prepare cash from operating activities using the indirect method. (LO 5).* Use the information from E9-36B to prepare the cash from operating activities section of the statement of cash flows using the indirect method. Then, compare it with the statement you prepared for E9-36B. What are the similarities? What are the differences? Which statement do you find most informative?

E9-38B. *Calculate change in cash. (LO 1, 5).* Given the following information, calculate the change in cash for the year:

Cash received from sale of company equipment	$ 20,000
Cash paid for salaries	8,500
Cash paid for other operating expenses	12,250
Cash paid for purchase of treasury stock	16,000
Cash paid for rent	12,000
Cash received from issuance of bonds	125,000
Cash collected from customers	45,000
Cash paid to do a major repair of delivery van to prolong its useful life for five more years	21,820

E9-39B. *Calculate cash from operating activities. (LO 2, 5).* Use the information given for Pro Consultants, Inc., to calculate the following:
  a. Cash paid for utilities
  b. Cash paid for interest
  c. Cash paid for inventory items
  d. Cash collected from customers
  e. Cash proceeds from stock issue

From the Financial Statements for Pro Consultants, Inc.

	Income Statement Amount for the Year	Balance Sheet Beginning of the Year	Balance Sheet End of the Year
Sales revenue	$105,050		
Accounts receivable		$ 10,000	$ 16,500
Utilities expense	8,700		
Utilities payable		2,000	3,500
Cost of goods sold	35,500		
Inventory		10,500	5,500
Accounts payable		2,000	500
Interest expense	2,550		
Interest payable		400	325
Common stock and additional paid-in capital		175,000	260,000

E9-40B. *Prepare cash from operating activities section of statement of cash flows and determine the method used. (LO 2, 4).* Use the information from E9-39B to calculate the cash flow from operating activities for Pro Consultants, Inc. Based on the information provided, which method of preparing the statement of cash flows does Pro Consultants, Inc., use?

E9-41B. Calculate cash flows from investing and financing activities. *(LO 1, 6)*. The following events occurred at Electric Research, Inc., during the year ended June 30, 2010:

July 25	Signed a note with Local First Bank for $25,000
August 8	Purchased equipment for $50,000 cash
October 15	Sold old equipment for $20,100, resulting in a $100 gain
January 24	Issued bonds for $150,000
March 20	Purchased new delivery vehicles for $32,000 cash
April 15	Paid cash dividends of $2,500
June 30	Paid interest expense with $2,300 cash to Local First Bank

Compute Electric Research, Inc.'s net cash flow from (1) investing activities and from (2) financing activities for the year ended June 30, 2010.

E9-42B. *Calculate cash from operating activities using the direct method. (LO 1, 4).* The following information applies to Change Corporation:

> **Change Corporation**
> **Income Statement**
> **For the Year Ended December 31, 2010**

Sales	$ 55,000
Cost of goods sold	(17,250)
Gross margin	37,750
Rent expense	(5,750)
Net income	$ 32,000

1. Accounts receivable started the year with a balance of $1,050 and ended the year with a balance of $2,250.
2. The beginning balance in accounts payable (to vendors) was $650, and the ending balance was $1,550. Inventory was $1,000 less at the end of the year than it was at the beginning of the year.
3. The company started the year with $2,000 of prepaid rent and ended the year with $1,500 of prepaid rent.

Determine the following cash flows:
   a. Cash collected from customers for sales during the year
   b. Cash paid to vendors for inventory during the year
   c. Cash paid for rent during the year

E9-43B. *Calculate cash from operating activities using the indirect method. (LO 5).* Anika Book Distributors, Inc., reported net income of $415,000 for 2009. The company also reported depreciation expense of $75,000 and a gain of $6,250 on the sale of machinery. The comparative balance sheet shows an increase in accounts receivable of $1,500 for the year, a $4,100 increase in accounts payable, and a $2,175 decrease in prepaid expenses. Prepare the cash from operating activities section of the statement of cash flows for 2009 using the indirect method.

E9-44B. *Calculate cash from operating activities using the indirect method. (LO 5).* The following information was taken from Hive Marketing, Inc.'s balance sheets at June 30, 2010 and 2011:

	2011	2010
Current assets		
Cash	$ 71,000	$ 65,000
Accounts receivable	50,000	45,000
Inventory	75,000	61,000
Prepaid expenses	$ 35,000	$ 41,000
Total current assets	$231,000	$212,000

Current liabilities		
Accrued expenses payable	$ 9,000	$10,000
Accounts payable	62,000	81,000
Total current liabilities	$ 71,000	$91,000

Net income for the year ended June 30, 2011, was $62,000. Depreciation expense was $12,750.

Prepare the cash provided by operating activities section of the company's statement of cash flows for the year ended June 30, 2011, using the indirect method.

E9-45B. *Calculate cash from operating activities using the direct method. (LO 4).* Health Spa Corporation completed its first year of operations on December 31, 2012. The firm's income statement for the year showed revenues of $210,000 and operating expenses of $78,000. Accounts receivable was $45,000 at year end and payables related to operating expense were $28,750 at year end. Compute net cash from operating activities using the direct method.

E9-46B. *Calculate cash from operating activities using the direct method. (LO 1, 4).* During the fiscal year ended September 30, 2010, Whitehouse Data, Inc., engaged in the following transactions:
   a. Collected $75,000 on accounts receivable
   b. Paid $125,000 on accounts payable related to operating expenses
   c. Made cash sales of $275,000
   d. Declared a 3-for-1 stock split
   e. Paid salaries of $35,000
   f. Recorded depreciation expense of $17,250
   g. Issued common stock for $25,000
   h. Repaid principal of mortgage for $295,000
   i. Sold land for $150,000
   j. Paid interest on mortgage in the amount of $17,800
   k. Purchased new equipment for cash of $61,500
   l. Paid operating expenses of $55,000

Using the relevant transactions, prepare the cash from operating activities section of the statement of cash flows using the direct method.

E9-47B. *Prepare the statement of cash flows using the indirect method. (LO 2, 5).* Use the following information for Professional Athletics, Inc., to prepare a statement of cash flows for the year ended June 30, 2009, using the indirect method:

Professional Athletics, Inc.
Comparative Balance Sheets

	June 30, 2009	June 30, 2008
Assets		
Cash	$ 110,000	$ 47,000
Accounts receivable	156,000	128,000
Inventories	360,000	338,000
Land	270,000	210,000
Equipment	700,000	520,000
Accumulated depreciation	(180,000)	(120,000)
Total assets	$1,416,000	$1,123,000
Liabilities and Shareholders' Equity		
Accounts payable	$ 70,000	$ 80,000
Bonds payable	370,000	430,000
Common stock and additional paid-in capital	450,000	350,000
Retained earnings	526,000	263,000
Total liabilities and shareholders' equity	$1,416,000	$1,123,000

Additional information follows:

    a. Net income for the fiscal year ended June 30, 2009, was $290,000.

    b. The company declared and paid cash dividends.

    c. The company redeemed bonds payable amounting to $60,000 for cash of $60,000.

    d. The company issued common stock for $100,000 cash.

E9-48B. *Analyze a statement of cash flows. (LO 7).* The following information was taken from the most recent statement of cash flows of Innovative Electronics Company:

Net cash provided by operating activities	$ 845,000
Net cash used by investing activities	$ (530,000)
Net cash provided by financing activities	$1,675,000

1. What information do these subtotals from the statement of cash flows tell you about Innovative Electronics Company?
2. What additional information would you want to see before you analyze Innovative Electronics Company's ability to generate positive operating cash flows in the future?
3. Did Innovative Electronics have a positive net income for the period? What information would you like to see to help you predict next year's net income?

All of the A problems can be found within MyAccountingLab, an online homework and practice environment.

Problems
Set A

P9-49A. *Prepare the statement of cash flows (direct or indirect method). (LO 2, 3, 4, 5, 6, 7).* The income statement for the year ended December 31, 2011, and the balance sheets at December 31, 2010, and December 31, 2011, for Craig's Service Company are presented here.

Craig's Service Company
Income Statement
For the Year Ended December 31, 2011

(amounts in thousands, except earnings per share)

Service revenue		$92,000
Expenses:		
Wages and salaries	$60,000	
Advertising	10,000	
Rent	4,800	
Depreciation	3,600	
Supplies	5,200	
Total expenses		83,600
Income before taxes		$ 8,400
Income taxes		2,940
Net income		$ 5,460
Earnings per share		$ 0.55

Craig's Service Company
Comparative Balance Sheets

	December 31, 2011	December 31, 2010
(amounts in thousands)		
Assets:		
Current assets:		
Cash	$ 6,910	$ 3,500
Accounts receivable	12,000	14,000
Supplies	200	370
Prepaid advertising	800	660
Total current assets	$19,910	$18,530
Property, plant, and equipment		
Equipment $44,000		$40,000
Less: accumulated depreciation 21,600		18,000
Total property, plant, and equipment	22,400	22,000
Total assets	$42,310	$40,530
Liabilities and Stockholders' Equity:		
Current liabilities:		
Wages and salaries payable	$ 2,700	$ 3,300
Taxes payable	1,900	1,780
Total current liabilities	$ 4,600	$ 5,080
Stockholders' equity:		
Common stock $30,000		$30,000
Retained earnings 7,710		5,450
	$37,710	$35,450
Total liabilities and stockholders' equity	$42,310	$40,530

Requirements

1. Prepare a statement of cash flows for the year ended December 31, 2011, using (a) the direct method and (b) the indirect method.
2. Why is the statement of cash flows important to the company and to parties external to the company?
3. As a user, which format would you prefer—direct or indirect—and why?
4. Evaluate the way in which the company spent its cash during the year. Do you think the company is in a sound cash position?
5. Calculate the firm's free cash flow for the most recent year.

P9-50A. *Calculate cash from operating activities using the indirect method. (LO 5).* The following information is from the comparative balance sheets of Discovery Tech Corporation at June 30, 2011 and 2010:

(in thousands) At June 30	2011	2010
Current assets:		
Cash	$2,750	$2,115
Accounts receivable	3,000	2,750
Inventory	1,700	1,025
Prepaid insurance	270	320
Total current assets	$7,720	$6,210

Current liabilities:		
Accounts payable	$1,800	$1,750
Salaries payable	$3,750	$3,150
Total current liabilities	$5,550	$4,900

Net income for the year ended June 30, 2011, was $425,000. Depreciation expense of $105,000 was included in the operating expenses for the year.

Requirement

Use the indirect method to prepare the *cash from operations* section of the statement of cash flows for Discovery Tech Corporation for the year ended June 30, 2011.

P9-51A. *Calculate cash from operating activities using the indirect method. (LO 5).* The following information comes from the balance sheets of Moonlight Spa Treatments, Inc., at March 31, 2011 and 2010:

(in thousands)	2011	2010
Current assets:		
Cash	$3,765	$3,005
Accounts receivable	989	1,050
Inventory	1,500	1,000
Prepaid rent	125	250
Total current assets	$6,379	$5,305
Current liabilities:		
Accounts payable	$1,475	$1,105
Wages payable	1,700	1,960
Total current liabilities	$3,175	$3,065

Net income for the year ended March 30, 2011, was $105,700. Included in the operating expenses for the year was depreciation expense of $98,000.

Requirement

Prepare the *cash from operating activities* section of Moonlight Spa Treatments, Inc.'s statement of cash flows for the year March 31, 2011. Use the indirect method.

P9-52A. *Calculate cash from operating activities using the indirect method. (LO 5).* Burke Landscaping Company had the following information available for the year ended June 30, 2009:

	July 1, 2008	June 30, 2009
Accounts receivable	$356,000	$302,000
Prepaid insurance	76,000	32,000
Inventory	132,000	142,000

Burke Landscaping Company reported net income of $675,000 for the year ended June 30, 2009. Depreciation expense, included on the income statement, was $60,500.

Requirement

Assume that the preceding information is all the information relevant to the statement of cash flows. Use the indirect method to prepare the *cash flows from operating activities* section of Burke Landscaping Company's statement of cash flows for the year ended June 30, 2009.

P9-53A. *Calculate investing and financing cash flows. (LO 6).* To prepare its statement of cash flows for the year ended December 31, 2010, Sweet Confections, Inc., gathered the following information:

Gain on sale of land	$ 25,000
Proceeds from sale of land	170,000
Proceeds from bond issue (face value $150,000)	135,000
Amortization of bond discount	3,500
Dividends declared	34,000
Dividends paid	32,000
Issuance of common stock	50,000

Requirements

1. Prepare the *cash from investing* section of the statement of cash flows.
2. Prepare the *cash from financing* section of the statement of cash flows.

P9-54A. *Calculate investing and financing cash flows. (LO 6).* To prepare its statement of cash flows for the year ended June 30, 2011, Glavine Sports Products, Inc., gathered the following information:

Loss on sale of automobile	$ 5,000
Proceeds from sale of automobile	7,500
Purchase of automobile	42,000
Dividends declared	10,000
Dividends paid	5,000
Proceeds from sale of treasury stock	65,000
Repayment of loan principal	17,500
Payment of interest on loan	500

Requirements

1. Prepare the *cash from investing* section of the statement of cash flows.
2. Prepare the *cash from financing* section of the statement of cash flows.

P9-55A. *Calculate investing and financing cash flows. (LO 6).* To prepare its statement of cash flows for the year ended December 31, 2012, McKinney Carterette Cataloging Specialists, Inc., gathered the following information:

Dividends paid	$ 17,750
Purchase of treasury stock	25,000
Proceeds from bank loan	55,000
Gain on sale of equipment	15,000
Proceeds from sale of equipment	30,000
Proceeds from sale of common stock	175,000

Requirements

1. Prepare the *cash from investing* section of the statement of cash flows.
2. Prepare the *cash from financing* section of the statement of cash flows.

P9-56A. *Analyze a statement of cash flows. (LO 5, 6, 7).* Use the following statement of cash flows for the Matlock Company to answer the required questions:

Matlock Company
Statement of Cash Flows
For the Year Ended December 31, 2010

(amounts in thousands)

Cash flows from operating activities:		
Net income		$1,500
Depreciation expense	$ 210	
Decrease in accounts receivable	320	
Increase in inventory	(70)	
Increase in prepaid rent	(10)	
Increase in accounts payable	150	600
Net cash provided by operating activities		$2,100
Cash flows from investing activities:		
Purchase of equipment	$(1,000)	
Proceeds from sale of old equipment	200	
Net cash used by investing activities		(800)
Cash flows from financing activities:		
Repayment of long-term mortgage	$(1,350)	
Proceeds from sale of common stock	500	
Payment of cash dividends	(200)	
Net cash used by financing activities		(1,050)
Net increase in cash during 2010		$ 250
Cash balance, January 1, 2010		346
Cash balance, December 31, 2010		$ 596

Requirements

1. How did Matlock Company use the majority of its cash during 2010?
2. What information does this give you about Matlock Company?
3. What was Matlock Company's major source of cash during 2010?
4. Is this an appropriate source of cash for the long run? Explain.
5. Calculate Matlock's free cash flow for 2010.

Set B

P9-57B. *Prepare the statement of cash flows (direct or indirect method). (LO 2, 3, 4, 5, 6, 7).* Following are the income statements for Ocoee Oil Company for the year ended December 31, 2011, and the balance sheets at December 31, 2010 and 2011.

Ocoee Oil Company
Income Statement
For the Year Ended December 31, 2011

Sales revenue		$150,000
Cost of goods sold		63,000
Gross margin		87,000
Other expenses:		
Wages and salaries	$32,000	
Depreciation and depletion	4,500	
Miscellaneous	12,400	
Total other expenses		48,900
Income before taxes		38,100
Income taxes		8,200
Net income		$ 29,900

Ocoee Oil Company
Comparative Balance Sheets

		December 31, 2011		December 31, 2010
Assets				
Current assets:				
Cash		$ 0		$ 6,400
Accounts receivable		2,900		2,700
Inventory		60,000		42,000
Total current assets		$ 62,900		$51,100
Property, plant, and equipment			$ 39,000	
Equipment	$ 82,300			
Less: accumulated depreciation	(20,100)		(15,600)	
Total property, plant, and equipment		62,200		23,400
Total assets		$125,100		$74,500
Liabilities and shareholders' equity				
Current liabilities:				
Accounts payable	$ 6,400		$ 5,700	
Salaries payable	1,500		1,300	
Taxes payable	1,900		2,100	
Total current liabilities	$ 9,800		$ 9,100	
Notes payable	30,000		10,000	
Total liabilities		$ 39,800		$19,100
Shareholders' equity				
Common stock	$ 40,000		$ 40,000	
Retained earnings	45,300		15,400	
Total shareholders' equity		85,300		55,400
Total liabilities and shareholders' equity		$125,100		$74,500

Requirements

1. Prepare a statement of cash flows for the year ended December 31, 2011, using (1) the direct method and (2) the indirect method.
2. Why is the statement of cash flows important to the company and to parties external to the company?
3. As a user, which format—direct or indirect—would you prefer and why?
4. Evaluate the way in which the company spent its cash during the year. Do you think the company is in a sound cash position?
5. Compute the firm's free cash flow.

P9-58B. *Calculate cash from operating activities using the indirect method. (LO 5).* The following information is from the comparative balance sheets of Runnels Cosmetics Company at March 31, 2010 and 2009:

(in thousands) At March 31	2010	2009
Current assets:		
Cash	$4,050	$3,720
Accounts receivable	3,500	3,150
Inventory	1,550	1,800
Prepaid rent	450	520
Total current assets	$9,550	$9,190
Current liabilities:		
Accounts payable	$3,000	$2,275
Salaries payable	3,900	4,700
Total current liabilities	$6,900	$6,975

Net income for the year ended March 31, 2010, was $157,000. Depreciation expense of $54,000 was included in the operating expenses for the year.

Requirement

Use the indirect method to prepare the *cash from operations* section of the statement of cash flows for Runnels Cosmetics Company for the year ended March 31, 2010.

P9-59B. *Calculate cash from operating activities using the indirect method. (LO 5).* The following information comes from the balance sheets of Expert Continuing Education, Inc., at June 30:

(in thousands)	2011	2010
Current assets:		
Cash	$4,075	$3,980
Accounts receivable	2,500	2,250
Inventory	675	725
Prepaid insurance	700	485
Total current assets	$7,950	$7,440
Current liabilities:		
Accounts payable	$4,600	$4,265
Wages payable	1,505	1,869
Total current liabilities	$6,105	$6,134

Net income for the year ended June 30, 2011, was $315,000. Included in the operating expenses for the year was depreciation expense of $134,000.

Requirement

Prepare the *cash from operating activities* section of Expert Continuing Education, Inc.'s statement of cash flows for the year ended June 30, 2011. Use the indirect method.

P9-60B. *Calculate cash from operating activities using the indirect method. (LO 5).* Fitness Elite Corporation had the following information available for 2012:

	January 1	December 31
Accounts receivable	$160,000	$152,000
Prepaid insurance	96,000	52,000
Inventory	152,000	120,000

Fitness Elite Corporation reported net income of $275,000 for the year. Depreciation expense, included on the income statement, was $35,400.

Requirement

Assume that the preceding information is all the information relevant to the statement of cash flows. Use the indirect method to prepare the cash flows from operating activities section of Fitness Elite Corporation's statement of cash flows for the year ended December 31, 2012.

P9-61B. *Calculate investing and financing cash flows. (LO 6).* To prepare its statement of cash flows for the year ended June 30, 2011, Purified Water Company gathered the following information:

Proceeds from bond issue (face value $500,000)	$350,000
Amortization of bond premium	2,750
Dividends declared	19,000
Dividends paid	14,000
Purchase of treasury stock	35,000
Loss on sale of equipment	10,000
Proceeds from sale of equipment	45,000

Requirements

1. Prepare the *cash from investing* section of the statement of cash flows.
2. Prepare the *cash from financing* section of the statement of cash flows.

P9-62B. *Calculate investing and financing cash flows. (LO 6).* To prepare its statement of cash flows for the year ended December 31, 2012, N.C. Lewis Technology International, Inc., gathered the following information:

Dividends declared	$25,000
Dividends paid	18,000
Proceeds from sale of treasury stock	55,000
Repayment of loan principal	27,000
Payment of interest on loan	270
Loss on sale of machinery	1,500
Proceeds from sale of machinery	6,000
Purchase of machinery	48,700

Requirements

1. Prepare the *cash from investing* section of the statement of cash flows.
2. Prepare the *cash from financing* section of the statement of cash flows.

P9-63B. *Calculate investing and financing cash flows. (LO 6).* To prepare its statement of cash flows for the year ended June 30, 2010, Linds Cloud Soft Bedding Company gathered the following information:

Proceeds from bank loan	$225,000
Loss on sale of machinery	5,000
Proceeds from sale of machinery	10,000
Proceeds from bond issuance	275,000
Dividends paid	45,200
Purchase of treasury stock	125,000

Requirements

1. Prepare the *cash from investing* section of the statement of cash flows.
2. Prepare the *cash from financing* section of the statement of cash flows.

P9-64B. *Analyze a statement of cash flows. (LO 5, 6, 7).* Use the following statement of cash flows for the SS&P Company to answer the required questions:

SS&P Company
Statement of Cash Flows
For the Year Ended December 31, 2011

(amounts in thousands)

Cash from operating activities:		
Net income		$ 2,500
Depreciation expense	$ 510	
Decrease in accounts receivable	720	
Increase in inventory	(90)	
Increase in prepaid rent	(20)	
Decrease in accounts payable	(150)	970
Net cash provided by operating activities		$ 3,470
Cash from investing activities:		
Purchase of equipment	$(3,000)	
Proceeds from sale of old equipment	900	
Net cash used by investing activities		(2,100)
Cash from financing activities:		
Repayment of long-term mortgage	$(7,500)	
Proceeds from sale of common stock	2,100	
Payment of cash dividends	(1,200)	
Net cash used by financing activities		$(6,600)
Net increase (decrease) in cash during 2011		(5,230)
Cash balance, January 1, 2011		10,580
Cash balance, December 31, 2011		$ 5,350

Requirements

1. How did SS&P Company use the majority of its cash during 2011?
2. What information does this give you about SS&P Company?
3. How did SS&P Company obtain the majority of its cash during 2011?
4. Is this an appropriate source of cash for the long run? Explain.
5. Calculate SS&P's free cash flow for 2011.

Financial Statement Analysis

FSA9-1. *Analyze a statement of cash flows. (LO 7).* Use the financial statements for Borders Group, Inc., which can be found at www.borders.com, to answer the following questions:

1. What were the major sources and uses of cash during the most recent fiscal year? What does this indicate about Borders' cash position?
2. What evidence, if any, is there that Borders is expanding?

FSA9-2. *Analyze a statement of cash flows. (LO 2, 7).* The following statements of cash flows are from First Solar, Inc.'s 2008 annual report:

FIRST SOLAR, INC., AND SUBSIDIARIES
Consolidated Statements of Cash Flows

(in thousands)	December 27, 2008	December 29, 2007	December 30, 2006
Cash flows from operating activities:			
Cash received from customers	$1,203,822	$ 515,994	$ 110,196
Cash paid to suppliers and associates	(723,123)	(276,525)	(111,945)
Interest received	19,138	19,965	2,640
Interest paid, net of amounts capitalized	(4,629)	(2,294)	(712)
Income taxes paid, net of refunds	(1,975)	(19,002)	—
Excess tax benefit from share-based compensation arrangements	(28,661)	(30,196)	(45)
Other	(1,505)	(1,991)	(710)
Net cash provided by (used in) operating activities	463,067	205,951	(576)
Cash flows from investing activities:			
Purchases of property, plant and equipment	(459,271)	(242,371)	(153,150)
Purchase of marketable securities	(334,818)	(1,081,154)	—
Proceeds from maturities of marketable securities	107,450	787,783	—
Proceeds from sales of marketable securities	418,762	—	—
Increase in restricted investments	(15,564)	(6,008)	(6,804)
Investment in related party	(25,000)	—	—
Acquisitions, net of cash acquired	—	(5,500)	—
Other investments in long-term assets	—	—	(40)
Net cash used in investing activities	(308,441)	(547,250)	(159,994)
Cash flows from financing activities:			
Proceeds from issuance of common stock	—	365,969	302,650
Proceeds from notes payable to a related party	—	—	36,000
Repayment of notes payable to a related party	—	—	(64,700)
Repayment of long-term debt	(41,691)	(34,757)	(135)
Other equity contributions	—	—	30,000
Proceeds from stock options exercised	16,036	10,173	100
Proceeds from issuance of debt, net of issuance costs	138,887	49,368	130,833
Excess tax benefit from share-based compensation arrangements	28,661	30,196	45
Proceeds from economic development funding	35,661	9,475	16,766
Other financing activities	(5)	(3)	(9)
Net cash provided by financing activities	177,549	430,421	451,550
Effect of exchange rate changes on cash and cash equivalents	(20,221)	7,050	391
Net increase in cash and cash equivalents	311,954	96,172	291,371
Cash and cash equivalents, beginning of year	404,264	308,092	16,721
Cash and cash equivalents, end of year	$ 716,218	$ 404,264	$ 308,092

Answer the following questions:

1. What was First Solar's main source of cash for the most recent fiscal year?
2. Is First Solar expanding its business? What evidence on the statement of cash flows supports your opinion?
3. Did the company issue any new stock during the most recent fiscal year? Any new debt?
4. When a firm uses the direct method, it must also provide a reconciliation of net income to net cash from operating activities. What does this mean? Do you think this requirement discourages the use of the direct method?

FSA9-3. *Analyze a statement of cash flows. (LO 7, 8).* The statement of cash flows for Chico's FAS, Inc., for the years ended January 31, 2009, February 2, 2008, and February 3, 2007, appears on the following page.

CHICO'S FAS, INC., AND SUBSIDIARIES
CONSOLIDATED STATEMENTS OF CASH FLOWS

	Fiscal Year Ended		
(in thousands)	January 31, 2009	February 2, 2008	February 3, 2007
CASH FLOWS FROM OPERATING ACTIVITIES			
Net (loss) income	$ (19,137)	$ 88,875	$ 166,636
Adjustments to reconcile net (loss) income to net cash provided by operating activities —			
Depreciation and amortization, cost of goods sold	8,782	10,386	7,564
Depreciation and amortization, other	88,790	81,593	61,840
Deferred tax benefit	(20,507)	(6,635)	(22,324)
Stock-based compensation expense, cost of goods sold	2,769	4,909	6,004
Stock-based compensation expense, other	9,821	12,171	15,237
Excess tax benefit from stock-based compensation	(100)	(209)	(2,365)
Deferred rent expense, net	6,060	9,508	6,867
Goodwill impairment	—	—	6,752
Gain on sale of investment	—	(6,833)	—
Impairment of long-lived assets	13,691	—	—
Loss (gain) on disposal of property and equipment	761	(908)	826
Decrease (increase) in assets —			
Receivables, net	3,766	(18,770)	(4,517)
Income tax receivable	12,267	—	—
Inventories	11,847	(32,388)	(14,696)
Prepaid expenses and other	4,224	(3,958)	(3,676)
(Decrease) increase in liabilities —			
Accounts payable	(22,488)	24,119	7,532
Accrued and other deferred liabilities	(1,100)	46,787	57,314
Total adjustments	118,583	119,772	122,358
Net cash provided by operating activities	99,446	208,647	288,994
CASH FLOWS FROM INVESTING ACTIVITIES:			
Purchases of marketable securities	(569,358)	(1,212,894)	(162,690)
Proceeds from sale of marketable securities	587,809	1,190,761	325,894
Purchase of Fitigues assets	—	—	(7,527)
Purchase of Minnesota franchise rights and stores	—	(32,896)	—
Acquisition of other franchise stores	—	(6,361)	(811)
Proceeds from sale of land	—	13,426	—
Proceeds from sale of investment	—	15,090	—
Purchases of property and equipment	(104,615)	(202,223)	(218,311)
Net cash used in investing activities	(86,164)	(235,097)	(63,445)
CASH FLOWS FROM FINANCING ACTIVITIES:			
Proceeds from issuance of common stock	306	3,533	6,402
Excess tax benefit from stock-based compensation	100	209	2,365
Cash paid for deferred financing costs	(629)	—	—
Repurchase of common stock	(311)	(694)	(200,148)
Net cash (used in) provided by financing activities	(534)	3,048	(191,381)
Net increase (decrease) in cash and cash equivalents	12,748	(23,402)	34,168
CASH AND CASH EQUIVALENTS, Beginning of period	13,801	37,203	3,035
CASH AND CASH EQUIVALENTS, End of period	$ 26,549	$ 13,801	$ 37,203
SUPPLEMENTAL DISCLOSURES OF CASH FLOW INFORMATION:			
Cash paid for interest	$ 159	$ 461	$ 107
Cash paid for income taxes, net	$ 13,591	$ 74,563	$ 105,646
NON-CASH INVESTING AND FINANCING ACTIVITIES:			
Receipt of note receivable for sale of land	—	$ 25,834	—
Receivable from sale of equity investment	—	$ 2,161	—

The accompanying notes are an integral part of these consolidated statements.

Answer the following questions:

1. Does Chico's use the direct or the indirect method of preparing the statement of cash flows?
2. Did receivables increase or decrease during the most recent fiscal year?
3. Why is depreciation, a noncash expense, included on the statement of cash flows?
4. On two of the three years' statements, inventory is shown as a negative number (subtracted). Describe what happened to the balance in the inventory account during each of those years.
5. Did the balance in accounts payable increase or decrease during the most recent year? Explain.
6. Do you think Chico's is expanding? Find some numbers to support your answer.
7. Calculate Chico's free cash flow for all three years. What do these values indicate?
8. Do you see any particular risks indicated by Chico's cash flow patterns?

Critical Thinking Problems

Risk and Control

To be successful, a company must anticipate its cash flows. What evidence would help you evaluate whether or not a company does adequate cash planning? Is there any information not available in the company's annual report that would help you make this evaluation?

Ethics

After two years of business, the Lucky Ladder Company decided to apply for a bank loan to finance a new store. Although the company had been very successful, it had never prepared a cash budget. The owner of Lucky Ladder Company used the information from the first two years of business to reconstruct cash forecasts. He presented these new forecasts with his financial statements as though they had been prepared as part of the company's planning. Do you think this behavior was ethical? What would you do in similar circumstances? Why?

Group Assignment

To prepare the class for a debate about the format of the statement of cash flows, assign the direct method to half of the groups in the class and the indirect method to the other half of the groups. Have each group prepare arguments about the superiority of its assigned method of presenting the operating section of the statement of cash flows. Think about both theoretical and practical aspects of the methods. Refer to the cash flow information from First Solar, Inc., provided in FSA9-2.

Internet Exercise: Carnival Corporation

Carnival Corporation prides itself on being "The Most Popular Cruise Line in the World®"—a distinction achieved by offering a wide array of quality cruise vacations. Go to www.carnival.com and locate About Carnival: Investor Relations. You should be able to find the firm's SEC filings. Find the firm's 10-K filed on January 29, 2009, for its 2008 fiscal year.

IE9-1. Use the entire 10-K to answer the following questions:

1. Carnival Corporation operates several cruise lines. Find and list three of them.
2. Within the past five years, how many new ships has Carnival put into service?
3. Are the payments for ships considered capital expenditures or revenue expenditures? On the statement of cash flows, which business activity category will report these payments?

IE9-2. Find the annual statement of cash flows (page F-3 of the 2008 10-K) to answer the following questions:

1. Does Carnival use the direct or the indirect method to prepare the statement of cash flows? How can you tell? Which activity section is affected by this choice of method?
2. For the most recent year, list the amount of net cash inflow or outflow from each of the three major types of activities reported on the statement of cash flows. Which type of activity is providing the most cash? Is this considered favorable or unfavorable?

3. For the most recent year, what amount is reported for net income and net cash from operating activities? Are these amounts the same? Explain why or why not.

4. For the most recent year, did Carnival report cash inflows or outflows for capital expenditures? Is this considered favorable or unfavorable? Explain why. What do you think these capital expenditures are primarily for? What was the net amount of the capital expenditure? Which activity section reports this information?

5. For the most recent year, what amount of cash dividends did Carnival pay out? For the most recent year did Carnival issue or retire any common stock? What was the net amount issued or retired? For the most recent year did Carnival issue or retire any long-term debt? What was the net amount issued or retired? Which activity section reports this information?

6. Does this statement of cash flows indicate a strong or weak position with regard to cash and liquidity? Explain.

10

Using Financial Statement Analysis to Evaluate Firm Performance

LEARNING OBJECTIVES

When you are finished studying Chapter 10, you should be able to:

1. Recognize and explain the components of net income.

2. Perform and interpret a horizontal analysis and a vertical analysis of financial statement information.

3. Perform a basic ratio analysis of a set of financial statements and explain what the ratios mean.

4. Recognize the risks of investing in stocks and explain how to control those risks.

5. (Appendix 10A) Define comprehensive income and explain how it changes.

6. (Appendix 10B) Explain how a firm's investments in other firms' marketable securities are valued and reported.

ETHICS Matters

Getting It Right the First Time

Accounting information is an important part of the financial information investors use to evaluate a firm's performance. As an investor, you need to feel confident in a firm's reported earnings. We count on the people who prepare the financial statements as well as the independent auditors to produce reliable financial information. However, mistakes are inevitable. When a firm has made an error, earnings may need to be restated. Good news for investors: The number of corporate financial restatements dropped from 1,235 in 2007 to 869 in 2008. This was the second year in a row that the number of restatements declined. The number of restatements hit its lowest level since before the passage of the Sarbanes-Oxley Act of 2002. The time period covered by the restatement (479 days) and the size of the required adjustment ($6.1 million on average) were also much lower than in the two previous years.

You might think this very significant improvement in restatement statistics is related to the provisions of the Sarbanes-Oxley Act, which requires firms to have effective internal controls over financial reporting. Maybe it is related to the law's requirements for a code of ethics for managers or to the requirement that firms have a whistle-blower hotline for reporting suspected fraud. Whatever the reasons, this is a trend that brings some welcome favorable news related to corporate accounting and reliable financial statements.

L.O.1
Recognize and explain the
components of net income.

A Closer Look at the Income Statement

You have learned a great deal about the basic financial statements and how accountants record, summarize, and report transactions. There is information you can easily see in the financial statement, but there is also information that is difficult to see. It is important to look beyond the size and source of the numbers to see what the numbers *mean*. We have been examining the individual parts of the financial statements. Now we will examine all of the financial statements together to answer the following questions: What information do financial statements provide? What does the information mean? How can we use it?

Before beginning the detailed analysis of the financial statements, we need to take a closer look at some of the characteristics of the income statement. Because earnings—net income—is the focus of financial reporting, companies worry about how current and potential investors will interpret the announcement of earnings each quarter. It is not uncommon for companies to be accused of manipulating their earnings to make them appear higher than they actually are. In an effort to make the components of earnings clear and to represent exactly what they should to financial statement users, the Financial Accounting Standards Board (FASB) requires that two items be separated from the regular earnings of a company. The major reason for segregating these items is that they should not be considered as part of the ongoing earnings of the firm. Reported earnings is an amount used to predict future earnings, but the following two items are not expected to be repeated in the future:

1. Discontinued operations
2. Extraordinary items

Discontinued Operations

If you pay attention to the financial news, you are bound to hear about a company selling off a division. During 2006, 2007, and 2008, Darden Restaurants, Inc., showed discontinued operations on its income statement. During those years, the firm sold its Smokey Bones restaurants and closed a number of Bahama Breeze restaurants. The gains or losses from these kinds of transactions are shown separately on the income statement. Firms are always evaluating the contribution that the various divisions make to the profits of the firm. If a division is not profitable or no longer fits the strategy of the firm, a firm may sell it to remain profitable or change the firm's focus. Parts of a company's operations that are eliminated are called **discontinued operations**.

Discontinued operations are those parts of the firm that a company has eliminated by selling a division.

When a firm eliminates a division, the financial implications are shown separately from the regular operations of the firm under both U.S. generally accepted accounting principles (GAAP) and International Financial Reporting Standards (IFRS). Why would this separation be useful? Earnings is an important number because it is used to evaluate the performance of a firm and to predict its future performance. To make these evaluations and predictions more meaningful, it is important that one-time transactions be separated from recurring transactions. This separation allows investors to see one-time transactions as exceptions to the normal operations of the firm. In addition to any gain or loss from the sale, the earnings or loss for the accounting period for the discontinued operations must also be shown separately. The tax effects of these items are shown with each individual item rather than being included with the rest of the firm's income taxes. This presentation is called *net of tax*. We will look at an example of a firm with discontinued operations.

In 2010, Muzby Manufacturing sold off a major business segment, the crate-production division, because the firm wanted to focus its operations on its core business, which did not include the crate division. The current year's income or loss from the crate-production division and the gain or loss from the sale of that division is shown separately on the income statement. Suppose the following:

1. Muzby Manufacturing's income from continuing operations before taxes was $395,600, and taxes related to that income were $155,000.
2. The discontinued segment contributed income of $12,000 during the year, and taxes related to that income were $1,900.
3. The discontinued segment was sold for a gain of $63,000, and taxes related to that gain were $28,000.

The first highlighted section of Exhibit 10.1 shows how this information would be presented on the income statement for Muzby Manufacturing.

EXHIBIT 10.1

Showing Discontinued Operations and Extraordinary Items on the Income Statement

The first highlighted portion of the income statement shows how amounts related to discontinued operations are presented, and the second highlighted portion shows how extraordinary items are presented.

Muzby Manufacturing
Income Statement
For the Year Ended December 31, 2010

Income from continuing operations before income taxes		$ 395,600
Income tax expense		155,000
Income from continuing operations		240,600
Discontinued operations		
Income from discontinued crate-production segment (net of taxes of $1,900)	$10,100	
Gain on disposal of crate-production segment (net of taxes of $28,000)	35,000	45,100
Income before extraordinary item		$ 285,700
Loss on extraordinary item		
Expropriation of foreign operation (net of taxes of $67,000)		(133,000)
Net income		$ 152,700

Extraordinary Items

You have learned that the effect of discontinued operations is the first item that accountants disclose separately on the income statement. The second item is the financial effect of any event that is *unusual* in nature and *infrequent* in occurrence. The financial effects of such events are called **extraordinary items** under U.S. GAAP. (IFRS do not allow extraordinary items.) To qualify as extraordinary, the events must be abnormal and must *not* be reasonably expected to occur again in the foreseeable future. There is a great deal of judgment required to decide if an event should be considered extraordinary. Examples of occurrences that have been considered extraordinary include eruptions of a volcano, a takeover of foreign operations by the foreign government, and the effects of new laws or regulations that result in a one-time cost to comply. Each situation is unique and must be considered in light of the environment in which the business operates. Note that the income tax effects of extraordinary items are also reported separately from the rest of the firm's income taxes.

> **Extraordinary items** are events that are unusual in nature and infrequent in occurrence.

Suppose Muzby Manufacturing has a factory in a foreign country, and the government of that country decides to take possession of all American businesses. The value of the lost factory is $200,000. U.S. tax law allows companies to write off this type of extraordinary loss, which means that the company receives a tax savings. Suppose the applicable tax savings is $67,000. The second highlighted portion of Exhibit 10.1 shows how Muzby Manufacturing would present the information on its income statement for the year.

What does it mean for a company to show discontinued operations and extraordinary items *net of tax*? What would be the alternative?

Your Turn 10-1

Horizontal and Vertical Analysis of Financial Information

Now that you are prepared to recognize extraordinary items and discontinued operations that may appear on the income statement, you are ready to analyze an entire statement or set of statements. There are three primary ways to analyze financial information: horizontal analysis, vertical analysis, and ratio analysis.

> **L.O.2**
> Perform and interpret a horizontal analysis and a vertical analysis of financial statement information.

Horizontal Analysis

Horizontal analysis is a
technique for evaluating financial
statement items across time.

Horizontal analysis is a technique for evaluating a financial statement item over a period of time. The purpose of horizontal analysis is to express the change in a financial statement item in percentages rather than in dollars. Financial statement users can spot trends more easily with horizontal analysis than by simply looking at the raw numbers. Consider the cash flows for General Mills, Inc. According to its 2009 10-K, General Mills made the following cash expenditures for property, plant, and equipment:

General Mills, Inc.: Capital Expenditures					
For Fiscal Years Ended on the Last Sunday in May					
(in millions of dollars)					
	2009	**2008**	**2007**	**2006**	**2005**
	$562.6	$522.0	$460.2	$360.0	$434.0

Often, the analyst selects one of the years, called the base year, as the reference point. The amounts reported for the other years are expressed as a percentage of the chosen base year. Suppose we choose 2005 as the base year. Then, we subtract the 2005 capital expenditures ($434.0) from 2006 capital expenditures ($360.0) and divide by the base year number ($434.0).

$$\frac{\$360.0 - \$434.0}{\$434.0} = -17.1\%$$

Our calculation shows that during the fiscal year ended in May 2006, General Mills decreased its capital expenditures by 17.1% of the base year's capital expenditures. The calculation is done the same way for each year. The percentage change from the base year to 2007 is calculated as follows:

$$\frac{\$460.2 - \$434.0}{\$434.0} = 6.0\%$$

General Mills, Inc.					
Capital Expenditures Comparison—Base Year 2005					
(in millions of dollars)					
	2009	**2008**	**2007**	**2006**	**2005**
Capital expenditures	$562.6	$522.0	$460.2	$360.0	$434.0
% change	29.6%	20.3%	6.0%	−17.1%	100%

There is more than one way to do a horizontal analysis. Frequently, the analysis is done by comparing one year with the next, rather than using a fixed base year. For example, we could compare the capital expenditures for 2009 with those for 2008. In this case, there would be an increase. How much? Less than 8%, as shown next:

$$\frac{\$562.6 - \$522.0}{\$522.0} = 7.8\%$$

It is usually difficult to understand the significance of a single item such as capital expenditures when viewing the raw numbers. To make trends more apparent, it may be useful to express the changes in spending in percentage form. Horizontal analysis shows the changes in investment in General Mills, Inc.'s property, plant, and equipment in a way that makes it easy to see what's happening.

Suppose Watts Company has sales for the past five years as follows:

Your Turn 10-2

2012	2011	2010	2009	2008
$142,600	$138,500	$125,900	$134,500	$125,000

Use 2008 as the base year and perform a horizontal analysis. What does it tell you about the firm's sales for this five-year period?

Vertical Analysis

Vertical analysis is similar to horizontal analysis, but this analysis involves items on a single year's financial statement. Each item on a financial statement is expressed as a percentage of a selected base amount. This is also called **common-sizing** a financial statement. For example, to perform a vertical analysis on the balance sheet, you would take every amount on the statement and convert it to a percentage of total assets. For a vertical analysis of an income statement, sales is almost always used as the base amount because almost all of a firm's expenditures depend on the level of sales. Each amount on the statement is expressed as a percentage of sales. This type of analysis can point out areas in which the costs might be too large or growing without an obvious cause. For example, if managers at General Mills see that certain costs, as a percentage of sales, are increasing, they can investigate the increase and, if necessary, take action to reduce the firm's costs in that area. Internally, General Mills would do a vertical analysis with much more detail. For investors, vertical analysis also allows the meaningful comparison of companies of different sizes. Exhibit 10.2 shows a vertical analysis for General Mills' income statements for the fiscal years ended May 31, 2009, and May 25, 2008.

Vertical analysis is a technique for comparing items on a financial statement in which all items are expressed as a percent of a common amount.

Common-sizing involves converting all amounts on a financial statement to a percentage of a chosen value on that statement; also known as *vertical analysis*.

EXHIBIT 10.2

Vertical Analysis

The analysis for a single year provides some information, but the comparison of two years reveals more about what's going on with General Mills, Inc. The percentages look very consistent across these two years. What item(s) stands out in the analysis? The notes to the financial statements are the first place to look for additional information whenever an analysis reveals something interesting or unusual.

> **General Mills, Inc.**
> **Consolidated Statements of Earnings**
> (dollars in millions)

	For the Year Ended			
	May 31, 2009		May 25, 2008	
Net sales	$14,691.30	100.00%	$13,652.10	100.00%
Cost of sales	9,457.80	64.38%	8,778.30	64.30%
Selling, general, and administrative expenses	2,953.90	20.11%	2,625.00	19.23%
Other (gain), net	(84.90)	−0.58%	0	
Restructuring, impairment, and other costs	41.60	0.28%	21.00	0.15%
Operating profit	2,322.90	15.81%	2,227.80	16.32%
Interest, net	390.00	2.65%	421.70	3.09%
Earnings before income taxes and after-tax				
earnings from joint ventures	1,932.90	13.16%	1,806.10	13.23%
Income taxes	720.40	4.90%	622.20	4.56%
After-tax earnings from joint ventures	91.90	0.63%	110.80	0.81%
Net earnings	$ 1,304.40	8.88%	$ 1,294.70	9.48%

Your Turn 10-3

Use the income statements for 2010 and 2009 from Brothers Company to perform a vertical analysis using sales as the base. What information does the analysis provide?

Brothers Company
Income Statements

	For the Year Ended	
	March 31, 2010	March 31, 2009
Sales revenue	$10,000	$8,000
Expenses:		
Cost of goods sold	3,200	2,800
Operating expenses	300	275
Bad debts expense	100	90
Insurance expense	200	200
Rent expense	600	600
Depreciation expense	250	250
Interest expense	75	75
Total expenses	4,725	4,290
Net income	$ 5,275	$3,710

L.O.3
Perform a basic ratio analysis of a set of financial statements and explain what the ratios mean.

Ratio Analysis

As you have read, a financial ratio is a comparison of different amounts on the financial statements. Throughout this book, you have learned that ratio analysis uses information in the financial statements to formulate specific values that determine some measure of a company's financial position. We will review all the ratios you have learned and then look at an additional category of ratios, market indicators.

A Review of All Ratios

There are four general categories of ratios, named for what they attempt to measure:

Liquidity ratios are used to measure the company's ability to pay its current bills and operating costs.

- **Liquidity ratios:** These ratios measure a company's ability to pay its current bills and operating costs—obligations coming due in the next fiscal year. We have previously discussed the current ratio (Chapter 2), the accounts receivable turnover ratio (Chapter 4), and the inventory turnover ratio (Chapter 5). In this chapter, we will learn an additional liquidity ratio: cash from operations to current liabilities.

Solvency ratios are used to measure the company's ability to meet its long-term obligations and to survive over a long period of time.

- **Solvency ratios:** These ratios measure a company's ability to meet its long-term obligations, such as its long-term debt (bank loans), and to survive over a long period of time. We previously discussed the debt-to-equity ratio (Chapter 7).

Profitability ratios are used to measure the operating or income performance of a company.

- **Profitability ratios:** These ratios measure the operating or income performance of a company. Remember, the goal of a business is to make a profit, so this type of ratio examines how well a company is meeting that goal. We've read about the profit margin ratio (Chapter 3), return on assets (Chapter 6), asset turnover ratio (Chapter 6), and return on equity (Chapter 8).

Market indicators are ratios that relate the current market price of the company's stock to earnings or dividends.

- **Market indicators:** These ratios relate the current market price of the company's stock to earnings or dividends. In this chapter, you'll learn about the price–earnings ratio and the dividend payout ratio.

Exhibits 10.3A on page 467 and 10.3B on page 468 show the three types of ratios you learned about in earlier chapters. Exhibit 10.3B, on page 468, also includes these two new ratios called

EXHIBIT 10.3A

Common Ratios

Ratio	Definition	How to use the ratio	Chapter where you studied the ratio
LIQUIDITY			
Current ratio	$\dfrac{\text{Total current assets}}{\text{Total current liabilities}}$	To measure a company's ability to pay current liabilities with current assets. This ratio helps creditors determine if a company can meet its short-term obligations.	2
Cash from operations to current liabilities	$\dfrac{\text{Net cash from operating activities}}{\text{Average current liabilities}}$	To measure a company's ability to meet its short-term obligations. This ratio is similar to the current ratio. However, only cash generated from operating activities is considered as available to pay the current liabilities.	10
Inventory turnover ratio	$\dfrac{\text{Cost of goods sold}}{\text{Average inventory}}$	To measure how quickly a company is selling its inventory.	5
Accounts receivable turnover ratio	$\dfrac{\text{Net credit sales}}{\text{Average net accounts receivable}}$	To measure how quickly a company collects the cash from its credit sales.	4
SOLVENCY			
Debt-to-equity ratio	$\dfrac{\text{Total liabilities}}{\text{Total shareholders' equity}}$	To compare the amount of debt a company has with the amount the owners have invested in the company.	7

Note: Turnover ratios are sometimes called efficiency ratios.

market indicators. Keep in mind that the ratios introduced in this book are just a few of the dozens of ratios used in the analysis of financial statements.

Suppose General Mills has a current ratio greater than one and pays off a current liability with cash. What effect would this have on the company's current ratio?

Your Turn 10-4

Liquidity Ratio with Cash Flows

The current ratio (current assets divided by current liabilities) was introduced in Chapter 2; it is the most commonly used ratio for measuring liquidity. The new liquidity ratio introduced here uses net cash from operating activities, from the statement of cash flows, in the numerator and average current liabilities in the denominator. This ratio is directed specifically at the amount of cash a firm is generating from its operations to pay its current liabilities. The ratio is called **cash from operations to current liabilities**, and the calculation is straightforward:

$$\frac{\text{Net cash provided by operating activities}}{\text{Average current liabilities}}$$

Cash from operations to current liabilities ratio is the net cash from operating activities divided by average current liabilities.

EXHIBIT 10.3B

Ratio	Definition	How to use the ratio	Chapter where you studied the ratio
PROFITABILITY			
Return on assets	$\dfrac{\text{Net income}}{\text{Average total assets}}$	To measure a company's success in using its assets to earn income for owners and creditors, those who are financing the business. Average total assets are the average of beginning assets and ending assets for the year.	6
Asset turnover ratio	$\dfrac{\text{Net sales}}{\text{Average total assets}}$	To measure how efficiently a company uses its assets.	6
Return on equity	$\dfrac{\text{Net income} - \text{preferred dividends}}{\text{Average common shareholders' equity}}$	To measure how much income is earned with the common shareholders' investment in the company.	8
Profit margin ratio	$\dfrac{\text{Net income}}{\text{Net sales}}$	To measure the amount from each dollar of sales that is bottom-line profit.	3
Gross profit ratio	$\dfrac{\text{Gross profit}}{\text{Net sales}}$	To measure a company's profitability. It is one of the most carefully watched ratios by management because it describes the percentage of the sales price that is gross profit. A small shift usually indicates a big change in the profitability of the company's sales.	5
Earnings per share	$\dfrac{\text{Net income} - \text{preferred dividends}}{\text{Weighted average number of shares of common stock outstanding}}$	To calculate net income per share of common stock.	8
MARKET INDICATORS			
Price–earnings ratio	$\dfrac{\text{Market price per common share}}{\text{Earnings per share}}$	To calculate the market price for $1 of earnings.	10
Dividend yield ratio	$\dfrac{\text{Dividend per share}}{\text{Market price per share}}$	To calculate the percentage return on the investment in a share of stock via dividends.	10

Your Turn 10-5

Company A has a gross profit ratio of 30% and Company B has a gross profit ratio of 60%. Can you tell which company is more profitable? Why or why not?

Market Indicator Ratios

The market price of a share of stock is what an investor is willing to pay for the stock. There are two ratios that use the current market price of a share of stock to help potential investors predict what they might earn by purchasing that stock. One ratio is the **price–earnings (P/E) ratio**. This ratio is defined by its name: It is the price of a share of stock divided by the company's current earnings per share.

Price–earnings (P/E) ratio is the market price of a share of stock divided by that stock's earnings per share.

$$\text{P/E ratio} = \frac{\text{Market price per share}}{\text{Earnings per share}}$$

Investors and financial analysts believe the P/E ratio indicates future earnings potential. A high P/E ratio indicates that the company has the potential for significant growth. When a new firm has no earnings, the P/E ratio has no meaning because the denominator is zero. For the first several years of business Amazon.com had no earnings but a rising stock price. Analysts have varying opinions about the information contained in the P/E ratio.

The other market indicator ratio is the **dividend yield ratio**. This ratio is the dividend per share divided by the market price per share. You may find that the values for the dividend yield ratio are quite low compared to the return an investor would expect on an investment. Investors are willing to accept a low dividend yield when they anticipate an increase in the price of the stock.

Dividend yield ratio is dividend per share divided by the current market price per share.

Stocks with low growth potential, however, may need to offer a higher dividend yield to attract investors.

$$\text{Dividend yield ratio} = \frac{\text{Dividend per share}}{\text{Market price per share}}$$

Exhibit 10.4 shows the earnings per share, the dividends per share, and the market price per share for Google Inc. and for ExxonMobil. Which stock would be a better buy for long-term growth? Which would be best if you needed regular dividend income?

For fiscal years ended	Google Inc. December 31, 2008	ExxonMobil Corporation December 31, 2008
Earnings per share	$ 13.46	$ 8.78
Dividends per share	$ 0.00	$ 1.55
Ending market price per share	$448.89	$79.83
Price/earnings ratio	33.35	9.09
Dividend yield ratio	n/a	1.94%

EXHIBIT 10.4

Price/Earnings and Dividend Yield Ratios

The types of stock that will appeal to an investor depend on the investor's preferences for income and growth. A young investor, for example, will not need dividends from retirement funds invested in stocks. These long-term investors would prefer to invest in companies with high growth potential, no matter what the dividend yield. Google might be more attractive, with its high P/E ratio of 33.35 (last day of 2008), than ExxonMobil, with its lower P/E ratio of 9.09 (last day of 2008). A retiree who needs dividend income for living expenses will be more concerned with the size of the dividend yield of an investment and less concerned with the investment's long-term growth. For that investor, ExxonMobil would be better than Google for dividends, because ExxonMobil pays regular dividends and Google has never paid a dividend to its shareholders.

These two market-related ratios are very important to management and to investors because analysts and investors use them in evaluating firms' stock. If you examine a company's annual report, you are likely to see these ratios reported, usually for the most recent two or three years.

Understanding Ratios

A ratio by itself does not give much information. To be useful, a ratio must be compared to the same ratios from previous periods, ratios of other companies in the industry, or industry averages. Keep in mind that, with the exception of earnings per share (EPS), the calculations to arrive at a specific ratio may vary from company to company. There are no standard or required formulas to calculate a ratio. One company may calculate a debt ratio as *debt* to *equity*, whereas another company may calculate a debt ratio as *debt* to *debt plus equity*. An analyst can create any ratio that he or she believes will be useful in the analysis of a company's financial statements. When interpreting and using any company's ratios, be sure you know how those ratios have been computed. When you are computing ratios, be sure to be consistent in your calculations so you can make meaningful comparisons among them.

Even though the only ratio that must be calculated and presented as part of the financial statements is EPS, which is shown on the income statement, a firm typically includes many of the ratios we have discussed in this chapter in its annual report. When these ratios are not shown as part of the financial statements, they may be included in other parts of the annual report, often in graphs depicting trends over several years.

Any valuable financial statement analysis requires more than a cursory review of ratios. The analyst must look at trends, components of the values that are part of the ratios, and other information about the company that may not even be contained in the financial statements.

Using Ratio Analysis

We will compute some of the ratios shown in Exhibits 10.3A and 10.3B for Abercrombie & Fitch Co. (A&F) using the company's 2008 annual report. Exhibit 10.5 shows the income statements for three years, and Exhibit 10.6 shows the balance sheets for two years.

EXHIBIT 10.5

Income Statements for Abercrombie & Fitch Co.

Abercrombie & Fitch Co.
Consolidated Statements of Net Income
(Thousands, except per share amounts)

	2008	2007	2006*
NET SALES	$3,540,276	$3,749,847	$3,318,158
Cost of Goods Sold	1,178,584	1,238,480	1,109,152
GROSS PROFIT	2,361,692	2,511,367	2,209,006
Stores and Distribution Expense	1,511,511	1,386,846	1,187,071
Marketing, General & Administrative Expense	419,659	395,758	373,828
Other Operating Income, Net	(8,864)	(11,734)	(9,983)
OPERATING INCOME	439,386	740,497	658,090
Interest Income, Net	(11,382)	(18,828)	(13,896)
INCOME BEFORE INCOME TAXES	450,768	759,325	671,986
Provision for Income Taxes	178,513	283,628	249,800
NET INCOME	$ 272,255	$ 475,697	$ 422,186
NET INCOME PER SHARE:			
BASIC	$ 3.14	$ 5.45	$ 4.79
DILUTED	$ 3.05	$ 5.20	$ 4.59
WEIGHTED-AVERAGE SHARES OUTSTANDING:			
BASIC	86,816	87,248	88,052
DILUTED	89,291	91,523	92,010
DIVIDENDS DECLARED PER SHARE	$ 0.70	$ 0.70	$ 0.70

*Fiscal 2006 was a 53-week year.

Other information needed for the analysis follows:

- Net cash from operating activities is $490,836,000 for fiscal year 2008 and $817,524,000 for fiscal year 2007.
- Market price per share at the close of fiscal year is approximately $17.85 per share at January 30, 2009 (the 2008 fiscal year end) and $82.06 per share at February 1, 2008 (the 2007 fiscal year end).
- Dividends declared are shown on the face of the income statement.

The computations for the ratios are shown in Exhibits 10.7A on page 472 and 10.7B on page 473. Even though two years of ratios do not give us enough information for making decisions, use this as an opportunity to practice how to calculate the ratios.

Ratios are relatively easy to calculate; the difficulty comes in interpreting them. Books have been written to try to teach people to do this, and analysts can be paid very large salaries for their expertise in financial statement analysis. In each chapter of this book in which a ratio was introduced, you will find information about how the ratio is calculated, interpreted, and used. Following are some examples of how ratios are related and how information can be gained from looking at them in conjunction with each other.

Liquidity Ratios

CURRENT RATIO. Often, a current ratio greater than one is viewed as adequate, meaning that a firm has enough current assets to meet its current obligations (current liabilities) in the coming year. Recall, however, that the ratio captures current assets and current liabilities at a moment in time—the

EXHIBIT 10.6

Balance Sheets for Abercrombie & Fitch Co.

Abercrombie & Fitch Co.
Consolidated Balance Sheets
(Thousands, except share amounts)

	January 31, 2009	February 2, 2008
ASSETS		
CURRENT ASSETS:		
Cash and Equivalents	$ 522,122	$ 118,044
Marketable Securities	—	530,486
Receivables	53,110	53,801
Inventories	372,422	333,153
Deferred Income Taxes	43,408	36,128
Other Current Assets	93,763	68,643
TOTAL CURRENT ASSETS	1,084,825	1,140,255
PROPERTY AND EQUIPMENT, NET	1,398,655	1,318,291
MARKETABLE SECURITIES	229,081	—
OTHER ASSETS	135,620	109,052
TOTAL ASSETS	$2,848,181	$2,567,598
LIABILITIES AND SHAREHOLDERS' EQUITY		
CURRENT LIABILITIES:		
Accounts Payable	$ 92,814	$ 108,437
Outstanding Checks	56,939	43,361
Accrued Expenses	241,231	280,910
Deferred Lease Credits	42,358	37,925
Income Taxes Payable	16,455	72,480
TOTAL CURRENT LIABILTIES	449,797	543,113
LONG-TERM LIABILITIES:		
Deferred Income Taxes	34,085	22,491
Deferred Lease Credits	211,978	213,739
Debt	100,000	—
Other Liabilities	206,743	169,942
TOTAL LONG-TERM LIABILITIES	552,806	406,172
SHAREHOLDERS' EQUITY:		
Class A Common Stock—$.01 par value: 150,000,000 shares authorized and 103,300,000 shares issued at January 31, 2009 and February 2, 2008, respectively	1,033	1,033
Paid-In Capital	328,488	319,451
Retained Earnings	2,244,936	2,051,463
Accumulated Other Comprehensive (Loss) Income, net of tax	(22,681)	7,118
Treasury Stock at Average Cost 15,664,385 and 17,141,116 shares at January 31, 2009, and February 2, 2008, respectively	(706,198)	(760,752)
TOTAL SHAREHOLDERS' EQUITY	1,845,578	1,618,313
TOTAL LIABILITIES AND SHAREHOLDERS' EQUITY	$2,848,181	$2,567,598

The accompanying notes are an integral part of these consolidated financial statements.

end of the last day of the fiscal year. A&F has a current ratio of 2.41. In isolation, this appears to be quite adequate. However, it is very useful to look at the other liquidity ratios in conjunction with the current ratio to see how quickly A&F is converting its receivables and inventory into cash. If a current ratio is high because of high values in accounts receivable and inventory, rather than cash, the rate at which those current assets are converted into cash, which is what is needed to pay current liabilities, becomes important. Another way to approach that question of adequate cash is to look at the amount of cash the company is generating from its operating activities.

CASH FROM OPERATIONS TO CURRENT LIABILITIES RATIO. For A&F, this ratio has declined. Having a ratio of less than 1 indicates that A&F has more current liabilities, on average, than the cash it generates from its operations. If this is a problem, we should try to identify more specifically why the company is not generating sufficient cash. That takes us to the turnover ratios.

EXHIBIT 10.7A

Ratio Analysis for Abercrombie & Fitch Co.

As you evaluate the ratios, keep in mind that even two years' worth of ratios is rarely enough information to come to any conclusions. Most annual reports provide the data for ten years' worth of ratios. Often, ratio analysis is useful for identifying potential problem areas. No problems are obvious for Abercrombie & Fitch Co. from this analysis.

Ratio	Definition	Computation	Computation	Interpretation
LIQUIDITY		FYE January 31, 2009	FYE February 2, 2008	
Current ratio	$\dfrac{\text{Total current assets}}{\text{Total current liabilities}}$	$\dfrac{\$1,084,825}{\$449,797} = 2.41$	$\dfrac{\$1,140,255}{\$543,113} = 2.10$	Excellent current ratio. Industry (apparel retailers) average is 1.37.
Cash from operations to current liabilities	$\dfrac{\text{Net cash from operating activities}}{\text{Average current liabilities}}$	$\dfrac{\$490,836}{(\$543,113 + \$449,797)/2}$ $= 0.99$	$\dfrac{\$817,524}{(\$510,627^* + \$543,113)/2}$ $= 1.55$ * From the 2007 balance sheet not shown here	The significant decline in this ratio is troublesome. The serious decline in cash generated by operations deserves further analysis.
Inventory turnover ratio	$\dfrac{\text{Cost of goods sold}}{\text{Average inventory}}$	$\dfrac{\$1,178,584}{(\$333,153 + \$372,422)/2}$ $= 3.34$	$\dfrac{\$1,238,480}{(\$427,447^* + \$333,153)/2}$ $= 3.26$ * From the 2007 balance sheet not shown here	The company is turning its inventory over only a little more than 3 times per year. Industry average is 3.3 times per year in 2008.
Accounts receivable turnover ratio	$\dfrac{\text{Net sales}}{\text{Average net accounts receivable}}$	$\dfrac{\$3,540,276}{(\$53,801 + \$53,110)/2} = 66.23$	$\dfrac{\$3,749,847}{(\$43,240^* + \$53,801)/2}$ $= 77.28$ * From the 2007 balance sheet not shown here	The company is turning over its receivables over 66 times per year. When cash and credit card sales are included in the numerator, it inflates this ratio, so it isn't very meaningful without more information.
SOLVENCY				
Debt-to-equity	$\dfrac{\text{Total liabilities}}{\text{Total equity}}$	$\dfrac{\$449,797 + \$552,806}{\$1,845,578} = 0.54$	$\dfrac{\$543,113 + \$406,172}{\$1,618,313} = 0.59$	The firm has made a small decrease in the amount of debt in its capital structure.

INVENTORY TURNOVER RATIO. At first glance, it appears that this is an area that could be a problem for A&F. Turning over inventory only 3.34 times per year translates into over 109 days in inventory. Remember that you can calculate the average number of days in inventory by dividing 365 (days in the year) by the turnover ratio. In other words, it takes, on average, 109 days to sell an inventory item. While this sounds like very slow moving inventory, we'll need more information to reach any conclusion. The Retail Owners Institute (http://retailowner.com) provides some relevant industry data. The average inventory turnover for clothing and accessories stores was 3.4 in 2007 and 3.3 in 2008. As a matter of fact, in 2004 the average was only 3.1. It appears that inventory turnover is not a particular problem for A&F considering the industry. However, improving that ratio could help A&F's cash flow.

ACCOUNTS RECEIVABLE TURNOVER RATIO. As mentioned in the table, the accounts receivable turnover ratio for a retail store is always high due to the large number of sales made with cash and bank credit cards. Even this ratio has declined for A&F, which is not a good sign. Taken

EXHIBIT 10.7B

PROFITABILITY		FYE January 31, 2009	FYE February 2, 2008	
Return on assets	$\dfrac{\text{Net income}}{\text{Average total assets}}$	$\dfrac{\$272{,}255}{(\$2{,}567{,}598 + \$2{,}848{,}181)/2}$ $= 10.1\%$	$\dfrac{\$475{,}697}{(\$2{,}248{,}067^* + \$2{,}567{,}598)/2}$ $= 19.8\%$ * From the 2007 balance sheet not shown here	The effect of the recession can easily be seen in this decrease in the firm's ROA.
Asset turnover ratio	$\dfrac{\text{Net sales}}{\text{Average total assets}}$	$\dfrac{\$3{,}540{,}276}{(\$2{,}567{,}598 + \$2{,}848{,}181)/2}$ $= 1.31$	$\dfrac{\$3{,}749{,}847}{(\$2{,}248{,}067^* + \$2{,}567{,}598)/2}$ $= 1.56$ * From the 2007 balance sheet not shown here	The firm's use of its assets to generate sales has decreased. Again, this is not surprising in the economic climate of this particular year.
Return on equity	$\dfrac{\text{Net income} - \text{preferred dividends}}{\text{Average common shareholders' equity}}$	$\dfrac{\$272{,}255}{(\$1{,}618{,}313 + \$1{,}845{,}578)/2}$ $= 15.7\%$	$\dfrac{\$475{,}697}{(\$1{,}405{,}297^* + \$1{,}618{,}313)/2}$ $= 31.5\%$ * From the 2007 balance sheet not shown here	Again, we see the large decrease in ROE. Still, the return to shareholders is good.
Profit margin ratio	$\dfrac{\text{Net income}}{\text{Net sales}}$	$\dfrac{\$272{,}255}{\$3{,}540{,}276} = 7.7\%$	$\dfrac{\$475{,}697}{\$3{,}749{,}847} = 12.7\%$	Not only have sales decreased, the amount of each sales dollar that makes it all the way to the bottom line has decreased. This indicates increasing costs.
Gross profit ratio	$\dfrac{\text{Gross profit}}{\text{Sales}}$	$\dfrac{\$2{,}361{,}692}{\$3{,}540{,}276} = 66.7\%$	$\dfrac{\$2{,}511{,}367}{\$3{,}749{,}847} = 67.0\%$	This ratio has not changed much, so the increasing costs indicated by the profit margin ratio are not due to the cost of the inventory.
Earnings per share	$\dfrac{\text{Net income} - \text{preferred dividends}}{\text{Weighted average \# of common shares outstanding}}$	$\dfrac{\$272{,}255}{86{,}816^*} = \$3.14$ *Disclosed on the income statement	$\dfrac{\$475{,}697}{87{,}248^*} = \$5.45$ *Disclosed on the income statement	The calculation is shown here, but remember that you will not need to calculate this ratio if you have the income statement. It will be shown on the face of the statement.
MARKET INDICATORS				
Price-earnings ratio	$\dfrac{\text{Market price per share}}{\text{Earnings per share}}$	$\dfrac{\$17.85}{\$3.14} = 5.68$	$\dfrac{\$82.06}{\$5.45} = 15.06$	Earnings have decreased significantly, and the stock price has plummeted. At the beginning of the 2008 fiscal year, investors were willing to pay $15.06 for every dollar of earnings. By year end, they were only willing to pay $5.68 for a dollar of earnings.
Dividend yield	$\dfrac{\text{Dividend per share}}{\text{Market price per share}}$	$\dfrac{\$0.70}{\$17.85} = 3.9\%$	$\dfrac{\$0.70}{\$82.06} = 0.9\%$	Dividends have remained stable, so the yield will vary with stock price. These are the stock prices at fiscal year end.

together, these liquidity ratios indicate that A&F can meet its short-term obligations but that both inventory and accounts receivable could be areas where A&F could increase its efficiency.

Profitability Ratios

Return ratios—ROA and ROE—measure the relationship between the firm's income and the amount of investment that a specific group has made in the company. ROA, for example, measures the return to all investors, both debt and equity holders. ROE, on the other hand, measures the return to common equity investors only. Our analysis showed that A&F had an ROA of 10.1% and an ROE of 15.7% for the 2008 fiscal year. Unfortunately, both have gone down significantly from the 2007 fiscal year (ROA was 19.8% and ROE was 31.5%). Industry data for 2007 indicates that the industry average for apparel (retail) was 11.9 for ROA and 21.4 for ROE (Standard and Poor's Industry Surveys, February 12, 2009). In both cases, A&F's return ratios exceeded the industry averages in 2007.

   As you can see, ratio analysis is not an easy task. There are many resources to help you, often provided online or in your school's library. However, there is no substitute for understanding the company you are analyzing. A company's financial history, its market, its management, its strategy, and the general state of the economy all play a role in the interpretation of financial information.

Financial Statement Analysis—More than Numbers

You have probably noticed the following sentence at the end of every actual financial statement you have ever seen, "The accompanying notes are an integral part of these financial statements." Some analysts believe there is more real information about the financial health of a company in the notes than in the statements themselves. Go to the back of the book where you will find the financial statements for Books-A-Million, Inc. Look at the detailed and extensive notes that accompany the statements. The more you learn about analyzing and evaluating a company's performance, whether in subsequent courses or in actual business experience, the more you will understand the information in the notes to the financial statements. When you are comparing two or more firms, you need to know the accounting choices those firms have made—such as depreciation and inventory methods—to make valid comparisons. Often, analysts compute new

---

UNDERSTANDING

Business

What is EBITDA?

If you read much about financial statements and earnings, you will eventually come across the expression "EBITDA" (pronounced ïba duh). It is an acronym for *earnings before interest, taxes, depreciation, and amortization*. EBITDA can be calculated from information on the income statement (earnings, taxes, and interest) and the statement of cash flows (depreciation and amortization—added back to net income when calculating cash from operating activities). Eliminating these items—because they involve management discretion and estimates—can make it easier to compare the financial health of various firms. Because it is a result of management's financing choices (debt rather than equity), eliminating interest takes away the effect of a firm's capital structure.

   Even though EBITDA has become a popular measure of a firm's performance, it does not tell the whole story. According to Investopedia.com, there are at least four reasons to be wary of EBITDA.

1. There is no substitute for cash flows. No matter what EBITDA is, a firm cannot operate without sufficient cash.
2. The items that are eliminated from earnings are not avoidable, so ignoring them can be misleading.
3. EBITDA ignores the quality of earnings. You will learn more about that in Chapter 11.
4. Using EBITDA to calculate a price–earnings ratio could make a firm look cheaper than it actually is.

   The bottom line is that EBITDA is useful, but it is only one of many measures of a firm's performance. Remember that EBITDA is NOT defined by GAAP, so firms may measure EBITDA in different ways.

amounts using a different method than the one the firm used so that the amounts can be meaningfully compared to those of another firm. For example, if one company uses LIFO and another uses FIFO, an analyst would convert the LIFO values to FIFO values using the disclosures required in the notes of firms that use LIFO.

To better appreciate the role of accounting information in business, look at a business plan. A business plan is a detailed analysis of what it would take to start and maintain the operation of a successful business. Anyone writing a business plan includes a sales forecast, expense estimates, and prospective financial statements. These are "what-if" financial statements, forecasts that are part of the business plan. Banks often require these statements before they will lend money to a new firm.

Because accounting is such an integral part of business, accounting principles will continue to change as business changes. Each year, the FASB and the SEC add and change the rules for valuing items on the financial statements. FASB is also concerned with the continued usefulness and reliability of the accounting data from electronic transactions, e-business, and real-time access to financial data. As competition takes on new dimensions, particularly due to new technology, the scrutiny of a firm's financial information will increase. With the influence of the financial scandals of the early 2000s and the recession that began in 2008, the financial information needed for good decision making will continue to grow in importance.

Business Risk, Control, and Ethics

L.O.4
Recognize the risks of investing in stocks and explain how to control those risks.

We already discussed, in Chapter 1, the risks associated with starting a business. Now we will take the perspective of an investor. After all, you are very likely to buy stock in a publicly-traded company sometime in your life. Many working people have money in retirement funds that are invested in the stock of publicly-traded companies. Additionally, the movement of the stock market affects a large number of firms and individual investors. How should you, as an investor, minimize the risks associated with stock ownership? That risk, of course, is losing your money!

First, you should be diligent about finding a financial advisor or financial analyst to help you, or you should become an expert from your own study and analysis of available stocks. You also need to know and understand some financial accounting and financial statement analysis, which you have been exposed to in this course. However, being knowledgeable or consulting an expert does not give an investor complete protection against losses.

Between September 30, 2007, and March 6, 2009, the stock market lost 56% of its value, a decline of about $13 trillion.

Source: The Urban Institute, Fact Sheet on Retirement Policy, March 9, 2009.
http://www.urban.org/retirement_policy/url.cfm?ID=411847

That leads to the second and most effective way to minimize the risks associated with stock ownership: diversify. In everyday usage, to diversify means to vary or expand. In the language of investment, diversify means to vary the investments you make—to expand beyond a narrow set of investments. Diversification means not putting all of your eggs in one basket. A diversified set of investments allows an investor to earn a higher rate of return for a given amount of risk.

There is no way to eliminate all of the risks of stock ownership, but having many different types of investments will help you minimize your risk or, equivalently, increase your return for a given amount of risk. Part of diversification is investing in assets other than stocks. As you might recall from Chapter 7, investors also purchase corporate bonds. Investing in bonds and other debt securities is part of a sound diversification strategy. Real estate is another example of an investment that is often included in a diversified portfolio. The composition of a person's investment portfolio depends on how much risk that person is willing to take. According to Bank One, "A diversified portfolio does not concentrate in one or two investment categories. Instead, it includes some investments whose returns zig while the returns of other investments zag."

Chapter Summary Points

- Components of net income include income from continuing operations, discontinued operations, and extraordinary items. Gains and losses from discontinued operations and from extraordinary items are segregated from other revenues and expenses so that an investor can easily separate these nonrecurring items from those expected to recur in the future.
- Horizontal analysis compares a specific financial statement item across time, often with reference to a chosen base year. A vertical analysis, also known as common-sized statements, shows every item on a single year's financial statement as a percentage of one of the other financial statement items. Most often, a vertical analysis of the income statement calculates all items as a percentage of sales, and a vertical analysis of the balance sheet calculates all items as a percentage of total assets.
- Ratio analysis is a tool used by anyone who wants to evaluate a firm's financial statements. Remember that a ratio is meaningful only when it is compared to another ratio.
- Investing in a firm as an owner, by purchasing a firm's stock, can create risks. The biggest risk is that the firm will not do well and its stock price will decrease. The best protection for an investor is to have a diversified portfolio. That is, buy a variety of stocks and other investments, such as bonds and real estate, so that a decrease in the price of one asset may be offset by an increase in the price of another.

Chapter Summary Problems

Instructions

Use the information on the following income statement and balance sheet for Apple Inc. to perform a ratio analysis on the two most recent fiscal years. Use Exhibits 10.7A and 10.7B as a model. Comment on your results.

Apple Inc.
Consolidated Statements of Operations

(In millions, except share amounts, which are reflected in thousands and per share amounts)

Three Fiscal Years Ended September 27, 2008	2008	2007	2006
Net sales	$ 32,479	$ 24,006	$ 19,315
Cost of sales	21,334	15,852	13,717
Gross margin	11,145	8,154	5,598
Operating expenses:			
Research and development	1,109	782	712
Selling, general, and administrative	3,761	2,963	2,433
Total operating expenses	4,870	3,745	3,145
Operating income	6,275	4,409	2,453
Other income and expense	620	599	365
Income before provision for income taxes	6,895	5,008	2,818
Provision for income taxes	2,061	1,512	829
Net income	$ 4,834	$ 3,496	$ 1,989
Earnings per common share:			
Basic	$ 5.48	$ 4.04	$ 2.36
Diluted	$ 5.36	$ 3.93	$ 2.27
Shares used in computing earnings per share:			
Basic	881,592	864,595	844,058
Diluted	902,139	889,292	877,526

Apple Inc.
Consolidated Balance Sheets
(In millions, except share amounts)

	September 27, 2008	September 29, 2007
ASSETS:		
Current Assets:		
Cash and cash equivalents	$11,875	$ 9,352
Short-term investments	12,615	6,034
Accounts receivable, less allowances of $47 in each period . . .	2,422	1,637
Inventories	509	346
Deferred tax assets	1,447	782
Other current assets	5,822	3,805
Total current assets	34,690	21,956
Property, plant, and equipment, net	2,455	1,832
Goodwill	207	38
Acquired intangible assets, net	285	299
Other assets	1,935	1,222
Total assets	$39,572	$25,347
LIABILITIES AND SHAREHOLDERS' EQUITY:		
Current liabilities:		
Accounts payable	$ 5,520	$ 4,970
Accrued expenses	8,572	4,310
Total current liabilities	14,092	9,280
Non-current liabilities	4,450	1,535
Total liabilities	18,542	10,815
Commitments and contingencies		
Shareholders' equity:		
Common stock, no par value; 1,800,000,000 shares authorized; 888,325,973 and 872,328,972 shares issued and outstanding, respectively	7,177	5,368
Retained earnings	13,845	9,101
Accumulated other comprehensive income	8	63
Total shareholders' equity	21,030	14,532
Total liabilities and shareholders' equity	$39,572	$25,347

See accompanying Notes to Consolidated Financial Statements.

Additional information you will need (dollars in millions) follows:

Total assets at September 27, 2006	$17,205
Inventory at September 27, 2006	$ 270
Net accounts receivable at September 27, 2006	$ 1,252
Total current liabilities at September 27, 2006	$ 6,443
Total shareholders' equity at September 27, 2006	$ 9,984
Net cash from operating activities for FYE September 27, 2007	$ 5,470
Net cash from operating activities for FYE September 27, 2008	$ 9,596
Market price of stock on September 27, 2007	$153.47
Market price of stock on September 27, 2008	$128.24

Solution

Ratio	Definition	Computation	Computation	Interpretation
LIQUIDITY		FYE September 27, 2008 (dollars in millions)	FYE September 27, 2007 (dollars in millions)	
Current ratio	$\dfrac{\text{Total current assets}}{\text{Total current liabilities}}$	$\dfrac{34,690}{14,092} = 2.46$	$\dfrac{21,956}{9,280} = 2.37$	Apple has no problem meeting its short-term obligations.
Cash from operations to current liabilities	$\dfrac{\text{Net cash from operating activities}}{\text{Average current liabilities}}$	$\dfrac{\$9,596}{(\$9,280 + \$14,092)/2} = 0.82$	$\dfrac{\$5,470}{(\$6,443^* + \$9,280)/2} = 0.70$ * From the 2006 balance sheet not shown here	The ratio appears to be a bit low, but it has increased during the most recent year.
Inventory turnover ratio	$\dfrac{\text{Cost of goods sold}}{\text{Average inventory}}$	$\dfrac{\$21,334}{(\$346 + \$509)/2} = 49.90$	$\dfrac{\$15,852}{(\$270^* + \$346)/2} = 51.47$ * From the 2006 balance sheet not shown here but provided with the given data	Apple turns over its inventory quickly. For 2008, the average number of days in inventory was only 7.31 days (365/49.90).
Accounts receivable turnover ratio	$\dfrac{\text{Net sales}}{\text{Average net accounts receivable}}$	$\dfrac{\$32,479}{(\$1,637 + \$2,422)/2} = 16.00$	$\dfrac{\$24,006}{(\$1,252^* + \$1,637)/2} = 16.62$ * From the 2006 balance sheet not shown here but provided with the given data	Apple collects its receivables in a reasonable amount of time. Average days to collect AR in 2008 was 22.81 days (365/16.00).
SOLVENCY				
Debt-to-equity	$\dfrac{\text{Total liabilities}}{\text{Total equity}}$	$\dfrac{\$18,542}{\$21,030} = 0.88$	$\dfrac{\$10,815}{\$14,532} = 0.74$	While this looks like a high debt ratio, notice that Apple has very little long-term debt. Some sources will use only long-term debt in the numerator of this ratio.

PROFITABILITY				
Return on assets	$\dfrac{\text{Net income}}{\text{Average total assets}}$	$\dfrac{\$4,834}{(\$25,347 + \$39,572)/2}$ $= 14.89\%$	$\dfrac{\$3,496}{(\$17,205^* + \$25,347)/2}$ $= 16.43\%$ * From the 2006 balance sheet not shown here but provided with the given data	Good ROA, although decreasing slightly; not surprising given the recession during this year
Asset turnover ratio	$\dfrac{\text{Net sales}}{\text{Average total assets}}$	$\dfrac{\$32,479}{(\$25,347 + \$39,572)/2}$ $= 1.00$	$\dfrac{\$24,006}{(\$17,205^* + \$25,347)/2}$ $= 1.13$ * From the 2006 balance sheet not shown here but provided with the given data	This change indicates a decrease in the efficiency with which the firm's assets are generating sales.
Return on equity	$\dfrac{\text{Net income} - \text{preferred dividends}}{\text{Average common shareholders' equity}}$	$\dfrac{\$4,834}{(\$14,532 + \$21,030)/2}$ $= 27.19\%$	$\dfrac{\$3,496}{(\$9,984^* + \$14,532)/2}$ $= 28.52\%$ * From the 2006 balance sheet not shown here	This is an excellent ROE, decreasing only very slightly even in a recession.
Profit margin ratio	$\dfrac{\text{Net income}}{\text{Net sales}}$	$\dfrac{\$4,834}{\$32,479} = 14.88\%$	$\dfrac{\$3,496}{\$24,006} = 14.57\%$	This is an excellent profit margin ratio. It shows Apple is controlling its costs quite well.
Gross profit ratio	$\dfrac{\text{Gross profit}}{\text{Sales}}$	$\dfrac{\$11,145}{\$32,479} = 34.31\%$	$\dfrac{\$8,154}{\$24,006} = 33.97\%$	The slight increase is excellent, especially considering the economy at this time.
Earnings per share	$\dfrac{\text{Net income} - \text{preferred dividends}}{\text{Average \# of common shares outstanding}}$	$\dfrac{\$4,834,000}{881,592^*} = \$5.48$ * Disclosed on the income statement. Notice that NI was given in millions while number of shares was given in thousands. Three zeros are added to the net income number to put the numerator and denominator in the same units.	$\dfrac{\$3,496,000}{864,595^*} = \$4.04$ * Disclosed on the income statement	The calculation is shown here, but remember that you will not need to calculate this ratio if you have the income statement. It will be shown on the face of the statement.
MARKET INDICATORS				
Price–earnings ratio	$\dfrac{\text{Market price per share}}{\text{Earnings per share}}$	$\dfrac{\$128.24}{\$5.48} = 23.40$	$\dfrac{\$153.47}{\$4.04} = 37.99$	Even though earnings have gone up, the market price at year end has decreased significantly during this time. That has resulted in a significant decrease in the PE ratio.
Dividend yield	$\dfrac{\text{Dividend per share}}{\text{Market price per share}}$	N/A Apple did not pay any dividends.		

Key Terms for Chapter 10

Available-for-sale securities (p. 508)

Cash from operations to current liabilities ratio (p. 467)

Common-sizing (p. 465)

Comprehensive income (p. 505)

Discontinued operations (p. 462)

Dividend yield ratio (p. 468)

Extraordinary items (p. 463)

Held-to-maturity securities (p. 507)

Horizontal analysis (p. 464)

Liquidity ratios (p. 466)

Market indicators (p. 466)

Price–earnings (PE) ratio (p. 468)

Profitability ratios (p. 466)

Solvency ratios (p. 466)

Trading securities (p. 507)

Unrealized gain or loss (p. 507)

Vertical analysis (p. 465)

Answers to YOUR TURN Questions

Chapter 10

Your Turn 10-1

Those items must be shown after the tax consequences have been subtracted because this method of reporting the items net of taxes keeps the tax implications of these items separate from the company's regular tax expense. The alternative is to show the items before the tax implications and then to include the tax savings or tax increases in the company's regular tax expense.

Your Turn 10-2

2008	2009	2010	2011	2012
100%	7.6%	0.7%	10.8%	14.1%

Every year the firm's sales have exceeded sales in the base year. Except for 2010, the percentage increase has been good and continues to increase.

Your Turn 10-3

Brothers Company
Income Statements

	For the Year Ended			
	March 31, 2010		March 31, 2009	
Sales revenue	$10,000	100.0%	$8,000	100.0%
Expenses:				
Cost of goods sold	3,200	32.0%	2,800	35.0%
Operating expenses	300	3.0%	275	3.4%
Bad debts expense	100	1.0%	90	1.1%
Insurance expense	200	2.0%	200	2.5%
Rent expense	600	6.0%	600	7.5%
Depreciation expense	250	2.5%	250	3.1%
Interest expense	75	0.8%	75	0.9%
Total expenses	4,725	47.3%	4,290	53.6%
Net income	$ 5,275	52.8%	$3,710	46.4%

The company's performance has improved in almost all areas. The higher net income is not just due to the increase in sales. The cost of goods sold as a percentage of sales has gone down, and all the expenses have also decreased as a percent of sales.

Your Turn 10-4

This payoff would increase the current ratio. We can use a simple example to illustrate why: Suppose current assets were $500 million and current liabilities were $250 million. The current ratio would be 2. Now suppose $50 million worth of current liabilities were paid off with current assets. Then current assets would be $450 million, and current liabilities would be $200 million.

The current ratio is now 2.25. When a fraction is greater than 1 and both the numerator and the denominator of a fraction are reduced by the same amount, the value of the fraction will increase.

Your Turn 10-5

No, the gross profit ratio does not tell which company is more profitable because one company may have higher sales than the other. For example 30% of a large number is better than 60% of a small number. Also, the amount of costs the companies must cover beyond the cost of goods sold is unknown. The gross profit ratio is most useful for comparing companies in the same industry or evaluating performance of a single company across time.

Questions

1. Define the items that the Financial Accounting Standards Board requires a firm to report separately on the income statement. Why is this separation useful?
2. What criteria must be met for an event to be considered extraordinary? Give an example of an event that would be considered extraordinary.
3. What does it mean to show an item net of tax? Where is this done and why?
4. What is horizontal analysis? What is the purpose of this method of analysis?
5. What is vertical analysis? What is the purpose of this method of analysis?
6. What is liquidity? Which ratios are useful for measuring liquidity and what does each measure?
7. What is solvency? Which ratios are useful for measuring solvency and what does each measure?
8. What is profitability? Which ratios are useful for measuring profitability and what does each measure?
9. What are market indicators? Which ratios are market indicators and what does each measure?
10. How are financial ratios used to determine how successfully a company is operating?

Multiple-Choice Questions

1. Suppose a firm had an extraordinary loss of $300,000. If the firm's tax rate is 35%, how will the loss be shown in the financial statements?
   a. On the income statement, below income from operations, net of tax savings, for a net loss of $195,000
   b. On the income statement as part of the calculation of income from operations, before taxes, for a loss of $300,000
   c. As supplementary information in the notes to the financial statements
   d. As a cash outflow from financing on the statement of cash flows
2. Current assets for Kearney Company are $120,000 and total assets are $600,000. Current liabilities are $80,000 and total liabilities are $300,000. What is the current ratio?
   a. 2.00
   b. 2.50
   c. 1.90
   d. 1.50
3. Ritchie Company sold some fixed assets for a gain of $100,000. The firm's tax rate is 25%. How would Ritchie Company report this transaction on its financial statements?
   a. On the income statement as part of the calculation of income from continuing operations, net of tax, in the amount of $75,000
   b. As an extraordinary item, net of tax, in the amount of $75,000
   c. As discontinued operations, net of tax, in the amount of $75,000
   d. On the income statement as part of the calculation of income from continuing operations at the before tax amount of $100,000
4. Gerard Company reported sales of $300,000 for 2010; $330,000 for 2011; and $360,000 for 2012. If the company uses 2010 as the base year, what were the percentage increases for 2011 and 2012 compared to the base year?
   a. 10% for 2011 and 10% for 2012
   b. 120% for 2011 and 120% for 2012
   c. 110% for 2011 and 110% for 2012
   d. 10% for 2011 and 20% for 2012

5. On June 30, Star Radio reported total current assets of $45,000; total assets of $200,000; total current liabilities of $42,000; and total liabilities of $80,000. What was the current ratio on this date?
   a. 0.56
   b. 2.50
   c. 1.07
   d. 0.93

6. Talking Puppet Company reported a P/E ratio of 50 on the last day of the fiscal year. If the company reported earnings of $2.50 per share, how much was a share of the company's stock trading for at that time?
   a. $20 per share
   b. $125 per share
   c. $50 per share
   d. $47.50 per share

7. Singleton Company had sales of $2,000,000, cost of sales of $1,200,000, and average inventory of $400,000. What was the company's inventory turnover ratio for the period?
   a. 3.00
   b. 4.00
   c. 5.00
   d. 0.33

8. Suppose a firm had an inventory turnover ratio of 20. Suppose the firm considers a year to be 360 days. How many days, on average, does an item remain in the inventory?
   a. 5.56 days
   b. 18 days
   c. 20 days
   d. 360 days

9. Suppose a new company is trying to decide whether to use LIFO or FIFO in a period of rising inventory costs. The CFO suggests using LIFO because it will give a higher inventory turnover ratio. Is the CFO correct?
   a. Yes, the average inventory will be lower (the ratio's denominator) and the cost of goods sold (the ratio's numerator) will be higher than if FIFO were used.
   b. No, the average inventory would be the same because purchases are the same no matter which inventory method is chosen.
   c. The inventory method has no effect on the inventory turnover ratio.
   d. Without specific inventory amounts, it is not possible to predict the effect of the inventory method.

10. If a firm has $100,000 debt and $100,000 equity, then
    a. the return on equity ratio is 1.
    b. the debt-to-equity ratio is 1.
    c. the return on assets ratio is 0.5.
    d. the firm has too much debt.

MyAccountingLab

Short Exercises
Set A

SE10-1A. *Discontinued operations. (LO 1).* In 2010, Earthscope Company decided to sell its satellite sales division, even though the division had been profitable during the year. During 2010, the satellite division earned $54,000 and the taxes on that income were $12,500. The division was sold for a gain of $750,000, and the taxes on the gain amounted to $36,700. How would these amounts be reported on the income statement for the year ended December 31, 2010?

SE10-2A. *Extraordinary items. (LO 1).* Sew and Save Company suffered an extraordinary loss of $30,000 last year. The related tax savings amounted to $5,600. How would this tax savings be reported on the income statement?

SE10-3A. *Horizontal analysis. (LO 2).* Olin Copy Corporation reported the following amounts on its 2012 comparative income statement:

(in thousands)	2012	2011	2010
Revenues	$6,400	$4,575	$3,850
Cost of sales	3,900	2,650	2,050

Perform a horizontal analysis of revenues and cost of sales in both dollar amounts and in percentages for 2012 and 2011, using 2010 as the base year.

SE10-4A. *Vertical analysis. (LO 2).* Bessie's Quilting Company reported the following amounts on its balance sheet at December 31, 2010:

Cash	$ 5,000
Accounts receivable, net	40,000
Inventory	35,000
Equipment, net	120,000
Total assets	$200,000

Perform a vertical analysis of the assets of Bessie's Quilting Company. Use total assets as the base. What information does the analysis provide?

SE10-5A. *Ratio analysis. (LO 3).* Fireworks Company reported current assets of $720,000 and a current ratio of 1.2. What were current liabilities?

SE10-6A. *Ratio analysis. (LO 3).* A five-year comparative analysis of Low Light Company's current ratio follows:

	2008	2009	2010	2011	2012
Current ratio	1.19	1.85	2.50	3.40	4.02

What has been happening to the liquidity of Low Light Company over the five years presented?

SE10-7A. *Ratio analysis. (LO 3).* Suppose Company A has an inventory turnover ratio of 25 and a gross margin ratio of 10%, while Company B has an inventory turnover ratio of 3.5 and a gross margin of 50%. Which company is more likely to be a grocery store and which is more likely to be a clothing boutique? Explain why.

Set B

SE10-8B. *Discontinued operations. (LO 1).* In 2011, Office Products decided to sell its furniture division because it had been losing money for several years. During 2011, the furniture division lost $140,000. The tax savings related to the loss amounted to $25,000. The division was sold at a loss of $350,000, and the tax savings related to the loss on the sale was $50,000. How would these amounts be reported on the income statement for the year ended December 31, 2011?

SE10-9B. *Extraordinary items. (LO 1).* RM Inc. suffered an extraordinary loss of $50,000 last year. The related tax savings amounted to $8,600. How would this tax savings be reported on the income statement?

SE10-10B. *Horizontal analysis. (LO 2).* Use the following information about the capital expenditures of Andes Company to perform a horizontal analysis, with 2009 as the base year:

(in millions)	2012	2011	2010	2009
Capital expenditures	$41,400	$45,575	$43,850	$50,600

What information does this provide about Andes Company?

SE10-11B. *Vertical analysis. (LO 2).* Perform a vertical analysis on the following income statement, with sales as the base amount:

Sales	$35,000
Cost of goods sold	14,000
Gross margin	21,000
Other expenses	7,000
Net income	$14,000

What other information would you need to make this analysis meaningful?

SE10-12B. *Ratio analysis. (LO 3).* Ronca Company reported current liabilities of $720,000 and a current ratio of 1.2. What were current assets?

SE10-13B. *Ratio analysis. (LO 3).* The following is a five-year comparative analysis of Accent Company's return on assets and return on equity:

	2007	2008	2009	2010	2011
Return on assets	8%	7.5%	7.12%	6.54%	6%
Return on equity	20%	21%	21.8%	22.2%	23%

1. What does this analysis tell you about the overall profitability of Accent Company over the five-year period?
2. What does this analysis tell you about what has happened to Accent's amount of debt over the past five years?

SE10-14B. Ratio analysis. *(LO 3).* Do you think that Macy's or Wal-Mart has the higher inventory turnover ratio? Why? Which company do you think has the higher gross margin ratio? Why? (Find these firms' financial statements on the Internet and see if you are correct.)

Exercises
Set A

E10-15A. *Discontinued operations. (LO 1).* Use the following information to construct a partial income statement beginning with income from continuing operations:

Income from continuing operations	$230,000
Loss during the year from operating discontinued operations	60,000
Tax benefit of loss	9,500
Loss from sale of discontinued operations	128,500
Tax savings from loss on the sale	31,000

E10-16A. *Extraordinary items. (LO 1).* Devon's Central Processing Agency suffered a $560,000 loss due to a disaster that qualifies as an extraordinary item for financial statement purposes. The tax benefit of the loss amounts to $123,000. If income from continuing operations (net of tax) amounted to $1,300,500, what is net income?

E10-17A. *Horizontal analysis. (LO 2).* Conway Furniture reported the following amounts for its sales during the past five years:

2010	2009	2008	2007	2006
$30,000	$28,400	$26,300	$24,200	$25,400

Using 2006 as the base year, perform a horizontal analysis. What information does the analysis provide that was not apparent from the raw numbers?

E10-18A. *Vertical analysis. (LO 2).* Use the following income statement from Color Copy to perform a vertical analysis with sales as the base:

Color Copy, Inc.
Income Statement
For the Year Ended September 30, 2011

Sales revenue		$10,228
Cost of goods sold		5,751
Gross profit		4,477
Operating expenses:		
Depreciation—buildings and equipment	$ 100	
Other selling and administrative	2,500	
Total expenses		2,600
Income before interest and taxes		1,877
Interest expense		350
Income before taxes		1,527
Income taxes		150
Net income		$ 1,377

E10-19A. *Current ratio. (LO 3).* Calculate the current ratio for Suzanne's Hotels for the years given in the following comparative balance sheets:

Suzanne's Hotels, Inc.
Balance Sheets

	December 31, 2011	December 31, 2010
Current assets:		
Cash	$ 98,000	$ 90,000
Accounts receivable, net	110,000	116,000
Inventory	170,000	160,000
Prepaid expenses	18,000	16,000
Total current assets	396,000	382,000
Equipment, net	184,000	160,000
Total assets	$580,000	$542,000
Total current liabilities	$206,000	$223,000
Long-term liabilities	119,000	117,000
Total liabilities	325,000	340,000
Common stockholders' equity	90,000	90,000
Retained earnings	165,000	112,000
Total liabilities and stockholders' equity	$580,000	$542,000

Although two years is not much of a trend, what is your opinion of the direction of this ratio?

E10-20A. *Debt-to-equity ratio. (LO 3).* Use the balance sheets from Suzanne's Hotels in E10-19A to compute the debt-to-equity ratio for 2011 and 2010. Suppose you calculated a debt ratio using debt plus equity as the denominator. Which ratio—debt-to-equity or debt-to-debt plus equity— seems easiest to interpret? As an investor, do you view the "trend" in the debt-to-equity ratio as favorable or unfavorable? Why?

E10-21A. *Ratio analysis. (LO 3).* Zap Electronics reported the following for the fiscal years ended January 31, 2011, and January 31, 2010:

January 31	2011	2010
(in thousands)		
Accounts receivable	$ 36,184	$ 24,306
Inventory	106,754	113,875
Current assets	174,369	154,369
Current liabilities	71,616	68,001
Long-term liabilities	12,316	35,200
Shareholders' equity	121,851	198,935
Sales	712,855	580,223
Cost of goods sold	483,463	400,126
Interest expense	335	709
Net income	11,953	4,706

Assume all sales are on credit and the firm has no preferred stock outstanding. Calculate the following ratios:

1. Current ratio (for both years)
2. Accounts receivable turnover ratio (for 2011)
3. Inventory turnover ratio (for 2011)
4. Debt-to-equity ratio (for both years)
5. Return on equity ratio (for 2011)

Do any of these ratios suggest problems for the company?

E10-22A. *Ratio analysis. (LO 3).* Corner Grocers reported the following for its two most recent fiscal years:

December 31	2012	2011
Cash	$ 25,000	$ 20,000
Receivables (net)	60,000	70,000
Merchandise inventory	55,000	30,000
Plant assets (net)	280,000	260,000
Total assets	$420,000	$380,000
Accounts payable	45,000	62,000
Long-term notes payable	75,000	100,000
Common stock	135,000	122,000
Retained earnings	165,000	96,000
Total Liabilities and Shareholders' Equity	$420,000	$380,000
Net income for the year ended 12/31/12	$ 75,000	
Sales (all sales were on account)	450,000	
Cost of goods sold	210,000	
Interest expense	1,500	

Calculate the following for the year ended December 31, 2012:

1. Current ratio
2. Accounts receivable turnover ratio
3. Inventory turnover ratio
4. Return on assets
5. Return on equity

E10-23A. *Ratio analysis. (LO 3).* Furniture Showcase reported the following for its fiscal year ended June 30, 2010:

Sales	$530,000
Cost of sales	300,000
Gross margin	230,000
Expenses	113,000
Net income	$117,000

At the beginning of the year, the company had 50,000 shares of common stock outstanding. At the end of the year, there were 40,000 shares outstanding. The market price of the company's stock at year end was $20 per share. The company declared and paid $80,000 of dividends near year end.

Calculate earnings per share and the price–earnings ratio for Furniture Showcase.

Use the following balance sheets and income statements for Campbell Soup Company for E10-24A through E10-27A:

Campbell Soup Company
Consolidated Balance Sheets
(Millions, except per share amounts)

	August 3, 2008	July 29, 2007
Current Assets		
Cash and cash equivalents	$ 81	$ 71
Accounts receivable (Note 15)	570	581
Inventories (Note 15)	829	775
Other current assets (Note 15)	172	151
Current assets held for sale	41	—
Total current assets	1,693	1,578
Plant Assets, Net of Depreciation (Note 15)	1,939	2,042
Goodwill (Note 5)	1,998	1,872
Other Intangible Assets, Net of Amortization (Note 5)	605	615
Other Assets (Note 15)	211	338
Non-current Assets Held for Sale	28	—
Total assets	$ 6,474	$ 6,445
Current Liabilities		
Notes payable (Note 11)	$ 982	$ 595
Payable to suppliers and others	655	694
Accrued liabilities (Note 15)	655	622
Dividend payable	81	77
Accrued income taxes	9	42
Current liabilities held for sale	21	—
Total current liabilities	2,403	2,030
Long-term Debt (Note 11)	1,633	2,074
Other Liabilities (Note 15)	1,119	1,046
Non-current Liabilities Held for Sale	1	—
Total liabilities	5,156	5,150
Shareowners' Equity (Note 13)		
Preferred stock; authorized 40 shares; none issued	—	—
Capital stock, $.0375 par value; authorized 560 shares; issued 542 shares	20	20
Additional paid-in capital	337	331
Earnings retained in the business	7,909	7,082
Capital stock in treasury, 186 shares in 2008 and 163 shares in 2007, at cost	(6,812)	(6,015)
Accumulated other comprehensive loss	(136)	(123)
Total shareowners' equity	1,318	1,295
Total liabilities and shareowners' equity	$ 6,474	$ 6,445

Campbell Soup Company
Consolidated Statements of Earnings
(millions, except per share amounts)

	2008 53 Weeks	2007 52 Weeks	2006 52 Weeks
Net Sales	$7,998	$7,385	$6,894
Costs and expenses			
Cost of products sold	4,827	4,384	4,100
Marketing and selling expenses	1,162	1,106	1,033
Administrative expenses	608	571	552
Research and development expenses	115	111	103
Other expenses/(income) (Note 15)	13	(30)	9
Restructuring charges (Note 7)	175	—	—
Total costs and expenses	6,900	6,142	5,797
Earnings Before Interest and Taxes	1,098	1,243	1,097
Interest expense (Note 15)	167	163	165
Interest income	8	19	15
Earnings before taxes	939	1,099	947
Taxes on earnings (Note 10)	268	307	227
Earnings from continuing operations	671	792	720
Earnings from discontinued operations	494	62	46
Net Earnings	$1,165	$ 854	$ 766
Per Share—Basic			
Earnings from continuing operations	$ 1.80	$ 2.05	$ 1.77
Earnings from discontinued operations	1.32	.16	.11
Net Earnings	$ 3.12	$ 2.21	$ 1.88
Weighted average shares outstanding—basic	373	386	407
Per Share—Assuming Dilution			
Earnings from continuing operations	$ 1.76	$ 2.00	$ 1.74
Earnings from discontinued operations	1.30	.16	.11
Net Earnings	$ 3.06	$ 2.16	$ 1.85
Weighted average shares outstanding—assuming dilution	381	396	414

E10-24A. *Horizontal analysis. (LO 2).* Use the statements of earnings for Campbell Soup Company to perform a horizontal analysis for each item reported for the year from July 29, 2007, to August 3, 2008. What does your analysis tell you about the operations of Campbell Soup Company for the year?

E10-25A. *Vertical analysis. (LO 2).* Use the statements of earnings for Campbell Soup Company to perform a vertical analysis for each item reported for the last two fiscal years using net sales as the base. What does your analysis tell you about the operations for the years reported?

E10-26A. *Liquidity ratios. (LO 3).* Use the financial statements for Campbell Soup Company to calculate the following liquidity ratios for FYE August 3, 2008:

1. Current ratio
2. Inventory turnover ratio
3. Accounts receivable turnover ratio (Assume all sales are credit sales.)

What information does this provide about the firm's liquidity?

E10-27A. *Solvency and profitability ratios. (LO 3).* Use the financial statements for Campbell Soup Company to calculate the following solvency and profitability ratios for FYE August 3, 2008:

1. Debt-to-equity ratio
2. Return on assets
3. Return on equity

4. Gross margin percentage
5. Profit margin percentage

What information does this provide about the firm's solvency and profitability?

Set B

E10-28B. *Discontinued operations. (LO 1).* Use the following information to construct a partial income statement beginning with income from continuing operations:

Income from continuing operations	$310,000
Loss during the year from operation of discontinued operations	75,000
Tax benefit of loss	19,400
Loss from sale of discontinued operations	105,750
Tax savings from loss on the sale	32,000

E10-29B. *Extraordinary items. (LO 1).* Tropical Vacations suffered a $1,070,000 loss due to a tsunami, which qualifies as an extraordinary item for financial statement purposes. The tax benefit of the loss amounts to $155,000. If income from continuing operations (net of tax) amounted to $1,861,250, what is net income?

E10-30B. *Horizontal analysis. (LO 2).* Sunny's Umbrellas reported the following amounts for sales during the past five years:

2012	2011	2010	2009	2008
$27,925	$30,400	$33,525	$26,250	$30,300

Using 2008 as the base year, perform a horizontal analysis. What information does the analysis provide that was not apparent from the raw numbers?

E10-31B. *Vertical analysis. (LO 2).* Use the following income statement from Designers Discount, Inc., to perform a vertical analysis with sales as the base:

Designers Discount, Inc.
Income Statement
For the Year Ended December 31, 2010

Sales revenue		$16,374
Cost of goods sold		7,985
Gross profit on sales		$ 8,389
Operating expenses:		
Depreciation—buildings and equipment	$ 265	
Other selling and administrative	3,750	
Total expenses		4,015
Income before interest and taxes		$ 4,374
Interest expense		254
Income before taxes		$ 4,120
Income taxes		1,236
Net income		$ 2,884

E10-32B. *Current ratio. (LO 3).* Calculate the current ratio for Mike & Kat Racing Company for the years given in the following comparative balance sheets:

Mike & Kat Racing Company
Balance Sheets

	December 31, 2010	December 31, 2009
Current assets:		
Cash	$186,000	$192,000
Accounts receivable, net	94,000	85,000
Inventory	185,000	170,500
Prepaid expenses	17,000	14,000
Total current assets	482,000	461,500
Equipment, net	215,000	195,000
Total assets	$697,000	$656,500
Total current liabilities	$267,000	$269,000
Long-term liabilities	185,000	190,000
Total liabilities	452,000	459,000
Shareholders' equity	163,750	148,250
Retained earnings	81,250	49,250
Total liabilities and shareholders' equity	$697,000	$656,500

Although two years will not show a significant trend, what is your opinion of the direction of this ratio?

E10-33B. *Debt-to-equity ratio. (LO 3).* Use the balance sheets from Mike & Kat Racing Company in E10-32B to compute a debt-to-equity ratio for 2010 and 2009. Suppose you calculated a debt ratio using debt plus equity as the denominator. Which ratio—debt-to-equity or debt-to-debt plus equity—seems easiest to interpret? As an investor, do you view the "trend" in the debt-to-equity ratio as favorable or unfavorable? Why?

E10-34B. *Ratio analysis. (LO 3).* Crystal Cromartie's Frozen Foods reported the following for the fiscal years ended September 30, 2011, and September 30, 2010:

September 30 (in millions)	2011	2010
Accounts receivable	$ 21,265	$ 13,802
Inventory	45,692	47,682
Current assets	185,716	155,716
Current liabilities	80,954	72,263
Long-term liabilities	15,251	17,852
Shareholders' equity	21,871	58,035
Sales	88,455	70,223
Cost of goods sold	60,463	52,750
Interest expense	21.5	43.2
Net income	1,842	1,006

Assume there is no outstanding preferred stock and all sales are credit sales. Calculate the following ratios:

1. Current ratio (for both years)
2. Accounts receivable turnover ratio (for 2011)
3. Inventory turnover ratio (for 2011)
4. Debt-to-equity ratio (for both years)
5. Return on equity (for 2011)

Do any of these ratios suggest problems for the company?

E10-35B. *Ratio analysis. (LO 3).* Hudson Coffee Shops reported the following for the two most recent fiscal years:

December 31	2010	2009
Cash	$ 34,000	$ 17,000
Receivables (net)	85,000	80,000
Merchandise inventory	74,000	48,000
Fixed assets	365,000	324,000
Total assets	$558,000	$469,000
Accounts payable	65,000	83,000
Long-term notes payable	82,000	112,000
Common stock	176,000	144,000
Retained earnings	235,000	130,000
Total liabilities and shareholders' equity	$558,000	$469,000
Net income for the year ended 12/31/10	$115,000	
Sales (all sales were on account)	620,000	
Cost of goods sold	284,000	
Interest expense	3,000	

Calculate the following for the year ended December 31, 2010:

1. Current ratio
2. Accounts receivable turnover ratio
3. Inventory turnover ratio
4. Return on assets
5. Return on equity

E10-36B. *Ratio analysis. (LO 3).* International Imports Corporation reported the following for its fiscal year ended June 30, 2011:

Sales	$640,000
Cost of sales	470,000
Gross margin	170,000
Expenses	94,000
Net income	$ 76,000

At the beginning of the year, the company had 50,000 shares of common stock outstanding and no preferred stock. At the end of the year, there were 50,000 common shares outstanding and no preferred stock. The market price of the company's stock at year end was $20 per share. The company declared and paid $25,000 of dividends near year end.

Calculate earnings per share, the price–earnings ratio, and dividend yield for International Imports.

Use the following balance sheets and income statements for GameStop Corp. for E10-37B through E10-40B:

GameStop Corp.
Consolidated Balance Sheets
(In thousands)

	January 31, 2009	February 2, 2008
ASSETS		
Current assets:		
Cash and cash equivalents	$ 578,141	$ 857,414
Receivables, net	65,981	56,019
Merchandise inventories, net	1,075,792	801,025
Deferred income taxes — current	23,615	27,481
Prepaid expenses	59,101	48,915
Other current assets	15,411	3,863
Total current assets	1,818,041	1,794,717
Property and equipment:		
Land	10,397	11,870
Buildings and leasehold improvements	454,651	378,611
Fixtures and equipment	619,845	538,738
Total property and equipment	1,084,893	929,219
Less accumulated depreciation and		
amortization	535,639	417,550
Net property and equipment	549,254	511,669
Goodwill, net	1,862,107	1,402,440
Other intangible assets	247,790	14,214
Deferred taxes	—	26,332
Other noncurrent assets	35,398	26,519
Total noncurrent assets	2,694,549	1,981,174
Total assets	$4,512,590	$3,775,891
LIABILITIES AND STOCKHOLDERS' EQUITY		
Current liabilities:		
Accounts payable	$1,047,963	$ 844,376
Accrued liabilities	514,748	416,181
Total current liabilities	1,562,711	1,260,557
Senior notes payable, long-term portion, net . . .	545,712	574,473
Other long-term liabilities	104,486	78,415
Total long-term liabilities	650,198	652,888
Total liabilities	2,212,909	1,913,445
Commitments and contingencies		
(Notes 10 and 11)		
Stockholders' equity:		
Preferred stock — authorized 5,000 shares; no		
shares issued or outstanding	—	—
Class A common stock — $.001 par value;		
authorized 300,000 shares; 163,843 and		
161,007 shares issued and outstanding,		
respectively	164	161
Additional paid-in-capital	1,307,453	1,208,474
Accumulated other comprehensive		
income (loss)	(28,426)	31,603
Retained earnings	1,020,490	622,208
Total stockholders' equity	2,299,681	1,862,446
Total liabilities and stockholders' equity	$4,512,590	$3,775,891

See accompanying notes to consolidated financial statements.

GameStop Corp.
Consolidated Statements of Operations
(In thousands, except per share data)

	52 Weeks Ended January 31, 2009	52 Weeks Ended February 2, 2008	53 Weeks Ended February 3, 2007
Sales	$8,805,897	$7,093,962	$5,318,900
Cost of sales	6,535,762	5,280,255	3,847,458
Gross profit	2,270,135	1,813,707	1,471,442
Selling, general and administrative expenses	1,445,419	1,182,016	1,021,113
Depreciation and amortization	145,004	130,270	109,862
Merger-related expenses	4,593	—	6,788
Operating earnings	675,119	501,421	333,679
Interest income	(11,619)	(13,779)	(11,338)
Interest expense	50,456	61,553	84,662
Debt extinguishment expense	2,331	12,591	6,059
Earnings before income tax expense	633,951	441,056	254,296
Income tax expense	235,669	152,765	96,046
Net earnings	$ 398,282	$ 288,291	$ 158,250
Net earnings per common share — basic	$ 2.44	$ 1.82	$ 1.06
Weighted average shares of common stock — basic	163,190	158,226	149,924
Net earnings per common share — diluted	$ 2.38	$ 1.75	$ 1.00
Weighted average shares of common stock — diluted	167,671	164,844	158,284

E10-37B. *Horizontal analysis. (LO 2).* Use the statements of income for GameStop Corp. to perform a horizontal analysis for each item reported for the year from February 2, 2008, to January 31, 2009. What does your analysis tell you about the operations of GameStop Corp. for the years reported?

E10-38B. *Vertical analysis. (LO 2).* Use the statements of income for GameStop Corp. to perform a vertical analysis for each item reported for the two most recent years using sales as the base. What does your analysis tell you about the operations of GameStop Corp. for the years reported?

E10-39B. *Liquidity ratios. (LO 3).* Use the financial statements for GameStop Corp. to calculate the following liquidity ratios for the most recent fiscal year:

1. Current ratio
2. Inventory turnover and average days in inventory
3. Accounts receivable turnover and average days to collect AR

What do these ratios tell you about the firm?

E10-40B. *Solvency and profitability ratios. (LO 3).* Use the financial statements for GameStop Corp. to calculate the following solvency ratios and profitability for the most recent fiscal year and provide an interpretation for each ratio:

1. Debt-to-equity ratio
2. Profit margin ratio
3. Return on assets
4. Return on equity
5. Gross margin percentage

All of the A problems can be found within MyAccountingLab, an online homework and practice environment.

Problems
Set A

P10-41A. *Discontinued operations and extraordinary items. (LO 1).* Each of the following items was found on the financial statements for Hartsfield Company for the year ended December 31, 2011:

Net income from continuing operations	$136,500
Gain on the sale of a discontinued segment, net of taxes of $42,000	140,000
Loss from operation of discontinued segment, net of taxes of $24,000	(80,000)
Gain on sale of land	65,000
Extraordinary loss, net of taxes of $6,000	(20,000)

Requirements

1. For the items listed, indicate the financial statement and appropriate section, where applicable, on which each would appear.
2. Provide a description of each item and give as many details of each item's financial statement presentation as possible.
3. Based on the data provided, what is Hartsfield Company's tax rate?

P10-42A. *Prepare an income statement. (LO 1).* The Pops Corporation reported the following for the year ended December 31, 2010:

Sales	$575,000
Cost of goods sold	230,000
Interest income	10,000
Gain on sale of equipment	8,000
Selling and administrative expenses	12,000
Interest expense	5,000
Extraordinary gain	15,000
Loss from discontinued segment operations	(10,500)
Gain on disposal of discontinued segment	28,000

Requirement

Assume the corporation is subject to a 30% tax rate. Prepare an income statement for the year ended December 31, 2010.

P10-43A. *Prepare an income statement. (LO 1).* The following balances appeared in the general ledger for Hacky Sak Corporation at fiscal year end September 30, 2011:

Selling and administrative expenses	$ 15,000
Other revenues and gains	40,000
Operating expenses	65,000
Cost of goods sold	125,000
Net sales	385,000
Other expenses and losses	25,000

In addition, the following occurred during the year:
   a. On April 10, a tornado destroyed one of the company's manufacturing plants, resulting in an extraordinary loss of $55,000.
   b. On July 31, the company discontinued one of its unprofitable segments. The loss from operations was $25,000. The assets of the segment were sold at a gain of $15,000.

Requirements

1. Assume Hacky Sak's income tax rate is 35%; prepare the income statement for the year ended September 30, 2011.
2. Calculate the earnings per share the company would report on the income statement assuming Hacky Sak had a weighted average of 200,000 shares of common stock outstanding during the year and paid no preferred dividends.

P10-44A. *Prepare horizontal and vertical analysis. (LO 2).* Following are the income statements for Alpha Company:

Alpha Company			
Income Statements			
(in thousands)			

	For the Year Ended December 31,		
	2010	2009	2008
Net sales	$5,003,837	$4,934,430	$4,881,103
Cost of goods sold	2,755,323	2,804,459	2,784,392
Gross profit	2,248,514	2,129,971	2,096,711
Selling, general, and administrative			
expenses	1,673,449	1,598,333	1,573,510
Operating income	575,065	531,638	523,201
Interest expense	61,168	71,971	80,837
Interest and net investment			
expense (income)	(5,761)	(6,482)	(8,278)
Other expense—net	29,540	26,046	23,365
Income before income taxes	490,118	440,103	427,277
Income taxes	186,258	167,239	166,663
Net income	$ 303,860	$ 272,864	$ 260,614

Requirements

1. For each of the years shown, prepare a vertical analysis, using sales as the base. Write a paragraph explaining what the analysis shows.
2. Using 2008 as the base year, prepare a horizontal analysis for sales and cost of goods sold. What information does this analysis give you?

P10-45A. *Calculate and analyze financial ratios. (LO 3).* Following is information from a firm's financial statements:

	Year Ended December 31		
	2011	2010	2009
Net sales (all on account)	$5,003,837	$4,934,430	
Cost of goods sold	2,755,323	2,804,459	
Gross profit	2,248,514	2,129,971	
Interest expense	61,168	71,971	
Income taxes	186,258	167,239	
Net income	303,860	272,864	
Cash and cash equivalents	18,623	19,133	3,530
Accounts receivable, less allowance	606,046	604,516	546,314
Total current assets	1,597,377	1,547,290	1,532,253
Total assets	4,052,090	4,065,462	4,035,801
Total current liabilities	1,189,862	1,111,973	44,539
Long-term liabilities	1,163,696	1,237,549	
Total shareholders' equity*	1,698,532	1,715,940	1,592,180

*The firm has no preferred stock.

Requirements

1. Calculate the following ratios for 2011 and 2010:
   a. Current ratio
   b. Accounts receivable turnover ratio
   c. Debt-to-equity ratio
   d. Profit margin ratio

    e. Return on equity

    f. Gross profit percentage

2. Suppose the changes from 2010 to 2011 in each of these ratios were consistent with the direction and size of the change for the past several years. For each ratio, explain what the trend in the ratio would indicate about the company.

P10-46A. *Calculate and analyze financial ratios. (LO 3).* The following financial statements were taken from the 2010 annual report of Presentations Company:

Presentations Company
Balance Sheets
(in thousands)

	December 31, 2010	December 31, 2009
ASSETS		
Current assets:		
Cash	$ 1,617	$1,220
Accounts receivable	1,925	3,112
Merchandise inventory	2,070	966
Prepaid expenses	188	149
Total current assets	$ 5,800	$5,447
Plant and equipment:		
Buildings, net	$ 4,457	$2,992
Equipment, net	1,293	1,045
Total plant and equipment	$ 5,750	$4,037
Total assets	$11,550	$9,484
LIABILITIES		
Current liabilities:		
Accounts payable	$ 1,817	$1,685
Notes payable	900	1,100
Total current liabilities	2,717	2,785
Long-term liabilities	3,500	2,000
Total liabilities	$ 6,217	$4,785
STOCKHOLDERS' EQUITY		
Common stock, no par value	$ 3,390	$3,042
Retained earnings	1,943	1,657
Total stockholders' equity	5,333	4,699
Total liabilities and stockholders' equity	$11,550	$9,484

Presentations Company
Income Statement
For the Year Ended December 31, 2010

Sales revenue	$12,228
Cost of goods sold	8,751
Gross profit on sales	3,477
Operating expenses:	
Depreciation—buildings and equipment	102
Other selling and administrative	2,667
Total expenses	2,769
Income before interest and taxes	708
Interest expense	168
Income before taxes	540
Income taxes	114
Net income	$ 426

Requirements

1. Calculate the following ratios for the year ended December 31, 2010.
   a. Debt-to-equity ratio
   b. Gross margin percentage
   c. Current ratio
   d. Profit margin ratio
2. What do the ratios indicate about the success of Presentations? What additional information would help you analyze the overall performance of this company?

P10-47A. *Calculate and analyze financial ratios. (LO 3).* The financial statements of For the Kitchen include the following items:

	At June 30, 2011	At June 30, 2010	At June 30, 2009
Balance sheet:			
Cash	$ 17,000	$ 12,000	$ 14,000
Investments (in trading securities)	10,000	16,000	20,000
Accounts receivable (net)	54,000	50,000	48,000
Inventory	75,000	70,000	73,000
Prepaid expenses	16,000	12,000	10,000
Total current assets	172,000	160,000	165,000
Total current liabilities	$140,000	$ 90,000	$ 75,000
Income statement for the year ended	June 30, 2011	June 30 2010	
Net credit sales	$420,000	$380,000	
Cost of goods sold	250,000	225,000	

Requirements

1. Compute the following ratios for the years ended June 30, 2011, and whenever possible for the year ended June 30, 2010. For each, indicate if the direction is favorable or unfavorable for the company.
   a. Current ratio
   b. Accounts receivable turnover
   c. Inventory turnover ratio
   d. Gross profit percentage (assume net credit sales = total sales)
2. Suppose the industry average for similar retail stores for the current ratio is 1.7. Does this information help you evaluate For the Kitchen's liquidity?

P10-48A. *Calculate and analyze financial ratios. (LO 3).* You are interested in investing in Teddy Company, and you have obtained the following balance sheets for the company for the past two years:

Teddy Company
Balance Sheets

	June 30, 2011	June 30, 2010
Current assets:		
Cash	$198,000	$ 90,000
Accounts receivable, net	210,000	116,000
Inventory	270,000	160,000
Prepaid rent	15,000	16,000
Total current assets	693,000	382,000
Equipment, net	280,000	260,000
Total assets	$973,000	$642,000
Total current liabilities	$306,000	$223,000
Long-term liabilities	219,000	117,000
Total liabilities	525,000	340,000
Common stockholders' equity	150,000	90,000
Retained earnings	298,000	212,000
Total liabilities and stockholders' equity	$973,000	$642,000

The following amounts were reported on the income statement for the year ended June 30, 2011:

Sales	$450,000
Cost of goods sold	215,000
Net income	80,000

Requirements

1. Compute as many of the financial statement ratios you have studied as possible with the information provided for Teddy Company. Some ratios can be computed for both years and others can be computed for only one year.
2. Would you invest in Teddy Company? Why or why not? What additional information would be helpful in making this decision?

Set B

P10-49B. *Discontinued operations and extraordinary item. (LO 1).* Each of the following items was found on the financial statements for Edge Company for the year ended December 31, 2011:

Income from continuing operations	$125,000
Gain on the sale of discontinued segment, net of taxes $9,000	50,000
Loss from operation of discontinued segment, net of taxes of $9,500	(34,500)
Gain on sale of equipment	10,000
Extraordinary loss from earthquake, net of taxes $45,000	(120,000)

Requirements

1. For each item listed, indicate the financial statement and appropriate section, if applicable, on which each would appear.
2. Provide a description of each item and give as many details of each item's financial statement presentation as possible.

P10-50B. *Prepare an income statement. (LO 1).* The Blues Corporation reported the following for the year ended December 31, 2011:

Sales	$425,000
Cost of goods sold	185,000
Interest income	4,000
Gain on sale of equipment	6,000
Selling and administrative expenses	18,000
Interest expense	2,000
Extraordinary gain	23,000
Loss from discontinued segment operations	(9,500)
Gain on disposal of discontinued segment	34,000

Requirement

Assume the corporation is subject to a 30% tax rate. Prepare an income statement for the year ended December 31, 2011.

P10-51B. *Prepare an income statement. (LO 1).* The following balances appeared in the general ledger for Ski Daddle Corporation at fiscal year end December 31, 2012:

Selling and administrative expenses	$ 45,000
Other revenues and gains	80,000
Operating expenses	110,000
Cost of goods sold	185,000
Net sales	325,000
Other expenses and losses	8,000

In addition, the following occurred during the year:

a. On August 20, a fire destroyed one of the company's warehouses resulting in an extraordinary loss of $35,000.
b. On October 31, the company discontinued one of its unprofitable segments. The loss from operations was $35,000. The assets of the segment were sold at a gain of $19,000.

Requirements

1. Assume Ski Daddle Corporation's income tax rate is 30%; prepare the income statement for the year ended December 31, 2012.
2. Calculate the earnings per share the company would report on the income statement assuming Ski Daddle had 100,000 shares of common stock outstanding during the year and paid preferred dividends of $15,000.

P10-52B. *Perform horizontal and vertical analysis. (LO 2).* Following are the income statements from Nappy's recent annual report:

Nappy Company
Income Statements

	For the Year Ended December 31,		
	2010	2009	2008
Net revenue	$26,971	$25,112	$23,512
Cost of sales	12,379	11,497	10,750
Selling, general, and administrative expenses	9,460	8,958	8,574
Amortization of intangible assets	145	138	165
Other expenses	204	224	356
Operating profit	4,783	4,295	3,667
Income from investments	323	280	160
Interest expense	(163)	(178)	(219)
Interest income	51	36	67
Income before income taxes	4,994	4,433	3,675
Income taxes	1,424	1,433	1,244
Net income	$ 3,570	$ 3,000	$ 2,431

Requirements

1. For each of the years shown, perform a vertical analysis, using sales as the base. Write a paragraph explaining what the analysis shows.
2. Using 2008 as the base year, perform a horizontal analysis for net revenue and cost of sales. What information does this analysis give you?

P10-53B. *Calculate and analyze financial ratios. (LO 3).* Macy's reported the following results in its 2008 10-K:

Macy's, Inc.		
Consolidated Balance Sheets		
(millions)		

	January 31, 2009	February 2, 2008
ASSETS		
Current Assets:		
Cash and cash equivalents	$ 1,306	$ 583
Receivables	439	463
Merchandise inventories	4,769	5,060
Supplies and prepaid expenses	226	218
Total Current Assets	6,740	6,324
Property and Equipment — net	10,442	10,991
Goodwill	3,743	9,133
Other Intangible Assets — net	719	831
Other Assets	501	510
Total Assets	$22,145	$27,789
LIABILITIES AND SHAREHOLDERS' EQUITY		
Current Liabilities:		
Short-term debt	$ 966	$ 666
Merchandise accounts payable	1,282	1,398
Accounts payable and accrued liabilities	2,628	2,729
Income taxes	28	344
Deferred income taxes	222	223
Total Current Liabilities	5,126	5,360
Long-Term Debt	8,733	9,087
Deferred Income Taxes	1,119	1,446
Other Liabilities	2,521	1,989
Shareholders' Equity:		
Common stock (420.1 and 419.7 shares outstanding)	5	5
Additional paid-in capital	5,663	5,609
Accumulated equity	2,008	7,032
Treasury stock	(2,544)	(2,557)
Accumulated other comprehensive loss	(486)	(182)
Total Shareholders' Equity	4,646	9,907
Total Liabilities and Shareholders' Equity	$22,145	$27,789

Macy's, Inc.
Consolidated Statements of Operations
(millions, except per share data)

	2008	2007	2006
Net sales	$ 24,892	$ 26,313	$ 26,970
Cost of sales	(15,009)	(15,677)	(16,019)
Inventory valuation adjustments – May integration	–	–	(178)
Gross margin	9,883	10,636	10,773
Selling, general and administrative expenses	(8,481)	(8,554)	(8,678)
Division consolidation costs and store closing related costs	(187)	–	–
Asset impairment charges	(211)	–	–
Goodwill impairment charges	(5,382)	–	–
May integration costs	–	(219)	(450)
Gains on the sale of accounts receivable	–	–	191
Operating income (loss)	(4,378)	1,863	1,836
Interest expense	(588)	(579)	(451)
Interest income	28	36	61
Income (loss) from continuing operations before income taxes	(4,938)	1,320	1,446
Federal, state and local income tax benefit (expense)	135	(411)	(458)
Income (loss) from continuing operations	(4,803)	909	988
Discontinued operations, net of income taxes	–	(16)	7
Net income (loss)	$ (4,803)	$ 893	$ 995
Basic earnings (loss) per share:			
Income (loss) from continuing operations	$ (11.40)	$ 2.04	$ 1.83
Income (loss) from discontinued operations	–	(.04)	.01
Net income (loss)	$ (11.40)	$ 2.00	$ 1.84
Diluted earnings (loss) per share:			
Income (loss) from continuing operations	$ (11.40)	$ 2.01	$ 1.80
Income (loss) from discontinued operations	–	(.04)	.01
Net income (loss)	$ (11.40)	$ 1.97	$ 1.81

Requirements

1. Calculate the following ratios for the most recent fiscal year:
    a. Current ratio
    b. Accounts receivable turnover ratio (Uses total sales in the numerator.)
    c. Debt-to-equity ratio
    d. Return on assets
    e. Return on equity
2. Comment on the results of your analysis.

P10-54B. *Calculate and analyze financial ratios. (LO 3).* The following information was taken from the annual report of ROM. The account balances are as of December 31, 2011.

Cash	$ 1,220
Accounts receivable	3,112
Merchandise inventory	966
Prepaid expenses	149
Buildings, net	2,992
Equipment, net	1,045
Accounts payable	1,685
Notes payable	1,100
Long-term liabilities	2,000
Common stock, no par value	3,042
Retained earnings	1,657
Sales for the year	10,200
Cost of goods sold	6,750
Net income	2,500

Requirements

1. Calculate the following ratios for 2011:
   a. Debt-to-equity ratio
   b. Gross profit percentage
   c. Current ratio
   d. Profit margin ratio
2. What do the ratios indicate about the success of ROM? What additional information would be useful to help you analyze the overall performance of this company?

P10-55B. *Calculate and analyze financial ratios. (LO 3).* The financial statements of Builder Bob's include the following items:

From the balance sheet:	At September 30, 2010	At September 30, 2009
Cash	$ 27,000	$ 22,000
Investments (short-term)	15,000	12,000
Accounts receivable (net)	44,000	40,000
Inventory	85,000	75,000
Prepaid rent	6,000	2,000
Total current assets	$177,000	$151,000
Total current liabilities	$120,000	$ 80,000

The income statement for the year ended September 30, 2010, includes the following:

Net credit sales*	$320,000
Cost of goods sold	150,000

*Assume all sales are credit sales.

Requirements

1. Compute the following ratios for the year ended September 30, 2010, and September 30, 2009:
   a. Current ratio (2009 and 2010)
   b. Accounts receivable turnover (2010 only)
   c. Inventory turnover ratio (2010 only)
   d. Gross margin percentage (2010 only)
2. Which financial statement users would be most interested in these ratios?
3. Suppose the industry average for similar retail stores for the current ratio is 1.2. Does this information help you evaluate Builder Bob's liquidity?

P10-56B. *Calculate and analyze financial ratios. (LO 3).* You are interested in investing in Apples and Nuts Company, and you have obtained the following balance sheets for the company for the past two years:

Apples and Nuts Company
Balance Sheets

	December 31, 2012	December 31, 2011
Current assets:		
Cash	$ 98,000	$ 90,000
Accounts receivable, net	310,000	216,000
Inventory	275,000	170,000
Prepaid rent	10,000	6,000
Total current assets	693,000	482,000
Equipment, net	180,000	258,000
Total assets	$873,000	$740,000
Total current liabilities	$206,000	$223,000
Long-term liabilities	219,000	217,000
Total liabilities	425,000	440,000
Common stockholders' equity	250,000	190,000
Retained earnings	198,000	110,000
Total liabilities and stockholders' equity	$873,000	$740,000

Net income for the year ended December 31, 2012, was $100,000.

Requirements

1. Compute as many of the financial statement ratios you have studied as possible with the information from Apples and Nuts Company. (Compute 2012 ratios.)
2. Would you invest in this company? Why or why not? What additional information would be helpful in making this decision?

Critical Thinking Problems

Risk and Control

Think about the risks of investing in a company and about the information provided by the financial ratios you studied in this chapter. Which financial ratios do you believe might give you information about the risks of investing in a company? Comment on those ratios from Apple Inc., which you calculated at the end of the chapter in the Chapter Summary Problem.

Ethics

Atlantis Company sells computer components and plans on borrowing some money to expand. After reading a lot about earnings management, Andy, the owner of Atlantis, has decided he should try to accelerate some sales to improve his financial statement ratios. He has called his best customers and asked them to make their usual January purchases by December 31. Andy told the customers he would allow them, until the end of February, to pay for the purchases, just as if they had made their purchases in January.

1. What do you think are the ethical implications of Andy's actions?
2. Which ratios will be improved by accelerating these sales?

Group Assignment

In groups, try to identify the type of company that is most likely indicated by the ratios shown next. The four types of companies represented are as follows: retail grocery, heavy machinery, restaurant, and drug manufacturer. Make notes on the arguments to support your position so that you can share them in a class discussion.

	Gross Margin Ratio	(Long-Term) Debt-to-Equity Ratio	Accounts Receivable Turnover Ratio	Inventory Turnover	Return on Equity Ratio
1	82.9%	25%	5.5 times	1.5 times	22.9%
2	33.7%	134%	49.3 times	11.2 times	3.6%
3	25.3%	147%	2.3 times	5.0 times	5.0%
4	37.4%	62%	34.9 times	32.9 times	15.7%

Internet Exercise: Papa John's International

Papa John's Pizza has become a widely recognized name in pizza. Papa John's 3,000 restaurants (about 75% are franchised) are scattered across the United States and 10 other countries. Examine how Papa John's compares with its competition.

IE10-1. Go to www.papajohns.com and click on Company Info at the bottom of the main page. Then select About Us and explore Papa John's Story and Our Pizza Story. What differentiates Papa John's from its competition?

IE10-2. Go to http://moneycentral.msn.com and get the stock quote for PZZA, Papa John's stock symbol. Identify the current price-to-earnings ratio and dividend yield ratio. What do these market indicators mean for Papa John's?

IE10-3. Go to http://moneycentral.msn.com and look up the information for Papa John's. Then, Select Financial Results from the menu on the left, and then select Key Ratios.
   a. Select Financial Condition from the list. Find the current ratio for Papa John's and the industry. Who would find these ratios of primary interest? Identify the debt-to-equity ratio for Papa John's and the industry. Is Papa John's primarily financed by debt or equity? How can you tell?
   b. Select Investment Returns from the list. Identify return on equity and return on assets for Papa John's and the industry. What do these ratios measure?
   c. Select Ten-Year Summary from the list. Review the information provided for return on equity and return on assets. What additional information is revealed about Papa John's financial position? Is this information helpful?

IE10-4. Review the information recorded earlier. Does Papa John's compare favorably with industry averages? Support your judgment with at least two observations.

Appendix 10A

Comprehensive Income

In the chapter, you learned that the Financial Accounting Standards Board (FASB) has defined two items that companies need to separate from regular earnings on financial statements: discontinued operations and extraordinary items. There is a third item—**comprehensive income**.

Even though most transactions that affect shareholders' equity are found on the income statement—revenues and expenses—there are a small number of transactions that affect shareholders' equity that are excluded from the calculation of net income. We already know about two of them:

1. Owners making contributions (paid-in capital)
2. Owners receiving dividends

In addition to these two, there are several other transactions that affect equity without going through the income statement. The most common examples of these transactions are (1) unrealized gains and losses from foreign currency translations and (2) unrealized gains and losses on certain investments. Rather than including either of these kinds of gains and losses on the income statement, they are reported as a direct adjustment to equity. The reason is that these items do not really reflect a firm's performance, so firms have lobbied to have them kept out of the calculation of earnings. To keep these transactions from getting lost among all the financial statement numbers, the FASB requires the reporting of net income plus these other transactions that affect shareholders' equity in an amount called comprehensive income. Comprehensive income includes all changes in shareholders' equity during a period except those changes in equity resulting from contributions by shareholders and distributions to shareholders. There are two parts of comprehensive income: net income and *other comprehensive income*. We know what types of transactions are included in net income—revenues, expenses, discontinued operations, and extraordinary items. Items included in other comprehensive income include unrealized gains and losses from foreign currency translation and unrealized gains and losses on certain types of investments. Exhibit 10A.1 on the following page shows all of the items that affect shareholders' equity.

L.O.5
Define comprehensive income and explain how it changes.

Comprehensive income is the total of all items that affect shareholders' equity except transactions with the owners; comprehensive income has two parts: net income and other comprehensive income.

What is the purpose of having a statement of comprehensive income rather than a simple income statement?

Your Turn 10A

EXHIBIT 10.A1

Comprehensive Income

The items in the left column appear on the financial statements in the equity classifications shown in the right column.

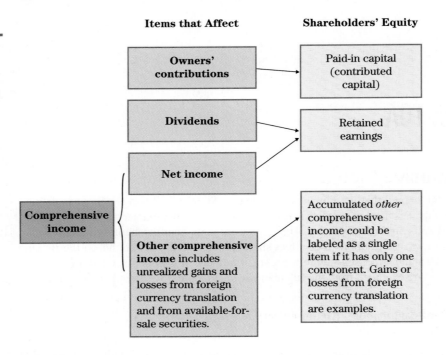

Solution to YOUR TURN Appendix 10A:

The FASB wants to make the changes to shareholders' equity that do not affect net income more apparent to financial statement users.

Short Exercises

SE10A-1A. *Comprehensive income. (LO 5).* Give an example of a gain or loss that would be excluded from the income statement and shown directly on the balance sheet as part of accumulated other comprehensive income.

SE10A-2B. *Comprehensive income. (LO 5).* Give an example of an item (other than a gain or loss) that would be excluded from the income statement and shown directly on the balance sheet as part of accumulated other comprehensive income.

Appendix 10B

Investments in Securities

You have learned that certain gains and losses related to investments may be included in other comprehensive income (Appendix 10A). We will take a closer look at how a firm accounts for its investments in the securities of another firm. You will see how gains and losses on some of these investments are reported as part of comprehensive income.

In addition to assets that a firm uses in its main line of business, a firm will often invest its extra cash in investments in other firms. For example, Apple's 2008 balance sheet shows over $12.6 billion of short-term investments. These are investments in the stocks of other firms. For example, Apple may want to own some stock in Intel. Like individual and other investors, firms can go to the stock market and purchase any of the stocks trading in that market. Firms can have both short- and long-term investments, depending on how long they plan to keep the investments. Although our focus in this chapter has been on long-term assets, we'll take a brief look at both short-term and long-term investments.

When interest rates are low, a company's extra cash—cash not immediately needed—may earn more in the stock market or bond market than it would in a bank savings account or certificate of deposit. That is one reason a company buys stocks and bonds of other companies with its extra cash. For entities such as banks and insurance companies, investing cash in other companies is a crucial part of managing their assets. Stocks are called equity securities and bonds are debt securities. Both may be purchased with a company's extra cash. When a company buys another company's debt securities or less than 20% of its equity securities, the accounting rules require firms to classify their investments in securities into one of three categories: held to maturity, trading, or available for sale.

Held-to-Maturity Securities

Sometimes a company purchases debt securities and intends to keep them until they mature. Bonds have a maturity date, but equity securities do not. If a company has the intention of keeping the debt securities until maturity and their financial condition indicates that they should be able to do this, the securities will be classified as **held-to-maturity securities**. Such investments are recorded at cost, and they are reported on the balance sheet. No matter how much held-to-maturity investments are worth on the market, a company will always report them at cost when preparing its balance sheet.

Trading Securities

If a company buys the securities solely to trade them and make a short-term profit, the company will classify them as **trading securities**. The balance sheet shows trading securities at their market value. A company obtains the current value of the investments from the *Wall Street Journal* or a similar source of market prices. Those values are then shown on the balance sheet. Updating the accounting records to show the securities at their market value is called *marking to market*. If the securities' cost is lower than market value, then the company will record the difference as an unrealized gain. If the securities' cost is higher than market value, then the company will record the difference as an unrealized loss. Remember, *realizing* means actually getting something. Any gain or loss on an investment the company is holding (holding means *not* selling) is something the company does not get (a gain) or does not give up (a loss) until the company sells the securities. **Unrealized gains or losses** are gains or losses on securities that have not been sold. Such a

Held-to-maturity securities are investments in debt securities that the company plans to hold until they mature.

Trading securities are investments in debt and equity securities that the company has purchased to make a short-term profit.

Unrealized gain or loss is when an increase or decrease in the market value of a company's investments in securities is recognized either on the income statement (for trading securities) or in other comprehensive income in the equity section of the balance sheet (for available-for-sale securities) when the financial statements are prepared, even though the securities have *not* been sold.

gain or loss may also be called a *holding gain* or *loss*. The unrealized gains and losses from trading securities are reported on the income statement.

For example, suppose Avia Company has invested $130,000 of its extra cash in securities—stocks and bonds traded on the stock and bond markets. At the end of the year, the securities that cost Avia $130,000 have a market value of $125,000. On the income statement for the year, Avia will show an unrealized loss of $5,000. The loss is recorded as an adjustment made before the financial statements are prepared.

The securities' new value of $125,000 (originally $130,000 minus loss of $5,000) has replaced their original cost. Now, $125,000 will be the "cost" and will be compared to the market value on the date of the next balance sheet. Remember, the company purchased these trading securities as investments to trade in the short run, so the firm's investment portfolio is likely to look very different at the next balance sheet date.

Available-for-Sale Securities

Sometimes a company is not sure how long it will keep the securities it has purchased. If the company does not intend to sell the securities in the short term for a quick profit or does not intend to hold them until maturity, the company will classify the securities as **available for sale**. Every year, when it is time to prepare the annual balance sheet, the cost of this group of securities is compared to the market value at the balance sheet date. The book value of the securities is then adjusted to market value, and the corresponding gain or loss is reported in shareholders' equity. Such a gain or loss is called an *unrealized* or *holding* gain or loss, just as it is called for trading securities. But these gains and losses do not go on the income statement. Instead, they are included as part of accumulated other comprehensive income in the shareholders' equity section of the balance sheet.

> **Available-for-sale securities** are investments the company may hold or sell; the company's intention is not clear enough to use one of the other categories—*held to maturity* or *trading*.

Your Turn 10B

A corporation has invested $50,000 in the securities of other companies. At the end of the year, that corporation's portfolio has a market value of $52,000. Describe where these securities would be shown on the annual financial statements and at what amount under each of the conditions described.

1. The investment is classified as trading securities.
2. The investment is classified as available for sale.
3. The investment is classified as held to maturity.

Suppose Avia Company classified its portfolio of securities that cost $130,000 as available for sale. If the market value of the securities is $125,000 at the date of the balance sheet, the securities must be shown on the balance sheet at the lower amount. In this case, the unrealized loss will *not* be shown on the income statement. Instead of going through net income to retained earnings, the loss will go directly to the shareholders' equity section of the balance sheet. The loss will be shown after retained earnings, either alone and labeled as an unrealized loss from investments in securities, or combined with other non-income statement gains and losses and labeled as *accumulated other comprehensive income*.

Impairment

When any asset's value has declined permanently below its book value, it must be written down. This is true no matter how the asset is classified. As you know, accountants do not want to overstate assets. This is where the real problem with valuing investments has come in the last few years. Firms with large investments in mortgage-related securities have had to reduce the value of those assets on their balance sheets. The balancing part of the transaction in the accounting equation is a charge to income (i.e., a loss). Both the FASB and the IASB have grappled with this issue, and they have relaxed the rules forcing the write-down of some of these securities.

What happens when the securities stop trading in active markets? How does a firm calculate securities' value for the balance sheet? Should the loss go on the income statement or should it go directly to shareholders' equity? How do you determine if the decline in value is permanent? These are important questions that both the FASB and the IASB continue to debate, and they point out that accounting is not exact. It involves many crucial judgments. Keep an eye out for developments on this topic in the financial press.

Selling the Securities

When a firm sells any of these securities—trading, available for sale, or held to maturity—the gain or loss on the sale is calculated like other accounting gains and losses. The book value of the security at the time of the sale is compared to the selling price. The selling price is often called the proceeds from the sale. If the book value is greater than the proceeds, the firm will record a loss on the sale. If the book value is less than the proceeds, the firm will record a gain on the sale. Gains and losses from the actual sale of the securities are both *realized* (the sale has actually happened) and *recognized* (the relevant amounts are shown on the income statement).

Solution to YOUR TURN Appendix 10B:

1. The securities will be shown in the current asset section of the balance sheet at a value of $52,000. The write-up will be balanced with a $2,000 unrealized gain on the income statement.
2. The securities will be shown in either the current asset or the long-term asset section of the balance sheet (depending on a firm's intent) at a value of $52,000. The write-up will be balanced with a $2,000 unrealized gain that will go directly to equity, as part of accumulated other comprehensive income.
3. The securities will be shown at their cost of $50,000 in the long-term asset section of the balance sheet (unless the debt securities are maturing in the coming year, in which case they would be current assets).

Short Exercises

All of the A exercises can be found within MyAccountingLab, an online homework and practice environment.

SE10B-1A. *Investments. (LO 6).* In January 2010, Bowers Company had some extra cash and purchased the stock of various companies with the objective of making a profit in the short run. The cost of Bowers' portfolio was $36,500. On December 31, 2010, the date of the balance sheet, the market value of the portfolio was $25,200. How would this decrease in value be reflected in Bowers' financial statements for the year ended December 31, 2010?

SE10B-2B. *Investments. (LO 6).* In April 2011, Convey Company had some extra cash and purchased the stock of various companies with the objective of making a profit in the short run. The cost of Convey's portfolio was $79,450. At December 31, 2011, the date of the balance sheet, the market value of the portfolio was $85,200. How would this increase in value be reflected in Convey's financial statements for the year ended December 31, 2011?

Exercises
Set A

E10B-3A. *Investments. (LO 6).* Omicron Corporation invested $125,000 of its extra cash in securities. Under each of the following independent scenarios, (a) calculate the amount at which the investments would be valued for the year-end balance sheet, and (b) indicate how the effect of these scenarios should be reported on the other financial statements, if at all.
1. All the securities were debt securities, with a maturity date in two years. Omicron will hold the securities until they mature. The market value of the securities at year end was $123,000.
2. Omicron purchased the securities for trading, hoping to make a quick profit. At year end the market value of the securities was $120,000.
3. Omicron is uncertain about how long it will hold the securities. At year end the market value of the securities is $126,000.

E10B-4A. *Investments. (LO 6).* Kinsey Scales invested $164,000 of its extra cash in securities. Under each of the following independent scenarios, (a) calculate the amount at which the investments would be valued for the year-end balance sheet, and (b) indicate how these scenarios should be reported on the other financial statements, if at all.

1. All the securities were debt securities, with a maturity date in two years. Kinsey will hold the securities until they mature. The market value of the securities at year end was $158,000.
2. Kinsey purchased the securities for trading, hoping to make a quick profit. At year end the market value of the securities was $162,000.
3. Kinsey is uncertain about how long it will hold the securities. At year end the market value of the securities is $167,000.

Set B

E10B-5B. *Investments. (LO 6).* During 2010, Nike invested $500,000 of extra cash in securities. Of the total amount invested, $275,000 was invested in bonds that Nike plans to hold until maturity (the bonds were issued at par value); $165,000 was invested in various equity securities that Nike plans to hold for an indefinite period of time; and $60,000 was invested in the stock of various companies that Nike intends to trade to make a short-term profit. At the end of the year, the market value of the held-to-maturity securities was $200,000; the market value of the trading securities was $145,000; and the market value of the available-for-sale securities was $75,000. Use the accounting equation to record all adjustments required at year end, and indicate how the effects of each group of securities will be reported on the financial statements.

E10B-6B. *Investments. (LO 6).* During 2009, Arctic Fans & Blowers invested $245,000 of extra cash in securities. Of the total amount invested, $115,000 was invested in bonds that Arctic plans to hold until maturity (the bonds were issued at par); $55,000 was invested in various equity securities that Arctic plans to hold for an indefinite period of time; and $75,000 was invested in the stock of various companies that Arctic intends to trade to make a short-term profit. At the end of the year, the market value of the held-to-maturity securities was $108,000; the market value of the trading securities was $52,000; and the market value of the available-for-sale securities was $85,000. Use the accounting equation to record all adjustments required at year end and indicate how the effects of each group of securities will be reported on the financial statements.

11

Quality of Earnings, Corporate Governance, and IFRS

ETHICS Matters

Would You Blow the Whistle on Fraud?

Would you blow the whistle on fraud? In 2002, Sherron Watkins of Enron, Cynthia Cooper of WorldCom, and Coleen Rowley of the FBI were *Time* magazine's "People of the Year." These women were credited with blowing the whistle on fraud in their respective organizations. The Sarbanes-Oxley (SOX) Act of 2002 requires that firms have a hotline to make it easier for whistle-blowers to anonymously report any suspicious actions or behavior going on in the company, particularly as it pertains to financial information. However, a study conducted to evaluate the effectiveness of this part of the law found that the number of frauds detected by employees blowing the whistle declined from 21% before SOX to 16% five years later. Why? According to the study, "Who Blows the Whistle on Corporate Fraud?" 82% of the cases with named employees resulted in the whistleblower being fired, quitting under duress, or having his or her responsibilities significantly changed as a result of the disclosure of the fraud. Clearly, there is a disincentive to disclosing your identity when it comes to being a whistleblower. In addition to requiring the availability of an anonymous hotline for reporting fraud, SOX also prohibits a company from demoting, firing, threatening, or harassing someone for the legal act of disclosing suspected fraud in the company. As you have observed, however, sometimes a person or a company does not abide by the law. Would you blow the whistle on fraud? It's a matter of ethics.

Source: *"Study: Sarbox Curbs Fraud Whistleblowing,"* by Sara Johnson. CFO.com, February 13, 2007.

LEARNING OBJECTIVES

When you are finished studying Chapter 11, you should be able to:

1. Explain Wall Street's emphasis on earnings and the potential problems that result from this emphasis.

2. Define quality of earnings and explain how it is measured.

3. Recognize the common ways that firms can manipulate earnings.

4. Describe the corporate accounting failures of the early 2000s.

5. Explain the requirements of the Sarbanes-Oxley Act of 2002.

6. Evaluate a firm's corporate governance.

7. Describe the differences between IFRS and U.S. GAAP.

511

L.O.1
Explain Wall Street's
emphasis on earnings and
the potential problems that
result from this emphasis.

Why Are Earnings Important?

You have learned about the four basic financial statements and the notes to the financial statements. To wrap up your introduction to financial accounting, we are going to step back and look at the big picture. What do investors focus on when they evaluate a firm's financial statements? How accurate is the information? Who, or what, stands behind the information to assure investors that it is truthful and reliable? These are just a few of the questions we will consider in this chapter. We start with the market's focus on earnings, which appears on the income statement.

How often have you read or heard about a firm's earnings? Managers estimate earnings and disclose those estimates to the public. Financial analysts study managements' earnings estimates and announce their own expected earnings for the firm. Among the hundreds of measurements that investors consider—gross domestic product (GDP), housing starts, interest rates, unemployment figures, and budget deficits, to name a few—there is one number that Wall Street simply calls "the number." A firm's stock price moves up when earnings exceed analysts' forecasts and down when reported earnings do not meet the forecasts. According to Alex Berenson, a financial reporter for the *New York Times* and author of *The Number: How the Drive for Quarterly Earnings Corrupted Wall Street and Corporate America*, "Earnings per share is the number for which all other numbers are sacrificed." As you know, accountants define *earnings per share* as net income divided by the weighted average number of outstanding shares of (common) stock.

As Berenson points out, earnings alone cannot accurately reveal the state of a firm's financial performance. A narrow focus on a single number can result in serious miscommunication between the firm and its investors. However, reported earnings have a real effect on a firm's stock price.

Your Turn 11-1

Describe why earnings is such an important number.

L.O.2
Define quality of earnings
and explain how it is
measured.

The Quality of Earnings

As you have learned, investors typically use earnings per share to evaluate a firm's performance. How accurate and reliable is this number? **Quality of earnings** is a term accountants use to describe how well a reported earnings number communicates the firm's true performance. The quality of earnings is a subjective concept, and few people agree on the definition. Bernstein and Wild, two accounting authors,[1] identify three ways to evaluate the quality of earnings.

Quality of earnings refers to
how well a reported earnings
number communicates the firm's
true performance.

1. Firms that make more conservative choices of accounting principles often have a higher quality of earnings.
2. Firms that face fewer internal and external risks that threaten their survival and profitability often have a higher quality of earnings.
3. Firms that recognize revenue early or postpone recognition of expenses often have a lower quality of earnings.

Sometimes the accounting choices managers make are classified as conservative or aggressive. Conservative choices are those that reduce net income and assets or increase liabilities. Aggressive choices are those that increase net income and assets or decrease liabilities. Potentially understating income or assets is more conservative than potentially overstating income or assets. Can you see why this is true? If a firm overstates earnings, shareholders may sue the firm and its auditors, but if a firm understates earnings, shareholders are less likely to be disappointed. Higher-quality earnings are associated with more conservative accounting choices. Here are some examples.

Recall that a firm must estimate the useful life and salvage value of depreciable assets, make inventory cost flow assumptions such as LIFO or FIFO, and estimate bad debts expense. Each of these choices will affect the quality of the firm's reported earnings. Consider a capital-intensive company in the manufacturing sector. Firms such as General Motors and Dow Chemical have huge investments in property, plant, and equipment. The income statements for these firms will have a significant amount of depreciation expense for manufacturing facilities and equipment.

---

[1]Bernstein, L. and J. Wild. 2000. *Analysis of Financial Statements*. New York: McGraw-Hill.

The amount of that expense will depend on how management estimates the useful lives and salvage values of the assets. What kind of choices would make earnings appear larger? The longer the estimated useful lives of property, plant, and equipment, and the larger the estimated salvage values, the smaller the annual depreciation expense. The smaller the depreciation expense, the larger the reported earnings. In cases such as depreciation, the more discretion management has, the more potential there is for a lower quality of the related earnings. Having more depreciable assets means more estimates and potentially a lower quality of earnings because managers can make choices that increase or decrease earnings.

In other cases, a manager views a particular choice as producing higher-quality earnings than another. Consider inventory methods. When a company chooses FIFO, the older inventory costs are matched with the sales revenue on the income statement. When a company chooses LIFO, however, the more recent costs are shown on the income statement. Which method produces a higher quality of earnings number? While there is some disagreement about this and situations where it may not hold, analysts generally believe that LIFO produces a better income statement number because the costs used are more current. As a result LIFO produces a higher quality of earnings number than FIFO produces.

Next, we will discuss three common ways that firms can manipulate earnings, reducing the quality of their earnings. Then, we will turn to the Sarbanes-Oxley Act, the goal of which is to increase the quality of earnings and make financial reporting more transparent.

What makes one firm's earnings higher in quality than another's?

Your Turn 11-2

Common Ways to Manipulate Earnings

You have learned that investors are concerned about the quality of firms' earnings. After studying basic financial accounting, you should be able to see that many of the amounts on the financial statements are estimates. A great deal of judgment goes into the calculations, and that often results in questions about the truthfulness and reliability of the financial statements. Whenever judgment is involved, there is the potential for someone to take advantage of the opportunity to make self-serving decisions. It is important that the users of financial statements study those statements with healthy skepticism. Keep in mind, however, that the vast majority of firms' managers and accountants do their best to make sound, ethical judgments.

To help you increase your understanding of the numbers on the financial statements, we will look at three specific accounting procedures that often reduce the quality of earnings. Unfortunately, firms may use these procedures to "cook the books." **Cooking the books** is a slang term that means to manipulate or falsify the accounting records to make the company's financial performance look better than it actually is. Although there are numerous activities used to manage earnings, many of which can be very complicated, the Securities and Exchange Commission identifies three activities that deserve special attention when you are evaluating a company's financial performance:

1. Big bath charges
2. Cookie jar reserves
3. Revenue recognition

Big Bath Charges

The expression "big bath charges" was made famous among accountants in a 1998 speech by then chairman of the SEC, Arthur Levitt, to the New York University Center for Law and Business. According to the **big bath** theory of corporate financial reporting, one way to manage earnings is to maximize a current loss by recording expenses that actually belong on future income statements.

When a firm is not going to meet its earnings expectations, the firm's managers "clean up" the balance sheet by writing off any asset that looks like it may need to be written off in the next few years. This is, of course, a clear violation of the matching principle. The reasoning goes something like this: As long as our firm is going to be punished by Wall Street for missing our

L.O.3
Recognize the common ways that firms can manipulate earnings.

Cooking the books is a slang expression that means to manipulate or falsify the firm's accounting records to make the firm's financial performance or position look better than it actually is.

Big bath is an expression that describes a violation of GAAP's matching principle in which more expenses are taken in a bad year than are actually justified, so fewer expenses can be taken in future years.

earnings number, we might as well go ahead and miss it big. Moving as many expenses as we can from future periods into the current period will help us in the future.

Accounting researchers have found evidence to support this practice by studying firms that either exceed or miss the analysts' forecasts. A significant number of firms just make their earnings forecast by a very small margin. However, when a firm misses its earnings forecast, the amount by which it misses is larger, on average, than the margin for firms that make their forecasts. This is consistent with the idea of taking a *big* bath as long as you are getting in the tub.

How can you identify the big bath type of accounting practice? Read the following material when you are evaluating a company's earnings:

- Several years of financial statements rather than just a single year; look for unusual expenses and write-offs that appear out of step with previous years
- The notes to the financial statements
- Management's discussion and analysis about the company's performance in newspaper and business magazines

Cookie Jar Reserves

> **Cookie jar reserves** is an expression that describes an account, usually a liability, that is established by recognizing an estimated expense inaccurately. When the expenditures actually occur, the firm charges them against the reserve rather than against income. This practice is a violation of the matching principle.

Another way to manage earnings is to use reserve accounts to record expenses early and make future earnings look good. This is called using **cookie jar reserves**. Using reserve accounts is a way to stash away amounts that can help the firm increase earnings in the future if and when the earnings are needed to meet earnings forecasts. The word *reserve* is used in many ways, so be aware of its ambiguity when you see it in a firm's financial statements or in the financial press. Usually it does *not* involve cash. If you want to know if a reserve is a cash amount, look for the term *cash reserve* rather than simply *reserve*.

One example of something that might be called a reserve is related to accounts receivable. You learned about the allowance method for estimating bad debts. A firm with a significant amount of uncollectible accounts must estimate future bad debts related to current sales so that the bad debts expense can be recorded in the same period as the sales to which it relates. As you know, bad debts expense is an estimate, and the corresponding amount is recorded in an account called the allowance for bad debts (or uncollectible accounts). This is often called a reserve for bad debts. Banks, for example, might mention loan loss reserves in their financial statements. This accounting rule creates an opportunity for a firm to "manage" one of its expenses and, consequently, manipulate earnings.

Suppose a firm had credit sales of $1,000,000 in Year 1 and estimated that related bad debts would be 5% of sales, or $50,000. The firm would record the following:

Assets	=	Liabilities	+	Shareholders' equity		
				Contributed capital	+	Retained earnings
Allowance for bad debts (50,000)						Bad debts expense (50,000)

This would reduce income by $50,000 in Year 1. During Year 2, as the actual customers who will not pay are identified and written off, no bad debts expense is recorded. Instead, the accounts are written off against the allowance for bad debts. Suppose that during Year 2, $48,000 worth of accounts are written off, leaving a balance of $2,000 in the allowance for bad debts. Now, at the end of Year 2, the firm must estimate its future bad debts from credit sales in Year 2. Whatever the estimate, the bad debts expense recorded for Year 2 will be $2,000 less than the estimate because the reserve—the allowance for bad debts—still has $2,000 left over from Year 1. (This example assumes the firm uses the accounts receivable method of estimating bad debts expense.)

Now go back to Year 1 and suppose that the firm is having a very poor year and it will definitely miss the analysts' earnings forecasts for the year. When the firm's accountant is recording the bad debts expense for the year, there may be a temptation to record an amount that exceeds the actual estimate. Why? As long as Year 1 is a bad year, the firm might as well take as many expenses as possible, leaving fewer for future accounting periods. Again, this is a clear violation of the matching principle.

Suppose the firm recorded $60,000 worth of bad debts expense at the end of Year 1. The same amount will be recorded in the allowance for bad debts. Now if $48,000 worth of bad debts are actually written off in Year 2, the balance in the allowance for bad debts at the end of Year 2 will be $12,000 rather than $2,000—if the allowance for bad debts had been recorded at the correct estimate of $50,000. The firm now has a cushion of $12,000 to reduce Year 2's bad debts expense if it needs it to increase earnings in Year 2. Using a reserve such as the allowance for bad debts to manipulate or to smooth earnings is a common way to use cookie jar reserves.

Cookie jar reserves and big bath charges are both ways for firms to allocate expenses to the wrong accounting periods to provide the most benefit. Sometimes a firm has a goal of smoothing earnings—keeping them from having big fluctuations; at other times a firm wants to shift expenses from the future to the present to improve future earnings.

How can you tell if a firm is using cookie jar reserves? Watch for trends in the reported amounts for these reserves. Often, the specific amounts are not shown in the statements but are given in the detailed notes to the financial statements. Analyzing changes in ratios related to the reserves may also be helpful.

Revenue Recognition

A third way to manage earnings is to use improper revenue recognition techniques. In the first few chapters, you learned that generally accepted accounting principles (GAAP) allow a firm to recognize revenue when (1) the firm has earned it and (2) collection is reasonably assured. This accounting principle leaves some room for interpretation and judgment. A firm might violate this principle by recognizing revenue prematurely or by creating totally fictitious revenue. Improperly recognizing revenue can help a firm to meet analysts' earnings forecasts and to keep the firm's stock price rising. There are cases of executives making millions of dollars by selling their stock in the firm when the stock price was inflated due to fraudulent earnings.

Here are some examples of how firms have improperly recognized revenue:

- Recorded sales of merchandise at the end of the quarter despite the fact that the goods were not delivered to the customer until the beginning of the following quarter
- Routinely kept their books open after the end of the accounting period to continue recording sales until the sales goals for the period were met
- Recorded sales of merchandise shipped to customers who had not placed orders for the merchandise
- Shipped goods to salespeople in the field and recorded the sales even though the salespeople had not delivered the goods to customers
- Shipped goods off-site to locations they controlled and recorded those shipments as sales revenue
- Created fictitious documents for both the purchase of goods and the subsequent sale of those goods to fictitious customers

When you analyze a firm's financial statements, how can you identify these types of revenue recognition problems? First, firms disclose their revenue recognition policies in the first note of the notes to the financial statements. If a firm has recently changed its revenue recognition policy, you should study the reasons and review the prior years' revenue patterns. Analyzing the relationship between sales and accounts receivable is quite useful in identifying early or fictitious revenue recognition. If accounts receivable as a percentage of sales is increasing, you should investigate the cause. Every industry or business sector has its own type of revenue recognition problem. You need to understand the way revenue is recognized in your company's accounting system to know the potential for problems with early or late revenue recognition.

What We Learned from the Business Scandals of the Early 2000s

L.O.4
Describe the corporate accounting failures of the early 2000s.

Even with the concern over quality of earnings and managers' potential to manipulate earnings with a big bath, cookie jar reserves, or improper revenue recognition, Congress has rarely interfered with accounting standards. Until early this century, the 1933 and 1934 Securities Acts were the governing laws for publicly-traded firms and their auditors. However, the scandals and financial failures of the early 2000s prompted Congress to pass the Sarbanes-Oxley Act of 2002. Sponsored by Senator Paul Sarbanes of Maryland, now retired, and Congressman Michael Oxley of Ohio, the act brought the topic of corporate governance into the headlines. Even a decade later, the Sarbanes-Oxley Act continues to be at the forefront of financial reporting.

Corporate governance has many definitions. Simply stated, it is the way a firm governs itself, as executed by the board of directors. **Corporate governance** has been defined as a process carried out by the board of directors to provide direction and oversight on behalf of all the company's stakeholders—owners, suppliers, and customers. The term has also been defined as a set of relationships between the board of directors, management, shareholders, auditors, and any others with a stake in the company. Corporate governance is not a new concept—corporations have been governing themselves for years. However, accounting scandals bring the topic to the attention of the media, government officials, and the general public.

Accounting scandals and the resulting business failures are not a modern-day phenomenon. One of the biggest business failures in history occurred in 1931, when Insull Utility Investment collapsed under the weight of a complex corporate structure held together by creative accounting. At the time, the press dubbed Insull the biggest business failure in the history of the world. Fast forward to 2001 (the collapse of one of the world's largest energy companies, Enron) and to 2002 (the bankruptcy of WorldCom). These failures were huge and had an enormous impact on our economy and the employees of the companies, but failures are not new. However, there are lessons to be learned from them.

See if you can find a recent update on the scandals shown in Exhibit 1.18 in Chapter 1. One of the best ways you can be an intelligent investor, manager, or employee is to stay up to date. Read current financial publications and keep up with news events. One of the positive things to come out of these business failures and scandals is the increased attention the news media gives business issues.

What have we learned from the business failures of the past decade? Following is just a sampling:

> **Corporate governance** is the way a firm governs itself, as executed by the board of directors. Corporate governance is also described as the set of relationships between the board of directors, management, shareholders, auditors, and any others with a stake in the company.

1. Some corporate executives will do almost anything to meet earnings expectations and keep the firm's stock price stable or rising. Often, the goal is one of personal enrichment through the executives' exercise of options and the sale of company stock. This problem typically arises when executive compensation is specifically linked to stock performance or when executives receive significant stock options for the firm's stock.
2. The ethical climate in a firm is set by top management. Chief executive officers and chief financial officers must establish and demand the integrity of the firm's disclosures—both financial and nonfinancial.
3. External auditors and their clients can get too close. An auditor's independence is a necessary condition for a meaningful audit, and auditing firms need to take a close look at the relationship(s) between a firm and its external auditors.
4. Application of GAAP is subject to significant management discretion, and firms must make their earnings more transparent.
5. No matter how good or how effective the accounting principles are, there is no way for accounting standards to stop fraud. Auditors and the SEC, however, may be able to make some progress in reducing fraud.
6. Financial statements are only part of the information investors and creditors need to evaluate a company's past, present, and future. Overreliance on a single amount—earnings per share—can be a disaster.

As it did in the 1930s with the passage of the Securities Acts of 1933 and 1934, Congress responded to the corporate failures that came to light in the early 2000s with legislation—the Sarbanes-Oxley Act of 2002. As you read about the law, think about the problems it is meant to address. Consider, too, the effects of the recession of 2008–2009 on Congressional action.

Your Turn 11-3   What do you think auditors learned from the financial failures of the 2000s?

The Sarbanes-Oxley Act of 2002

L.O.5
Explain the requirements
of the Sarbanes-Oxley Act
of 2002.

No one will be able to navigate successfully in the business world without some knowledge of the Sarbanes-Oxley Act of 2002. All publicly-traded companies and any international companies that trade on the U.S. stock exchanges must comply with this law. Exhibit 11.1 on the following page summarizes the key provisions of the law. We will look at the major groups affected by the Sarbanes-Oxley Act and discuss how the law affects them.

Key Players in Corporate Governance

The Sarbanes-Oxley (SOX) Act has significant implications for the following four groups:

1. Management
   - The Chief Executive Officer (CEO) and Chief Financial Officer (CFO) are responsible for the firm's internal controls. The SOX Act requires the company to include with its annual report a separate report on the effectiveness of the company's internal controls. The firm's external auditors must attest to the accuracy of the internal control report.
   - Management has the ultimate responsibility for the accuracy of the financial statements and the accompanying notes. In most firms, that responsibility is delegated to lower-level managers, but top management cannot escape ultimate legal responsibility. SOX requires the CEO and the CFO to certify the annual financial statements—they will swear that they have reviewed the statements and that, based on their knowledge, the report does not contain any false statements and does not omit any significant facts.
   - As you read earlier in the chapter, firms must provide a mechanism for the anonymous reporting of fraudulent activities in the company, including a hotline for the reporting. Whistle-blower protection is extended to company employees who lawfully disclose information that the employee reasonably believes constitutes a violation of securities laws or any law that deals with fraud against shareholders. According to SOX, no officer or agent of the company may "discharge, demote, suspend, threaten, harass, or in any other manner discriminate against an employee in the terms and conditions of employment because of any lawful act done by the employee." That means that the company cannot punish a person in any way for blowing the whistle—disclosing suspected fraud in the company.

2. The board of directors (BOD)
   - These are the people who are elected by stockholders to establish general corporate policies and make decisions on major company issues, such as dividend policies. Members of the board are elected by the shareholders to represent the interests of shareholders.
   - The part of the board of directors responsible for overseeing the financial matters of the firm is the audit committee. Members of this committee are concerned with the firm's controls over financial reporting and with overseeing the external auditors.
   - SOX requires the audit committee to be made up of independent directors from the board of directors. Company managers cannot be on the committee. The audit committee is responsible for hiring, compensating, and overseeing the work of any public accounting firm hired by the company.

3. External auditors
   - These are accountants specifically trained to examine the firm's financial statements and financial controls and report on the statements to the shareholders. External auditors give an opinion on whether or not the firm's financial statements fairly present the financial position and the results of operations in accordance with GAAP. As you know, the SEC requires all publicly-traded firms to have an annual audit of the financial statements by external auditors.
   - SOX requires that auditors remain independent of their clients to ensure objectivity. The SEC has always had rules about auditor independence, but the law strengthens these rules. For example, auditors can no longer provide information processing or bookkeeping services to their audit clients.
   - SOX also requires that the auditor report to the client's audit committee, which is part of the board of directors, rather than to the client's management team.

EXHIBIT 11.1

Key Provisions of the Sarbanes-Oxley Act of 2002

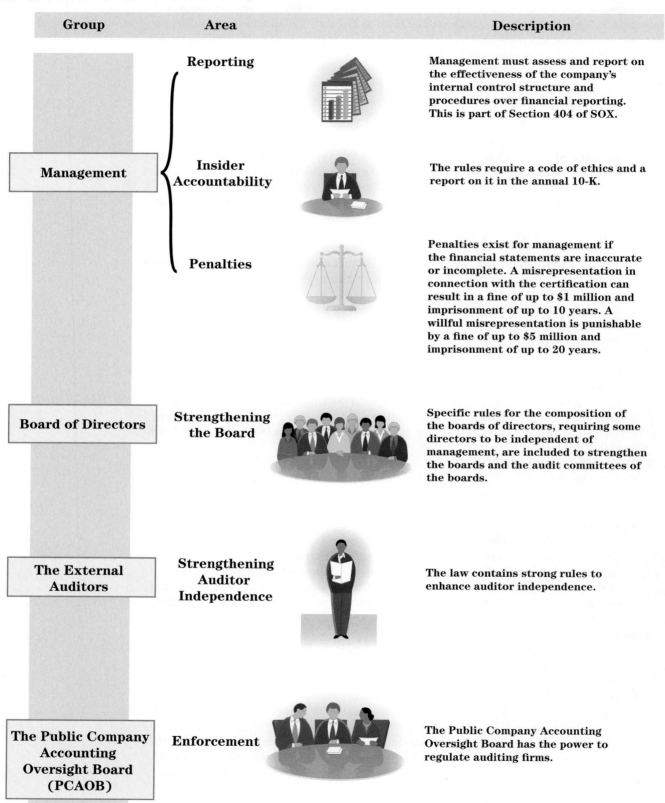

Group	Area		Description
Management	Reporting		Management must assess and report on the effectiveness of the company's internal control structure and procedures over financial reporting. This is part of Section 404 of SOX.
	Insider Accountability		The rules require a code of ethics and a report on it in the annual 10-K.
	Penalties		Penalties exist for management if the financial statements are inaccurate or incomplete. A misrepresentation in connection with the certification can result in a fine of up to $1 million and imprisonment of up to 10 years. A willful misrepresentation is punishable by a fine of up to $5 million and imprisonment of up to 20 years.
Board of Directors	Strengthening the Board		Specific rules for the composition of the boards of directors, requiring some directors to be independent of management, are included to strengthen the boards and the audit committees of the boards.
The External Auditors	Strengthening Auditor Independence		The law contains strong rules to enhance auditor independence.
The Public Company Accounting Oversight Board (PCAOB)	Enforcement		The Public Company Accounting Oversight Board has the power to regulate auditing firms.

4. Public Company Accounting Oversight Board (PCAOB)
- This regulatory group was established by the SOX Act. Members are appointed by the SEC in consultation with the chairman of the Board of Governors of the Federal Reserve System and the secretary of the treasury.
- The purpose of the PCAOB is to regulate the auditing profession.
- All accounting firms that audit publicly-traded companies must register with the PCAOB and follow its rules.
- The SEC must approve any rules set by the PCAOB.
- As this book goes to press, the United States Supreme Court has agreed to review a case that addresses the constitutionality of the creation of the PCAOB. According to a lawsuit filed by Free Enterprise Fund, the existence of the PCAOB violates the separation-of-powers principle.

The purpose of the Sarbanes-Oxley Act is to strengthen financial reporting and the corporate governance of publicly-traded companies. However, there are some potential disadvantages of the law's requirements. Most of the arguments against the law center on the high cost of implementing Section 404, the requirement for firms to implement and document internal controls related to their financial reporting systems. Some people argue that the real problem in corporate America is the lack of high moral and ethical values, which cannot be solved with this legislation.

Since the passage of the Sarbanes-Oxley Act of 2002, non-audit fees have gone from 51% of audit firm revenues to just 21%. Experts view this as evidence that the law has been effective in increasing auditor independence.

Source: "*Since Sarbox, Non-audit Fees Dove from 51% to 21%,*" by David M. Katz, CFO.com, May 7, 2009.

Outlook for the Future

We are living in a time when the way companies do business is changing. The importance of accounting and financial reporting is unquestionable. The financial crisis and resulting recession that began in 2008 underscore the significance of accounting. All business managers—marketing managers, production managers, human resource managers, operations managers—must be able to understand financial information and the way it is gathered and reported. All business managers must identify risks for their specific areas and create internal controls to manage those risks. For example, a marketing manager must be aware of how the accounting is done for sales commissions in order to evaluate the accuracy of a salesperson's weekly sales report. Perhaps the accounting department pays the salespeople their commissions each Monday for sales submitted by noon on the previous Friday. There is a risk that the salesperson will include sales that are scheduled to be completed by the end of the day on Friday so that the Friday afternoon sales will be included in Monday's payment. A control for this would be to match the salesperson's report of sales to the shipping department's weekly shipments. Recall that, in general, revenue is not recognized until the goods are shipped. Commissions to the salespeople should be paid on amounts of revenue the firm has actually earned.

Firms spend a tremendous amount of money to comply with the Sarbanes-Oxley Act's rules and regulations. According to a 2007 study by Financial Executives International, costs of complying with Section 404, the most expensive part of implementing the Sarbanes-Oxley Act, have dropped every year since the law's passage. Between 2005 and 2007, costs dropped by 23%—to an average cost of $2.9 million—for the set of firms surveyed (large companies with average revenues of $6.8 billion). Most people believe costs will continue to decline for the next several years as firms gain efficiency and new software to help document internal controls is developed.

The current and expected future increases in regulation in the accounting and finance area have resulted in a surge in employment opportunities for accounting and auditing firms. According to the Federal Bureau of Labor Statistics, the number of accounting jobs is expected to increase by as much as 18% between 2006 and 2016, which is faster than the average for all occupations (7%–13%). According to a 2009 survey by Robert Half International, the world's largest specialized staffing firm, most CFOs plan to maintain the current level of employment in their accounting and finance departments, in spite of the recession. Twenty-five percent of the CFOs in the survey cited accounting positions as the most difficult to fill.[2]

Your Turn 11-4

Explain why internal controls are so important to firms and their auditors.

L.O.6

Evaluate a firm's corporate governance.

Evaluating Corporate Governance

The Sarbanes-Oxley Act of 2002 changed the way corporations govern themselves in the United States. The roles of the firm's board of directors, CEO, CFO, and its shareholders are frequently the topic of articles in the popular financial press. It is difficult, however, to find the answer to a very important question: What is *good* corporate governance?

Defining and Measuring Good Corporate Governance

Most experts—managers, the SEC, and academic researchers—agree that the most important factor in good corporate governance is an ethical climate, which top management sets. Other attributes of good governance include

1. an independent board of directors made up of high-quality directors with a variety of backgrounds.
2. a CEO who encourages board involvement in the review of major management and financial decisions.
3. financial information for shareholders that is transparent—easily understandable, simple, and straightforward.
4. strong and independent external auditors.

Little research exists to confirm that these, or any other, elements of corporate governance actually prevent fraud. But even if you agree that these are desirable elements, can you see how difficult it might be to measure them?

Neither lack of supporting research nor measurement difficulty has stopped the development of corporate governance rating systems. Some of the companies involved in developing rating systems for corporate governance are RiskMetrics, GovernanceMetrics International, and the Corporate Library. A study by professors at Stanford University's Rock Center for Corporate Governance found these commercial governance ratings "have either limited or no success in predicting firm performance or other outcomes of interest to shareholders."[3]

How Can We Evaluate a Firm's Corporate Governance?

There are two key ways to find out about a firm's corporate governance:

1. Web sites
2. Annual reports or 10-Ks

Many large firms post their corporate governance policies on their Web sites, where you can find menus for corporate governance guidelines, codes of ethics, and various committees of the board of directors. On some Web sites, you will find information about each member of the board and of the audit, compensation, and nominating committees.

You read earlier in the chapter that one of the requirements of SOX is that management must report on the effectiveness of the company's system of internal controls. This report is included in the company's 10-K. Also, the external auditors must attest to and issue a report on management's assessment of internal controls. This, too, can be found in the firm's 10-K.

Just as the financial statements alone are insufficient to come to a conclusion about the value of a company, the corporate governance information provided by a company is not sufficient to

---

[2]Taub, S. 2009. Hiring Standstill: It Could Be Worse. *CFO.com*. March 10, 2009.

[3]Dainer, R., I. Gow, and D. Larcker. 2008. Rating the Ratings: How Good Are Commercial Governance Ratings? Working paper. Rock Center for Corporate Governance, Stanford University.

draw any definite conclusions about the integrity and honesty of the company and its management. However, as information about how a company's corporate governance policies are working becomes more readily available, it will be easier to evaluate this area of the company.

Name two characteristics of good corporate governance.

Your Turn 11-5

International Financial Reporting Standards (IFRS)

L.O.7
Describe the differences between IFRS and U.S. GAAP.

Throughout this book, you have read about IFRS and the potential adoption of these standards in the United States. While U.S. GAAP and IFRS have much in common, there are both minor and major differences between the two. The overall difference between the two sets of standards is the approach they take with respect to detailed guidance for the preparation of financial statements. U.S. GAAP are commonly described as rule based, while IFRS are commonly described as principle based. This is demonstrated by the fact that U.S. GAAP have over 160 Financial Accounting Standards, and IFRS include fewer than 50 International Reporting Standards.

If this book or the course you are taking is your first exposure to accounting, you may have thought that U.S. GAAP give *too many* alternatives for accounting for a specific type of transaction. Why not mandate that every company use FIFO for inventory or straight-line depreciation? Why are there a variety of ways to account for something? The reason for these choices is directly related to the purpose of financial information: to be useful for decision making. No firm is exactly like another. Because a firm wants to express its financial performance and condition in the most realistic and useful way possible, one firm may make accounting choices that are different from those of another firm. To fairly present its financial condition, one firm may depreciate a building for 30 years, while another may have an identical building being depreciated over 40 years. Why? The firm chooses the number of years based on its assessment of useful life. The building may be used in different ways by the two firms, and the choice of useful life should reflect the amount of time the firm plans to use the building. To mandate a specific number of years for depreciating a building would decrease the usefulness of the information on the financial statements. There are dozens, if not hundreds, of other examples of how providing choices improves the quality of the resulting information. While you may read about those who take advantage of the availability of choices, remember that the vast majority of business people, including accountants and auditors, are doing their best to communicate financial information honestly and ethically.

There is significantly less detailed guidance in IFRS than in U.S. GAAP. This means that a switch to IFRS will require a new approach to the preparation of the financial statements. In particular, auditors will have to be prepared to exercise more judgment in their task of providing an opinion on the fair presentation of the firm's financial statements. The world's largest accounting firms are preparing already, even though it is unlikely that IFRS will be fully implemented in the United States before 2014. Additionally, these firms already have a great deal of expertise in IFRS because they currently audit many firms in other countries where IFRS are the authoritative set of standards.

Both sets of standards have similar goals—to provide useful information for the users of financial statements. Both are accrual basis, and both require an income statement, a balance sheet, and a statement of cash flows. The composition of these statements is quite similar, although the format of the statements can certainly be different. The balance sheet for Cadbury, which is one of the world's largest confectionery companies and which is based in the United Kingdom, is shown in Exhibit 11.2 on the following page. The firm's financial statements are prepared in accordance with IFRS. One of the first things you'll notice is that the statement begins with long-term assets, which IFRS call non-current assets. Liabilities, however, start with the current liabilities. Also, notice that the liabilities are shown as negative amounts. The form of the accounting equation on which this balance sheet is based is Assets – Liabilities = Equity. These are just a few of the more obvious differences. To review the firm's entire annual report, which includes its financial statements and notes, go to www.Cadbury.com.

Exhibit 11.3 on page 523 provides some of the more specific differences between U.S. GAAP and IFRS. These examples are ones you will likely be able to understand. There are many others that apply to more advanced accounting topics. If you wish to learn more about

EXHIBIT 11.2

Cadbury: An Example of a Balance Sheet Prepared Under IFRS

Cadbury
Comparative Balance Sheets

Notes		At December 31, 2008 £m*	At December 31, 2007 £m
	Assets		
	Non-current assets		
14	Goodwill	2,288	2,805
15	Acquisition intangibles	1,598	3,378
15	Software intangibles	87	149
16	Property, plant, and equipment	1,761	1,904
17	Investment in associates	28	32
17	Investment in subsidiaries	—	—
24	Deferred tax assets	181	124
25	Retirement benefit assets	17	223
20	Trade and other receivables	28	50
18	Other investments	2	2
		5,990	8,667
	Current assets		
19	Inventories	767	821
	Short-term investments	247	2
20	Trade and other receivables	1,067	1,197
	Tax recoverable	35	41
	Cash and cash equivalents	251	493
27	Derivative financial instruments	268	46
		2,635	2,600
21	Assets held for sale	270	71
	Total assets	8,895	11,338
	Liabilities		
	Current liabilities		
22	Trade and other payables	(1,551)	(1,701)
	Tax payable	(328)	(197)
27	Short-term borrowings and overdrafts	(1,189)	(2,562)
23	Short-term provisions	(150)	(111)
32	Obligations under finance leases	(1)	(21)
27	Derivative financial instruments	(169)	(22)
		(3,388)	(4,614)
	Non-current liabilities		
22	Trade and other payables	(61)	(37)
27	Borrowings	(1,194)	(1,120)
25	Retirement benefit obligations	(275)	(143)
	Tax payable	(6)	(16)
24	Deferred tax liabilities	(121)	(1,145)
23	Long-term provisions	(218)	(61)
32	Obligations under finance leases	(1)	(11)
		(1,876)	(2,533)
21	Liabilities directly associated with assets classified as held for sale	(97)	(18)
	Total liabilities	(5,361)	(7,165)
	Net assets	3,534	4,173
	Equity		
28	Share capital	136	264
28	Share premium account	38	1,225
28	Other reserves	850	(4)
28	Retained earnings	2,498	2,677
28	Equity attributable to equity holders of the parent	3,522	4,162
29	Minority interests	12	11
	Total equity	3,534	4,173

*Notice that the statements are in British currency, pounds sterling. The m after the pound sign signifies that the amounts are in millions.

EXHIBIT 11.3

U.S. GAAP versus IFRS

ACCOUNT(S)	TOPIC	U.S. GAAP POSITION	IFRS POSITION	IMPLICATIONS OF SWITCH TO IFRS
Inventory (*Asset*) **and Cost of Goods Sold** (*Income Statement*)	Inventory Costing	Companies can choose to use LIFO inventory costing, if desired. Many use LIFO for its tax benefits.	LIFO is not allowed under any circumstances.	LIFO could be eliminated for financial accounting purposes. Companies could still choose to use the FIFO, average cost, or specific identification inventory costing methods.
Inventory (*Asset*)	Lower-of-Cost-or-Market (LCM)	Market is usually determined to be the replacement cost of inventory. LCM write-downs cannot be reversed.	Market is always net realizable value (essentially, the selling price) of inventory. Under certain circumstances, LCM write-downs can potentially be reversed.	LCM write-downs may become less common, as selling prices are usually greater than replacement costs. Some of these write-downs might be reversed over time.
Property, Plant, and Equipment (*Assets*)	Asset Impairment and Revaluation	If long-term assets are impaired, they are written down. Such write-downs cannot be reversed.	Long-term assets may be written down, based on fair market values (appraisals). Such adjustments can potentially be reversed.	The cost principle might not apply to long-term assets as strongly. Assets could be evaluated by independent appraisers and adjusted either up or down to new fair market values.
Research and Development (*Income Statement/ Assets*)	Development Costs	All research and development costs are expensed. The only exception is for computer software development costs, which can be capitalized and amortized over future sales revenues.	All research is expensed, but all development costs are capitalized and amortized over future sales revenues.	The standards already developed by U.S. GAAP might be extended to apply to all development costs, not just to computer software development.
Intangible Assets (*Assets*)	Capitalization and Recognition of Intangible Assets	U.S. GAAP are reluctant to recognize intangible assets. Such assets are only recognized when they are purchased. Internally-developed intangible assets (such as brand names and patents) are not recognized as assets on the balance sheet.	Intangible assets are recognized if their future benefit is probable and reliably measurable (the standard U.S. GAAP are currently used for contingent liabilities). These assets may be purchased or internally generated.	More intangible assets could be shown on balance sheets. These assets could be adjusted for amortization or impairment over time.
Contingent Liabilities (*Liabilities*)	Recording of Contingent Liabilities	Probable contingent liabilities are recorded in formal accounting records. Reasonably possible contingent liabilities are disclosed in financial statement notes.	Both probable and reasonably possible contingent liabilities are recorded in the formal accounting records.	More liabilities could be recorded. Some of these liabilities could be reversed in future years if the obligations do not come to pass.
Extraordinary Items (*Income Statement*)	Recording of Extraordinary Items	U.S. GAAP allow extraordinary items (that is, items that are both unusual and infrequent) to be reported separately on the income statement as a component of income after continuing operations.	Extraordinary items do not have special treatment. Even "unusual and infrequent" items are reported on the income statement as ordinary income from continuing operations.	Extraordinary items may disappear from the income statement to be reclassified as "ordinary" revenues and expenses.
Interest Revenue and Interest Expense (*Income Statement*)	Classification of Interest on the Statement of Cash Flows	Cash received and cash paid for interest (revenue and expense) are classified as cash from operating activities on the statement of cash flows.	Interest received may be classified as an operating or an investing activity. Interest paid may be classified as an operating or a financing activity.	Interest revenue and expense may be reported in different places on the cash flows statement.

IFRS, you can find plenty of information. Start with the Web sites of the four largest accounting firms (www.ey.com, www.kpmg.com, www.pwc.com, www.deloitte.com) where you will find free publications that address all aspects of international accounting standards and the adoption of IFRS by the United States.

You Have Come a Long Way

As you finish this study of financial accounting, look back and see how far you have come. When you started Chapter 1, you probably did not know a balance sheet from an income statement. Now you know the elements of the four basic financial statements and the principles that accountants use to prepare these statements. You have learned that the statements alone do not provide sufficient information for investors. The accompanying notes that you often see referenced at the bottom of each statement are an integral part of the financial statements. You have learned that companies can "cook the books," but also remember that the vast majority of accountants, managers, and business executives are honest people who are doing their best, often in difficult situations.

Chapter Summary Points

- Analysts and investors use earnings per share (EPS) to evaluate a firm's performance, often putting excessive weight on this amount.
- Quality of earnings refers to how well a particular earnings number communicates a firm's true performance.
- Three common ways a firm can manipulate earnings are by (1) using big bath charges—writing off as many expenses as possible in a bad year to minimize expenses in the future, (2) using cookie jar reserves to increase or decrease earnings as desired, and (3) recognizing revenue too soon.
- The corporate accounting failures of the early 2000s were the result of accounting frauds. The result was legislation—the Sarbanes-Oxley Act of 2002—to improve corporate governance.

Key Terms for Chapter 11

Big bath (p. 513)
Cookie jar reserves (p. 514)

Cooking the books (p. 513)
Corporate governance (p. 516)

Quality of earnings (p. 512)

Answers to YOUR TURN Questions

Chapter 11

Your Turn 11-1

Earnings are used by investors to evaluate a firm's performance. The price of a firm's stock often goes up if the firm meets earnings expectations and down if the firm doesn't meet earnings expectations.

Your Turn 11-2

Earnings are a function of the choices managers make in reporting earnings. Some choices—such as LIFO for inventory in a period of rising prices—lead to a higher quality of earnings than others.

Your Turn 11-3

There are several possible answers to this question. Two important ones are (1) independence, both actual and perceived, is crucial to doing an effective and credible job, and (2) high ethical values and personal integrity are essential—in auditing and life.

Your Turn 11-4

Managers must report on the firm's internal controls and their effectiveness. Some firms may need new ways to gather information about the effectiveness of the firm's controls. The auditors must attest to management's report, which means that the auditors must gather sufficient evidence to give their opinion on the truthfulness of management's report. These are added responsibilities for the firm's managers and the firm's auditors.

Your Turn 11-5

Here are a few characteristics: (1) a board of directors (BOD) with a majority of independent directors, (2) a BOD with a chairman who is not the firm's CEO, (3) a reputable and reliable internal audit function, (4) independent external auditors, (5) a strong code of ethics, with the top management setting the tone, and (6) a compensation system that does not place too much reliance on the stock price but does reward increasing the firm's underlying value.

Questions

1. What determines the quality of earnings?
2. Why are earnings so important?
3. What events motivated Congress to pass the Sarbanes-Oxley Act of 2002?
4. What is the role of the Public Company Accounting Oversight Board (PCAOB)?
5. Who is responsible for establishing auditing standards for audits of public companies? Who is responsible for establishing accounting standards for public companies? Explain these two sets of standards.
6. What provisions of Sarbanes-Oxley should increase auditor independence? Explain how.
7. What changes does Sarbanes-Oxley require for a company's board of directors?
8. What are internal controls and who is responsible for their effectiveness?
9. What is the responsibility of the audit committee of the board of directors?
10. Who is responsible for certifying the financial statements filed with the SEC?
11. What is a cookie jar reserve, and how is it used?
12. What is the big bath theory?
13. When should a company recognize revenue?

Multiple-Choice Questions

1. Which of the following is a problem resulting from the emphasis on earnings?
   a. Managers may ignore sales forecasts.
   b. Internal controls may deteriorate.
   c. Quality of earnings may suffer.
   d. Responsibilities of lower-level managers may increase.
2. A publicly-traded firm must have
   a. a functioning board of directors.
   b. a CFO with significant accounting experience.
   c. a specific time each week to meet with employees regarding potential fraud.
   d. an ethics committee.
3. The audit committee is
   a. part of the internal audit function.
   b. a subset of directors who must be independent.
   c. no longer part of corporate governance.
   d. chaired by a CPA.
4. Who is responsible for selecting, hiring, and compensating the external auditors?
   a. CEO
   b. CFO
   c. Audit committee of the BOD
   d. All of the above
5. High-quality earnings are those that
   a. fluctuate widely between periods.
   b. provide accurate and reliable information about a firm's earnings.
   c. exceed $1 per share.
   d. are found in the shareholders' equity section of the balance sheet.

Short Exercises

SE11-1. *Importance of earnings. (LO 1).* What is the most important number a firm reports in the opinion of Wall Street analysts? What problems has this created?

SE11-2. *Quality of earnings. (LO 2).* How do you think analysts evaluate the quality of a firm's earnings? Do you think higher-quality earnings translate into higher stock prices?

SE11-3. *Big bath theory. (LO 3).* Describe the big bath theory and give some examples of items that could be written off early.

SE11-4. *Revenue recognition. (LO 3).* What types of companies might have problems with revenue recognition? How can investors learn about the revenue recognition policies of a company?

SE11-5. *Corporate failures. (LO 4).* Some of the scandals of the early 2000s were the result of misapplying accounting principles, and others were the result of questionable accounting principles. Which do you think describes the WorldCom failure? Why? Do you think good accounting principles can eliminate financial failures like Enron and WorldCom? Have any of the corporate failures from 2008–2009 been related to accounting? If so, describe how.

SE11-6. *Sarbanes-Oxley Act. (LO 5).* Discuss the costs and benefits of requiring managers to report on the company's internal controls. Do you think it is necessary for the external auditor to attest to management's report? Why or why not?

SE11-7. *Sarbanes-Oxley Act. (LO 5).* One of the requirements of the Sarbanes-Oxley Act is that the lead auditor or coordinating partner and the reviewing partner must rotate off the audit every five years. In your opinion, what is the purpose of this requirement? Do you think it will be achieved?

SE11-8. *Corporate governance. (LO 5, 6).* What is the advantage of having a financial expert on the board of directors? Are there any drawbacks?

SE11-9. *Corporate governance. (LO 5, 6).* Discuss the advantages and disadvantages of having the audit committee deal directly with the external auditors.

SE11-10. *Corporate governance. (LO 6).* Do you think that good corporate governance can be measured? Would you use it in a decision to invest in a specific company?

SE11-11. *IFRS vs. GAAP. (LO 7).* In the most general sense, what is the difference between IFRS and U.S. GAAP? What is a general similarity?

SE11-12. *IFRS vs. GAAP. (LO 7).* How does U.S. GAAP differ from IFRS in the way inventory may be recorded?

SE11-13. *IFRS vs. GAAP. (LO 7).* How does U.S. GAAP differ from IFRS in the way property, plant, and equipment may be valued on the balance sheet?

Exercises

E11-14. *Quality of earnings. (LO 2).* Suppose Company A is quite similar to Company B in most respects—same size, same industry—but Company A uses the allowance method for bad debts and Company B does not. Which company do you believe has the higher quality of earnings and why?

E11-15. *Quality of earnings. (LO 2).* Loder Company had a good year, and recorded a large gain on the sale of a discontinued business segment. Bates Company, on the other hand, had no discontinued business segments on its income statement. Otherwise, both income statements were very similar. Loder Company announced earnings of $1.25 per share and Bates announced earnings of $1.20 per share. Your friend Bob tells you that you should invest in Loder because it has higher quality earnings because it is larger. What is your response?

E11-16. *Big bath theory. (LO 3).* Mismatch Company had a terrible year and will definitely have a net loss for the year. Give two examples of some accounting adjustments in which estimates could be changed so that Mismatch could make the loss even larger this year to make the subsequent years more positive.

E11-17. *Cookie jar reserves. (LO 3).* Chip Company is making estimates of bad debts and warranties at year end, December 31, 2009. The firm believes that it will have declining revenue in 2010, so the accounting manager suggests the firm record $50,000 for bad debts expense this year, even though the aging schedule indicates that only $30,000 needs to be recorded. Explain how doing that could help net income in 2010.

Internet Exercises

IE11-1. Go to Google and type in "corporate governance." How many hits did you get? Check out a few of the links to see what type of information is available on the topic of corporate governance.

IE11-2. Go to the PCAOB Web site at www.pcaobus.org. According to its Web site, what is the mission of the PCAOB? So far, do you believe it is accomplishing this mission? Why or why not?

IE11-3. Go to the Walt Disney Company Web site at www.disney.com. Follow the link at the bottom to *Corporate Info* and then to *Investor Relations*. Finally, select *Corporate Governance*. What information is available about the company's corporate governance? See if you can find out how many times the board of directors meets each year. Do you think that is a sufficient number of meetings? Why or why not?

IE11-4. Select a pair of companies in the same industry—such as Wal-Mart and Target, Hershey Foods and Tootsie Roll, or The Home Depot and Lowe's. For the two companies you select, go to their Web sites and locate the information about corporate governance. Summarize the information you found. How does the information for the two companies compare? Did you find any surprising similarities or differences? Do you think investors are interested in this information?

IE11-5. In August 2009, General Electric Corporation agreed to pay $50 million to settle a suit filed by the SEC that said the company "used improper accounting methods to increase its reported earnings or revenue and avoid reporting negative financial results" (From the SEC press release 2009-178, found at http://www.sec.gov/news/press/2009/2009-178.htm). Go to GE's Web site at www.ge.com and read about the company's corporate governance (under Our Company). What is your impression of its governance, particularly in light of the SEC settlement?

IE11-6. Go to Cadbury's Web site at www.cadbury.com, and find the link to its most recent annual report. Then, locate the financial statements and notes.

1. Look in the notes and find where the firm discusses its accounting methods. Can you tell what accounting standards the firm uses? How about currency denomination?
2. What firm serves as the external auditors for Cadbury?
3. On the firm's balance sheet (in Exhibit 11.2) and income statement (provided on the following page), find five things you recognize as non-GAAP.

Cadbury
Consolidated Income Statements

		For the Year Ended December 31	
			Re-presented (restated)
Notes		2008 £m*	2007 £m
	Continuing operations		
2	Revenue	5,384	4,699
3	Trading costs	(4,803)	(4,258)
4	Restructuring costs	(194)	(165)
5	Non-trading items	1	2
	Profit from operations	388	278
17	Share of result in associates	10	8
	Profit before financing and taxation	398	286
9	Investment revenue	52	56
10	Finance costs	(50)	(88)
	Profit before taxation	400	254
11	Taxation	(30)	(105)
	Profit for the period from continuing operations	370	149
31	Discontinued operations		
	(Loss)/profit for the period from discontinued operations	(4)	258
	Profit for the period	366	407
	Attributable to:		
	Equity holders of the parent	364	405
	Minority interests	2	2
		366	407
	Earnings per share from continuing and discontinued operations		
13	Basic	22.6p	19.4p
13	Diluted	22.6p	19.2p
	From continuing operations		
13	Basic	22.8p	7.0p
13	Diluted	22.8p	7.0p

*Pounds sterling, in millions

Appendix A
Selection from
Books-A-Million
2009 Annual Report

BOOKS·A·MILLION
2009 Annual Report

COMPANY PROFILE

Books-A-Million is one of the nation's leading book retailers and sells on the Internet at *www.booksamillion.com*. The Company presently operates 220 stores in 21 states and the District of Columbia. The Company operates two distinct store formats, including large superstores operating under the names Books-A-Million and Books & Co. and traditional bookstores operating under the names Books-A-Million and Bookland.

FIVE-YEAR HIGHLIGHTS

(In thousands, except per share amounts, ratios and operational data)	1/31/09	2/2/08	2/3/07[1]	1/28/06	1/29/05
Statement of Income Data	**52 weeks**	52 weeks	53 weeks	52 weeks	52 weeks
Net revenue	**$513,271**	$535,128	$520,416	$503,751	$474,099
Net income	**10,574**	16,522	18,887	13,067	10,199
Earnings per share - diluted	**0.68**	1.01	1.12	0.77	0.59
Weighted average shares - diluted	**15,609**	16,302	16,805	16,888	17,178
Capital investment	**19,806**	16,878	14,907	11,297	14,923
Dividends per share - declared	**0.28**	3.36	0.33	0.23	0.23
Balance Sheet Data					
Property and equipment, net	**$ 58,038**	$ 53,514	$ 51,471	$ 51,001	$ 55,946
Total assets	**279,292**	284,833	304,037	311,659	300,812
Long-term debt	**6,720**	6,975	7,100	7,200	7,500
Stockholders' equity	**104,494**	99,051	157,034	145,009	134,859
Other Data					
Working capital	**$ 62,145**	$ 58,785	$117,737	$ 106,637	$ 95,382
Debt to total capital ratio	**0.18**	0.26	0.04	0.05	0.05
Operational Data					
Total number of stores	**220**	208	206	205	206
Number of superstores	**200**	184	179	173	168
Number of traditional stores	**20**	24	27	32	38

(1) The year ended February 3, 2007 included an extra week and $2.3 million of gift card breakage from prior periods.

BOOKS·A·MILLION®
2009 Annual Report

To Our Stockholders:

Fiscal Year 2009 brought extraordinary challenges. The economic downturn that began developing in the fourth quarter of fiscal 2008 gained momentum and dramatically affected our sales in the second half of the year. The downturn was most pronounced in the third quarter. We did manage a modest improvement during the holiday season, outperforming our key competitors in comparable store sales.

The sales challenge was felt broadly across most departments of our stores as low consumer confidence led to decreased traffic. The core book business, while down, did have some bright spots as Teen and the phenomenal success of Stephanie Meyer's *Twilight* saga drove customers to the stores in December. Books related to the election season, faith based titles such as William Young's *The Shack* and media driven bestsellers like Glenn Beck's *The Christmas Sweater* also performed well. A price conscious consumer contributed to strong growth in our bargain book category and we aggressively expanded and promoted our assortment to take advantage of this trend.

Another positive trend was the growth of sales of general merchandise. Gifts, toys, games and book accessories all had solid increases as our investment in inventory delivered results, particularly in the fourth quarter.

We closed Fiscal Year 2009 with an improved balance sheet and a focus on expense control. During the fiscal year, we reduced our inventory balance by $2.5 million and reduced debt by $12.5 million.

We opened 16 new stores during the year. We expect to open three to five new stores in the coming year. This anticipated reduction in new stores is the result of a severe economic climate and the lack of quality real estate opportunities.

We will undoubtedly continue to face an unsettled economic climate in the year ahead. However, we are determined to maintain our disciplined approach to the fundamentals of our business both to deliver the best possible results in the short term and to position our company for the opportunities to come in a recovering economy.

Clyde Anderson

Clyde B. Anderson
Chairman and Chief Executive Officer

FINANCIAL HIGHLIGHTS
(In thousands, except per share amounts)

	Fiscal Year Ended	
	1/31/09	2/2/08
Net revenue	$513,271	$535,128
Operating profit	18,890	27,420
Net income	10,574	16,522
Net income per share – diluted	0.68	1.01
Dividends per share – declared	0.28	3.36

(In thousands)

	As of	
	1/31/09	2/2/08
Working capital	$ 62,145	$ 58,785
Total assets	279,292	284,833
Stockholders' equity	104,494	99,051

BOOKS·A·MILLION
2009 Annual Report

SELECTED CONSOLIDATED FINANCIAL DATA

			Fiscal Year Ended		
(In thousands, except per share data)	1/31/09	2/2/08	2/3/07	1/28/06	1/29/05
Statement of Operations Data:	52 weeks	52 weeks	53 weeks	52 weeks	52 weeks
Net revenue	$513,271	$535,128	$520,416	$503,751	$474,099
Cost of products sold, including warehouse distribution and store occupancy costs	361,934	376,580	363,688	357,166	339,012
Gross profit	151,337	158,548	156,728	146,585	135,087
Operating, selling and administrative expenses	116,648	117,079	112,227	108,945	98,870
Impairment Charges	1.351	60	333	215	337
Gain on insurance recovery	--	--	--	1,248	--
Depreciation and amortization	14,448	13,989	14,069	15,636	17,788
Operating profit	18,890	27,420	30,099	23,037	18,092
Interest expense, net	1,920	1,346	105	1,441	1,874
Income from continuing operations before income taxes	16,970	26,074	29,994	21,596	16,218
Provision for income taxes	6,396	9,552	11,107	8,545	6,001
Income from continuing operations	10,574	16,522	18,887	13,051	10,217
Discontinued operations:					
Income (Loss) from discontinued operations (including impairment charge)	--	--	--	27	(29)
Income tax provision (benefit)	--	--	--	11	(11)
Income (Loss) from discontinued operations	--	--	--	16	(18)
Net income	$ 10,574	$ 16,522	$ 18,887	$ 13,067	$ 10,199
Net income per common share:					
Basic:					
Net income per share	$ 0.70	$ 1.03	$ 1.16	$ 0.80	$ 0.62
Weighted average number of shares outstanding - basic	15,219	16,089	16,352	16,275	16,453
Diluted:					
Net income per share	$ 0.68	$ 1.01	$ 1.12	$ 0.77	$ 0.59
Weighted average number of shares outstanding - diluted	15,609	16,302	16,805	16,888	17,178
Dividends per share – declared	$ 0.28	$ 3.36	$ 0.33	$ 0.23	$ 0.23
Balance Sheet Data:					
Property and equipment, net	$ 58,038	$ 53,514	$ 51,471	$ 51,001	$ 55,946
Total assets	279,292	284,833	304,037	311,659	300,812
Long-term debt	6,720	6,975	7,100	7,200	7,500
Deferred Rent	8,554	8.079	8,706	8,637	12,622
Liability for uncertain tax positions	2,032	2.174	--	--	--
Stockholders' investment	104,494	99,051	157,034	145,009	134,859
Other Data:					
Working capital	$ 62,145	$ 58,785	$117,737	$106,637	$ 95,382

BOOKS·A·MILLION®
2009 Annual Report

MANAGEMENT'S DISCUSSION & ANALYSIS OF FINANCIAL CONDITION & RESULTS OF OPERATIONS

General

The Company was founded in 1917 and currently operates 220 retail bookstores concentrated primarily in the southeastern United States. Of the 220 stores, 200 are superstores that operate under the names Books-A-Million and Books & Co., and 20 are traditional stores that operate under the Bookland and Books-A-Million names. In addition to the retail store formats, the Company offers its products over the Internet at *www.booksamillion.com*. As of January 31, 2009, the Company employed approximately 5,300 full and part-time employees.

The Company's growth strategy is focused on opening superstores in new and existing market areas, particularly in the Southeast. In addition to opening new stores, management intends to continue its practice of reviewing the profitability trends and prospects of existing stores and closing or relocating under-performing stores. During fiscal 2009, the Company opened sixteen stores, closed four stores and relocated seven stores.

The Company's performance is partially measured based on comparable store sales, which is similar to most retailers. Comparable store sales are determined each fiscal quarter during the year based on all stores that have been open at least 12 full months as of the first day of the fiscal period. Any stores closed during a fiscal period are excluded from comparable store sales as of the first day of the fiscal period in which they close. Remodeled and relocated stores are also included as comparable stores. The factors affecting the future trend of comparable store sales include, among others, overall demand for products the Company sells, the Company's marketing programs, pricing strategies, store operations and competition.

Current Economic Environment

The United States and global economies are presently experiencing extremely challenging times and it is possible that general economic conditions could deteriorate further. The Company believes that these conditions have had and will continue to have an adverse impact on spending by the Company's current retail customer base and potential new customers. Because of these significant challenges, we are continuously reviewing and adjusting our business activities to address the changing economic environment. We are carefully managing our inventory and liquidity and enforcing expense controls while working diligently and prudently to grow our business. Despite overall store number growth in fiscal 2009, the Company reduced its year-end inventory balance by $2.5 million as of January 31, 2009 to $204.3 million, as compared to the fiscal year-end 2008 balance of $206.8 million. In addition, we reduced our outstanding loan balance at fiscal year-end 2009 under the Company's revolving credit facility, that allows for borrowings up to $100.0 million, to $15.8 million. This credit facility had a balance of $28.0 million at February 2, 2008. The Company was also able to reduce its selling and administrative expenses during fiscal 2009 by $0.4 million as compared to fiscal 2008. The Company opened 16 new stores in fiscal 2009. Due to current economic conditions, we will not open as many new stores in fiscal 2010 as were opened in fiscal 2009. Because of the uncertainty in the overall economic environment, the unpredictability of consumer behavior and the concern as to whether current conditions will improve, it is very difficult for us to predict how our business may be affected in the future. Our business and financial performance may be adversely affected by current and future economic conditions that cause a further decline in business and consumer spending, including a reduction in the availability of credit, increased unemployment levels, higher energy and fuel costs, rising interest rates, financial market volatility and long-term recession. These conditions could have a negative impact on the earnings, liquidity and capital resources of the Company.

Executive Summary

The purpose of this section is to provide a brief summary overview of the 52-week period ended January 31, 2009. Additional detail about the income statement and balance sheet is provided in the pages following this summary.

Income Statement

For the 52-week period ended January 31, 2009, Books-A-Million reported net income of $10.6 million. This represents a 36.0% decrease from the 52-week period ended February 2, 2008. The decrease is attributable to severe macro-economic conditions in fiscal 2009 and the impact of the release of *Harry Potter and the Deathly Hallows*, the final book in the Harry Potter series, in the prior year. *Harry Potter and the Deathly Hallows* contributed $7.3 million in sales during the 52-week period ended February 2, 2008.

Consolidated net revenue decreased $21.9 million, or 4.0%, in the 52-week period ended January 31, 2009, compared to the 52-week period ended February 2, 2008. Comparable store sales decreased 7.2% in fiscal year 2009 compared to the 52-week period ended February 2, 2008. The decrease is due to severe macro-economic conditions in fiscal 2009 and the impact of the release of *Harry Potter and the Deathly Hallows* in the prior year as detailed above.

Gross profit, which includes cost of sales, distribution costs and occupancy costs, decreased $7.2 million, or 4.5%, in the 52-week period ended January 31, 2009, compared to the 52-week period ended February 2, 2008. Gross profit as a percentage of sales decreased from 29.6% to 29.5% over the same period. The decrease is attributable to higher occupancy costs offset by improved sales of higher margin items, lower promotional discounts and lower markdowns.

Operating, selling and administrative expenses decreased $0.4 million, or 0.04%, in the 52-week period ended January 31, 2009, compared to the 52-week period ended February 2, 2008. The decrease was attributable to reduced salary, bonus, 401(k) and payroll tax expense, reduced advertising expenses and reduced bad debt expense, partially offset by increased credit card fees, travel, insurance and new store expenses.

Impairment charges increased $1.3 million in the 52-week period ended January 31, 2009, compared to the 52-week period ended February 2, 2008. The increase was attributable to $0.7 million in impairment charges taken on leasehold improvements at various stores and a $0.7 million impairment of goodwill.

Consolidated operating profit was $18.9 million for the 52-week period ended January 31, 2009, compared to $27.4 million for the 52-week period ended February 2, 2008, a decrease of $8.5 million. This decrease was attributable to decreased sales and gross margin, along with an increase in operating selling and administrative expenses.

Balance Sheet
Current assets decreased $7.7 million, or 3.4%, in fiscal year 2009 compared to fiscal year 2008. The decrease is attributable to a $2.5 million decrease in inventory, a $1.4 million decrease in prepaid expenses and a $3.7 million decrease in accounts and related party receivables. The reduction in inventory is attributable to a tight focus on inventory reduction and control in both our stores and our warehouses in response to difficult macro-economic conditions. This reduction was accomplished despite the addition of sixteen new stores. The decrease in prepaid expenses is attributable to reduced prepayments of rent, supplies and import duties. The decrease in accounts and related party receivables is the result of reduced sales.

Current liabilities decreased $11.0 million, or 6.8%, in fiscal year 2009 compared to fiscal year 2008. The decrease is attributable to a $12.2 million decrease in short-term borrowings and a $6.0 million decrease in accrued expenses, partially offset by a $5.5 million increase in accounts payable. The decrease in short-term borrowings is the result of cost control, a reduction in inventory and an increase in accounts payable leverage. The reduction in accrued expenses is the result of reduced accruals for bonuses, insurance, returns and capital expenditures. Accounts payable increased due to more effective management of payment terms.

Critical Accounting Policies
General
Management's Discussion and Analysis of Financial Condition and Results of Operations discusses the Company's consolidated financial statements, which have been prepared in accordance with accounting principles generally accepted in the United States of America. The preparation of these financial statements require management to make estimates and assumptions in certain circumstances that affect amounts reported in the accompanying consolidated financial statements and related footnotes. In preparing these financial statements, management has made its best estimates and judgments of certain amounts included in the financial statements, giving due consideration to materiality. The Company believes that the likelihood is remote that materially different amounts will be reported related to actual results for the estimates and judgments described below. However, application of these accounting policies involves the exercise of judgment and use of assumptions as to future uncertainties and, as a result, actual results could differ from these estimates.

Property and Equipment
Property and equipment are recorded at cost. Depreciation on equipment and furniture and fixtures is provided on the straight-line method over the estimated service lives, which range from three to seven years. Depreciation of buildings and amortization of leasehold improvements, including remodels, is provided on the straight-line basis over the lesser of the assets estimated useful lives (ranging from five to 40 years) or, if applicable, the periods of the leases. Determination of useful asset life is based on several factors requiring judgment by management and adherence to generally accepted accounting principles for depreciable periods. Judgment used by management in the determination of useful asset life could relate to any of the following factors: expected use of the asset; expected useful life of similar assets; any legal, regulatory, or contractual provisions that may limit the useful life; and other factors that may impair the economic useful life of the asset. Maintenance and repairs are charged to expense as incurred. Improvement costs are capitalized to property accounts and depreciated using applicable annual rates. The cost and accumulated depreciation of assets sold, retired or otherwise disposed of are removed from the accounts, and the related gain or loss is credited or charged to income.

BOOKS·A·MILLION
2009 Annual Report

Other Long-Lived Assets

The Company's other long-lived assets consist of property and equipment which include leasehold improvements. At January 31, 2009, the Company had $58.0 million of property and equipment, net of accumulated depreciation, accounting for approximately 20.8% of the Company's total assets. The Company reviews its long-lived assets for impairment whenever events or changes in circumstances indicate that the carrying amount of an asset may not be recoverable in accordance with Statement of Financial Accounting Standards (SFAS) No. 144, *"Accounting for the Impairment or Disposal of Long-Lived Assets."* The Company evaluates long-lived assets for impairment at the individual store level, which is the lowest level at which individual cash flows can be identified. When evaluating long-lived assets for potential impairment, the Company will first compare the carrying amount of the assets to the individual store's estimated future undiscounted cash flows. If the estimated future cash flows are less than the carrying amount of the assets, an impairment loss calculation is prepared. The impairment loss calculation compares the carrying amount of the assets to the individual store's fair value based on its estimated discounted future cash flows. If required, an impairment loss is recorded for that portion of the asset's carrying value in excess of fair value. Impairment losses, excluding goodwill impairment, totaled $0.7 million, $0.1 million and $0.3 million in fiscal 2009, 2008 and 2007, respectively. For all years presented, the impairment losses related to the retail trade business segment.

Goodwill

At January 31, 2009, the Company had $0.7 million of goodwill, accounting for approximately 0.3% of the Company's total assets. SFAS No. 142, "Goodwill and Other Intangible Assets," requires that goodwill and other unamortizable intangible assets be tested for impairment at least annually or earlier if there are impairment indicators. The Company performs a two-step process for impairment testing of goodwill as required by SFAS No. 142. The first step of this test, used to identify potential impairment, compares the estimated fair value of a reporting unit with its carrying amount. The second step (if necessary) measures the amount of the impairment. The Company completed its annual impairment test on the goodwill during the fourth quarter of fiscal 2009 and determined that an impairment charge was required. As a result, impairment charges of $0.7 million were recorded the fourth quarter of fiscal 2009, which are the direct result of declining market conditions.

Closed Store Expenses

Management considers several factors in determining when to close or relocate a store. Some of these factors are: decreases in store sales from the prior year, decreases in store sales from the current year budget, annual measurement of individual store pre-tax future net cash flows, indications that an asset no longer has an economically useful life, remaining term of an individual store lease, or other factors that would indicate a store in the current location cannot be profitable.

When the Company closes or relocates a store, the Company charges unrecoverable costs to expense. Such costs include the net book value of abandoned fixtures and leasehold improvements, lease termination costs, costs to transfer inventory and usable fixtures, other costs in connection with vacating the leased location, and a provision for future lease obligations, net of expected sublease recoveries. Costs associated with store closings of $0.4 million, $0.6 million and $0.4 million during fiscal 2009, 2008 and 2007, respectively, are included in selling and administrative expenses in the accompanying consolidated statements of income.

Inventories

Inventories are taken throughout the fiscal year. Store inventory counts are performed by an independent inventory service, while warehouse inventory counts are performed internally. All physical inventory counts are reconciled to the Company's records. The Company's accrual for inventory shortages is based upon historical inventory shortage results.

Cost is assigned to store and warehouse inventories using the retail inventory method. Using this method, store and warehouse inventories are valued by applying a calculated cost-to-retail ratio to the retail value of inventories. The retail method is an averaging method that is widely used within the retail industry. Inventory costing also requires certain significant management estimates and judgments involving markdowns, the allocation of vendor allowances and shrinkage. These practices affect ending inventories at cost as well as the resulting gross margins and inventory turnover ratios.

The Company estimates and accrues shrinkage for the period between the last physical count of inventory and the balance sheet date. The accrual is calculated based on historical results. As this estimate is based on historical experience, the variances between the estimate of shrinkage and the adjustment resulting from physical inventories are traditionally not significant.

Reserves for markdowns are estimated based upon the Company's history of liquidating non-returnable inventory.

The Company utilizes the last-in, first-out (LIFO) method of accounting for inventories. The cumulative difference between replacement and current cost of inventory over stated LIFO value is $2.9 million as of January 31, 2009 and $2.5 million as of February 2, 2008. The estimated replacement cost of inventory at January 31, 2009 is the current first-in, first out (FIFO) value of $207.2 million.

Vendor Allowances
The Company receives allowances from its vendors from a variety of programs and arrangements, including merchandise placement and cooperative advertising programs. Effective February 3, 2002, the Company adopted the provisions of Emerging Issues Task Force ("EITF") No. 02-16, *Accounting by a Customer (Including a Reseller) for Certain Consideration Received from a Vendor*, which addresses the accounting for vendor allowances. As a result of the adoption of this statement, vendor allowances in excess of incremental direct costs are reflected as a reduction of inventory costs and recognized in cost of products sold upon the sale of the related inventory.

Accrued Expenses
On a monthly basis, certain material expenses are estimated and accrued to properly record those expenses in the period incurred. Such estimates include those made for payroll and employee benefits costs, occupancy costs and advertising expenses among other items. Certain estimates are made based upon analysis of historical results. Differences in management's estimates and assumptions could result in accruals that are materially different from the actual results.

Income Taxes
The Company recognizes deferred tax assets and liabilities for the expected future tax consequences of events that result in temporary differences between the amounts recorded in its financial statements and tax returns. Under this method, deferred tax assets and liabilities are determined based on the differences between the financial statement and tax bases of assets and liabilities using enacted tax rates in effect for the year in which the differences are expected to reverse.

Results of Operations
The following table sets forth statement of income data expressed as a percentage of net sales for the periods presented.

	Fiscal Year Ended		
	1/31/09	2/2/08	2/3/07
	52 weeks	52 weeks	53 weeks
Net revenue	**100.0%**	100.0%	100.0%
Gross profit	**29.5%**	29.6%	30.1%
Operating, selling, and administrative expenses	**23.0%**	21.9%	21.6%
Impairment charges	**0.3%**	0.0%	0.1%
Depreciation and amortization	**2.8%**	2.6%	2.7%
Operating profit	**3.7%**	5.1%	5.8%
Interest expense, net	**0.4%**	0.3%	0.0%
Income from continuing operations before income taxes	**3.3%**	4.9%	5.8%
Provision for income taxes	**1.2%**	1.8%	2.2%
Income from continuing operations	**2.1%**	3.1%	3.6%
Net income	**2.1%**	3.1%	3.6%

Fiscal 2009 Compared to Fiscal 2008
Consolidated net revenue decreased $21.8 million, or 4.0%, to $513.3 million for the 52-week period ended January 31, 2009 from $535.1 million for the 52-week period ended February 2, 2008.

Comparable store sales for the 52-week period ended January 31, 2009 decreased 7.2% when compared to the same 52-week period in the prior fiscal year. The decrease in comparable store sales was attributable to severe macro-economic conditions and the positive impact of the release of *Harry Potter and the Deathly Hallows* on sales in the prior year.

Our core book department business was down for the year. However, several categories performed well. Teen, faith based titles and election related titles demonstrated strength. The teen category was positively impacted by the success of Stephanie Meyer's *Twilight* series. Titles such as William Young's *The Shack* and Glenn Beck's *The Christmas Sweater* also had a positive impact. Bargain books and gifts continue to increase year over year driven by the broader economic climate and better assortments.

BOOKS·A·MILLION®
2009 Annual Report

The Company opened sixteen new stores during fiscal 2009 resulting in partial year sales of $13.9 million and closed four stores during fiscal 2009 with partial year sales of $1.4 million. The Company also converted one traditional store to a superstore during fiscal 2009 with partial year sales of $1.3 million.

Net sales for the retail trade segment decreased $20.4 million, or 3.9%, to $508.3 million in the 52-week period ended January 31, 2009, from $528.6 million in the 52-week period ended February 2, 2008. The decrease is due to the 7.2% decrease in comparable store sales as described above, partially offset by the impact of sales from new stores opened in fiscal 2008 and fiscal 2009.

Net sales for the electronic commerce segment decreased $1.8 million, or 6.8%, to $25.2 million in the 52-week period ended January 31, 2009, from $27.0 million in the 52-week period ended February 2, 2008. The decrease in net sales for the electronic commerce segment was due to severe macro-economic conditions and decreased business-to-business sales.

Gross profit, which includes cost of sales, distribution costs and occupancy costs (including rent, common area maintenance, property taxes, utilities and merchant association dues), decreased $7.2 million, or 4.5%, to $151.3 million in the 52-week period ended January 31, 2009, from $158.5 million in the 52-week period ended February 2, 2008. Gross profit as a percentage of net sales decreased to 29.5% in the 52-week period ended January 31, 2009, from 29.6% in the 52-week period ended February 2, 2008. The decrease is attributable to higher occupancy costs offset by higher club card membership income and lower markdowns.

Operating, selling and administrative expenses decreased $0.4 million, or 0.04%, to $116.6 million in the 52-week period ended January 31, 2009, from $117.1 million in the 52-week period ended February 2, 2008. Operating, selling and administrative expenses as a percentage of net sales increased to 22.7% in the 52-week period ending January 31, 2009 from 21.9% in the 52-week period ended February 2, 2008. The decrease was attributable to reduced salary, bonus, 401(k) and payroll tax expense, reduced advertising expenses and reduced bad debt expense, partially offset by increased credit card fees, travel, insurance and new store expenses.

Impairment charges increased $1.3 million to $1.4 million in the 52-week period ended January 31, 2009, compared to the 52-week period ended February 2, 2008. The increase was attributable to $0.7 million in impairment charges taken on leasehold improvements at various stores and a $0.7 million impairment of goodwill.

Depreciation and amortization increased $0.5 million, or 3.3%, to $14.5 million in fiscal 2009, from $14.0 million in fiscal 2008. Depreciation and amortization as a percentage of net sales increased to 2.8% in fiscal 2009, from 2.6% in fiscal 2008, due to new store growth in fiscal years 2009 and 2008.

Consolidated operating profit was $18.9 million for the 52-week period ended January 31, 2009, compared to $27.4 million for the 52-week period ended February 2, 2008. This 31.1% decrease was attributable to decreased store sales for the reasons set forth above, which resulted in lower gross profit for fiscal 2009. Operating profit as a percentage of sales was 3.7% for fiscal 2009. Operating profit was 5.1% of sales for fiscal 2008. The decrease as a percentage of sales from fiscal 2008 is attributable to the decrease in gross margin as a percent of sales plus the increase in operating, selling and administrative expenses and depreciation as outlined above. Operating profit for the electronic commerce segment was $1.5 million in each of fiscal 2009 and 2008. Operating profit for the electronic commerce segment was flat from last year in spite of a $1.8 million decrease in net sales. This was caused by improved gross margin through less discounting and greater sales of higher margin items such as gifts and bargain books.

Net interest expense increased $0.6 million, or 42.6%, to $1.9 million in fiscal 2009, from $1.3 million in fiscal 2008, due to higher average debt in fiscal 2009 partially offset by lower average interest rates. Average debt for the 52-week period ended January 31, 2009 was $41.3 million compared to $27.8 million for the 52-week period ended February 2, 2008. The increase in average debt is attributable to reduced sales, additional share repurchases in fiscal 2009 and the impact of the special dividend paid on July 5, 2007.

The effective rate for income tax purposes was 37.7% for fiscal 2009 and 36.6% for fiscal 2008. The increase in the effective tax rate was due to a higher effective state tax rate in the current fiscal year, as well as the impact of more favorable federal tax credits in fiscal 2008.

The Company did not close any stores in fiscal 2009 in a market where the Company does not expect to retain the closed stores' customers at another store in the same market. Two such stores were closed in fiscal 2008. The financial impact of these closings was not reported as discontinued operations in the financial statements as the impact was immaterial.

Fiscal 2008 Compared to Fiscal 2007

Consolidated net revenue increased $14.7 million, or 2.8%, to $535.1 million for the 52-week period ended February 2, 2008 from $520.4 million for the 53-week period ended February 3, 2007. Two events occurred in the year ended February 3, 2007 that increased total net revenue when compared to the year ended February 2, 2008. First, the 2007 fiscal year included one more week than the 2008 fiscal year. This additional week produced $9.0 million in net sales. Second, the 2007 fiscal year included one-time additional sales income of $2.3 million related to the recognition of gift card breakage from prior years. Consolidated net revenue increased $25.9 million, or 5.1%, to $535.1 million for the 52-week period ended February 2, 2008, when compared with $509.3 million during the period ending February 3, 2007 on a 52-week operating basis (which excludes the $9.0 million of additional sales from the 53rd week of the 2007 fiscal year and the one-time additional sales income of $2.3 million in fiscal 2007 related to gift card breakage from prior years).

Comparable store sales for the 52-week period ended February 2, 2008 increased 1.4% when compared to the same 52-week period in the prior fiscal year. The increase in comparable store sales was attributable to a strong performance in our best sellers and promotional items. During the second quarter of the year ended February 2, 2008, Harry Potter and the Deathly Hallows was released and added to our comparable store sales increase.

Consolidated net revenue included $1.4 million of gift card breakage income for the 52-week period ended February 2, 2008 compared to $3.2 million for the 53-week period ended February 3, 2007. The 53-week period ended February 3, 2007 included $2.3 million, $1.4 million net of taxes, of gift card breakage income related to periods prior to fiscal 2007. In fiscal 2007 the Company formed a gift card subsidiary, Books-A-Million Card Services ("Card Services"), and began recording gift card breakage income for those cards for which the likelihood of redemption is deemed to be remote (after 24 months of inactivity) and which there is no legal obligation to remit the value of such redeemed gift cards to the relevant jurisdictions. The primary function of Card Services is to administer the Company's gift card program and to provide a more advantageous legal structure. The $2.3 million related to periods prior to fiscal 2007 represents a change in estimate in the escheat liability due to operational changes related to the creation of Card Services.

Our core book department business was down slightly for the year. However, sales of fiction titles were very strong, driven by sales of commercial fiction titles and the January publication of John Grisham's *The Appeal* and Stephen King's *Duma Key*. Biography titles experienced the success of Elizabeth Gilbert's memoir, *Eat, Pray Love*. We also built on the positive sales trends in teen titles, graphic novels and our Faithpoint inspirational titles. Sales of children's books sales increased over prior year due to sales of *Harry Potter and The Deathly Hallows* setting new records and the ongoing growth of children's titles generally. Our stores produced solid gains in bargain books and gifts with toys and games experiencing gains over prior periods.

The Company opened nine new stores during fiscal 2008 resulting in partial year sales of $6.4 million and closed seven stores during fiscal 2008 with partial year sales of $1.2 million. The Company also converted one traditional store to a superstore during fiscal 2008 with partial year sales of $1.0 million.

Net sales for the retail trade segment increased $15.6 million, or 3.0%, to $528.6 million in the 52-week period ended February 2, 2008, from $513.0 million in the 53-week period ended February 3, 2007. When compared to the same 52-week period last year, the retail trade segment increased $23.8 million, or 4.7%. In addition to the factors discussed above, the increase in net sales for the retail trade segment was due to new stores opened in fiscal 2008.

Net sales for the electronic commerce segment increased $1.0 million, or 3.6%, to $27.0 million in the 52-week period ended February 2, 2008, from $26.0 million in the 53-week period ended February 3, 2007. When compared to the same 52-week period last year, the electronic commerce segment increased $1.7 million, or 6.7%. The increase in net sales for the electronic commerce segment was due to increased business to business sales.

Gross profit, which includes cost of sales, distribution costs and occupancy costs (including rent, common area maintenance, property taxes, utilities and merchant association dues), increased $1.8 million, or 1.2%, to $158.5 million in the 52-week period ended February 2, 2008, from $156.7 million in the 53-week period ended February 3, 2007. Gross profit as a percentage of net sales decreased to 29.6% in the 52-week period ended February 2, 2008 from 30.1% in the 53-week period ended February 3, 2007. Excluding the extra week and gift card breakage recorded in fiscal 2007, gross profit as a percentage of net sales decreased 0.2% in fiscal 2008. The decrease is the result of higher occupancy and warehouse costs partially offset by lower promotional discounts, lower markdowns, improvements in store inventory shrinkage and higher club card membership income.

BOOKS·A·MILLION
2009 Annual Report

Operating, selling and administrative expenses increased $4.5 million, or 4.1%, to $117.1 million in the 52-week period ended February 2, 2008, from $112.6 million in the 53-week period ended February 3, 2007. Operating, selling and administrative expenses as a percentage of net sales remained relatively flat at 21.9% in the 52-week period ending February 2, 2008 compared to 21.6% in the 53-week period ended February 3, 2007. Excluding the extra week recorded in fiscal 2007, operating, selling and administrative expenses as a percentage of net sales increased 0.2% in fiscal 2008. The increase was due to an increase in health care expense, promotional expense for our club card program and a revision of the franchise tax estimate.

Depreciation and amortization decreased $0.1 million, or 0.6%, to $14.0 million in fiscal 2008, from $14.1 million in fiscal 2007. Depreciation and amortization as a percentage of net sales decreased to 2.6% in fiscal 2008, from 2.7% in fiscal 2007, due to the impact of certain assets becoming fully depreciated during the prior year.

Consolidated operating profit was $27.4 million for the 52-week period ended February 2, 2008, compared to $30.1 million for the 53-week period ended February 3, 2007. Excluding the extra week and gift card breakage recorded in fiscal 2007, operating profit increased $0.6 million during fiscal 2008. This increase was attributable to increased store sales for the reasons set forth above, which resulted in higher gross profit for fiscal 2008. Operating profit as a percentage of sales was 5.1% for fiscal 2008. Excluding the extra week and the gift card breakage recorded in fiscal 2007, operating profit was 5.3% of sales for fiscal 2007. The decrease as a percentage of sales from fiscal 2007 is attributable to the decrease in gross margin as a percent of sales plus the increase in operating, selling and administrative expenses offset by the reduction in depreciation as outlined above. The operating profit for the electronic commerce segment was $1.5 million, compared to $1.4 million in fiscal 2007. The improvement in operating results was due to higher gross margin partially offset by higher customer service payroll, an adjustment to our gift card reserves, software maintenance and bad debt.

Net interest expense increased $1.2 million, or 1185.8%, to $1.3 million in fiscal 2008, from $0.1 million in fiscal 2007, due to borrowing from our revolving credit facility as a result of the special dividend paid on July 5, 2007 and our share repurchase program. During fiscal 2008, the Company purchased 1.4 million shares of its common stock at a total cost of $20.0 million under its share repurchase program.

The effective rate for income tax purposes was 36.64% for fiscal 2008 and 37.0% for fiscal 2007. The decrease in the effective tax rate was due to federal tax credits for prior year returns taken in fiscal 2008.

The Company closed two stores in fiscal 2008 in a market where the Company does not expect to retain the closed stores' customers at another store in the same market. The store's sales and operating results for fiscal 2008 have not been included in discontinued operations because the impact on the financial statements was immaterial. The Company continues to report in discontinued operations for prior year stores closed where the Company does not expect to retain the closed stores' customers at another store. One such store was closed in fiscal 2007. The financial impact of these closings was reported as discontinued operations in the financial statements, but had a minimal impact on the financial results of the Company.

Presented below is certain financial information for the fiscal year ended February 3, 2007 on a 52-week "operating basis," the effect of which is to exclude the financial results for the final week of the fiscal period and to exclude the effect of prior year gift card breakage income. This information is presented because the fiscal year ended February 3, 2007 was one week longer than the fiscal year ended February 2, 2008 and included gift card breakage income related to periods prior to fiscal 2007.

Management uses these non-GAAP financial measures because it believes that they are important to investors in comparing the Company's financial performance in one fiscal period against a prior fiscal period in circumstances where the fiscal periods are of a different duration or include a material non-recurring item such as a change in estimate. As noted above, the fiscal year ended February 3, 2007, was one week longer than the fiscal year ended February 2, 2008 and included $2.3 million, $1.4 million net of taxes, of prior year gift card breakage income.

These non-GAAP financial measures have limitations as analytical tools, and you should not consider them in isolation or as substitutes for results determined in accordance with GAAP. Additionally, other companies in the retail industry may not exclude portions of a fiscal period from the financial results for such period, limiting their usefulness as a comparative measure. The following table reconciles the non-GAAP measures from the fiscal year ended February 3, 2007, with the comparable financial measure calculated and presented in accordance with GAAP.

BOOKS·A·MILLION
2009 Annual Report

REPORT OF INDEPENDENT REGISTERED PUBLIC ACCOUNTING FIRM

Board of Directors and Stockholders
Books-A-Million, Inc.

We have audited the accompanying consolidated balance sheets of Books-A-Million, Inc. and subsidiaries (the "Company") as of January 31, 2009 and February 2, 2008 and the related consolidated statements of income, stockholders' equity, and cash flows for each of the three years in the period ended January 31, 2009. These financial statements are the responsibility of the Company's management. Our responsibility is to express an opinion on these financial statements based on our audits.

We conducted our audits in accordance with the standards of the Public Company Accounting Oversight Board (United States). Those standards require that we plan and perform the audits to obtain reasonable assurance about whether the financial statements are free of material misstatement. An audit includes examining, on a test basis, evidence supporting the amounts and disclosures in the financial statements. An audit also includes assessing the accounting principles used and significant estimates made by management, as well as evaluating the overall financial statement presentation. We believe that our audits provide a reasonable basis for our opinion.

In our opinion, the consolidated financial statements referred to above present fairly, in all material respects, the financial position of the Company as of January 31, 2009 and February 2, 2008, and the results of its operations and its cash flows for each of the three years in the period ended January 31, 2009 in conformity with accounting principles generally accepted in the United States of America.

We also have audited, in accordance with the standards of the Public Company Accounting Oversight Board (United States), the Company's internal control over financial reporting as of January 31, 2009, based on criteria established in Internal Control—Integrated Framework issued by the Committee of Sponsoring Organizations of the Treadway Commission (COSO) and our report dated April 14, 2009 expressed an unqualified opinion.

/s/ GRANT THORNTON LLP

Atlanta, Georgia
April 14, 2009

BOOKS·A·MILLION
2009 Annual Report

REPORT OF INDEPENDENT REGISTERED PUBLIC ACCOUNTING FIRM

Board of Directors and Stockholders
Books-A-Million, Inc.

We have audited Books-A-Million, Inc.'s and subsidiaries (the "Company") internal control over financial reporting as of January 31, 2009, based on criteria established in Internal Control—Integrated Framework issued by the Committee of Sponsoring Organizations of the Treadway Commission (COSO). The Company's management is responsible for maintaining effective internal control over financial reporting and for its assessment of the effectiveness of internal control over financial reporting, included in the accompanying Management's Report on Internal Controls Over Financial Reporting. Our responsibility is to express an opinion on the Company's internal control over financial reporting based on our audit.

We conducted our audit in accordance with the standards of the Public Company Accounting Oversight Board (United States). Those standards require that we plan and perform the audit to obtain reasonable assurance about whether effective internal control over financial reporting was maintained in all material respects. Our audit included obtaining an understanding of internal control over financial reporting, assessing the risk that a material weakness exists, testing and evaluating the design and operating effectiveness of internal control based on the assessed risk, and performing such other procedures as we considered necessary in the circumstances. We believe that our audit provides a reasonable basis for our opinion.

A company's internal control over financial reporting is a process designed to provide reasonable assurance regarding the reliability of financial reporting and the preparation of financial statements for external purposes in accordance with generally accepted accounting principles. A company's internal control over financial reporting includes those policies and procedures that (1) pertain to the maintenance of records that, in reasonable detail, accurately and fairly reflect the transactions and dispositions of the assets of the company; (2) provide reasonable assurance that transactions are recorded as necessary to permit preparation of financial statements in accordance with generally accepted accounting principles, and that receipts and expenditures of the company are being made only in accordance with authorizations of management and directors of the company; and (3) provide reasonable assurance regarding prevention or timely detection of unauthorized acquisition, use, or disposition of the company's assets that could have a material effect on the financial statements.

Because of its inherent limitations, internal control over financial reporting may not prevent or detect misstatements. Also, projections of any evaluation of effectiveness to future periods are subject to the risk that controls may become inadequate because of changes in conditions, or that the degree of compliance with the policies or procedures may deteriorate.

In our opinion, the Company maintained, in all material respects, effective internal control over financial reporting as of January 31, 2009, based on criteria established in Internal Control—Integrated Framework issued by COSO.

We also have audited, in accordance with the standards of the Public Company Accounting Oversight Board (United States), the consolidated balance sheets of the Company as of January 31, 2009 and February 2, 2008, and the related consolidated statements of income, stockholders' equity, and cash flows for each of the three years in the period ended January 31, 2009 and our report dated April 14, 2009 expressed an unqualified opinion on those financial statements.

/s/ GRANT THORNTON LLP

Atlanta, Georgia
April 14, 2009

BOOKS·A·MILLION
2009 Annual Report

Consolidated Balance Sheets

	As of	
(Dollars in thousands, except per share amounts)	**1/31/09**	2/2/08
Assets		
Current Assets:		
Cash and cash equivalents	$ **5,529**	$ 5,595
Accounts receivable, net of allowance for doubtful accounts of $354 and $741, respectively	**5,431**	6,450
Related party receivables	**1,133**	3,780
Inventories	**204,305**	206,836
Prepayments and other	**3,239**	4,678
Total Current Assets	**219,637**	227,339
Property and Equipment:		
Land	**628**	628
Buildings	**6,915**	6,915
Equipment	**79,003**	76,653
Furniture and fixtures	**88,999**	84,843
Leasehold improvements	**58,086**	53,071
Construction in process	**536**	398
Gross Property and Equipment	**234,167**	222,508
Less accumulated depreciation and amortization	**176,129**	168,994
Net Property and Equipment	**58,038**	53,514
Deferred Income Taxes	**463**	2,452
Other Assets:		
Goodwill	**653**	1,368
Other	**501**	160
Total Other Assets	**1,154**	1,528
Total Assets	**$279,292**	$284,833
Liabilities and Stockholders' Equity		
Current Liabilities:		
Accounts payable:		
Trade	$ **94,418**	$ 88,994
Related party	**2,321**	2,213
Accrued expenses	**35,554**	41,539
Accrued income taxes	**848**	995
Deferred income taxes	**8,591**	6,846
Short-term borrowings	**15,760**	27,967
Total Current Liabilities	**157,492**	168,554
Long-term Debt	**6,720**	6,975
Deferred Rent	**8,554**	8,079
Liability for Uncertain Tax Positions	**2,032**	2,174
Total Non-current Liabilities	**17,306**	17,228
Commitments and Contingencies		
Stockholders' Equity:		
Preferred stock, $.01 par value; 1,000,000 shares authorized, no shares outstanding	-	-
Common stock, $.01 par value; 30,000,000 shares authorized, 21,236,218 and 20,850,611 shares outstanding at January 31, 2009 and February 2, 2008, respectively	**212**	209
Additional paid-in capital	**91,432**	89,752
Treasury stock at cost (5,455,720 shares at January 31, 2009 and 5,216,951 shares at February 2, 2008, respectively)	**(46,258)**	(44,468)
Retained earnings	**59,108**	53,558
Total Stockholders' Equity	**104,494**	99,051
Total Liabilities and Stockholders' Equity	**$279,292**	$284,833

The accompanying notes are an integral part of these consolidated statements.

BOOKS·A·MILLION

2009 Annual Report

CONSOLIDATED STATEMENTS OF INCOME

(In thousands, except per share data)	Fiscal Year Ended		
	1/31/09	2/2/08	2/3/07
	52 weeks	52 weeks	53 weeks
Net revenue	$513,271	$535,128	$520,416
Cost of products sold, including warehouse distribution and store occupancy costs	361,934	376,580	363,688
Gross profit	151,337	158,548	156,728
Operating, selling and administrative expenses	116,648	117,079	112,227
Impairment charges	1,351	60	333
Depreciation and amortization	14,448	13,989	14,069
Operating profit	18,890	27,420	30,099
Interest expense, net	1,920	1,346	105
Income before income taxes	16,970	26,074	29,994
Provision for income taxes	6,396	9,552	11,107
Net Income	$ 10,574	$ 16,522	$ 18,887
Net income per common share:			
Basic			
Net income per share	$ 0.70	$ 1.03	$ 1.16
Weighted average number of shares outstanding – basic	15,219	16,089	16,352
Diluted			
Net income per share	$ 0.68	$ 1.01	$ 1.12
Weighted average number of shares outstanding – diluted	15,609	16,302	16,805
Dividends per share – declared	$ 0.28	$ 3.36	$ 0.33

The accompanying notes are an integral part of these consolidated statements.

2009 Annual Report

CONSOLIDATED STATEMENTS OF CHANGES IN STOCKHOLDERS' EQUITY

(In thousands)	Common Stock		Additional Paid-In Capital	Treasury Stock		Retained Earnings	Accumulated Other Comprehensive Income (Loss)	Total Stockholders' Equity
	Shares	Amount		Shares	Amount			
Balance, January 28, 2006	19,764	$198	$79,509	3,287	$(16,954)	$82,263	$(7)	$145,009
Net income						18,887		18,887
Unrealized gain on accounting for derivative instruments, net of tax provision of $4							7	7
Subtotal comprehensive income								18,894
Purchase of treasury stock, at cost				531	(7,460)			(7,460)
Dividends paid						(5,303)		(5,303)
Issuance of restricted stock	148	1	1,558					1,559
Issuance of stock for employee stock purchase plan	9		88					88
Exercise of stock options	540	6	1,674					1,680
Tax benefit from exercise of stock options			2,567					2,567
Balance, February 3, 2007	20,461	$205	$85,396	3,818	$(24,414)	$95,847	$ --	$157,034
Net income						$16,522		$16,522
Subtotal comprehensive income								$16,522
FIN 48 Adjustment						(1,987)		(1,987)
Purchase of treasury stock, at cost				1,399	$(20,054)			(20,054)
Dividends paid						(56,824)		(56,824)
Issuance of restricted stock	155	$2	$1,464					1,466
Issuance of stock for employee stock purchase plan	8		118					118
Exercise of stock options	226	2	1,136					1,138
Tax benefit from exercise of stock options			1,638					1,638
Balance, February 2, 2008	20,850	$209	$89,752	5,217	$(44,468)	$53,558	$ --	$99,051
Net income						$10,574		$10,574
Subtotal comprehensive income								$10,574
Purchase of treasury stock, at cost				239	$(1,790)			(1,790)
Dividends paid						(5,024)		(5,024)
Issuance of restricted stock	374	$3	$1,887					1,890
Issuance of stock for employee stock purchase plan	12		132					132
Tax decrement from stock based compensation			(339)					(339)
Balance, January 31, 2009	21,236	$212	$91,432	5,456	$(46,258)	$59,108	$ --	$104,494

The accompanying notes are an integral part of these consolidated statements

BOOKS·A·MILLION®
2009 Annual Report

CONSOLIDATED STATEMENTS OF CASH FLOWS

	Fiscal Year Ended		
(In thousands)	**1/31/09**	2/2/08	2/3/07
	52 Weeks	52 Weeks	53 Weeks
Cash Flows from Operating Activities:			
Net income	**$10,574**	$16,522	$18,887
Adjustments to reconcile net income to net cash provided by operating activities:			
Depreciation and amortization	**14,448**	13,989	14,069
Stock-based compensation	**1,890**	1,466	1,559
Loss on impairment of assets	**1,351**	60	336
Loss on sale of property and equipment	**271**	479	228
Deferred income tax provision	**3,734**	2,933	465
Excess tax benefit of stock based compensation	**339**	(1,638)	(2,567)
Bad debt expense	**93**	430	254
(Increase) decrease in assets:			
Accounts receivable	**926**	644	1,890
Related party receivables	**2,647**	(1,133)	(1,513)
Inventories	**2,531**	(6,559)	4,512
Prepayments and other	**1,439**	(315)	(25)
Noncurrent assets (excluding amortization)	**(412)**	(3)	(124)
Increase (decrease) in liabilities:			
Accounts payable	**5,424**	5,575	(14,752)
Related party payables	**108**	(775)	297
Accrued income taxes	**(486)**	(1,719)	880
Accrued expenses	**(5,654)**	4,537	(3,090)
Total adjustments	**28,649**	17,971	2,419
Net cash provided by operating activities	**39,223**	34,493	21,306
Cash Flows from Investing Activities:			
Capital expenditures	**(19,819)**	(16,878)	(16,191)
Proceeds from sale of property and equipment	**13**	--	15
Net cash used in investing activities	**(19,806)**	(16,878)	(16,176)
Cash Flows from Financing Activities:			
Borrowings under credit facilities	**236,125**	174,212	2,850
Repayments under credit facilities	**(248,587)**	(146,370)	(2,950)
Proceeds from exercise of stock options and issuance of common stock under employee stock purchase plan	**132**	1,257	1,768
Purchase of treasury stock	**(1,790)**	(20,054)	(7,460)
Payment of dividends	**(5,024)**	(56,824)	(5,303)
Excess tax benefit from stock based compensation	**(339)**	1,638	2,567
Net cash used in financing activities	**(19,483)**	(46,141)	(8,528)
Net Decrease in Cash and Cash Equivalents	**(66)**	(28,526)	(3,398)
Cash and Cash Equivalents at Beginning of Year	**5,595**	34,121	37,519
Cash and Cash Equivalents at End of Year	**$5,529**	$5,595	$34,121
Supplemental Disclosures of Cash Flow Information:			
Cash paid during the year for:			
Interest	**$2,013**	$1,907	$ 910
Income taxes, net of refunds	**$3,319**	$6,666	$ 7,199
Supplemental Disclosures of Non Cash Investing Activities:			
Capital expenditures in accrued expenses	**$ (833)**	$ (368)	$(1,284)
Like-kind exchange of assets	**$1,600**	--	--

The accompanying notes are an integral part of these consolidated statements.

NOTES TO CONSOLIDATED FINANCIAL STATEMENTS

1. Summary of Significant Accounting Policies

Business

Books-A-Million, Inc. and its subsidiaries (the "Company") are principally engaged in the sale of books, magazines and related items through a chain of retail bookstores. The Company presently operates 220 bookstores in 21 states and the District of Columbia, which are predominantly located in the southeastern United States. The Company also operates a retail Internet website. The Company presently consists of Books-A-Million, Inc. and its three wholly owned subsidiaries, American Wholesale Book Company, Inc., Booksamillion.com, Inc. and BAM Card Services, LLC. All inter-company balances and transactions have been eliminated in consolidation. For a discussion of the Company's business segments, see Note 8.

Fiscal Year

The Company operates on a 52 or 53-week year, with the fiscal year ending on the Saturday closest to January 31. Fiscal year 2009 and fiscal year 2008 were each 52-week periods. Fiscal year 2007 was a 53-week period.

Use of Estimates in the Preparation of Financial Statements

The preparation of financial statements in conformity with accounting principles generally accepted in the United States of America requires that management make estimates and assumptions that affect the reported amounts of assets and liabilities, the disclosure of contingent assets and liabilities at the date of the financial statements and the reported revenues and expenses during the reporting periods. Actual results could differ from those estimates.

Revenue Recognition

The Company recognizes revenue from the sale of merchandise at the time the merchandise is sold and the customer takes delivery. Returns are recognized at the time the merchandise is returned and processed. At each period end, an estimate of sales returns is recorded. Sales return reserves are based on historical returns as a percentage of sales activity. The historical returns percentage is applied to the sales for which returns are projected to be received after period end. The estimated returns percentage and return dollars have not materially changed in the last several years. Sales tax collected is recorded net and is not recognized as revenue and is included on the consolidated balance sheets in accrued expenses.

The Company sells its Millionaire's Club Card, which entitles the customer to receive a ten percent discount on all purchases made during the twelve-month membership period, for a non-refundable fee. The Company recognizes this revenue over the twelve-month membership period based upon historical customer usage patterns. Related deferred revenue is included in accrued expenses.

The Company sells gift cards to its customers in its retail stores. The gift cards do not have an expiration date. Income is recognized from gift cards when: (1) the gift card is redeemed by the customer; or (2) the likelihood of the gift card being redeemed by the customer is remote (gift card breakage) and there is no legal obligation to remit the value of the unredeemed gift cards to the relevant jurisdictions. The gift card breakage rate is determined based upon historical redemption patterns. Based on this historical information, the likelihood of a gift card remaining unredeemed can be determined after 24 months of card inactivity. At that time, breakage income is recognized for those cards for which the likelihood of redemption is deemed to be remote and for which there is no legal obligation to remit the value of such unredeemed gift cards to the relevant jurisdictions. In fiscal 2007, the Company formed a gift card subsidiary, Books-A-Million Card Services, now known as BAM Card Services, LLC ("Card Services"), to administer the Company's gift card program and to provide a more advantageous legal structure. During fiscal 2009, the Company recognized $1.7 million of gift card breakage income. Breakage income for fiscal 2008 was $1.4 million. Breakage income for fiscal 2007 was $3.2 million, of which $2.3 million relates to periods prior to fiscal 2007. The $2.3 million represents a change in estimate in the escheat liability due to operational changes related to the creation of Card Services. Gift card breakage income is included in revenue.

Vendor Allowances

The Company receives allowances from its vendors from a variety of programs and arrangements, including placement and co-operative advertising programs. Effective February 3, 2002, the Company adopted the provisions of Emerging Issues Task Force ("EITF") No. 02-16, *Accounting by a Customer (Including a Reseller) for Certain Consideration Received from a Vendor*, which addresses the accounting for vendor allowances. As a result of the adoption of this statement, vendor allowances in excess of incremental direct costs are reflected as a reduction of inventory costs and recognized in cost of products sold upon the sale of the related inventory.

BOOKS·A·MILLION
2009 Annual Report

Accounts Payable

The Company classifies its checks written but not yet cleared by the bank in Accounts Payable since the right to offset does not exist as of January 31, 2009 as described in the provisions of FASB Interpretation No. 39, *Offset Amounts Related to Certain Contracts.* Checks are only written once approved by management. Amounts included in Accounts Payable representing checks written but not yet cleared as of January 31, 2009 and February 2, 2008 were $19.5 million and $25.0 million, respectively.

Inventories

Inventories are valued at the lower of cost or market, using the retail method. Market is determined based on the lower of replacement cost or estimated realizable value. Using the retail method, store and warehouse inventories are valued by applying a calculated cost to retail ratio to the retail value of inventories.

The Company currently utilizes the last-in, first-out (LIFO) method of accounting for inventories. The cumulative difference between replacement and current cost of inventory over stated LIFO value was $2.9 million as of January 31, 2009 and $2.5 million as of February 2, 2008. The estimated replacement cost of inventory is the current first-in, first-out (FIFO) value of $207.2 million.

Physical inventory counts are taken throughout the course of the fiscal period and reconciled to the Company's records. Accruals for inventory shortages are estimated based upon historical shortage results.

Inventories were:

	Fiscal Year Ended	
(In thousands)	**January 31, 2009**	February 2, 2008
Inventories (at FIFO)	**$207,217**	$209,314
LIFO reserve	**(2,912)**	(2,478)
Net inventories	**$204,305**	$206,836

Property and Equipment

Property and equipment are recorded at cost. Depreciation of equipment and furniture and fixtures is provided on the straight-line method over the estimated service lives, which range from three to seven years. Depreciation of buildings and amortization of leasehold improvements, including remodels, is provided on the straight-line basis over the lesser of the assets' estimated useful lives (ranging from five to 40 years) or, if applicable, the periods of the leases. Determination of useful asset life is based on several factors requiring judgment by management and adherence to generally accepted accounting principles for depreciable periods. Judgment used by management in the determination of useful asset life could relate to any of the following factors: expected use of the asset; expected useful life of similar assets; any legal, regulatory, or contractual provisions that may limit the useful life; and other factors that may impair the economic useful life of the asset. Maintenance and repairs are charged to expense as incurred. Improvement costs, which extend the useful life of an asset, are capitalized to property accounts and depreciated over the asset's expected remaining life. The cost and accumulated depreciation of assets sold, retired or otherwise disposed of are removed from the accounts, and the related gain or loss is credited or charged to income.

Long-Lived Assets

The Company's long-lived assets consist of property and equipment which includes leasehold improvements. At January 31, 2009, the Company had $58.0 million of property and equipment, net of accumulated depreciation, accounting for approximately 20.8% of the Company's total assets. The Company reviews its long-lived assets for impairment whenever events or changes in circumstances indicate that the carrying amount of an asset may not be recoverable in accordance with Statement of Financial Accounting Standards (SFAS) No. 144, *"Accounting for the Impairment or Disposal of Long-Lived Assets."* The Company evaluates long-lived assets for impairment at the individual store level, which is the lowest level at which individual cash flows can be identified. When evaluating long-lived assets for potential impairment, the Company will first compare the carrying amount of the assets to the individual store's estimated future undiscounted cash flows. If the estimated future cash flows are less than the carrying amount of the assets, an impairment loss calculation is prepared. The impairment loss calculation compares the carrying amount of the assets to the individual store's fair value based on its estimated discounted future cash flows. If required, an impairment loss is recorded for that portion of the asset's carrying value in excess of fair value. Impairment losses on long-lived assets, excluding goodwill impairment, totaled $0.7 million, $0.1 million and $0.3 million in fiscal 2009, 2008 and 2007, respectively, and were recorded in impairment charges. For all years presented, the impairment losses related to the retail trade business segment.

Goodwill

At January 31, 2009, the Company had $0.7 million of goodwill, accounting for approximately 0.2% of the Company's total assets. SFAS No. 142, *"Goodwill and Other Intangible Assets,"* requires that goodwill and other indefinite life intangible assets be tested for impairment at least annually or earlier if there are impairment indicators. The Company performs a two-step process for impairment testing of goodwill as required by SFAS No. 142. The first step of this test, used to identify potential impairment, compares the estimated fair value of a reporting unit with its carrying amount. The second step (if necessary) measures the amount of the impairment.

The valuation approaches are subject to key judgments and assumptions that are sensitive to change such as judgments and assumptions about appropriate sales growth rates, operating margins, weighted average cost of capital ("WACC"), and comparable company market multiples. When developing these key judgments and assumptions, the Company considers economic, operational and market conditions that could impact the fair value of the reporting unit. However, estimates are inherently uncertain and represent only management's reasonable expectations regarding future developments.

The Company completed its latest annual impairment test on goodwill during the fourth quarter of fiscal 2009 and determined that an impairment charge was required. As a result, an impairment charge of $0.7 million was recorded in the fourth quarter of fiscal 2009, which was the direct result of declining market conditions.

Deferred Rent

The Company recognizes rent expense by the straight-line method over the lease term, including lease renewal option periods that can be reasonably assured at the inception of the lease. The lease term commences on the date when the Company takes possession and has the right to control use of the leased premises. Also, funds received from the lessor intended to reimburse the Company for the cost of leasehold improvements are recorded as a deferred credit resulting from a lease incentive and are amortized over the lease term as a reduction of rent expense. As of January 31, 2009, deferred rent totaled $8.6 million compared to $8.1 million as of February 2, 2008.

Loss from Discontinued Operations

The Company periodically closes under-performing stores. The Company believes that a store is a component under SFAS No. 144. Therefore, each store closure would result in the reporting of a discontinued operation unless the operations and cash flows from the closed store could be absorbed in some part by surrounding Company stores(s) within the same market area. Management evaluates certain factors in determining whether a closed store's operations could be absorbed by surrounding store(s); the primary factor considered is the distance to the next closest Books-A-Million store. When a closed store results in a discontinued operation, the results of operations of the closed store include store closing costs and any related asset impairments. See Note 7 for discontinued operations disclosures.

Store Opening Costs

Non-capital expenditures incurred in preparation for opening new retail stores are expensed as incurred.

Store Closing Costs

The Company continually evaluates the profitability of its stores. When the Company closes or relocates a store, the Company incurs unrecoverable costs, including net book value of abandoned fixtures and leasehold improvements, lease termination payments, costs to transfer inventory and usable fixtures and other costs of vacating the leased location. Such costs are expensed as incurred and are included in selling, general and administrative costs. During fiscal 2009, 2008 and 2007, the Company recognized store closing costs of $0.4 million, $0.6 million and $0.4 million, respectively.

Advertising Costs

The costs of advertising are expensed as incurred. Advertising costs, net of applicable vendor reimbursements of $1.8 million, $1.8 million and $1.4 million, are charged to operating, selling and administrative expenses, and totaled $3.3 million, $3.8 million and $3.6 million for fiscal years 2009, 2008 and 2007, respectively.

Insurance Accruals

The Company is subject to large deductibles under its workers' compensation and health insurance policies. Amounts are accrued currently for the estimated cost of claims incurred, both reported and unreported.

Income Taxes

The Company recognizes deferred tax assets and liabilities for the expected future tax consequences of events that result in temporary differences between the amounts recorded in its financial statements and tax returns. Under this method, deferred tax assets and liabilities are determined based on the differences between the financial statement and tax basis of assets and liabilities using enacted tax rates in effect for the year in which the differences are expected to reverse.

BOOKS·A·MILLION
2009 Annual Report

Accounts Receivable and Allowance for Doubtful Accounts

Receivables represent customer, landlord and other receivables due within one year and are net of any allowance for doubtful accounts. Net receivables were $6.6 million and $10.2 million for January 31, 2009 and February 2, 2008, respectively. Trade accounts receivable are stated at the amount the Company expects to collect and do not bear interest. The collectability of trade receivable balances is regularly evaluated based on a combination of factors such as customer credit-worthiness, past transaction history with the customer, current economic industry trends and changes in customer payment patterns. If it is determined that a customer will be unable to fully meet its financial obligation, such as the case of a bankruptcy filing or other material events impacting its business, a specific reserve for doubtful accounts is recorded to reduce the related receivable to the amount expected to be recovered.

Cash and Cash Equivalents

For purposes of the consolidated statements of cash flows, the Company considers all short-term, highly liquid investments with original maturities of 90 days or less to be cash equivalents.

Sales and Use Tax Contingencies

The Company is subject to potential ongoing sales and use tax audits, income tax audits and other tax issues for both its retail and electronic commerce segments. It is the policy of the Company to estimate any potential tax contingency liabilities based on various factors such as ongoing state and federal tax audits, historical results of audits at the state or federal level and specific tax issues. Accruals for potential tax contingencies are recorded by the Company when they are deemed to have a probable likelihood of a liability and the liability can be reasonably estimated.

Stockholders' Equity

Basic net income per common share ("EPS") is computed by dividing income available to common shareholders by the weighted-average number of common shares outstanding for the period. Diluted EPS reflects the potential dilution, using the treasury stock method that could occur if stock options are exercised or restricted stock granted to employees vested and resulted in an increase of common stock that then shared in the earnings of the Company. Diluted EPS has been computed based on the average number of shares outstanding including the effect of outstanding stock options and restricted stock, if dilutive, in each respective year. A reconciliation of the weighted average shares for basic and diluted EPS is as follows:

	Fiscal Year Ended		
(In thousands)	**1/31/09**	2/2/08	2/3/07
Weighted average shares outstanding:			
Basic	**15,219**	16,089	16,352
Dilutive effect of unvested restricted stock outstanding	**390**	213	453
Diluted	**15,609**	16,302	16,805

In March 2004, the Board of Directors authorized a common stock repurchase program for up to 1.6 million shares, or 10% of the outstanding stock (the "March 2004 Plan"). Under the March 2004 Plan, the Company repurchased a total of 1,452,000 shares at a cost of $13.7 million. This plan is now discontinued.

On June 8, 2006, the Board approved a new stock repurchase program (the "June 2006 Plan"). The program authorized the repurchase of up to $10 million in shares of the Company's common stock over the following twelve months, but no specific number of shares was approved. Under the June 2006 Plan, the Company repurchased a total of 300,000 shares at a cost of $4.4 million. This stock repurchase program replaced the March 2004 Plan.

On August 23, 2006, the Board approved an additional stock repurchase program (the "August 2006 Plan"). This program authorized the repurchase of up to an additional $25 million in shares of the Company's common stock over the following eighteen months. This program is in addition to the June 2006 Plan to repurchase up to $10 million in shares of common stock. Under the August 2006 Plan, the Company repurchased 1,399,000 shares at a cost of $20.1 million during the fiscal year ended February 2, 2008. This plan expired on February 23, 2008.

On March 26, 2008, the Board of Directors authorized a new common stock repurchase program (the "March 2008 Plan") for up to $5 million in shares of common stock through the expiration of this plan on April 30, 2009. Under the March 2008 Plan, the Company repurchased 239,000 shares at a cost of $1.8 million during the fiscal year ended January 31, 2009.

On March 26, 2009, the Board of Directors authorized a new common stock repurchase program for up to $5 million in shares of common stock through the expiration of this plan on April 30, 2010.

Disclosure of Fair Value of Financial Instruments

Cash and cash equivalents, accounts receivable, accounts payable and accrued liabilities are reflected in the accompanying financial statements at cost, which approximates fair value because of the short-term maturity of these instruments. Based on the borrowing rates currently available to the Company for bank loans with similar terms and maturities at January 31, 2009 and February 2, 2008, the Company's debt approximates fair value.

Stock-Based Compensation

On January 29, 2006, the Company adopted the provisions of SFAS No. 123(R), *"Share-Based Payment,"* which revises SFAS No. 123, *"Accounting for Stock-Based Compensation,"* and supersedes APB Opinion 25, *"Accounting for Stock Issued to Employees."* SFAS No. 123(R) requires the Company to recognize expense related to the fair value of its stock-based compensation awards, including employee stock options.

Prior to the adoption of SFAS No. 123(R), the Company accounted for stock-based compensation awards using the intrinsic value method as required by APB Opinion 25. Accordingly, the Company did not recognize compensation expense in the statement of income for options granted that had an exercise price equal to or greater than the market value of the underlying common stock on the date of grant. However, the Company did record compensation expense related to restricted stock units based on the market value of its stock at the date of grant. As required by SFAS No. 123, the Company also provided certain pro forma disclosures for stock-based awards as if the fair-value-based approach of SFAS No. 123 had been applied.

The Company used the modified prospective transition method as permitted by SFAS No. 123(R) and, therefore, did not restate its financial results for prior periods. Under this transition method, the Company applied the provisions of SFAS No. 123(R) to new awards and to awards modified, repurchased or cancelled after January 29, 2006. In addition, the Company will recognize compensation cost for the portion of awards for which the requisite service has not been rendered (unvested awards) that are outstanding as of January 29, 2006, as the remaining service was rendered. The compensation cost recorded for these awards was based on their grant-date fair value as calculated for the pro forma disclosures required by SFAS No. 123.

The Company's pre-tax compensation cost for stock-based employee compensation was $1.9 million ($1.2 million net of taxes), $1.5 million ($0.9 million net of taxes) and $1.6 million ($1.0 million net of taxes) for the years ended January 31, 2009, February 2, 2008 and February 3, 2007, respectively, and were recorded in operating, selling and administrative expenses.

Under the 2005 Incentive Award Plan, employees are entitled to receive dividends on non-vested restricted stock. Pursuant to Emerging Issues Task Force ("EITF") No 06-11, Accounting for Income Tax Benefits of Dividends on share based payment awards, the Company has recorded a tax benefit on these dividends of $48,000, $463,000 and $32,000 for fiscal 2009, 2008 and 2007, respectively.

Comprehensive Income (Loss)

Comprehensive income (loss) is net income or loss, plus certain other items that are recorded directly to stockholders' equity. The only such items currently applicable to the Company are the unrealized gains (losses) on the derivative instruments explained in Note 3.

Recently Adopted Accounting Pronouncements

In September 2006, the FASB issued SFAS No. 157, *"Fair Value Measurements"* ("SFAS No. 157"), which defines fair value, establishes a framework for measuring fair value in accordance with generally accepted accounting principles in the United States ("GAAP") and expands disclosures about fair value measurements. For financial assets and liabilities, this statement is effective for fiscal periods beginning after November 15, 2007 and does not require any new fair value measurements. In February 2008, FASB Staff Position No. 157-2 was issued which delayed the effective date of SFAS No. 157 to fiscal years ending after November 15, 2008 for nonfinancial assets and liabilities, except for items that are recognized or disclosed at fair value in the financial statements on a recurring basis (at least annually). The adoption of SFAS No. 157, effective February 3, 2008, did not have a material effect on the Company's consolidated financial statements.

In February 2007, the FASB issued SFAS No. 159, *"The Fair Value Option for Financial Assets and Financial Liabilities —* including an amendment of FASB Statement No. 115." This statement permits entities to choose to measure many financial instruments and certain other items at fair value. This statement is effective for financial statements issued for fiscal years beginning after November 15, 2007, including interim periods within that fiscal year. The Company did not elect the fair value option for any of its existing financial instruments as of February 3, 2008 and the Company has not determined whether or not it will elect this option for financial instruments it may acquire in the future.

BOOKS·A·MILLION

2009 Annual Report

Recently Issued Accounting Pronouncements Not Yet Adopted

In December 2007, the FASB issued SFAS No. 141 (revised), *"Business Combinations"* ("SFAS No. 141R"). The objective of this statement is to improve the relevance, representational faithfulness and comparability of the information that a reporting entity provides in its financial reports about a business combination and its effects. SFAS No. 141R is effective for the Company on February 1, 2009 and its adoption is not expected to have a significant impact on the Company's financial statements.

In December 2007, the FASB issued SFAS No. 160, *"Noncontrolling Interests in Consolidated Financial Statements—an amendment of ARB No. 51"* ("SFAS No. 160"). The objective of this statement is to improve the relevance, comparability and transparency of the financial information that a reporting entity provides in its consolidated financial statements by establishing accounting and reporting standards for the noncontrolling interest in a subsidiary and for the deconsolidation of a subsidiary. SFAS No. 160 is effective for the Company on February 1, 2009 and its adoption is not expected to have a significant impact on the Company's financial statements.

In February 2008, the FASB issued FASB Staff Position (FSP) FAS 157-1, *"Application of FASB Statement No. 157 to FASB Statement No. 13 and Other Accounting Pronouncements that Address Fair Value Measurements for Purposes of Lease Classification or Measurement under Statement 13,"* and FSP FAS 157-2, *"Effective Date of FASB Statement No. 157."* These FSPs:

- Exclude certain leasing transactions accounted for under FASB Statement No. 13, Accounting for Leases, from the scope of FASB Statement No. 157, "Fair Value Measurements" (Statement 157). The exclusion does not apply to fair value measurements of assets and liabilities recorded as a result of a lease transaction but measured pursuant to other pronouncements within the scope of Statement 157.

- Defer the effective date in Statement 157 for one year for certain nonfinancial assets and nonfinancial liabilities, except those that are recognized or disclosed at fair value in the financial statements on a recurring basis (at least annually).

FSP FAS 157-1 is effective upon the initial adoption of Statement 157. FSP FAS 157-2 is effective February 12, 2008. The Company adopted the provisions of FSP 157-1 and 157-2 in the first quarter of 2008. See Note 8 for details regarding the impact of adoption on the Company.

In March 2008, the FASB issued FASB Statement No. 161, *"Disclosures about Derivative Instruments and Hedging Activities"* ("SFAS No. 161"). The new standard is intended to improve financial reporting about derivative instruments and hedging activities by requiring enhanced disclosures to enable investors to better understand their effects on an entity's financial position, financial performance and cash flows. It is effective for financial statements issued for fiscal years and interim periods beginning after November 15, 2008, with early application encouraged. Based on current conditions, the Company does not expect the adoption of SFAS No. 161 to have a significant impact on its results of operations or financial position.

In May 2008, the FASB issued FASB Statement No. 162, *"The Hierarchy of Generally Accepted Accounting Principles"* ("SFAS No. 162"). SFAS No. 162 identifies the sources of accounting principles and the framework for selecting the principles used in the preparation of financial statements of nongovernmental entities that are presented in conformity with GAAP. SFAS No. 162 will become effective 60 days following the SEC's approval of the Public Company Accounting Oversight Board's amendments to AU Section 411, The Meaning of Present Fairly in Conformity With Generally Accepted Accounting Principles. The Company does not expect the adoption of SFAS No. 162 to have a significant impact on its results of operations or financial position.

In June 2008, the FASB ratified EITF Issue No. 08-3, *"Accounting for Lessees for Maintenance Deposits Under Lease Arrangements"* ("EITF No. 08-3"). EITF No. 08-3 requires that all nonrefundable maintenance deposits be accounted for as a deposit with the deposit expensed or capitalized in accordance with the lessee's maintenance accounting policy when the underlying maintenance is performed. Once it is determined that an amount on deposit is not probable of being used to fund future maintenance expense, it is to be recognized as additional expense at the time such determination is made. EITF No. 08-3 is effective for the Company as of the beginning of its fiscal year that begins on February 1, 2009. The adoption of EITF No. 08-3 will not have a material effect on the Company's consolidated financial statements.

In September 2008, the FASB issued FSP No. FAS 133-1 and FIN 45-4, *"Disclosures about Credit Derivatives and Certain Guarantees – An Amendment of FASB Statement No. 133 and FASB Interpretation No. 45; and Clarification of the Effective Date of FASB Statement No. 161."* This FSP amends SFAS No. 133, *"Accounting for Derivative Instruments and Hedging Activities,"* to require disclosures by sellers of credit derivatives, including credit derivatives embedded in a hybrid instrument. This FSP also amends FASB Interpretation No. (FIN) 45, *"Guarantor's Accounting and Disclosure Requirements for Guarantees, Including Indirect Guarantees of Indebtedness of Others,"* to require an additional disclosure about the current status of the payment/performance risk of a guarantee. Further this FSP clarifies the FASB's intent about the effective date of SFAS No. 161, "Disclosures about Derivative Instruments and Hedging Activities." The provisions of this FSP that amend SFAS No. 161 and FIN 45 are effective for reporting periods ending after November 15, 2008 and the clarification of the effective date of SFAS No. 161 is effective upon issuance of this FSP. The Company adopted FSP FAS 133-1 and FIN 45-4 in the fourth quarter of 2008 and has concluded that it does not have a material effect on its consolidated financial statements.

In October 2008, the FASB issued FASB Staff Position (FSP) No. FAS 157-3, *"Determining the Fair Value of a Financial Asset When the Market for That Asset Is Not Active."* FSP 157-3 clarifies the application of SFAS No. 157, *"Fair Value Measurements ,"* in a market that is not active and provides an example to illustrate key considerations in determining the fair value of a financial asset when the market for that financial asset is not active. The FSP stipulates that determining fair value in a dislocated market depends on the facts and circumstances and may require the use of significant judgment when evaluating individual transactions or broker quotes which are some of the sources of the fair value measurement. In addition, FSP FAS 157-3 states that if an entity uses its own assumptions to determine fair value, it must include appropriate risk adjustments that market participants would make for nonperformance and liquidity risks. FSP FAS 157-3 is effective upon issuance, including prior periods for which financial statements have not been issued. The Company adopted FSP FAS 157-3 in the third quarter of 2008 and has concluded that it does not have a material effect on its consolidated financial statements.

2. Income Taxes

A summary of the components of the income tax provision is as follows *(in thousands)*:

	Fiscal Year Ended		
	1/31/09	2/2/08	2/3/07
Current:			
Federal	**$2,398**	$6,304	$10,089
State	**264**	314	553
	$2,662	$6,618	$10,642
Deferred:			
Federal	**$3,388**	$2,481	$ 338
State	**347**	453	127
	$3,734	$2,934	$ 465
Provision for income taxes	**$6,396**	$9,552	$11,107

A reconciliation of the federal statutory income tax rate to the effective income tax rate is as follows:

	Fiscal Year Ended		
	1/31/09	2/2/08	2/3/07
Federal statutory income tax rate	**35.0%**	35.0%	35.0%
State income tax provision	**3.2%**	2.1%	1.7%
Nondeductible meals and entertainment expense	**0.5%**	0.3%	0.2%
Other	**--**	0.1%	0.1%
FIN 48 unrecorded tax benefit adjustment	**(0.8%)**	--	--
Federal tax credits	**(0.2%)**	(0.9%)	--
Effective income tax rate	**37.7%**	36.6%	37.0%

BOOKS·A·MILLION

2009 Annual Report

Temporary differences (in thousands) which created deferred tax assets (liabilities) at January 31, 2009 and February 2, 2008, are as follows:

	As of 1/31/09		As of 2/2/08	
	Current	Noncurrent	Current	Noncurrent
Depreciation	$ --	$ (2,175)	$ --	$ (628)
Accruals	1,507	--	1,646	-
Inventory	(10,494)	--	(8,672)	--
State net operating loss carry forwards	--	28	--	--
Deferred Rent	631	2,547	695	3,418
Prepaids	(1,196)	--	(1,435)	--
Amortization	--	(77)	--	(358)
Allowance for bad debts	143	--	305	--
State tax	--	140	--	20
Stock Compensation	818	--	615	--
	(8,591)	463	(6,846)	2,452
Less: Valuation allowances	--	--	--	--
Deferred tax asset (liability)	$(8,591)	$463	$(6,846)	$2,452

In July 2006, the FASB issued FASB Interpretation No. 48, "*Accounting for Uncertainty in Income Taxes*—an interpretation of FASB Statement No. 109" ("FIN 48"), which provides criteria for the recognition, measurement, presentation and disclosure of uncertain tax positions. The Company adopted the provisions of FIN 48 on February 4, 2007. As a result of the implementation of FIN 48, the Company has recognized an increase of $2.0 million in the liability for unrecognized tax benefits, which was accounted for as a decrease to the balance of retained earnings. The Company evaluates these unrecognized tax benefits each reporting period. As of January 31, 2009, the total amount of unrecognized tax benefits that, if recognized, would affect the effective tax rate is $2.0 million. A reconciliation of the beginning and ending amount of unrecognized tax benefits is as follows:

	1/31/09	2/2/08
Balance at Beginning of Year	2,174	2,227
Additions based on tax positions related to current year	120	350
Reductions for tax positions of previous year	(262)	(403)
Balance at End of Year	2,032	2,174

The Company and its subsidiaries are subject to United States federal income tax as well as income tax of multiple state jurisdictions. In many cases these uncertain tax positions are related to tax years that remain subject to examination by the relevant taxing authorities. The Company has operations in various state jurisdictions that are currently under audit for years ranging from 2001 through 2006. With few exceptions, we are no longer subject to U.S. federal, state or local, or non-United States, income tax examinations for years prior to 2005.

It is reasonably possible that the amount of unrecognized tax benefits will increase or decrease in the next twelve months. These changes may be the result of settlement of ongoing state audits. It is expected that certain state audits will be completed in the next 12 months resulting in a reduction of the liability for unrecognized tax benefits of $60,000. It is also expected that the statute of limitations for certain unrecognized tax benefits will expire in the next 12 months resulting in a reduction of the liability for unrecognized tax benefits of $345,000. Depending on the outcome of these audits, the reduction of the liability for unrecognized tax benefits discussed above may affect the effective tax rate.

The Company's policy is to record interest and penalties related to income tax matters in income tax expense. Accrued interest and penalties were $0.83 million and $0.68 million as of January 31, 2009 and February 2, 2008, respectively. During fiscal year 2009 the Company recognized no interest or penalties.

A valuation allowance was established at the end of fiscal 2007 for net deferred taxes for a wholly-owned subsidiary. As of January 31, 2009, that entity was merged into the parent company. As a result, the net operating losses of that subsidiary are no longer available, and a valuation allowance is deemed unnecessary, as the realization of the remaining net operating losses is considered more likely than not. All remaining net operating losses relate to entities that were not merged.

3. Debt and Lines of Credit

The Company's current credit facility allows for unsecured borrowings up to $100 million for which no principal payments are due until the facility expires in July 2011. Availability under the facility is reduced by outstanding letters of credit issued there under. Interest on borrowings under the credit facility is determined based upon applicable LIBOR rates and the Company's rate spread, which varies depending on the maintenance of certain covenants. The credit facility contains financial and non-financial covenants, the most restrictive of which is the maintenance of a minimum fixed charge coverage ratio. Additionally, the covenants restrict the amount of dividends that can be paid if a certain amount of equity is not maintained. The Company was in compliance with all covenants during fiscal 2009 and as of January 31, 2009. The outstanding balance under this credit facility as of January 31, 2009 and February 2, 2008, was $15.8 million and $28.0 million, respectively, and the face amount of letters of credit issued under the facility was $2.2 million and $2.4 million, respectively. The maximum and average outstanding borrowings under the credit facility (excluding the face amount of letters of credit issued thereunder) during fiscal 2009 were $58.5 million and $41.3 million, respectively. The outstanding amount is considered short-term in the financial statements because all borrowings under the credit facility are completed under tranches that are due in 12 months or less, as allowed under the facility.

During fiscal 1996 and fiscal 1995, the Company acquired and constructed certain warehouse and distribution facilities with the proceeds of loans made pursuant to an industrial development revenue bond (the "Bond"), which was secured by a mortgage interest in these facilities. As of January 31, 2009 and February 2, 2008, there were $6.7 million and $7.0 million of borrowings outstanding, respectively, under these arrangements, which bear interest at variable rates (1.50% as of January 31, 2009). The Bond has a maturity date of December 1, 2019, with a purchase provision obligating the Company to repurchase the Bond, unless extended by the bondholder. In fiscal 2007, an unrelated bank purchased the Bond from the existing bondholder, and the new bondholder extended the date of the Company's purchase obligation of the Bond until July 1, 2011 and did not require a mortgage interest to secure the bond. Such an extension may be renewed annually by the bondholder, at the Company's request, to a date no more than five years from the renewal date. The Company entered into a $7.5 million interest rate swap in May 1996 that expired on June 7, 2006 and effectively fixed the interest rate on the Bond during that period at 8.73% (the "Bond Hedge"). The Company did not replace the Bond Hedge when it expired.

The Company's hedges were designated as cash flow hedges because they are interest rate swaps that convert variable payments to fixed payments. Cash flow hedges protect against the variability in future cash outflows of current or forecasted debt and related interest expense. The changes in the fair value of these hedges are reported on the balance sheet with a corresponding adjustment to accumulated other comprehensive income (loss) or in earnings, depending on the type of hedging relationship. Over time, the amounts held in accumulated other comprehensive income (loss) were reclassified to earnings if the hedge transaction became ineffective.

Prior to its expiration, the Bond Hedge was reported as a liability in the accompanying consolidated balance sheets at a fair value of $61,000 as of February 3, 2007. For the fiscal years ended January 31, 2009, February 2, 2008 and February 3, 2007, adjustments of $0, $0, and $7,000 were recorded as unrealized gains in accumulated other comprehensive income (loss), after tax.

4. Leases

The Company leases the premises for its retail bookstores under operating leases, which expire in various years through the year 2022. Many of these leases contain renewal options and require the Company to pay executory costs (such as property taxes, maintenance, and insurance). In addition to fixed minimum rentals, some of the Company's leases require contingent rentals based on a percentage of sales. The Company also has minimal operating leases for equipment and trailer trucks.

Minimum future rental payments under non-cancelable operating leases having remaining terms in excess of one year as of January 31, 2009 are as follows *(in thousands)*:

Fiscal Year	Future Minimum Rent
2010	$ 39,633
2011	33,310
2012	26,151
2013	20,857
2014	16,990
Subsequent years	49,905
Total	$186,846

BOOKS·A·MILLION
2009 Annual Report

Rental expense for all operating leases consisted of the following *(in thousands)*:

	Fiscal Year Ended		
	1/31/09	2/2/08	2/3/07
Minimum rentals	$37,483	$35,347	$33,205
Contingent rentals	90	(25)	53
Total	$37,573	$35,322	$33,258

5. Employee Benefit Plans

401(k) Profit-Sharing Plan

The Company and its subsidiaries maintain a 401(k) plan covering all employees who have completed six months of service and who are at least 21 years of age, and permit participants to contribute from 1% to 15% of compensation and participants over 50 years of age are allowed to make catch-up contributions. Limits to contributions by employees are established by the Internal Revenue Code. Company matching and supplemental contributions are made at management's discretion. Company matching contributions were 50%, 50% and 70% for fiscal 2009, 2008 and 2007, respectively. The employer contributions are made on employee contributions up to a maximum of 6% of the employee's salary. The expense under this plan was $389,000, $744,000 and $472,000 in fiscal 2009, 2008 and 2007, respectively.

2005 Incentive Award Plan

On June 1, 2005, the stockholders of the Company approved the adoption of the Books-A-Million, Inc. 2005 Incentive Award Plan (the "2005 Plan") for a total of 300,000 shares. On June 8, 2006, the stockholders of the Company approved an additional 300,000 shares to be awarded under the Plan, and on May 29, 2008, the stockholders of the Company approved an additional 600,000 shares to be awarded under the Plan. An aggregate of 1,200,000 shares of common stock may be awarded under the 2005 Plan. From June 1, 2005 through January 31, 2009, awards under the 2005 Plan consisted solely of awards of restricted stock. Each year the compensation committee makes awards to the Company's officers and key employees pursuant to the terms of the plan. In addition, directors who have served eleven consecutive months are eligible for awards as well as new directors appointed to the Board. Shares granted under the 2005 Plan (net of cancellations) were 309,583, 81,475 and 161,800 in fiscal 2009, 2008 and 2007, respectively. The compensation expense related to these grants is being expensed over the vesting period for the individual grants. The Company has recorded $1,890,000, $1,425,000 and $643,000 of stock-based compensation for the restricted stock grants in fiscal 2009, 2008 and 2007 respectively.

There are two types of restricted stock awards to employees. The first type of restricted stock award is "career based shares." Career based shares are completely unvested until the last day of the third or fifth fiscal year after the date of the grant (as applicable based on the service period specified) whereupon such career based shares vest in full if the employee who received the grant is then employed by the Company. The compensation expense for these shares is recognized ratably over the three-year or five-year requisite service period. The second type of restricted stock award is "performance based shares." Performance based shares are earned based on the achievement of certain performance goals for the fiscal year in which they are granted. If the performance goals are met, the performance based shares vest in 50% increments at the end of the first and second fiscal years after the fiscal year in which they were granted if the employee who received the grant is then employed by the Company. Compensation expense for these shares is recognized ratably over the period beginning on the date the Company determines that it is probable the performance goals will be achieved and ending on the last day of the vesting period.

Additionally, there are annual restricted stock grants to directors. Each director who has served at least eleven consecutive months as of the Company's annual meeting of stockholders receives a restricted stock grant, which shares of restricted stock vest in one-third increments on each of the first, second and third anniversaries of the grant date. The expense related to the directors' grants is recognized ratably over the three-year vesting period.

Executive Incentive Plan

The Company maintains an Executive Incentive Plan (the "Incentive Plan"). The Incentive Plan provides for awards to certain executive officers of either cash or shares of restricted stock. The Company has historically issued awards only in the form of restricted stock. Issuance of awards under the Incentive Plan is based on the Company achieving pre-established performance goals during a three consecutive fiscal year performance period. Awards issued under the Incentive Plan for a particular performance period vest on the third anniversary of the last day of such performance period if the recipient remains employed by the Company on such vesting date. Awards under the Incentive Plan are expensed ratably over the period from the date that the issuance of such awards becomes probable through the end of the restriction period. Awards granted under the Incentive Plan for the performance period ended February 3, 2007 totaled $100,000 (6,707 shares). The final grant for the Incentive Plan was awarded in March 2006 for the January 28, 2006 three-year performance period. There will be no future awards under the Incentive Plan.

BOOKS·A·MILLION®
2009 Annual Report

Restricted Stock Table
A combined summary of the status of restricted stock grants to employees and directors under the 2005 Incentive Award Plan and the Executive Incentive Plan is as follows *(shares in thousands):*

	Fiscal Year Ended			
	January 31, 2009		February 2, 2008	
		Weighted Average Grant Date		Weighted Average Grant Date
	Shares	Fair Value	Shares	Fair Value
Shares at beginning of period	271	$12.44	281	$11.56
Shares granted	377	$ 6.82	87	$14.16
Shares vested	(114)	$11.04	(92)	$11.35
Shares forfeited	(3)	$11.67	(5)	$13.14
Shares at end of period	531	$ 8.49	271	$12.44

Stock Option Plan
In April 1999, the Company adopted the 1999 Amended and Restated Employee Stock Option Plan (the "Stock Option Plan") which provided for option grants to executive officers, directors, and key employees. Upon the approval of the 2005 Incentive Award Plan by the Company's stockholders at the Company's annual meeting held in June 2005, the board determined that no more awards would be made under the Stock Option Plan. Options previously issued under the Stock Option Plan remain valid. All options granted prior to January 9, 2001 vested over a five-year period and expired on the sixth anniversary of the date of grant, and all options granted on and after January 9, 2001 vest over a three-year period and expire on the tenth anniversary of the date of grant. All options have exercise prices equal to the fair market value of the common stock on the date of grant. A summary of the status of the Company's stock option plan is as follows *(shares in thousands)*:

	Fiscal Year Ended					
	January 31, 2009		February 2, 2008		February 3, 2007	
		Weighted Average Exercise		Weighted Average Exercise		Weighted Average Exercise
	Shares	Price	Shares	Price	Shares	Price
Outstanding at beginning of year	43	$5.31	270	$5.09	814	$3.77
Granted	--	--	--	--	--	N/A
Exercised	--	--	(226)	5.05	(540)	3.11
Forfeited	--	--	(1)	5.76	(4)	4.80
Outstanding at end of year	43	$5.31	43	$5.31	270	$5.09
Exercisable at end of year	43	$5.31	43	$5.31	268	$5.08

During fiscal years 2009, 2008 and 2007, the Company recognized tax benefits related to the exercise of stock options in the amount of $(339,000), $1,638,000 and $2,567,000, respectively. The tax benefits were credited to paid-in capital in the respective years.

The total intrinsic value of stock options exercised during the year ended January 31, 2009 was $0.

The following table summarizes information about stock options outstanding as of January 31, 2009 *(shares in thousands)*:

	Options Outstanding			Options Exercisable	
Range of Exercise Price	Number Outstanding at January 31, 2009	Weighted Average Remaining Contractual Life (Years)	Weighted Average Exercise Price	Number Exercisable at January 31, 2009	Weighted Average Exercise Price
$1.69 - $ 2.37	11	3.82	$2.31	11	$2.31
$2.68 - $ 5.85	7	3.00	$3.04	7	$3.04
$6.13 - $9.62	25	5.21	$7.25	25	$7.25
Totals	43	4.51	$5.31	43	$5.31

The aggregate intrinsic values of outstanding options and exercisable options under the Stock Option Plan at January 31, 2009 were $0 and $0, respectively because the exercise price of the options outstanding was higher than the Company's stock price on January 31, 2009.

BOOKS·A·MILLION

2009 Annual Report

Other Information

As of January 31, 2009 the Company has $4,780,000 of total unrecognized compensation cost related to non-vested awards granted under our various share-based plans, which it expects to recognize over the following fiscal years:

Fiscal Year	Stock-based Compensation Expense
2010	$1,809,000
2011	$1,857,000
2012	$1,112,000
2013	$ 2,000
Total	$4,780,000

The Company received cash from options exercised during the fiscal years 2009, 2008 and 2007 of $0, $1,139,000, and $1,680,000 respectively. The impact of these cash receipts is included in financing activities in the accompanying Consolidated Statements of Cash Flows.

The number of shares of common stock currently reserved under the 2005 Plan for stock-based compensation programs as of January 31, 2009 is 498,544 shares.

Employee Stock Purchase Plan

The Company maintains an employee stock purchase plan under which 400,000 shares of the Company's common stock are reserved for purchase by employees at 85% of the fair market value of the common stock at the lower of the market value for the Company's stock as of the beginning of the fiscal year or the end of the fiscal year. Of the total reserved shares, 289,031, 276,732 and 268,167 shares have been purchased as of January 31, 2009, February 2, 2008 and February 3, 2007, respectively.

Executives' Deferred Compensation Plan

During fiscal 2006, the Board adopted the Books-A-Million, Inc. Executives' Deferred Compensation Plan (the "Executives' Deferred Compensation Plan"). The Executives' Deferred Compensation Plan provides a select group of management or highly compensated employees of the Company and certain of its subsidiaries (the "Participants") with the opportunity to defer the receipt of certain cash compensation. Each Participant may elect to defer under the Executives' Deferred Compensation Plan a portion of his or her cash compensation that may otherwise be payable in a calendar year. A Participant's compensation deferrals are credited to the Participant's bookkeeping account (the "Account") maintained under the Executives' Deferred Compensation Plan. Each Participant's Account is credited with a deemed rate of interest and/or earnings or losses depending upon the investment performance of the deemed investment option.

With certain exceptions, a Participant's Account will be paid after the earlier of: (1) a fixed payment date, as elected by the Participant (if any); or (2) the Participant's separation from service with Company or its subsidiaries. Participants may generally elect that payments be made in a single sum or installments in the year specified by the Participant or upon their separation from service with the Company. Additionally, a Participant may elect to receive payment upon a Change of Control, as defined in, and to the extent permitted by, Section 409A of the Internal Revenue Code of 1986, as amended.

Directors' Deferred Compensation Plan

During fiscal 2006, the Board adopted the Books-A-Million, Inc. Directors' Deferred Compensation Plan (the "Directors' Deferred Compensation Plan"). The Directors' Deferred Compensation Plan provides the Non-Employee Directors with the opportunity to defer the receipt of certain amounts payable for serving as a member of the Board (the "Fees"). A Non-Employee Director's Fee deferrals are credited to the Non-Employee Director's bookkeeping account (the "Account") maintained under the Directors' Deferred Compensation Plan. Each participating Non-Employee Director's Account is credited with a deemed rate of interest and/or earnings or losses depending upon the investment performance of the deemed investment option.

With certain exceptions, a participating Non-Employee Director's Account will be paid after the earlier of: (1) a fixed payment date, as elected by the participating Non-Employee Director (if any); or (2) the participating Non-Employee Director's separation from service on the Board. The participating Non-Employee Director may generally elect that payments be made in a single sum or installments in the year specified by the participating Non-Employee Director or upon the Non-Employee Director's separation from service on the Board. Additionally, a participating Non-Employee Director may elect to receive payment upon a Change of Control, as defined in, and to the extent permitted by, Section 409A of the Internal Revenue Code of 1986, as amended.

6. Related Party Transactions

Certain stockholders and directors (including certain officers) of the Company have controlling ownership interests in other entities with which the Company conducts business. Transactions between the Company and these various other entities ("related parties") are summarized in the following paragraphs:

The Company purchases a substantial portion of its magazines as well as certain seasonal music and newspapers from a subsidiary of Anderson Media Corporation ("Anderson Media"), an affiliate through common ownership. During fiscal 2009, 2008 and 2007, purchases of these items from Anderson Media totaled $22,674,000, $25,514,000 and $24,702,000, respectively. The Company purchases certain of its collectibles, gifts and books from Anderson Press, Inc. ("Anderson Press"), an affiliate through common ownership. During fiscal 2009, 2008 and 2007, such purchases from Anderson Press totaled $1,577,000, $2,284,000 and $1,423,000, respectively. The Company purchases certain of its greeting cards and gift products from C.R. Gibson, Inc., which was an affiliate through common ownership until November 7, 2007. C.R. Gibson, Inc was sold on November 7, 2007, ending its relationship with the Company as a related party. The purchases of these items in fiscal 2008 and 2007 were $346,000 and $447,000, respectively. The Company utilizes import sourcing and consolidation services from Anco Far East Importers Limited ("Anco Far East"), an affiliate through common ownership. The total paid to Anco Far East was $1,863,000, $2,622,000 and $2,391,000 for fiscal 2009, 2008 and 2007, respectively. These amounts paid to Anco Far East included the actual cost of the product, as well as fees for sourcing and consolidation services. All other costs, other than the sourcing and consolidation service fees, were passed through from other vendors. Anco Far East fees, net of the passed-through costs, for fiscal years 2009, 2008 and 2007 were $130,000, $184,000 and $167,000, respectively.

The Company sold books to Anderson Media in the amounts of $1,347,000, $3,653,000 and $2,430,000 in fiscal 2009, 2008 and 2007, respectively.

The Company leases its principal executive offices from a trust, which was established for the benefit of the grandchildren of Mr. Charles C. Anderson, a former member of the Board of Directors. The lease term is month to month. During fiscal 2009, 2008 and 2007, the Company paid rent of $151,000, $141,000, and $137,000, respectively, to the trust under this lease. Anderson & Anderson LLC ("A&A"), which is an affiliate through common ownership, also leases three buildings to the Company. During fiscal 2009, 2008 and 2007, the Company paid A&A a total of $455,000, $428,000, and $448,000, respectively, in connection with such leases. There were no future minimum rental payments on any of the four leases at January 31, 2009. The Company subleases certain property to Hibbett Sports, Inc. ("Hibbett"), a sporting goods retailer in the southeastern United States. One of the Company's directors, Albert C. Johnson, and Terry Finley, President of Books-A-Million, Inc.'s Merchandising Group, are members of Hibbett's board of directors. Additionally, the Company's Executive Chairman, Clyde B. Anderson, served on Hibbett's board of directors until June 2, 2008. During fiscal 2009, 2008 and 2007, the Company received $208,000, $236,000, and $191,000, respectively, in rental payments from Hibbett.

The Company, A&A, Anderson Promotional Events, Inc. and Anderson Press co-own two airplanes that are used by the Company in its business. The Company owns a 26% interest in each of these airplanes. Prior to July 1, 2008, the Company held a 49.9% interest in one airplane co-owned by the Company and A&A. In an effort to reduce operating and administrative expenses, on July 1, 2008 the Company entered into a like-kind exchange transaction whereby it transferred 23.9% of its interest in the one airplane in exchange for a 26% interest in another airplane co-owned by A&A, Anderson Promotional Events, Inc., Anderson Press and certain other parties (the "Co-Ownership Group"). The value of the airplane interests transferred and received by the Company in this exchange was approximately $1.6 million. No cash traded hands in this exchange. Through June 30, 2008, the Company maintained administrative control and rented the original airplane to other affiliated companies at rates that covered all variable costs and a portion of the fixed costs of operating the airplane. The total amount received from affiliated companies for use of the plane during fiscal 2009 through June 30, 2008 was $486,000. Of that amount, $128,000 was received from Anderson Growth Partners, of which Ms. Sandra Cochran and Mr. Clyde Anderson are partners. From July 1, 2008 to January 31, 2009, the Company was billed $407,000 by the Co-Ownership Group under the new cost sharing arrangement for the Company's use of the two airplanes. The expenses the Company pays for airplane use covers all of the variable costs attributable to the Company's use of the plane and a portion of the fixed costs. In addition, the Company paid amounts to other affiliated companies for the Company's use of their planes in the amount of $233,000.

7. Income or (Loss) from Discontinued Operations

The Company did not close any stores in a market where the Company does not expect another of its existing stores to absorb the closed store customers during fiscal 2009. The Company continues to report in discontinued operations stores closed in prior years where the Company does not expect to retain the closed stores' customers at another store.

BOOKS·A·MILLION

2009 Annual Report

The Company closed one store in fiscal 2008 in a market located in Georgia and one store in a market located in Indiana where the Company does not expect another of its existing stores to absorb the closed store customers. The store sales and operating results for fiscal 2008 have not been included in discontinued operations because the impact on the financial statements was immaterial. For fiscal 2008 the closed stores had sales of $1.5 million and pretax operating loss of $382,000.

The Company closed one store in fiscal 2007 in a market located in Georgia where the Company does not expect another of its existing stores to absorb the closed store customers. The store sales and operating results for fiscal 2007 have not been included in discontinued operations because the impact on the financial statements was immaterial. For fiscal 2007 the closed store had sales of $139,000 and pretax operating loss of $90,000.

In November 2004, the Emerging Issues Task Force ("EITF") issued EITF No. 03-13, *"Applying the Conditions in Paragraph 42 of FASB No. 144 in Determining Whether to Report Discontinued Operations."* EITF No. 03-13 addresses how an ongoing entity should evaluate whether the operations and cash flows of a disposed component have been or will be eliminated from the ongoing operations of the entity and the types of continuing involvement that constitute significant continuing involvement in the operations of the disposed component. EITF No. 03-13 became effective with the fiscal year beginning January 30, 2005. Prior to the effective date of EITF No. 03-13, the Company was already reporting certain closed stores as discontinued operations (see footnote 7). Therefore, adopting this new guidance did not impact the Company's financial position, results of operations or cash flows.

8. Business Segments

The Company has two reportable operating segments, as defined by SFAS No. 131, Disclosures about Segments of an Enterprise and Related Information: retail trade and electronic commerce trade. These reportable operating segments reflect the manner in which the business is managed and how the Company allocates resources and assesses performance internally.

Our chief operating decision maker is our Chairman and Chief Executive Officer. The Company is primarily a retailer of book merchandise. The Company's two reportable segments are two distinct businesses units, one a traditional retailer of book merchandise and the other a seller of book merchandise primarily over the Internet. The electronic commerce trade segment is managed separately due to divergent technology and marketing requirements. The retail trade reportable segment also includes the Company's distribution center operations, which predominantly supplies merchandise to our retail stores. Through the distribution center operations the Company sells books to outside parties on a wholesale basis. These sales are not material.

The Company evaluates the performance of the retail trade and electronic commerce trade segments based on profit and loss from operations before interest and income taxes. Certain intersegment cost allocations have been made based upon consolidated and segment revenues. Shipping income related to Internet sales is included in net sales, and shipping expense is included in cost of sales.

Both the retail trade and electronic commerce trade reportable segments derive revenues primarily from the sale of book merchandise through sales in our retail stores and over the Internet, respectively.

Segment information *(in thousands)*	1/31/09	Fiscal Year Ended 2/2/08	2/3/07
Net Sales			
Retail Trade	$508,253	$528,606	$512,967
Electronic Commerce Trade	25,166	26,992	26,048
Intersegment Sales Elimination	(20,148)	(20,470)	(18,599)
Net Sales	$513,271	$535,128	$520,416
Operating Profit			
Retail Trade	$ 18,276	$ 26,911	$ 29,223
Electronic Commerce Trade	1,541	1,462	1,400
Intersegment Elimination of Certain Costs	(927)	(953)	(524)
Total Operating Profit	$ 18,890	$ 27,420	$ 30,099
Assets			
Retail Trade	$277,896	$283,452	$303,110
Electronic Commerce Trade	1,396	1,381	927
Intersegment Sales Elimination	--	--	--
Total Assets	$279,292	$284,833	$304,037

Sales as a percentage of net sales by merchandise category is as follows:

	1/31/09	2/2/08	2/3/07
Books and Magazines	83.0%	83.9%	83.7%
General Merchandise	8.1%	7.8%	7.6%
Other	8.9%	8.3%	8.7%
Total	100%	100%	100%

General merchandise consists of gifts, cards, collectibles and similar types of products. Other products include café, music, DVD, E-Book and other products.

9. Commitments and Contingencies

The Company is a party to various legal proceedings incidental to its business. In the opinion of management, after consultation with legal counsel, the ultimate liability, if any, with respect to those proceedings is not presently expected to materially affect the financial position, results of operations or cash flows of the Company.

From time to time, the Company enters into certain types of agreements that require the Company to indemnify parties against third party claims. Generally, these agreements relate to: (a) agreements with vendors and suppliers, under which the Company may provide customary indemnification to its vendors and suppliers in respect of actions they take at the Company's request or otherwise on its behalf, (b) agreements with vendors who publish books or manufacture merchandise specifically for the Company to indemnify the vendors against trademark and copyright infringement claims concerning the books published or merchandise manufactured on behalf of the Company, (c) real estate leases, under which the Company may agree to indemnify the lessors for claims arising from the Company's use of the property, and (d) agreements with the Company's directors, officers and employees, under which the Company may agree to indemnify such persons for liabilities arising out of their relationship with the Company. The Company has Directors and Officers Liability Insurance, which, subject to the policy's conditions, provides coverage for indemnification amounts payable by the Company with respect to its directors and officers up to specified limits and subject to certain deductibles.

The nature and terms of these types of indemnities vary. The events or circumstances that would require the Company to perform under these indemnities are transaction and circumstance specific. The overall maximum amount of obligations cannot be reasonably estimated. Historically, the Company has not incurred significant costs related to performance under these types of indemnities. No liabilities have been recorded for these obligations on the Company's balance sheet at each of January 31, 2009 and February 2, 2008, as such liabilities are considered de minimis.

10. Cash Dividend

On March 19, 2009, the Board of Directors declared a quarterly dividend of $0.05 per share to be paid on April 16, 2009 to stockholders of record at the close of business on April 2, 2009. The Company intends to pay quarterly dividends in the future, subject to availability of funds and Board approval.

11. Accrued Expenses

Accrued expenses consist of the following (*in thousands*):

	As of 1/31/09	As of 2/2/08
Accrued expenses:		
Salaries, wages and employee benefits	$5,705	$7,756
Giftcard liabilities to customers	9,730	10,273
Deferred club card income	6,550	6,623
Taxes, other than income	4,698	5,734
Rent	2,263	2,237
Other	6,608	8,916
	$35,554	$41,539

BOOKS·A·MILLION
2009 Annual Report

12. Summary of Quarterly Results (Unaudited)

The following tables set forth certain unaudited financial data for the quarters indicated:

	Fiscal Year Ended January 31, 2009				
(In thousands, except per share amounts)	First Quarter	Second Quarter	Third Quarter	Fourth Quarter	Total Year
Net revenue	$115,481	$122,803	$110,952	$164,035	$513,271
Gross profit	33,924	35,089	29,075	53,249	151,337
Operating profit (loss)	2,018	1,580	(2,858)	18,150	18,890
Net income (loss)	907	645	(2,187)	11,209	10,574
Net income (loss) per share – basic	0.06	0.04	(0.14)	0.74	0.70
Net income (loss) per share – diluted	0.05	0.04	(0.14)	0.73	0.68

	Fiscal Year Ended February 2, 2008				
(In thousands, except per share amounts)	First Quarter	Second Quarter	Third Quarter	Fourth Quarter	Total Year
Net revenue	$116,318	$132,802	$117,696	$168,312	$535,128
Gross profit	33,759	37,692	32,095	55,002	158,548
Operating profit (loss)	3,454	4,865	(524)	19,625	27,420
Net income (loss)	2,111	3,100	(555)	11,866	16,522
Net income (loss) per share – basic	0.13	0.19	(0.03)	0.77	1.03
Net income (loss) per share – diluted	0.13	0.19	(0.03)	0.76	1.01

13. Fair Value Measurements

Effective February 3, 2008, the Company adopted SFAS No. 157, which defines fair value as the exchange price that would be received for an asset or paid to transfer a liability (an exit price) in the principal or most advantageous market for the asset or liability in an orderly transaction between market participants at the measurement date. SFAS No. 157 establishes a three-level fair value hierarchy that prioritizes the inputs used to measure fair value. This hierarchy requires entities to maximize the use of observable inputs and minimize the use of unobservable inputs when measuring fair value. As of January 31, 2009 the Company had no assets or liabilities which are required to be disclosed under the provisions of SFAS No. 157.

Therefore, there was no cumulative effect of adoption related to SFAS No. 157, and the adoption did not have an impact on the Company's financial position, results of operations, or cash flows.

The carrying amounts of other financial instruments reported in the balance sheet for current assets and current liabilities approximate their fair values because of the short maturity of these instruments.

At January 31, 2009, there was $15,760,000 outstanding under our revolving line of credit agreement and $6,720,000 outstanding under our long-term debt agreement. The borrowings under our revolving line of credit agreement and our long-term debt agreement bear interest at the variable rate described in Note 3 and therefore approximate fair value at January 31, 2009.

Appendix B
The Mechanics of an Accounting System

LEARNING OBJECTIVES

When you are finished studying Appendix B, you should be able to:

1. Define the general ledger system and explain how it works.

2. Explain and perform the steps in the accounting cycle.

3. Identify the adjustments needed before preparing financial statements and make those adjustments.

4. Describe the closing process and explain why it is necessary.

Accounting Information Systems

Throughout the chapters of this book, you have been keeping track of Team Shirts' transactions using an accounting equation work sheet. We can do that in a simple world with a small number of transactions. In the real world, that wouldn't work very well. A company in the real world needs a better system to keep track of the large number of transactions represented in the four basic financial statements. A company may have an accounting system that gathers *only* accounting information—just recording the information that applies to the financial statements—and other information systems gathering information for marketing, production, and other parts of the company. Alternatively, a company may have a single, integrated information system in which all company information is recorded—data about suppliers, employees, operations; and the accounting information is simply a small part.

The firm's accounting information is kept in the firm's **general ledger**. The general ledger is the collection of a company's accounts where the amounts from the firm's transactions are organized and stored. You can think of it as a big book with a page for every asset, liability, equity, revenue, and expense account. Later in this appendix, you will learn how transactions get recorded in a company's general ledger. For years, the **general ledger system** was maintained by the accounting department as a separate information system; and the other functional areas of the business—marketing, production, sales, etc.—each had its own system for keeping track of the information it needed. Since the development of computers and software programs that can manage large amounts of information, more and more companies are using a single, integrated information system. Thus, instead of keeping their data separately, accountants may get

The **general ledger** is the collection of the company's accounts where the information from the financial transactions is organized and stored.

The **general ledger system** is the accountant's traditional way of keeping track of a company's financial transactions and then using those records to prepare the basic financial statements.

their information from the company's overall information system—often referred to as an **enterprise-wide resource planning system (ERP)**.

No matter how it is related to the rest of a firm's information system, the accounting system is still called the general ledger system. The same financial statements are produced with both the general ledger and the integrated types of information systems. In this appendix, we will use the general ledger system, which was designed as a manual system, to demonstrate how transactions are recorded, classified, and summarized for the financial statements.

An **enterprise-wide resource planning system (ERP)** is an integrated software program used by large firms to manage all of a firm's information.

The General Ledger Accounting System

L.O.1

Define the general ledger system and explain how it works.

Keeping track of financial information with a traditional record-keeping system is often called *bookkeeping*. As transactions occur, they are recorded chronologically by a bookkeeper in a book called a **journal**. When we prepare an accounting equation work sheet showing the effect of each transaction on the accounting equation, we are doing something similar to recording a transaction in a journal. The resources exchanged are shown with their dollar amounts. The journal contains a record of each transaction as it occurs. An example is shown in Exhibit B.1. In the next section, you'll learn how the "debits" and "credits" columns are used. For now, just notice that all of the accounts affected by the transaction are used in a journal entry. Most companies use more than one journal; each department may have its own journal. Common journals are the (1) sales journal, (2) cash receipts journal, and (3) cash disbursements journal. For simplicity, we'll use a single, general journal for all our transactions.

Business transactions are first recorded in a **journal**. Then they are transferred to accounts in the general ledger through a process called posting.

EXHIBIT B.1

An Example of a Journal

Page 4: General Journal

Ref.	Date	Journal entry	Debits	Credits
J-1	June 1	Cash	65,000	
		Sales		65,000
		To record the collection of cash for sales.		
J-2	June 4	Equipment	20,600	
		Cash		20,600
		To record the purchase of equipment for cash.		

The journal entries are recorded chronologically. Then, the individual items are "regrouped" by account as they are posted to the general ledger. Trace the cash amounts in the journal entries to the general ledger cash account shown in Exhibit B.2 on page 566. The amounts for sales and equipment will be posted to their own general ledger accounts.

Because a company may have hundreds or even thousands of transactions during an accounting period, it would be difficult, probably impossible, to try to gather and use the information from a chronological record such as the journal. To be useful, the information needs to be reorganized, grouping together transactions that involve the same account. For example, when all the transactions that involve cash are grouped together, then the company's cash balance can be easily determined. As you can see from that example, it is useful for similar transactions to be grouped together. The transactions from the journal or journals are transferred to another book called the general ledger through a process called **posting** the transactions to the general ledger. Posting is done periodically; it could be daily, weekly, or monthly, depending on the size of the company.

The general ledger is the primary record of the financial information of the business. It is organized by accounts. As you read earlier in this book, an account is the basic classification unit of accounting information. You can think of each financial statement item as an account, and each account as a page in the general ledger. On the page for a particular account, we record all the additions to, and deductions from, that account.

For example, one account in the general ledger is cash. On the cash page in the general ledger, we find every cash collection and every cash disbursement made by the company. If there are more disbursements or collections than can fit on one page, they will be recorded on as many following pages as needed, all comprising the cash account. To make it easy to find the amount

Posting is the process of recording the transactions from the journal into the firm's general ledger so that the transactions will be organized by accounts.

of cash on hand, the cash account has a running balance. That means a new balance is calculated after every entry. Think about your own checkbook—that's the record you keep of each check you write (a subtraction); each deposit you make (an addition); and the resulting total remaining in your checking account (that's your running balance). If you keep a running balance, it is much faster to find out how much cash you have in your account. (Have you discovered what happens when you fail to keep your checkbook balance current?)

Accounts in the general ledger include cash, accounts receivable, inventory, prepaid insurance, equipment, accumulated depreciation, accounts payable, notes payable, contributed capital, and retained earnings. (Notice, these are given in the order in which they appear on the balance sheet.) How many accounts does a company have? Every company is different, and the number of accounts depends on the detail the company wants in its financial records. For example, one company could have an account called utilities expenses in which many different utility-related expenses could be accumulated. Another company might prefer to have a separate account for each type of utility expense—a separate page in the general ledger for electricity expense, gas expense, water expense, etc. The number of accounts is determined by the amount of detail a company wants to be able to retrieve from its records. If a company uses very little gas or water, it would be a waste of time and space to keep a separate account for those expenses. A company that uses water in its production process, on the other hand, would definitely want to keep a separate account for water purchases.

Companies also have subsidiary ledgers. These are detailed records that support the balances in the general ledger. For example, the *accounts receivable subsidiary ledger* will have details about the credit customers—sales, receipts, and account balances for every customer. The total dollar amount of accounts receivable in the accounts receivable subsidiary ledger will be the total in the general ledger.

Most companies have a large number of accounts, and they combine the similar ones for the financial statements. When we look at the financial statements, we can't really tell how many individual accounts a company has in its general ledger. Many smaller accounts may be combined for financial statement presentation.

Anyone in the firm with access to the accounting records who wants to know the balance in any account at any time can find it by looking in the general ledger. A list of the balances in all the accounts of a company is called a **trial balance**.

> A **trial balance** is a list of all the accounts of a company with the related balance.

Before the financial statements can be prepared, adjustments to the records must be made. We discussed those adjustments and how to make them in Chapter 3. Adjustments are needed because of the nature of accrual accounting. On the financial statements, we need to include revenues that have been earned and expenses that have been incurred, even if we have not yet received the cash earned or paid the cash for the expenses incurred during the accounting period. These adjustments are called accruals. The action has taken place, but the dollars have not been exchanged.

We also need to be sure to include on the income statement for the period any revenue we've earned or expenses we've incurred for which the dollars were exchanged at a previous time. These are called deferrals. The dollars were already exchanged, and we recorded the receipt of the cash when we received the cash. However, we did not recognize any revenue or expense at that time. At the end of the accounting period, we have to recognize any revenue we have earned and any expenses that we've incurred.

No matter what kind of accounting system a company uses, the information produced by that system must be adjusted before the financial statements can be prepared. After the adjustments are made, the financial statements are prepared. We have actually done all this—recording the transactions, making the adjustments, and preparing the financial statements—using the accounting equation work sheet. The general ledger system is simply a more feasible way to do it in an actual business.

Debits and Credits

To use the general ledger system and to understand the information it makes available, we must learn a bit more accounting language. Don't panic over the terms **debit** and **credit**. You will find them easy to understand, but only if first you get rid of any notions of what you already think debit and credit mean. In accounting, each term has a very specific meaning that should not be confused with its more general meaning.

> **Debit** means left side of an account.

> **Credit** means right side of an account.

In accounting, when we say *debit,* we mean the left side; when we say *credit,* we mean the right side. (This should be easy to remember.) Left is the only thing that the word *debit* means and right is the only thing that the word *credit* means—unless we apply the terms to specific accounts.

A general ledger has been traditionally composed of a multicolumn page, similar to the one shown in Exhibit B.2. The Debit column on the right shows the running balance in the cash account. You would almost never see a credit balance in this account. The general ledger is often computerized in a similar format.

EXHIBIT B.2

The General Ledger

Account: **Cash**					Account No. 1002	
					Balance	
Date	Item	Jrnl. ref.	Debit	Credit	Debit	Credit
2011						
June 1		J–1, p. 4 65,000		....	**65,000**	
June 4		J–2, p. 4		20,600	**44,400**	

This is the **Cash** account. The cash amounts from all the journal entries are posted here. Trace these amounts back to the journal entries shown in Exhibit B.1.

In the balance columns, the column on the left is called the debit (DR) column, and the column on the right is called the credit (CR) column. As a shortcut to using formal preprinted two-column paper, accountants often draw a T-account to represent a page in the general ledger. T-accounts shown in Exhibit B.3 are our representation of the general ledger shown in Exhibit B.2.

EXHIBIT B.3

Debits and Credits in T-Accounts

Asset		Liability		Shareholders' Equity	
Debit increases (normal balance)	Credit decreases	Debit decreases	Credit increases (normal balance)	Debit decreases	Credit increases (normal balance)

Revenue		Expense	
Debit decreases	Credit increases (normal balance)	Debit increases (normal balance)	Credit decreases

One T-account such as cash, shown next, represents a single page in the general ledger. The left side of a T-account is the debit side, and the right side of a T-account is the credit side.

Cash

Debit	Credit

Numbers we put on the left side of the account are called debits, and putting a number in the left column is called *debiting* an account. *Debit* is a wonderful word that can be an adjective, a noun, or a verb. The same goes for the word *credit*. The right side of the account is called the credit side, the numbers we put on the right side are called credits, and putting a number in the right column is called *crediting* an account.

In the fifteenth century, a monk named Fra Luca Paccioli wrote about a system that uses debits and credits with the accounting equation. In his system, the accounting equation stays in balance with each transaction *and* the monetary amounts of debits and credits are equal for each transaction. Here's how it works:

1. For the accounting equation, the balance in the accounts on the left side of the equation (*assets*) will increase with debits; and the balance in the accounts on the right side of the equation (*liabilities* and *shareholders' equity*) will increase with credits. It follows that the balance in an asset account will decrease with credits. Liability and equity account balances decrease with debits. Putting that together,

- asset accounts are increased with debits and decreased with credits.
- liability and shareholders' equity accounts are increased with credits and decreased with debits.

This means that when we want to add an amount to our cash balance, we put the number of that amount on the left (in the left column of the two columns in the general ledger account for cash)—so that's a debit. When we disburse cash and want to subtract the amount disbursed from the cash account, we put the number of that amount on the right side—so that's a credit. The *increase* side of an account is called its "normal" balance. Cash has a normal debit balance. Because we put the cash we receive on the debit side and the cash we disburse on the credit side, it makes sense that our cash account will normally have a debit balance. (It's not normal to disburse more cash than you have—it's pretty unusual.)

In accounting, we do not literally *add* and *subtract* from an account balance—we debit and credit an account to accomplish the same thing. If we make an error, we do not erase the mistake and replace it with the correct answer. Instead, we debit or credit the account to correct the error and make the account balance correct. When accounting records are kept by hand, all entries are made in ink so that no entries can be erased or changed. This has been traditional in accounting to keep the records from being altered. Recording every increase to, and decrease from, an account balance gives a complete record of every change made to the account.

2. Because shareholders' equity is increased with credits, all accounts that increase shareholders' equity will increase with credits. Revenue accounts increase with credits and decrease with debits. When we make a sale, we *credit* the sales account.

3. Because shareholders' equity is *decreased* with debits, all accounts that decrease shareholders' equity work in the opposite way as revenue accounts work. For example, expense accounts—where a list of our expenses is kept—increase with debits. As we incur expenses, we put the amounts on the left side of expense accounts.

Indicate whether each of the following accounts normally has a debit (DR) or credit (CR) balance and what type of account it is.

Your Turn `B-1`

Account Title	Expense	Revenue	Asset	Liability	Shareholders' Equity
Accounts payable				CR	
Accounts receivable					
Advertising expense					
Cash					
Depreciation expense					
Furniture and fixtures					
Accumulated depreciation					
Unearned fees					
Salary expense					
Common stock					
Rent expense					
Retained earnings					
(Earned) fees					
Land					
Building					

A summary of the use of debits and credits is shown in Exhibit B.3. Remember, it's just a clever system to be sure that, when we record a transaction, the accounting equation is kept in balance and, at the same time, debits = credits with every transaction. This system is called double-entry bookkeeping.

L.O.2
Explain and perform the
steps in the accounting cycle.

The **accounting cycle** begins with the transactions of a new accounting period. It includes recording and posting the transactions, adjusting the books, preparing financial statements, and closing the temporary accounts to get ready for the next accounting period.

The Accounting Cycle

The process that starts with recording individual transactions, produces the four basic financial statements, and gets our general ledger ready for the next accounting period is called the **accounting cycle**. Some of the steps in the accounting cycle won't make any sense to you yet, but this appendix examines each in detail. By the end of this appendix, you should be able to explain and perform each step. The steps in the accounting cycle follow:

1. Record transactions in the journal, the chronological record of all transactions, from source documents such as invoices. These are called journal entries.
2. Post the journal entries to the general ledger.
3. At the end of the accounting period, prepare an unadjusted trial balance.
4. Prepare adjusting journal entries and post them to the general ledger.
5. Prepare an adjusted trial balance.
6. Prepare the financial statements.
7. Close the temporary accounts.
8. Prepare a postclosing trial balance.

Let's look at each of these steps in detail.

Step 1: Recording Journal Entries

In the normal course of business, many transactions must be recorded in the accounting system. Let's look at how the transactions for a company's first year of business would be recorded in a journal. The transactions for the first year of Clint's Consulting Company, Inc., are shown in Exhibit B.4.

EXHIBIT B.4

Transactions for Clint's Consulting Company, Inc., during 2011

Date	Transaction
January 2	Clint contributes $2,000 of his own money to the business in exchange for common stock.
January 10	Clint's Consulting, Inc., borrows $4,000 from a local bank to begin the business.
February 4	Clint's buys supplies for $400 cash.
April 10	Clint's hires a company to prepare and distribute a brochure immediately for the company for $500 cash.
July 12	Clint's provides consulting services and earns revenue of $9,000 cash.
August 15	Clint's pays someone to do some typing, which costs $350 cash.
October 21	Clint's repays the $4,000 note along with $150 interest.
December 10	Clint's Consulting, Inc., makes a distribution to Clint, the only shareholder, for $600.

The first transaction in Clint's first year of business is his own contribution of $2,000 to the business in exchange for common stock. What a journal entry looks like on a journal page follows:

Date	Transaction	Debit	Credit
January 2, 2011	Cash	2,000	
	Common stock		2,000
	To record owner's cash contribution in exchange for common stock		1–1[a]

[a]This is a number we'll use to help us trace journal entries to the general ledger.

The cash account is increased by $2,000, so Clint's would debit the cash account for $2,000. Shareholders' equity is increased, so Clint's would credit common stock for $2,000. Notice, in this case two accounts are increased—one with a debit and one with a credit. In some transactions, both accounts are increased; in others, one account can be increased and one account can be decreased; or two accounts can be decreased. The only requirement for a journal entry is that the dollar amount of debits must equal the dollar amount of credits.

In the second transaction, Clint's Consulting Company borrows $4,000 from a local bank. Again, two different accounts are increased—one with a debit and one with a credit—in this transaction. Notice, debits ($4,000) = credits ($4,000).

Date	Transaction	Debit	Credit
January 10, 2011	Cash	4,000	
	Notes payable		4,000
	To record the loan from the bank		1-2

Debits are always listed first; credits are listed after all the debits—sometimes there is more than one account to debit or credit—and the accounts being credited are indented like the first sentence of a paragraph. Each page of the journal has a reference number that is used to trace journal entries to the general ledger. We'll see this number again when we post the journal entries to the general ledger.

The third transaction is the purchase of supplies for $400 cash. This is recorded with a debit to supplies and a credit to cash.

Date	Transaction	Debit	Credit
February 4, 2011	Supplies	400	
	Cash		400
	To record the purchase of supplies		1-3

Notice, this transaction increases one asset account (supplies) and decreases another asset account (cash). Because supplies is an asset, it is increased with a debit.

The fourth transaction is Clint's hiring a company to prepare and distribute a brochure immediately for its new consulting business. Clint's pays $500 for this service.

Date	Transaction	Debit	Credit
April 10, 2011	Advertising expense	500	
	Cash		500
	To record the cost of the brochures		1-4

In this transaction, an expense account, advertising expense, is increased by $500. Because expense accounts are eventually deducted from shareholders' equity, they increase with debits, the opposite of the normal balance in shareholders' equity accounts. Cash, an asset account, is decreased with a credit of $500.

Next, the company provides consulting services for $9,000 cash.

Date	Transaction	Debit	Credit
July 12, 2011	Cash	9,000	
	Consulting fees		9,000
	To record consulting revenue		1-5

In this transaction, cash is increased with a $9,000 debit. Consulting fees, a revenue account that will eventually be added to shareholders' equity, is increased with a $9,000 credit.

Clint has one employee who types for him occasionally, and he pays this person $350 for typing during his first year of business. This is an expense, which Clint categorizes as salary expense. Cash is reduced with a $350 credit, and salary expense is increased with a $350 debit.

Date	Transaction	Debit	Credit
August 15, 2011	Salary expense	350	
	Cash		350
	To record the cost of an employee to type		1-6

Next, the company repays the loan to the bank, with interest. The principal of the loan—the amount borrowed—was $4,000; the interest—the cost of using someone else's money—was $150. The journal entry for this transaction is an example of an entry with more than one debit.

Date	Transaction	Debit	Credit
October 21, 2011	Notes payable	4,000	
	Interest expense	150	
	Cash		4,150
	To record the repayment of a note plus interest		1-7

The debit to notes payable reduces the balance in that account. Before this transaction, it had a balance of $4,000. Now, when this debit is posted, the account will have a zero balance. The interest expense account will increase by $150 because expense accounts increase with debits. Cash is reduced by $4,150.

The final transaction of Clint's Consulting Company's first year of business is a $600 distribution to Clint, the only shareholder. In a sole proprietorship, a distribution is also called a **withdrawal**. Because Clint's Consulting Company is a corporation, the distribution is called a **dividend**. Corporations often use a special account to hold the amounts for dividends declared until it is time to prepare financial statements. The account is simply called dividends. The dividends account has a debit balance and will eventually reduce retained earnings. Paying a dividend reduces the cash balance. Remember, a dividend payment is not an expense.

> A distribution to the owner of a sole proprietorship is called a **withdrawal**; in a corporation, distributions to the shareholders are called **dividends**.

Date	Transaction	Debit	Credit
December 10, 2011	Dividends	600	
	Cash		600
	To record a dividend payment		1-8

Step 2: Posting Journal Entries to the General Ledger

Each of the journal entries a company makes must be posted to the general ledger. How often this is done depends on the number of journal entries a company normally makes. Some computerized systems post every journal entry automatically when it is entered into the system. Other companies post transactions to the general ledger daily or weekly.

The accounts for Clint's Consulting Company, Inc., all begin with a zero balance, because this is Clint's first year of business. Each journal entry has the reference number from the journal with it when the entry is posted in the general ledger. This provides a way to trace every entry in the general ledger back to the original record of the transaction in the journal. After all the journal entries are posted, it is easy to calculate the balance in any account. The accounts, shown in Exhibit B.5, are listed in the following order: assets, liabilities, shareholders' equity, revenues, and expenses.

Step 3: Prepare an Unadjusted Trial Balance

A trial balance is a list of all the accounts in the general ledger, each with its debit or credit balance. The reasons for preparing a trial balance are to confirm that debits equal credits and to have a way to quickly review the accounts for needed adjustments. Exhibit B.6 shows the unadjusted trial balance for Clint's Consulting at December 31, 2011.

Step 4: Adjusting Journal Entries

> **L.O.3**
> Identify the adjustments needed before preparing financial statements and make those adjustments.

Recording journal entries as transactions occur and posting them to the general ledger are routine accounting tasks. When a company gets ready to prepare financial statements at the end of the accounting period, there are more journal entries needed. These are not routine journal entries; they are called adjusting journal entries. As we discussed in Chapter 3, there are four situations

EXHIBIT B.5

Clint's Consulting Company, Inc., T-Accounts

ASSETS	=	LIABILITIES	+	SHAREHOLDER'S EQUITY

Cash
(asset)

1-1	2,000	400	1-3
1-2	4,000	500	1-4
1-5	9,000	350	1-6
		4,150	1-7
		600	1-8
EB*	9,000		

Supplies
(asset)

1-3	400	
EB	400	

Notes payable
(liability)

1-7	4,000	4,000	1-2
		0	EB

Common stock
(shareholder's equity)

	2,000	1-1
	2,000	EB

Dividends
(a special temporary account)

1-8	600	
EB	600	

Consulting fees
(revenue)

	9,000	1-5
	9,000	EB

Advertising expense
(expense)

1-4	500	
EB	500	

Salary expense
(expense)

1-6	350	
EB	350	

Interest expense
(expense)

1-7	150	
EB	150	

*EB = ending balance

Account	DR	CR
Cash	$ 9,000	
Supplies	400	
Notes payable		$ 0
Common stock		2,000
Dividends	600	
Consulting fees		9,000
Advertising expense	500	
Interest expense	150	
Salary expense	350	
	$11,000	$11,000

EXHIBIT B.6

Clint's Consulting Company, Inc., Unadjusted Trial Balance at December 31, 2011

that require adjustments before the financial statements are prepared. We need to adjust our records for *accrued revenues, accrued expenses, deferred revenues,* and *deferred expenses.* Let's look at an example of each of those adjustments in a general ledger system.

ACCRUALS. **Accrued Revenue.** Suppose Clint's Consulting Company did some consulting for a fee of $3,000, but the company has not billed the client yet so the revenue has not been recognized—when it is recognized, it is put on the income statement. At December 31, Clint's will adjust the company's records to recognize this revenue, even though the company has not collected the cash. First, notice the effect of the adjustment on the accounting equation.

Assets	=	Liabilities	+	Contributed capital (CC)	+	Retained earnings
+3,000 Accounts receivable						+3,000 Consulting fees

The transaction increases assets—accounts receivable (AR). That means Clint's would debit AR, because assets are increased with debits. Clint's has also increased a revenue account, consulting fees. (The $3,000 is recorded in a revenue account, not directly into the retained earnings account. However, the revenue will end up increasing retained earnings on our balance sheet.) Revenue accounts increase with credits, so we would credit the revenue account consulting fees for $3,000. The accounting equation is in balance *and* debits = credits for our transaction. Here's what the journal entry would look like:

Date	Transaction	Debit	Credit
December 31, 2011	Accounts receivable	3,000	
	Consulting fees		3,000
	To accrue revenue earned in 2011		A-1

Accrued Expenses Another situation that requires an adjustment is accrued expenses. If we have incurred an expense (the dollar amount that *will* be paid for an item or a service that has already been used to produce revenue), the matching principle requires us to put that expense on the same income statement as the revenue it helped generate.

Sometimes matching an expense with a specific revenue is impossible to do. In that case, we record the expense in the time period when the expense item was used. For example, it is often impossible to match an employee's work with specific revenue the company earns. So the cost of the work done by an employee is put on the income statement as an expense in the accounting period when the work was done.

Let's look at an example of recording salary expense in the period in which the work was done. When companies pay their employees—on normal paydays during the year—they debit the account *salary expense* and credit the account *cash*. The salary expense account may have a significant balance at year end because the company has been recording salary expense as the employees have been paid throughout the year. To make sure we've included *all* the salary expense for the year, we must examine the time our employees have worked near the end of the year. The purpose is to be sure to include the cost of *all* work done during a year in the salary expense on that year's income statement.

If we owe employees for work done in December 2011, but we will not pay them until January 2012, we have to accrue salary expense when we are adjusting our accounts at December 31, 2011. Suppose Clint's owes its employee $50 for work done in 2011, but the next payday is in 2012. To get this salary expense on the income statement for the year, Clint's must debit salary expense for $50 and credit salaries payable for $50. The salary expense on the income statement for the year ended December 31, 2011, will now include this $50. Salaries payable on the balance sheet at December 31, 2011, will show the $50 obligation. Look at the adjustment in the accounting equation, and then look at the journal entry. Notice that in the adjusting entry, just like in a routine journal entry, debits = credits. The accounting equation remains in balance.

Assets	=	Liabilities	+	CC	+	Retained earnings
		+50 Salaries payable				(50) Salary expense

Date	Transaction	Debit	Credit
December 31, 2011	Salary expense	50	
	Salaries payable		50
	To accrue salary expense at year end		A-2

Suppose a company owes employees $300 on December 31, 2010, the date of the financial statements; and the next payday is January 3, 2011. Give the adjusting journal entry necessary on December 31, 2010. How much salary expense will the company recognize when it actually pays the $300 to the employees on January 3, 2011? Give the journal entry for the payment on January 3, 2011. (Ignore payroll taxes.)

DEFERRALS. **Deferred Revenue** Deferred revenue is revenue that hasn't been earned yet, so it is recorded as a liability in a company's records—an obligation—when the cash is collected. Because cash has been collected, it must be recorded; but the goods or services have not yet been provided. The company must defer—put off—recognizing the revenue. When the cash is received, the company increases cash and increases a liability called unearned revenue. In a general ledger system, the amount of cash received is recorded in the cash account, where it is shown as a debit—that's an increase because assets are increased with debits. The journal entry is balanced with a credit to unearned revenue—that's an increase because liabilities are increased with credits.

Suppose Clint's had received $4,000 on May 1 for consulting services to be provided over the next 16 months. This is how the receipt of the $4,000 cash for services to be provided in the future affects the accounting equation, followed by the journal entry for the receipt of the $4,000 cash:

Assets	=	Liabilities	+	CC	+	Retained earnings
+4,000 cash		+4,000 Unearned consulting fees				

Date	Transaction	Debit	Credit
May 1, 2011	Cash	4,000	
	Unearned consulting fees		4,000
	To record the receipt of cash for services to be provided		1-9

Notice that this is *not* an adjusting entry; it's a regular journal entry—made when it occurs during the year—to record the receipt of cash. When we look at the T-accounts again, we'll see it posted with the transactions we posted previously.

Whenever a company has recorded unearned revenue during the year, an adjustment will be necessary at year end to recognize the portion of the revenue that has been earned during the time between when the cash was received and year end. If, on that basis, any of the unearned revenue becomes earned revenue by year end, the unearned revenue account will be decreased and the revenue account will be increased with an adjustment. In terms of debits and credits, the unearned revenue account, which is a liability, will be decreased with a debit. In Clint's case, the credit corresponding to that debit will go to consulting fees, which means that the earned revenue will now show up on the income statement with the other consulting fees Clint's has earned during the year. This adjustment is necessary to be sure all the earned revenue for the year is recognized—meaning, put on the income statement. Suppose Clint's had earned half of the unearned revenue at year end. The adjustment in the accounting equation and the corresponding journal entry for this adjustment follow:

Assets	=	Liabilities	+	CC	+	Retained earnings
		(2,000) Unearned consulting fees				+2,000 Consulting fees

Date	Transaction	Debit	Credit
December 31, 2011	Unearned consulting fees	2,000	
	Consulting fees		2,000
	To record earned revenue at year end		A-3

DEFERRED EXPENSES. Deferred expenses may need to be adjusted before the financial statements are prepared. Recall, a deferred expense is something the company paid for in advance. One example is supplies, discussed in Chapter 3. Clint's paid $400 for supplies during the year, and the company recorded them as an asset. At the end of the year, the company must determine how many supplies are left and how many were used. Clint's counts the supplies on hand and then subtracts that amount from the amount purchased. Suppose Clint's finds that there is $75 worth of supplies left in the supply closet on December 31. Since the company purchased $400 worth, that means $325 worth of supplies must have been used during the year. Clint's wants to show supplies expense of $325 on the year's income statement; and the corresponding asset should show $75 on the balance sheet at year end. This is the adjustment to get the accounts to their correct year-end balances, first in the accounting equation and then as a journal entry:

Assets	=	Liabilities	+	CC	+	Retained earnings
(325) Supplies						(325) Supplies expense

Date	Transaction	Debit	Credit
December 31, 2011	Supplies expense	325	
	Supplies		325
	To record supplies expense for the year		A-4

The T-accounts with the adjusting entries posted to them are shown in Exhibit B.7.

Steps 5 and 6: Preparing the Adjusted Trial Balance and the Financial Statements

After all the adjusting entries have been posted to the general ledger accounts and new balances have been computed in the general ledger, an **adjusted trial balance** is prepared. An adjusted trial balance is simply a list of all the general ledger accounts and their balances, to verify that debits = credits for all the company's accounts after all the adjustments have been made. The trial balance is an internal document, used in the process of preparing financial statements. Preparing an adjusted trial balance—and making sure it actually balances—helps ensure the accuracy of the recording process. If the adjusted trial balance *is* in balance—debits = credits—it can be used to prepare the financial statements.

The adjusted trial balance is shown in Exhibit B.8, and the financial statements are shown in Exhibit B.9 on page 576.

After the financial statements are prepared, we are *almost* ready to begin another accounting cycle. First, we must get our general ledger ready for a new fiscal year.

> A trial balance is a list of all the accounts, each with its debit balance or its credit balance. An unadjusted trial balance is prepared before any adjustments have been made. An **adjusted trial balance** is prepared after adjustments have been made, and it can be used to prepare the financial statements.

Step 7: Prepare Closing Entries

Revenue accounts, expense accounts, and dividends are **temporary accounts**. The balances in those accounts will be transferred to retained earnings at the end of each period; therefore, they will start each new period with a zero balance.

Think about the accounting equation and the work sheet we've been using throughout this book to record transactions. We've been listing the revenues and expenses in the retained earnings column, because they increase and decrease the owner's claims to the assets of the business. The balance sheet will balance only when the revenue and expense amounts are incorporated into the retained earnings balance. The net amount of revenues minus expenses—net income—is incorporated into retained earnings when we prepare the statement of changes in shareholders' equity.

> **L.O.4**
> Describe the closing process and explain why it is necessary.

> **Temporary accounts** are the revenue, expense, and dividends accounts.

EXHIBIT B.7

Adjusted T-Accounts for Clint's Consulting Co., Inc.

ASSETS	=	LIABILITIES	+	SHAREHOLDER'S EQUITY

Cash
(asset)

1-1	2,000	400	1-3
1-2	4,000	500	1-4
1-5	9,000	350	1-6
1-9	4,000	4,150	1-7
		600	1-8
EB	13,000		

Accounts receivable
(asset)

A-1	3,000	
EB	3,000	

Supplies
(asset)

1-3	400	325	A-4
EB	75		

Notes payable
(liability)

1-7	4,000	4,000	1-2
		0	EB

Unearned consulting fees
(liability)

A-3	2,000	4,000	1-9
		2,000	EB

Salaries payable
(liability)

		50	A-2
		50	EB

Common stock
(shareholder's equity)

	2,000	1-1
	2,000	EB

Dividends
(a special temporary account)

1-8	600	
EB	600	

Consulting fees
(revenue)

	9,000	1-5
	3,000	A-1
	2,000	A-3
	14,000	EB

Advertising expense
(expense)

1-4	500	
EB	500	

Salary expense
(expense)

1-6	350	
A-2	50	
EB	400	

Interest expense
(expense)

1-7	150	
EB	150	

Supplies expense
(expense)

A-4	325	
EB	325	

Account	DR	CR
Cash	$13,000	
Accounts receivable	3,000	
Supplies	75	
Notes payable		$ 0
Salaries payable		50
Unearned consulting fees		2,000
Common stock		2,000
Dividends	600	
Consulting fees		14,000
Advertising expense	500	
Interest expense	150	
Salary expense	400	
Supplies expense	325	
	$18,050	$18,050

EXHIBIT B.8

Adjusted Trial Balance for Clint's Consulting Company, Inc., for the Year 2011

EXHIBIT B.9

Financial Statements for Clint's Consulting Company, Inc., for 2011

Clint's Consulting Company, Inc.
Income Statement
For the Year Ended December 31, 2011

Revenue		
Consulting fees		$14,000
Expenses		
Advertising	$500	
Salaries	400	
Supplies	325	
Interest	150	
Total expenses		1,375
Net income		$12,625

Clint's Consulting Company, Inc.
Statement of Changes in Shareholder's Equity
For the Year Ended December 31, 2011

Beginning common stock	$ 0	
Common stock issued during the year	2,000	
Ending common stock		$ 2,000
Beginning retained earnings	$ 0	
Net income for the year	12,625	
Dividends	(600)	
Ending retained earnings		12,025
Total shareholder's equity		$14,025

Clint's Consulting Company, Inc.
Balance Sheet
At December 31, 2011

Assets		Liabilities and Shareholder's Equity	
Current Assets		Current Liabilities	
Cash	$13,000	Salaries payable	$ 50
Accounts receivable	3,000	Unearned consulting fees	2,000
Supplies	75	Total current liabilities	2,050
		Shareholder's equity	
		Common stock	2,000
Total assets	$16,075	Retained earnings	12,025
		Total shareholder's equity	14,025
		Total liabilities and	
		shareholder's equity	$16,075

Clint's Consulting Company, Inc.
Statement of Cash Flows
For the Year Ended December 31, 2011

Cash from operating activities		
Cash collected from customers	$13,000	
Cash paid for supplies	(400)	
Cash paid for interest	(150)	
Cash paid to employees	(350)	
Cash paid for advertising	(500)	
Net cash from operating activities		$11,600
Cash from investing activities		0
Cash from financing activities		
Cash from issue of stock	$ 2,000	
Proceeds from bank loan	4,000	
Repayment of bank loan	(4,000)	
Cash dividends paid	(600)	
Net cash from financing activities		1,400
Net increase in cash		$13,000
Beginning cash balance		$ 0
Ending cash balance		$13,000

From a bookkeeping perspective, **closing the accounts** is done—meaning to bring their balances to zero—with journal entries. Each account receives a debit or a credit to close it. For example, if a revenue account has a balance of $300—which would be a credit balance—the account is closed with a debit for $300. The corresponding credit in that closing journal entry is to retained earnings. Thus, closing the revenue account increases retained earnings. On the other hand, closing an expense account will decrease retained earnings. For example, if an expense account has a balance of $100—which would be a debit balance—the accounts is closed with a credit for $100. The corresponding debit for that closing journal entry is to retained earnings. Closing the expense accounts decreases retained earnings.

Keep in mind the reason for having revenue accounts and expense accounts. For a single accounting period, usually a year, the revenues and expenses are recorded separately from retained earnings so that we can report them on the year's income statement. Then we want those amounts included in retained earnings, and we want the revenue and expense accounts to be "empty" so they can start over, ready for amounts that will come during the coming year. Remember, the income statement covers a single accounting period. We don't want to mix up last year's revenue with this year's revenue in our revenue accounts or last year's expenses with this year's expenses in our expense accounts. The process of bringing these accounts to a zero balance is called closing the accounts, and the journal entries are called closing entries. We cannot close the revenue accounts and expense accounts until we have prepared the financial statements.

Asset accounts, liability accounts, and shareholders' equity accounts are **permanent accounts**, or **real accounts**. A balance in any of these accounts is carried over from one period to the next. For example, the amount of cash shown in the cash account will never be zero (unless we spend our last cent). Think about your own personal records. If you keep track of your cash (like your checking account), you will have a continuous record of your cash balance. On the date of a personal balance sheet, you would see how much cash you have on that particular date. As the next year begins, you still have that cash. It doesn't go away because a new year begins.

To get a better idea of what we mean by the continuous record in a permanent account, let's consider a simple example of a *temporary* account. Suppose you were keeping a list of your grocery expenses for the year. At the end of the year, after you have reported the amount of those expenses on your annual income statement, you would want to start a new list for the next year. Because an income statement reports expenses for a period of time—a year, in this example—your grocery expenses for one year would be reported on *one* income statement, but those expenses would not apply to the following year. You would want the grocery expense account to be empty when you begin the next year. Expense amounts must apply to a specific time period for them to make sense.

Exhibit B.10 shows the closing journal entries for Clint's Consulting, which are recorded after the financial statements are prepared.

Closing the accounts means bringing the balances in the temporary accounts to zero.

Permanent accounts or **real accounts** are accounts that are never closed. They are the asset, liability, and shareholders' equity accounts.

EXHIBIT B.10

Closing Entries

Ref.	Date	Journal entry	DR	CR
c-1	12/31	Consulting fees	14,000	
		Retained earnings		14,000
		To close revenue account		
c-2	12/31	Retained earnings	1,375	
		Advertising expense		500
		Salary expense		400
		Supplies expense		325
		Interest expense		150
		To close the expense accounts		
c-3	12/31	Retained earnings	600	
		Dividends		600
		To close dividends		

Your Turn B-3

Simple Company has one revenue account with a balance of $5,000 at year end and one expense account with a balance of $3,000. Prepare the closing journal entries for Simple Company.

MORE ABOUT CLOSING ENTRIES AND THE RELATIONSHIP BETWEEN THE INCOME STATEMENT AND THE BALANCE SHEET. Why do we bother with closing entries? They set the stage for the next accounting period by zeroing out the balances of all the temporary accounts. This is necessary because these accounts keep track of amounts that go to the income statement, which gives us the net income figure for *one specific period*. Without zeroing out the accounts, net income would include revenues or expenses for more than one period. Closing entries transfer the period's net income (or loss) to the retained earnings account (or to the owner's capital account in a sole proprietorship), so closing entries are the means by which net income flows downstream from the income statement through the statement of changes in shareholders' equity to the balance sheet.

Here's how the revenue amounts and expense amounts flow through the financial statements:

- *Income statement.* We present the details of net income—the revenues and expenses—on the income statement. The bottom line is net income.
- *Statement of changes in shareholders' equity.* We show net income as an addition to shareholders' equity on the statement of changes in shareholders' equity.
- *Balance sheet.* We present the total amount of shareholders' equity—which includes net income—on the balance sheet.

After we've used the revenue account balances and the expense account balances to prepare the income statement and after that information has flowed through to the balance sheet, we are ready to close the revenue accounts and expense accounts. That's the formal way of getting the correct balance in retained earnings. Here are the steps in detail to record closing entries:

1. Transfer all credit balances from the revenue accounts to retained earnings. This is done with a closing entry. The closing journal entry will have a debit to each of the revenue accounts for the entire balance of each—to bring them to a zero balance. The corresponding credit will be to retained earnings for the total amount of the period's revenue.

2. Transfer all debit balances from the expense accounts to retained earnings. This is done with a closing entry. The closing journal entry will have a debit to retained earnings and credits to all the expense accounts for their entire balances to bring them to a zero balance. The debit to retained earnings will be for the total amount of the period's expenses.

3. Transfer the dividends account balance to retained earnings. When a distribution is made to the shareholders of a corporation, a special account—dividends—is often used. This account is a temporary account that carries a debit balance. (When the dividends are declared and paid, dividends is debited and cash is credited.) The dividends account is closed directly to retained earnings. The amount of the dividends is not included on the income statement, but it is shown on the statement of changes in shareholders' equity. The journal entry to close this account will have a credit to dividends and a debit to retained earnings.

Look at the closing entries posted to Clint's T-accounts, shown in bold print in Exhibit B.11. Notice how the revenue and expense accounts have a zero balance.

When closing is done, there is one step left to completing our record keeping for the year. That step is preparing a postclosing trial balance.

Step 8: Preparing a Postclosing Trial Balance

A **postclosing trial balance** is a list of all the accounts and their debit balances or credit balances, prepared after the temporary accounts have been closed. Only balance sheet accounts will appear on the postclosing trial balance.

The final step in the accounting cycle is to prepare a **postclosing trial balance**. Remember, *post* means *after* (like *pre* means *before*). After the temporary accounts are closed, preparing a trial balance—a list of all the accounts with their debit or credit balances—accomplishes two things:

- It is a final check of the equality of debits and credits in the general ledger.
- It confirms that we are ready to start our next period with only real (permanent) accounts.

The postclosing trial balance for Clint's Consulting is shown in Exhibit B.12.

EXHIBIT B.11

T-Accounts with Closing Entries for Clint's Consulting Company, Inc.

ASSETS	=	LIABILITIES	+	SHAREHOLDER'S EQUITY

ASSETS

Cash
(asset)

1-1	2,000	400	1-3
1-2	4,000	500	1-4
1-5	9,000	350	1-6
1-9	4,000	4,150	1-7
		600	1-8

EB* 13,000

Supplies
(asset)

1-3	400	325	A-4
EB	75		

Accounts receivable
(asset)

A-1	3,000	
EB	3,000	

LIABILITIES

Notes payable
(liability)

1-7	4,000	4,000	1-2
		0	EB

Unearned consulting fees
(liability)

A-3	2,000	4,000	1-9
		2,000	EB

Salaries payable
(liability)

		50	A-2
		50	EB

SHAREHOLDER'S EQUITY

Common stock
(shareholder's equity)

		2,000	1-1
		2,000	EB

Retained earnings
(shareholder's equity)

C-2	1,375	C-1	14,000
C-3	600		
		EB	12,025

Dividends
(a special temporary account)

1-8	600	C-3	600

Consulting fees
(revenue)

		9,000	1-5
		3,000	A-1
		2,000	A-3
C-1	14,000	14,000	EB

Advertising expense
(expense)

1-4	500	C-2	500

Salary expense
(expense)

1-6	350		
A-2	50	C-2	400

Interest expense
(expense)

1-7	150	C-2	150

Supplies expense
(expense)

A-4	325	C-2	325

*EB=ending balance

Account	DR	CR
Cash	$13,000	
Accounts receivable	3,000	
Supplies	75	
Notes payable		$ 0
Salaries payable		50
Unearned consulting fees		2,000
Common stock		2,000
Retained earnings		12,025
Totals	$16,075	$16,075

EXHIBIT B.12

Postclosing Trial Balance for Clint's Consulting Company, Inc., at December 31, 2011

Review and Summary of the Accounting Cycle

To summarize, there are several steps in the process of preparing financial statements using a traditional general ledger system. Together, they are called the *accounting cycle.*

1. Record the transactions in the journal.
2. Post the journal entries to the ledger.
3. Prepare an unadjusted trial balance.
4. Adjust the accounts at the end of the period—record the adjusting journal entries and post them to the general ledger.
5. Prepare an adjusted trial balance.
6. Prepare the financial statements.
7. Close the temporary accounts to get ready for the next accounting period.
8. Prepare a postclosing trial balance.

UNDERSTANDING → # Business

Enterprise Resource Planning Systems

Enterprise resource planning (ERP) systems are changing the way businesses manage, process, and use information. ERP systems are computer-based software programs designed to process an organization's transactions and integrate information for planning, production, financial reporting, and customer service. It is estimated that the majority of companies with annual revenues exceeding $1 billion have implemented ERP systems.

Exactly how ERP systems operate varies from company to company, depending on the company's needs.

- ERP systems are packaged software designed for business environments, both traditional and Web based. *Packaged software* means that the software is commercially available—for purchase or lease—from a software vendor, as opposed to being developed in-house.
- An ERP system is composed of modules relating to specific functions. There are modules for *accounting,* including financial, managerial, and international accounting; *logistics,* including materials requirement planning, production, distribution, sales management, and customer management; and *human resources,* including payroll, benefits, and compensation management.
- All the modules work together with a common database. This creates an enterprise-wide system instead of separate, independent systems for each function of the business.
- ERP systems are integrated in terms of software, but not hardware. So, even though two companies may buy ERP packages from the same vendor, the way the system is used will likely be very different.
- Because of their popularity and growth, the large ERP vendors are familiar to many of us—SAP, Oracle,

PeopleSoft, J.D. Edwards, and BAAN. Together these vendors hold a major share of the ERP market and provide their system packages along with training to their clients around the world.

Companies implement ERP systems to do the following:

- Consolidate their systems and eliminate redundant data entry and data storage
- Decrease their computer operating costs
- Better manage their business processes
- Accommodate international currencies and international languages
- Standardize policies and procedures
- Enhance and speed up financial reporting
- Improve decision making
- Improve productivity
- Improve profitability

In spite of all the potential benefits of ERP systems, there are drawbacks. ERP systems are costly to implement, with total implementation costs running into the millions of dollars. Switching to a new system requires extensive and costly training for those who will use the system.

Given the widespread adoption of ERP systems, it is apparent that the market perceives the ERP system benefits to outweigh the costs. Therefore, whether you choose to go into accounting, information technology, finance, marketing, or management, it is likely that you will encounter an ERP system. However, given the speed with which technology changes, the ERP systems that you will encounter will be even more complex with greater capacities than the ones in existence today.

Team Shirts Transactions for March 2010 in a General Ledger System

We've already analyzed the transactions for Team Shirts for the third month of business, and prepared the financial statements for March in Chapter 3. Let's repeat the accounting cycle for the same month, this time using debits and credits. The transactions for March are shown in Exhibit B.13. Each transaction is recorded as an entry in the general journal, chronologically as it occurs during the company's business activity. Then each transaction is posted to the general ledger (we'll use T-accounts). At March 31, we'll post the adjusting entries needed to prepare the four financial statements. After following along through the adjusted T-accounts, you will prepare the financial statements.

EXHIBIT B.13

Transactions for Team Shirts for March

March 1	Purchased computer for $4,000 with $1,000 down and a three-month, 12% note for $3,000. The computer is expected to last for three years and have a residual value of $400.
March 10	Paid the rest of last month's advertising bill, $50.
March 15	Collected accounts receivable of $150 from customers from February.
March 20	Paid for February purchases—paying off the accounts payable balance—of $800.
March 24	Purchased 250 shirts for the inventory @ $4 each for cash, $1,000.
March 27	Sold 200 shirts for $10 each, all on account, for total sales of $2,000.

To use a general ledger system, we need to set up the accounts with their balances on March 1, 2010. Exhibit B.14 on the following page shows all the accounts with their beginning balances (indicated with BB). Those accounts, in the Team Shirts general ledger, will remain with the beginning balances until we post journal entries from the month's transactions.

The first step in the accounting cycle is to record each transaction in chronological order in the journal—as each occurs in the business. Look at each transaction and its corresponding journal entry in Exhibit B.15 on page 583. Notice, for each journal entry there is the following:

- The date of the transaction
- The account names
- Equality between the debits and credits—in every journal entry
- A brief explanation of the transaction

Study each journal entry to make sure you understand how the transaction was recorded.

The remaining steps in the accounting cycle begin with posting journal entries to the general ledger. Some computerized accounting systems automatically do this. Because we are using T-accounts to represent the general ledger, that's where we will start. Here are the remaining steps to take us to the financial statements:

1. Post the journal entries for March using the T-accounts shown in Exhibit B.14.
2. Then prepare an unadjusted trial balance at March 31.
3. Make the necessary adjusting journal entries at March 31 and post them to the T-accounts. For Team Shirts, three adjustments need to be made before the financial statements can be prepared. The adjustments are as follows:
   a. Depreciation expense for the computer: $100
   b. Interest payable on the note: $30
   c. Insurance expense for the month: $50
4. Prepare an *adjusted* trial balance at March 31, 2010.
5. Use the adjusted trial balance to prepare the four basic financial statements.

EXHIBIT B.14

T-Accounts for Team Shirts at the Beginning of March

ASSETS	=	LIABILITIES	+	SHAREHOLDER'S EQUITY

Cash
(asset)

BB* 6,695 |

Accounts payable
(liability)

| 800 **BB**

Common stock
(shareholder's equity)

| 5,000 **BB**

Accounts receivable
(asset)

BB   150 |

Other payables
(liability)

| 50 **BB**

Retained earnings
(shareholder's equity)

| 1,220 **BB**

Inventory
(asset)

BB   100 |

Notes payable
(liability)

Sales
(revenue)

Prepaid insurance
(asset)

BB   125 |

Interest payable
(liability)

Cost of goods sold
(expense)

Computers
(asset)

Insurance expense
(expense)

Accumulated depreciation
(contra asset)

Interest expense
(expense)

Depreciation expense
(expense)

*BB = beginning balance

Journal Entries for March 2010

Ref.	Date	Journal entry	DR	CR
3-1	3/01/10	Computer	4,000	
		Cash		1,000
		Notes payable		3,000
		To record the purchase of a computer with a cash payment of $1,000 and a note payable of $3,000		
3-2	3/10/10	Other payables	50	
		Cash		50
		To record the payment of a liability for last month's advertising expense		
3-3	3/15/10	Cash	150	
		Accounts receivable		150
		To record the collection of accounts receivable		
3-4	3/20/10	Accounts payable	800	
		Cash		800
		To record payment to vendor for last month's purchase		
3-5	3/24/10	Inventory	1,000	
		Cash		1,000
		To record the purchase of 250 T-shirts at $4 each, paid for in cash		
3-6a	3/27/10	Accounts receivable	2,000	
		Sales		2,000
		To record the sale of 200 T-shirts, on account		
3-6b	3/27/10	Cost of goods sold	800	
		Inventory		800
		To record the expense *cost of goods sold* and reduce the inventory by 200 × $4		

Here are the details for each step:

1. T-accounts are shown in the answer to part (3).
2.

Team Shirts
Unadjusted Trial Balance
March 31, 2010

Cash	$ 3,995	
Accounts receivable	2,000	
Inventory	300	
Prepaid insurance	125	
Computer	4,000	
Notes payable		$ 3,000
Common stock		5,000
Retained earnings		1,220
Sales		2,000
Cost of goods sold	800	
Totals	*$11,220*	*$11,220*

3. Adjusting journal entries and explanations follow:
   a. The computer has been used for one full month, so you must record depreciation expense. The cost was $4,000, an estimated residual value of $400, and a three year useful life. Each year the equipment will be depreciated by $1,200 [($4,000 – $400)/3 years]. That makes the depreciation expense $100 per month.

Date	Transaction	Debit	Credit
March 31, 2010	Depreciation expense	100	
	Accumulated depreciation		100
	To record the depreciation expense for March		Adj-1

   b. Team Shirts signed a $3,000 note on March 1 to purchase the computer. A month has passed, and Team Shirts needs to accrue the interest expense on that note in the amount of $30 ($3,000 × 0.12 × 1/12).

Date	Transaction	Debit	Credit
March 31, 2010	Interest expense	30	
	Interest payable		30
	To record the interest expense for March		Adj-2

   c. In mid-February, Team Shirts purchased three months of insurance for $150, which is $50 per month. On the March 1 balance sheet, there is a current asset called prepaid insurance in the amount of $125. A full month's worth of insurance expense needs to be recorded for the month of March. That amount will be deducted from prepaid insurance.

Date	Transaction	Debit	Credit
March 31, 2010	Insurance expense	50	
	Prepaid insurance		50
	To record the insurance expense for March		Adj-3

Following are the T-accounts with adjustments for March 2010 posted. (Ending balances in each account are shown with a double underline.)

ASSETS	=	LIABILITIES	+	SHAREHOLDER'S EQUITY

ASSETS

Cash
(asset)

*BB	6,695	1,000	3-1
		50	3-2
3-3	150	800	3-4
		1,000	3-5
**EB	3,995		

Accounts receivable
(asset)

BB	150	150	3-3
3-6a	2,000		
EB	2,000		

Inventory
(asset)

BB	100		
3-5	1,000	800	3-6b
EB	300		

Prepaid Insurance
(asset)

BB	125	50	Adj-3
EB	75		

Computers
(asset)

3-1	4,000	
EB	4,000	

Accumulated depreciation
(contra asset)

	100	Adj-1
	100	EB

LIABILITIES

Accounts payable
(liability)

3-4	800	800	BB
		0	EB

Other payables
(liability)

3-2	50	50	BB
		0	EB

Notes payable
(liability)

	3,000	3-1
	3,000	EB

Interest payable
(liability)

	30	Adj-2
	30	EB

SHAREHOLDER'S EQUITY

Common stock
(shareholder's equity)

	5,000	BB
	5,000	EB

Retained Earnings
(shareholder's equity)

	1,220	BB
	1,220	EB

Sales
(revenue)

	2,000	3-6a
	2,000	EB

Cost of goods sold
(expense)

3-6b	800	
EB	800	

Insurance expense
(expense)

Adj-3	50	
EB	50	

Interest expense
(expense)

Adj-2	30	
EB	30	

Depreciation expense
(expense)

Adj-1	100	
EB	100	

*BB = beginning balance
**EB = ending balance

4.

Team Shirts Adjusted Trial Balance March 31, 2010		
Cash	$ 3,995	
Accounts receivable	2,000	
Inventory	300	
Prepaid insurance	75	
Computer	4,000	
Accumulated depreciation		$ 100
Interest payable		30
Notes payable		3,000
Common stock		5,000
Retained earnings		1,220
Sales		2,000
Cost of goods sold	800	
Insurance expense	50	
Depreciation expense	100	
Interest expense	30	
Totals	$11,350	$11,350

5. The financial statements are as follows:

Team Shirts Income Statement For the Month Ended March 31, 2010

Sales revenue		$2,000
Expenses		
Cost of goods sold	$800	
Depreciation expense	100	
Insurance expense	50	
Interest expense	30	980
Net income		$1,020

Team Shirts Statement of Changes in Shareholder's Equity For the Month Ended March 31, 2010

Beginning common stock	$5,000	
Common stock issued during the month	0	
Ending common stock		$5,000
Beginning retained earnings	$1,220	
Net income for the month	1,020	
Dividends declared	0	
Ending retained earnings		2,240
Total shareholder's equity		$7,240

Team Shirts
Balance Sheet
At March 31, 2010

Assets		Liabilities and Shareholder's equity	
Current assets		**Current liabilities**	
Cash	$ 3,995	Interest payable	$ 30
Accounts receivable	2,000	Notes payable	3,000
Inventory	300	Total current liabilities	3,030
Prepaid insurance	75	**Shareholder's equity**	
Total current assets	6,370	Common stock	5,000
Computer (net of $100		Retained earnings	2,240
accumulated depreciation)	3,900	Total shareholder's equity	7,240
		Total liabilities and	
Total assets	$10,270	shareholder's equity	$10,270

Team Shirts
Statement of Cash Flows
For the Month Ended March 31, 2010

Cash from operating activities:		
Cash collected from customers	$ 150	
Cash paid to vendors	(1,800)	
Cash paid for advertising	(50)	
Net cash from operating activities		$(1,700)
Cash from investing activities:		
Purchase of computer*	$(1,000)	(1,000)
Cash from financing activities:		0
Net increase (decrease) in cash		$(2,700)
Beginning cash balance		6,695
Ending cash balance		$ 3,995

*Computer was purchased for $4,000. A note was signed for $3,000 and cash paid was $1,000.

You have seen these exact financial statements before. When we used the accounting equation to keep track of the transactions in Chapter 3, the results were the same as using the general ledger system here. No matter how we do the record keeping, the financial statements are the same. The mechanics of any accounting system—stand-alone or integrated with an enterprise resource planning system—must be designed to produce the information needed for the basic financial statements according to GAAP.

Key Terms for Appendix B

Accounting cycle (p. 568)
Adjusted trial balance
  (p. 574)
Closing the accounts (p. 577)
Credit (p. 565)
Debit (p. 565)
Dividend (p. 570)

Enterprise-wide resource
  planning system (ERP)
  (p. 564)
General ledger (p. 563)
General ledger system (p. 563)
Journal (p. 564)
Permanent accounts (p. 577)

Postclosing trial balance
  (p. 578)
Posting (p. 564)
Real accounts (p. 577)
Trial balance (p. 565)
Temporary accounts (p. 574)
Withdrawal (p. 570)

Answers to YOUR TURN Questions

Your Turn B-1

Account title	Expense	Revenue	Asset	Liability	Shareholders' equity
Accounts payable				CR (Credit)	
Accounts receivable			DR		
Advertising expense	DR				
Cash			DR		
Depreciation expense	DR				
Furniture and fixtures			DR		
Accumulated depreciation			(Contra) CR		
Unearned fees				CR	
Salary expense	DR				
Common stock					CR
Rent expense	DR				
Retained earnings					CR
(Earned) Fees		CR			
Land			DR		
Building			DR		

Your Turn B-2

Date	Transaction	Debit	Credit
December 31, 2010	Salaries expense	300	
	Salaries payable		300
	To accrue salary expense for December 2010		

No expense will be recognized in January 2011. It was recognized in December 2010, but will be paid in January 2011.

Date	Transaction	Debit	Credit
January 3, 2011	Salaries payable	300	
	Cash		300
	To record the cash payment of salaries payable		

Your Turn B-3

Date	Transaction	Debit	Credit
December 31, 2010	Revenue account	5,000	
	Retained earnings		5,000
	To close the revenue account to retained earnings		

Date	Transaction	Debit	Credit
December 31, 2010	Retained earnings	3,000	
	Expense account		3,000
	To close the expense account to retained earnings		

Questions

1. What is the general ledger system and what are its advantages?
2. What is an account?
3. What is the trial balance?
4. Which accounts are permanent and which are temporary?
5. What is the normal balance in each of these accounts?

> Accounts receivable
> Accounts payable
> Common stock
> Retained earnings
> Sales revenue
> Salary expense
> Cash
> Supplies expense
> Distributions (dividends)
> Inventory
> Bonds payable
> Cost of goods sold

6. What are the basic steps in the accounting cycle?
7. Can accounting transactions be recorded directly into the general ledger accounts? What is the advantage of using a journal first?
8. Is a credit a good thing or a bad thing? Explain.
9. What are adjusting entries and why are they necessary?

Multiple-Choice Questions

1. Evans Company completes a service engagement and bills a customer $50,000 on June 19, 2010. Included in the journal entry to record this transaction will be a:
   a. debit to cash, $50,000.
   b. credit to cash, $50,000.
   c. credit to accounts receivable, $50,000.
   d. credit to service revenue, $50,000.
2. A trial balance is a:
   a. list of all the accounts with a six-digit account number used by a business.
   b. place to record increases and decreases to a particular financial statement item's balance.
   c. chronological list of all recorded transactions.
   d. list of all the accounts used by the business along with each account's debit or credit balance at a point in time.
3. Bob Frederick, the owner of a delivery business, wants to know the balance of cash, accounts receivable, and sales on April 15 of the current period. Bob should look at what part of his accounting system?
   a. The journal
   b. The ledger
   c. The balance sheet
   d. The subsidiary journal
4. What is accomplished by preparing an unadjusted trial balance?
   a. A firm can make sure the debits equal the credits in the accounting system.
   b. A firm can make sure there are no errors in the accounting system.
   c. A firm can identify accruals and deferrals.
   d. All of the above
5. The data needed to prepare a trial balance comes from the
   a. journal.
   b. ledger.
   c. balance sheet.
   d. post-closing income statement.

6. If the income statement includes revenues earned even if the cash has not been collected from customers yet, it means that the
    a. closing entries have not been completed yet.
    b. journal has errors in it.
    c. accrual basis of accounting is being used.
    d. adjusting entries have not been done yet.
7. Myers Company pays its employees every Friday for a five-day workweek (Monday through Friday). The employees earn $3,000 per day of work. If the company pays the employees $15,000 on Friday, October 2, 2009, the entry into the journal would include
    a. a debit to wages expense for $15,000.
    b. a debit to cash for $15,000.
    c. a credit to wages payable for $15,000.
    d. a debit to cash for $3,000.
8. Jules, Inc., had a June 1, 2010, balance of office supplies of $100. During June, the company purchased $900 more of the office supplies in exchange for cash. On June 30, 2010, the supplies were counted and it was determined that $200 worth of office supplies were left unused. The adjusting journal entry should include a
    a. debit to supplies expense of $800.
    b. debit to office supplies of $900.
    c. credit to cash for $200.
    d. credit to supplies expense of $800.
9. Why should closing entries be completed at the end of each period?
    a. Certain accounts are not needed in the future.
    b. It allows the trial balance and financial statements to be prepared.
    c. All accounts must begin the next period at zero.
    d. Temporary accounts need to start the next period with a zero balance.
10. Which of the following accounts should NOT be closed?
    a. Accounts receivable
    b. Interest revenue
    c. Sales revenue
    d. Wages expense

MyAccountingLab

All of the A exercises can be found within MyAccountingLab, an online homework and practice environment.

Short Exercises
Set A

SEB-1A. *Normal account balances. (LO 1).* Given the following accounts, tell whether the normal balance of each account is a debit (DR) or a credit (CR):

1. _____ Supplies
2. _____ Insurance expense
3. _____ Income tax expense
4. _____ Salaries payable
5. _____ Retained earnings

SEB-2A. *Recognize revenue and record journal entries. (LO 1, 2, 3).* Indicate which of the following events would result in recognizing revenue for the year in which the described event takes place; indicate the amount and the account. Give the journal entry that would be made in each case. (Take the selling company's point of view.)

1. Seminole Boosters has received $75,000 in advanced ticket sales for next year's football games.
2. Comcast Cable collected several accounts that were outstanding from last year. Usually accounts are collected in advance; but in this case, the customer received the cable services last year but didn't pay until this year.
3. Customers paid $6,500 in advance for services to be rendered next year.

SEB-3A. *Recognize expenses and record journal entries. (LO 1, 2, 3).* Indicate which of the following events would result in recognizing expenses for the year in which the described event takes place; give the journal entry. (Take the company's point of view.)

1. Bright Shirts, Inc., sold 1,500 T-shirts to the FSU Bookstore for $16,500 cash. Bright originally paid $4,500 for the shirts.
2. Home Industries, Inc., received a utility bill for the last month of the year in the amount of $575 but won't actually pay it until next year.
3. Waterline, Inc., paid $8,600 for a two-year insurance policy—for the current year and for next year.

SEB-4A. *Relate the accounting equation to debits and credits. (LO 1).* Following are selected transactions for Ralph's Surfshop, Inc., that occurred during the month of December. For each transaction, tell which accounts will be affected and how (debit or credit).

1. The company paid $650 cash for a truck rental for December.
2. The company purchased inventory for $4,500 on account.

SEB-5A. *Record journal entries. (LO 1).* The following selected transactions for ABC, Inc., occurred during the month of April. Give the journal entry for each.

1. The company incurred operating expenses for $800, paid in cash.
2. The company purchased supplies for $500 cash, to be used during May.

SEB-6A. *Effect of transactions on cash. (LO 1).* How do the following transactions affect Jolly, Inc.'s cash account? (Tell if the result would be a debit or a credit.)

1. The firm gave customers $1,500 cash for returned merchandise.
2. The firm issued stock to investors for $7,750 cash.

SEB-7A. *Effect of transactions on the liability and shareholders' equity accounts. (LO 1).* How do the following transactions affect the liability and shareholders' equity accounts for Slow Pokes, Inc., during 2010? (Tell if the result would be a debit or a credit.)

1. The company earned $12,000 in sales for the year.
2. An estimated $2,500 will be due for yearly income taxes, payable in 2011.

SEB-8A. *Effect of transactions on accounts. (LO 1).* Determine how the accounts would be affected (increase or decrease and debit or credit) for the following transactions occurring in April 2011 for Computer Solutions, Inc.:

1. The company paid $4,500 for next year's rent.
2. The company paid $2,000 of its accounts payable, owed for previously purchased inventory.
3. The company declared and distributed $500 of dividends.

SEB-9A. *Determine permanent or temporary accounts. (LO 4).* For each of the following accounts, tell whether it is a permanent account or a temporary account:

1. _____ Merchandise inventory
2. _____ Insurance expense
3. _____ Interest expense
4. _____ Income taxes payable
5. _____ Common stock

Set B

SEB-10B. *Normal account balances. (LO 1).* Given the following accounts, tell whether the normal balance of each account is a debit (DR) or a credit (CR):

1. _____ Interest receivable
2. _____ Accounts payable
3. _____ Common stock
4. _____ Service revenue
5. _____ Prepaid rent

SEB-11B. *Recognize revenue and record journal entries. (LO 1, 2, 3).* Indicate which of the following events would result in recognizing revenue for the year in which the described event takes place; indicate the amount and the account. Give the journal entry that would be made in each case. (Take the selling company's point of view.)

1. Dell Inc. sold a computer system worth $10,000; the customer financed the purchase because he didn't have any cash.
2. Steel USA is producing 3 tons of steel for American Cans. It costs $4,500 per ton to produce, but American Cans has promised to pay $7,750 per ton when it receives the steel. Steel USA will probably ship it in the near future.

SEB-12B. *Recognize expenses and record journal entries. (LO 1, 2, 3).* Indicate which of the following events would result in recognizing expenses for the year in which the described event takes place; give the journal entry. (Take the T-shirt company's point of view.)

1. T-Shirts Plus, Inc., paid employees $6,000 for work performed during the prior year.
2. T-Shirts Plus, Inc., purchased 15,000 T-shirts for its inventory for $30,000 on account.
3. T-Shirts Plus, Inc., paid the factory cash for the 15,000 shirts purchased.

SEB-13B. *Relate the accounting equation to debits and credits. (LO 1).* Following are selected transactions for Jenna Enterprises, Inc., that occurred during the month of December. For each transaction, tell which accounts will be affected and how (debit or credit).

1. The company issued common stock to investors for $15,000 cash.
2. The company paid $1,500 cash for December rent for a warehouse.

SEB-14B. *Record journal entries. (LO 1).* The following selected transactions for Wilson's Consulting, Inc., occurred during the month of April. Give the journal entry for each.

1. The firm provided services to customers for $10,000. Seventy percent was paid with cash and thirty percent was on account.
2. The firm paid $1,000 for part of a $3,000 purchase made in March on account.

SEB-15B. *Effect of transactions on cash. (LO 1).* How do the following transactions affect Toys, Toys, Toys, Inc.'s cash account? (Tell if the result would be a debit or a credit.)

1. The company purchased $6,000 of baby cribs for cash.
2. The company sold one of its buildings, allowing the buyer to give it a short-term note for $135,000.
3. The employees were paid $5,400 cash in sales commissions.

SEB-16B. *Effect of transactions on the liability and shareholders' equity accounts. (LO 1).* How do the following transactions affect the liability and shareholders' equity accounts for Fast Signs, Inc., during 2010? (Tell if the result would be a debit or a credit.)

1. The company paid the remainder of a $3,000 loan.
2. The company obtained a loan for $10,000.

SEB-17B. *Effect of transactions on accounts. (LO 1).* Determine how the accounts would be affected (increase or decrease and debit or credit) for the following transactions occurring in January 2009 for Networking Solutions, Inc.:

1. The company received $25,000 cash from the owner in exchange for common stock.
2. The company purchased $10,000 of new office computers on account.
3. The company sold $2,500 of inventory for cash.

SEB-18B. *Determine permanent or temporary accounts. (LO 4).* For each of the following accounts, tell whether it is a permanent account or a temporary account:

1. _____ Cash
2. _____ Accounts payable
3. _____ Common stock
4. _____ Sales revenue
5. _____ Prepaid rent

Exercises
Set A

All of the A exercises can be found within MyAccountingLab, an online homework and practice environment.

EB-19A. *Record transactions to T-accounts. (LO 1, 2).* Record the following transactions for Bradford, Inc., in T-accounts and tell how each affects assets, liabilities, or stockholders' equity. The year end for Bradford, Inc., is June 30.

1. On September 1, the company issued a $6,000 note at 4%, both interest and principal due in one year.
2. On October 1, the company rented a copy machine and paid one year of rent in advance at a rate of $300 per month.
3. On December 30, the company purchased an insurance policy for a term of one year, beginning immediately. The cost was $600, paid in cash.
4. On March 1, the company purchased $600 worth of supplies for cash. The company started the year with $100 worth of supplies on hand.
5. Over the course of the year, the company earned $75,000 of service revenue, collected in cash.

EB-20A. *Record adjustments to T-accounts. (LO 1, 2, 3).* Use the information from EB-19A, including your answers to 1–5, to make the necessary adjustments to Bradford's accounts in preparation for the year-end financial statements. The company had $75 worth of supplies on hand at the end of the fiscal year.

EB-21A. *Record transactions to T-accounts and prepare an unadjusted trial balance. (LO 1, 2).* Matt opened a bookstore on April 1, 2011, selling new and used books. Matt contributed $4,000 in exchange for common stock to start the business, Matt's Books. Record each of the following transactions into T-accounts for the new company. Calculate the account balances and prepare an unadjusted trial balance at June 30, 2011.

1. On April 1, the company bought $2,000 of new books from its supplier with cash.
2. On April 30, customers brought in used books and the company purchased them for $550 cash.
3. On June 30, $1,000 of new books were sold for $3,000. Half of these sales were on account.
4. On June 30, the company sold all the used books for $1,500 cash.

EB-22A. *Record transactions to T-accounts and prepare an unadjusted trial balance. (LO 1, 2).* The trial balance of Whisper Lane Productions, Inc., on March 1, 2012, lists the company's assets, liabilities, and shareholders' equity on that date.

	Trial Balance	
Account Title	Debit	Credit
Cash	$15,000	
Accounts receivable	5,700	
Accounts payable		$ 3,200
Common stock		9,000
Retained earnings		8,500
Total	$20,700	$20,700

During March, Whisper Lane completed the following transactions:

1. The company borrowed $6,000 from the bank with a short-term note payable.
2. Whisper Lane paid cash of $12,000 to acquire land.
3. The company performed service for a customer and collected the cash of $3,500.
4. Whisper Lane purchased supplies on account, $225.
5. The company performed service for a customer on account, $1,800.

Set up T-accounts for the accounts given in the March 1 trial balance. Then post the preceding transactions to the accounts. Calculate the account balances and prepare an unadjusted trial balance at March 31.

EB-23A. *Recognize adjusting and closing entries. (LO 3, 4).* Use the information from EB-22A to identify the accounts that will likely need to be adjusted before the monthly financial statements are prepared. What additional information would you need in each case to make the appropriate adjustment? Which accounts will need to be closed at the end of the accounting period and why?

EB-24A. *Record closing entries and compute net income. (LO 4).* Given the following adjusted trial balance, record the appropriate closing entries. What is net income for the year?

Brett's Bait & Tackle, Inc.
Adjusted Trial Balance
June 30, 2011

	Debit	Credit
Cash	$ 13,000	
Accounts receivable	20,000	
Prepaid rent	28,000	
Supplies	21,500	
Equipment	20,000	
Accumulated depreciation		$ 9,000
Land	64,000	
Accounts payable		23,000
Notes payable		25,000
Interest payable		2,000
Common stock		51,000
Retained earnings		29,500[a]
Dividends	4,000	
Sales		94,000
Cost of goods sold	45,000	
Depreciation expense	3,000	
Salary expense	15,000	
Totals	$233,500	$233,500

[a]Retained earnings at July 1, 2010. (No accounts have been closed.)

EB-25A. *Record journal entries, record adjusting entries, and explain the accounting cycle. (LO 1, 2, 3, 4).* The Problem Solvers Consulting Corporation began business in 2010. The following transactions took place during January:

January	1	The owners invested $75,000 in exchange for common stock.
	1	The company borrowed $10,000 from a local bank with a 3% note and a six-month term. Both the principal and interest will be repaid in six months.
	1	The company purchased computer equipment for $13,200 cash. It should last four years, with no residual value.
	6	Supplies were purchased on account for $500.
	8	Office rent of $700 for January was paid in cash.
	20	The company received $3,150 from a customer for services to be performed in February.
	31	Consulting services performed during January on account totaled $12,000.

31 The company paid salaries of $6,500 to employees.

31 The company paid $300 to the supplies vendor as part of the $500 owed to the vendor from the purchase on January 6. The company only paid part of the invoice because it only used $300 worth of the supplies in January.

Give the journal entry for each transaction. Provide the reason for each entry. Then, make the necessary adjusting entries at January 31, 2010. What else should be done to finish the accounting cycle for the month?

EB-26A. *Record journal entries, post to T-accounts, and prepare an unadjusted trial balance. (LO 1, 2).* Ray & Peters CPAs decided to open its own tax practice, Tax Specialists, Inc. The following transactions are the events that occurred during May, the company's first month:

May 1 Ray and Peters each donated $20,000 cash in exchange for common stock. They also signed a note with National Bank for $25,000.

2 Tax Specialists paid $28,000 prepaid rent for the first year.

11 Office equipment was purchased on account for $17,500.

16 The company purchased insurance for two years with $6,500 cash. The policy was effective June 1.

18 A discolored piece of office equipment arrived and the supplier agreed to remove $3,500 from Tax Specialists' account.

25 The company purchased some office furniture on sale worth $10,000 on account.

28 Tax Specialists paid off balance owed on the equipment.

30 An office manager was hired at a rate of $110 a day. The start date is June 1.

Give the journal entry for each transaction. Set up the required T-accounts and post the entries to these accounts. Prepare an unadjusted trial balance.

Set B

EB-27B. *Record transactions to T-accounts. (LO 1, 2).* Record the following transactions for Krall Pianos, Inc., in T-accounts and tell how each affects assets, liabilities, or shareholders' equity. The year end for Krall Pianos, Inc., is December 31.

1. On March 1, Krall Pianos issued a $15,000 note at 6%, both interest and principal due in one year.
2. On May 1, Krall Pianos rented a warehouse and paid $6,750 for two years of rent in advance.
3. Krall Pianos purchased an insurance policy for a term of three years on July 1, beginning immediately. The cost was $5,400, paid in cash.
4. The company purchased $475 worth of supplies for cash on November 1. The company started the year with $375 worth of supplies on hand.
5. Over the course of the year, Krall Pianos earned $54,500 for cash sales of $15,000 worth of inventory, collected in cash. The company started the year with $20,000 in inventory.

EB-28B. *Record adjustments to T-accounts. (LO 1, 2, 3).* Use the information from EB-27B, including your answers to 1–5, to make the necessary adjustments to Krall Pianos' accounts in preparation for the year-end financial statements. At year end, there were $175 worth of supplies on hand.

EB-29B. *Record transactions to T-accounts and prepare an unadjusted trial balance. (LO 1, 2).* Flynt Freedman opened Flynt's Brew, Inc., on March 1, 2010, selling gourmet coffees, teas, and desserts. Flynt contributed $5,500 in exchange for common stock to start the business. Record the following transactions into T-accounts for Flynt's. Calculate the account balances and prepare an unadjusted trial balance at March 31, 2010.

1. On March 1, the company purchased $2,750 of inventory from the supplier with cash.
2. The company purchased equipment for $350 cash on March 15.
3. On March 30, the company paid $500 for operating expenses.
4. By the end of the month, the company had earned sales revenue of $6,500 by selling $2,000 of inventory. Cash sales were $6,000 and a local business who purchased items for a conference still owed Flynt's $500.

EB-30B. *Record transactions to T-accounts and prepare an unadjusted trial balance. (LO 1, 2).* The trial balance of Jewel's Diamond Dazzles, Inc., on November 1, 2011, lists the company's assets, liabilities, and shareholders' equity on that date.

Trial Balance

Account title	Debit	Credit
Cash	$18,000	
Accounts receivable	6,500	
Inventory	7,500	
Accounts payable		$11,700
Common stock		8,800
Retained earnings		11,500
Total	$32,000	$32,000

During November, Diamond Dazzles completed the following transactions:

1. The company borrowed $5,000 from the bank with a short-term note payable.
2. Diamond Dazzles paid cash of $8,500 to acquire land.
3. The company sold $5,000 of inventory to customers and collected the cash of $15,000.
4. Diamond Dazzles purchased supplies on credit, $375.
5. The company sold $1,000 of inventory to customers for $2,500 on account.

Set up T-accounts for the accounts given in the November 1 trial balance. Then post the preceding transactions to the accounts. Calculate the account balances and prepare an unadjusted trial balance at November 30.

EB-31B. *Recognize adjusting and closing entries. (LO 3, 4).* Use the information from EB-30B to identify the accounts that will likely need to be adjusted before the monthly financial statements are prepared. What additional information would you need in each case to make the appropriate adjustment? Which accounts will need to be closed at the end of the accounting period and why?

EB-32B. *Record closing entries and compute net income. (LO 4).* Given the following adjusted trial balance, record the appropriate closing entries. What is net income for the year?

SR Ski Shop, Inc.
Adjusted Trial Balance
December 31, 2011

	Debit	Credit
Cash	$ 15,000	
Accounts receivable	23,000	
Prepaid rent	19,600	
Supplies	21,750	
Equipment	18,000	
Accumulated depreciation		$ 10,000
Land	72,000	
Accounts payable		27,650
Notes payable		30,000
Interest payable		3,610
Common stock		45,500
Retained earnings		26,370[a]
Dividends	2,000	
Sales		69,220
Cost of goods sold	15,000	
Depreciation expense	5,000	
Salaries expense	21,000	
Totals	$212,350	$212,350

[a]Retained earnings at January 1, 2011. (No accounts have been closed.)

EB-33B. *Record journal entries, record adjusting entries, and explain the accounting cycle. (LO 1, 2, 3, 4).* Health & Nutrition Importance, Inc., began business July 1, 2012. The following transactions took place during July:

July 1   The owners invested $75,000 in exchange for common stock.

     1   The company borrowed $15,000 from a local bank with a 4% note and a six-month term. Both the principal and interest will be repaid in six months.

     1   The company purchased health equipment for $28,500 cash. It should last five years, with no residual value.

     5   The company purchased supplies on account for $750.

   15   The company paid rent of $675 for July in cash.

   23   The company received $3,500 in customer dues (service revenues) for the month of August.

   31   The company performed consulting services during July on account that totaled $15,000.

   31   The company paid salaries of $6,000 to employees.

   31   The company paid $500 to the supplies vendor as part of the $750 owed to the vendor from the purchase on July 5. The company only paid part of the invoice because it only used $500 worth of the supplies in July.

Give the journal entry for each transaction. Provide the reason for each entry. Then, make the necessary adjusting entries at July 31, 2012. What else should be done to finish the accounting cycle for the month?

EB-34B. *Record journal entries, post to T-accounts, and prepare an unadjusted trial balance. (LO 1, 2).* Julie Jones decided to open her own dry cleaning shop, Prestige Dry Cleaners, Inc. The following transactions are the events that occurred during April 2013, the company's first month:

April 1   Julie contributed $45,000 cash in exchange for common stock. She also signed a note with 1st Regional Bank for $30,000.

     3   The company rented a store at a shopping center and paid $14,400 prepaid rent for the first year.

   10   The company purchased dry cleaning equipment on account for $21,250.

   19   The company purchased insurance for three years with $5,400 cash. The policy was effective May 1.

   21   Part of the equipment purchased on April 10 was damaged. The supplier agreed to remove $3,150 from Prestige Dry Cleaners' account.

   24   The company purchased furniture for $6,000 for Julie's office on account.

   27   The company paid off the balance owed on the equipment.

   30   Three employees were hired at a rate of $56 a day each. Their start date is May 1.

Give the journal entry for each transaction. Set up the required T-accounts and post the entries to these accounts. Prepare an unadjusted trial balance.

Problems
Set A

PB-35A. *Prepare a trial balance and financial statements. (LO 1, 2).* The following is account information for Vision Corporation as of December 31, 2011, after all adjustments have been made:

Revenue	$20,000
Prepaid rent	1,000
Equipment	12,500
Accumulated depreciation, equipment	3,000
Common stock	4,000
Retained earnings	2,500[a]
Accounts receivable	5,000
Accounts payable	2,000
Salaries expense	2,000
Depreciation expense	1,000
Cash	1,000
Inventory	8,000
Dividends	1,000

[a]Balance at January 1, 2011.

Requirement

Prepare a trial balance at December 31, 2011, income statement and statement of changes in shareholders' equity for the year ended December 31, 2011, and balance sheet at December 31, 2011.

PB-36A. *Record journal entries, post to T-accounts, and prepare an unadjusted trial balance. (LO 1, 2).* Architectural Design and Associates, Inc., began business on May 1, 2011. The following transactions were entered into by the firm during its first two months of business, May and June:

May	1	Common stock was issued to investors in the amount of $275,000.
	1	Architectural Design signed a long-term note with 1st Regional Bank for $65,000.
	9	The company purchased an office building with cash for $130,500.
	13	Equipment was purchased on account for $35,000.
	20	Supplies worth $3,500 were purchased with cash.
	27	Architectural Design paid for equipment that was purchased on May 13.
	30	The company purchased a two-year insurance policy that began on June 1 with cash for $4,800.
	30	The city utility bill for $675 was received by Architectural Design. The utility bill is always due the 15th of the following month and will be paid then.
June	1	Architectural Design purchased some inventory on account for $50,000.
	3	The company purchased some advertising in a local newspaper and on a local radio station for $5,000 cash.
	15	May's utility bill for $675 was paid. (Note that the bill was recorded as a payable in May.)
	30	June salaries of $12,500 were owed to employees who started during the month. Salaries are always paid the last day of the month earned.
	30	Architectural Design earned service revenues of $60,000 for the month, of which $15,000 were on account.
	30	Architectural Design received the city utility bill for $625.

Requirements

1. Give the journal entry for each transaction.
2. Post each transaction to T-accounts.
3. Prepare an unadjusted trial balance.

PB-37A. *Prepare closing entries and financial statements. (LO 3, 4).* Tia's Cotton Fabrics, Inc., has the following account information on its adjusted trial balance:

Tia's Cotton Fabrics, Inc.
Adjusted Trial Balance
March 31, 2012

	Debit	Credit
Cash	$ 24,000	
Accounts receivable	28,000	
Prepaid rent	9,500	
Supplies	15,250	
Equipment	25,000	
Accumulated depreciation		$ 7,500
Land	44,000	
Accounts payable		24,805
Notes payable		17,650
Interest payable		2,175
Common stock		23,650[a]
Retained earnings		35,000[b]
Dividends	4,000	
Sales		97,675
Gain on sale of equipment		7,450
Cost of goods sold	51,475	
Depreciation expense	2,500	
Salaries expense	12,180	
Totals	$215,905	$215,905

[a]Balance at April 1, 2011. (No common stock has been issued during the year.)
[b]Balance at April 1, 2011. (No closing entries have been made.)

Requirement

Prepare the necessary closing entries and the income statement, statement of changes in shareholders' equity for the year ended March 31, 2012, and balance sheet as of March 31, 2012.

PB-38A. *Record adjusting journal entries, post to T-accounts, and prepare closing entries. (LO 1, 2, 3, 4).* Gourmet Teas & Coffee, Inc., has the following account balances at December 31, the end of the fiscal year:

Prepaid insurance	$ 4,000
Rental income	35,670
Unearned rental income	3,800
Accumulated depreciation	7,625
Salaries payable	5,550
Property tax expense	4,398
Depreciation expense	7,625
Salaries expense	10,400

The following information is available at the end of the year:
a. $1,000 worth of the prepaid insurance has not yet expired.
b. Of the unearned rental income only $1,500 remains unearned.
c. The business actually owes salaries of $5,500; the accountant recorded $50 extra by mistake.
d. The company owes an additional $4,700 in property taxes, not yet recorded.
e. Due to a clerical error, the depreciation expense amount is incorrect. It has been recalculated, and the total depreciation expense should be $8,750 for the year.

Requirements

1. Prepare the journal entries necessary to adjust the accounts.
2. Use T-accounts to compute and present the balances in these accounts after the adjustments have been posted.
3. Prepare the closing entries.

PB-39A. *Record business transactions and prepare financial statements. (LO 1, 2, 3, 4).* Sally opened a tropical fish store as a corporation and called it Exotic_Aquatics.com, selling only via the Internet. During 2011, the first year of business, Sally's company had the following transactions:

   a. The business was started with Sally's contribution of $16,500 in exchange for common stock on January 1.
   b. The company borrowed $10,000 from First American Bank at 7.5% for 12 months on January 1.
   c. The company purchased $6,000 in inventory for cash on February 15.
   d. The company paid $3,600 of rent to a Webmaster on June 30 for use of a maintained Web site for two years starting July 1.
   e. The company had cash sales of $11,100 for 2011 with cost of goods sold of $2,500.
   f. The company paid $1,050 in advertising fees.

Requirements

1. Post the preceding transactions to T-accounts to determine the balance of each account on December 31, 2011; include any adjusting entries necessary.
2. Prepare the adjusted trial balance at December 31, 2011, the income statement, statement of changes in shareholders' equity, and a statement of cash flows for the year ended December 31, 2011, and the balance sheet at December 31, 2011.
3. Prepare the closing entries and the postclosing trial balance at December 31, 2011.

PB-40A. *Record business transactions. (LO 1, 2, 3, 4).* A partial list of transactions from We Do Windows Company during 2010 follows:

   a. In January, Keith and Rachel each donated $22,500 in exchange for common stock to start the business.
   b. On February 1, the company paid $6,000 for two years rent in advance.
   c. During the year, the company purchased $10,000 of supplies for cash.
   d. On March 15, 2010, the shop obtained necessary equipment for $12,000 cash. The equipment should last for five years. The company will take a full year of depreciation in 2010.
   e. On April 1, 2010, the shop paid an annual insurance premium of $1,000, for coverage beginning April 1.
   f. On June 1, 2010, to increase business, the company paid for a year of advertising for $1,020.
   g. On November 1, 2010, the company obtained a three-month loan for $30,000 at 4.5% from Three Rivers Bank payable on February 1, 2011.
   h. As of December 31, 2010, cash revenues totaled $30,000.
   i. In December, the company entered into a contract with a local rental company to do all its window washing in 2011 for $8,000, payable in four installments. The first installment was collected from the rental company in December 2010.
   j. On December 31, the company paid $1,000 in cash dividends.
   Note: at the end of the year, remaining supplies totaled $2,000.

Requirements

1. Give the journal entries for the transactions; include any adjusting entries.
2. Post the transactions to T-accounts and prepare the adjusted trial balance at December 31, 2010.
3. Prepare the closing entries and post-closing trial balance for We Do Windows Company at December 31, 2010.

PB-41A. *Analyze business transactions and prepare financial statements. (LO 1, 2, 3, 4).* The accounting department for Fun in the Great Outdoors Resort, Inc., recorded the following journal entries for 2012, the first year of business:

	Description	Debit	Credit
a.	Cash	50,000	
	Common stock		50,000
b.	Office supplies	300	
	Accounts payable		300
c.	Prepaid rent	12,000	
	Cash		12,000
d.	Building	225,000	
	Note payable		225,000
e.	Cash	5,000	
	Unearned rent revenue		5,000
f.	Utilities expense	225	
	Cash		225
g.	Accounts payable	300	
	Cash		300
h.	Cash	12,000	
	Rent revenue		12,000
i.	Unearned rent revenue	3,000	
	Rent revenue		3,000
j.	Supplies expense	130	
	Supplies		130
k.	Rent expense	6,000	
	Prepaid rent		6,000
l.	Interest expense	100	
	Interest payable		100
m.	Depreciation expense	1,500	
	Accumulated depreciation—building		1,500
n.	Dividends	5,000	
	Cash		5,000
o.	Salary expense	1,200	
	Salaries payable		1,200

Fun in the Great Outdoors generates revenue by renting mountainside cottages to vacationers to the area. When a reservation is made in advance, Fun in the Great Outdoors collects half the week's rent to hold the reservation; however, Fun in the Great Outdoors does not require reservations, and sometimes customers will come in to rent a unit the same day. These types of transactions require that Fun in the Great Outdoors' accounting department record some cash receipts as unearned revenues and others as earned revenues.

Requirements

1. Explain the transaction or event that resulted in each journal entry.
2. Post entries (a) through (o) to T-accounts and calculate the balance in each account.
3. Did Fun in the Great Outdoors generate net income or net loss for the period ending December 31, 2012? How can you tell?
4. Prepare the four financial statements required at year end.
5. Prepare the closing entries.

PB-42A. *Record business transactions and prepare financial statements. (LO 1, 2, 3, 4).* The accounting records for Shelby & Sammy Pet Boarders, Inc., contained the following balances as of January 1, 2011:

Assets		Liabilities and Shareholders' Equity	
Cash	$40,000	Accounts payable	$17,000
Accounts receivable	16,500	Common stock	45,000
Land	20,000	Retained earnings	14,500
Totals	$76,500		$76,500

The following accounting events apply to Shelby & Sammy Pet Boarders, Inc.'s 2011 fiscal year:

January	1	The company acquired an additional $20,000 cash from the owners by issuing common stock.
	1	Pet Boarders purchased a computer that cost $15,000 for cash. The computer had no salvage value and a three-year useful life.
March	1	The company borrowed $10,000 by issuing a one-year note at 12%.
May	1	The company paid $2,400 cash in advance for a one-year lease for office space.
June	1	The company made a $5,000 cash distribution to the shareholders.
July	1	The company purchased land that cost $10,000 cash.
August	1	Cash payments on accounts payable amounted to $6,000.
	1	Pet Boarders received $9,600 cash in advance for 12 months of service to be performed monthly for the next year, beginning on receipt of payment.
September	1	Pet Boarders sold land for $13,000 cash. The land originally cost $13,000.
October	1	Pet Boarders purchased $1,300 of supplies on account.
November	1	Pet Boarders purchased a one-year, $20,000 certificate of deposit at 6%.
December	31	The company earned service revenue on account during the year that amounted to $40,000.
	31	Cash collections from accounts receivable amounted to $44,000.
	31	The company incurred other operating expenses on account during the year of $6,000.
	31	Salaries that had been earned by the sales staff but not yet paid amounted to $2,300.
	31	Supplies worth $200 were on hand at the end of the period.
	31	Based on the preceding transaction data, there are five additional adjustments that need to be made before the financial statements can be prepared.

Requirement

Post the journal entries directly to T-accounts, make the appropriate adjustments, prepare an adjusted trial balance, and prepare the financial statements (all four) for 2011. Then prepare the closing entries and the postclosing trial balance.

Set B

PB-43B. *Prepare a trial balance and financial statements. (LO 1, 2).* The following account information pertains to Dean Furniture, Inc., as of December 31, 2010, after adjustments:

Sales	$22,000	Other revenue	$13,000
Prepaid advertising	2,000	Equipment (net)	20,000
Common stock	14,000	Accounts receivable	2,500
Accounts payable	3,000	Cost of goods sold	11,000
Operating expenses	5,500	Cash	11,300
Inventory	15,200	Dividends	2,000
Retained earnings	17,500		

Requirement

Prepare a trial balance at December 31, 2010, income statement and statement of changes in shareholders' equity for the year ended December 31, 2010, and balance sheet as of December 31, 2010.

PB-44B. *Record journal entries, post to T-accounts, and prepare an unadjusted trial balance. (LO 1, 2).* Emerging Electronics, Inc., began business on February 1, 2012. The following transactions occurred during its first two months of business, February and March:

February	1	Common stock was issued to investors in the amount of $305,000.
	1	The company signed a long-term note with National Bank for $70,000.
	8	The company purchased a building with cash for $125,000.
	12	The company purchased equipment on account for $45,000.
	20	The company purchased supplies worth $4,300 for cash.
	28	The company paid for the equipment that was purchased on February 12.
	29	The company purchased a two-year insurance policy that began on March 1 with cash for $5,000.
	29	The company received the city utility bill for $475. The utility bill is always due the 12th of the following month and will be paid then.
March	1	The company purchased inventory on account for $65,000.
	3	The company purchased some advertising in a local newspaper and on a local radio station for $3,500 cash.
	12	February's utility bill for $475 was paid (note that the bill was recorded as a payable in February).
	31	The company paid employees for work done, $14,150 cash.
	31	The company earned sales revenues of $125,000 for the month, of which $35,000 were on account. Cost of inventory sold was $31,250.
	31	The company received the city utility bill for $425.

Requirement

Give the journal entry for each transaction. Post each transaction to T-accounts. Prepare an unadjusted trial balance at March 31, 2012.

PB-45B. *Prepare closing entries and financial statements. (LO 3, 4).* Following is an adjusted trial balance from Village Lighting Solutions, Inc.:

Village Lighting Solutions, Inc.
Adjusted Trial Balance
December 31, 2011

	Debit	Credit
Cash	$ 31,655	
Accounts receivable	52,000	
Prepaid rent	11,250	
Prepaid insurance	5,800	
Equipment	40,000	
Accumulated depreciation		$ 10,000
Land	25,755	
Salaries payable		1,250
Notes payable		16,875
Interest payable		1,820
Common stock		25,000[a]
Retained earnings		44,000[b]
Dividends	3,500	
Sales		151,595
Cost of goods sold	45,880	
Rent expense	13,000	
Insurance expense	1,200	
Depreciation expense	5,000	
Salaries expense	15,500	
Totals	$250,540	$250,540

[a]Balance at January 1, 2011. (No common stock has been issued during the year.)
[b]Balance at January 1, 2011. (No closing entries have been made.)

Requirement

Prepare the necessary closing entries, the income statement, and the statement of changes in share-holders' equity for the year ended December 31, 2011, and balance sheet as of December 31, 2011.

PB-46B. *Record adjusting journal entries, post to T-accounts, and prepare closing entries. (LO 1, 2, 3, 4).* Medical Massage, Inc., has the following account balances at the end of the year (partial list of accounts):

Service revenue	$34,320
Prepaid insurance	$4,000
Unearned service revenue	3,200
Salaries payable	2,550
Equipment	40,000
Accumulated depreciation	12,000
Taxes expense	3,650
Depreciation expense	5,000
Salaries expense	8,250

The following information is also available:
a. The company accountant forgot to depreciate a new deluxe massage table that was purchased at the beginning of the year. The table cost $4,000, has a useful life of four years, and has no expected residual value.
b. The unearned service revenue consists of gift certificates sold during the year. Medical Massage has lost track of customers redeeming certificates, but only $1,200 of the gift certificates have not been redeemed.
c. The company currently owes employees $200 of salaries in addition to the amount already recorded.
d. The company owes $1,075 in real estate taxes in addition to the taxes already recorded.
e. Half of the $4,000 insurance policy has expired.

Requirements

1. Prepare the adjusting journal entries necessary at year end.
2. Use T-accounts to compute and present the balances in these accounts after the adjustments have been posted.
3. Prepare the closing journal entries.

PB-47B. *Record business transactions and prepare financial statements. (LO 1, 2, 3, 4).* Gigi and Sue started Granny Apple Delicious, Inc., on January 1, 2011, to sell their famous applesauce. The following transactions occurred during the year:
a. Gigi and Sue started the business by contributing $15,000 each in exchange for common stock on January 1.
b. Also on January 1, the company borrowed $20,000 from Local Bank at 5.5%. The loan was for one year.
c. The company purchased $10,000 worth of apples and other inventory for cash during the year.
d. The company grew and needed to rent a shop. It paid $27,000 for rent on the shop for 18 months, beginning July 1.
e. Granny Apple Delicious, Inc., sold $36,000 worth of applesauce for cash during the first fiscal year. Of the inventory purchased in item (c) only $1,000 remained at year end.
f. During the year, Granny Apple Delicious, Inc., paid $1,525 in operating expenses.

Requirements

1. Post the preceding transactions to T-accounts to determine the balance of each account on December 31, 2011; include any adjusting transactions necessary.
2. Prepare the adjusted trial balance, the income statement, statement of changes in shareholders' equity, balance sheet, and a statement of cash flows at year end.
3. Prepare the closing entries and the postclosing trial balance at year end.

PB-48B. *Record business transactions. (LO 1, 2, 3, 4).* The following information is a partial list of transactions from Home Cleaning Service, Inc.:

   a. Tina, Don, and Daly each donated $5,000 in exchange for common stock to start the business on January 1, 2011.

   b. On March 1, Home Cleaning paid $3,000 cash for a two-year insurance policy that was effective immediately.

   c. On March 15, the company purchased $8,000 of supplies on account.

   d. On April 5, the company purchased some cleaning equipment for $10,000 cash. The equipment should last for five years with no residual value. Home Cleaning will take a full year of depreciation in 2011.

   e. On May 1, Home Cleaning purchased a year's worth of advertising in a local newspaper for $1,200 cash.

   f. On September 1, Home Cleaning obtained a nine-month loan for $15,000 at 5% from City National Bank, with interest and principal payable on June 1, 2012.

   g. On December 31, Home Cleaning paid $5,000 of what it owed on account for supplies from item (c); the company had $2,000 of the supplies still on hand at the end of the year.

   h. For the year ended December 31, 2011, Home Cleaning had revenues of $26,225. The cash had been received for all but $3,000.

   i. Home Cleaning paid $2,000 in cash dividends on December 31, 2011.

Requirements

1. Give the journal entries for the transactions; include any adjusting entries.
2. Post the transactions to T-accounts and prepare the adjusted trial balance at December 31, 2011.
3. Prepare the closing entries and post-closing trial balance for Home Cleaning Service, Inc., at December 31, 2011.

PB-49B. *Analyze business transactions and prepare financial statements. (LO 2, 3, 4).* The accounting department for Entertainment Activities, Inc., recorded the following journal entries for the fiscal year ended June 30, 2012:

	Description	Debit	Credit
a.	Cash	150,000	
	Common stock		150,000
b.	Office supplies	475	
	Accounts payable		475
c.	Prepaid rent	18,000	
	Cash		18,000
d.	Building	375,000	
	Note payable		375,000
e.	Cash	16,000	
	Unearned ticket revenue		16,000
f.	Utilities expense	525	
	Cash		525
g.	Accounts payable	475	
	Cash		475
h.	Cash	50,000	
	Ticket revenue		50,000
i.	Unearned ticket revenue	10,000	
	Ticket revenue		10,000
j.	Office supplies expense	300	
	Office supplies		300
k.	Rent expense	7,000	
	Prepaid rent		7,000
l.	Interest expense	225	
	Interest payable		225

m.	Depreciation expense	2,000	
	Accumulated depreciation—building		2,000
n.	Dividends	7,500	
	Cash		7,500
o.	Salary expense	5,500	
	Salaries payable		5,500

Entertainment Activities generates revenue by selling tickets for local events such as concerts, fights, and sporting events. Sometimes tickets are sold in advance and sometimes customers will purchase their tickets the same day as the event. These types of transactions require that Entertainment Activities' accounting department record some cash receipts as unearned revenues and others as earned revenues.

Requirements

1. Explain the transaction or event that resulted in each journal entry.
2. Post entries (a) through (o) to T-accounts and calculate the balance in each account.
3. Did Entertainment Activities generate net income or net loss for the fiscal year ended June 30, 2012? How can you tell?
4. Prepare the four financial statements required at year end.
5. Prepare the closing entries.

PB-50B. *Record business transactions and prepare financial statements. (LO 1, 2, 3, 4).* The accounting records for Juan Electric Corporation contained the following balances as of December 31, 2010:

Assets		Liabilities and Shareholders' Equity	
Cash	$50,000	Accounts payable	$17,500
Accounts receivable	26,500	Common stock	48,600
Prepaid rent (through April 30, 2011)	3,600	Retained earnings	24,500
Land	10,500		
Totals	$90,600		$90,600

The following accounting events apply to Juan Electric Corporation's 2011 fiscal year:

January	1	Juan Electric purchased a computer that cost $18,000 for cash. The computer had no salvage value and a three-year useful life.
March	1	The company borrowed $20,000 by issuing a two-year note at 3%.
May	1	The company paid $6,000 cash in advance for an eight-month lease for office space. The lease started immediately.
June	1	The company paid cash dividends of $2,000 to the shareholders.
July	1	The company purchased land that cost $15,000 cash.
August	1	Cash payments on accounts payable amounted to $6,000.
	1	Juan Electric received $6,000 cash in advance for 12 months of service to be performed monthly, beginning on receipt of payment.
September	1	Juan Electric sold land for $13,000 cash. The land originally cost $15,000.
October	1	Juan Electric purchased $1,300 of supplies on account.
November	1	Juan Electric purchased a one-year, $10,000 certificate of deposit at 3%.
December	31	The company earned service revenue on account during the year that amounted to $50,000.
	31	Cash collections from accounts receivable amounted to $46,000.
	31	The company incurred other operating expenses on account during the year that amounted to $6,000.
Also:		Salaries that had been earned by the sales staff but not yet paid amounted to $2,300.
		There were $200 worth of supplies on hand at the end of the period.
		Based on the preceding transaction data, there are some additional adjustments that need to be made before the financial statements can be prepared.

Requirements

1. Give the journal entries for the transactions; include any adjusting entries.
2. Post the journal entries to T-accounts, prepare an adjusted trial balance, and then prepare the income statement, statement of changes in shareholders' equity, and statement of cash flows for the year ended December 31, 2011, and the balance sheet at December 31, 2011. Then, prepare the closing entries and the postclosing trial balance.

Financial Statement Analysis

Use the selection from the annual report of Books-A-Million, Inc., in Appendix A to answer the following questions:

1. When you look at the financial statements for Books-A-Million, can you tell if the company uses a general ledger accounting system? Explain.
2. Find at least four pieces of quantitative information contained in the selection from Books-A-Million's annual report that would not be found in a general ledger system.
3. Who are the auditors for Books-A-Million?
4. How does having an audit affect a firm's riskiness?

Critical Thinking Problem

Ethics

Companies often try to manage earnings by either recognizing revenue before it is actually earned according to GAAP or by deferring expenses that have been incurred. For example, to meet the targeted earnings for a specific period, a company may capitalize a cost that should be expensed. Read the following scenario and then decide how you would handle this opportunity to manage earnings.

You are a division manager of a large public company. Your bonus, as well as the bonuses of several of your best employees, is calculated on your division's net income targets that you must meet. This year that target is $1.5 million. You are authorized to sign off on any decision made within your division.

On December 15, 2011, your division of the company ordered $150,000 worth of supplies in anticipation of the seasonal rush. Most of them will be used by year end. These supplies were delivered on the evening of December 27. (Note that your company generally expenses supplies when purchased.) If you record this supplies expense this year, your net income will be $1.45 million and you will not meet the target and will therefore not receive your bonus of $25,000 that you have worked hard for. In addition, some of your key employees will not receive their bonuses. What would you do and why?

Glossary

A

Accelerated depreciation is a depreciation method in which more depreciation expense is taken in the early years of the asset's life and less in the later years.

The **accounting cycle** begins with the transactions of a new accounting period. It includes recording and posting the transactions, adjusting the books, preparing financial statements, and closing the temporary accounts to get ready for the next accounting period.

Accounts payable are amounts that a company owes its vendors. They are liabilities and are shown on the balance sheet.

Accounts receivable is a current asset that arises from sales on credit; it is the total amount customers owe the firm.

The **accounts receivable (AR) turnover ratio** is a ratio that measures how quickly a firm collects its accounts receivable. It is defined as credit sales divided by average accounts receivable.

An **accrual** is a transaction in which the revenue has been earned or the expense has been incurred, but no cash has been exchanged.

Accrual basis accounting refers to the way we recognize revenues and expenses. Accountants do not rely on the exchange of cash to determine the timing of revenue recognition. Firms recognize revenue when it is earned and expenses when they are incurred—no matter when the cash is received or disbursed. Accrual accounting follows the matching principle.

The **accumulated depreciation** is the reduction to the cost of the asset. Accumulated depreciation is a contra-asset, deducted from the cost of the asset for the balance sheet.

Activity method of depreciation is the method of depreciation in which useful life is expressed in terms of the total units of activity or production expected from the asset, and the asset is written off in proportion to its activity during the accounting period.

An **adjusted trial balance** is a list of all accounts with their debit and credit balances, prepared after adjustments have been made.

Adjusting the books means to make changes in the accounting records, at the end of the period, just before the financial statements are prepared, to make sure the amounts reflect the financial condition of the company at that date.

An **aging schedule** is an analysis of the amounts owed to a firm by the length of time they have been outstanding.

The **allowance for uncollectible accounts** is a contra-asset account, the balance of which represents the total amount the firm believes it will not collect from its total accounts receivable.

The **allowance method** is a method of accounting for bad debts in which the amount of the uncollectible accounts is estimated at the end of each accounting period.

Amortization means to write off the cost of a long-term asset over more than one accounting period.

Amortization schedule is a chart that shows the amount of principal and the amount of interest that make up each payment of a loan.

An **annuity** is a series of equal cash receipts or cash payments over equally spaced intervals of time.

Asset turnover ratio measures how efficiently a company is using its assets to generate sales. It is defined as net sales divided by average total assets.

Assets are economic resources owned or controlled by the business.

Authorized shares are shares of stock that are available for a firm to issue per its corporate charter.

Available-for-sale securities are investments the company may hold or sell; the company's intention is not clear enough to use one of the other categories—*held to maturity* or *trading*.

The **average days in inventory** is the number of days it takes, on average, to sell an item of inventory.

B

Bad debts expense is the expense to record uncollectible accounts receivable.

The **balance sheet** shows a summary of each element of the accounting equation: assets, liabilities, and shareholders' equity.

A **bank reconciliation** is a comparison between the cash balance in the firm's accounting records and the cash balance on the bank statement to identify the reasons for any differences.

A **bank statement** is a summary of the activity in a bank account sent each month to the account holder.

Big bath is an expression that describes a violation of the GAAP matching principle in which more expenses are taken in a bad year than are actually justified, so fewer expenses can be taken in future years.

A **bond** is an interest-bearing, long-term note payable issued by corporations, universities, and governmental agencies.

Bonds issued at a discount are bonds issued for an amount less than the face value of the bond. This happens when the market rate of interest is greater than the bond's stated rate of interest.

Bonds issued at a premium are bonds issued for an amount more than the face value of the bond. This happens when the market rate of interest is less than the bond's stated rate of interest.

Bonds issued at par are bonds issued for the face value of the bond. This happens when the market rate of interest is equal to the bond's stated rate of interest.

The **book value** of an asset is the cost minus the accumulated depreciation related to the asset.

The **books** are a company's accounting records.

C

Capital is the name for the resources used to start and run a business.

A **capital expenditure** is a cost that is recorded as an asset, not an expense, at the time it is incurred. This is also called *capitalizing* a cost.

Capital structure is the combination of debt and equity that a firm uses to finance its business.

To **capitalize** is to record a cost as an asset rather than to record it as an expense.

Carrying value is another expression for book value.

The **carrying value** of a bond is the amount that the balance sheet shows as the net value of the bond, similar in meaning to the carrying value of a fixed asset. It is equal to the face value of the bond minus any discount or plus any premium.

Cash basis accounting is a system based on the exchange of cash. In this system, revenue is recognized only when cash is collected, and an expense is recognized only when cash is disbursed. This is not an acceptable method of accounting under GAAP.

Cash equivalents are highly liquid investments with a maturity of three months or less that a firm can easily convert into a known amount of cash.

The **cash from financing activities** section of the statement of cash flows includes transactions related to how a business is financed. Examples include contributions from owners and amounts borrowed using loans.

The **cash from investing activities** section of the statement of cash flows includes transactions involving the sale and purchase of long-term assets used in the business.

The **cash from operating activities** section of the statement of cash flows includes cash transactions that relate to the everyday, routine transactions needed to run a business.

Cash from operations to current liabilities ratio is the net cash from operating activities divided by average current liabilities.

A **certified public accountant (CPA)** is someone who has met specific education and exam requirements set up by individual states to make sure that only individuals with the appropriate qualifications can perform audits. To sign an audit report, an accountant must be a CPA.

A **classified balance sheet** shows a subtotal for many items, including current assets and current liabilities.

Closing the accounts means bringing the balances in the temporary accounts to zero.

Common stock is the most widespread form of ownership in a corporation; common shareholders have a vote in the election of the firm's board of directors.

Common-sizing involves converting all amounts on a financial statement to a percentage of a chosen value on that statement; also known as *vertical analysis*.

Comparative balance sheets are the balance sheets from consecutive fiscal years for a single company. The ending balance sheet for one fiscal year is the beginning balance sheet for the next fiscal year.

Comprehensive income is the total of all items that affect shareholders' equity except transactions with the owners; comprehensive income has two parts: net income and other comprehensive income.

A **contra-asset** is an amount that is deducted from an asset.

A **contra-revenue** is an account that is an offset to a revenue account and therefore deducted from the revenue for the financial statements.

Contributed capital is an owner's investment in a company.

Cookie jar reserves is an expression that describes an account, usually a liability, that is established by recognizing an estimated expense inaccurately. When the expenditures actually occur, the firm charges them against the reserve rather than against income. This practice is a violation of the matching principle.

Cooking the books is a slang expression that means to manipulate or falsify the firm's accounting records to make the firm's financial performance or position look better than it actually is.

A **copyright** is a form of legal protection for authors of "original works of authorship," provided by U.S. law.

Corporate governance is the way a firm governs itself, as executed by the board of directors. Corporate governance is also described as the set of relationships between the board of directors, management, shareholders, auditors, and any others with a stake in the company.

A **corporation** is a special legal form for a business in which the business is a legal entity separate from the owners. A corporation may have a single owner or a large number of owners.

Cost of goods available for sale is the total of beginning inventory plus the net purchases made during the period (plus any freight-in costs).

Cost of goods sold is the total amount paid by a firm for the goods sold during the period.

Credit means right side of an account.

Current assets are the assets the company plans to turn into cash or use to generate revenue in the next fiscal year.

Current liabilities are liabilities the company will settle— pay off—in the next fiscal year.

Current ratio is a liquidity ratio that measures a firm's ability to meet its short-term obligations.

D

Debit means left side of an account.

Debt-to-equity ratio compares the amount of a firm's liabilities to the amount of its equity, an indication of solvency.

Declining balance depreciation is an accelerated depreciation method in which depreciation expense is based on the declining book value of the asset.

A **deferral** is a transaction in which the cash is exchanged *before* the revenue has been earned or the expense has been incurred.

Definitely determinable liabilities are obligations that can be measured exactly.

Depletion is the amortization of a natural resource.

A **deposit in transit** is a bank deposit the firm has made but is not included on the month's bank statement because the deposit did not reach the bank's record-keeping department in time to be included on the current bank statement.

Depreciation is a systematic and rational allocation process to recognize the expense of long-term assets over the periods in which the assets are used.

The **depreciation expense** is the expense for each period.

The **direct method** shows every cash inflow and outflow to prepare the statement of cash flows.

The **direct write-off method** is a method of accounting for bad debts in which they are recorded as an expense in the period in which they are identified as uncollectible.

Discontinued operations are those parts of the firm that a company has eliminated by selling a division.

Discount on bonds payable is a contra-liability that is deducted from bonds payable on the balance sheet; it is the difference between the face value of the bond and its selling price when the selling price is less than the face (par) value.

The **discount rate** is the interest rate used to compute the present value of future cash flows.

Discounting means to compute the present value of future cash flows.

Dividend yield ratio is dividend per share divided by the current market price per share.

Dividends are the distribution of a corporation's earnings to the owners or shareholders of the corporation.

E

Earnings per share (EPS) is a commonly used measure of firm performance, defined as net income minus preferred dividends divided by the weighted average number of common shares outstanding.

An **enterprise-wide resource planning system (ERP)** is an integrated software program used by large firms to manage all of a firm's information.

Estimated liabilities are obligations that have some uncertainty in the amount, such as the cost to honor a warranty.

Expenses are the costs incurred to generate revenue.

Extraordinary items are events that are unusual in nature and infrequent in occurrence.

F

The **Financial Accounting Standards Board (FASB)** is the group that sets accounting standards. It gets its authority from the SEC.

Financial leverage is the use of borrowed funds to increase earnings.

Financial services companies deal in services related to money.

First-in, first-out (FIFO) is the inventory cost flow method that assumes the first items purchased are the first items sold.

A **fiscal year** is a year in the life of a business. It may or may not coincide with the calendar year.

FOB (free on board) destination means that the vendor (selling firm) pays the shipping costs, so the buyer has no freight-in cost.

FOB (free on board) shipping point means the buying firm pays the shipping costs. The amount is called freight-in and is included in the cost of the inventory.

A **for-profit firm** has the goal of making a profit for its owners.

A **franchise** is an agreement that authorizes someone to sell or distribute a company's goods or services in a certain area.

Free cash flow is equal to net cash from operating activities minus dividends and minus capital expenditures.

The **full-disclosure principle** means that the firm must disclose any circumstances and events that would make a difference to the users of the financial statements.

G

The **general ledger** is the collection of the company's accounts where the information from the financial transactions is organized and stored.

The **general ledger system** is the accountant's traditional way of keeping track of a company's financial transactions and then using those records to prepare the basic financial statements.

Generally accepted accounting principles (GAAP) are the guidelines for financial reporting.

The **going-concern assumption** means that, unless there is obvious evidence to the contrary, a firm is expected to continue operating in the foreseeable future.

Goodwill is the excess of cost over market value of the net assets when one company purchases another company.

Gross profit ratio is equal to the gross profit (sales minus cost of goods sold) divided by sales. It is a ratio for evaluating firm performance.

H

Held-to-maturity securities are investments in debt securities that the company plans to hold until they mature.

The **historical-cost principle** means that transactions are recorded at actual cost.

Horizontal analysis is a technique for evaluating financial statement items across time.

I

Impairment is a permanent decline in the fair market value of an asset such that its book value exceeds its fair market value.

The **income statement** shows all revenues minus all expenses for an accounting period—a month, a quarter, or a year.

The **indirect method** starts with net income and makes adjustments for items that are not cash to prepare the statement of cash flows.

Intangible assets are rights, privileges, or benefits that result from owning long-lived assets that do not have physical substance.

The **interest** is the cost of borrowing money—using someone else's money.

Interest payable is a liability. It is the amount a company owes for borrowing money (after the time period to which the interest applies has passed).

Internal controls are a company's policies and procedures designed to protect the assets of the firm and to ensure the accuracy and reliability of the accounting records.

The **Internal Revenue Service (IRS)** is the federal agency responsible for federal income tax collection.

The **International Accounting Standards Board (IASB)** is the group that sets international financial reporting standards.

The **International Financial Reporting Standards (IFRS)** are international guidelines for financial reporting, used in many places around the world.

The **inventory turnover ratio** is defined as cost of goods sold divided by average inventory. It is a measure of how quickly a firm sells its inventory.

Issued shares are shares of stock that have been offered and sold to shareholders.

J

Business transactions are first recorded in a **journal**. Then they are transferred to accounts in the general ledger through a process called posting.

L

Last-in, first-out (LIFO) is the inventory cost flow method that assumes the last items purchased are the first items sold.

Liabilities are the obligations of a business; amounts owed to creditors.

Liquidity is a measure of how easily an asset can be converted to cash. The more liquid an asset is, the more easily it can be turned into cash.

Liquidity ratios are used to measure the company's ability to pay its current bills and operating costs.

Long-term assets are assets that will last for more than a year.

Long-term liabilities are liabilities that will take longer than a year to settle.

The **lower-of-cost-or-market (LCM) rule** is the rule that requires firms to use the lower of either the cost or the market value (replacement cost) of its inventory on the date of the balance sheet.

M

The **maker** of a note is the person or firm making the promise to pay.

A **manufacturing company** makes the goods it sells.

Market indicators are ratios that relate the current market price of the company's stock to earnings or dividends.

The **market rate of interest** is the interest rate that an investor could earn in an equally risky investment.

The **matching principle** says that expenses should be recognized—shown on the income statement—in the same period as the revenue they helped generate.

A **merchandising company** sells a product to its customers.

Modified accelerated cost recovery system (MACRS) is the method that the IRS requires firms to use to depreciate its assets for tax purposes.

The **monetary-unit assumption** means that the items on the financial statements are measured in monetary units (dollars in the United States).

A **multistep income statement** starts with sales and subtracts cost of goods sold to get a subtotal called gross profit on sales, also known as gross margin. Then, other operating revenues are added and other operating expenses are deducted. A subtotal for operating income is shown before deductions related to nonoperating items and taxes are deducted. Then, income taxes are subtracted, leaving net income.

N

Net income equals all revenues minus all expenses for a specific period of time.

Net profit equals all revenues minus all expenses.

Net realizable value is the amount of its accounts receivable balance that the firm expects to collect.

Noncurrent assets, or long-term assets, are assets that will last for more than a year.

Noncurrent liabilities, or long-term liabilities, are liabilities that will take longer than a year to settle.

A **not-for-profit firm** has the goal of providing goods or services to its clients.

Notes to the financial statements are information provided with the four basic statements that describe the company's major accounting policies and provide other disclosures to help external users better understand the financial statements.

O

On account means *on credit*. The expression applies to either buying or selling on credit.

An **ordinary annuity** is an annuity whose payments are made at the end of each interval or period.

An **outstanding check** is a check the firm has written but that has not yet cleared the bank. That is, the check has not been presented to the bank for payment yet.

Outstanding shares are shares of stock that are owned by stockholders.

P

Paid-in capital, another name for contributed capital, is the owner's investment in the business.

Par value is the monetary amount assigned to a share of stock in the corporate charter. It has little meaning in today's business environment.

A **partnership** is a company owned by two or more individuals.

A **patent** is a property right that the U.S. government grants to an inventor "to exclude others from making, using, offering for sale, or selling the invention throughout the United States or importing the invention into the United States for a specified period of time."

The **payee** of a note is the person or firm receiving the money.

The **periodic inventory system** is a method of record keeping that involves updating the inventory account only at the end of the accounting period.

Permanent accounts or **real accounts** are accounts that are never closed. They are the asset, liability, and shareholders' equity accounts.

The **perpetual inventory system** is a method of record keeping that involves updating the inventory account at the time of every purchase, sale, and return.

A **postclosing trial balance** is a list of all the accounts and their debit balances or credit balances, prepared after the temporary accounts have been closed. Only balance sheet accounts will appear on the postclosing trial balance.

Posting is the process of recording the transactions from the journal into the firm's general ledger so that the transactions will be organized by accounts.

Preferred stock is stock that represents a special kind of ownership in a corporation. Preferred shareholders do not get a vote but they do receive dividends before the common shareholders.

Premium on bonds payable is an adjunct-liability that is added to bonds payable on the balance sheet; it is the difference between the face value of the bond and its selling price, when the selling price is more than the face (par) value.

Prepaid insurance is the name for insurance a business has purchased but not yet used. It is an asset.

Prepaid rent is an asset. It represents amounts paid for rent not yet used. The rent expense is deferred until the rented asset has actually been used—when the time related to the rent has passed.

The **present value** is the value today of a given amount to be invested or received in the future, assuming compound interest.

Price–earnings (P/E) ratio is the market price of a share of stock divided by that stock's earnings per share.

The **principal** of a loan is the amount of money borrowed.

Proceeds are the amount of cash the bond issuer collects from the bondholders when the bonds are issued.

Profit margin on sales is a ratio that measures how much of the firm's sales revenue actually makes its way to the bottom line—net income. To calculate this ratio, simply divide net income by net sales.

Profitability ratios are used to measure the operating or income performance of a company.

A **promissory note** is a written promise to pay a specified amount of money at a specified time.

The **Public Company Accounting Oversight Board (PCAOB)** is a group formed to oversee the auditing profession and the audits of public companies. Its creation was mandated by the Sarbanes-Oxley Act of 2002.

A **purchase discount** is a reduction in the price of an inventory purchase for prompt payment according to terms specified by the vendor.

A **purchase order** is a record of the company's request to a vendor for goods or services. It may be referred to as a P.O.

Purchase returns and allowances are amounts that decrease the cost of inventory due to returned or damaged merchandise.

Q

Quality of earnings refers to how well a reported earnings number communicates the firm's true performance.

R

Realized means the cash is collected. Sometimes revenue is *recognized* before it is *realized.*

Recognized revenue is revenue that has been recorded so that it will show up on the income statement.

Relative fair market value method is a way to allocate the total cost for several assets purchased together to each of the individual assets. This method is based on the assets' individual market values.

Replacement cost is the cost to buy similar items in inventory from the supplier to replace the inventory.

Residual value, also known as salvage value, is the estimated value of an asset at the end of its useful life. With most depreciation methods, residual value is deducted before the calculation of depreciation expense.

Retained earnings is the total of all net income amounts minus all dividends paid in the life of the company. It is descriptively named—it is the earnings that have been kept (retained) in the company. The amount of retained earnings represents the part of the owner's claims that the company has earned (i.e., not contributed). Retained earnings is *not* the same as cash.

Return on assets is a ratio that measures how well a company is using its assets to generate income. It is defined as net income divided by average total assets.

Return on equity (ROE) measures the amount of income earned with each dollar of common shareholders' investment in the firm. To calculate ROE, take net income minus preferred dividends divided by average common shareholders' equity.

Revenue is the amount the company has earned from providing goods or services to customers.

The **revenue-recognition principle** says that revenue should be recognized when it is earned and collection is reasonably assured.

A **risk** is a danger—something that exposes a business to a potential injury or loss.

S

A **sales discount** is a reduction in the sales price of a product offered to customers for prompt payment.

Sales returns and allowances is an account that holds amounts that reduce sales due to customer returns or allowances for damaged merchandise.

Salvage value (also known as *residual value*) is the estimated value of an asset at the end of its useful life.

The **Securities and Exchange Commission (SEC)** is the governmental agency that monitors the stock market and the financial reporting of the firms that trade in the market.

Segregation of duties means that the person who has physical custody of an asset is not the same person who has record-keeping responsibilities for that asset.

The **separate-entity assumption** means that the firm's financial records and financial statements are completely separate from those of the firm's owners.

A **service company** does something for its customers.

Shareholders' equity—the owners' claims to the assets of the company. There are two types: contributed capital and retained earnings.

Shares of common stock are the units of ownership in a corporation.

A **single-step income statement** groups all revenues together and shows all expenses deducted from total revenue.

A **sole proprietorship** is a company with a single owner.

Solvency ratios are used to measure the company's ability to meet its long-term obligations and to survive over a long period of time.

The **specific identification method** is the inventory cost flow method in which the actual cost of the specific goods sold is recorded as cost of goods sold.

The **statement of cash flows** shows all the cash collected and all the cash disbursed during the period. Each cash amount is classified as one of three types: cash from operating activities, cash from investing activities, or cash from financing activities.

The **statement of changes in shareholders' equity** starts with the beginning amount of contributed capital and shows all changes during the accounting period. Then the statement shows the beginning balance in retained earnings with its changes. The usual changes to retained earnings are the increase due to net income and the decrease due to dividends paid to shareholders.

Stock dividends are new shares of stock that are distributed to the company's current shareholders.

A **stock exchange** is a marketplace where buyers and sellers exchange their shares of stock. Buying and selling shares of stock can also be done on the Internet.

The **stock market** is the name for a collection of stock exchanges. It is a term generally used to designate any place where stock is bought and sold.

A **stock split** is the division of the current shares of stock by a specific number to increase the number of shares outstanding.

Stockholders or **shareholders** are the owners of the corporation.

Straight-line depreciation is a depreciation method in which the depreciation expense is the same each period.

In general, **supplies** are not called inventory. Supplies are miscellaneous items used in the business. When purchased, supplies are recorded as an asset. Supplies expense is recognized after the supplies are used. *Inventory* is a term reserved for the items a company purchases to resell.

T

Tangible assets are assets with physical substance; they can be seen and touched.

Temporary accounts are the revenue, expense, and dividends accounts.

The **time-period assumption** means that the life of a business can be divided into meaningful time periods for financial reporting.

Timing differences arise when revenues are earned in one accounting period and collected in a different accounting period. They also arise when expenses are incurred in one accounting period and paid for in another.

A **trademark** is a symbol, word, phrase, or logo that legally distinguishes one company's product from any others.

Trading securities are investments in debt and equity securities that the company has purchased to make a short-term profit.

Treasury stock is stock that has been repurchased by the issuing firm.

A **trial balance** is a list of all the accounts of a company with the related balance.

U

Unearned revenue is a liability. It represents the amount of goods or services that a company owes its customers. The cash has been collected, but the action of *earning* the revenue has not taken place.

Unrealized gain or loss is when an increase or decrease in the market value of a company's investments in securities is recognized either on the income statement (for trading securities) or in other comprehensive income in the equity section of the balance sheet (for available-for-sale securities) when the financial statements are prepared, even though the securities have *not* been sold.

V

Vertical analysis is a technique for comparing items on a financial statement in which all items are expressed as a percent of a common amount.

W

Weighted average cost is the inventory cost flow method in which the weighted average cost of the goods available for sale is used to calculate the cost of goods sold and the ending inventory.

A distribution to the owner of a sole proprietorship is called a **withdrawal**; in a corporation, distributions to the shareholders are called **dividends**.

X

XBRL (Extensible Business Reporting Language) is a technology that enables firms to report information in a standardized way that makes the data immediately reusable and interactive.

Index

MyAccountingLab

◄ MyAccountingLab is web-based, tutorial and assessment accounting software that not only gives students more "I Get It" moments, but gives instructors the flexibility to make technology an integral part of their course. It's also an excellent supplementary resource for students.

■ For Instructors

MyAccountingLab provides instructors with a rich and flexible set of course materials, along with course-management tools that make it easy to deliver all or a portion of your course online.

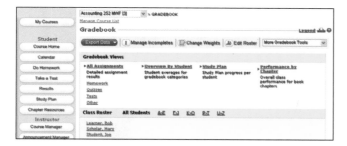

◄ Powerful Homework and Test Manager

Create, import, and manage online homework assignments, quizzes, and tests. Create assignments from online exercises directly correlated to your textbook. Homework exercises include guided solutions to help students understand and master concepts. You can choose from a wide range of assignment options, including time limits, proctoring, and maximum number of attempts allowed.

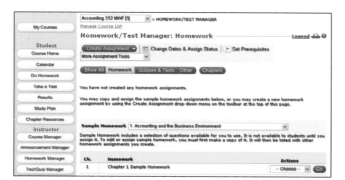

◄ Comprehensive Gradebook Tracking

MyAccountingLab's online gradebook automatically tracks your students' results on tests, homework, and tutorials and gives you control over managing results and calculating grades. All MyAccountingLab grades can be exported to a spreadsheet program, such as Microsoft® Excel. The MyAccountingLab Gradebook provides a number of student data views and gives you the flexibility to weigh assignments, select which attempts to include when calculating scores, and omit or delete results for individual assignments.

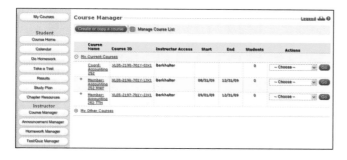

◄ Department-Wide Solutions

Get help managing multiple sections and working with Teaching Assistants using MyAccountingLab Coordinator Courses. After your MyAccountingLab course is set up, it can be copied to create sections or "member courses." Changes to the Coordinator Course ripple down to all members, so changes only need to be made once.